CAL FLYN is a freelance journalist from the Highlands of Scotland. She has written for the *Sunday Times* and *Daily Telegraph*, and been a contributing editor at *The Week* magazine. Her work has appeared widely across the media and she won the 2013 Bradt/*Independent on Sunday* travel-writing prize. She has an MA in Experimental Psychology from Lady Margaret Hall, Oxford, and a postgraduate certificate in newspaper journalism from Lambeth College. *Thicker Than Water* is her first book.

D1579306

THICKER THAN WATER

History, Secrets and Guilt: A Memoir

CAL FLYN

WILLIAM COLLINS

William Collins
An imprint of HarperCollins*Publishers*
1 London Bridge Street
London SE1 9GF
WilliamCollinsBooks.com

First published in Great Britain by William Collins in 2016
This William Collins paperback edition published in 2017

1

This book has been written with the assistance of
Creative Scotland and Arts Trust Scotland

A catalogue record for this book is
available from the British Library

ISBN 978-0-00-812662-9

Printed and bound in Great Britain by
Clays Ltd, St Ives plc

Page ii: unknown Aboriginal man, Gippsland, c. 1858–9
Page iii: Angus McMillan, c. 1860

Map by John Gilkes

MIX
Paper from
responsible sources
FSC® C007454

To my parents,
who make everything possible

Contents

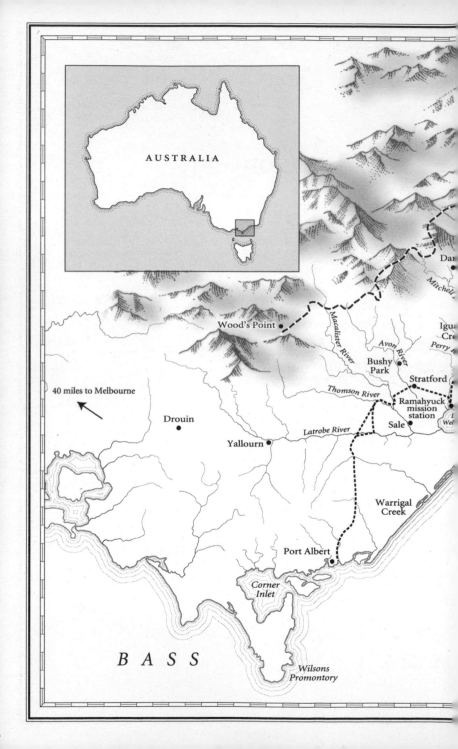

AUSTRALIA

Dar

Mitchell

Wood's Point

Macalister River

Avon River

Perry

Igua
Cre

Bushy
Park

Stratford

Thomson River

40 miles to Melbourne

Ramahyuck
mission
station

Drouin

Latrobe River

Sale

Wel

Yallourn

Warrigal
Creek

Port Albert

Corner
Inlet

BASS

Wilsons
Promontory

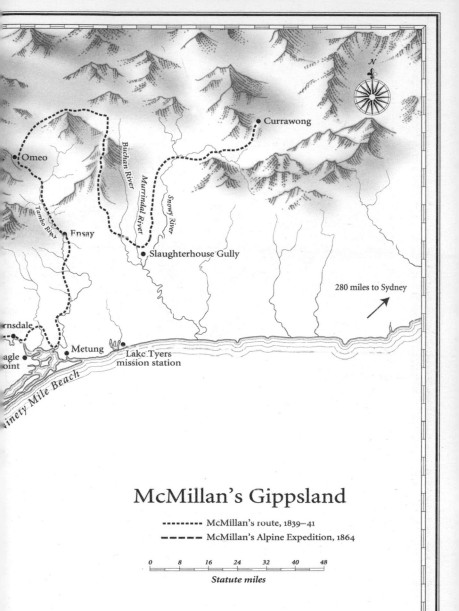

Currawong

Omeo

Buchan River

Murrindal River

Snowy River

Tambo River

Ensay

Slaughterhouse Gully

280 miles to Sydney

...nsdale

...agle
...oint

Metung

Lake Tyers
mission station

Ninety Mile Beach

McMillan's Gippsland

·········· McMillan's route, 1839–41

━ ━ ━ ━ McMillan's Alpine Expedition, 1864

0   8   16   24   32   40   48

Statute miles

STRAIT

Prologue

Gippsland, Victoria. July 1843

Ronald Macalister was dead. The blacks had killed him.

Angus McMillan's stablehand found the body at the side of the track a half-mile from Alberton, a mess of blood and gore. They had dragged the lad from his horse. Dragged him flailing and yowling to the dust, dispatched him with their wooden clubs, and later, once he was dead, they had cut him.

Though Angus knew Ronald well — had known him for years, in fact, since he'd worked for the dead man's uncle — he had barely recognised him. The corpse had been stripped naked, the face disfigured, the insides left spewing out upon the ground. There were slashes in the gut where the Gunai attackers had cut the fat from around his kidneys.

All the settlers were in uproar; this time the blacks had gone too far. Not a sheep, nor a bullock, not even a shepherd or a stockman; this time they had killed the nephew of the big man Lachlan Macalister himself, and a crime of this magnitude could not go unpunished. There must be reprisals. Angus felt the heavy weight of responsibility settling down upon his shoulders.

1

For who else could lead the men of Gippsland? He was the founding father, the man who had led the way from the withered plains of the colony over the Great Dividing Range. He was the one who had hacked through the snarls of stringybark and tea tree and finally guided them down into these green and fertile pastures. He had gathered his countrymen around him in the new land and shown them the way they must now live. There was no one else.

In the end, retribution was not so difficult to organise. The men were fired up, just waiting for the touchpaper to be lit. It didn't take much persuasion to amass a hunting party; by the next morning every Scotsman in the district with a gun and a sound horse was assembled, ready for the off, baying like the hounds. Baying for blood. They called themselves the Highland Brigade.

A cry went up and the mob were off. The horses skittered under them, sensing but not understanding the tension in their riders, whose reins were short and faces set as they cursed in their native Gaelic, guttural and emphatic, and struggled for control. And all the time their eyes flitted along the skyline, searching for sign of the Gunai.

Overnight every one of the Aboriginal workers had melted away into the bush, abandoning their posts on the homesteads and the cattle stations. They were as spooked as the horses by the strange charge in the air, the rumbling among their workmates and masters. The murder of Ronald Macalister had set something in motion that they couldn't yet predict, but they didn't want to be around to find out what it was.

Word spread amongst the Highlanders that the blacks had been gathering down by the coast, where the sea pummelled its soft fists into the silver sweep of Ninety Mile Beach. Someone had heard that natives had been seen wearing the clothes of poor dead Ronald, clothes they must have stripped from the lifeless body before the blades were drawn. Clothes that would be spattered with the dead man's blood.

Another said that when the attackers were disturbed they were squatting down beside the body, with the clear intention of eating the man's flesh. They were inhuman, said someone, and they all agreed. They were dangerous, murderous vermin that needed exterminating.

Later it would never be clear who had said exactly what to whom; at that moment they were of one body and one mind. They looked around and saw only brothers and equals united in pursuit of a common enemy. This was more than revenge: it was about securing the safety of their homes, the virtue of their women and a future for their children. It was white against black, good versus evil, the triumph of civilisation over barbarism.

It would be impossible to identify the culprits of the Macalister killing, for what separated one black from another? Each was as murderous as the next. And was not the life of a Macalister worth ten, or twenty, of the natives? The loss of a Macalister must be answered with whatever punishment was necessary to ensure that no white man would ever find harm at the hands of the blacks again.

The Highlanders were armed, organised and angry. When suddenly they came upon the Aboriginal encampment, on a flat by a waterhole nestled in a wide bend of the creek, no one needed to tell them what to do. They advanced stealthily towards the camp, fanning out in a line until they stretched between the banks of the creek on either side, like the string of a bow. It was a fine trap: when the first shots were fired there was nowhere for the Gunai tribesmen to run to.

Crack. Crack. Rifles fired into the centre of the camp, scattering men, women, children. Some of them clutched infants to their chests, as if their frail bodies could protect them from firepower.

Crack. Crack. Bullets began to rain down upon the Gunai. The screams of shock and fright would soon intermingle with the wails of the wounded.

Crack. Crack. The Scots advanced, bloodlust in their eyes. Those still able to run, ran. They ran blindly from the muzzles of the guns, tumbling down the steep banks and into the waterhole. Others made a desperate break through the line of horsemen, eyes fixed on the cover offered by the scrub beyond.

Crack. Crack. The deep water offered solace, but only temporarily. The terror and chaos were contained in another room. Underwater even the gunfire sounded different: a distant drumroll, more felt than heard, and the strange suction sounds of bullets through water.

Lungs burning, the fleeing Gunai were forced to raise their heads to breathe. As they surfaced, the Highlanders fired again. Again and again, until there was no one left to fire at.

The water was red with blood. Fresh blood, vivid and unreal. Thick and opaque, like the paint in a pot. It swirled and eddied, leaching from the corpses, flecked with a white frothy scum where the water had churned up.

When all was quiet, Angus stepped forward to inspect his men's work. There were too many dead blacks to count: dozens of them. Warriors, shamans, hunters, gatherers, fathers, mothers, sons, daughters, infants, elders, all dead. One of the Scotsmen pulled a young Aboriginal boy from the water. He was around twelve or thirteen, and still living, although he had been hit in one eye with a shotgun slug. Later they would christen him 'Bung Eye'.

On, ordered Angus. Let's move on.

They marched Bung Eye ahead, made him lead the way. There must be other camps, they said. Take us to the other camps. They waved their guns in his face. He didn't have much choice.

They walked on across endless flat land under an endless flat sky, pushing through the starburst heads of kangaroo grass that grew up as high as their stirrup irons. Three miles to the south they found another camp, on another flat by another waterhole. The midden nearby attested to a long residency: layers upon layers of discarded shells. A handful each from every meal, built up over hundreds of years.

Again the Gunai were surrounded. Again the shotguns fired. Crack. Crack. Crack. And on again, Bung Eye! Lead on! Once more they advanced across the plain, to another creek, another waterhole.

Crack. Crack. Crack.

The massacre at Warrigal Creek was one of the bloodiest episodes on the very bloody Australian frontier. In all, somewhere between eighty and two hundred Gunai people were slaughtered that day, wiping out in a single assault a substantial portion of the southern Bratowooloong clan.

The leader of the Highland Brigade, Angus McMillan, was a Scot who had fled the horror of the Highland

Clearances, during which thousands of his countrymen were forced from their land to make way for sheep, only to re-enact brutal clearances of his own upon this new land: Gippsland, the south-eastern corner of Australia.

He was a tough man, a pious man, a lonely man. A man who had struggled through miles of unknown territory, built new homes with bare hands, met tribes who had never seen or even known of white skin. He was a man who cut tracks, fought bushfires, felled trees, shot strangers dead.

He was 'the Butcher of Gippsland'.

He was my great-great-great uncle.

1

Blood Relatives

I've spent the last decade of my life scrambling for foot-holds and handholds, pulling myself ever onward, ever upwards. Shift – move – adjust – and shift again. It was only when my bough began to bend, and creak under my own weight, that it occurred to me to think: How did I get here? Where did I come from? Who is behind me?

The summer I turned twenty-five was the first time I felt the wobble. On paper everything seemed ideal. I had landed my dream job as a reporter on a national newspaper, and since then I spent my days high on adrenaline, making bad-tempered phone calls, arguing with lawyers and scanning the news wires for excitement. My nights were spent blowing off steam in East End bars, nights fuelled by alcohol and enthusiasm that could fire off in any direction at any time, end up anywhere. It was exciting. *I* felt exciting.

But more and more I was feeling something else as well. Everything seemed very precarious somehow, as if, when I next turned to take hold of all the strands of my life, my hands might slip through space, finding nothing solid to grip onto. I had a mounting sense of dread.

For despite the business cards and the security passes and the smart-casual work wardrobes, it wasn't working out quite the way I'd planned. Over the past three years I'd seen too many of my contemporaries slipping suddenly from their rungs and sliding down the snakes back to the start. Pumped up by the big talk of the graduate recruiters, we had graduated right into the worst of the financial crisis, and all the overconfidence – ours, theirs, everyone's – was coming crashing down around us.

The easy, breezy lives we'd been promised at those Magic Circle, Big Four, get-rich-quick corporate-sponsored drinks parties had vanished in a puff of smoke; after all the champagne hysteria the next few years had come on in a flood of disappointment and stifled ambition. One of my university peers spent weeks in the papers as a photo of her, looking dishevelled but fragilely beautiful as she carried a cardboard box of belongings from the Lehman Brothers office, was wheeled out by the picture editors again and again. The face of the recession, of hubris, of financial calamity; we recognised her.

London had seemed a shining city of hopes and dreams, but now it had transformed into a dark and terrifying place, where jobs stuttered and vanished but the rents were still rising up in front of us like a drawbridge. I had no security. None of us had any security. And for the first time in my life I was scared. Low-level and not such low-level anxiety buzzed in the background of all my thoughts.

On the one hand, I was lucky. I had a job, and I held it tight. But everyone knew that newspapers were a doomed industry. The internet was rendering us obsolete. It was all we talked about, in hushed voices in the office. 'Get out now while you can,' senior reporters told me in harsh whispers. 'It's too late for me. I'm too old to retrain. Save yourself.'

After work I wandered through the docks, looking at all the yachts and skyscrapers and cocktail bars, and I couldn't remember what I was doing there. I picked up my phone. Dialled.

'Can I come home for a while?'

'Of course,' said my mother. 'Whenever you want.'

Home for me is the Highlands. This is a detail about myself that has always been a disproportionately large source of pride and the basis for a bizarre game of one-upmanship I play secretly, constantly, with everyone else, smiling quietly to myself as others recount with self-deprecating humour the banality of their suburban roots in Luton or Wolverhampton or Wigan.

Never mind that I fled at eighteen, as soon and as fast as education allowed – first to India and later to university in England, both in their own way the most antithetical environments to the Highlands that I could imagine – or that by now I'd lived for so long away from 'home' that my accent had slipped so low as to be imperceptible. They say that ex-pats make the best patriots, and I believe them. I can't help it. I love the place.

My childhood summers were spent paddling with Highland ponies in the biting cold waters of Loch Ness, then charging – kicking their barrel sides and flapping my reins – together up the muddy tracks in the hills above. In the autumn I walked home across the field, gorging on brambles, stumbling through nettles. We swam in the loch behind my house, climbing into a rowing boat at its centre and jumping off again until our fingers turned blue. When we were older my friends and I threw parties in fields, drinking cheap cider amid clouds of midges, lying back on our jackets to watch shooting stars. And in the winter, if we were lucky, the northern lights.

The Highlands are a place where it's easy to escape and walk out all alone, except for the sheep and the honey-sweet aroma of the gorse. It's a place where you can go entire days, even in the middle of summer, without seeing another soul. To me it seems the only place to be from.

Now it was to the Highlands that I had the urge to return. I was suddenly grateful for the grandeur of the landscape and the reassurance of family, newly appreciative of the importance of knowing and understanding my place in the world. Fed up with being a lone wolf, I was turning tail back to the den.

With two weeks' leave to play with, I set off with my mother on a jaunt around the island haunts of her youth. From our home on the Black Isle we headed west, through the green pastures of the east coast and up into the bleak stretches of heather moor that characterise the north and west, skirting the lochs that split the country along its weakest fault. Mum's a nervous passenger, and she clutched the door handle and held her breath on the corners, but between the bends we talked about family, her family — all these vivid characters to whom I am bound inextricably but have never met, the people who define so much of my identity.

When my grandmother was still alive we would make this journey often, rushing to catch the ferry from Kyle and rumbling the car down the concrete slip and onto the diamond plate of the metal ramp. I would peer out at the other cars, crammed together like a herd of cows, and the big metal rivets that held the walls together. Everything that went on and off the island came via that ferry – horses kicking the backs of their boxes, sheep packed two-storey into trailers with their ears poking through the air vents, lorries bearing food and supplies that shifted the balance of the ferry perceptibly as they came on board.

Once aboard we had to leave the car and clamber up the metal ladder to the wet-sprayed deck or the striplit waiting room in case the vehicles started moving around during the voyage. It was just a short jump by Hebridean standards. You could see our destination, Kyleakin, across the water, and the hills of Skye, whose southerly arm, Sleat, loomed up in front of us as the little ferry set off gamely across the waves. After twenty minutes we all trooped back down the ladder and into the cars to drive off up the ramp. It was my favourite part of the trip.

Now the ferry is gone, replaced by a road bridge that skims across the water like a stone, shooting straight out from the mainland and skipping off Eilean Bàn – 'the White Island' – barely missing the lighthouse and its keeper's cottage, the impact sending it arching in a high parabolic path above the sea before alighting on the Skye coast.

Skye is central to my family's history. It's where my mother grew up, and where her father's family was from, and it's also where my parents met, when my father came to work with my maternal grandfather in the Portree court. We drove north along the edge of the island, stopping at sites of family significance. 'That was my granny's house,' said my mother as we reached Breakish, a scattering of crofthouses set back from the road. She pointed to a whitewashed cottage with a neatly hatched slate roof. Triangular dormer windows poked through the tiles at the front like eyes, in the local vernacular.

Across the road sat the family croft — a narrow strip of land stretching away towards the sea, a traditional island smallholding held under an unusual form of Scots law, whereby tenants rent the land from the local estate, build their own houses on it, and pass on the tenancy when they die. Mum's brother Myles was still the official tenant, although the grass was quietly being grazed by a neighbour's bedraggled sheep in his absence. We stopped to look, but I felt odd and underwhelmed. The croft is a ghostly, wordless presence in many of our family's discussions of Skye, a reference point around which stories and lives rotate. But in reality, there was nothing marking it out as ours.

I had heard that it didn't have any buildings on it any more, that the house had been sold off separately decades ago, but I hadn't really processed that. Seeing it in person for the first time in years, this soggy paddock didn't feel much different from any of the others around it, or the thousands we'd passed on the drive. Still, I felt that it meant something to have gone there, that it existed. There was a link between our family and this rocky patch of earth, something more material than memory alone.

A track led down from the road across a flat expanse of reeds and heather to the Breakish graveyard, where my forebears lay quietly on a rise overlooking the beach, dark kelp drawn up tight over the sand like a blanket.

I remembered this place from my childhood: windswept, the black sea bottomless under a sombre sky. Cattle standing on the track. The large cartoony petals of carnations in their metal colanders and the fabric flowers stabbed into oasis foam, cloth leaves fluttering in the cold wind.

We laid flowers at the graves of my grandparents and of my uncle Niall, who died when I was young. Afterwards we drifted through the kissing gate into the oldest section of the graveyard, behind a low dry-stone wall. Here the gravestones were larger, monumental, almost Gothic. Marble angels crouched with heads bent, in mourning for entire families. Celtic crosses stood proudly; a row of neat matching stones remembered unnamed sailors.

There were family stones here for us too. We browsed, looking for the name.

'Wait — here.'

It was a neat grey stone, almost as tall as me, the stone left rough along its edges. Engraved ivy climbed up the left side. 'In loving memory of Myles McMillan, died 14th December 1899 ...' began a roll-call of the deceased. There, at the foot of the list, came '... and Angus, Christina, who died in Australia'.

I had a camera in my hand. I lifted it, focused on the stone. Snap.

Portree was a thirty-mile drive north from Breakish along the coast, through the seaside village of Broadford and darting between the feet of the red Cuillins — Beinn na Caillich, 'the hill of the old woman', with her grizzled and scree-strewn face, then Marsco and finally the perfect, conical Glamaig. The black Cuillin ridgeline loomed up in the west beyond, jagged and forbidding.

To our right we looked out across the water to the tiny isle of Pabay and her big sister Scalpay, then the south end of Raasay rose out of the water, with the familiar shorn crown of Dun Caan, flat like a tabletop.

Portree is a small town – a big village, really – clasped between the three steep sides of a fishing harbour. We wandered along the water's edge between stacks of green-stringed lobster creels and the neat cottages that line the quayside; painted baby-blue and rose, sage-green and amber. The evening sun caught the sides of the fishing boats and buoys that speckled the sea loch further out, and burnished the rocky slopes of the isles beyond.

On the way back through the village we passed the butcher's ('New recipe!!! Irn Bru sausages: £6.98/kg', a handwritten sign promised) and then the courthouse where my grandfather – my mother's father – was the procurator fiscal for many years. Her family lived just outside Portree in a big, chaotic house of brothers and sisters and animals.

Heading north out of town towards the house, we rounded a bend and the Old Man of Storr swung suddenly into view – a startling pinnacle of rock jutting from the hillside so abruptly it seemed almost to stand up.

'There –' said Mum, knocking me out of my reverie. She slowed the car and craned her head to look past me out of the passenger window. 'Our house was just behind those trees.' But it wasn't there any more: the line of trees turned out to screen a cul-de-sac of modern bungalows. We stopped the car.

'Creag an Iolaire,' I read aloud from the street sign. Craig an yo-lara. Eagle Rock.

'That was the name of my house,' she said, and stopped as if to catch her breath. 'I remember when they planted those trees.'

At the top of the little street, her former driveway, on the site of the family home, was a stubby, white-harled block of flats. A sign outside declared it 'Macmillan House', after my mother's maiden name.

You often hear about people who return after long absences to their childhood homes and knock on the door to ask if they can have a look around. They try to remember what it looked like under the coats of paint, the new wallpaper, before the extension was built. The house is the same, but not the same, as if one day you had miscounted the steps and walked into a neighbour's home: in the image of your own, but the colours all wrong, and everything in the wrong place. What a curious sense of loss this is, when we know that things cannot stay the same.

We drove on glumly, past the Storr and along the coast road, echoing the curve of the ridge, until Portree and the cul-de-sac were long behind us. The land there is stark and bleak, grass holding to the slopes where it can, wrinkles in the hillside where the earth has slipped and settled again, peaty water settled in the clefts levelling the uneven pitch of the ground. Further out on the headland, white cottages cling on to the rocks like limpets.

We spent the night in a B&B that sat out alone on the heather near Staffin. The scale of the place unsettled me – the great malevolent forces that shaped the earth writ large across the land. And the colours too: the vegetation was not green, but crimson and orange and gold. 'Like the surface of Mars,' said Mum.

It was late by the time we arrived, the sky the strange dusky twilight it will stay all night this far north in the summer, and we realised we hadn't brought anything for dinner. There was not a shop or pub for miles around. Too embarrassed to beg for food from the landlady, we pooled our resources and split a pack of breath mints and a cellophane gift bag of tablet between us in a bedspread picnic. All that was missing were the plastic cups and the cuddly toys.

I noticed with relief that I had no signal on my phone. For the first time in months I felt safe.

Back in Portree, we found ourselves drawn in by an A4 poster promising an exhibition on the Skye diaspora in the new archive centre, in the old boys' boarding house at the high school.

The exhibition was small – photocopied documents pinned up on blue felt display boards, black-and-white photos of kilted Highlanders in their brave new worlds: America, Canada, Africa, India – and the archive smelt of carpet tiles and the chlorine from the school swimming pool across the carpark, but we dallied, reading each label slowly, waiting for the rain to die down outside.

There were aged, curling registers in glass cases that recalled in long lists the names of those who sailed from the west coast of Scotland in the eighteenth and early nineteenth centuries in search of a new life. They were the refugees from the Highland Clearances, an agricultural revolution that saw the removal of thousands upon thousands of Highlanders from their traditional land by their clan chiefs. In Gaelic they call this time *Fuadaich nan Gàidheal*: the expulsion of the Gael.

From Skye, most left for Nova Scotia, Canada, where even now one can still hear the lilt of Gaelic song and the beat of the bodhran – almost a third of its population still self-identify as ethnically 'Scottish', as opposed to Canadian. But not all. The emigrants fired off in every direction, and the displays in front of me charted how the thin tendrils of kinship stretched out from this island across the world.

I was enchanted by a copy of an old, hand-drawn map, a segment of coastline blown up on the photocopier to cover an A3 sheet. Seas and rivers had been delicately shaded blue by some devoted archivist with a pencil. A mountain range stretched across the top of the page, coloured purple, and a set of unknown straight-edged boundaries upon the land had been rendered in green.

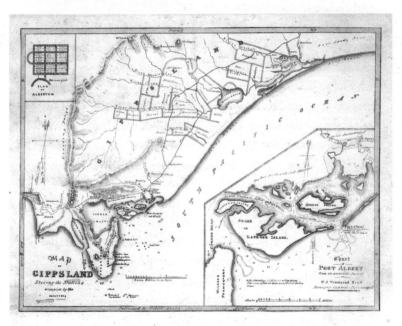

The 1845 map of Gippsland on display at the Portree exhibition.

There was something fantastical about it, like a real-life treasure map, with names straight out of J.M. Barrie's imagination: 'Snake Island', 'Shoal Lagoon', 'Mount

Useful', 'Sealer's Cove'. But there were names I recognised too: one peak was labelled 'Ben Cruachan', like a mountain in Argyllshire; a settlement called 'Glengarry', like the Lochaber village; another called 'Tarradale' – wasn't that in Ross-shire? The green squares too bore names I knew: Campbell, Macalister, Cunningham.

I couldn't identify the country by its coastline. In thick copperplate, carefully traced and filled in with a pink coloured pencil, the words SOUTH PACIFIC OCEAN rose out of the empty space of the sea.

I gave up, let myself check the information tag: 'Robert Dixon's map of Gippsland, Australia, showing the stations occupied by the squatters, 1845 ... The detailed insert shows the Macalister River, named by explorer Angus McMillan after Captain Lachlan Macalister (1797–1858), a grandson of Alexander of Strathaird. Angus McMillan was born in Glenbrittle, Skye in 1810.' There was a monochrome portrait of the explorer stapled to the board alongside: a sober, severe-looking man with strong features and a white chinstrap beard. He wore a tweed three-piece and cravat, and looked off into the middle distance from under heavy brows.

I smiled, watching the rain lash against the windowpane. I tried to imagine sailing all the way from Skye to the South Pacific. Landing on Snake Island.

'Angus McMillan,' came Mum's voice from behind me. 'He's a relative of ours.'

I wasn't listening. The thought was still turning itself over in my head. 'Get on a boat here, and don't get off until you get to Australia,' it went. 'Sealer's Cove,' it said. 'Mount Useful.'

'What?' I asked, belatedly.

'He's a relative of ours,' she said again. 'I remember my father telling us about him when we were children. He was very proud of it. Angus was an explorer in Australia when it was first being settled. There are whole areas named after him. You'll have to ask your uncle Myles, he'll know more about it.'

'Huh.' I looked at the map again, impressed. There was a mountain in the north-west corner of the map that had been labelled 'Mount Angus'. I drew this small source of fuzzy pride close to my chest, like an otter with a clam shell.

Until this moment I had never understood the appeal of family history, the draw for all those anoraks poring over their bloodlines in the back rooms of libraries. I knew it would be hard to explain the significance of my discovery, in the same way that the relating of last night's dream is never as interesting for the audience as it is for the teller. Sheer self-indulgence. Yet it was strange how much this revelation had cheered me. How this whole trip had cheered me.

I couldn't be sure why it had affected me so much to learn of this swashbuckling relative. His story, after all, did not appear to have had much bearing on my life thus far. But, I told myself, wasn't it this sense of context that I was seeking when I returned to Skye? Of course our lives should stand alone, to be considered on their own merits, but didn't it add something to step back and see myself as the latest episode in a longer series? As part of a family epic, whose themes reverberate down the generations?

There is a certain comfort, I realised, in accepting the existence of some kind of folk destiny, wherein the predecessors' achievements confer some inherent advantage, some easing of paths on the present generation; the very simplest form of predestation. One can almost imagine the nods of approval from the family portraits in the great hall ...

For this reason I was glad that McMillan was an explorer. I could use this familial detail as a hook to hang my wanderlust from – the yearning for escape that rears up in me even in the most pleasant of circumstances, the restlessness that has driven me from gainful employment and fulfilling relationships and onto aeroplanes instead, time and again, to hike along the Yangtze, or cruise the backwaters of Kerala, or snowshoe in the Arctic. With this new information, I could reimagine myself as the latest in a line of notable wanderers, rather than a deadbeat who simply found it hard to settle down to work.

I have often daydreamed of how I too would have been an explorer, had I been born into another century. It grieves me that there is now so little on earth to explore, truly explore – only the final dark crevices of deep-water trench and polar crevasse. Meanwhile the breaching of the new frontiers, beyond our own planet (stars spinning past the portholes, one-way trips to Mars), remains decades away.

What I'd give to touch down on a strange beach and walk out into unknown land. To draw the first map and write on it my own names for what I saw.

I was in the habit of following leads, so I called my uncle Myles, as my mother had suggested. He lives in London now, in a terraced house with a Greek wife and two young sons who speak with English accents, but the white walls bear his oil paintings of the Skye landscape in red-browns and mustard yellow and the deep blue slate of the Atlantic.

Myles's reluctance to give up the tenancy of the croft at Breakish reflected a wider reluctance in both him and his wife Eleny to accept that they would stay in London, despite having lived there for nearly thirty years. Every time I visit, one or the other of them is apt to mention some new scheme they've been discussing recently – a house swap with a Highland family, perhaps, or a new start somewhere on the English coast. Something, anyway, that would pitch them directly from inner city to remote location. The boys do not want to go.

For my uncle, that croft kept up a tie between him – and, by association, the whole family – and Skye like an umbilical cord, a legal paper trail of personal heritage that signified so much, but in actuality boiled down to only a strip of scrappy pasture that we don't even own. I was a Skye man, it said. And, although I've changed, at any point I could return to this place and be a Skye man again.

Myles did know more about the family explorer. Angus was his great-grandfather Martin's uncle, he said. 'He discovered a region in Australia and opened it up for the British. The area he discovered was called Gippsland, after Sir George Gipps, the governor then. You might have to go and find out all about it.'

I made a non-specific sound. 'Maybe I should.'

'The McMillans were a big family, and most of them went abroad. Dad was always telling us stories about their adventures. Martin was a captain on the clippers sailing round the Horn and back with wool. One brother took ill with measles on board ship and died. He was put ashore and buried on Tierra del Fuego.'

I smiled wistfully to myself, visualising and then weighing the phrase 'latest in a long line of adventurers' in my mind.

Myles also seemed wistful. He was a wanderer too, in his youth, a traveller who carried his home on his back. 'Personally I've always yearned to see Australia. To see the coral, swim around the Great Barrier Reef. Those red deserts ... Angus has a statue somewhere over there, apparently. I'd like to see that too.'

'Where?'

'In Gippsland, which I'm told is in Victoria ... More research needed, I think, before you go booking any tickets.'

More research needed. I took it as an order, and started to read.

It started promisingly, with the entry in *The Australian Dictionary of Biography*:

Angus McMillan (1810–1865), explorer and pioneer pastoralist, was born on 14 August 1810 at Glenbrittle, Isle of Skye, Scotland, the fourth son of Ewan McMillan ... He arrived in January 1838 with letters of introduction to Captain Lachlan Macalister, who made him ... manager at Currawang in the Maneroo (Monaro) country and he began there in February 1839. In this year he learned much bushcraft, befriended Aboriginal tribes and after an eventful journey in May climbed Mount McLeod and glimpsed the plain and lakes country of Gippsland.

McMillan pioneered Gippsland and spent the rest of his life contributing to its welfare ... He died while extending the boundaries of the province he had discovered. Although he received little wealth from Gippsland, his journals and letters and those of his contemporaries reveal him as courageous, strong and generous, with a great love for his adopted country.

I read the entry with a thrill of pride, printed it out and basked in the reflected glory. Soon after, I stumbled upon a second-hand copy of Ken Cox's florid hagiography, *Angus McMillan: Pathfinder*, online ('the story of one man's battle against natural obstacles'), and when it arrived I pored over it like a gospel, underlining the most flattering passages.

On the inside cover I found a ballpoint inscription declaring the book the property of 'Cllr Robinson, Port Albert', and a map of the first European explorers' routes through and around the state of Victoria and its surrounds, showing McMillan's explorations in their proper context.

Each was given a different mark to denote their routes. The first forays into the region were confined to the coast. The earliest, marked COOK 1770 and characterised by a trail of dots and crosses, was shown to swoop in from New Zealand to the south-east, hit the Gippsland coast at Point Hicks, turn and follow the coast round Cape Howe and north towards Botany Bay, in the southern suburbs of modern-day Sydney.

Cook was not the first European to encounter this mysterious continent – a series of seamen working for the Dutch East India Company had sailed along the northern coast and skiffed the underside of Tasmania over the previous century – but his expedition would prove crucial to the future of the new land. Evidence submitted to

Parliament by members of his party (notably the onboard botanist Joseph Banks) would lead to the founding of the first convict colony in 1788.

Short choppy dashes showed BASS 1797 sailing south from Sydney in a whaleboat as he sought to prove the existence of a strait separating Van Diemen's Land (now Tasmania) from the mainland. He skimmed Wilsons Promontory, where the tiny Little Penguins come ashore, briefly touched land at Western Port Bay, before shooting back the way he came.

Then came GRANT 1800 (long, confident dashes), the first to sail Bass Strait from west to east, and MURRAY 1801 (the dot-dash, dot-dash of Morse code), discoverer of Port Phillip Bay, a shallow inlet leaping with dolphins and whales, on the shores of which Melbourne would later be founded.

Inland, it was another twenty-three years before HUME AND HOVELL 1824–25 (Xs and dashes) made the first inroads into Victoria, hiking south with a party of convicts from the former's home at Lake Hume, trying and failing to cross the Great Dividing Range at what they christened Mount Disappointment, before finally forcing their way over and down to the coast at Port Phillip.

From the Monaro plains of New South Wales, McKILLOP 1835 shortly came tripping down in a line of tiny cross-stitches, coming to a halt at Lake Omeo. Then HUTTON 1838, represented as the noughts to McKillop's crosses, edged in along the coast from the east, reaching the golden shore of Lake King before turning back. Despite these incursions, an enormous stretch of land between these lakes and Port Phillip Bay remained – to the Western colonists – entirely unknown and unexplored.

At last, the name I was looking for: McMILLAN 1839–41. In dense black dashes he was shown tumbling down the Snowy River gorge to Mount Macleod, where he was pulled up short by the hard going and the threat of hostile tribes, turning north to McKillop's outpost at Omeo, then immediately south again along the banks of the Tambo River. Finally successful, he headed west, fording rivers as he went, then south across flat plains to hit the coast at Port Albert. He did not know it then, but this fertile country would become his adopted home, where he would shoot from obscurity to high society.

A final set of marks – circles separated by lines – shows STRZELECKI 1840 piggybacking along McMillan's tracks to the Macalister River, before striking off towards Western Port Bay. The so-called Polish 'Count' Paweł Strzelecki's overlapping journey and rival claim to the title of 'discoverer of Gippsland' would come to trouble my relation greatly in his latter years.

I devoured the book in a couple of days, a fanciful portrait of a daring hero that even I found overblown, and turned back to the internet for more. My appetite for information was limitless. But there was plenty to find: photos of cairns built in his memory, a panoramic painting of the view from his homestead (lush grassland, blue-tinged mountains far behind, Aboriginal children playing on a fallen tree) by the Austrian-born artist Eugene von Guérard, and facts, facts, facts, each sending me spinning off on another internet spiral.

But one too many searches brought me finally to an uncomfortable discovery. It started with a single, sobering sentence in a news report dated 2005.

A Scottish pioneer revered as one of Australia's
foremost explorers faces being erased from maps
amid accusations that he was responsible for the
cold-blooded murder of hundreds of aborigines.

I skimmed it quickly, expecting more praise, more admiration, and didn't digest the words completely until an odd dropping sensation alerted me to the new discovery. I recognised the feeling at once, an uncomfortable, visceral reaction I've had sometimes while working on investigations – a new scrap of incriminating evidence, perhaps a footnote in a company's accounts or an unexpected name on a title deed, will set my nervous system clanging like the sounding of a gong before I've even realised what I've found.

'Wait, what?' I thought, sending my eyes spinning back up the way they came.

I read the sentence again, and felt a gradual unspooling inside me. The next paragraph hammered the point home:

The aborigines are calling for the electoral district
of McMillan in the southern state of Victoria to be
renamed out of respect for the men, women and
children they say were slaughtered by Angus
McMillan and his 'Highland Brigade' in the
massacre of Warrigal Creek. The 1843 massacre
was one of several attributed to McMillan,
originally from Glenbrittle, Skye, and his band of
Scottish settlers, who ... are accused of carrying
out a genocidal campaign against the aborigines for
a decade.

'Oh,' I thought. Just: 'Oh'. Not sadness or disappointment or the trundling, wondering, what-does-this-mean? All of that came later. I was simply stopped short. I opened up the search bar again and began to type. 'Angus McMillan', I started, then paused to assemble my thoughts. As I hesitated, a list of suggestions popped up unbidden:

Angus McMillan Gippsland
Angus McMillan explorer
Angus McMillan massacres

I clicked the third option, with a thrill of anxiety. Soon I had drawn up a list of dates and places and sketchy details of what, I learned, have become known as 'the Gippsland Massacres'. The placenames alone invoked a chill.

1840–41, Nuntin: Angus McMillan and his men kill unknown numbers of Gunai people in skirmishes during 'the defence of Bushy Park'

1840, Boney Point: During one such skirmish, 'a large number' of blacks pursued and shot down at confluence of Perry and Avon rivers by McMillan's men

1841, Butchers Creek: McMillan's stockmen chase and shoot down 'a party of blacks' at a headland to the north of Bancroft Bay

1842, Skull Creek: Unknown number shot down west of Lindenow in reprisal for death of two white shepherds

1843, Warrigal Creek: More than 80 (as many as 200) shot down by Angus McMillan and his men following the death of Ronald Macalister

1844, Maffra: Unknown number killed in rumoured
skirmish
1846–47, central Gippsland: 'At least 50' shot
during the search for a white woman supposedly
held captive by Gunai people
1850, Slaughterhouse Gully: 16 thought to have
been shot down near the 'Pyramids' rock
formation by the McLeod family and their men
1850, Brodribb River: Unknown number shot
down during 'hunt' along riverside

I realised that I had stumbled upon a dark secret. Far from
the romance of our family folklore, Angus McMillan
appeared to be a dark character responsible for some truly
terrible deeds. And more than that: over recent years, his
name has come to symbolise some of the very worst
excesses of Australia's violent colonial past.

It is easy, as a Scot, to assume a certain martyr complex.
Historically speaking, we have been cast as the plucky
victims who struggled bravely on in a fight that was
weighted against us from the start. And without thinking,
I had absorbed the national story as my own.

Every past injustice is hammered home in history lessons
at school: wars upon wars in which our plaid-wrapped
men ran fearlessly to their deaths, armed only with clay-
mores and shields, their throaty war cries harmonising
with the skirl of the bagpipes and the shrieks of the bloody
and bruised in the great symphony of battle.

We remember the sacrifices of our people *en masse* at
every football match, every rugby match, at the end of

concerts and parties, with voices raised and quavering with emotion:

> O Flower of Scotland
> when will we see
> your like again,
> That fought and died for
> that wee bit Hill and Glen
> and stood against him.

We remember our scorn for the colonising English, who took our land, stole our freedom and stamped on our culture as well, suppressing traditional music, our national dress, the Gaelic language. But, we tell ourselves, we have not been cowed. Our national pride, our *hunger* for freedom, for self-determination, remains:

> But we can still rise now,
> and be the nation again
> that stood against him.

The belief in our nationhood is as strong as ever, our indignation still bubbling. We are proud still, and angry, and self-righteous. And quite right too.

But, as in everything, the full story of the Scots is complex. It is full of threads that will not tie neatly together, and details that do not always flatter that sense of self-righteousness. Even the Battle of Culloden – the great slaughter that finally crushed the Jacobite rising in 1746, so often invoked as a symbol of the triumph of the ammunition of the English over the courage of the Scots – was the culmination of what was as much a civil war as a war between nations, as clan turned against clan, seduced by the sophisticated south or the desire to settle old scores.

Many of the most enthusiastic proponents of the British Empire would emerge from among the Scots. Only a year after the bloodbath of Culloden, Prime Minister Henry Pelham declared that 'every Scotch man who has zeal and abilities to serve the King should have the same admission with the administration as the subject of England had'. It was a shrewd move on the part of the British government, and one that would see the colonial administration becoming increasingly Scotch in character over the following decades.

Britain sent at least forty governors of Scottish descent to America before it declared independence in 1776, including General John Campbell, governor general of Virginia and commander-in-chief of British forces in North America during the Seven Years' War (he was later replaced by James Abercrombie, another Scot).

As the American colony grew restless, it was Pitt the Younger's Edinburghian right-hand man Henry Dundas – bitterly nicknamed 'the uncrowned king of Scotland' – who called most vocally for the harsh punishment of the rebels. He also devoted much time and energy to blocking attempts to outlaw the slave trade – according to one estimate, he single-handedly delayed its abolition in the British Empire by ten or fifteen years through his 'skilful obstructions'.

As Home Secretary, Dundas acted to open India to his fellow Scots, and they soon came to dominate the administration of the colony and the East India Company. The first three governors general of India were Scots, and later, seven of the twelve viceroys. Others, like Sir Arthur

Hamilton-Gordon, son of the Fourth Earl of Aberdeen, skipped from colony to colony, serving as governor of Trinidad, Mauritius, Fiji, New Zealand, and finally Ceylon (modern-day Sri Lanka).

Thus in America, India, the Caribbean and the Pacific, the hand of empire stretched out in the form of opportunistic Scots, as the colonised became the colonisers. In Gippsland, Australia, Angus McMillan wreaked destruction upon the indigenous people in the name of British expansion.

I had known – however vaguely – that men like him had existed. Men who had fled a homeland made miserable by colonisation, then made it their lives' work to extend the empire, some of them, like McMillan, killing wholesale in its name. But whereas previously they had been aberrations, incongruous footnotes to a rousing narrative, now here he was, right there in the family tree. Part of my story, part of my heritage, part of *me*.

I returned to London determined to put the whole sorry business out of my mind. I took another job, at another paper, and tried to concentrate on fitting in and getting on. But I couldn't forget what had been, for me, a momentous discovery. It rolled around in the back of my head, unsettling me. All my easy assumptions about my heritage had proved to be flimsy.

What I was feeling reminded me of a concept I'd once stumbled across in a book: 'intergenerational guilt'. It described a generation of Germans who felt a profound sense of guilt and remorse for their nation's role in the Holocaust, although they had not been born at the time it took place. At the time I had flicked through the pages with indifferent curiosity, but now I rolled back through their reasoning. I couldn't help but wonder: what responsibility for our ancestors' actions do we all unwittingly take on?

It seemed to me that McMillan's story sat at the very crossroads of what makes a person victim or aggressor, good or evil. From my reading I had been presented with two characters: McMillan the hero – the hard-working, generous Scot honoured with plaques, portraits and cairns – and McMillan the villain – a bloodthirsty tyrant who rampaged through the bush, cutting down unarmed women and children. But what was the truth? I was left with the task of fitting both together to construct the image of one man, seen from two different directions.

Was it the views of his contemporaries or the harsh realities of life in the outback that had prompted such an apparent transformation – from virtuous Presbyterian lad to cold-blooded killer – or even the ravages of the landscape itself? I struck upon the idea of travelling to Australia to retrace his journey, as closely as I could, in search of the answer. Perhaps I might find it wandering still the rough tracks through the bush in the Snowy River gorge and the foothills of the Australian Alps. Perhaps it was grazing with the cattle in the Gippsland pastures.

There too I could confront the true legacy of McMillan's actions by seeking out the present-day representatives of the Aboriginal group he had terrorised. What state were they in? What could I do to help them? Would they want my pity? I had no way of knowing; I would have to go there to find out.

2

But for the Sea

It started with a departure, as so many stories do.

Friday, 8 September 1837. Angus McMillan stood on the dockside in Greenock, looking for the ship that would carry him across the ocean. All his goodbyes had been said, all his belongings stowed in sturdy wooden trunks. He was an emigrant – or rather, a would-be emigrant. All he needed was to secure his passage to the other end of the earth.

McMillan had a vessel in mind: the *Minerva*. His friend Allan MacCaskill was already booked to travel on it to the colony of New South Wales. Or 'New Holland', as McMillan still called it, an old name that conjured up some of the old mystery: unknown coastlines, islands of knowledge swimming in great seas of empty mapspace. He had seen her too, her great bulk at the quay, the bright flags flying, readying herself for flight. But there was no room, said MacCaskill. All her berths had been filled.

Half of Scotland seemed to have got there ahead of him, and they all seemed to have planned in advance. Men in plaid, cheekbones protruding like broken glass; hollow-eyed women with children hiding in amongst their skirts; families with everything they owned slung onto their backs. All desperate for passage on board, an escape, pouncing upon what tickets there were. They were rats from a sinking ship, and McMillan was one of them; paws scrabbling for purchase on polished decks as an entire country upended beneath them. Those who had lost their grip were flooding out through the ports across the ocean, looking for a new life in the New World: New Zealand, New South Wales, New York, Newfoundland. They'd go anywhere there was room to sit down.

He, like many of his compatriots, had mixed feelings. Sailing out from Barra, only three days previously, he had pressed himself against the rail to watch the retreating shores of the beloved island slipping away from him, *not for their sake*, as he told his journal, *but for the love of some of its ever to be remembered inhabitants.** Clear light danced on a rippling sea, flecked far off with the fins of basking sharks soaking up the late-summer sun. But none of this could cheer him, nor his friend Finlayson Kilbride. *Alas he had no cure for the deep wounds of my tortured heart.*

Still, it had been set in motion. The future beckoned, and however reluctantly, he had heeded its call. *O'er the blue waves I go.*

After a long day trudging the docks, from agent to ship and back again, McMillan retired to his inn and MacCaskill with no news to speak of. The ship's crew had only confirmed MacCaskill's warning: there were no second-class berths, and all the first-class cabins were already filled. *As for going in the hold*, he wrote, *I could never dream of it.* The *Minerva* had not long retired from her career as

---

* Italicised text is directly quoted from McMillan's own journals.

a transport for convicts, and conditions on board were little better now than they had been then. He could not face all those weeks below deck: the double layer of bunks down either side, no ventilation, no natural light. Two to a bed. For four months! God only knew the horrors of the hold, the filth and the lice and the disease that would whip through the steerage passengers as they lay packed together at night, waves slamming the hull by their feet. For all this they would pay £21 a head. No. He did not have much, but it had not come to that, not yet.

But what were the alternatives? A whole day's enquiry had turned up little else. There was space in the cabins on the *Bullant*, but that would cost £74 – his entire savings. Or he could try Liverpool, and spend yet more of his dwindling funds getting there, with no promise of a better offer. All around him, others were making the same calculation: what worth pride, when with every day their financial position was weakening? But then, to arrive ragged in the port at the other side, one of those pale, faceless hundreds – poor wretches – *that* could cost a man more than could be bought back at the other end.

McMillan at least was saved the trade-off. A breakthrough came that evening just as he undressed for bed, still wrangling with his own pride and preparing for another day of ships' agents and haggling. A gentleman arrived at the inn seeking him by name: the captain of the *Minerva*, he said, had sent him with a message. There was a berth in Captain Furlong's own cabin, which McMillan could have for £55.

The deal was done. Now there was little to do but write his last letters home, and wait with nervous anticipation as the *Minerva* finished her toilette. He bought copies of the New Testament in town, and sent them on a boat bound for the Western Isles to the young women of Barra: his sisters, Miss Finlayson Kilbride, and his *dear Miss Margaret* – his first love, who he was leaving behind. Oh, the agony of waiting! With every passing day he was forced to renew his resolve.

God's will be done. And God's will, he reminded himself, was that he must go. On Monday, seeking solace in prayer, he went to the kirk twice, both in the morning and in the afternoon. But it left him cold. *The clergymen I heard were strangers.*

Hold steady. Tuesday dawned and they filed aboard, heavy trunks stowed neatly under narrow bunks. Anchor up, sails unfurled. Course set for the south. After all the anticipation, all the hanging around, there was a carnival atmosphere. At night the steerage passengers ventured up onto the decks and danced under the stars in delight. But McMillan was in no mood for celebrations. *They should employ their time to better advantage*, he thought darkly, and retreated to his cabin to scribble in his journal and dwell on the dark coast that drifted ceaselessly by, inch by inch, behind him into the night.

He would never go home again.

At twenty-seven, he was already a man with some experience of the sea. An islander by birth, he had grown up in and around boats; he knew well the whip of the wind and salt spray on the face, the constant shifting of the deck beneath him.

He and his family had spent their lives skipping between the Hebridean islands, as his father Ewen sought out suitable positions to support his growing brood. Angus was the fourth of at least fourteen children, a large family even in those times; and though the McMillans were not poor, relatively speaking – Ewen was a tacksman, a sort of intermediary between clan chief and the peasantry, the closest equivalent to a middle class in traditional Highland society – their position was unstable.

The agricultural revolution sweeping Scotland was rendering the role of the tacksman obsolete as more and more English managers and 'land economists' were brought in to commercialise the vast Highland estates. Change was afoot; the McMillans kept on the move. They had started in Glen Brittle on the Isle of Skye, at the foot of the forbidding Cuillin ridge. It was the domain of Macleod of Macleod, the clan chief who – when not in London – lived at Dunvegan Castle, twenty miles to the north-west.

As tacksman Ewen had made a name for himself as a grafter and an innovator, importing new, improved breeds of sheep from the mainland, before he met and married Marion, a well-connected local girl both well educated and deeply devout. Their growing brood had been instilled with the importance of religion and education, of leading a moral life, and the skills for self-sufficiency necessary in a remote community.

But across the Macleod estate, rents were rising like the tide, and there was no extra money coming in to pay them with. When their nineteen-year lease came to an end, the family packed up and sailed west, first to South Uist, and then to Barra, a jewel of an island just to the south, where Angus spent his formative years. The then laird, General Roderick MacNeil, had converted from Catholicism, and brought numbers of Protestant outsiders onto the island after inheriting the estate in 1822; the industrious – and numerous – McMillans took to their subsidiary role as lay missionaries as energetically as MacNeil could have hoped.

It had been an outdoor, practical, windswept childhood; one spent trudging through rain and snow and hail, mending fences and lambing sheep, navigating small boats through the wild gales that howled their way down the Minch. So, on board the *Minerva*, he stared up at the sails and out to the horizon with a critical eye, and noted the ship's pace and progress in his journal each day. Within a few hours, his spirits began to sink: *our craft does not appear to be a good sailor*. But conditions were good, at least. The coast of Ireland appeared within the day, and then Wales. *Fine leading under single reef top sails*. The wind was behind them, blowing them straight down the Irish Sea, and out into the Atlantic Ocean.

I too was now twenty-seven. It had taken eighteen months to get things in order – or, more accurately, sufficiently disordered – so that I might head off in pursuit of Angus McMillan. I'd left my job, left London, amassed some (already dwindling) funds, and booked my own passage to Australia.

Before I left, I returned to Skye for a last look. I need to get closer to him; to nestle in close to the heart of this strange man and listen for his pulse. I was thinking of the tombstone with his name *in absentia*, of the black gabbro cliffs of the ragged-edged range that loomed over McMillan in his infancy. I wanted to see it all afresh, start at his beginning and work from there.

I had dragged my boyfriend with me. Well, 'dragged' is unfair. Alex loved the Highlands as much as I did – more, even. He was a Londoner who dreamed of moors and mountains, who saw the whole of Scotland as a sort of adventure playground of snow and rock, of peaks to be scaled and troughs to be traversed. He'd been dragging me to remote parts, to the tops of mountains and to icy trig points – fingers of cement rising out of the rock, shrouded in mist, encrusted in windsculpted ice – for months.

It was winter now; we'd been living together since the spring. Our reckless love, a whirlwind of promises and declarations, had culminated in a hasty move to the countryside. Each of us had seen in the other an easy solution to problems we had not yet been ready to voice. But now, in our house in a village in the north of England, each of us had been sitting in separate rooms, making separate plans for the coming months. We had made a deal: meet you back here in spring. 'We'll be fine,' we each said to each other. 'It's not so long.' And we smiled with our mouths but not with our eyes. This trip would be our swansong, but we were not yet ready to voice that thought either.

Since my visit with my mother, my brother Rory had moved to Skye with his wife to start a family. Mum and her siblings had been almost euphoric at the announcement; the family claim to the island had been shored up, brought from the academic into the actual and made solid again. Myles was in the process of handing over the family croft so my brother might build a house on it.

Alex and I drove north, the car packed with everything we owned, love blooming in my heart as the neat dry-stone-wall stitching of Cumbria gave way first to the long slow slopes of the Southern Uplands, and then to the bleaknesses and steepnesses of the Highlands. Winter was closing in, and with it came the all-encompassing dark. At Cluanie we slowed to a crawl, wary of the red deer that had come down off the hills to amass along the roadside, lantern eyes glinting in the darkness like some terrible premonition. I nosed the car into their midst, taking care not to touch one with the bumper and jolt this dream sequence into the real, and slid to a halt as the largest stag stood his ground in the centre of the road. He raised his head, many-pointed antlers silhouetted against the gloom like a great pair of wings opening. Then slowly, insolently, he turned and bounded down the bank, white rabbit-tail flashing in the shaft of headlight.

Poring over the map that night, my eyes alighted on a small grey square near a bay pockmarked with the stippled texture signifying pebble beach. 'Glenbrittle House', said the label. McMillan's childhood home. I waved Alex over, but his eyes snagged instead on the mass of contours to the near east: the Cuillin ridge, all tumbling crags and chutes of scree. He cared little for my murdering relative; he ached instead for the feel of cold rock under his hands. We made another deal.

In the morning we set off again for the hills, heating on full blast and rain blattering at the windscreen. Talking in undertones, still half asleep, we nearly didn't see the bird hunched in the middle of the road, watching our approach with wide yellow eyes as he guarded some small prey in his talons. Alex slammed on the brakes as the bird took off, but too late and in the wrong direction. He launched and flew directly into our path, glaring in at us through the windscreen. At the last moment he lifted, but not enough – he clipped the roof of the car with one wing. I shrieked and craned around to see him whirl and right himself in the air, wings outstretched and as unsteady as a drunk.

A golden eagle. I'd never seen one before, not in the wild. Only those depressed, scrawny specimens on their Astroturfed perches at game fairs, shackled at the ankle. 'Is that a good omen or a bad one?'

'Good,' said Alex definitively. 'He survived.'

'Yes,' I said. 'I hope so.'

The road wound a slalom path down into Glen Brittle, through a neat-penned conifer plantation. Stray larches pressed against the wire, stretching their feathery arms out between the strands. Dead pines swayed, monuments to themselves, bare of needles but shrouded entirely in thick white lichen like cobwebs, or lace – bridal somehow, so many Miss Havishams in their veils.

Snow had gathered in this sheltered nook, where ploughs rarely ventured. A single car had preceded us that morning, and its tracks wriggled down over the narrow strip of tarmac, bunny-hopping at places where the driver had nearly lost control. Neat heaps of grit had been left at five-yard intervals along the worst stretches by the council, so the locals could help themselves.

The Cuillin rose up on our left as we descended, recent snowfall exaggerating the terribleness of its crags, each crack picked out in the sharp black and white of a Victorian engraving; the jagged line of the ridge stretching above dark and forbidding, sharp enough to skewer a cloud to its highest peak. At its foot, the hillside was a magnificent technicolour of the clashing orange vegetation, darker bracken and flashes of bright, almost neon green where burns had overflowed and spilled out across the face of the slope.

We abandoned the car and hiked in to where the water rushing down off the mountains rumbled through a series of perfect turquoise ponds: the Fairie Pools. The noise was tremendous as the water crashed between levels, then slowed and stilled in the deep, dark channels between the rocks. I clambered down to a pool partway up the chain that had been split in two by an elegant underwater arch, and dipped an arm in up to the elbow. The water was gloriously, bitingly cold, numbing my fingers almost instantaneously.

Alex was impatient to be on his way, and set off alone towards the start of the ridge. I watched him go, then turned back towards the road, with the roar of the falls in my ears. Water was everywhere, slipping between the rocks, dripping on my forehead, resting in still pools and puddled on the ground, which was sodden as a dropped cloth. Where tributaries had cut down into the hillside, stripped birches huddled for warmth out of the wind, naked branches crimson. Erratic rocks dotted the burned-red hillside, teetering where they had sat so unsteadily for hundreds of years.

I waited at the car until I caught a glimpse of him silhouetted against the sky on the crest of the ridge, then drove down into the township along a single-track road, scattered with sheep-droppings. Here and there amongst the heather and peat bog that lined the foot of the glen clumps of hut circles nudged mushroom-like from the earth.

There wasn't much to Glenbrittle: a youth hostel, closed for winter; a mountain rescue base; a clutch of cottages, barely enough to call it a hamlet, where the glen opened up by the water's edge. Three lush fields, spotted with heavy-set sheep, led down to a dark pebble beach. The landscape was stark and unforgiving, the colours rich: the burgundy of the heather, the rusting bracken, the bare purple birch, the hawthorn's scarlet berries, the gleaming white snow of the peaks.

Glenbrittle House was easy to identify; a somewhat tumbledown, but nicely proportioned stone building, its grey-harl façade patched up in places with concrete. I was hovering outside, considering my options, when a young man stamped across the puddled road, enveloped in thick, kelpy green oilskins.

'Excuse me,' I blurted out, stupidly. 'Do you know which one is Glenbrittle House?'

He paused. 'The big grey one.'

I nodded and made to leave, but he spoke again. 'Do you mind me asking why you want to know? Only, it's my granny's house.' He was friendly enough, and about my age, with dark hair crammed under a beanie hat. He led me up the garden path and peeled off his waterproofs at the door as if shedding his skin, leaving his trousers cinched into his rubber boots. 'I'll fetch her for you. She often doesn't hear the bell.'

I stood politely on the doorstep in the rain, craning my neck to get a look inside. The interior was big and roomy, but dated – the hallway papered with photo-detail brick-work. Finally the owner came out, and blinked at me, cautious. She clutched a copy of the *West Highland Free Press* in one hand, holding it to her breast like a shield.

'Angus McMillan?' she said. 'Oh, no. I don't know. When was this?' She was a tiny, white-haired woman.

'1810?' I hazarded. She batted the air, letting out a puff of air – ho! – as if to say, 'Well, I'm not that old!' and her grandson and I laughed.

'It's been in our family, the MacRaes, for seventy years now,' she told me. 'Though it's not ours, you realise. We're tenant farmers. The whole lot belongs to Macleod of Macleod at Dunvegan.'

I nodded. Some things never change. 'Who else lives round here?'

She considered. 'There's just us, really. Our family.' She looked fondly at her grandson. 'There's a few moved in from elsewhere, but' – a bit disapprovingly – 'all just holiday homes.'

Down on the beach, I picked my way across the coloured pebbles and the seaweed lying thick and variegated as autumn leaves. Hailstones drew a white-rim tideline along the shore, like foam swept in off the sea. A band of rain drew across the bay like a curtain.

It was such an isolated spot. A man with thirteen siblings – perhaps more: records from that period are very partial – would never be lonely. But his parents would have been instrumental in the formation of his character. They were his only role models.

Out across the water I could make out the faint outline of the island of Canna. Directly behind it, unseen in this weather, was South Uist, the family's next stop, and to its south, McMillan's beloved Barra. Each of these islands has its own personality. South Uist, the flat sandy isle, tucks its head down out of the wind, its back grown thick with a fur of wildflowers upon the machair in summer: eyebright and lady's bedstraw, harebells and butterfly orchids, corn marigolds and sea bindweed, field gentian and red clover. Barra is a rougher, readier sort of place, its one green peak looming from the sea, slipping the earth from its shoulders like a shawl, smooth rocks poking through the slopes like clavicles, smoothed by the wind.

I visited Barra too, alone this time, and camped on a silver cockle beach unseen by any other; then, tramp-like, on a grass verge on the outskirts of Castlebay, the only village. I cycled the circumference of the island on a borrowed bike, otter-spotting, calling out in greeting to the curious seals that followed me along the water's edge, singing them nonsense songs and the scraps of pop music that popped into my head.

The McMillans' solid Georgian farmhouse at Eoligarry, on the north end of the island, has long been demolished, but I cycled up anyway, finding the tide out and the enormous expanse of white sand now employed as a runway for the tiny airport. Wind battering my face, I watched a twelve-seater propeller plane land, wheels bouncing on the sand, sending salt water up behind it in a sheet, carrying the post and groceries. Five figures ventured down the steps and out into the rain, bent double against the wind. Even today, I thought, this is a remote outpost of humanity.

Angus McMillan never explicitly explained in his journals why he left the Hebrides, but it is not hard to paint a picture of the prevailing tides that swept him from their shores. Scotland at that time was in crisis, both financial and existential. In the century since the union with England the ancient clan system had been dissolving, and dissatisfaction among the poor was growing.

Historically, the clan chiefs had held a position of paternalist responsibility over their subjects in a subsistence economy. However, since the advent of the United Kingdom, the lairds were becoming increasingly embedded in the moneyed society south of the border, frequenting the gentlemen's clubs of Mayfair and dabbling in Westminster politics. Keenly aware of their aristocratic status in Highland society, but without the vast incomes of the English landed gentry, they began to turn their attentions to generating new profits from their estates.

There has been much discussion of the motivations that underlay the turmoil of the subsequent decades, but whether the chiefs' decisions were driven by personal greed or simply market forces, the transition to capitalism would be a painful one. The great Highland estates underwent a seismic shift which saw unprofitable tenants, who had depended on the lairds for their livelihoods, displaced – initially to provide a workforce for the burgeoning kelp industry, and later to make way for sheep. To the peasantry, these upheavals were a profound betrayal of the trust they had placed in their traditional patriarchs.

Between 1780 and 1880, an estimated half a million people left the Highlands – some under their own steam, many under duress – permanently skewing the country's demographics towards the newly urban south and sending tens of thousands across the oceans to the New World.

It was not only the destitute who left, although many were destitute. For many young men like Angus McMillan, this was a chance to better themselves in new, more egalitarian countries, where land was cheap, or even free.

Coming from a culture where land equated to power more than money ever had, this was a startling opportunity.

Australia in particular was becoming a hub of migration from the Hebrides. Visiting Skye in 1840, the novelist Catherine Sinclair commented that every family she met seemed to have a member settled in or en route there. In Angus McMillan's immediate family, for example, it is known that four of the brothers lived at some stage in Australia: Angus himself, and his brothers John, William and Donald – who had also lived in Jamaica for some years before he joined Angus in Gippsland. A fifth brother, Norman, travelled to South America, only to drown in the Amazon.

The newspapers of the day were full of advertisements for cheap passages to the US, Canada and the new colonies of the far-off Southern Ocean, Australia and New Zealand. Some offered government assistance towards the cost. One such advert from 1835, placed by the Colonization Committee of South Australia, noted, 'Commissioners are also prepared to receive applications from such intending Settlers as may wish to have their Servants or Labourers conveyed to the Colony FREE OF CHARGE by means of the Emigration Fund.'

As the rural population dwindled, entire villages fell empty and were abandoned to the elements and to the blackfaced sheep that now grow fat on the grass that grows high amid the ruins. Huge round stones slip one by one from their places in crumbling walls to the ground; roof-less buildings shrink and sink as they are reclaimed by the land.

*

Balnabodach is one such village. It lies on the north-west edge of Barra, four miles from the pier at Castlebay, overlooking a tiny pebbled cove. I spotted it from the road as I cycled back from the airport, left my bike unlocked on the verge, shimmied under the fence where the sheep had got through, and headed down to inspect. A fat-rumped roan pony watched me uninterestedly as I waded through drifts of sphagnum moss, thigh-deep in places, as wet and as soft as a cloud. Within seconds my feet were squelching in their boots, peaty water oozing between my toes, my jeans soaked to the crotch.

The remains of the old village were rendered in texture and colour, most house sites made visible only by the changes in vegetation – rectangles of sheep-cropped grass gleaming amidst crowds of dark, rubbery reeds and the burned-out orange of the bracken. A single cottage was roofless but otherwise almost perfectly preserved, with a doorway and shoulder-height walls, the rocks dry-stacked, slotted together perfectly, its good condition a testament to the skill of its builder. Its windows had been sealed with rocks sometime in the distant past – the mark of the plague.

Across a stream and up a bank huddled four or five more ruins, in poorer condition. The walls had tumbled many years before; now grown over, but sitting proud to the ground, the same rounded humps of old graves.

It is a lonely prospect. In Angus McMillan's time – the 1820s and '30s – this would have been a busy, bustling township: a tight huddle of one-roomed blackhouses thatched with reeds, cattle penned at their backs as dogs and chickens roamed loose between the walls. But now there was nothing. Less than nothing; a palpable absence. A negative.

In the course of those two decades, a financial drama unfolded that would see the island's ownership fall from the hands of the MacNeils of Barra, who had held the title since the eleventh century. General MacNeil, who had brought the McMillans to the island, found he had inherited an estate shackled by legalities and weighted with liabilities. Although he had served with distinction at the Battle of Waterloo, this had apparently not been enough to impress his father, Colonel Roderick, whose lack of faith in his son's financial acumen had manifested itself in the imposition of a deed of entail upon the estate before his death to prevent its being sold off piecemeal; it had then been further bound with a large number of settlements to the colonel's other children. At the time of his death it was already foundering.

That same year, 1822, the bottom fell out of the Scottish kelp industry when the lifting of import restrictions after the defeat of Napoleon saw the market flooded with cheaper European alternatives. Until then, lairds had been able to produce a ton of kelp for around £3 – gathering seaweed from the beaches and burning it down to create soda ash – and sell it on as fertiliser for £20. By these vertiginous profits the MacNeil accounts had been buoyed. Without them, it sank without trace.

MacNeil the younger turned to ever more desperate means of staying afloat. He established an alkali works, so the kelp could be processed on the island and thus sold at a higher price, at which the islanders were forced to work. It failed miserably. He threatened local fishermen with eviction if they sold their catch in Glasgow or to passing boats rather than at Castlebay, where he could take his cut. He seized his tenants' cattle, and later their sheep.

There was not much else to take: 'The poverty of the people is beyond description,' their parish priest wrote in 1831.

For all of the islanders it was a time of enormous stress and uncertainty. Even the tacksmen, like Angus's father, were not safe: his counterpart in the south was evicted from his farm at Vatersay, which had been passed down in his family for generations.

The estate reached crisis point in 1837, when the general finally admitted defeat. As MacNeil was facing bankruptcy and preparing to sell up, Angus McMillan packed his bags and sailed for the mainland with the intention of joining his friend Allan MacCaskill on the boat to New South Wales. He was not alone. That same year, 1,253 other emigrants left Scottish ports for Australia, 2,391 for the American colonies (including Nova Scotia), and 1,130 for the United States.

This sorry tale forms the backdrop to McMillan's departure. He was, however, fortunate to have left in time to miss the very worst the Clearances had to throw at the island.

The Barra estate was sold to an outsider, Colonel John Gordon of Cluny. Gordon was a notoriously ruthless man of vast means – 'the richest commoner in the kingdom' – who on his death would leave £2 million and numerous estates scattered across Scotland as well as lucrative plantations on Tobago. Over the following decade the destitute tenants would be pushed from the estate, initially in a trickle and finally in a great torrent now regarded as one of the most brutal clearances of the period.

During the 1840s, a series of crop failures left the island in a constant state of near-famine. In one particularly bleak period, the minister reported 'a scene of horror' as starving families scratched in the sand for cockles, without which 'there would have been hundreds dead this day'. Gordon found that, far from the estate being an investment, he was now responsible for supporting the majority of its two-thousand-strong population. And so he began to evict them.

By the winter of 1850, the piteous state of Gordon's expelled tenants had attracted the concerned attention of the Lord Provost of Edinburgh, who heard reports that a number of families from Barra had arrived in the city 'in a state of absolute starvation'. A few months earlier, 132 families had been removed from their crofts, a feat accomplished by 'demolishing their cottages, and then, after they were cast out desolate on the fields, getting them shipped off the island'. None 'could speak a word of English' – only the heavily accented Gaelic of the island.

These wretched families had been dumped on the island of Mull, and from there some had struggled to Edinburgh in the hope of appealing to the colonel himself, who kept his headquarters there. But Gordon was not to be found.

Even if he had been present to meet his former tenants, it is unlikely that compassion would have been forthcoming. The next year he would call his poorest tenants to a public meeting to 'discuss rents and arrears', with a threatened £2 fine for non-attendance. The meeting was a ruse: 1,700 people from Barra and nearby South Uist were forced – begging, pleading and struggling – onto an emigrant ship bound for Quebec. Those resisting were dragged from the caves and mountains and handcuffed together on a boat that carried them from the tiny, wind-swept island to a vast, unknown wilderness of dense, dark forest and frozen wastes. When, finally, they were let loose on dry land there was an ocean between them and everything they had ever known.

In Balnabodach, all eight families still resident were forced on board ship, with only the clothes they had on. Not one of those recorded as living there in 1841 was to be found in the census of 1851. Today the name Balna-bodach can still be found on maps – a label for the smat-tering of modern white-harled cottages set high and apart along the road, far back from the ruins at the water's edge, to house people who have come here for the peace, the quiet, the tranquillity.

Standing there in the dell, out of sight, I realised that I had not spoken to another person all day. For the first time I appreciated the bittersweet nature of that Highland solitude I had thought so quintessential, so central to its character. Many of the most silent spots in the Highlands and Islands today were once the most densely populated – indeed, the devastating impact of the crop failures and the kelp-industry collapse had been attributed by some commentators to overcrowding. The emptiness of the glens is as artificial as once was its congestion.

I was alone that trip, but I had not felt lonely until now.

These lost generations maintain a presence in Scottish culture more than 150 years later. Songs and poetry writ-ten in the times of the Clearances circulate and recirculate, the hot breath of each singer taken in by the next, a constant oral reliving of that turbulent age.

The most famous, perhaps, is Sorley MacLean's 1954 Gaelic poem 'Hallaig', an elegy for an abandoned village on the author's native island of Raasay (*'Mura tig 's ann theàrnas mi a Hallaig/a dh'ionnsaigh Sàbaid nam marbh,/far a bheil an sluagh a' tathaich,/gach aon ghinealach a dh'fhalbh'*; 'I will go down to Hallaig,/to the Sabbath of the dead,/ where the people are gathered,/every single generation gone'). Or perhaps it is The Proclaimers' hit 1987 song 'Letter from America', which addresses the emigrants directly ('I've looked at the ocean/tried hard to imagine/ the way you felt the day you sailed/from Wester Ross to Nova Scotia').

They are songs of loss, of heartbreak, of the pain of being left behind. The departed wrote songs too, songs filled with the crash of the sea and the tug of the heart. Thoughts of home pull from deep inside, behind the navel, somewhere delicate and bruised and inarticulate. The emigrants are rootless, anchorless, their homesickness trailing like a long lead behind them, with no one holding on to it. Oh! for our dispossessed brothers. Oh! for the land of bleak beauty. Oh! for the touch of soft rain on the skin, for the peat smoke from the hearth, for the mud of the well-trodden path.

They have a saying in Nova Scotia, an expression of longing: *Ach an cuan* – But for the sea. But for the sea we'd be together again.

At Sabhal Mòr Ostaig, the Gaelic college in Skye, I watched a group of singers who stood stiff-armed at the centre of the dance floor; their leader alone at first, tapping her foot, eyes to the ceiling, harsh Gaelic consonants chopping through the low, rich tones of her voice.

Thoir mo shoraidh dhan taobh tuath
Eilean Sgithanach nam buadh
'N t-eilean sin dan tug mi luaidh
Àit' is bòidhche fo na neòil
Thoir mo shoraidh dhan taobh tuath.

Bear my greetings to the north
To the Isle of Skye and all its graces
That island to whom I gave my love
The most beautiful place under the clouds
Bear my greetings to the north.

From those exiled abroad, this song had crossed the miles and the years to pop up among us like a message in a bottle. Heard now afresh, it was a mournful keening to a long-lost homeland which sat only a few miles to my north, behind the Cuillin ridge, the Macleod estate: Dunvegan, Duirinish, Glenbrittle. The land of Angus McMillan's childhood.

A sharp intake of breath, and then the others were singing too, the warbling, flat-noted melody calling to mind the nasal tone of the chanter. And then, all around me, one by one, the voices of the audience were coming together too, soaring loud and clear and high up into the rafters above:

B'fheàrr leam fhìn na mìle crùn
Mi bhith nochd air tìr san Dùn
Mi gun coisicheadh le sùnnd
Rathad ùr aig clann MhicLeòid
Thoir mo shoraidh dhan taobh tuath.

54

I'd pay a thousand crowns
To be tonight ashore in Dunvegan
I would happily walk
Clan MacLeod's new road
Bear my greetings to the north.

Many of the singers that night had themselves travelled from what was once the New World back to the Old World, to rediscover their lost links to the Highlands. So many studying at the college were Canadians, Australians, New Zealanders, with names like MacDonald, Fraser and Munro.

They felt a tie, they confided by the bar late at night, a complex bond that is difficult to explain or understand. They felt compelled to return to a homeland they had never seen. Thousands of the diaspora return to Scotland every year; I watched them in my childhood, trooping through the village in their tour groups, keeping the tweed shop in business, cheering for the pipe band. Many are better-informed on the ins and outs of Scottish history than Scots themselves. Clan membership, particularly, is now dominated by overseas members who trade notes on the minutiae of family trees that have spread their branches across continents. Perhaps the locals feel they have nothing to prove; the visitors, with their foreign accents and long-lensed cameras, much.

But it was hard too for those left behind – those left standing in empty glens, watching first as the thatch of the empty homes collapsed, and then the walls. Imagine the desolation of the empty township, the abandoned schools, the silent churches. In Croik church in Sutherland, the dispossessed scratched messages in the glass of the windows as they sought shelter from the driving rain: 'Glencalvie people, the wicked generation'. They thought they were being punished for their sins.

The old ways were dissolving under their feet. The warriors who had once commanded fear amongst even the most stout-hearted Englishmen now found their skills and courage in battle repurposed for the furthering of the British Empire. What else could they do to earn money, in a world that now seemed to revolve around it? They knew of no other way to live.

The old tongue too was in the process of being phased out. Since the seventeenth century, the Highland nobility had been obliged by law to send their children to English-speaking schools in the south; more recent attempts to Anglicise the wild and rebellious population of the Highlands and Islands had resulted in the prohibition of the Gaelic language in schools, even in solely Gaelic-speaking areas – a ludicrous policy resulting only in classrooms filled with uncomprehending faces and dire literacy rates.

By Angus McMillan's time, Lowland policy had been relaxed somewhat, in that it allowed the teaching of the scriptures in Highlanders' mother tongue, so as not to inhibit their religious education at least. As a result Gaelic had begun to take on the quality of a spiritual mode of communication, a speaking in tongues. It was the vernacular of the church and the home, an unwritten language of confession, of conviction, of off-the-record conversation, while English became established as the language of the learned, the landed, the future.

But only the old language has the vocabulary to describe that particular flavour of Highland melancholy. Edward Dwelly's great dictionary, *Faclair Gàidhlìg* (1911), records forty-nine different words for sadness, each with its own special quality. *Snigheadh* sadness: also the act of falling in drops, the shedding of tears. *Mùig* sadness: darkness of mood, gloom, also snot, snivelling nose. *Mì-fhuran*: a churlish sadness, joylessness, a disinclination to welcome or congratulate. *Aithridh*: the sadness of repentance.

Longing finds twenty-four ways of expressing itself. In *fonn*, a carnal longing, also land, earth, plain, the drone of a bagpipe. *Leid*: uncomfortable longing, also a shake-down or bed made on the floor, a temporary fireplace. *Deòthas*: the longing for a loved one, as of a calf for its mother.

There are other words too, more subtle descriptions of a land that finds itself emptied of life.

Aibheis (noun): An expanse of sea or air, an abyss; a place full of fairies, or in ruins or unkempt.

Tannasgach (adjective): Abounding in spectres or ghosts.

Sporthail (noun): A subdued rattling noise, such as is made by a stone wall about to fall.

3

The Fever Ship

A month passed. Time moved slowly.

The *Minerva* was making heavy work of the voyage, and McMillan grew bored with watching sails appear on the horizon behind them only to speed by with demoralising ease, leaving the *Minerva* in their wake. He wished he had gone in another ship.

Daily he stared out at the sea, calculating their progress, growing impatient in his impotence: *Wind is fair this day, also E by S, steering SW, going about 5½ miles an hour. Lat 20 59 Long 22½°. Very warm.* They were surrounded by ocean on all sides, with nothing but their own company as they chased the horizon across its infinite expanse. McMillan's eyes raked the skyline as a man walking out at night casts around the circle of light given out by his lantern; he was watching for the coasts of new lands, the masts of strange ships that dipped in and out of sight on their unknown courses.

Four days before, they'd seen the Canary Islands, specks of rock in the far distance, but they hadn't sighted land since. Shoals of flying fish skimmed the surface of the waves, driving themselves into the air with slashing tails, then smoothly soaring on stained-glass wings. The heavily laden *Minerva* sat low in the water, and as the fish glided unseeingly forward they grazed the tops of the rails and came in to land, gasping, on the deck. They tasted like mullet, fat and sweet.

The shores of Cape Verde lay still a few days to the south, somewhere over the horizon, unseen. The passengers were listless, settling heavy as sand into the rhythm of life on board: biscuit and salt pork, lime juice, the strictly rationed water grown stale in its barrels, inertia. The stutter and sigh of conversation drying up. A Sunday service in the German missionary's stilted English marked off the weeks like the tally on a prison wall. But although his body was confined, McMillan's mind roamed free across the ocean, coasting on the thermals like a seabird; forward into the unknown, then inevitably backwards, to the comforts and the consolations of home.

He retreated to his cabin, braced himself against the rolling of the ocean, dipped a pen, and opened his journal. *Bright fancy brings me to the distant shores of green Barra, for my heart will throb with warm affection at the mention of thy ever remembered name. Often do I think of thee amid this wilderness of water, when nothing is heard but the roar of the tempest and nothing visible beyond our back but the lowering heaven and the rolling sea.* He knew that the lives of those he had left behind would still be rolling on without him as he trod water and stewed on his present condition: his past choices, his future chances, his lost love.

For McMillan the journey was uneventful. But below him, in the hold, the mass of his fellow passengers ran the full gamut of human experience. A young man, *in a poor state of health*, disappeared from his bed one day and was

59

never seen again; over the side, presumably, but who could say for sure? His poor wife, who had left his side only to prepare him a drink, would pass the rest of the journey scouring the ship in desperation. The German missionary held a funeral, in case. Afterwards, McMillan turned back to the ocean to regard the *merciless wave* afresh. He did not want to die, he thought, not without ever seeing his home again.

The German held another ceremony, a wedding for a young couple from Kintyre. Afterwards, McMillan eyed the lovers fondly as they danced on deck long into the night. He envied them. They would arrive in the New World together, secured to each other, and linked too by the other to their former existence. As for him, he would have to face the future alone: *I must own my weakness on thinking of dear — that loved me while I lived near her, and I hope will preserve my memory while in a foreign clime and under the heat of a tropical sun.*

He mourned the loss of his old life, with no aspect of the new one yet in view. He wrote to his brothers, his sisters, his mother, his father, his *Miss Margaret*, but the *Minerva* made no stop at any port, and the letters sat, unsent and unread, in his cabin. By the time they were sent, by the time he heard back, the news would be long out of date: they had been split apart like firewood, and there would be no putting them back together.

Time passed in an interminable haze of sorrow and introspection. He resolved that on arrival at his destination he would be a better man, *hereafter to do whatever I think to do my duty and work for the good and advantage of mankind. To be sweet and benevolent, quiet, peaceably contented, generous, easy company, humble, meek, diligent and industrious, charitable even of aliens.* He cleaned and waxed his boots. He set himself arithmetic problems. He wished for a faster ship. He prayed.

Though progress was slow, it was constant. Celestial signposts marked their advance: every day the sun rose higher in the sky; by now it was nearly directly overhead at midday. Constellations whirled in nightly dance, slipping down and down, taking their leave as they reached the edge of the dance floor, allowing new sets to take their places from the opposite horizon.

He grieved for things it had not occurred to him that he would miss. *Last night there was an eclipse of the moon. Totally eclipsed about 10 for it was quite dark then and the stars appeared beautifully, but I've almost lost sight of my friend the Great Bear.* He took the time to examine every facet of the life he had left behind and store it carefully in a file marked *home.*

It is not only distance that creates lags in communication. A gulf between my boyfriend and me had begun to grow even in the moments when we lay next to each other in bed. In the rush to clear our house and catch my plane, we had left important conversations unspoken and said a goodbye more ambiguous than I'd expected.

It had been a sorry parting, and one that I felt guilty to be causing. Before we left the house I had pressed my forehead to his chest and promised everything I had, and made him promise too, again and again. But this much I knew: all our belongings were either in our backpacks or in the boxes stowed away in my childhood bedroom awaiting a plan of action, of which we had none.

Still, I was on my way. And when I found myself safe in my seat on the first of several flights, uncontactable, in transit, my initial reaction was one of relief. Out of touch, out of office, out of sync with the world, I have always found the still point at my centre. My mind is always steadiest when my body is in motion.

It was late morning when I took off from London, but there was barely time for lunch before the dark came upon us and we flew on into the night. Lights were dimmed and blinds pulled low. The frequent fliers put their eyemasks on and tried to catch up with the world we were heading towards. Twelve hours later I was reluctantly awake in the gilded purgatory of Dubai International Airport, swilling the milky dregs of a double-strength coffee and watching the flights on the departures board tick up and up and up.

Unlike in McMillan's time, when it was a tangible and gruelling process, travel today is experienced in the abstract. On board a plane, the passenger moves extraordinary distances with relative immediacy, while signing over all autonomy to the cabin staff. One has no need to worry about food, or water, or even amusing oneself, while in the hands of these unreliable timekeepers who slow or speed the passage of the day depending on the direction in which you are flying: skipping from breakfast to dinner, or working their way down the aisles shutting out the light, heralding in the artificial night even as the sun burns fiercely upon the fuselage outside

I ate what food I was offered, drank what wine was given to me, slept whenever my eyes fluttered closed. I got drunk and confused, got off one plane and onto another, drank more wine. I passed out across a bank of empty seats, then snapped at the hostess when she woke me for my meal. Breakfast again. How long had I been travelling? It was an unedifying state of affairs. At least on a ship, as the mercury of the thermometer inches up degree by degree, and the stars slip from view to the underside of the earth, there is time for adjustment. Time to come to terms with the distance, both mentally and physically.

They understood time differences in McMillan's day — the disparity between the 'noon' of a clock set to Greenwich Mean Time and the actual noon observed from on board the ship had been used as a navigational tool since the seventeenth century — but in the nineteenth century it was not so pressing a reality as it is today, given the lack of immediate communication and the slow speed of travel. To those on board, it would not have been apparent that day by day their body clocks were adjusting themselves, that day was becoming night and night becoming day — that they were not, in fact, staring together with their loved ones up at the same moon every evening.

Jet lag began with the advent of high-speed travel, and it is hard, or at least it is hard while suffering from its effects, not to interpret it as nature's payback for tampering with the natural way of things: that long-distance travel should be appropriately protracted. It put me in mind of an aside in Douglas Adams's *The Hitchhiker's Guide to the Galaxy*, which quotes 'an ancient Arcturan proverb': 'However fast the body travels, the soul travels at the speed of an Arcturan Mega-Camel.' This would mean, it adds, 'in these days of hyperspace and Improbability Drive, that most people's souls are wandering unprotected in deep space in a state of some confusion; and this would account for a lot of things'.

Certainly, I arrived in Australia in a state of physiological and emotional confusion, my sense of purpose and understanding of my mission trailing some way behind, perhaps over Eurasia, certainly a considerable distance from civilisation.

I tottered through the streets of Melbourne, made top-heavy by rucksacks strapped to both my back and my front, navigating the gridiron central business district where tall glass skyscrapers jostled for space in their neat plantations. I was used to tangled, sprawling old cities, had always thought of the 'central business district' as a construct of urban development rather than as an actual physical location. But here it was, in poker-straight rows and columns like a computer simulation, every corner tipped with pedestrian signals at each axis, emitting a low, rhythmic chirrup in stereo from all around. In turn, they rose from their drumbeat in a crescendo of solid noise, cicadas taking the air on a remote hillside. In the still night streets it was disconcerting. At least navigation was easy: walk four blocks, turn, walk four blocks. Addresses here were like a game of battleships.

The hostel was an enormous, elderly institution close to the Queen Victoria Market. Downstairs was very jolly, all neon colours and glossy posters, but the bedrooms on the fourth floor had the atmosphere of a Victorian boarding house. At home, I calculated, it would nearly be time to get up. I lay sleepless on a metal cot in a cell-like room, and waited for the clock to tick round and the sun to right itself.

Angus McMillan, I thought. I need to find Angus McMillan, and then tie our lives together again.

*

McMillan and his fellow voyagers came in the second wave of immigrants to New South Wales: free men, who had decided to make the journey to the convict colony of their own accord.

Those aboard the *Minerva* were for the most part law-abiding, conscientious men and women, many of whom had been inspired to travel to the far side of the world by the writing of John Dunmore Lang, the first Presbyterian minister in Sydney, who was presently in Glasgow seeking recruits with whom to improve the colony. Lang deplored the wickedness and sexual licentiousness he saw in Sydney; an inevitable result, he wrote, of its beginnings as a repository for the criminal outcasts of British society. In a series of convincing polemics he called for willing members of his flock to populate a country that was, to his eyes, rich in opportunity yet poor in virtue.

These 'very superior' immigrants were promised land, an improved standard of living, higher wages, and an escape from the destitution of their homeland. Lang secured sponsorship for 140 Scottish tradesmen, much in demand among the largely unskilled population of New South Wales, and persuaded around four thousand more to emigrate under their own steam over the course of a decade.

McMillan himself carried a copy of Lang's *An Historical and Statistical Account of New South Wales* when he boarded the *Minerva*, which he read from cover to cover over the course of the voyage. It was a *very flattering account* of the country, he thought, and he was taken with one of Lang's poems, which he copied out in full during a bout of homesickness.

Thicker Than Water

No parent, sister, brother
Can greet me now – nor other
Earthly friend.
The deep sea lies before thee
But Jehovah's shield is o'er me
To defend ...

McMillan's own writing reveals him to be as devout a recruit as Lang could have hoped for. At his weakest moments he turns his gaze to the heavens, prostrating himself before the Almighty, he *who has the boundless ocean in the palm of his hand.* He repeats his motto again, and again, until his mind is still: *God's will be done. God's will be done. God's will be done.*

When the sailors slaughtered a sheep on the Sabbath, the young Highlander was outraged. The German missionary too attracted his wrath when McMillan spotted him whistling on the poop deck after a sermon. It was not the Gaelic way, McMillan said. (It's true – it is not. Even today the Sabbath is widely observed throughout the Highlands and Islands, particularly in Eilean Siar, the Outer Hebrides, where on Sundays many still refuse to work, watch television, exercise or drive a car except to travel to church. On Lewis there were protests when ferries introduced Sunday sailings in 2009.)

He tried to arouse the indignation of the other passengers, but there were few takers. His neighbour Taylor quoted the apostle Paul: 'Whatsoever is set before you, eat, asking no question for conscience' sake.' The German himself only *took a slow look of me and left me to discuss my argument alone.*

66

McMillan felt angry and isolated aboard this ship of heathens. Were they not on a mission to improve an ungodly land? He shut himself in his cabin and refused the meat, turned his face from the world. The captain, *a moderate man*, tried to talk him down. He was older, made wise by experience. McMillan was quite right, of course, he assured him. *He'd defy any one on board to say otherwise as I have the word of God on my side.*

But the realities of life in a primitive colony might loosen McMillan's chokehold upon right and wrong, the captain warned. *He said if he met me 40 years hence I would be of a different opinion.*

I knew where to find him. His words, at least. His journals – kept during three crucial phases of his life – are held in the State Library of Victoria, a neoclassical pile on the corner of Swanston and La Trobe.

I was there as soon as the doors opened, filed my complicated request forms and waited in the drab manuscript room in the bowels of the building. They arrived quickly, in cream accordion envelopes tied with string, and I unpacked them, fingers quivering over creased, delicate documents in their protective plastic sleeves. At last, the insight I was looking for, file 268/1: 'Journal of a cruise from Greenock to New Holland, 5 September 1837–22 December 1837'. In flowing hand, on the tall, thin pages of a handbound notebook, the thoughts of the young McMillan. I had found him.

It was strange to think that his inner thoughts, scrawled down in a cabin on the raging sea, were present in the here and now, in this buzzing bright-lit room more than a century later. Did he ever consider that they would be read by anyone other than himself, never mind pored over and parsed phrase by phrase by generations of researchers? By me? I suppose we all must, we diarists. Otherwise, what would be the point of recording our thoughts at all? If it were merely the act of writing we seek, we could write upon a slate and then wipe it clean.

I read as fast as I could, my eyes straining to find words in the looping, old-fashioned cursive. When the library prepared to close I stood on a chair and photographed each page, of this and the two later documents, and retreated to my hostel to continue detangling his words from the screen of my laptop. It was my first insight into the character of this man I had hitched myself to.

Much had been made of the negative aspects of his character – his superiority, his outspoken piety ('sanctimonious, intolerant and churlish', as one historian has described him) – but I was unconvinced. They should read *my* diaries, I thought, if they're looking for a case study in intolerance and churlishness. There was something sturdy about him, his optimism and his faith; his resolve to devote himself to work and to the furthering of mankind.

And there was a romance to him that I had not anticipated. During a storm far out in the ocean he listened as the wind *moaned in most melancholy tone through the rigging*. Outside, *a dark haze extended itself over the whole southern sky*. As sail upon sail was taken in and hatches secured, McMillan headed out onto the deck to stand in the lashing rain. *I stood silent and alone, thinking of Him who overrules the deep as well as dry land and gladdens our weak hearts when infused with fear.*

He had a comic turn of phrase, too. In another such storm, as the ship rocked *most fearfully*, he noted how *some of the passengers were thrown on their beam ends and rolled from side to side, like so many seals.* His sketches of his dinner-table companions were lacerating: the captain was a *gentlemanly fellow*, but a skipper from Greenock travelling as a passenger was of *a very cannibal appearance.* The German missionary was a *fat greasy man*, whose wife was *so extensive in raising the little finger for I have seen her gulp five glasses of wine and a tumbler of beer before 3 o'clock. (Oh, for a Highland lady*, he mourned. She *would hardly put her rosy lips to the glass*.) An Englishman called Simpson came in for special criticism: *a down right ass and a fool of all the company.* A Mr Mitchell, on the other hand, was *no better than a guttural mumbler.*

Ha. Perhaps it was my tiredness, my sense of being out of sync with my surroundings, but his particular brand of misanthropy appealed to me. As I sat alone in the hostel's bar, adrift in a sea of backpacker hedonism, I found myself strangely drawn to him, so tightly bound by his standards and his islander integrity.

Endless streams of European youths filed out of the main doors into the Melbourne streets, only to be replaced by yet more backpackers coming in, weighed down like packhorses with their rucksacks and carrier bags looped through and over every arm. Girls slept sprawled on the bar sofas, their backpacks like totem poles in every corner. The PA stuttered into life from the speaker above my head every few minutes with the Australian call to prayer. 'Come on down to the bar,' a disembodied voice wheedled. 'Half-price vodka, free beer pong until 10 p.m.'

'I can't wait for tomorrow night,' a Brummie lad told a pretty Czech girl beside me. She smiled blandly back at him, inviting explanation. 'I'm going to get muntered.'

In my tired, cantankerous frame of mind, I was enjoying McMillan's catty remarks and his Eeyore-like air. *This life*, he reminded me, in schoolmasterly reprimand, *is only a scene of variety which soon passeth away and affords no solid satisfaction, but in the consciousness of doing well, and in the hope of another life.* He was a strange, earnest young man. If he were to exist in the here and now, I reflected, he might have been sitting with me, nursing a glass of wine, glowering at all the fun-havers with as much venom as I was. The thought gave me heart.

Across the room, a rowdy drinking game came to some orgiastic conclusion as a stocky young man reared up and half-ran, half-fell out of his seat while his companions roared and heckled. He barged sideways, unseeing, into the nearest sofa, lost his balance and tipped bodily over the back and onto one of the sprawling sleeping girls. Pandemonium. The girl, thrust suddenly from dream into alarming reality, screamed in shock and fear. Strangers clapped and catcalled. The PA coughed again, theme and variation: 'Come to the bar before 10 p.m. tonight for free beer pong and half-price jugs!'

'McMillan,' I couldn't help thinking, 'if only you were here to see this.'

I turned back to my screen, read again McMillan's response to the captain's warning that in forty years he would have reconsidered the rigidity of his beliefs. McMillan would have none of it: *I answered, if I was spared to see another forty years that I hoped to be guided by the same guide.*

His comment came down upon me like a weight. Forty years later, I knew, McMillan would be dead. Within five, he would already have the blood of innumerable innocents on his hands.

I felt myself pulled by a complex tug of emotions. I'd come looking for a killer, and had instead found an earnest, headstrong man of my own age, full of ideals and expectations. What happened to him?

They had crossed the equator and found the earth upside down. Each change rang through him with a piercing tone: the new moon, when it appeared, had inverted. It looked strange, but also just the same. The southern sky at least was beautiful. At night he lay on his back on the boards and traced his finger down the sweep of the Milky Way, joined the dots of the Southern Cross, smoothed the smudges that marked the Magellanic Clouds.

And across that glorious sky in the daytime came *great flocks of birds*. Birds of all stripes: sea swallows and storm petrels; fowl of a sort the sailors called the stormy pheasant — *they put me in mind of the common plover, but much brighter in colour* — and another they called the castle pigeon, its back spotted with black and white. Albatrosses too, in their dozens, their six-foot wingspans *in beautiful dun colours*, dark eyes rimmed with white.

But while McMillan's eyes turned upwards, death stalked the deck, and down below, in the hold, all hell was breaking loose. Fever was taking root among the steerage passengers, spreading from bunk to bunk. McMillan was right not to have travelled there: they were dropping like flies. Almost every other day seemed to herald a new death.

The first victim, a three-month-old child, had died a month into the voyage. All the passengers had attended the service as the tiny body was consigned to the deep. A few days later, more bad news – the young woman who had been married on board was sick: *our surgeon reports her to be in a dangerous way.*

By the end of November, McMillan reported that ten of the steerage passengers were ill. He fretted that they must be suffering from a contagious fever, though the ship's surgeon assured him it was 'only a cold'. *I am grieved to say that I cannot rely much on his judgement. Fearful consideration if it proves infectious – no one has a chance to escape its ravages.*

And so it proved. A young unmarried man from Greenock was the next to die, and within hours another, a shepherd, laid low *by the strong arm of the King of Terrors.* McMillan worried for their souls – *how poor a time to meet God, when the mind is infected with disease* – and prayed that there would be no more deaths. But to no avail. The surgeon soon grew to regret his earlier confidence, as first his own father and then his mother were taken. *His oldest sister, by every appearance, is on the brink of the grave.*

By late December, another sixteen or seventeen were confined to the hospital. Far from help, the *Minerva* sailed on. They were far out in the Indian Ocean, thousands of miles from dry land. McMillan was running out of paper. He used his last scraps to prepare himself for the worst, and to reassert his faith. *If it is thy holy will to call me Lord, grant that all who are dear to me may be forever united in thy kingdom. Thy will be done and may I be submissive to it.*

He was resigned to his fate, whatever it might be. He crammed his last entry into the bottom corner of the page on 22 December 1837, still a month's journey from Sydney: *It is a beautiful day.*

*

72

The Fever Ship

The *Minerva* finally staggered into port on 23 January 1838. 'THE FEVER SHIP', as Lang's newspaper the *Colonist* greeted it, had by then lost fourteen to typhus fever, while eighty-six of the 198 steerage passengers had contracted the disease, including the surgeon, who was in 'a dangerous state'.

At that time it was not known how typhus was spread (via lice), but an inspector saw enough to attribute the cause of the sickness to the 'overcrowded state of the 'tween decks', where the steerage passengers slept crammed together. 'I am informed,' he added, 'that when the vessel left Scotland, the space between decks was [also] crowded to excess with lumber, which was made a receptacle of refuse provision, and filth of every description.'

McMillan and all the others travelling in the cabins had escaped its grip, but were obliged to spend three weeks in quarantine on board the ship, under a yellow flag in Spring Cove, before they were finally allowed to disembark.

Arrival in Sydney would have been a shock to the system for a good Presbyterian boy from Skye. In 1838 the colony was celebrating its fiftieth anniversary, but while Sydney and Parramatta were now under stable government, the rougher edges maintained a lawless, frontierland air. Around a third of the population still were serving prisoners but, in terms of numbers, the dominant group was now the former convicts who had served out their sentences. Unable to afford the return fare, they were marooned indefinitely in a continent-sized prison. Many were now pursuing their own interests, searching for suitable land on the margins of the colony

There, conversation tended towards the coarse, and justice towards the brutal. Survival required cunning and

73

self-interest, with little call for manners or sympathy for one's fellows. New arrivals often wrote home shocked by the discovery of how the realities of Antipodean life had robbed the colonists of human decency.

The very earliest arrivals had had the worst time of it. They had been dispatched from Britain in 1787 as a matter of urgency after the American Declaration of Independence in 1776 halted transportation of convicts there, generating enormous pressure on British jails. In Westminster, politicians watched with concern as elderly vessels were anchored in the Thames for use as prison ships, and convened an emergency parliamentary investigation: where could all these convicts go?

Evidence submitted by those aboard Captain Cook's expedition in 1770 – the first European encounter with Australia's eastern seaboard – was enough to convince the desperate policy-makers to send a fleet of boats carrying around 1,500 passengers, roughly half of whom were convicts, to establish what is now Sydney.

Incredibly, due to the time constraints, these reluctant colonists were sent out without any further reconnaissance. It took a gruelling eight months to reach Botany Bay, the proposed site of the new settlement, and perhaps another ten minutes after that to realise that this was not the green and pleasant land so stirringly evoked by Cook's botanist in the oak-panelled committee rooms of the Palace of Westminster, but instead a dry and alien habitat where the plants were unrecognisable, the soil arid, the climate treacherous and the animals unknown and often venomous.

They might have arrived on the surface of Mars for all they knew or understood about their new environment, and they were woefully ill-suited to master it. As the art critic and historian Robert Hughes has explained, 'The colony that would have to raise its own crops in unknown soil had only one professional gardener, and he was a raw youth of twenty. It would need tons of fish, but had only one fisherman. There were only two brickmakers, two bricklayers and a mason for all the houses that would need building [and] no sawyers.'

It was, to put things mildly, a very uncomfortable few years for those first arrivals, who struggled by on starvation rations as their crops failed year after year. Watkin Tench, an officer whose account of the colony's founding was published by Debrett's, wrote of those first, desperate months: 'Famine ... was approaching with giant strides, and gloom and dejection overspread every countenance. Men abandoned themselves to the most desponding reflections.'

The arrival of these incompetent pioneers had been met with surprising good humour by the local Aboriginal population. The Eora people, who populated the Sydney basin, had made some show of aggression on first contact, gathering in great numbers on the clifftops to brandish their spears and chant threateningly. ('*Warra warra*,' they shouted. '*Warra warra*.' Go away.) But they were intrigued by the new arrivals, and soon came down to investigate, leading to a scene of some geniality. 'They came round ye boats & many little things were given them,' the future governor Philip Gidley King recorded in his journal. 'Hatts was more particularised by them, their admiration of which they expressed by very loud shouts, whenever one of us pulled our hatts off.'

This initial bonhomie would soon give way to anger and resentment as boatload upon boatload of the British

75

began to arrive: the Second Fleet in June 1790, the Third Fleet in July of the next year. Thus began the trickle, which became the flood. In all, 825 convict ships were sent to Australia, averaging around two hundred prisoners aboard each. These white interlopers spread inland from Port Jackson like a plague, occupying the most fertile land and encroaching upon a culture that had successfully existed in its present form for tens of thousands of years.

It is impossible to overstate the disruptive effects that these settlers would go on to have upon the lives of the Aboriginal people. Of these, disease would be the most devastating, jumping from tribe to tribe, racing across the continent far in advance of even the most adventurous Europeans. Of the Aboriginal nations of south-east Australia, only the Gunai people of what became Gippsland and their neighbours the Ngarico avoided the smallpox epidemics that cut down their countrymen like scythes, first in 1789 and again between 1829 and 1831. They were probably saved by their hostile outlook and lack of interaction with rival tribes. How sad, then, that they would be so devastated by the Gippsland pioneers led by Angus McMillan.

Today's Sydney, with its clean, breezy streets, gleaming skyscrapers and iconic harbour, is unrecognisable from the fleapit that McMillan encountered, but it is still a mecca for travellers and immigrants. Arrivals at Central Station are faced with a street of towering youth hostels and hotels, while nearby George Street, where dim sum and noodle restaurants vastly outnumber any other type of shop – apart from, perhaps, the backpackers' travel agents offering budget tours – has a distinctly international feel.

I stopped there overnight, still brooding on the future that beckoned to the serious young man I had encountered in the journals. But I felt calm. I had direction again – I was back on a path he had beaten before me. From his arrival at the quayside, he turned inland into the dry interior, and set about learning the skills for life in the fledgling colony.

I paused just long enough to take in the sights – but like Angus, I wasn't stopping long. I was off in search of cowboy country.

4

The Cattle Station

The train line from Sydney wended through mangrove swamps and bays toothed with sharp island outcrops before twisting in on itself and heading north-west into the dry interior.

I had booked onto the New South Wales railway as I would a plane: handed over ID, checked in my luggage, printed out a boarding ticket in advance. The whole aesthetic evoked 1960s air travel: wide, blocky reclining seats, cup holders, metal ashtrays carved into cubby holes in the walls. The buffet car served hot canteen lunches: roast chicken with vegetables or spaghetti bolognaise, $9 each and served in foil-covered TV-dinner trays, ordered from the conductor before 11 a.m. and picked up in person at noon.

My carriage was nearly empty, but an uppity lady steward paced the train, checking and rechecking that no one had moved from their assigned seat or carelessly allowed their belongings to spill into the empty place beside them, as if the headmaster had recently offered her the chance to prove herself as bus monitor. Her silver bob was scraped back under a black velvet Alice band, lending her a waspish look. Every ten minutes she spoke in chiding tones into the intercom. 'For anyone who was planning to hop out at the next stop for a cigarette – smoking in train stations is *prohibited*.'

North of Newcastle the lush, thickety vegetation petered out and the land opened out into a wide plain. Abandoned buildings scattered the landscape, collapsed in on their withered beams like elephant carcasses picked over by scavengers. Corrugated-iron roofs were striped with rust the deep red of clotted blood. In the middle of nowhere we came upon an enormous stopped freight train made up of dozens upon dozens of linked cars, an endless centipede of industry. A mining company was stripping the earth of her jewellery. The Australian heartland may be bleak on the surface, but underneath there is endless wealth. Each year mining companies unearth more than A$100 billion (£50 billion)-worth of iron ore, bauxite, uranium, natural gas and other resources.

Outside, the temperature was floating somewhere over 40°C, warping the tracks and limiting our progress to two-thirds of the normal speed. We trundled listlessly through a succession of towns whose names aroused confused pangs of recognition in me: Lochinvar, Aberdeen, Scone. A route map on the side of the carriage told me that the track would terminate at Armadale. The settlers' habit of naming their new homes after their old homes struck me as oddly poignant; the reassuring familiarity of the names immediately offset by the clanging disparity between the two places.

I looked out at wide, sun-bleached avenues and backyard swimming pools, but thought of the razor winds of the North Sea, and the rain that slices horizontally through the granite city. I thought of the Armadale ferrymen whiling away long workless days in hotel bars as a freezing gale outside whips the ocean into an impassable fury. What would prompt someone to link these places with those? What a strange and illogical way to help yourself feel at home.

Even weeks later I still felt that odd shock of recognition on spotting familiar names on road signs, the way you feel on meeting someone who shares a name with your brother, or the school bully, or a childhood pet. It doesn't dissipate; the associations are too deeply ingrained. Mark, an English friend of my brother's who I met for brunch in Melbourne, had laughed when I mentioned this. 'Yes, it's so strange. The names are all so incongruous. Chelsea here is down and out, it's Camberwell that's full of the ladies who lunch. Croydon is north of Bayswater. We're through the looking glass.'

'And there's St Kilda,' I added, referring to the beach-side suburb in south Melbourne, newly fashionable after decades of infamy as the city's red-light district.

He raised his eyebrows, inviting me to continue, so I told him about the tiny, wave-battered island that sits alone far off the west coast of Scotland, about the odd hobbit people who lived there for generations, scrambling barefoot over the rocks, stealing gannets' eggs and wrenching up limpets, until the British government finally evacuated the island in 1930. The stench of seafowl and rotting fish.

'Well,' he said, 'maybe that one's not so different.'

I disembarked at Tamworth, the self-appointed 'country music capital' of Australia, whose main attractions are an annual music festival and the oversized golden guitar on the outskirts of town. The festival was long gone; the streets were deserted. The few human figures I spotted outside were eerie metal statuettes of country musicians making themselves comfortable on benches or mooching on street corners.

I was to be picked up the next day by Tim Skerritt, the owner of a cattle station an hour's drive out of town. Tim's 1,280-acre property offered greenhorns and travellers an opportunity to learn the skills required for station work: aspiring station hands (or 'jackaroos' and 'jillaroos') might try their hands at mustering sheep and cattle, learn the basics of field and fence care, and take away the all-important letter of recommendation to show potential employers. These incomers would help to fill a growing shortfall of capable station hands in areas where many of the local youngsters have been lured away by the six-figure salaries available in the mines – not so much a brain drain as a brawn drain.

Stockwork is still vital for the Australian economy, which was founded on the proceeds of the wool trade, and it lies too at the heart of the self-image of a country that owes so much of its creation to the never-ending wanderlust of the cattlemen.

When Angus McMillan arrived in Australia he came armed with a letter of introduction of his own, which quickly secured him work as a station manager on the Clifton cattle run owned by a fellow Highlander, Captain Lachlan Macalister, near Camden, New South Wales.

McMillan's link to Macalister was fortunate: the captain was a prominent settler, local magistrate and former head of the mounted police who had been granted this extensive tract of land in what was then known as the valuable 'Cowpastures' district, around fifty miles south-west of Sydney, as a reward for his distinguished military service. He had also acquired a 16,300-acre estate further south, near Goulburn, which he named 'Strathaird' after the peninsula on Skye where both he and McMillan were born.

By this time, 1838, the colony of New South Wales had outgrown its original boundaries and spilled over the Blue Mountains to the west into the vast plains the settlers found beyond. The colony was still a wild place, but with increasing numbers of free settlers arriving in their boat-loads, drawn by promises of land and opportunity, a fledgling bourgeoisie was forming, and society was beginning to settle into its component layers. Three classes were emerging: the convicts at the bottom, still to be spotted in unhappy rows working the roads, shackled together under the baking sun; the 'Emancipists', former convicts who had worked out their sentences; and finally the 'Exclusives', free men who had been posted abroad, or had even *paid* for the privilege of moving to Australia, and who were now at pains to distinguish themselves from the other sorry lot.

Camden, the nearest outpost of civilisation to Macalister's property, was moulded by the pretensions of the Exclusives. Today it is a town of 50,000 people, and the sort of place Australians like to prefix with the word 'historic' on road signs: full of redbrick post offices, ornamental street lamps and two-storey, net-curtained, bay-windowed houses. Later, I stopped by for an afternoon out of curiosity, parking my hire car by the public pool, and a sports field and Victorian grandstand neatly enclosed by white post-and-rail fencing like a racecourse.

There was still a steamy, colonial feel to the place. In town, Whiteman's Arcade sat in unfortunate placement across the high street from White Lady Funerals. A backstreet lined with rows of old brick agricultural stores led to the equestrian park, Cobbitty Pony Club and Miss L. Davies' Town Farm Community Gardens, where oddly stylish scarecrows decked out in dresses, straw hats and necklaces were crowding between the lavender rows and tangled English roses.

The streets were lined with weeping willows, elms and apple trees, all reassuringly familiar to European eyes in a country where nothing looks or works quite the way you expect. As one early settler wrote, in Australia the 'swans are black, the eagles white, the cod fish is found in rivers and perch in the sea, the valleys are cold and the mountain tops warm, the trees shed their bark annually instead of their leaves'. Another wrote of 'birds without wings, as large as deer, their bodies covered with hair instead of feathers; [and] beasts with the beaks of birds'.

For Angus McMillan there was a lot to learn about this baffling country, which could not have been more different from his beloved green Hebrides. The industrious Scot set to work at Clifton with gusto, and soon marked himself out to his employer as a man of solid constitution, steadfastness and Presbyterian work ethic. In short, he showed great promise. Before long he found himself Macalister's right-hand man.

But McMillan also found himself on the precipice of the class divide. There was no true 'upper class' in New South Wales in the traditional sense, but men like Macalister and the pastoralist John Macarthur, owner of the adjoining Camden Park estate, sat on the very surface of society like gold leaf. They were becoming very, very rich men, and much of this success had been gifted to them. Not only had the land they called their own arrived in the form of a government grant, they had also been assigned a steady supply of unpaid labour in the form of the convicts.

By this time more than 75,000 offenders had been deposited in New South Wales, many of whom had since been funnelled out of the chain gangs and into private enterprise. Convicts assigned to work on cattle and sheep stations had often started their sentences in the gangs, before being 'promoted' to an assignment following good behaviour. But the experiences of assigned convicts were very mixed. Some unlucky souls found their new bosses at least as merciless as the officers supervising the chain gangs, and were rendered 'nearly stupid from hard toil and cruel treatment' at the hands of 'demon incarnate' masters.

An abolitionist described one superintendent as 'in the habit of putting handcuffs and leg irons on them, and throwing them into a dungeon on the estate, where they remained generally for three days without meat or drink … [he had] drawn as much blood from the flogged backs of his assigned men, as would make him to swim in human gore'. And for some, the psychological challenges of remote work were at least as harmful as the lash. Shepherds were expected to wander for months in the bush, on foot and without even the company of a sheepdog, struggling back and forth under darkness each night to collect their meagre rations. Alone in the bush, guarding his flocks and listening to the howls of the dingoes, a man could quickly lose his mind.

It seems that the masters on Macalister's station at Clifton were of the less compassionate sort, for McMillan found the treatment of the convicts unsettling, once even testifying in court about their abuse. An entire work squad had been put on trial for refusing to work during a thunderstorm. McMillan relayed the outcome of the case to a newspaper: 'I was put in the witness box, and on giving my evidence that I would not ask anyone to work on such a day, the police magistrate at once announced that his men were at work, and there could not be such heavy rain as sworn to within five miles of his place, and sentenced the men to fifty lashes each. His children were dismissed from school to enable them to enjoy the torture of their fellow creatures, and I believe his wife also attended the flagellation.'

Sickened by this 'inhuman' conduct, McMillan requested a move further from the heart of this 'accursed colony', and towards the straggly edges of the map, where each day the frontier drifted further into unknown country.

Cattle drovers, pushed forward by a constant need for fresh grazing, were effectively the new explorers. Although legislation limited settlement to within a rough arc around Sydney of about two hundred miles – the so-called 'Nineteen Counties' – there was not much the government could do to prevent these itinerant men roving ever further inland; self-sufficient, bush-wise, always on the move, they slept under the stars in the swags they carried and laid claim to new pasture with makeshift huts constructed from slabs of bark. As Don Watson described in his book *Caledonia Australis* (1984), they were the 'factotums of white civilization in Australia, in a sense the flux in the transition from black to white occupation of the interior'.

These rough and ready pioneers retain a special place in Antipodean folklore. Much of Australian literature, well into the twentieth century, revolves around heroic accounts of their 'battling against' harsh landscapes, the movement of the cattle and lives lived around the billycan on the campfire. 'Pioneers' by Banjo Paterson, the best-known of the 'bush poets', is a good example of the genre:

They came of bold and roving stock that would not
fixed abide;
They were the sons of field and flock since e'er
they learnt to ride,
We may not hope to see such men in these
degenerate years
As those explorers of the bush – the brave old
pioneers.

'Twas they who rode the trackless bush in heat and
storm and drought;
'Twas they who heard the master-word that called
them farther out;
'Twas they who followed up the trail the mountain
cattle made,
And pressed across the mighty range where now
their bones are laid.

McMillan's year on Macalister's cattle station was an education that taught him the skills that would serve him well as an explorer and pioneer pastoralist: how to muster cattle on horseback; how to build a bark hut; which of these unknown plants were edible; which of these unknown animals were venomous; how to navigate steep, bush-tangled slopes that spread out into the distance, unmarked by track or trail.

Tim arrived in Tamworth in a spluttering, aged minibus to take me and his latest batch of trainees to the farm. I recognised him immediately: a strong, capable Crocodile Dundee lookalike in a wide-brimmed bush hat and torn jeans. His shirt was dirt-coloured and the top buttons long lost, revealing the skin below in a swatch of deep brick.

The homestead was half an hour by road out of town, followed by a long drive up an unfinished track through sharply rolling landscape. The orange-gold of scorched grass was interrupted only by the occasional irrigated garden, neat fenced-off patches made luminous with life. The earth of the steep banks and bare patches was red, but at the bottom of the empty, weed-strewn creekbeds the rocks were a dull steel-grey. The few animals around seemed oddly sleek and healthy for this desiccated environment: piebald magpies disregarding a scarecrow in jeans and an old bush hat, gleaming stockhorses flicking at the flies with their tails, and cattle ripping greedily at the last scraps of edible grass. A dead fox lay baking at the side of the road, red fur luxurious against the dust.

Within a couple of hours we were saddled up and riding onto the high ridgeline looking for Aberdeen Angus cattle. After a brief quizzing and a quick lookover Tim had teamed me with a pretty chestnut mare called She Oak. 'She's fast,' said George, one of the stockmen, when I asked about her. 'Just let her go if she wants to go, don't grab at her mouth. And watch her with the other horses. She's a bitch.'

I loved her on sight. She Oak had a silken, unpulled mane, a white snip set at an angle across her nose and three white ankle socks, like a naughty schoolgirl who'd let the other slip down. She wore a home-made rope bridle – a big knot at each cheek holding the bit in her mouth – and an Australian stock saddle equipped with solid knee blocks and a high cantle to keep the rider secure in rough terrain or on a difficult mount. A leather breastplate held the saddle in place as we shinned up terrifyingly steep gradients. She tackled hills with brio, breaking into a trot or a canter if I let her, her ears pricked forward as the sweat lathered where the reins touched against her neck. No matter how long we were out, she was always ready to pull ahead and run and run and run.

She Oak and her colleagues were Australian stock horses, a breed derived from horses imported by the British, starting with the nine carried over on the First Fleet in 1788. The stock-horse blood originated largely among English thoroughbreds, Welsh mountain ponies, Arabians and the sturdy little ponies from nearby Indonesian islands. They have the delicacy and dished faces of Arabs, the hardiness of polo ponies, the lucky-dip colouring – buckskin, roan, blanket-spotted, leopard-spotted, wall-eyed – of the American quarter horse.

The type is nicely characterised in another of Banjo Paterson's works, his classic 'The Man from Snowy River':

> He was something like a racehorse undersized,
> With a touch of Timor pony – three parts
> thoroughbred at least –
> And such as are by mountain horsemen prized.

> He was hard and tough and wiry — just the sort
> that won't say die —
> There was courage in his quick impatient tread;
> And he bore the badge of gameness in his bright
> and fiery eye,
> And the proud and lofty carriage of his head.

The skill of the riders forms a core to the pioneer mythology; the man from Snowy River races up and down the gullies until his horse's sides are heaving, and bloody 'from hip to shoulder from the spur'. In McMillan's time, the English settler John Pettit wrote of the stockmen of Gippsland: 'In riding in horses and cattle they go full gallop thro' the Bush no matter how thick the trees turning sharp around them almost touching, jumping over all fallen logs in the most astonishing manner going over such ground as would capsize any horse not up to it.'

At Tim's the riding conditions were no better, but I found myself desperate to prove myself to this terrifyingly capable man, particularly when I heard that the jobs generally available to female trainees in the outback were as nannies or cooks. Tim himself had three young men tasked with the livestock and landcare and riding, while the three girls' main jobs seemed to be cooking, cleaning and looking after the two children he'd fathered with a young woman more than twenty years his junior, originally hired to do his admin.

The macho outback culture owes much to the days of the pioneers, when men were *real men* and women were scarce (in 1838, the year of McMillan's arrival, white men outnumbered white women in rural New South Wales by seventeen to one). I was already becoming used to the slow, patronising blink of the Australian male as I grappled with uncooperative sheep and heaved my own bags into the back of the ute. But then, I've always liked a challenge.

I'm a strong rider, so I pushed myself forward in the mustering, looking for approval. Coming down the steep, stony hillsides I sat ramrod straight, reins held loosely in one hand, heels down, hips jerking side to side with She Oak's steps. Whenever a calf or cow made a break for it, I urged her into a canter, looping wide around the escapee, then walking calmly back towards it, hooting long low notes that curved up in glissando to a high whoop that I'd copied from the stockmen.

Tim Skerrit musters cattle on horseback at his station near Tamworth.

We gathered the cattle from every corner of the property and brought them down towards the yard, funnelling them into two small paddocks with a tall metal fence and a crush separating them. I jumped down to help split the calves from the heifers, whipping long sticks into the dirt to spook them and drive them apart, grabbing the small ones and pushing them bodily through the gate. Sweat soaked my shirt and beaded in unexpected places – my neck, my cheeks, the smooth skin on the inside of my forearms.

I was rewarded when, after a long day under a merciless sun, Tim eyed me approvingly and asked what I would be doing the next week. 'Heading to Gippsland,' I reminded him. 'Following the old exploratory paths.'

'Ah, yeah?' He'd clearly forgotten the entire reason I was there. I didn't really mind. Actually, I was hoping he was about to ask me to throw it all in and help them with the mustering all season, but instead he nodded once and turned back to the cattle. 'Get the branding iron,' he said to the boys.

On our return to the homestead each afternoon we shed our sweaty clothes onto the ground and jumped into the dam beyond the fence – a small artificial reservoir that collected rainwater. The water was mud-coloured and refreshing, warm on top but deadly cold in the deep. When we swam we set it swirling, cold fronts whipped up from below and sent spinning across the surface like a typhoon.

A wooden walkway jutted out into the empty air above our heads, a clear indication of how far the water level had fallen since winter. We took it in turns to jump off, legs wheeling in mid-air as we fell ten feet into the water. I felt my feet press into the spongey bottom and pushed off, surfacing with a gasp, lungs burning. 'Look out for yabbies,' said one of the boys. 'Got pincers like lobsters. Sometimes you feel them brushing against your legs.'

We staggered back to the yard in our bare feet, dodging dry cowpats and the thorniest of the weeds to drink bush tea by the fire from a billycan, brewed until it was bitter and chalky from the milk whitener. There were fat wedges of damper – a basic milk-bread stuffed with raisins and baked around a tin can so it came out shaped like a Bundt cake with a thick golden crust – made in the fire using a thick-lidded pot. One night we ate fried bullock testicles, fatty globs of gore we had cut off with a scalpel earlier that day and gathered in a hat for safekeeping.

To a sun-starved Scot it was glorious: clear skies, forty degrees, no phone reception and no internet. I was enjoying being carefree and cut off. The books I'd brought were sitting unread at the end of my bunk; I'd half-forgotten Angus McMillan and the rest of my quest. But to those living on the station, the heavenly weather was beginning to cause some concern. 'It's the driest summer since the sixties,' said Tim. 'At least. My da reckons it's the driest he's ever seen, and he's seen a few. He's ninety this year.'

By Wednesday evening the torridity was coming to a head. It had been muggy and hot all day, but clouds had crept in unnoticed with the dusk, quietly fading in as if they had been there all along. The thunder cleared its throat, then the flash of first lightning came from somewhere over the hill out of sight. A tiny spattering of rain. 'Not enough,' warned one of the Australians. 'The lightning could start a fire, and this rain wouldn't be heavy enough to put it out.'

The pasture where Tim's horses grazed was golden with close-cropped grasses that lent a velvety fuzz to the curve of the hill. It was so dry the blades would crunch and break under your soles as you walked. Further up, the bush grew in grey-green knots of spindle-armed trees and the creepers that choked them, the earth pale and sandy between their roots. Everywhere the ground was littered with the long, slender limbs of the gums that seemed simply to have let go; huge branches, half the tree sometimes, would have peeled themselves off and crashed to the ground. The long curved leaves of the eucalyptus, the size and shape of kukri knives, gold, tan and greenish brown, curled in the heat and piled up like tinder, ready to go up at any moment.

The Australian ecosystem has been sculpted by flame. Many plants thrive in or depend upon fire at key points of their life cycle; the release of the seeds of the saw banksia and the flowering of the grass tree are both triggered by bushfire. Others are simply highly flammable: the ubiquitous eucalypt, for example, whose resinous sap and paper-like bark are perfectly designed to catch and spread fire.

Bushfires have the effect of stripping out younger, less established plants and providing breathing room to the biggest trees. These brutes are then free to grow tall and strong and freestanding, lending the land the appearance of an English country estate, a feature made much of in the writing of the earliest arrivals. Sydney Parkinson, a draughtsman on Captain Cook's 1770 voyage along the eastern coast of Australia, wrote of his surprise at the pleasant, cared-for aspect of the newfound 'wilderness' of New South Wales: 'The country looked very pleasant and fertile; and the trees, quite free from under-wood, appeared like plantations in a gentleman's park.'

There is a false impression that Aboriginal people lived an idyllic lifestyle, 'in harmony' with the environment, hunting and gathering at such low intensity that they left no trace on the landscape. In fact, it was their continent-wide habit of 'firestick farming' – burning out the scrub, grasses and under-canopy of the forests in complex rotation to encourage new growth or lure larger fauna into better hunting ground – that resulted in this distinctive habitat. It killed off fire-sensitive plants and selected for the fire-friendly – in effect, it altered the entire ecosystem of the continent. As Edward Curr, one of the earliest settlers along the Murray, wrote: 'It may perhaps be doubted whether any section of the human race has exercised a greater influence on the physical condition of any large portion of the globe than the wandering savages of Australia.'

Man-made fire was still widespread at the end of the eighteenth century – making its first appearance in English literature in the verse of Thomas Muir, one of the 'Scottish martyrs' transported to New South Wales for their Jacobin sympathies in 1794:

> To clear the forest's dark impervious maze
> The half-starv'd Indian lights a hasty blaze
> Then lifts the Torch, and rushing o'er the Strand
> High o'er his head he waves the flaming Brand
> From Bush to Bush with rapid steps he flies
> Till the whole forest blazes to the skies.

The arrival of the European settlers was followed by a sudden fall in the bushfire. Those who build houses and farms rather than temporary shelters flinch from the destruction that such fires bring. As a result, the fire-friendly plants have been growing in their thickets ever since – fuel for the fires builds over years, just waiting for a spark. The result has been some of the most destructive fires in human history. In 1851, 'Black Thursday' raged through five million hectares of Victoria, killing twelve people and more than a million sheep; 'Ash Wednesday' in 1983 killed seventy-five and razed 2,500 buildings; most recently 'Black Saturday' of 2009 killed 173 and left an estimated seven thousand homeless.

Two years before my arrival, a bushfire swept through the hill behind Tim's homestead, barely missing the buildings. Tim packed his wife, children and female staff off to a neighbour's property, away from the flames, but stayed on with the other men to fight the fire with hoses, buckets and whatever water they could get their hands on.

They saved the house, but the burned-out trees still stood in swathes, poking limbless from the ground like fenceposts. Close up, I saw that their blackened trunks were wreathed in new sweet, green leaves, bursting through from the living tree underneath all the way up their lengths. And so the Australian flora regenerates.

On Thursday night the weather finally broke. I was swimming in the dam, racing the dogs to sticks that Mariánne, a Norwegian girl on the jillaroo course, was throwing in from the water's edge. Lightning was flickering again, somewhere in the corner of my vision, and the thunderclaps were growing louder and more frequent, until they came so close together they might have been simultaneous. Heavy drops began to hit the water around my head and shoulders, spot-spotting at first, before suddenly the sky unzipped and they came down on us in a torrent.

We whooped in delight, girlish squeals that sent the dogs skittering in the shallows, delighted by our excitement. A flash, the boom of the thunder again, directly above us now. I howled happily up into the sky like a wolf, rain splashing my face.

'You guys?' It was Tim's wife. 'You'd better get out of the water before you get fried.'

It was the droughts of New South Wales that finally sent the settlers south over the Australian Alps. By May 1839, less than a year and a half after McMillan's arrival at Clifton, conditions were growing desperate.

The *South Australian Gazette and Colonial Register* reported that 'the present year must be looked upon as the most calamitous the colony has ever experienced, occasioned by the long continued drought'. It carried extracts of reports from across New South Wales (a title which at that time referred to the entirety of the mainland colony, from present-day Brisbane in the north to Melbourne on the south coast, with a pocket of uncharted land – Gippsland – beyond the Australian Alps in the south-east), noting that 'the state of the interior is represented as deplorable in the extreme':

> Bathurst – The drought continues, and no words
>   can express the miserable appearance of the
>   country; there is not supposed to be enough

wheat left for seed – no milk – no cheese, and no vegetables.

Patrick's Plains – There is neither food for man nor beast; the plains are as destitute of grass as a turnpike road.

Paterson, Hunter's River – The country is in a desponding state for want of rain; there will be no maize. God knows what will become of us all if some change does not take place very soon.

Port Phillip – The country is altered much for the worse; all the grass is burnt up, and the greatest difficulty is experienced in procuring food for the cattle. Several of the well-known fords of the rivers Hume and Ovens are quite dry, and the rivers have become a chain of ponds.

King – The drought continues with unabating severity, stock of every description are beginning to fall off for want of pasturage; things are in a dreadful state.

Murrumbidgee – The river has decreased so considerably as to become dry in many places, and fish may be seen lying in a putrid state on the bed of the river.

Wellington – The country is burnt up; sheep are dying by hundreds; the cattle have all long since been dead. For the last twelve months there has not been rain for two consecutive days.

This drought did not only affect the settlers, of course. The hard times were driving the British and Aboriginal populations into competition over the meagre supplies. One correspondent from Port Phillip, the large bay where

Melbourne had been founded four years previously, reported: 'The blacks have killed forty head of cattle belonging to Mr. Faithfull, and thirty six sheep of Colonel White's since you left. You may expect to hear shortly of some wild work taking place here, the blacks are so continually encamping near us.'

The dark allusion to 'wild work' was in fact a euphemism for what might, in modern terminology, be described as an ethnic cleansing. The previous year, 'great numbers' of the Kamilaroi people of New South Wales – the group indigenous to the Tamworth area – had been killed over the course of several months in what the local magistrate described as 'a war of extirpation' (*extirpation* – to pull up by the roots). The bloodiest episode, the Waterloo Creek massacre, took place in January 1838, when the officer in charge, Major James Nunn, claimed to have killed between two and three hundred Kamilaroi (although later estimates have placed the upper limit at around seventy).

The infamous Myall Creek massacre took place the same year, about a hundred miles north of Tim's homestead, when twenty-eight unarmed members of the Kamilaroi's Wirrayaraay tribe were tied to a rope, marched from their camp and slaughtered. Witnesses later described how the children had been beheaded, before the adults were forced to run as three stockmen brandishing swords slashed at their bodies.

The Wirrayaraay victims were well-known to their killers – many had been given English nicknames: Charlie, Davey, Martha, Old Joey, 'King' Sandy – but the extent of the betrayal and brutality is not what has singled out the Myall Creek incident; rather it is the only massacre in Australian history following which white Europeans were tried and executed for their role in frontier killings of Aboriginal people. In all, eleven settlers were tried for murder, of whom seven were found guilty and hanged: Charles Kilmeister, James Oates, Edward Foley, John Russell, John Johnstone, William Hawkins and James Parry. An eighth, John Blake, was cleared but later committed suicide.

The Myall Creek trials and hangings caused enormous controversy in their time. The defendants argued that they had not realised that killing an Aboriginal man was a crime, so common was the sport on the frontier. The newspapers took up the cause of the settlers: 'The whole gang of black animals,' argued the *Sydney Herald*, 'are not worth the money the colonists will have to pay for printing the silly court documents.'

But the judge reminded the court that the law made no distinction between the murder of an Aboriginal man and that of a white man. For the Kamilaroi this was a rare glimmer of justice. It must have seemed that finally the lives of the black population would be valued and protected. It must have seemed like a turning point. It wasn't. The effect of the prosecutions was to foster a culture of silence among the settlers. The killings did not stop, but instead became concealed in layers of secrecy and doublespeak. Settlers realised that talking openly about massacres and murders was no longer safe; that boasting of your kills could bring about your own execution.

Living in rural New South Wales through 1838 and into 1839, Angus McMillan could not have been unaware of the Myall Creek trial and its outcome. He would have discussed it among his fellow workers over a dram, even as the drought drew the settlers and the Aboriginal tribes into ever-closer conflict.

I was discussing the events of Myall Creek over a drink myself one evening when one of the girls on the course, a pretty, strong-looking teenager, overheard me and volunteered the fact that she had an Aboriginal father.

'Oh,' I said, surprised. 'I suppose you have the colouring for it.' She had a golden, sunkissed glow about her, a sweet snub nose, dark eyes under unexpectedly fair hair.

She nodded. 'I don't usually tell people. It's not something to be proud of.' I raised an eyebrow. 'They've got a pretty bad reputation. Drink. Drugs. Hitting their women. You know?'

I shook my head. 'Not really.'

'Have you not heard about Palm Island? It's off the coast of Queensland, where I'm from, an Aboriginal settlement. Pretty famous. Mad stuff goes on. Fighting, drugs, rioting, no control. Had to send commandos in one time after they set the police station on fire. It's one of the most dangerous places in the world.'

Her boyfriend was nodding at me, eyes wide, as she spoke. 'Yeah, man,' he chimed in. 'Shit gets pretty crazy in the settlements.'

'Anyway,' she added, 'I didn't know my dad ever anyway. Didn't stick around. They don't, usually.'

Tim was working nearby, checking some heavy tools. He inspected each one before piling them into the back of the ute.

I called over. 'Hey, Tim? Are there still Aboriginal people living in the Tamworth area?'

He half-turned as he considered his answer. 'Some,' he said, a noncommittal Australian tic which can mean anything from wild understatement to reluctant accedence. There was a pause while I waited for him to elaborate, but he didn't.

'Where might I find them?'

'The pub.' He waited until I feigned the required snort of amusement, before giving me a slow smile. 'Ah, there's a few. But I've probably got darker skin than the lot of them. They're all half-white, or most of them. I reckon I could claim welfare about as well as them. Go into the bars on Friday night and ask around and you'll find them.'

After a week on the cattle station, wearing the same filthy shirt and torn jeans every day, I quite fancied an evening out in any case. Mariánne the Norwegian was a willing accomplice. She'd just been offered a job at one of the neighbouring stations, and this would be her last chance to hit the town for months.

By 10 p.m. we were a bottle of wine down each, and feeling confident in our conversational skills. We stalked the main streets, trailing from empty bar to empty bar in search of new friends, finally alighting on the thump thump thump of dance music we could hear on the still night air as our final destination. The only club in Tamworth! We had to go there.

We weren't the only clubbers in Tamworth, but it was a close-run thing. A lone DJ stood on the stage, pluckily pumping up the volume as red and white spotlights strobed the empty dancefloor in the manner of school discos everywhere. Mariánne and I took to the floor without hesitation, on the basis that the lack of other dancers meant all the more space for us, but we were finally forced to submit to the downward pull of entropy as our aggressive pointing gave way to shoulder shimmying, in turn degenerating to the head bob, until finally we found ourselves sitting in garden chairs out the back, speaking to a red-faced station hand of indeterminate age in a waxed leather hat and Blundstones.

The fact that he had somehow ended up entertaining both of the only two unaccounted-for women in the bar seemed to have aroused a great hilarity among the other regulars, who kept stopping by our table to slap him on the shoulder in congratulatory fashion, or to ask us if this man was bothering us. After a while the music was turned off and the main lights on, but rather than throw us out, the bar manager, DJ and doorman came to join us out back with drinks in hand.

'Where are all the Aboriginal people in Tamworth?' I asked. 'I haven't seen any.'

'They're here,' the doorman assured me. 'But they don't hang out in this bar.'

'Where do they hang out?'

They exchanged glances. 'Not bars that *you* want to go to,' the doorman said, eyeing my bare shoulders, following the line of my clavicles with an expression I wasn't entirely comfortable with. 'There's parts of town that they all live ... but not the nice parts.' A beat passed. 'Why do you want to know?'

I hesitated, then dived in. I was just passing through, I told them, on my way to Gippsland to investigate the massacres led by a relative of mine, generations ago. I wasn't sure what I thought about it yet. But I felt strangely guilty, as if some of the responsibility for the current poor state of the Australian Aboriginal population lay at my feet. And much more so, here in person, now that I realised how ghettoised that population really was.

It was late, and we were all drunk, and I wasn't really sure how well I was explaining myself. Partway through my speech I felt a surge of self-censure for ruining the mood. But after a pause for consideration, the doorman rose to the occasion.

'That's a really dangerous thing,' he said finally. 'Taking on that responsibility. I don't think that helps anything. Actually, it makes it worse. Accepting blame. The problem with the Aboriginals is that they're always blaming other people for the way it is now.'

I must have been frowning, because he held up an appeasing hand. 'Think about it. I don't care if your great-great-grandfather killed my great-great-grandfather because my great-grandfather speared one of your great-great-grandfather's sheep. It's not good that it happened, obviously. But that doesn't mean that *you* are in any way to blame for all the failures in *my* life now. It's nothing to do with you.'

It was an argument I had heard before – a simple refusal to accept collective debt. Not a denial of the past, but a shrugging of shoulders. Many contemporary Australians feel that being assigned responsibility for their forebears' actions is not only unjust, but could lead to costly reparations and a revival of ill feeling that should have been laid to rest long ago. It is time to move on, not – as the controversial historian Keith Windschuttle has argued – to 'add fuel to the politics of permanent grievance on which the hard men of Aboriginal activism have long thrived'.

'But doesn't it make you feel bad?' I persisted, not willing to let it drop. 'To be a member of the group that's at such an advantage? An advantage gained at the expense of the others?'

'Yes, but ...' He thought about it. 'But that's life. Some people are born rich. Some people poor. We all have to work with what we've got.'

'It really fucks me off,' the DJ burst in, 'the way the Abos are always blaming white people for the shit that goes on in their community. As if it's our fault if they're drunk, or that their kids aren't going to school, or whatever. They're blaming us for their shit lives, their shit houses, their shitty behaviour. But that's not my fault. I didn't make it this way. And they can change it. No one's stopping them going to school. Nobody's stopping them getting jobs.'

He was swaying slightly. I wasn't sure how he'd managed to get quite so drunk in the short interval since the music stopped. Around us and above us the disco lights continued to spin and churn to an unheard beat, bringing a strange, hallucinatory tinge to the whole scene.

There was an awkward silence. I had the sense that although the other men agreed in principle, the drunk man had put it more bluntly than they were willing to.

'Hey,' he said suddenly, as if something completely wonderful and unexpected had just occurred to him. 'Do you want to have another drink?'

Mariánne and I looked at each other. She raised her eyebrows at me, shrugged.

'Sure,' I said. 'I'll have a gin and tonic.'

5

First In, Best Dressed

Jeannie Haughton was a playwright. I'd first come across her online, in an ABC segment on a play she'd written about Angus McMillan: *Salute the Man*. A scathing take-down of him, by all accounts. She was pictured looking rather stern on the verandah of his former homestead, which has now been relocated and reconstructed in an odd mixed-period 'heritage park' fifty miles away to the south-east.

I'd emailed a few months back, not knowing what I wanted from her. Just to make contact – as if McMillan was a friend we had in common. 'I'm thinking of coming to Gippsland,' I wrote. 'Perhaps we could meet up?' My mission had taken more concrete form even as I typed the words onto the page.

Her reply came like a gift. She'd always wanted to follow McMillan's trail herself, she said. Perhaps we could travel together, as a sort of investigative unit, and her husband could drive us from site to site. 'We have maps, a four-by-four, a caravan and a tent.' It was an offer I couldn't refuse.

Jeannie met me off the train at Drouin, on the eastern edge of Gippsland. She was a statuesque, bohemian-looking woman with a cloud of red corkscrew curls and a multicoloured coat. 'Haughts is delighted,' she said, meaning her husband, Ian. 'He's always looking for an excuse to get out in the caravan, and I'll never go with him.' Ian turned out to be a wiry, bald fellow, particular about order and systems, and quick to laugh. Jeannie was right, he *was* delighted, greeting me like an old friend.

'Make yourself at home,' said Jeannie. 'Sorry about the wall.' She gestured vaguely towards a gaping hole in the front of the house where an extension was being built, over which a tarpaulin flapped weakly.

'You can lock the door if you like,' cracked Ian, 'but there's not much point.'

I lingered in the house for a couple of days as Jeannie crammed in a last few appointments. The waiting was not unpleasant. I was patient, expectant. We were in 'the McMillan electorate', said Jeannie, and this relaxed me. I was already getting closer. I leafed dreamily through books, watched king parrots and rainbow parakeets bicker and preen in the garden, wandered the roads nearby.

It was greener here in Drouin than in New South Wales. I was captivated by the eucalypts: gum trees, the Australians call them, although they didn't look like any trees that I knew. They had lissome, flyaway branches that struck off at haphazard angles then curled in unexpected directions, silvery white and gleaming in the hazy morning light. Above, the delicate slips of the leaves – clouds of them, showers of them. They came down in the wind like confetti, or feathers discarded

Lower down, around their trunks, the bark grew in thicker layers that were shed to fall down like shadows made real, each species disrobing in its own style to

106

reveal the slender white limbs underneath, fresh and clean, and as wrinkled as newborns. Long strands peeled off in streamers and gathered in bundles in the joints of branches below, hanging over the road like bead curtains. Or in small islands, leaving pale fresh patches behind, an impressionist painting made up of blotches of unexpected, overlapping colours: sage, dove-grey, a pale primrose auburn. On others, layers upon layers of bark unfurled, old books falling open, their curling pages coming loose at the seams.

I began to read the second diary, McMillan's expedition journals from his exploratory years. In fact, there were several versions – I'd located the original copy in the state archives, ink on blue paper, browned and blotchy after all those years but still legible, the others written for assorted periodicals during his lifetime. Each gave slightly different insights. I read and cross-referenced them against each other.

Jeannie had printed out a nineteenth-century map that showed the routes of the early explorers. McMillan's path had been picked out in a lurid yellow. I pored over it, trying to match his journal entries against first this, then a modern road map. His party started somewhere called Currawong, which did not seem to correspond to anywhere on the present-day map, before looping somewhat haphazardly through the mountainous region north of the Snowy River, reasserting their purpose and finally charging south into Gippsland along a river called the Tambo.

It was this latter phase that Jeannie suggested we retread. 'A lot of this,' she said, waving her arm airily across the top half of my map, 'is still very rough country. Very remote. If you want to head into these mountains for bushwalking and other young-person stuff, you can do that later.'

As we prepared to leave, Ian gave me a tour of his four-wheel-drive, which was kitted out ready for the full Aussie off-road experience: safari snorkel, double-sized diesel canisters, a battery-powered fridge that slid into the boot like a drawer. I was amused by the prospect of heading out on a caravanning tour, but Ian advised me solemnly as he started the engine and rolled down the drive that the caravan scene was different in Australia from in Britain, more extreme.

'Have you heard of the grey nomads? There's a trend here for older couples to hit the road after their children have left home. Take early retirement. Sell the house, the furniture, the whole caboodle, then spend that money on a good motorhome, or a top-class caravan at the very least, and head out on the road – and they don't come back.

'This is a huge country, Cal. You can just get out on the road and drive and drive and drive and always be covering new ground. Up to the Kimberley for the dry season, down through Western Australia in time for the wildflowers. Just pull over whenever you're tired of driving, no worries about finding a campsite or anything – you've got your fridge, your cooker, your water tank, about a hundred litres of fuel ...'

I nodded, smiling. I understood his fervour. There is something thrilling about mammoth countries, the freedom of having nothing hemming you in for thousands of miles in any direction. The Americans have an equivalent name for itinerant pensioners like these, which I prefer: 'snowbirds'. These snowbirds migrate south in winter like geese taking flight on the bitter Arctic winds, picking their way south, seeking sun and a place to roost, usually in Florida or Arizona. Small desert towns find themselves dwarfed by the swathes of campervans that spring up on their outskirts in neat suburban rows, year after year.

Peck peck. Gobble gobble. They pass the winter picking bare the local stores. Come rainy season they pack up and drive back to where they came from, leaving only desert where once there was an endless white, plastic city.

'You could just drive and drive and drive,' Ian repeated. He glanced into the back seat hopefully, but Jeannie wasn't listening.

1839. With the colony of New South Wales racked by drought, ever more settlers flooded into the interior, looking for fresh land. It was the scramble for Australia: a race to annex the best pasture. Finders keepers – that was the rule. The settlers would occupy the land as 'squatters' and wait for the freehold to be formalised later, once they were too established to be removed. As they say locally: first in, best dressed.

By this time the dray track from Yass that stretched 350 miles to the 'huddle of huts' that comprised the newly founded Melbourne had transformed into a busy highway, where an estimated 20,000 cattle were so tightly crammed that 'great care [had to] be exercised to prevent the mixing of herds, and consequent annoyance and confusion', one drover recalled later. On arrival in this new portion of the colony the migrants would search for suitable 'vacant' pasture upon which they might graze their stock, but this was getting harder and harder.

It was a rushed game of hide and seek that they were joining late: everywhere they looked – under the bed, behind the curtain – someone had nestled themselves in before they got there. Their hunger for land was never-ending.

Gippsland, however, 14,000 square miles of fertile land tucked into the south-eastern corner of the continent, had so far survived the occupation unscathed. A few half-hearted attempts had been made to scale the Australian Alps to see what lay beyond them, but with no success. If there was grazing land to be found there, it was bounded by precipitous mountains to the north, steep gorges to the east, a tempestuous sea to the south, and an impenetrable forest of thorns to the west. It was a natural fortress, with no easy way in and no easy way back out.

But suspicions as to the region's potential were aroused when that winter the ship of James Macarthur, son of the pastoralist John, was blown off course while sailing in Bass Strait, and his party found themselves travelling parallel to the coast 'far to the west of Cape Howe'. Macarthur noted: 'Mr [George] Blaxland and I both observed that the mountains receded considerably inland towards Wilson's Promontory, and that it was likely a valuable grazing country existed between the mountains and the coast.'

They were so close, yet so far away. The beauty of the crescent beach, a scythe of white sand, belied the danger of their situation – uncharted rocks and reefs that lurked beneath the surface, unpredictable currents that whipped through the waves, the surf battering down upon the shore like so many slamming doors. Already this perilous stretch of water had claimed dozens of ships; there was no way to anchor and investigate. But they took note, made plans.

What lay in this hidden dell? It was a secret, held out like a promise.

Angus McMillan too had seen into the future, standing high upon the peaks to the north-east.

By February he had found himself manager on a station high up on the Monaro plateau, around a hundred miles to the south of where Canberra sits now. With a year of station work under his belt he had been tasked with seeking out fresh land by which his master Macalister's hungry stock might be spared, and his imagination began to drift south to the undiscovered land beyond the blue-tinged peaks.

Two months later, restless for action and fired with ambition, he climbed to the highest point of the Tingaringy ridge, *and to my great delight got a view of the sea.* He sat there for hours, comparing what he could see with Matthew Flinders' chart of the coast, and calculated that the mountain range he could see stretching off to the west must be set around thirty miles back from the beach. He knew at once, he wrote later, that he must one day penetrate this unknown region. *I looked to the S.W., and said here is a noble work for a bold and determined mountaineer, thinking all the time how I could accomplish the object in view.*

Seeking information, he visited a nearby Aboriginal camp. Its inhabitants – the Ngarico tribe of the Monaro – were the first indigenous people he had encountered at close quarters, and he found them helpful. *With a palpitating heart I listened until one of them, pointing to the S.W., cried out cabone benel which means a large plain. I then took both their hands in mine and expressed a wish to go there.*

But neither of the two Ngarico men who had seen the great lakes, plains and rivers of that hidden country with their own eyes were able to accompany him. They were old now, and too frail for the journey. Besides which, they were not keen to make contact with the natives of that land – the 'warrigals', as they called them: wild dogs. In Gippsland, they warned him, there were *plenty fish, plenty kangaroo, thousand duck, thousand swan, and thousand black-fellow, 'like it chumbug along o' plain'* – meaning that they *were as numerous as the sheep*. Nor would any of the white men in his party accompany him. He was too inexperienced a leader, the rumoured wild men too alarming.

But the Promised Land beyond the mountains became an obsession to McMillan. Finally, after many weeks of persuasion and a demonstration of his abilities with a shotgun, the elders consented to one of the younger members of the tribe accompanying him as a guide. The pair set off with four weeks' provisions on what turned out to be a bruising false start: a short-lived attempt to breach the fortress walls by way of the Snowy River gorge.

They were soon forced to turn back north, towards the high plains of Omeo, where McMillan's friend James MacFarlane had recently established a station at the furthest edge of white settlement. But not before he had clambered to the top of Mount Macleod for a bird's-eye view of what would become his kingdom. *To my unspeakable joy there was the low country at my feet – the lakes and plains extending to the W.S.W., as far as the eye could carry.*

*

We came into a huge, flat country where cattle grazed in vast yellowing meadows. It was flat as flat could be. Far off on the horizon to the north, the foothills of the Australian Alps could be seen, painted with the green-blue tinge of the eucalypts. They seemed so distant and out of keeping with our surroundings that they might have been sketched onto a backdrop and reeled across the skyline like the scenery for a play.

This was Gippsland. In 1839 it would have been lush, widely spaced woodland dotted with freshwater lagoons and punctuated with the curling smoke of the fires of innumerable Aboriginal encampments. Today it is a vast expanse of flat, fertile farmland, well occupied by contented herds of cattle that roam this grassland like wildebeest on the Serengeti, black as silhouettes and up to their bellies in flaxen grass heavy with seeds.

Irrigation channels offered the only contours, their existence proclaimed as proudly as latecomers to a ball – 'I announce the attendance of Boisdale Drainage Ditches nos. 1 and 2!' – and mobile sprinkler systems stretched motionless across the length of the fields, endless metal hoses lifted high in the air, snakes on skates.

The sun was almost directly overhead, the sky streaked through with cirrus harpstrings. I gazed out at the landscape as we flew by, reading the signs. They had a storybook ring – 'Cherry Tree Creek', 'Stringy Bark Cottages', 'Dirty Hollow'. Someone was selling wildflowers in bunches from a trolley at the side of the road. This *was* a huge country, I was realising afresh. From dot to dot on the map, barely a speck of the state, a distance I had rashly assumed too short to worry about – a short hop, nothing more – was apparently going to take us four hours' drive.

More signs, pleading now: 'Sore Eyes? Powernap Now', and 'The Only Cure for Tiredness is Sleep'. A campaign of persuasion aimed at all those cruise-control drivers speeding thousands of miles across the continent without a pause. As if on cue, I felt my eyelids flutter. Sleep roared up behind me, and overtook.

I woke up in the Wild West. Omeo had a dusty, frontier-land feel, like the set of a spaghetti western, the main street lined with clapboard shops with high, scroll-topped façades in an autumnal palette. Everything seemed to have closed early for the day, adding to the sense that there wasn't really anything behind the blinds except empty cardboard boxes and trestle tables bearing props. I half-expected John Wayne to come clattering out of a pair of saloon doors and whistle for his horse.

There was a butcher, a redbrick 'post and telegraph office' and a handful of old colonial-style boarding houses: Snug as a Bug (est. 1879) and Martin's Place, a cute wooden hut in peppermint green wearing a pretty copper windvane like a tiara. 'Survived Two Bush Fires', a sign out front boasted. The road continued north out of town past the Golden Age Motel towards Mount Bogong, where once Aboriginal groups would gather from miles around, every year, to feast on the fatty bogong moths during their spring migration. It is now a highly seasonal skiing destination; mismatched skis bleached in the window of the petrol station, while fluorescent orange snow-gates stood incongruously in the crisp dead grass by the petrol pumps.

We pitched our camp on the banks of Livingstone Creek, where sulphur-crested cockatoos were grazing like sheep in the shade of the trees. As we drove up they flew into the branches, noisily indignant, voices sharp and rasping and unexpectedly harsh, screeching criticism as I pitched my tent below. Jeannie and Ian unhitched their caravan and got the kettle on as I strolled back up the hill into town.

In some ways, the town and its surrounds had changed little since McMillan's days; the cattleman, or at least the legend of him, still reigns supreme. The placenames had a rough drovers' humour to them: a local paper informed me of a bushfire that had recently rushed through the valley between Terrible Hollow and Mount Buggery – Mount Buggery having apparently evaded the notice of the group of prudish surveyors who rechristened nearby Mount Arsehole as Mount Arthur in the 1930s. Posters in the windows advised that I had just missed a pioneer skills demonstration and 'late-night bush jam', but if I hung around for a few more weeks there would be whip-cracking, wood-chopping and the Great Australian Pack Horse Competition at the annual mountain cattlemen's festival.

Back in 1839, Omeo was in its most primitive state – no more than a few huts and shacks thrown together while the cattle wandered loose across the tablelands 'as wild as hares' – but to McMillan and his guide trekking up through the Cobberas range to the south-east it must have been a welcome sight. It was June, and bitterly cold in the mountains, hoarfrost clinging to the leaves of the snow gums, thick drifts high in the lee of the peaks. But lower down, where MacFarlane and his rivals were setting up shop, it was dry, brittle-grassed, a reminder of the droughts that still blighted the interior. It refocused McMillan upon his task. He didn't stay there long.

*

When I returned to the tent, feet wet from fording the creek, I found Jeannie and Ian itching to get back on the road. 'There's a viewpoint nearby called McMillan's Lookout,' said Jeannie, pointing it out on the map. 'I think you should see it.'

The view from the lookout, at 3,060 feet, was indeed spectacular. The land slid away from us down steep slopes choked with gnarled gums and tea trees that filled the air with their thick, medicinal aroma. Below us the plains radiated out from the dwindling waters of Lake Omeo, golden meadows carpeting a shallow, undulating basin hemmed in at the back by the three peaks of The Brothers. Here and there were the silver glimmers of the gums, slipping out of their clothes, pale bark falling to the ground like halos, their shadows lying long and lazy in the evening light.

The sky enormous above; the land enormous below. I could feel the curvature of the earth, and its endless possibility. Raw desire rose inside me, a yearning not only to read about this man, or even to read his words, but to see this brave new world through his eyes. I wanted his drive, his self-sufficiency. I wanted to star in my own epic.

This was just the starting point, I thought. This was only the beginning.

There was a low stone cairn raised on a plinth where an older couple were posing for photos. Ian ambled across to help out. 'Do you want a picture of you both together?'

They acquiesced, thanking him, the woman adding as an afterthought, 'You know, we're here visiting because my husband is a descendant of one of the original pioneers.'

We three laughed, unable to believe the coincidence. 'Really? Which one?'

'James MacFarlane. He set up the first cattle station,' said the man. He was a big, barrel-chested guy of around sixty-five, with silver hair and a kindly, academic air.

'But I know all about him!' I cried. 'I'm here to follow the trail of Angus McMillan, a relative of *mine*. He was one of the pioneers too – the explorer who opened up Gippsland.'

We regarded each other with pleasure. It was amusing to think that more than 150 years ago, our forebears could very well have been standing together in the same spot. This man and I were the same, drawn to a place we had never been, treading and retreading the paths of our forebears. Looking for significance, for recognition, for a sense of ourselves and of where we have come from. Of who we could be.

Finally, after a delay of months while he rushed back and forth to Currawong and Clifton to gather supplies and support from his employer, McMillan was ready to make a second attempt. First he established another run on behalf of Macalister, a jumping-off point twenty-five miles south of Omeo at a spot the local Ya-itma-thang people called Numbla Munjee, 'Blackfish Place'. Then he gathered his party of three men and his kit and they set off once more into the unknown.

The journey was tough going, through some of the worst country McMillan had ever seen: a hilly and broken landscape of rocky gullies and dense, thorny undergrowth. The party lost a packhorse early on when it slipped and fell on one of the steeper slopes, rolling until it was finally halted by a sturdy tree, *having staked itself in four or five places*. Eventually two Ya-itma-thang guides led the group to an ancient Aboriginal walking route along the river-banks – now reborn as the Great Alpine Road – where they saw the first evidence of the warrigals McMillan had been warned about: ashes from the *extinct fires of what must have been a numerous body of natives*.

At this point, little was known of the Gunai people except for the rumours retailed by the natives of the Monaro and at Omeo. They were a ferocious, warlike people, the guides warned them. Yet the first meeting did little to confirm that reputation. As McMillan rode on ahead, he was suddenly confronted by dozens of Gunai tribesmen who emerged noiselessly from the bush. They stopped a few yards away, and stared at him in open dismay. *When I dismounted, and moved my hands in friendly salutation they fled in all directions*. Not so fearless, then.

But they were not taken entirely by surprise by the arrival of the white man. They had heard reports of a new type of man, a pale-skinned man with the power of mlang-mri, 'lightning eye', flashing death to those who looked at him, and the ability to draw together the banks of a river so he might pass over it. Many other explorers and pioneer settlers had encountered remote tribes who seemed to be expecting them. The explorer and surveyor Thomas Mitchell, for example, reported in 1834 of how on encountering an unknown tribe in New South Wales his party were met by 'calls in various directions, and "white-fellow" pronounced very loudly and distinctly [which] appears to be their name for our race'.

For the Gunai, however, McMillan's horse came as a shock: *from the astonishment displayed at the circumstance of my dismounting from the horse, I fancied they took both man and horse to constitute one animal.*

The tribesmen were gone, disappeared back into the bush. But they had not gone far. *At a great distance we heard all day their cooeying, and the cries and wailing of women and children.* First contact: the Gunai had been found. Although, of course, they had never been lost.

Another cairn now marks the location of McMillan's Numbla Munjee homestead, a square base of rocks bound by rough mortar which rises to a blunt pyramid topped with shards of stone. I leapt out of the car to sniff around. Photos show me leaning chummily against the cairn, grinning inanely. I was getting into the swing of it now; the appeal of his celebrity was rubbing off on me.

This was the second in a series of cairns thrown up in his honour during a rush of nostalgic patriotism in the 1920s, like a trail of breadcrumbs that traces the route of the successful expedition from this spot south along the River Tambo and down into the shifting grasses of the alluvial plains. At Bruthen we came across another. A plaque on it read: 'Angus McMillan passed by here, 1839' – like schoolboy graffiti. This one was topped with a concrete pillar supporting a large stone ball. Cairns flew past like flags – one at Mossiface, at Sarsfield, at Lucknow. I was hot on his heels.

Down, down, we followed him. Into the flats. Into the deep rich earth of the floodplains. The word 'wide' could have been invented for this space. An enormous expanse, with everything open to the air. Long vistas to the Alps in the north, the ocean to the south.

Ceremony at a cairn commemorating McMillan's achievements, 1920s.

I had a copy of McMillan's expedition journal with me, and I read it aloud as we drove, trying to conjure what he had seen, then superimpose it upon the present day. *The country consists of beautiful open forest, and the grass was up to our stirrup-irons as we rode along, and was absolutely swarming with kangaroos and emus. The lake was alive with wild ducks, swans, and pelicans.*

To our right was the hill McMillan had climbed from which to survey his new domain. There he saw not only the magnificent body of water he called Lake Victoria, but the rivers that ran like arteries through the flesh of the land. To the Highlanders, struggling down from the parched, drought-stricken dustbowl of New South Wales, it must have seemed a land of milk and honey. It put him in mind, he wrote later, of another place entirely. Of Walter Scott's 'Land of the mountain and the flood'. A place he had been dreaming of and grieving for ever since he left its fair shores.

A vision came to McMillan as he looked out across this paradisiacal scene, something not unlike a religious experience. *It was then I keenly felt that I had a noble and glorious task to perform and that I was only an instrument in the hands of the Almighty to accomplish it. Here was a country capable of supporting all my starving countrymen lying dormant.*

I named it at that moment 'Caledonia Australis'.

No time to celebrate. Shortly after this, the party would turn back to prepare for the next phase, settlement — though not before another brief encounter with the Gunai. A hundred tribesmen fled into the scrub upon their approach, burning their camps as they went, but McMillan's party managed to catch up with an elderly man who trailed behind the rest of his tribe. They found him, chillingly, adorned by four dried human hands that hung from his neck like costume jewellery.

If they thought this a bad omen, they didn't say so. It was only onwards, ever onwards. Six weeks' backbreaking work cutting a road suitable for livestock. Next, another return to the Monaro to bring five hundred head of cattle down into the new country, this *Caledonia Australis*, to form a new station on a *delightful tract of country* by the Avon River as a base for further expansion.

It was a punishing lifestyle. The excitable young Matthew Macalister (nephew of Lachlan, and McMillan's assistant) kept a journal too, recording in more detail how they were constantly on the move through uneven terrain, fording rivers and slashing through thorny scrub. They slept in the open air or under roughly constructed bark shelters, and subsisted on rations and whatever could be scavenged. 'Emu eggs for breakfast (one each),' Macalister wrote one morning. 'Mr McMillan and I could not finish ours but Ross managed to get sight of the bottom of his.'

McMillan brushed over the strain in his own workman-like journals, save to note at one point that he had spent sixteen of the last twenty-four months sleeping on the ground *without even the luxury of a tent*. A letter by a contemporary, George Edward Mackay, who settled the Ovens River area around the same time, gives some insight into the physical travails: 'I may mention as a specimen of the fatigue undergone by the earlier squatters, that for six days and nights before I left the Ovens I never lay down,' he later recalled, 'being engaged all day in herding the cattle, and all night in walking round them.' He was alone all this time, he added, his men being either similarly employed with the sheep or in guarding the stores. 'As soon as the necessity for exertion ceased, I was seized with œdematous swelling of the legs and eyelids. I could neither see nor walk, and was carried back to the Hume on a dray.'

'Bushed on this trip,' admitted Macalister.

Angus McMillan would soon take his place among the notables of the district, but the following twelve months were a challenge. His patron was not as impressed as McMillan had hoped, telling him only that without a harbour to allow shipment of livestock to the markets in Hobart, all this beautiful pasturage might prove more trouble than it was worth.

McMillan was dispatched back to the south to find a suitable location for a port. In the meantime Macalister kept McMillan's discovery of this rich new land quiet, all the while applying more and more pressure. Months of false starts and failed missions culminated in a bad-tempered power struggle between McMillan and Lieutenant Ross, who had been dispatched by Macalister to replace him as leader, and had even – to McMillan's fury – mounted himself on McMillan's own grey horse, Clifton.

He was spitting mad. All his work, all these months of discomfort and labour seemed to count for little. When, finally, the instruction came through to abandon the country and sell the existing cattle in Melbourne, it was too much. Disobeying his orders, McMillan instead formed a party of five, took four weeks' provisions and set off with the intention *to do or die*.

On 11 February 1841, from a hill they named Tom's Cap, they at last got sight of the much-longed-for natural harbour of Corner Inlet. Three days later, on Valentine's Day, they struck the coast. The inlet was thickly lined with vegetation and heavy with the stink of the mangrove, but McMillan did not care. Its waters were sheltered and seven feet deep at low tide; finally they had found a safe harbour on this destructive stretch of coastline.

Triumph at last. The cautious Scot allowed himself a moment of unfettered joy, bathing his feet in the warm waters as he thanked his God. *This was a happy day. Having accomplished my object, I had great cause to be thankful to Him who guarded me and shielded me from many a danger.*

They called it Port Albert. Taking his axe to the bark of a fat gum near the water's edge, he cut his legend:

ANGUS MCMILLAN
14–2–1841

and turned back towards the interior. He had proven his worth as an explorer and as a man. Not only to his employer, but to himself.

This breakthrough could not have been more timely. Unknown to McMillan, Melbourne was already abuzz with the news of the glorious grazing land to the east. A second party financed by James Macarthur – he who had prophesied the existence of 'valuable grazing country' while swept off course in Bass Strait – had tailgated McMillan into the region, following his tracks for part of the way, before striking off and cutting west through dense forest towards Melbourne. It was led by the charming Polish adventurer 'Count' Paweł Strzelecki. Tales of his daring exploits and a near brush with death – the party had become disoriented in the near-impenetrable scrub, been forced to abandon their horses and only spared starvation thanks to the skills of their Aboriginal guide – were the talk of the town.

Then, coincidentally, the paddle steamer *Clonmel* had been stranded on a sandbar off the coast only a month previously, and those aboard had managed to row to Sealer's Cove, at the foot of Wilsons Promontory. Curious probing by boat around this region had already aroused some interest in the harbour in which McMillan now stood, carving his initials.

This constellation of events had primed the businessmen of Melbourne to the region's possibilities: news of Port Albert, and of McMillan's brand-new overland route from the north, spread quickly. All his faith in the project had been vindicated. But there was a small catch. As word of Strzelecki's expedition had got out first, many of the names suggested by the *foreign imposter* for prominent landmarks had already entered the local lexicon. This rankled with McMillan, who thought it little more than *piracy*; some of these names, like Lake King, he pointed out, could not be less appropriate for Queen Victoria's colony.

In the following years, as news of McMillan's primacy spread – and bitter proxy battles over the men's rival claims to the title of 'discoverer of Gippsland' were fought in the letters page of the *Port Phillip Herald* – some of Strzelecki's names were officially overturned in favour of McMillan's: Mount Gisborne reverted to Mount Wellington, the Macarthur River to the Mitchell, the River Riley to the Nicholson.

It was too late for the most significant, however: Strzelecki's name had stuck irrevocably. In honour of the governor of the day, Sir George Gipps – declared by the *Sydney Morning Herald* 'the worst Governor the colony has ever had' – *Caledonia Australis* and the grand vision it symbolised had been written over: it was Gipps' Land.

Port Albert's day in the sun is long over. Since the construction of the Princes Highway – from Sydney south-east along the coast through Melbourne and beyond – and the dimming of Hobart as a centre of commerce, there is no need of it as an agricultural port. Instead it is a pretty, somewhat overlooked little tourist town, a few yachts roped tightly to the jetty as their crews squint into the wind that batters in off the strait. We stopped by only briefly, listlessly perusing the models in the maritime museum then following a walking trail out of town to the spot where McMillan struck water, now known as McMillan Bay. The tree with its Valentine's carving was chopped down during his lifetime by the local commissioner Charles Tyers with the intention of preserving it as some kind of monument, but it is long lost. No matter.

We turned back north towards the site of the first station, that *delightful tract* on the banks of the Avon River, since grown into a town and renamed Stratford – thus becoming, incongruously, Stratford-upon-Avon. It makes the most of it: the local gallery displayed a jolly technicolour portrait of the Bard on the wall, copies of the collected works in the gift shop, and posters for the annual Shakespeare festival on the door, the result of what I could only presume to be an extended local in-joke taken root.

A few miles downriver was the site of McMillan's homestead, his much-beloved Bushy Park. It was here that he finally struck out alone in 1841, the quarrel with Macalister over the search for Corner Inlet having driven a wedge between them, and he found himself marking out land, laying claim in his own name for the first time.

Over the next twenty years McMillan amassed a steadily growing fortune, and from this new family seat oversaw a property empire that at its height extended to seven runs encompassing a total of 150,000 acres, an area ten times the size of Barra. Each run had its own accommodation, gardens and agricultural facilities. Bushy Park boasted a homestead, assorted outbuildings including stables and a 'ball room' where he held ceilidhs, a six-acre orchard and a further thirty acres under cultivation with wheat, oats and peas. Today such an estate would be worth many millions of dollars.

Von Guérard's *View of the Gippsland Alps, from Bushy Park on the River Avon.*

He had made the jump that his father had never managed, from tacksman to laird. As befitting a gentleman of his status he took to wearing tweed three-piece suits as well as his omnipresent tartan bonnet. He hosted visiting dignitaries, including the anthropologist Alfred Howitt, who would later diligently record the traditions of the vanishing Gunai, and the botanist Baron von Mueller. Eugene von Guérard, the most significant landscape artist of the period, stayed at Bushy Park too, and while there painted the panoramic view from the terrace: blue ranges skirting the horizon, horned bullocks lazing in the long grass, Aboriginal children playing on a fallen gum.

It was all McMillan's own. He was the Laird of Gippsland now. But he hadn't forgotten his roots. His brother Donald joined him at Bushy Park after a period in the West Indies. McMillan also arranged for newly emigrated Scots to stay at the Port Phillip Club in Melbourne at his expense until they had found suitable employment in the colony. He himself employed plenty of Highlanders; they flocked to him. He served the workers two drams of whisky a day. 'If hospitality be a virtue his was unbounded, and he exercised it continuously,' one contemporary recalled.

And his generosity was rewarded. He was made judge at the 'Green Wattle' races, highlight of the Gippsland social calendar, and was later elected by a landslide as Member of the Legislative Assembly for South Gippsland. The controversy over who had better claim to the discovery of the land – McMillan or Strzelecki – had died down: McMillan had stayed, while Strzelecki, attention-seeker that he was, had torn off in search of greater glory elsewhere. McMillan, everyone was agreed, was the true hero of Gippsland, and rightly deserved the title.

The first of a series of annual dinners in his honour was organised in 1856. Amid 'loud and repeated cheers' and toasts to the queen, McMillan was singled out for the highest of praise and prevailed upon to give a speech, the body of which was later reported in the Melbourne *Argus*:

Chairman and Gentlemen, – you have by your unexpected and unlooked for kindness this evening placed me in a position that nearly deprives me of the power of utterance. Little did I think when, in the performance of my duty to my employer, so many years ago, in forcing my way inch by inch through the wilds and fastnesses that bound this now fertile district, that my humble efforts would be thus so signally honoured by the inhabitants of this favoured territory ... It was a happy day to me when I found my way to the Old Port, but this indeed is the happiest hour of my life.

This version of the truth – the story of plucky Highlander made good – is what seems to have stuck, on the surface at least.

McMillan took to styling himself as a gentleman.

Near the site of his former homestead at Bushy Park we found the inevitable cairn, and a noticeboard outlining his achievements and legacy. No mention of any trouble. We drove the perimeter of the old estate along a long line of red gums that stood sentry on the verge – stained with dark clots where the trunks had been bruised, like blood on a grazed knee – and I hung my head out of the window, trying to identify the spot where von Guérard must have stood to paint his panorama.

This trip, I reflected, had so far been unexpectedly painless. I had come face to face with precisely no uncomfortable truths about the family legacy. It was almost as if no one had told anyone in Gippsland about all the ugly goings-on in their own history. Maybe, suggested a small voice, there's been some kind of misunderstanding. Maybe it wasn't as bad as all that. It's possible that I've got the wrong impression.

This growing suspicion – or was it hope? – did not abate when we visited McMillan's grave in Sale. The enormous graveyard was on the outskirts of town, 14,000 plots laid out in extravagant style in the form of a clover. At its centre, where the leaves branched off, a many-headed signpost directed each denomination to their own patch of sacred ground, like one of those humorous signs at tourist hotspots indicating that New York lies 3,796 miles in one direction and Moscow 1,435 in another.

We followed the 'PRESBYTERIAN >>>' arm to a decrepit section where rusted metal fences kept visitors from treading on the bare earth of the graves, the stones cracked and watermarked, their inscriptions barely legible. Some sat at drunken angles, set askew by rabbit holes dug directly underneath. The names I could make out were like the roll call at a Scottish school: Isabella and Archibald MacLachlan from Rothesay; Flora Macdonald Brown of Portree; Robert Alexander, native of Linlithgow; even a William Wallace ('loved husband of Bridget, RIP').

I searched fruitlessly for McMillan on all the headstones around a central obelisk that dwarfed them all, until finally I realised with a start that the obelisk was in fact the grave I was looking for. It too was fenced off, and a large sign bearing the logo of a local tourism initiative stood nearby, commemorating

THE DISCOVERY OF GIPPSLAND
by
ANGUS MCMILLAN
1810–1865

and bearing a blurb briefly outlining McMillan's achievements.

This grave, I learned later, had been the focus of an 'annual pilgrimage' of Sale residents from 1924 until the events of the Second World War overtook their nostalgic fervour. Local newspaper reports describe how dignitaries, well-wishers and schoolchildren gathered to commemorate the life of 'undoubtedly one of the greatest men Gippsland had ever known'. They gave speeches, recited poetry and sang songs written in his honour:

Let Onward, Onward, be the cry
Of each brave heart to-day.
There's land and room for all
Does not McMillan say.

(*Chorus*) Then come over the mountains,
Come where the green wattles grow;
Come where sweet birds are singing,
Come where the rivers flow.

Then Hurrah, Hurrah for the Pilot
That first set foot in Gippsland.
And three cheers for the boys that were with him
With our glass, our heart, and hand ...

On the way back into town we passed a turn-off for
McMillan Street. A few blocks down, McMillan Park. The
local college, I knew, had a McMillan campus. Later,
totally lost and searching for a place to camp, I would
stumble across an abandoned, overgrown campsite; an
entrance arch labelled it the property of the McMillan
County Scouts. It was almost eerie, the way a sort of
personality cult had grown up around him. Nowhere was
there mention of any massacres. I had come here expecting hushed voices and recriminations, but instead I had
found him canonised, immortalised at every corner.

What did that mean? I was struggling to understand
where I stood, distracted by the heaving of my push-me-
pull-you emotions. In one sense, if Angus McMillan wasn't
the villain I had understood him to be, then my entire trip
was nothing more than a self-congratulatory lap of victory
around the sites of my relative's achievements. At the

same time, I still felt the warm glow of reflected fame. I *wanted* it to be the truth. I *wanted* him to be every bit as good as they said he was.

I wanted him to be a hero.

We were late, horribly late. Jeannie and I came barrelling in through the doors, blurting our apologies.

Two representatives of the Maffra Historical Society, based near Bushy Park, had agreed to meet us in what was once a beet factory, now a makeshift museum exhibiting what seemed, to my eyes, a collection of the most incredible mundanity. Much wall space had been awarded to the 'rise, success, and eventual end' of the sugar-beet industry in the district, closely followed by a series of exquisitely detailed pen portraits of all the local farms and their homesteads circa 1890.

Perhaps this is the purpose of these odd, hyperlocal societies: to catalogue the past in such painstaking detail that only the residents themselves would be interested in doing so. In Boisdale, a nearby village, an equivalent group had sunk much time and thought into a series of bronze plaques logging the birth and career of almost every building – the butcher's, the post office, the brick cottages 'built to house the cheese and butter factory workers' – as if they couldn't bear even a single detail to be forgotten.

Taking this into account, I was all the more staggered by the inexplicable lack of information about those supposed massacres, some of which were alleged to have been committed only a few miles from this spot. Wouldn't a group of such evident diligence and focus have alighted breathlessly on a thrilling historical scandal in their very district? This, I thought, was *real history*, a meaty saga of ambition and butchery and the struggle for power – a more fertile patch for study, surely, than lists of factory workers and municipal planning through the decades.

Still, it was generous of them to have agreed to meet me at all, and they were well informed. They were delighted to discuss the local area, and had come prepared with a list of references I should look up in the local archive; but they were oddly taciturn on the subject of Angus McMillan and the massacres.

'Well,' said one of them cautiously, under close questioning, 'I'm not sure we have very much on McMillan. Although I know of him, of course.' She was a mumsy woman, with wire-rimmed spectacles and mouse-coloured hair. She blinked at me, then gestured to a small patch of wall space where McMillan was pictured hand in hand with two unidentified Aboriginal men. 'I think he was ... very much a man of his time. I think he did what he thought was best. It was all they could do at the time.'

Her companion, an older man, was more headstrong. 'When we learned about him at school, we never heard anything about this,' he said. 'All these claims originated from the research of one man,' he continued, opening his hands as if inviting me to reach my own conclusions. 'What some of these so-called historians come up with to sell their books!'

I knew who he was referring to: Peter Gardner, a local historian who had written a series of books in the 1980s in which he laid out much inflammatory evidence of bloodshed in the earliest years of settlement, causing quite a kerfuffle in the press and historical journals.

The woman chimed in again. 'Angus was a pioneer. He

was doing a job, clearing the land of whatever it was full of. We wouldn't be here without him. Maybe it was nasty at the beginning, but it's history now, and you just have to get on with things. You know, when Aboriginal people go on about ... Well. They're lucky it was the British, and not the Dutch or Germans. Then they'd *really* have been in trouble.'

That night we stayed with Cath and Mike, old friends of Jeannie and Ian's, retired teachers who lived in a low-slung, surprisingly spacious bungalow up a long, gum-lined drive on what was once the Boisdale run, Bushy Park's neighbour station, set up by McMillan on Macalister's behalf in 1840.

Cath welcomed me with a pile of books she had salvaged during a clear-out of her school library. 'Local history was on the curriculum, but it seems to have gone out of fashion,' she lamented. We sat on the terrace at the front of the house, where long tendrils of climbing plants stretched down to stroke our faces, kindly tentacles.

I was usually slightly deflated by Australian country homes, which even on the largest estates tend to make little impact on approach: almost inevitably single-storeyed, stretching off backwards like a maze. They are not grand, but it's the roof space that counts: almost everyone collects rainwater for their private supply, and many houses in the country are not attached to the mains supply at all. The gathering and filtration systems are a constant source of fascination, and at any rural gathering, as time goes on the probability of any two Australian men turning to the subject of water collection approaches one.

The house lay in a 'rain shadow', Mike informed me broodily at dinner. 'It looks great, good farmland, until there's a ten-year drought ... then it feels like it's never going to rain again.' On the wall was a frame holding a series of photos of their daughter bouncing on a trampoline, one a year, every year, for ten or fifteen years, as she grew through infancy and girlhood into her awkward teens. In the background the photographs unintentionally charted the state of the climate, the yearly rainfall tracked and coded by colour. In the early pictures the grass was green-yellow, then strawlike. A few years later, shorn short and so blond it was almost white.

'Our son got married here that summer,' said Cath, following my eyes. 'We had to lay a red carpet to make it a bit more presentable. The grass just turned to dust under your feet.'

'What about you, Cal?' Jeannie changed the subject. 'What about your partner? Doesn't he mind you disappearing off to the other side of the world for weeks at a time?'

I felt the eyes of the table on me. 'Not really!' I chirruped. 'He's off doing something else. Trekking in the desert. Counting leopards.'

'Oh. Then you understand each other.'

'Yes,' I said, at first pleased and then uneasy. Recently we seemed to have been misunderstanding each other more often than understanding. Or we had been, at least, until he went to the desert.

He'd emailed from a border town: 'I won't be able to message much after this.'

'That's fine,' I'd lied. 'I understand.' I hadn't heard from him since.

I smiled, falsely, breezily, around the table, and changed the subject again.

After dinner, head swimming, I excused myself and walked down the track in the dusk towards Maffra, the nearest town. An earlier squall of rain had soaked immediately into the thirsty earth, and the sky had opened up again above me, now awash with stars, the sweep of the Milky Way a veil drawn fast across its naked breast. The sliver of new moon hung hooklike, a bright satellite-star at its foot.

The air was still, but the night was alive with sound, which grew in pitch and volume as I veered off through the thick grass towards a shallow pool that reverberated with the rasping of frogs — some deep and percussive, others melodic, singsong, all falling quiet as I approached then resuming behind me when I moved on, in a bubble of silence.

I ran my hands along the smooth trunk of a fallen gum, tracing the silky folds where the limbs joined the trunk. They were sensual somehow. I'd been aching to touch them for days, slipping my fingers into the puckers in the bark that brought to mind thoughts of warm flesh, of wrists and ankles, of the creases between thumb and forefinger, the no-man's land between the curve of a jaw and the neck.

A flock of black birds sat massed in the bare branches of a dead tree above, watching and catcalling, dark menaces with long curving beaks and the hunched wings of vultures. Their shrieks were guttural, penetrating.

The dark drew in like a cloak, the wall of sound closing tight around me. I could imagine, now, the long, slow summer nights on the runs. The soundscape, the landscape, the pull on the heart of these wide-open spaces.

The catch of breath in the back of the throat at the sheer scale of the place.

Imagine tumbling off the boat with your bag of belongings and finding all this endless land stretching out before you, when at home they were being pushed from their tiny cliffside toeholds.

6

Black War

But of course it hadn't been lying there empty. The Gunai people were already there, had been there for tens of thousands of years.

McMillan may have taken umbrage at Strzelecki's renaming, his 'piracy', but the Gunai too had names for everything, long before his arrival. The disputed Lake King – or was it Lake Victoria? – had always been, to its residents, known as Narran, meaning 'moon'. To them, the river by which McMillan constructed his homestead was not the Avon, but the Dooyedang. And they did not see the land as McMillan saw it, in acres and yields, in heads of cattle, but through the prism of a complex system of mythology and tradition.

The deep waters of Corner Inlet and its surrounds – the mangroves and wetlands, the scattering of islands in the bay – were not a natural harbour at all, but a souvenir from the events of the Dreamtime. Long ago, legend had it, this region had been part of a land bridge connecting Gippsland to far-off Tasmania, but one day the frog spirit Tiddilik had drunk all of the water in the land and carried it around in his gut until finally, at Tarra Warackel (Port Albert), he spewed it all out in a great flood that washed away the land and left only islands and the perilous stretch of water of Bass Strait. These wetlands became the home of Boorun the pelican and Tuk the musk duck, the father and mother of all the Gunai peoples.

Further east, at Bung Yarnda (Lake Tyers), the sea-being Narkabungdha found himself tired from rushing over rocks and rolling back and forth across the sand, and came inland to rest. He found a quiet place among the shady gum trees where he fell asleep, creating those magnificent freshwater lakes that irrigate the fertile grasslands. To the north, the limestone caves that riddle the hillsides of Bukkanmunjie (Buchan) were home to the mischievous nyols, who stole the memory of those who visited them, and at Ngrung a Narguna (Den of Nargun) a huge living rock from the beginning of time sheltered behind a water-fall, waiting for stray children to snatch away.

These stories and beliefs were unique to Gunai culture, one of several hundred distinct Aboriginal nations that patchworked the Australian continent at the time of the arrival of the First Fleet. Together, these nations – who, in the southeast, refer to themselves collectively as Koories – comprised a total population estimated at between 700,000 and a million. Within what is now the state of Victoria alone there were dozens of Aboriginal nations – as many as thirty-nine, according to one estimate – each of which had its own language, culture and beliefs, and constantly shifting relations with its neighbours, as alliances formed and dissolved, territory was disputed and blood feuds fought.

Five linguistically similar groups around the Port Phillip area to the east, for example, had joined together to form the 'Kulin alliance'; they hated and despised the Gunai, who in turn terrorised the Ya-itma-thang and Ngarico peoples to their north and west. These bitter conflicts had played out over centuries, as each made incursions into the other's land to wage war in night-time raids – black-skinned men painted with ochre and clay emerging like phantoms from the darkness to kill or to steal away women. This was the backdrop of the warrigals' fearful reputation.

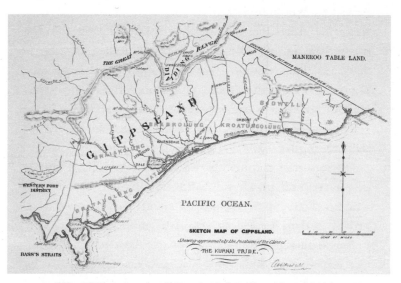

Alfred Howitt's map of Gippsland describing the territories held by each clan.

All of these nations were subdivided into smaller 'clan groups', each with a specific dialect and variants of tradition, and in turn these clans were divvied further into smaller family groups of perhaps a couple of dozen members each, who would come together for special ceremonial occasions. The Gunai nation was made up of five clans: the Brabawooloong, of the high country and central lowlands;

the Bratowooloong, who lived in the south; the Brayak-ooloong of the west; the Krowathunkooloong to the east; and the Tatungooloong of the coast and the lakes.

All lived a nomadic existence, moving with the seasons between a number of different sites, following the fluc-tuating sources of food and water, constructing their temporary shelters as they went from leaves or bark or branches, or simply commandeering caves among the rocks. As the hunter-gatherer lifestyle had proven suffi-cient for nutrition and shelter – tasks required for survival taking up only four or five hours of the day – there had been no need for agriculture or pastoralism. There were no fences then, or permanent structures; no marked boundaries between each clan's territory.

The first European arrivals in Australia were baffled by these eccentric natives, who had no yen for personal possessions nor any obvious leaders or hierarchy. Political power and land ownership had little relevance to them; as Captain Cook observed on his arrival in Botany Bay in 1770, 'all they seem'd to want was us to be gone'.

And it was the intangibility of the Aboriginal presence that initially lulled the colonists into the false sense that they were settling an unoccupied land. Cook, in fact, had originally been issued with instructions from the Admiralty that he should take possession of 'convenient situations' in the new country in the name of the king, 'with the consent of the natives'. But such agreements were never made concrete, unlike in New Zealand, where representatives of the Crown negotiated directly with Maori chiefs and recognised traditional ownership; put simply, the British could not identify any Aboriginal leaders with authority to negotiate, and so did not negotiate at all.

In later years, in misguided attempts to gain a foothold in the shifting sands of indigenous society, the settlers would crown Aboriginal 'kings', picking out the most cooperative elders and presenting them with curved copper breastplates, their names engraved upon them like a plaque for a wall, and the title 'KING OF THE ——' underneath. They were intended to act as handy name tags so other colonists might court these new, recognisable powers, but the policy met with mixed success. The recipients would sometimes trade away these 'king plates' to others, or as the Gippsland missionary John Bulmer later wrote, 'These fellows who have been given a brass plate wait at every steamer landing ... asking for sixpence to get grog with.'

Gunai encampment, 1870. The man on the right wears a king plate.

The only documented attempt to bargain directly with an Aboriginal group for ownership of the land took place many decades later, in 1835, when the explorer and pastoralist John Batman negotiated the 'purchase' of 600,000 acres of land in the Melbourne area from Kulin leaders, in return for an annual tribute of blankets, axes, knives, scissors, mirrors and assorted clothing. There have been a number of questions over the validity of the resulting document, not least because the Aboriginal 'translators' brought by Batman's party shared no common language with the Kulin – it is now thought that the Kulin leaders believed they were being offered gifts in exchange for safe passage through their land – but nevertheless this 'treaty' was perceived as enough of a threat to the Crown, which assumed ownership of all Australian land, for Governor Sir Richard Bourke to issue a proclamation declaring it null:

> every such treaty, bargain, and contract with the Aboriginal Natives ... for the possession, title, or claim to any Lands lying and being within the limits of the Government of the Colony of New South Wales ... is void and of no effect against the rights of the Crown ...

Any persons found in possession of such land 'will be considered as trespassers', he added. Thus Bourke made explicit the principle that had underpinned the actions of the British colonists up to this point, and that would become the explicit doctrine of the administration for more than 150 years: the concept of Australia as *terra nullius*, no-man's land. An empty place, belonging to no one. The Aboriginal people who wandered its tracks, picking its fruit, catching its fish, but not tilling the soil or grazing the plains, were considered as wild animals; they came with the territory, but could not be considered its owners. Without an owner, the land was there for the taking. And take it they did.

Driven first by drought, and then by the depression that hit Melbourne in the early 1840s, new settlers rushed for the new land. Those coming from the west were largely following the siren call of Strzelecki, who had very successfully spread word of the pleasures that awaited them in Gippsland, even going so far as to produce a (horribly inaccurate) map suggesting the most direct route into the region from Melbourne. Whether any of the incomers thought twice about taking directions from a man who had almost starved to death whilst undertaking the same journey I don't know, but certainly many of them ran immediately into trouble.

The area through which they must travel to reach the pastureland – a primeval forest of eucalypt, bonewood and towering mountain ash – was notoriously difficult going. William Odell Raymond, an English magistrate who would become McMillan's neighbour when he took up the Stratford run in 1842, found himself and his party caught in the dense, prickly undergrowth like flies in a web, 'suffering severely from the cuts we got getting through the scrub[,] our clothes and boots being completely torn off of us'.

The Gunai generally avoided the area, considering it subject to an ancient curse. They called it *Wea-wuk*: the bad country. Both the Gunai and the neighbouring Bun Wurrung clan of the Kulin believed that strangers who walked upon this cursed land were at risk of harm. To travel safely, it was thought, visitors had to travel in the company of the traditional owners (the Brayakooloong or

Bratowooloong clans of the Gunai), sleep on a layer of leaves so as to keep from touching the ground, and eat only what morsels their host brought them, pulling them from a skewer using their teeth.

Of course, the incoming European settlers knew none of this, only the extreme difficulties that many of their number suffered in their attempts to breach the 'fortress' of Gippsland. Henry Colden Harrison, 'the father of Australian Rules Football' and the son of a grazier, wrote many years later of his family's unsuccessful attempt to settle in Gippsland. Having set out with five hundred cattle and 'five or six thousand sheep', they managed to lose most of the former in the scrub. As for the latter, they were so thirsty that 'the poor animals, on seeing the sea, rushed into it, and many of them were attacked and killed by the sharks'. By the time the Harrisons finally got to their destination with the sad remnants of their livestock, they were out of luck: the choicest cuts of land had already been snapped up. At the Tarwin River, on the edge of Gippsland, they met future Victorian governor Charles La Trobe, who advised them to turn back, assuring them 'that there was not a yard of country left'.

From first discovery to 'not a yard left' took less than five years. It was a sea change, a transformation far too rapid in nature for colonial infrastructure to keep up with. With a scattered, autonomous and largely undocumented population came a total lack of governance: this was very much the Australian frontier – the Wild East, perhaps.

In the early years there was no state presence whatsoever. The first government representative, Commissioner Charles Tyers, arrived by boat in 1843 – following three failed attempts to enter overland, repulsed each time by the viciousness of the Bad Country – to find total chaos. The region was 'infested' with 'runaway convicts and other bad characters', he complained in a note to his superiors, adding an appeal to be provided with a unit of mounted police to help him keep order. The first resident minister, Reverend Willoughby Bean, found things little improved by 1848, when he reported on the 'disreputable and immoral class of persons' who continued to reside in the area, and quoted a local judge's pronouncement that the outskirts of Port Albert had become a 'pandemonium upon earth'.

It is hard, perhaps, for someone who has grown up in the security of a developed country to comprehend the vertigo felt by those who launched themselves out into this new land, only to find themselves floating in a stateless vacuum. As an unsupervised classroom will morph in minutes from quiet concentration into a seething mass of feral children, any community without effective government oversight is at risk of speedy descent into chaos and injustice. Henry Meyrick, a young English settler who travelled with his brother to the region in 1846, wrote home, overwhelmed by the experience. 'We have learned some wisdom in Gippsland,' he told his mother. 'It is a current saying that a man who has lived here can match the devil himself. It is certainly the most lawless place I have ever heard of.'

The sheer pace of change could be difficult for some of the earliest pioneers to come to terms with; the very first arrivals often reflected with mixed feelings upon the role they had played as harbingers of this change. Evelyn Sturt, an early settler in the Ovens River area, looked back two decades later with some nostalgia, remembering how on his arrival the country had been 'most beautiful – miles of it untrodden by stock, and indeed unseen by Europeans. Every creek abounded with wild fowl, and the quail sprang from the long kangaroo grass which waved to the very flaps of the saddle. It has often been a source of regret to me,' he added, 'that all the charms attending the traversing of a new country must give way to the march of civilization; the camp on the grassy sward is now superseded by the noisy road-side inn; the quart pot of tea by the bottle of ale. All the quiet serenity of an Australian bush, as we have known it, has yielded to the demands of population ... I look back to those days as some joyous scene of school-boy holidays.'

Theirs were not the only sets of eyes looking upon the evolving landscape in horror. The explorers had, at least, seen Western civilisation before; they recognised it, and had made it their lives' work to advance its interests. But imagine the same through the eyes of the Gunai. Imagine the shock of seeing your country, through which you had wandered unfettered all your life, re-form and mutate before your eyes: the ground left stubbled and raw as acres of bush were cleared; fences erected to contain hordes of alien beasts, those slack-jawed masticators; wooden shacks popping up like fungus in all the best camping spots by the rivers and waterholes, appearing one day and never moving off. And everywhere, now, these white-faced men.

The Gunai had a close relationship with the dead. They believed their departed kindred passed through the solid vault of the sky to live in the spirit-country, a land like their own, of tall eucalypts and fast-flowing rivers, but that they could send down ropes and revisit the land of the living. And so they stayed on, ever present but not always visible. They wandered among the sleeping bodies at night, conversed with the Gunai in dreams – counselled them, warned them, brought them offerings of song and charms to protect them from evil.

They were often friendly, but not always – evil spirits sometimes cursed or physically attacked the living – and the appearance of even the benevolent dead could be a portent of doom. The anthropologist Alfred Howitt relayed a story of an elderly Koorie man who reported that 'in the night, his father, his father's friend and a female spirit he could not recognize, had come to him and said that he would die next day, and that they would wait for him'. Howitt added that he could give many similar instances, 'and, strange to say, the dying man in all these cases kept his appointment with the ghosts to the very day'.

The Gunai therefore treated their dead with a respect bordering on veneration. As McMillan had already seen, they had a propensity to wear the hands of the deceased slung around their necks as a token of affection. 'They are beautifully preserved,' noted a later arrival, 'nails and flesh, with veins all perfect. Their mode of preserving them is by a curious process of stewing with hot stones.'

It was traditional to carry around the bodies of the dead for weeks or months, in a very literal interpretation of the grieving process. The corpse would be wrapped in a curl of bark as it decomposed, flesh liquefying, hair and teeth loosening. Every so often the bark would be unpeeled to reveal what was left of the body, and the grease exuding from the corpse applied to the mourners' skin. Finally, when the body had truly decayed, the fingers and other appendages were broken off and stuffed into a possum-skin bag for use as a pillow.

The Gunai too, under certain circumstances, would eat the flesh of warriors they had killed in combat – not for sustenance, but in a ceremonial act of conquest. They believed that by consuming the flesh of their enemies, particularly the fat from around the kidneys, they would gain the strength of the dead man. 'They said the flesh tasted better than beef,' reported Howitt. To roast human meat, they would cut sections from the corpse and pass a burning firestick over them. During this process the scorched outer layer of skin peeled off and the blood drained away, leaving the chunks of carcass an eerie white hue.

When the bushmen first encountered McMillan on the banks of the Tambo, they recognised the colour of his skin as the pallor of death. 'Mrart', they called the white man. Ghost.

It was an obvious assumption to make. Elsewhere in Victoria, the escaped convict William Buckley had been taken in by the Wathaurung Kulin, who thought him the returned spirit of a dead tribesman. The widow of the dead man had found Buckley wandering the bush holding a spear that had been used to mark the grave. She took him to be her husband and he was welcomed into the clan, with whom he lived for over thirty years.

But now, in Gippsland, the mrart's own people had come en masse to settle this country. All of them men, all of them white-faced, all of them speaking in tongues and spraying violence from the rods they raised to their lightning eyes. An invasion of ghosts, each with the power to strike a Gunai man down dead at a hundred paces with that sudden crack and a great fountain of blood.

The initial encounters between the two groups – notably McMillan's encounter with the elderly man bedecked with hands, who after receiving gifts of a knife and trousers from the party, shook hands with all its members then turned to the horses and *shook the bridles very heartily* – were fairly innocuous. But when the Gunai realised that their white visitors planned to set up home, they reacted strongly and negatively, and moved to repulse them.

In October 1840, after establishing the first station on the banks of the Avon, McMillan and five men made a third, failed attempt to fight their way to Corner Inlet. Foiled by a succession of marshes, thickets and torrential rivers, they were forced to admit defeat not twenty miles from the anticipated harbour, the existence of which they still had to confirm and locate before settlement of the region could begin in earnest. In ill spirits, and by this stage barely speaking to one another, the party turned towards home, with the uncomfortable sense that they were being watched.

The tribesmen kept their distance, flitting away through the bush faster than the heavily laden visitors and their horses could follow, but the group grew uneasy. At night they took it in turns to keep watch, eyes searching the formless dark beyond the circle of light cast by the fire, ears pricked for the sound of footsteps in the dark.

Finally, as they struggled across Clifton Morass – a mire where McMillan's *gallant grey* had once been so badly bogged they were obliged to parbuckle him to solid ground – their shadows revealed themselves. The party were suddenly surrounded on all sides by around eighty Gunai men, each brandishing a quartz-tipped spear and a carved wooden shield. Vastly outnumbered, and feeling his party in danger, McMillan *fired both barrels, but did not kill any of them*. It was enough: the Gunai took fright, and fled back into the scrub.

This was the first sign that all was not well.

Those dark faces, which had formerly seemed so innocent – fleeing the explorers' approach with such urgency that they would leave their belongings behind – now appeared threatening and unknowable. They had allowed their ghostly visitors to pass unscathed as they watched from the shadow of the bush, but now McMillan recalled the warnings of those infamous warriors conjured up by the Omeo blacks.

Leaving his men to their work, he hurried back along his old tracks to the Monaro and civilisation, where the nearest commissioner of Crown lands might be found. They needed assistance, fast, he told officials when he arrived. Could the commissioner spare men and firearms for the protection of settlers in the new district?

The appeal fell on deaf ears. Any settlers heading so far beyond the limits of the colony, the commissioner told him, were doing so at their own risk. McMillan's and his men's safety was entirely in their own hands.

Dejected, McMillan turned back once more, only to find on his return to Gippsland that his fears had been realised. While he had been away, wrangling with bureaucrats in the Monaro, the station on the Avon had been attacked. His men had escaped with their lives, but barely

– they had fled to Numbla Munjee with the Gunai in hot pursuit for the first twenty-five miles. The cattle, they said, had all been speared or dispersed.

It was a major setback, but McMillan was damned if he would give up now. Steeling himself for combat, he formed a party of eight men, armed them well and returned to Bushy Park, to find a hellish scene: the remains of their dead animals scattered all around, the one-roomed hut where once they'd slept reduced to ruins. They rebuilt it, further back from the creek this time, and hunkered down.

Each day they lit fresh fires to advertise their presence to the Gunai, then returned to the hut to wait it out. Time passed slowly. The sun rose, plateaued and fell again. Flies settled on faces and forearms, buzzing lazily away whenever the men raised a hand to shoo them, then setting down again as soon as the coast was clear. The nights were endless and oppressively hot. Finally, on the night of 22 December, the men were disturbed by noises from outside. McMillan's horse, Clifton, had come up close to the hut, showing the whites of his eyes; he had been spooked by movements in the dark. The men knew then that they must prepare for attack.

Dr Alexander Arbuckle, the first doctor to practise in Gippsland and a close friend of McMillan's, had been injured during the journey to the station, so they installed him in the fireplace, where he was told to load the spare guns in between volleys. The others cut loopholes in the hut's thin walls and waited for sunrise.

The day faded in. Birdsong; the sigh of the wind through the tall grass. Light crept through the valley, illuminating the figures of the Gunai men who circled the hut like a bad dream. An army, five or six hundred strong, all of them watching, waiting. The tension was unbearable. Then – movement, as the men crouched, fixed spears to their woomeras and prepared to let loose upon the hut. A voice sounded, low and urgent, in the dark interior: McMillan's. He told his men to prepare to fire. They were not to waste a bullet.

'There was a desperate fight,' the *Gippsland Times* reported later, 'but history is silent as to the casualties among the natives. The whites came through all right.'

*

I do hereby strictly forbid any of His Majesty's Subjects, resident or stationary in this Colony, from using any act of Injustice or wanton Cruelty towards the Natives, on pain of being dealt with in the same manner as if such act of Injustice or wanton Cruelty should be committed against the Persons and Estates of any of His Majesty's Subjects.

Proclamation by Governor King, 30 June 1802

The rules were clear enough. Thou shalt not kill. Thou shalt not torture. Thou shalt not inflict wanton cruelty. But the Sydney government's moralising grew further and further out of step with the reality of the frontier.

The Gunai were growing more troublesome as the settlers dug in. The white men, it seemed, were in infinite supply, and as their population began to multiply they were carving up every scrap of grazing land between them. The Gunai found their traditional campsites and hunting grounds occupied, and their prey animals – kangaroos, wallabies, emus – driven to the margins of the country and replaced by those strange swarms of four-legged creatures. Resentment grew on both sides.

With no concept of pastoralism or the 'ownership' of animals, the Gunai turned to hunting the settlers' stock, spearing the slow-moving cattle and eating what they could before the huge carcasses rotted. They drove flocks of sheep to remote spots, then broke their legs to restrain them, and thus keep their meat fresh. 'It is absurd to blame the aborigines for killing sheep and cattle,' the Gippsland court clerk George Dunderdale reflected. 'You might as well say it is immoral for a cat to catch mice.' Still, it drove the squatters, who had painstakingly driven the animals hundreds of miles, to distraction. Edward Bell, a pioneer in the Wimmera region during the period, remembered: 'I recollect a cow being brought into the stockyard stuck all over with spears, like a porcupine ... In tracking cattle I came upon a place where the blacks had within a few days camped some stolen sheep in bough-yards, and where the torn fleeces and broken legs and joints, since gnawed by wild dogs, told a tale of wasteful destruction.'

Many facing financial ruin turned, as McMillan had, to the government for support, and found none forthcoming. 'It was scarcely to be wondered at,' Bell wrote, 'that the settlers took the law into their own hands on such occasions.' So it proved in Gippsland. McMillan's 'defence of Bushy Park', as it came to be known, had set the tone for future encounters between the two peoples. The settlers were hardening their hearts.

New arrivals were confronted with a simple choice: beat a retreat, and seek out a less fertile location in some unexploited cranny in a less conflicted area of the colony; or face the Aboriginal threat and attempt to neutralise it. To most of them, the choice was simple. Within a very short space of time, they began to kill without compunction.

The second clash – perhaps more accurately, the second *known* clash – took place shortly after, when McMillan's same party is thought to have ridden down a group of Gunai to the marshy confluence of the Avon and Perry Rivers, where they were trapped and shot down in their dozens.

Later, George Augustus Robinson, Chief Protector of Aborigines for Port Phillip with the duty to 'protect and civilize' the besieged indigenes of Victoria, to which Gippsland had latterly been added, would – after a jolly evening's entertainment at Bushy Park – stumble upon 'many human bones and skulls' in the area, which lay bleaching in the grass for years to come. No doubt this was the source of the spot's macabre name: Boney Point.

Pastoral scene on banks of Lake Wellington. Boney Point, scene of the second clash, is not far away.

Most often the flashpoint would be the spearing of sheep or cattle; the squatters would retaliate by shooting dead the first Gunai they came across, usually with no evidence that the victims had been the culprits. Patrick Coady Buckley, one of McMillan's contemporaries, described such a scene in his journal: 'Walked out ... to scrub below House where blacks had taken some sheep evening before. On our way out saw five Blackfellows about one hundred and fifty yards ahead[.] Marshall and I fired at them and chased them but they got into the scrub ... Marshall and I had double barreled guns.'

The wronged Gunai would then wait for an opportunity to take their revenge. In a straight fight against an armed militia they stood little chance, but they were skilled practitioners of guerrilla warfare. For this *was* war. Unofficial and undeclared it may have been, but for a period of around a decade the two groups were in a state of total hostility.

It became unsafe to travel alone or unarmed in Gippsland. Wandering shepherds and lonely drovers were picked off in sudden raids or by carefully laid ambush. 'Unfair!' cried the settlers, without irony, and prepared their response. And thus was the bitter cycle inflamed.

It was a reprisal killing like this that led to by far the fiercest confrontation of the period, the massacre at Warrigal Creek. In July 1843 Lachlan Macalister's nephew Ronald was killed while out riding near Alberton, the fifth in a spate of recent black-on-white murders. Investigating later, Protector Robinson suggested that Macalister had been killed in retribution for an earlier incident, when 'some depraved white men had in a fit of drunkenness shot at and killed some friendly natives'.

When the corpse was discovered, all hell broke loose. Whether they had known it or not, by killing Ronald Macalister the culprits had landed a solid punch at the core of Gippsland society. The settlers united in a single, furious body with McMillan at its head, ready to strike down the next black face they saw. The nearest Gunai target lay a few miles along the coast, a long-standing encampment in a picturesque curve of the creek. They charged down there, waving pistols and crying obscenities, and let loose upon the unsuspecting tribesmen.

They were like madmen, these men of the 'Highland Brigade'. When the carnage at Warrigal Creek was not enough to quench their blood-thirst they rode on, marching an orphaned child guide ahead of them at gunpoint. They stalked the flats searching for quarry, even as the wails of the dying rang in their ears and the stink of blood-spatter hung in their noses.

The Bratowooloong clan targeted at Warrigal Creek and in subsequent attacks had once numbered between 330 and five hundred members. When they were next counted, in 1869, there were only seventeen. Afterwards there was no great outpouring of grief, for there was nearly no one left to grieve. The memory of those who had been killed was snuffed out and buried along with them, as an entire clan group collapsed in on itself like a black hole.

As race relations grew ever more antagonistic, the attacks became more one-sided, taking on an element of sport: the killing of the Gunai had become something like a culturally acceptable hobby. Letters of the time take on the air of match reports, thrumming with the rallying cries of the huntsmen — Hark forrard! Hark forrard! — as they call ever more hounds to the hunt. Even Crown Commissioner Tyers took part. 'A.M. — rain[,] P.M. — fine,' began one 1845 entry in his journal. 'In pursuit of blacks.'

The next year, Patrick Buckley recorded a tortuous episode when, after a series of cattle-spearings, he stumbled upon a young Gunai couple walking along the beach. He waited behind a dune until they drew near, then rode them down and forced them into the water at gunpoint. 'I had pistols with me and fired Blank Shots to keep them in the Sea which I did for about four hours,' he wrote later. The male fared worse; he seemed nearly drowned in the breakers. Buckley rode down into the surf, got a rein around his neck and pulled him up onto the sand. 'He pretended to be dead.'

What struck me most on reading these journals is how rarely their authors appear to be implicated in any actual killing. There are many, many accounts of 'shots fired' and 'pursuits' or 'chases', of storming Aboriginal encampments to 'take the natives by surprise'. Very few record the specifics of any actual deaths. But killing was certainly taking place; the young settler Henry Meyrick had been watching, wide-eyed, from the sidelines. 'The blacks are quiet here now poor wretches,' he wrote in 1846. 'No wild beast of the forest was ever hunted down with such unsparing perseverance as they are. Men, women and children are shot whenever they can be met with ... No consideration on earth would induce me to ride into a camp and fire on them indiscriminately, as is the custom whenever the smoke is seen.'

One does not have to look far for an explanation of the diarists' coyness. 'These things are kept very secret,' continued Meyrick, 'as the penalty would certainly be hanging.' Of course: the Myall Creek executions had shown that this was no empty threat. No further prosecutions had yet taken place, but who was to say they would not?

The culprits were educated men: landowners, justices of the peace, even the Crown Commissioner himself. They knew what could and could not be put down on paper. The clues are in what remains unsaid, the gaps in the accounts, the turning-away of heads.

A new vocabulary came into use. The Gunai did not commit 'crimes' or 'theft'. They perpetrated 'outrages', 'depredations' and 'barbarities'. By contrast, Aborigines were not 'killed' or 'murdered', they were 'dispersed'. Sometimes, following an 'outrage', they would be 'punished', or 'chastised'. Shots might be fired. It was never made clear where they landed.

The purpose of this new vocabulary was to obfuscate, and it did the job well. Meyrick reported what he knew of the massacres to William Thomas, the Assistant Protector, who recorded this 'most awful statement of doings', but noted the 'utter impossibility of bringing forward valid evidence to convict in a court of law'. His hands were tied, he said, 'yet the awful spectacle of human skeletons & packs of bones & reports of doings within the last 3 yrs, shows that the Aborigines have been cut off in awful numbers, & the residue left almost totally destitute'. And so the two men watched through their fingers as the Gunai were picked off like ducks in a shooting gallery.

If the written accounts of the period fail us in terms of objectivity, perhaps a set of figures tells the story more accurately, without the need for words. Commissioner Tyers, writing to Governor La Trobe in 1854, laid down his best estimates for the Gunai population at the time of his arrival (four years after McMillan) and at the present day:

GIPPSLAND: NUMBER OF ABORIGINES.
1843 — 1,800
1853 — 131
1854 (February) — 126

One of the oldest cultures in the world was being abruptly extinguished.

But secrets like this are very difficult to keep secret. It was far from the perfect crime. There are rumours, of course, and remains. Scraps of evidence that, when put together, form a convincing case for the prosecution.

To Bairnsdale. It was a low-slung town whose suburbs of wood-slat bungalows stretched out in a maze in all directions. The streets bore the names of early settlers: Pearson, Anderson, Nicholson, Wallace.

We had an appointment to meet Peter Gardner, the historian so disliked by my friend at the Maffra Historical Society. I knew his writing from a series of shocking exposés in historical journals of the massacres, but I had struggled to get hold of his three books, which had been published by a tiny local press with a minimal web presence.

He was, as he himself would admit, a subscriber to what is described by the Australian right wing as the 'black armband' school of thought. The term has emerged during the so-called 'history wars' which have drawn much public debate in Australia over recent decades, as academics and politicians of all stripes clash over what should be the proper interpretation of colonial history. Is it a daring tale of pioneers and plucky underdogs? Or is the truth to be found in the hidden lining, the dark recesses, that secret history that for the most part went unrecorded?

The most contentious area of debate centres on the dispossession of the Aboriginal population, and the significance that should be afforded to reports of violence on the frontier during this period. For many years, indigenous groups were simply not considered part of the grand narrative – writing in 1959, the historian John La Nauze observed that Aboriginal Australians had been little more than a 'melancholy anthropological footnote' to Australian history – but for some, the pendulum has now swung too far the other way.

Revisionist historians like Bill Stanner and Henry Reynolds did much to bring the Aboriginal experience of colonisation to light in the 1970s and 1980s, and their work has been very influential. Critics claim that this new school of thought paints an unnecessarily jaundiced picture, and achieves little other than creating a 'guilt industry' that has skewed modern politics and feeds the political correctness that ties it in knots. These criticisms have been levelled at Gardner too, as he waged what has been, a lot of the time, a one-man battle to get at the truth of the 'Black War' of Gippsland.

But he has persevered. 'The charge of "political correctness" has always been laughable,' he has written in response to his detractors. 'I first commenced my studies and writing in the early seventies. It wasn't until the mid-1980s ... that the question of frontier violence was even gener-

OUR LADY OF DUBLIN, an ancient statue of Our Lady and the Child Jesus, called the **Black Madonna**, because its tough oak was stained dark brown during the Reformation when . bright colours were forbidden in churches. It presides over the City as a sign of Mary's protection for her believing children who gather in faith.

SHRINE OF OUR LADY OF DUBLIN

Whitefriar Street Church,

The Carmelite Priory,

56 Aungier Street, Dublin 2. Tel. 758821

ally considered in Gippsland. Far from being politically correct, this work was new, somewhat controversial and challenged the status quo.'

Gardner moved to the region in 1973, initially working as a high-school teacher, and found his curiosity aroused by the paucity of information on the original inhabitants of the area. Some locals went so far as to deny the prior existence of any Aboriginal group – another claim he found 'laughable'. He immersed himself in Gippsland's history, fossicking in the archives, and began to piece together the uncomfortable reality. His earliest papers were published to a sometimes hostile audience – one local columnist dubbed the events Gardner described as the 'might-have-been' massacres – yet he stood resolute.

On paper I knew him to be bullish and self-assured, unafraid of controversy. His shocking conclusions were always backed up by quotes and figures, the veracity of which he had weighed and measured with clear-eyed exactitude. Conflicting voices were given short shrift: he declared Keith Windschuttle's claims that historians had falsified evidence to exaggerate the scale of frontier violence 'so much garbage'.

So it was with some surprise that I greeted the man who answered the door to us. He seemed quiet and non-confrontational, even shy. Tall and broad-shouldered, he was casually dressed, beard and ponytail grown long and slightly grey. He ushered us through to the kitchen table and put the kettle on, apparently discomfited by the atten-tion. His gaze skittered away to the window behind me whenever we made eye contact.

'It's a pleasure to meet you,' gushed Jeannie. 'You changed the way we think about history in Gippsland.'

'Uh,' he said, looking away. 'No. Not just me. Don Watson, of course –' the author of *Caledonia Australis* – 'and others.'

'You do seem to have done a lot of the heavy lifting,' I said, eliciting a rather awkward smile. 'So what next? Will you publish again?'

A shake of his head. 'I don't have the energy for it any more.' He gestured around the modest bungalow: its old-fashioned wallpaper, the squat bookcases full to overflowing. 'This place was my daughter's retirement plan for us. It has ... come to fruition a bit earlier than expected.' He sighed. 'I've handed over the copyright of the books to the local Aboriginal corporation. They can do what they want with them now. Reprint them. Sell them, if they can.'

He got up from the table without explanation, and disappeared into a back room. There was a pause while we waited. My eyes and Jeannie's met. We'd come expecting a firebrand, but instead we had found a tired man, a moderate who had fought hard and met a great deal of resistance. He reappeared holding a stack of his books. The publishing house *was* small, he agreed – it was his own. Struggling to find a publisher, he had decided to print them himself. He handed over the books I had been unable to locate. The topmost title made me wince: *Our Founding Murdering Father*. Underneath was the same picture of Angus McMillan I'd seen in the old beet factory at Maffra, hand in hand with two black men, one of whom seemed to be holding a spear.

'What I would say,' Gardner said, catching my dismay, 'is that this is one side of a debate.' He seemed to feel uncomfortable that his allegations might upset me.

'No, no,' I said, flicking the book open. 'I want to know.'

The books were forensic, yet at the same time tub-thumpingly polemical, carefully argued and backed with evidence filleted from early settlers' diaries and letters. His main sources – the cast of characters in a murky pastoral drama – were outlined with deftly drawn character sketches: the naïve Meyrick, the hapless protector Robinson, the gun-happy Buckley. The massacres themselves were neatly dissected: dates, locations, names of known participants, estimated death tolls. Asterisks marked the most likely locations on inky hand-drawn maps.

These were only a few of the known instances, Gardner was at pains to explain. Elsewhere he attempted a rough estimate of total Gunai deaths by white violence:

Warrigal Creek: range 60–150. My estimate 100.
Associated massacres (clashes following): range
    30–80. My estimate 50.
Boney Point: range 40–80. My estimate 60.
Butchers Creek: range 30–80. My estimate 50.
Slaughterhouse Gully: range 20–40. My estimate 30.
Milly Creek: range 20–40. My estimate 30.
Tambo Crossing: 'upwards of 70'. My estimate 70.
Estimated 20 further massacres (5 deaths or more):
    range 100–140. My estimate 120.
Estimated 30 other clashes (fewer than 5 deaths):
    range 60–140. My estimate 100.

Result –
Bottom estimate 430.
My estimate 610.
Top estimate 820.

This calculation roughly tied in with that made by Meyrick in a letter to his parents in 1846: 'I am convinced that not less than 450 have been murdered altogether.' Written several years before the conflict came to a close, it is not improbable that this figure would have grown to six hundred, or more.

And at the heart of it all: Angus McMillan, the Butcher of Gippsland.

McMillan's heroism was a myth of his own invention, wrote Gardner. At best, he can be seen as 'a fanatic – misguided in his beliefs, and more than slightly dishonest in his methods. At worst he can be considered a rogue of some stature ... If today McMillan is to be admired as a local hero, at the very least it should be known why this is so; that his popularity was originally, in large part, directly attributable to his brutal and violent suppression of the original inhabitants of the region.'

I came away chilled and unhappy. Essentially, Gardner's books seemed a character assassination. Every one of McMillan's achievements, so lauded in the annals of Gippsland, was called into doubt, every facet of his character redrawn in less flattering lines. 'Our Founding Murdering Father'. I repeated the phrase in my mind, again and again.

This fresh avalanche of criticism had hit me like a body-shock. It was strange. I had known that there were questions over McMillan's conduct, and more; that he had been implicated in a string of mass murders. And yet somehow, over the last few weeks I'd allowed myself to grow close to him. What with all the celebrity and celebration I'd become – what? – proud of him, I supposed, and the enormity of his fall from grace hit me afresh. I was now completely tied up in it all, I realised, emotionally speaking. But I didn't feel any closer to understanding what had happened.

For reasons that were unclear, I felt I wanted to go there, to the sites of the massacres, as if the places themselves might summon some homicidal insanity I might tap into and comprehend.

Boney Point was the closest. Jeannie, Ian and I made a short, poorly conceived trip down the long track that led to a carpark on the banks of the Perry River. The road stopped short several hundred yards from the site, an impassable mass of marshy scrub in between. Two men sat at the water's edge fishing, not speaking, empty tinnies littering the sandy soil behind them. No go.

I came back later, equipped with a borrowed kayak, and pushed down between the mangroves that crowded the edges of the river, trying to imagine the action unfolding in front of my eyes. But it was difficult. The view was obscured, the land hard to picture under all this growth. Did they ride along there? Did they shoot from here? Was that where they stumbled upon the bones? It was no use. After a few minutes I gave up and just sat alone on the water, the soft breath of the wind on my face as I let myself be slowly towed downstream. Pelicans swept by overhead, coming down in a graceful loop to land somewhere flat beyond the scrub.

The site of the Warrigal Creek massacre was on private land, but Peter Gardner had given me the phone number of the current owner, Elizabeth Balderstone. After a few hours I'd summoned up the courage to call her, but there had been no answer. I left a garbled message on her answer-phone, something along the lines of 'Hello! Do you have a massacre site on your land? Can I see it?!', then hung up, flustered. I could have kicked myself. The reporter in me knew that the best thing to do would have been to leave a cryptic message with my number, then get her talking when she called back. I had probably blown it. Why would she want her property to be known as a place of slaughter? Why would she open her doors to massacre tourists like us?

Hours ticked by, with no response. Jeannie and Ian were restless. They needed to get back home, so we began to make plans to return to Drouin. Yet we were reluctant to give up hope.

We drove to the area, holding Gardner's line map up to the GPS to get our bearings, and stopped at the closest point to the site that we could reach on public land. It was a bird reserve now, on the edge of Ninety Mile Beach. The wind was up, but we staggered out over the dunes and picked our way along the tideline. The beach was littered with hundreds of dead birds, half buried by sand.

'Shearwaters,' said Ian, nudging one with his foot. 'A mass death. It keeps happening. No one knows why.'

I wandered off alone, feeling sick to the core, and climbed high on the dunes to search for the mouth of the creek, where once the blood would have run down into the sea. Sand stretched off to either side as far as I could see. It was beautiful but bleak, the sky hazy and as heavy as my heart.

My phone rang. Elizabeth.

'I got your message. Come tomorrow.'

The next day dawned like a gospel. The sun was out, a light breeze ruffling the grass. We drove the three-mile driveway with the windows down. Sheep were scattered across enormous flat fields like marbles on a tabletop. A few twisted old gums stood guard along the track, warped by the wind. Closer to the house, freshly clipped sheep picked their way back from cream-gloss shearing sheds, bare and surprised-looking, woollen trackmarks circling their torsos, tufts of missed-a-bits poking as if through loosely wrapped bandages. The buzzing of the busy production line drifted through the open doors as we trundled past.

The homestead was at the far end, surrounded by mature gardens. It was a glorious two-storey house with a big terrace and a round brick well. Roses climbed the walls, branding irons sat in wooden barrels like lilies in a vase, mismatched cowbells hung from pegs by the door, as if carefully prepped for a lifestyle magazine shoot. It was stylish in a *European* way, I thought vaguely.

Elizabeth strode out to meet us with a nervous, alert smile. She was a fine-boned woman with a neat blonde bob, wearing a purple rugby shirt over jeans and work boots. She must have been in her fifties, but looked younger, glamorous somehow. 'Call me Libby,' she said.

She led us into the kitchen, where the high ceiling was ornamented with hammered tin tiles, the shelves stacked with bottles and jars of home-made preserves: plum sauce and Seville-orange marmalade. A blocky old-fashioned fridge was collaged with family photos: long-limbed daughters who laughed and rode horses, a handsome smiling man I tentatively identified as her late husband. After his early death she had kept the farm, she said, and now ran it on her own.

'The site you're looking for,' she said, locking eyes with me, 'is just beyond the house, in a bend of the creek.'

'Does it not feel strange, to live so close?'

She sighed. 'The way I always think about it is that I've taken on the role of a guardian. We fenced it off, you see, to keep people from walking on it. And if anyone wants to visit, to see it for themselves – well, of course they're welcome. There was some discussion that perhaps there should be a marker, or a memorial of some kind, but that's not a decision I feel I can take alone, and it's difficult to know exactly who needs to be asked. Would you like to see it?'

I nodded keenly, and we all trooped out through the garden. Two fat Labradors wrestling in the garden leapt to greet us, while spook-eyed kelpies, working dogs, watched us jealously from their kennels out the back.

'Here,' said Libby, gesturing beyond a thin-strand fence enclosing a flat area that had grown thick with brush and prickly grass.

I felt as if I'd been hollowed out. The others left me to it.

By now I'd read the accounts of the massacre so often I could play them like a film reel that unfolded over the pleasant pastoral scene in front of me. Yes, I thought, I can see it now. It was a beautiful spot for an encampment. A slope led down to a babbling brook feeding into a deep waterhole, where ducks swam in tight formation. I imagined children playing in the shallows, women digging for roots and weaving baskets, men sharpening their spearheads.

The gunmen would have stood *here*, I thought, pacing it out. Along this line. Then they would have advanced – I stepped forward, determined the necessary distance – and fired from *here*.

Crack, crack. The shots came like punches. The pause to reload, the rattle of shaky hands. The screams and the howls. The shuddering last breaths. The cries of children jerked awake, of tiny newborns dropped from lifeless hands. For the wounded, the final thud of the rifle butt to bash in their heads. The blow of mercy, or mercilessness.

The Highlanders were driven by rage and retribution. Their hearts were hardened by anger and grief. But oh – the things they must have seen that day. They must have known that this was wrong. They must have known it was wrong when they fished out that one surviving child, bleeding from the eye, and marched him on and on, in search of his people, so that they might kill them in front of him. They must have known this was wrong.

Later, the cover-up would begin. They came back, loaded the bodies into bullock drays, dumped them and burned them amid the dunes on the beach. Now they truly were a band of brothers, bonded together by their secret. They kicked the evidence over with sand, and tried to forget the whole thing. But how could they?

That night, when the bloodlust had subsided and they slunk home to their shabby bark huts, pulled their itchy wool blankets around them, the sights of the day must have played and replayed before their eyes. Such sights could not be shrugged off easily. Colin Maclaren, one of the participants, was asked years later by a young stockman whether he had 'shot plenty of blacks in his time', but Maclaren 'merely shut one eye and, screwing his features to that particular side, remained silent'. In his later years he retreated to an island in Lake Victoria where he lived as a hermit, alone with his remembrances.

To Angus McMillan the ringleader, lying awake as the kookaburras bounced their maniacal laugh between each other outside, it must have seemed a sort of madness. He must have seen the blood swirling, the water churning. The women turned flesh, the children turned meat. The crowding of the flies upon the bodies.

I'd been reading a lot about massacres lately. Phrases and images began to lurk in the shadowy parts at the back of my brain, slipping in and out at inappropriate moments. Shrink-wrapped meat in the supermarket took on a gruesome aspect; puddled footprints at the poolside were recast as trails of gore; visits to the toilet block at night became suffused with the psychological tension of a thriller. I had opened myself to the horrors of the past, and now its skeletons were taking up residence in my mind.

Perhaps this explained the dreams that had begun to interrupt my sleep. I would wake with a shock, having dreamed I was being chased by unknown, faceless men with guns. In these dreams, made dumb by fear, I would make pathetic attempts to hide, pulling leaves or blankets over myself like a child and waiting, heart hammering – *If I can't see you ...* – or I would run, fast, from the attackers, but they were faster, and they caught me they caught me they caught me.

Sometimes, if I was really deeply asleep, I would feel the bullets pass right through my body. And then I woke up.

7

The White Woman

A rumour was born. At first thin and insubstantial, it rose into the atmosphere like a ribbon of smoke from the tip of a cigarette. It emerged in the form of a letter to the editor of the *Sydney Herald*: a white woman had been spotted in Gippsland, lost in the bush. Held captive, reportedly, by a group of Gunai tribesmen.

Angus McMillan, as usual, was at the centre of it. It was his letter; his exploratory party, tramping through the unknown *fastnesses* of Gippsland, who came upon an Aboriginal encampment which, deserted by its panicked inhabitants on their approach, was found to be stocked with a vast assortment of European objects: checked shirts, moleskin trousers, shoemakers' awls, a lock of brown hair, coins, several English-language newspapers and a bible printed in Edinburgh two years previously. Out of context, many days' travel from the nearest station, the men found the hoard unsettling.

There was more to come. 'Enclosed in three kangaroo skin bags we found the dead body of a male child about two years old,' he wrote. 'Dr Arbuckle carefully examined [it] professionally, and discovered beyond doubt its being of European parents; parts of the skin were perfectly white not being in the least discoloured.'

In light of the dead child, the cache of incongruous belongings seemed altogether more ominous. The obvious conclusion, McMillan's men felt, was that tribesmen had attacked a party of Europeans nearby – perhaps a group of shipwreck survivors – and killed them all. The trinkets and the infant's body seemed to have been kept as souvenirs of some sort. With this grim notion in mind, the party reconsidered the events of the moments before as they approached the encampment, and agreed that they must have seen a survivor of this *melancholy catastrophe*:

> [As they fled] we observed the men with shipped spears driving before them the women, one of whom we noticed constantly looking behind her, at us, a circumstance which did not strike us much at the time, but on examining the marks and figures about the largest of the native huts we were immediately impressed with the belief that the unfortunate female is a European – a captive of these ruthless savages.

The letter was published in the *Herald* on 28 December 1840, six weeks after the event, and caused a minor stir among its readership. Not everyone was convinced; a few sceptics poured cold water over McMillan's interpretations of events, perhaps best demonstrated by a scathing editor's comment in the *Port Phillip Patriot*, added when it reproduced the letter a few days later:

> The clue to the foregoing mystery is doubtless to be found in the robbery of Mr. Jamieson's station at Western Port, which must have occurred very

shortly before the date of Mr. McMillan's excursion. The European dead child and living woman, are we suspect mere creatures of the imagination. – Ed.

And yet, something about these creatures of the imagination caught the public's attention. Their spectral forms rose up like smoke, eddied, and dissipated, but at their feet the source still burned. Cast aside in the dark undergrowth, the flames caught in the dry grass and began to spread. The fallout from this letter would cascade down through the next seven years, gathering pace as it went.

The mysterious white woman found sustenance in the social and political climate of the time. Fed by a dozen different agendas and motivations, she took on a life of her own. Interest rose to fever pitch; soon she had taken solid enough form in the minds of the public that rescue parties would tear off into the bush in a desperate bid to find and retrieve her, fuelled by the self-righteous fervour of the wronged.

That first glimpse of her, of that departing, insubstantial figure, would be reiterated endlessly over the coming years. Always fleeing, always fleeting, always almost out of sight.

Steve had chosen the bar. It was a trendy, gentrified sort of place in Fitzroy, an artfully dishevelled suburb of Melbourne where the buildings had been left to decay in a picturesque manner: paint peeled from the lacy filigree of the terraces, old posters from yesteryear slowly unhitched themselves, leaving only their traces, a spray of bright graffiti colours collaged in every alley.

I got there early and found a table, reflecting while I waited that I did not know precisely what I hoped to achieve with this meeting, nor what to expect; merely that Steve Paton, a young artist of Gunai descent, would be the first Aboriginal person I had met – or at least, the first who had identified himself as such.

In fact, there was scant evidence on what Australian television I had seen, or in the newspapers I had read, that a contemporary Aboriginal population even existed. Nor had I noticed obviously Aboriginal people 'around' – in the streets, in the bars, in the shops. It was strange, I felt: although I knew the Aboriginal community was a small minority, at roughly 3 per cent of the population nationally, that still worked out at one in every thirty or so individuals, or around 670,000 people – not an insignificant number. Their invisibility perplexed me.

Steve turned out to be my age, well-groomed, well-educated, and dressed as if he might be on his way to a pop-up tiki bar – which, incidentally, was exactly where he was planning to go later. He wore Ray-Bans and an ironic Hawaiian shirt, on which coiling lilies were picked out in muted shades. He had striking features – molasses-brown eyes set beneath a heavy brow, and a fairish complexion, more olive than black – with a hipster beard and shoulder-length hair pulled up into a bun at the back of his head.

We sipped our drinks tensely for a while as I fluttered around the issues of race and identity without landing. 'Look,' I started afresh, finally hitting solid ground. 'I suppose what I'm trying to get at is that it's not very clear to anyone outside Australia how current all of these issues I'm reading about are. Are there still two cultures, running alongside each other in parallel? Is one still in the process of being choked off by the other? I mean ...' I gestured vaguely at his shirt. 'I guess I can tell you're not really living a traditional lifestyle.'

No, he agreed. There *were* Aboriginal groups in Australia, he said, mainly in the remote north and west, living something closer in nature to the old ways – isolated from outside influences but combining elements of modern life such as cars, shopping and so on with hunting, foraging for 'bush tucker' and maintaining ancient beliefs and customs. But to him Aboriginal identity was now more about passing on what cultural knowledge was left, and ensuring that it was sufficiently acknowledged and respected.

As a youngster he'd had little interest in the past, but by the time he reached his mid- to late twenties he suddenly found himself passionate about researching his family's history and cultural heritage. I nodded in recognition.

Steve's family has been at the heart of Aboriginal affairs in Gippsland for decades. His grandfather, Uncle Albert Mullett, a respected elder, spearheaded the campaign to have the Gunai people's right to their traditional lands officially recognised (via a specialist field of Australian law known as 'native title'); other relatives have played prominent roles in furthering Gunai culture, including Steve's mother Doris, who had worked for many years to revive the Gunai language, and his aunt Jenny, a painter and ceramicist whose work is often inspired by Aboriginal history and folklore.

As part of an art project in 2012, Steve asked Uncle Albert to teach him and his cousins to build a bark canoe in the traditional style: cut from the tree in an enormous sheet, smoked, rolled up at the ends and sealed with clay. Then they brought the whole family together by the riverside and floated it on the water. Traditionally, knowledge of how to create a canoe like this – as well as a thousand other necessities for survival – would have been passed down to every young man during a period of initiation called the *jeraeil*. The canoe was a symbol, explained Steve, not only of the old lifestyle and values, but of the ancient origins of his people.

In Gunai folklore, Boorun, the first man, came down from the mountains in the form of a pelican, carrying his bark canoe on his head. As he came to the shores of Corner Inlet, he heard a tap-tap-tap coming from inside the canoe. Lowering it to the water, he found that he had carried a woman with him all that time. She was Tuk, the musk duck. Together they became the mother and the father of all the Gunai people.

Steve called his project 'Boorun's canoe'. It was the first time a bark canoe had been floated on the waters of Gippsland for a hundred years. To attempt it was a risk, he said – right up until the last second they feared that it might sink, and unwittingly become a terrible symbol of all the lost Gunai knowledge – but he didn't like the idea of it becoming yet another dusty old artefact sitting behind glass, unused, another aid for anthropologists, with which to teach *them* about the way their people had once lived, but then forgot. The canoe, and a series of photographs documenting the process taken by an old schoolfriend, Cameron Cope, were now on display in the Melbourne Museum.

I'd been to the museum already, and seen the canoe there. But something about the display had confused me.

Elsewhere I'd seen the name of Steve's people spelt a number of ways – 'Gunai', 'Ganai', 'Kurnai', 'Kurnay' – which I had loosely assumed to be due to some issue in rendering the language in the Latin alphabet. But in any official context, as in the museum's display, it was given instead as a weird double-barrelled name, 'Gunaikurnai'.

Steve pursed his lips when I mentioned this. 'Gunai,' he said. Then, 'Kurnai.' Almost indistinguishable. 'Say it with a guttural sound at the beginning ... To me, they're one and the same. But saying that, it's all tied up with an issue of identity.' Some families described themselves as Gunai, others as Kurnai. He sighed. 'It was a detail that became *political.*'

During Uncle Albert's land-rights campaign in the 1990s and 2000s, the faction identifying themselves as the Kurnai broke off to file a counter-claim, disputing the right of any others to the land. Their claim, later rejected by the courts after an exhaustive six-day hearing, was that due to a combination of tribal rules, only the descendants of a single, named Gunai (or rather, Kurnai) woman might be rightly considered heirs to the traditional lands.

It was an unpleasant episode of infighting which, among such a small community, could not help but become personal, and it was one too that sent its combatants spinning endlessly back into the past, only to return bearing more evidence of birthrights and superior bloodlines. This was not the first time such small differences in spelling have come to represent wider divisions within an ethnic group: in Canberra, for example, a bitter feud raged for many years between two groups which identified themselves as the Ngunnawal and the Ngunawal respectively, each disputing the other's claim to better represent the region's traditional custodians; similarly, in Melbourne, rival groups representing the Boon Wurrung/Bunurong people, each utilising a different spelling, have vied for recognition as the 'official' cultural body.

'This was a disagreement that arose after the process of Anglicisation, rather than an existing rift that pre-dated settlement,' explained Steve. In any case, it was an issue that had only been settled recently, and the compromise – running both names together: Gunaikurnai – was intended to provide a united identity through which to state their case.

'I suppose it's a bit like ...' He paused, and looked at me appraisingly. 'Do you know there are five subgroups, language groups, within the Gunai nation?'

I nodded, flicking through my notes and pointing to my list:

Bratowooloong
Brayakooloong
Tatungooloong
Krowathunkooloong
Brabawooloong

'Yes, exactly. Strictly speaking, I'm from this group – Tatungooloong – but really, there are so few of us left and it's all gotten so mixed up that we all just identify now as one group, the Gunai, or the Gunaikurnai.'

I'd been put in touch with Steve by his photographer schoolfriend Cam, with whom I had made plans to travel through the more remote sections of Gippsland – Jeannie's 'young-person stuff' – as we retraced Angus McMillan's journey back to its source in the Monaro plains.

'I thought I might come along with you for a bit,' said Steve. 'I've been thinking for a while about doing some artwork based on the Aboriginal experience of settlement.'

'If you like,' I replied, pleased. It would be useful to travel through Gunai country with someone with knowledge and an intuitive understanding of its traditional culture. 'The more the merrier.'

A band struck up on a small stage in the corner, in front of a backdrop painted with a kitsch frontier scene. Three men were silhouetted, on horseback, in ten gallon hats, rifles slung across their backs. A sunset had been rendered behind them in broad brushstrokes of orange and magenta and gold. Cowboys and Aborigines.

Cam picked me up for our road trip at Jeannie's house. He came straight from a work event in Melbourne; tall, fresh-faced, clean-cut in a suit and tie but driving a dusty old ute. We went to his mother's house, an airy, high ceilinged bungalow filled with treasures brought home by her sons from their foreign travels, like cats bringing offerings of mice to the doorstep. I laid my maps out across the kitchen table and we pored over them, plotting our way up into the high country, following McMillan's route as closely as possible, focusing on his initial failed attempt to enter the region from the Monaro. As we worked, Cam reeled off a list of books I should read, prefaced with a warning.

'Aboriginal folk won't always be impressed with what you've read or heard about from the "experts",' he said. 'They'll like that you take an interest, but they won't all have read the same books as you, necessarily, and what you've read might not tally with their own experience. People won't be pleased if *you* try to tell *them* about their own culture or history, if you see what I mean.'

I nodded.

'Just listen.'

We met Steve the next day, and drove slowly east through the Latrobe Valley towards Traralgon, first through the coalfields, the forest of cloud-height chimneys belching thick white smoke into the atmosphere. The columns themselves wore a certain leggy elegance, but the structures and machinery at their feet had a nasty look in their eyes. A retired coal-harvesting machine was parked up on the roadside, its mean metal teeth on a rotating device at the end of a long, crane-like neck, ludicrously outsized, something from science fiction or a real-life alien invasion.

'DREDGER 21' read a label at its base, like a name-tag at a mixer, above a list of its vital statistics: 'Manufactured 1952. Weight: 725 tonnes. Height: 23 metres.' The bucket-wheel dredgers in use today were much bigger in size and capacity, the sign continued, and had now grown too large to fit inside the Melbourne Cricket Ground. I imagined one trying and failing, scattering stadium seats, a scene of Armageddon unfolding behind.

The lookout point nearby offered the dispiriting vista of an enormous flooded crater: the Yallourn open-cut coal-mine. 'This was the site of the township Yallourn,' announced a sign cheerily, offering up a scale outline of the crater superimposed over a map of a 1920s model village – hospital, railway station, golf course, neat wooden houses with terracotta roofs – all carefully planned and purpose-built for energy workers and their families, before it was dismantled in the eighties so these sawtoothed monsters might get at the heavy, coal-rich ground beneath.

'Today the town no longer exists,' continued the sign, unnecessarily, indicating the scene of devastation behind. The sides of the mine were roughly terraced, hewn from the earth, its base flooded with mud and filthy water. The mud was scarred with trackmarks and silty, rust-like tide-lines. Somewhere there, now many feet above ground level, was Yallourn.

I was fascinated by this phantom town, whose access roads still led up to and off the edge of the cut. Of course, its inhabitants still exist somewhere – they were rehoused, 'rationalised' among a number of nearby towns – but even so, something, some collective identity, was lost. However humane, this dispossession must have had a profound psychological impact that left its people clawing for purchase on their former selves. The historian Peter Read has described how the town's citizens were haunted by the memory of their old home:

> Yallourn people bought their houses and re-erected them elsewhere, or hunted for them in nearby towns and photographed them. They dug out plants, they souvenired bits of their houses and public buildings, they bought the building supplies and laid their [new] paths with Yallourn bricks.

That identity, that Yallourn-ness that had gone, was something residents are still trying to keep alive, decades on. Later I stumbled across a version of Yallourn that lived on online. Setting the year to 1959, I strolled between computer-generated houses and wandered the main square. A database contained details of the sort that would never be recorded in any history book: the technical-school badge (a pylon and a book, the motto 'Knowledge is Power'), the recipe for Poulos' famous spaghetti bolognaise, a book of numbers for phones that no longer ring.

It was a virtual town built by rootless people, endlessly dreaming up an afterlife for their home. But no matter what they do, the experience of how this all fitted together to make Yallourn Yallourn – the smell of the theatre auditorium at night, the sound of voices echoing in the school canteen, the way the trees' long shadows would striate the empty streets in the low sun of the late afternoon – all that will die with their generation, and there is no way to keep it alive.

I wondered, disloyally, whether the Yallourn residents' attempts to keep their town alive might act too as some kind of parable for the Mullett family's own crusade to keep alive a culture that preceded them. Steve building a canoe that was no longer needed for fishing, his mother reviving a language that is no longer spoken. What drove their attempts to sustain a way of life that would otherwise disappear? How valid were the results of such efforts, if the participants had not lived that culture themselves? I didn't know the answers yet.

'That was the ugly bit of Gippsland,' the boys assured me as we roared on. 'We'll be past it soon.'

Golden Beach at dusk: an odd, empty seaside hamlet with a time-warp feel, like the set of a *Carry On* film. A spare Norfolk pine stood in the square, decked out in fairy lights that traced its trunk and branches, a child's drawing of a tree. A squat building offered hot showers for two dollars. Overhead an unlit revolving sign advertised GOLDEN BEACH FOODARAMA.

We drove on, and turned off down a track to a clearing between the trees, tucked in behind an enormous sand dune. It was so close to the shore that we could feel each incoming wave booming loudly down and then sighing in relief as it slunk back through the sand. I felt as if we were standing in an enormous pair of lungs, the sea's salty breath on the backs of our necks, ruffling the dry leaves above our heads.

A pit was still charred by the remains of the previous occupants' fire. Steve and Cam lit it afresh, using the dry seedpods of the banksia to get it going. They were woody toilet-brush heads, each harbouring dozens of horrid muppet mouths that gaped open like castanets to scatter their seeds when they came into contact with the flames. The straw-like fronds and wooden beaks caught quickly, and as the fire took hold their fat bodies gave off a red-hot glow like coals.

We erected our tents then sat on a tartan rug by the fire, drinking beer and wine from a cask, swatting at sand flies, squinting against the smoke. It was a nice spot, and we savoured it for a moment for what it was, talking lazily about inconsequential things, skirting the subject of what had brought us together.

At last Steve cleared his throat. He had an idea, he said, that he wanted my help with: a collaborative project that would explore settlement by reinterpreting the events of a key period of early Gippsland history from an Aboriginal point of view. 'I'm interested in exploring the myth of the

White Woman of Gippsland,' he said. 'Have you heard about this?'

The author and Steve around the campfire at Golden Beach.

I had, of course. It was a strange episode, one so rife with misinformation and misinterpretations that I did not know what to think of it. On the face of it, it seemed a simple story: the tale of a damsel in distress and her would-be rescuers. But the truth of her, and what she symbolised, was more complex. She may have been an unfortunate soul; she may have been merely a figment of the collective imagination. Either way, her arising, and the significance she was accorded, exposed the most vulnerable parts of the colonial mind to the air.

In the end it was this white woman, whose very existence has never been fully confirmed, who would bring black—white hostilities in Gippsland to a climax. The hunt for her would result in a renewal of the climate of fear, and a squall of Aboriginal deaths from which the Gunai would never truly recover.

For several years after her initial sighting, the trail had gone cold as the settlers turned their attention to more pressing matters: the building and the burning, the construction of the huts and the homesteads, the growing conflict with the Gunai.

The white woman made occasional cameo appearances, popping up in the footnotes of the period; unconfirmed sightings mentioned in the journals as she dipped and dived, ducking out of sight before rearing up again, her story told and retold in the Chinese whispers of frontier society.

But in May 1846, with the 'Black War' at its height, she made a glorious comeback, the ubiquitous Angus McMillan at her back. He reappeared in the newspaper, stirring the pot: he had 'captured the child of a young lady, whom the blacks stole away some years since, and for whom there is a reward of £1,000'. Proof! Or proof of sorts – the child was never mentioned again – but it was enough to catch the attention of a community that had by now become well primed to the dangers of the Gunai.

This mysterious creature who lurked in the darkest shadows of the bush soon became something of a *cause célèbre*. News of her tragic plight raced through the homesteads of the district and the smoking rooms of Melbourne, the fledgling city now thriving to the west. As hunger for action grew, so came a rallying call from the editor of the *Port Phillip Herald*: 'Will *no one* come forward and put the

Government to the blush by leading a party in search of this truly unfortunate lady?'

She formed a focus not only for the flexing of masculine bravado, but also for the increasing dissatisfaction with the colonial government. Melbourne was growing restless; soon it would strike off from New South Wales, taking the entire Port Phillip district with it, and establish itself as the capital of a new colony, Victoria. The white woman 'cause' formed a convenient rallying point for influential Melbourne figures, a symbolic crusade through which they might show up the Sydney administration as both apathetic and out of touch. If the government would not save this woman, they said, then they would do it themselves.

Press coverage, steered by calculating editors, began to heat up. Details from every sighting were endlessly rehashed as letters pages hosted a furious debate over every aspect of the tale: Who was she? Where had she come from? Why had they taken her? What were they doing to her?

This last question was the one that aroused the most lingering interest. With concern for her well-being as justification, the erotic imagination of the papers' overwhelmingly male readership was permitted to run riot. She was not only a captive, it was soon agreed, but was being held as a sexual slave, 'compelled to yield to the disgusting passions and desires of a set of black cannibals'. Deflowered at spearpoint, she was now concubine to a chief, and mother to his half-blood children. Pulses rose. Heavy-breathing conjecture was published uncritically under the heading of 'news'.

White men were enraptured by the plight and the penury of the white woman. They debated and deliberated over her best means of rescue. They fundraised and planned, prepared for action, all the while their minds whirring with horror and arousal and longing.

It is an episode which, to modern eyes, is distasteful in a number of ways.

To Steve, the entire basis of the outcry, specifically the assumptions behind it, was deeply offensive. The lost woman, of unknown character, was widely assumed to be whiter than white, a virginal *naif*; her unidentified Aboriginal 'captor' instinctively characterised as the most monstrous of fairytale villains.

These attitudes are clearly manifested in the language of the articles and letters about the white woman's disappearance. A poem written in her honour and published in the Melbourne *Argus* typifies the vocabulary and tone employed:

> Unhappiest of the fairer kind;
> Who knows the misery of thy mind?
> Compell'd to breathe the pois'nous breath
> Of a rank scented black;
> To yield to his abhorr'd embrace,
> To kiss his staring, ugly face,
> And listen to his clack.

'It's just so *vicious*,' said Steve. 'As if we [the Gunai] were a pack of rabid animals.'

To my eyes, the affair also threw the double standards to which women and men were then held into sharp relief. White society was clearly scandalised by the prospect of one of its women having sexual contact with an

Aboriginal man, despite implicitly acknowledging that its own men were regularly fornicating with Aboriginal women whenever they might be convinced or coerced to do so.

Sometimes, in Gunai society, sex with a wife or young female relative had been offered to visitors as a gesture of hospitality. Perhaps misinterpreting this generosity as indifference to the fate of their women, early settlers soon began to pass these 'gins' and 'lubras' between themselves. Some Aboriginal women rode as 'boys' among the cattlemen, keeping them warm at night, but they were not considered on a level with either the cattlemen themselves or European women, who were expected to adhere to higher moral standards. These women were sex objects, yes, but low-status ones, and when they returned to their own people they often took unwelcome gifts back with them in the form of sexually transmitted infections.

As a result, venereal disease rampaged through the frontier. Complications arising from gonorrhoea alone are estimated to have cut Aboriginal reproductive capacity by 40 per cent nationally between 1815 and 1855, while in Gippsland notes kept by a local physician between 1849 and 1852 show syphilis to be the most common ailment among his largely white, male, unmarried patients, who numbered among the most esteemed members of the community. Such infection rates went unremarked in the popular press.

Thus the settler men were free to mop up their lust with the native 'gins' without criticism, while the missing white woman, a placeholder for all of her fair-skinned peers, was winched by many hands up to a pedestal so high as to give the girl vertigo.

For the white woman stood for far more than her single lost soul. She was an icon for the life the settlers had left behind. She was a delicacy, an innocent who cringed from the horrors that lay in the no-man's land beyond the last station. By saving her they had a chance of redeeming themselves, of casting themselves as the heroes in a tale that had theretofore been lacking in moral character.

She was not the first of her kind. In fact, the idea of a white woman taken captive by 'primitives' was a well-worn trope in colonial societies. In America, a rich literature had already grown up around these women – 'captivity narratives', as they are known – loosely based on a number of real-life cases, including those of Mary Rowlandson the minister's wife; Eunice Williams, taken by the Mohawks aged seven; Mary Jemison, sold on by the Shawnee to the Seneca.

These unfortunates spawned a genre that fascinated the American public. Survivors' accounts of their captivity became bestsellers. Songs were written and dedicated 'to the white woman'. She would be drawn sometimes: stripped naked, roped roughly up against a tree, squirming as the light of the flames danced over her skin and the painted savages whirled and ululated around her helpless figure, leering, victorious, hungry.

In Gippsland they saw her similarly subjugated: unclothed, herded ahead of her captors at the point of their spears. If she slowed, one report claimed, they would plunge the spears into her ripe flesh. The commentariat outdid themselves in their florid portrayals of the carnal existence in which she now found herself. She was 'wandering about the bush in a state of nudity', they panted, 'a slave of savage lust and barbarous violence'.

The recurrence of the white woman motif – for it is better understood as a motif than as an isolated incident – shows us something of the psychological undercurrents in colonial culture. The settlers' task had been to civilise and make safe this new land for their future wives and children. Now, the loss of one of their own to the bush was an existential threat to their life and work. The real-life captives of America had acted as a lightning rod for the colonists' deepest fears; in Australia, the same terrors echoed.

To understand the fascination that she held, it helps to recall how scarce women were in the colony at this time. On his arrival in Melbourne in 1842, the settler Edward Curr commented upon the 'total absence of women from the streets'; the few who were there dodged harassment by avoiding the rabble of the town. Out on the frontier the numbers were thinner still, with hardly a white woman – wife or maid – to be found during the earliest years of settlement.

This was largely because the rough and ready work of pioneering was not seen as a suitable life for a woman – or at least a woman of refinement. Living in a bark hut in a troubled district was no place for a 'young lady', or a girl who had been 'well bro' up', as Gippsland settler John Pettit explained in his letters home. But the lack of women posed a palpable threat to the colony's future. During the following decades there would be a great push to bring unmarried women to the colony, poor Irish and Scotswomen for the most part – many of them speaking only the odd, heavily accented word of English – their fares covered by the government in the name of the continued existence of the colonial project.

Boatloads of them would disgorge upon the dockside, and men dressed in their Sunday best – ties uncomfortable around thick workmen's necks, belts pulled tight round scrawny waists, ragged fingernails scrubbed clean – worked the crowds of women, enquiring politely whether any in search of a husband might take them. Others simply allowed their employers to pick one out on their behalf. Soon, Pettit wrote, these women had disappeared 'like smoke'.

One of their number was Christina McNaughton, a farmer's daughter from Argyllshire who arrived in New South Wales in 1849 as one of a shipload of migrant women. She was barely literate, undoubtedly poor, certainly not one of Pettit's 'well bro' up' young ladies. Little is known of her in the first three years after her arrival; like smoke, she drifted through the colony without trace, until she popped up in Gippsland as housekeeper at Angus McMillan's Bushy Park homestead in 1852.

He had not propositioned her with marriage on the dockside. McMillan would have had his sights set on a more accomplished, refined woman, a wife befitting his status as landowner and respectable figure of Gippsland society. Perhaps even his *dear Miss Margaret* back on Barra, with whom he had continued to correspond for some years after his emigration. Nevertheless, two children followed, Ewen in 1858 and Angus in 1861.

Back in 1846, when the white woman made her re-appearance, all this was far in the future. Like so many other men in the colony, McMillan was starved of female company. More and more, his mind was taken up with the fragrant, ethereal figure of the lost woman. She lurked on the edge of the bush, on the edge of consciousness, like a siren, luring men in, haunting their dreams.

But who was she? That, no one could agree upon.

Each community put forward its own preferred candidate. The Irish suspected her of being a Mrs Capel. The English preferred Miss Lord. The Scots thought her Anne – or perhaps Anna – Macpherson. She was no one and anyone. She was an everywoman, a figure every settler could relate to, upon whose anonymous, unsullied face they might project their own particular brand of virtue.

The theory was that she had been the lone survivor of a shipwreck, that she had fetched up on Ninety Mile Beach, not far from where we were camping, either alone or as one of a party that was attacked and slaughtered by the hostile Gunai. The idea was not unfeasible: any number of ships had found themselves in difficulties in the treacherous waters of Bass Strait. The *Britannia*, for example, wrecked off the coast in 1839 en route to Sydney. And the *Britomart* a month later, bound for Hobart.

Either wreck could plausibly have left a white female survivor marooned in Gippsland in time for her first sighting in November 1840. A young Aboriginal boy known as Jackie Warren (sometimes Tackewarren), somewhat *too* coincidentally now living with McMillan at Bushy Park, attested to a shipwreck survivor having lived with a neighbouring tribe near the coast.

Once feasibility was established, certainty began to grow, and details of her identity embroidered. She was young, beautiful, educated – that was a given. She was the wife of a brewer, the daughter of a respectable Sydney merchant, the employee of a prominent Melbourne hotelier. She was all of these and none of them.

Jackie Warren/Tackewarren as a grown man in 1866.

But she was a true victim – that they could all agree upon. Anyone who dared suggest anything different was soon shouted down. The mayor of Melbourne, who suggested that, if she did exist, the white woman might have formed over her six years' captivity 'connections and ties with the blacks which she might not wish to dissever' (a reasonable argument, given the reactions of some American captives following 'rescue': Cynthia Ann Parker, for example, would reportedly die of heartbreak after her 'rescue' from the Comanches after twenty-four years) found himself 'denounced in forcible terms' at a public meeting. The continuing inaction of the government drew fervent criticism, targeted now at the superintendent specifically:

If Mr. La Trobe had a daughter situated as this friendless woman is, what would he not do to rescue her? ... Would not every energy be brought into play to relieve her? Would not the services of a dozen – aye, a hundred – parties be engaged in the pursuit of this savage tribe?

The controversy rose to a fever pitch. Public meetings were held, donations flooded in. By October 1846 two search parties had been dispatched, one state-sponsored, the other privately funded.

The private expedition, led by Christian de Villiers, consisted of five white and ten Aboriginal men, carrying provisions for four months and a great many white handkerchiefs printed with a message to the woman in both English and Gaelic, to be distributed among the tribes:

WHITE WOMAN! – There are fourteen [sic] armed men, partly White and partly Black, in search of you. Be cautious; and rush to them when you see them near you. Be particularly on the look out every dawn of morning, for it is then that the party are in hope of rescuing you. The white settlement is towards the setting sun.

The state-funded expedition, by contrast, consisted of twenty-five men, comprising twenty-three 'native police' (Aboriginal officers of the Wurundjeri and Bunurong Kulin)

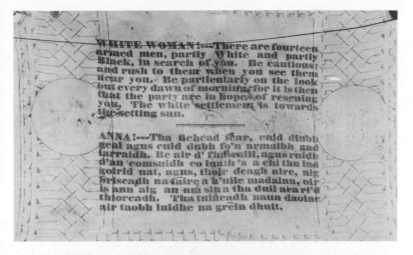

Both sides of the printed handkerchiefs distributed by de Villiers' party.

led by two white officers, William Dana and William Walsh. This was the first of three native police forces in Australia, all of which would become notorious for their heavy-handedness and cavalier use of violence as their indigenous members wielded new state-sanctioned power over their traditional tribal enemies. Dana's force tore off into the bush wielding firearms, the ghostly presence of the white woman enticing them ever onward, like a beacon on the horizon. They would cut down all in their path.

Later, Commissioner Tyers would estimate the official expedition to have been responsible for 'at least fifty' Gunai deaths during the hunt for the white woman, as they confronted ever more remote and hostile tribes. In one instance, they rushed upon an Aboriginal encampment on the banks of the Snowy River at night, a brutal incident that continued to be discussed among the Gunai in hushed undertones for years to come. De Villiers' party – whose leaders were of a more humanitarian bent, writing fascinated commentaries on the tribes they encountered for the *Port Phillip Herald* – inadvertently became witnesses to the aftermath of this attack when de Villiers and his deputy James Warman stumbled upon piles of black bodies riddled with bullets and a pair of escapees stumbling around shackled together at the ankle.

They reported these horrors, first to the authorities and then to the newspapers, denouncing the 'wanton barbarity' shown by 'those harpies of hell, *misnamed police*'. 'So long as such persons as Messrs W. Dana and Walsh are in command of the native police, nothing can stop [the Gunai's] extermination,' wrote Warman, adding, 'I should not wonder if we are subpoenaed to give evidence in the wholesale butchery at the Snowy River.'

Their allegations were published in January 1847, prompting the government to recall the native police to account for their behaviour. Dana denied everything. Nevertheless, he received a dressing-down from Governor FitzRoy, who deemed him to 'have acted with a great want of discretion, to say the least', and substituted a Sergeant Windridge in his place.

The hunt continued. Rumours of the woman were constantly reported by the Gunai they came across. She was the wife of a chief, the mother of two children. She 'cry plenty', and 'ask why did not the white men come and take her away'. Perhaps some of these reports were true, perhaps all of them. She danced ahead, tantalising her pursuers, always ever so slightly out of reach.

But they were gaining on her. They could taste her on the air.

By midsummer, the search parties had narrowed her abductors down to a single clan, of whom the warrior Bungelene was reputed to have taken her as a wife. De Villiers' party gathered titbits in every tribe they came across: she was 'tall, with a considerable stoop'. She was unable to suckle her children. She was very sick, others warned them, since Bungelene had been 'beating her about the head with a waddy'.

There was always some ambiguity when dealing with remote tribesmen. Due to the language barrier, much of the tracking depended upon a mime involving two paper cut-outs – both women, one shaded black – and asking the tribesmen to point to the figure who represented Bungelene's wife. This was not a failsafe method. One of de Villiers' party reported how a source 'shouted with delight, as much to say "I know what you want"', before racing off to his camp. He returned to the breathless party 'with a brace of sylvan nymphs, and presented one to me and one to Mr A.B.'.

Nevertheless, with a name for her captor, and a chase under way, the white woman's existence seemed more concrete. Any lingering doubts were forcefully countered by her supporters, not least by McMillan, who took to the pages of the *Herald* again in February 1847. 'As a proof,' he wrote, 'I am now willing to give my services to assist in her recovery.' The *Herald* judged this submission ('the decisive letter of Mr. McMillan – an old and most respectable settler') as itself another plank in a 'body of evidence [that] has now been established to prove the existence of the white woman among the blacks, as perfectly irresistible'.

Superintendent La Trobe disagreed: the evidence, he said, remained 'far from conclusive'. But the public believed it. What could La Trobe do? He authorised the search to continue 'without regard to expense'.

A few days later the *Port Phillip Patriot* waded in. 'FORCE MUST BE USED, AND OUGHT TO BE USED,' it thundered. 'There appears to exist a degree of sensitive apprehension for the safety of the savages,' yet 'the matter comes to this – the blacks declare that the woman shall not be given up unless captured by force ... Is then the woman to remain in their brutalizing dominion, until the *ultima ratio* be adopted?'

Force, then.

Bungelene and his two (Aboriginal) wives were rounded up by the obedient Windridge and his party, and taken into custody at the native police base in Narre Warren. His wives remaining there as security, Bungelene was then marched into the bush, charged with obtaining the white woman's release.

If she did exist, he did not lead them to her; the party was growing thoroughly frustrated by endless wandering and the spiral of lies and uncertainties that seemed to lie at the heart of the Bungelene theory. They 'upbraided him with his duplicity', and threatened to shoot him 'for leading us astray'.

But at last, in April 1847, the search party seemed on the edge of a breakthrough. They found themselves in the scrub on the edge of the beach, waiting breathlessly for the white woman to be brought out. After several days' wait and repeated false promises, she arrived with great ceremony, carried by her captors as if upon a sedan.

The white men gasped. She was bare-breasted, her body painted with the harsh rust-red of ochre. She was battered indeed; both arms had been cut off at the elbows.

She was the figurehead of a ship.

Imagine their dismay. Thousands of pounds had been squandered on the search, both state funds and public donations. Weeks of their lives had been lost out in the bush, sleeping rough and remonstrating with unfriendly tribes.

They had been like greyhounds, racing pell-mell around the track, jostling for position. And when finally they had grabbed the lure with their teeth, torn it roughly down, they had found it was not a rabbit at all, but an empty glove. And all around the voices of the spectators still rang out, yelling, screeching, cursing, crying out for a win.

Was this her? The fabled white woman, the angel of the south? There seemed no clear explanation.

Bungelene took the brunt of their disappointment, being returned to Narre Warren in disgrace and 'brutally chained to a gum tree for many days and nights', according to

Assistant Protector William Thomas. 'The old man is very uneasy,' noted Donald Mcleod, a member of both the private and the state expeditions. 'We have been telling him that the White people are Coming from Melbourne to Shoot the blacks on the Islands and the Mountains and that we are to bring him to Melbourne there to be hanged[,] all which he believes which makes him rather Down hearted and frightened.'

They did not shoot him, but nor did they set him free. He continued to be held without charge. By July, the day book records him as 'very menancolly being detained so long'. In November he died. 'Of grief', said the papers.

None of this grim business achieved anything in terms of clearing up the confusion surrounding the white woman. All that was obvious was that the whole affair was getting out of hand. Further, unofficial, parties made up of maverick young men had joined the hunt; anarchy and disorder loomed.

Finally, Commissioner Tyers prevailed upon Angus McMillan to stop the madness. And so, having been present at the birth of the white woman, he became witness to her death. He was inextricably tangled up in the affair from first to last.

An extraordinary edition of the *Herald* was published, headlined 'Murder of the Captive White Woman at Gipps Land', reporting intelligence conveyed 'from the station of Mr. McMillan'. A woman's body had been located, alongside that of what appeared to be a mixed-race child. Bungelene's brother was blamed for the deaths; he was supposed to have killed them in a revenge attack. Tyers had called McMillan and the good Dr Arbuckle to the inquest, at which it was determined that 'there could not be an atom of doubt of one of [the bodies] being that of a white female'. Thus the white woman was finally laid to rest.

What was McMillan's motivation in creating the myth? Was she a cynical ploy with which to stir up hatred of the Gunai? Did he think her resurrection a tactical strike? Or had it been based on an honest belief in the existence of a suffering woman in need of salvation?

Whatever the truth, it seems he had been convinced to back down. The white woman was dead.

There is something tragic in the observation that a woman who may or may not ever have existed, with no confirmed name or identity, became the most significant woman in the history of Gippsland. Hard-done-by wives, mistresses and housekeepers would continue with their home-making, spreading civilisation one household at a time, and raising children in often extraordinarily difficult circumstances, while in the newspapers, for decades to come, discussion continued to rage over the fate of the phantom woman and how she might have been saved.

In Angus McMillan's own homestead, Christina would bear two children before this pious man would deign to marry her, and only then after the local preacher prevailed upon him to stop living in sin. He signed the marriage certificate with a loose, careless autograph; his wife's signature, however, gives much away. In a laborious hand, Christina both reclaimed her place in polite society and misspelt her own name.

'C h r i s t i o n', she wrote.

*

Steve's idea for his project was simple. He envisaged a series of photographs depicting a modern-day re-enactment of the white woman affair. But, he suggested, told from an Aboriginal point of view, these events might be seen in a different light. He had in mind something like a love story, an outback *Romeo and Juliet*. 'What if she really did exist,' he floated, 'but she went of her own accord?'

I nodded along, not entirely following his train of thought. But a runaway bride, I later learned, would not seem so surprising to a person looking through Gunai eyes. The disappearance of the woman, the subsequent pursuit, the constant dodging – all of this bore a marked resemblance to the traditional courtship customs of the Gunai.

As the anthropologist Alfred Howitt explained: 'The young Kŭrnai man ... could acquire a wife in one way only, namely, by running off with her secretly and with her own consent.' Under cover of darkness, a young couple would make a break for it. 'Stealing round to the back of her parents' camp, in which she was sitting, he touched her with a long stick, and she being ready to run off pulled the end as a signal. He then left, and the girl, having her bag (*batung*) packed up, in fact, having her trousseau ready, flitted after him.'

After their departure, a sort of ritualised outrage would unfold. The young woman's father would beat his breast, gather a hunting party and set off in the couple's wake. If found quickly, they would be soundly beaten then packed off back to their separate homes, only to run off again at the next chance they got. And so it went on, again and again, until the outrage grew stale and the union was finally accepted by the clan. Better-prepared couples might successfully evade capture, sometimes staying away long enough for the woman to bear a child before they returned home (the pair attacked by Patrick Coady Buckley on Ninety Mile Beach were in all likelihood on such a 'honeymoon'). In these cases the match would be accepted more quickly, although a ceremonial fight between the groom and the bride's family would still take place upon their eventual return.

Though blood was drawn on these occasions, 'there can be no doubt that the old people of the Kŭrnai winked at this practice of marriage by elopement. In by far the greater number of cases, they themselves had obtained a wife or husband in this manner, and yet when their daughter married in the same way they were furious at it, and punished her with severity.'

And so, as the white woman made her break into the bush, hand in hand with her Gunai lover, an angry mob in hot pursuit, she could be confident in the knowledge that her mate was well-versed in the quick getaway, that they were following a well-trodden tradition of forbidden love in his culture.

This was the backstory that Steve imagined when he heard about the white woman. This was the story he wanted to tell, one that resolved not only his reservations about the traditional interpretation of the incident, but also mine. He planned a series of images portraying her flight, casting me in the role of the white woman – not as the damsel in distress, but a decision-making woman – and he as my Aboriginal captor, or rather companion, taking me by the hand.

Who knows what really happened? Perhaps she existed, perhaps she didn't. Perhaps she was stolen, perhaps she went willingly. Each scenario seemed to me as unlikely as any other. Increasingly, I was coming to the conclusion that whatever most had the appearance of truth tended to turn out to be the furthest from it.

We stood together knee-deep in the surf, squinting against the light. Ninety Mile Beach stretched off to either side like a smear of paint, silver sand bleached white as bone under an insistent sun. And behind us the ocean, enormous, restless, tugging at the hem of my dress, sucking at my feet, sand shifting with each stroke of the waves.

Cam was a hundred yards up the beach, staring intently through his lens as he tried to fit in the full sweep of the landscape: the endless ocean, the infinite sky. And us, two antlike figures, staging our own small drama in the bottom eighth of the frame. I shut my eyes, felt my hair lift

Steve and the author run from the waves on Ninety Mile Beach.

upwards on the breeze, like a seabird riding the thermals. I lifted my arms from my sides. Wings, I thought. Like wings.

'Stand closer!' Cam called, yelling to be heard over the surf. 'Can you face each other? Look at each other!'

I swivelled awkwardly and stepped forward, self-conscious now, keeping my face level with Steve's chest. After a moment I forced my eyes to dart up to his, and found him regarding me with what seemed to be barely suppressed amusement.

We chatted awkwardly as we stood arm's distance apart, like two dancers waiting for the music to begin, trying not to move our lips. 'Hands down!' ordered Cam. 'Shoulders square! Heads up!'

We subsided into silence, regarding each other obediently, humour slipping away. We were standing too close now to maintain eye contact. I let my eyes wander along Steve's jawline, keeping my expression neutral. I could feel the salt water soaking through my skirts, rising up from surface level towards its high tide.

'Okay?' Cam's voice was reedy, trembling in the wind. He raised an arm to signal.

'Okay?' asked Steve, turning to look at me. I nodded. He grasped my hand in his and we ran, careering through the shallows, leaving perfect footprints across the wet sand, which gleamed momentarily as the water retreated towards the withdrawing wave. When we crossed the tideline I stumbled as my feet flailed in the soft sand, but Steve's hand was clamped tight on mine and he pulled me upright, towed me along behind him. I was flying now, running faster than I had ever run, bare feet pedalling, hardly touching the ground. Reaching the foot of the dunes we scrambled up, powered by momentum, scrabbling at the ropelike roots of the spinifex with our free hands. We clambered and climbed, making our escape, we were away ...

Finally we came to rest, laughing, chests heaving, in the lee of the dunes.

Below us on the sand, Cam was already hollering more instructions.

'Come back down!' he yelled. 'Again. Try and run in step. Try to go when the wave has swept all the way back out.'

'Okay,' we called back. 'Okay.'

And we padded back along the wet sand, into the surf. My wet dress was sandy now, and sticking to my legs. We took each other's hands and waited for the signal to go.

8

Slaughterhouse Gully

It was time to take stock. I'd been on the trail of Angus McMillan for weeks now, amassing facts and stats and theories in my notepad: the what, the where and the how. I had attempted to crack open the mythology of the man to get at the truth of him, and at his less admirable achievements. I had mapped the course of his life from fresh-off-the-boat emigrant to landed laird, from sea level to highest peak. But though I now felt in possession of the facts, I still had not resolved my core question. I did not understand what could have pushed a man to such extreme behaviour, caused him to slip his moral moorings so completely.

I knew that he had started out a good man, if somewhat self-righteous. And I also knew that he seemed to come good again in the end: well-liked, well-respected, generous to a fault. And in the middle – what? A complete mental break?

Certainly the speed of his transformation was remarkable. In 1839 McMillan was railing against the mistreatment of the convicts at Camden; by 1841 he had taken up 'hunting blacks' as a favoured pastime. What could possibly have happened between his departure from the Monaro and setting up in Gippsland that could have hardened him so?

It seemed so incredibly out of character that to attribute it to some inherent evilness seemed a get-out somehow. Even Peter Gardner, McMillan's greatest critic, had backed away from such a conclusion.

I no longer knew what to feel. McMillan had become a sort of logic problem, and I didn't have enough information to solve it. Or rather, I had the answer, but I didn't understand the process by which it had been reached.

But this equation was common enough. Angus McMillan, I knew, was not the only man to have made such a transition. The same metamorphosis had taken place in homesteads across Gippsland, across Australia, across the colonial world. All these respectable men; all these cold-blooded killers.

I was mulling this over as we drove north, leaving the swell of the ocean far behind, heading into the hills, up into the Snowy gorge, towards Currawong and the Monaro plains. We were following McMillan's tracks upstream, back to the source.

Junction of the Buchan and Snowy Rivers, painted by
Eugene von Guérard in 1867.

210

The three of us were packed in the car along with our tents, water, fishing rods, a crossbow, sleeping bags, stoves and other outdoors paraphernalia. I sat wedged in the back, my feet resting on a pile of kindling and a small sheathed axe, listening to the boys talk, occasionally chiming in with a bit of information I'd read somewhere. Past Buchan – neat town square, the brilliant lavender-blue blossom of the jacarandas bursting over lawns like confetti – we lapsed into a companionable silence which Cam occasionally interrupted to read us passages from Peter Gardner's books.

'Listen to this,' he said. '"Some settlers gladly hailed the proposal of one who said, 'Let's take our guns, and go into the bush, and shoot a lot of blackfellows for a lark.' And they did it."'

He turned to look at me with an unreadable expression. It was unspeakably horrid. But also inexplicable, impossible to relate to. I screwed up my face, trying to think of a suitable response. But I had only questions. What on earth could have been going through those men's heads?

Perhaps, as Steve suggested, they simply didn't think of Aboriginal men as human. They did, after all, talk about them as if they were pests. Like kangaroos grazing wild upon the pasture, perhaps, or dingoes picking off the lambs at night. Even Henry Meyrick, the conscientious objector, admitted that 'if I caught a black actually killing my sheep I would shoot him with as little remorse as I would a wild dog'.

But it was more than that: killing was so normalised it had become a sort of entertainment. The journals of squatters of the time are peppered with episodes of such

211

senseless violence that they beggar belief: buckets of burning embers thrown onto tribesmen's bare feet; bags of flour laced with arsenic handed out to hungry women. What was the *point*? They were like little boys pulling the legs off butterflies, incinerating ants with a magnifying glass.

'Hang on,' Cam said suddenly. 'We're about to pass pretty close to Slaughterhouse Gully, one of the last massacres before the Gunai were effectively defeated. Not by McMillan and his men, but ... friends of his.' He read another passage aloud:

The blacks who were living in a wild state had been spearing cattle. [The local settlers] organized a party well armed and mounted, and according to my information cornered the Abos on a flat close to the Murrindale river and shot them down without mercy. Some escaped but many did not and for many years their bones lay bleaching on the ground, some of the victims I have been told were thrown into the river at a spot where the river flows under the hill.

There was a pause.

'Well,' said Steve. 'Shall we go there and see it for ourselves?'

To find Slaughterhouse Paddock we left the car on a verge and shinned over a gate marked 'Private', following a rough track down between a limestone quarry and a muddle of wooded hills. The cattle grazing there scattered, herding their calves before them, then stopped to look back at us, lowing, warning us off. We followed in their wake through the waves of long grass, crickets flying up in clouds with every step; the grass was moving with them, reactive.

The pitch of the land was wrinkled by dusty tracks where the cows had worn in the ground like an old pair of shoes. The karst landscape had left jagged grey stones protruding from the hillside like broken teeth in their gums. Ahead and above, the ground gradually rose to the Pyramids, a conspicuous limestone outcrop crowned with a tiara of stony needles.

I frowned, folding my copy of Gardner's *Gippsland Massacres* open at the hand-drawn map and holding it up to compare it to the scene in front of us. We were looking for a gully that was supposed to be nearby. According to Gardner it would be an 'appropriate site for a large number of Aboriginals to be trapped against the rugged bluff'. Somewhere between a dozen and two dozen of the Krowathunkooloong clan had been shot down as they cowered there, with no means of escape.

The boys frowned, distracted from the human tragedy for a moment by the difficulty of piecing together the historical accounts, of linking Gardner's line map to the place we stood in. We split up to cover more ground, me cursing my white dress – still stiff with salt from the waves at Ninety Mile Beach – which caught on the barbed-wire grass with every step. I had paused to pull the prickles from my hem, teasing them carefully with my fingers, when I spotted a wombat moving at great speed ahead of me, waddling a quick escape as Steve obliviously clambered up the slope above.

I grinned, ticking off another box in my mental list of quintessential Australian wildlife, and made to follow him. His fat little legs whirred as he rounded a bend and hopped down some terrace-like steps trodden in the hillside by sheep or cattle. I sped up, trying not to lose sight of him, quickly cornered a couple of thorny shrubs, then had to skid to a halt to stop myself from slipping into a deep fissure in the earth.

My mouth formed an 'O'. 'Come here!'

The wombat flinched at my voice but kept running, skipping down and into the hillside where the ground had been torn open to expose its layers of rocks: red-raw but delicate as *millefeuille*, the earth's coats of paint.

Steve and Cam came up behind me wordlessly, and peered down into the abyss. I read aloud from the book I still clutched in one hand: '"No bones have been found and not surprisingly as some of the cave holes in the area drop down to a great depth to underground streams."' I couldn't see the bottom, nor to the back of the chasm where it pierced deep into the hill – a natural mausoleum. We had to be close.

'We need to get higher,' ordered Steve. 'Get a bird's-eye view.'

We headed up the rocky slope, gravitating towards the natural crenellations at the peak: 'the Citadel', as some of the locals called it, and I liked that better. The land spread out below us, its hairshirt of matted gums clinging to every curve. Blowflies buzzed around noisily.

I flicked back through the pages, looking for descriptive passages. '"The avenging party came upon the aborigines who were feasting on the banks of a lagoon behind The Pyramids,"' I read aloud. '"Confronted by the white men and all chance of escape cut off by the steep cliffs of the Murrindal River, the tribe had no chance of escape and was annihilated by the bullets of the enraged whites."'

'There,' said Steve. He was craning over the edge to look down at a flat green pasture in the hook of the river, neatly hoed and streaked with perfect dotted lines of green leaves. It was directly below us, stopping at the edge of the water, before the rocks jutted straight up to where we were crowded at the top of the precipice.

'Right there. It has to be.'

'Is that the right road? Shaws Gully Road?' Cam craned around in his seat. 'Stop. Go back.'

We slewed sideways, made a clumsy three-point turn and pulled onto the rough track. A five-bar gate blocked the way. A sign hanging from the top bar read 'Locals only'.

As we considered, a red saloon car trundled across a cattle grid on the other side of the gate and pulled up. The driver got out, opened the gate, got back in, drove through and came to a halt alongside us. He eyed us suspiciously and wound down his window.

'Can I help you?'

'Uh ...' Steve started uncertainly. 'Can we get down to the Pyramids this way?'

The driver sucked through his teeth. We could try, he said, but he didn't fancy our chances. He reeled off a list of gates that we would find blocking our path, as if it were a gauntlet we would have to run. 'Why do you want to go there?'

'You know,' Cam piped up, avoiding the question, 'we've got a relation of Angus McMillan in the back.'

'Oh, *Angus*?' The man glanced at me, interested now. I flashed an awkward grin back. 'Well, there's an old lady down there that lives in the original homestead from the pioneer days. Still got the gun loops cut in the walls. You'll want to see that.' He was warming to his subject now. 'I probably shouldn't say this' – he lowered his voice and leaned out of the window – 'but there's a spot down there where the Aborigines were all chased down and killed.'

We feigned ignorance, making little noises of shock and sympathy. 'Gosh,' I said, though he couldn't hear me through the window. 'Really?'

'Although, you know,' he said, brightening, 'it's a real beautiful spot. Well – try, why don't you? If you see anyone, just say Jack said it was all right to look around.' He lifted a hand in farewell and drove off.

We nosed through the gate and headed the way he'd come, past the old homestead – a broad building whose corrugated-iron roof rose to a high peak, climbing plants choking the columns of the terrace – and down. The track wound on through the deep blue of the evening, past collapsing agricultural sheds and through a milling flock of sheep badly in need of shearing, wool hanging down behind them in filthy dreadlocks, tangling in the undergrowth.

The bush closed in around us. After four more gates and a fifteen-minute drive, the track came to an abrupt halt at a padlocked driveway. We stopped again, unsure, then got out of the car. 'No Trespassing', read another sign. 'No Shooting'.

My eyes began to adjust to the lowering dusk. The track led down to some polytunnels, a row of stakes, tidy lines of neat vegetables. Close by on our left, the ground banked up to what looked like an old drover's hut perched on a grassy mound. We got out of the car and stood by the gate, hemming and hawing, finally deciding that we'd come too far to turn back. We climbed over the fence.

Up close, it was clearly a cattleman's hut that had been renovated to make a small homestead: a stocky little shed with a steeply pitched roof, a crude corrugated-iron chimney, and a stubby verandah tacked onto the front, where waxed coats hung in rows like bats. I stepped forward and rapped on the door. No answer. There was a dog bowl on the mat, but no bark. Three pairs of boots sat coupled up along the wall. The place had the air of the *Mary Celeste*, as if the inhabitants had walked out halfway through dinner, pausing only to shut the door behind them.

'Look,' said Steve, his back to us. We turned.

From higher up we could see the curve of the paddock's edge, the arced path of the river. The muscled back of the rock rose beyond, silhouetted against the darkening sky, its three-pronged crown. An 'appropriate site for a large number of Aboriginals to be trapped against the rugged bluff'.

Another fragment from Gardner's book came unbidden to my mind: 'Here the offending tribe was so badly defeated that its power was definitely broken, and never after did any of its members molest the whites.'

'Yeah,' I said finally. I didn't have anything else left to say.

*

217

As the night came in, so came the fear.

We drove back the way we had come, before turning off at a side track in search of a camping spot. It was properly dark now, our headlights picking out little but the branches that closed in around us and the insects that flitted, disorientated, through the beams, flecking our view with chaotic light trails like a meteor shower. The track seemed long disused, grass grown up between the ruts. No one had driven here for some time.

The trees opened out into a small clearing. We pulled up in a square, flat spot that looked as if it had been cleared for a house that had never been built. To our left, an old shepherd's cabin squatted in the shadows. Planks had been nailed over its windows and doors at crazed angles, a rush job. I felt the hairs rise on the back of my neck.

I thought about McMillan and his men fighting 'the defence of Bushy Park', and other desperate night-time struggles from huts like this. Firing through the gun loops at unknown attackers. Battening down, blocking the doors, bracing themselves for the inevitable attack. It made me think of those militant Zionist settlers in the West Bank, hiding away in their fortified homes – shuttered windows, reinforced doors – alternately terrorising or terrorised by their neighbours. What sort of life was that?

Here the settlers had sat, locked inside their tiny, flimsy pockets of safety, heads bent in silent prayer, hands clasped around the shaft of a rifle, ears pricked for the signal that outside all hell was about to break loose. Why did they stay?

Oblivious to my growing unease, Cam got out and went to search for firewood at the edge of the clearing. I opened my mouth to call him back, but couldn't think of any protest that wouldn't sound ridiculous. The door slammed, leaving Steve and me alone in the car. We sat in silence for a moment.

'I get the feeling we're not welcome here,' said Steve finally. 'I just want to get as far away from this place as possible.'

His words hung in the air. It was the sort of statement I'd normally shoot down in flames, denounce as superstitious nonsense. But this time I couldn't find the words. I felt it too. A rising panic. An unidentifiable fear of the clearing, the hut, the woods, the faceless shadows between the trees. I turned to stare out of the window into the dark, the rational part of my brain struggling to maintain calm.

After a moment Steve spoke again. 'Aboriginal people believe that the spirits of the dead continue to communicate with the living long after death. Some people have got a special sensitivity to it.' He had it, he said, or he thought he did. While working on his canoe project his dreams had become filled with spirits, seeking him out from beyond the sky to whisper secrets in his ears. When, finally, the boat had been launched, he had paddled out alone into the gloaming. Wisps of mist had spun up from the lake's glassy surface. They walked towards him like ghosts, dawdled alongside, then blew straight through him.

As he spoke, two lights appeared on the hill opposite, like a torch reflecting off the backs of a pair of eyes. Well-spaced car headlamps facing us straight on. 'If we can see them,' I thought, madly, 'they can see us.'

'Switch off the lights,' I commanded. Steve did so without hesitation.

Darkness. Silence, except for the sound of our breath.

Suddenly the passenger door opened, flung open angrily. The interior lamp flicked on with it, flooding the car with light again.

'What are you doing?' Cam had an armful of sticks. 'I can't see a thing.'

Steve cleared his throat. 'I think we should camp somewhere else.'

Cam looked at Steve, then at me. Outnumbered, he sighed. 'Okay. Let's go.'

Fear is irrational, illogical, inexorable. It is more force of nature than fleeting emotion. It is a survival method, hardwired into our bodies by millions of years of evolution. It bubbles up, more often than not at night, when one is tired and alone. Night is when the large predators come out, under the cover of darkness, creeping unnoticed behind their prey until it is too late. Are you scared of the dark? Of course you are. We're programmed to be.

In situations that your brain perceives to be high-risk, a single unexpected sight or sound is enough to trigger a physiological response, sending the body into high alert. Senses become sharpened, scanning in every direction for threats unknown. The creaking of a house contracting at night becomes the footsteps of an intruder. Wardrobes and cupboards appear as lairs, for humans or otherwise. Faces and figures materialise from the gloom, out of falling water or drifting smoke. *Pareidolia*, they call this: finding form in the formless. Knowing what it's called doesn't blunt its power to frighten.

To me, those headlights in the dark appeared as eyes looking directly at me. For Steve, out in his bark canoe, those whirling columns of air and spray that had blown up from the water's surface had appeared as figures – 'willy willies', he'd called them. In Aboriginal mythology, willy willies are spirits that have taken earthly form: the dead elders, said Steve.

Aboriginal people, of course, are not alone in turning to the supernatural to explain natural phenomena. For the white settlers, too, there was much that they did not understand, and this uncertainty was frightening. Maps of the region from this time resemble preparatory sketches for some unfinished work: Port Albert a speckling on the southern edge; cart tracks like snail trails across expanses otherwise barren of detail; blank spaces labelled with Brechtian simplicity – 'unsurveyed country', 'indifferent land'.

The only thing they knew for certain about this emptiness was that nothing was impossible. All sorts of weird creatures had crawled out of the earth: beavers with beaks, spiders the size of saucepans – pioneers in the 'bad lands' of west Gippsland complained of earthworms that grew to six feet in length. The black swans that swam unruffled on the tides of Corner Inlet were symbol enough, were they not, of Old World assumptions that had been all too easily disproven?

Thus they took seriously the Aboriginal lore that told of 'bunyips', hulking, hairy creatures with 'eyes like live coals and tusks like a walrus' that lurked in billabongs waiting for unsuspecting passers-by. In Ararat, two hundred miles to the west, the natives had once supposedly caught one; they pulled it up onto the bank and traced its form in the mud, this record drawn and redrawn for generations as an incontrovertible proof. The Gunai spoke of 'dooligahs', yeti-type figures that haunted the forests of the high country. The white men joked about them, but hunted them too, and they and the risk they posed took up a strange semi-existence in the world of the settlers.

The danger posed by the Gunai, however, was not entirely imagined. It would be disingenuous to paint them as hapless victims, as they so often are in present-day tellings of the frontier clashes. Henry Reynolds' groundbreaking book *The Other Side of the Frontier*, first published in 1981, was the first to present the settlement of Australia as a white 'invasion' which faced a sustained Aboriginal resistance, rather than the traditional narrative of the peaceful settlement of a formerly 'wild' country.

The resistance was not so organised as to comprise a single, united movement, but certainly many tribes – including the Gunai – put up decades-long struggles, during which groups of what might best be described as freedom fighters engaged in a range of anti-white tactics, including massed attacks (as seen at the defence of Bushy Park), surveillance and the purposeful destruction of stock, horses and property in a form of economic warfare. Guerrilla tactics were at the core of the resistance. 'Their whole art of war', as one Tasmanian pioneer concluded, was 'a concealed, silent and treacherous attack'.

In pre-contact times, the Aboriginal methods characterised by early settlers as 'treachery' were an integral part of intertribal warfare. Sneaking up on a rival tribe in the middle of the night was a valid tactic; ruthless revenge might be taken months or years after an original slight. Warriors were revered for their displays of cunning and deceit. Now, disadvantaged in terms of firepower, this bent towards stealth and surprise was the Aboriginal warriors' only hope of success. They gathered in the dark and descended in force upon isolated homesteads; they ambushed lonely travellers. By necessity they were opportunistic, seeking out weakness and preying upon the vulnerable.

Correspondence of the time details an array of horrifying incidents. Shepherds were set upon while sleeping, their mutilated bodies discovered days later. Men in remote huts were found with pipes in their mouths, hands in their pockets, and an axe in the back of their heads. This is high-tension, horror-movie fare. So while it is certainly true that the white settlers had the upper hand, we must also accept that in the earliest years of settlement, despite the shows of bravado, much of the time they were scared out of their wits.

Alfred Thompson, writing about his time as a pioneer in the Mount Battery region around the same period, explained well how these terrors might worm their way into the heads of the squatters:

> The effect of these atrocities upon the minds of the men, perpetrated in a lonely, isolated spot, remote from assistance, and where nothing distracted their ideas or prevented their brooding upon the one subject, was great. Their fears magnified the danger to such an extent that they lived in a continual state

of anxiety, apprehension and alarm. The huts were loopholed to enfilade each other. They neither dined nor slept without their arms being within reach; the barking of a dog was a signal of danger which sent every man to his post; we had to place two shepherds with every flock, and when the hut-keeper went to the creek for water, a man was posted on the bank with a double-barrelled gun to guard him from the waddy of the ubiquitous aboriginal, who was supposed to lurk behind every gum-tree and to peer from every bush.

Facing this constant strain, and a shapeshifting opposition whose members seemed one day amiable, the next blood-thirsty, instilled in the settlers a hardened attitude as they ceased to regard the Gunai as individuals, but rather as a duplicitous mass. All Aboriginal people who had not yet come in from the cold to work as station hands or servants were seen as a potential threat, and viewed with a suspicion tinged with fear. They had ceased to be people, and were instead nameless, numberless members of the 'other side'.

A former British cavalry officer, a veteran of two tours of Afghanistan, once described a similar process to me. 'It wasn't soldiers versus soldiers out there,' he told me. 'That was the problem. Any Afghan walking around had the potential to be the enemy in hiding. Anyone who wasn't white, wasn't in uniform, was a threat. We were living in constant fear of suicide attack.' After a moment he spoke again. 'It gets to you, after a while, that kind of paranoia. So you hole up in your bases, you lock the gates, and you point your guns to the outside.'

The growing alienation between the groups – in socio-logical terms, the 'othering' of the Gunai – was reflected in descriptions of tribesmen of the time, which focused on characteristics the settlers found repulsive. A dispatch from James Warman, of de Villiers' white woman search party, is a good example. The tribesmen he met were all 'exceedingly dirty in their habits', he wrote, 'and the smell from their bodies is very disgusting; in their diet nothing goes amiss, they even eat the ant eggs, in short vermin of every description serves them for their meals; they are also cannibals, eating even the bodies of their own women'. They were naked, he added, 'strangers to shame', and what's more, 'their hair is suffered to grow long, and is matted together with grease'.

They made, in other words, a good bogeyman for the unoccupied mind to brood upon at night. It must have seemed a frightening world indeed, as bunyips lurked in every waterhole and stinking cannibals behind every bush. And fear can do funny things to a person.

Late afternoon. We rose into the mountains, weaving through the shining gums, tall, willowy women throwing their arms in the air, green-fronded fingers tickling the wind, brown fronds discarded, carpeting the floor. Dogwoods thrust their cream bouquets at the road like stallholders. Through Butchers Ridge, a one-horse town with a tumbledown metal shack and a goat on its front lawn. More gory names, more lost, unknowable stories.

Down into the thick undergrowth, red sand blowing across the road. Seldom Seen Creek. And up again. Wide, high country plains with blue mountains rising behind, layered upon each other like a watercolour, blue upon blue. Powder, periwinkle, cornflower, cobalt. The road snaked up between the trees, the tarmac came to an end and we shot on along a stony track. The trees were sparser here, silvery snow gums, splitting low, at ground level, and sending their slender limbs up where they gently parted to intermingle with their neighbours. The ground was rockier, the shrubs stunted and struggling.

High up the air was dense and humid, thick with the hazy antiseptic perfume of the eucalypt. Little River Gorge opened up like a crevasse to our right. Steve pulled over and we scrambled out to stare down into its depths – the rock tumbling away below us, the thin trickle of muddy water at its foot, thermals rushing up the rocky face like hot breath on our faces.

Difficult country, then, for an exploratory expedition.

It was down this way that Angus McMillan had made his first, failed attempt to reach Gippsland from the Monaro in 1839, and it was many years after that before a route through this region was found – before then, travellers had been forced to take McMillan's hundred-mile detour via Omeo. All attempts to find a way through this 'precipitous and broken country', wrote Tyers five years later, had failed 'in consequence of their horses being too jaded to proceed'.

McMillan had not helped his cause much by setting off in winter. In the highest mountain sections the horses waded through snow three feet deep, and the expedition was woefully ill-equipped. Jemmy Gibber, the Ngarico black who accompanied him as a guide, came barefoot and possibly bare-chested, and McMillan was travelling too light to be able to assist him much. He gave one half of his blanket to Gibber, but found he could not spare any clothes.

Alone with his Ngarico guide, who with every step into the unknown seemed to grow more distant, McMillan turned to his journal to pass the time. *Last night was bitter cold, having only one blanket, an old moulskin trouser and a blue shirt, and of course the luxury of a tent was never thought of. I felt cold indeed, and my companion, once he placed his strong body on the ground, could not be prevailed upon to put a piece of wood on the fire to warm his own frozen carcase. Very little riding today, hills rather steep, my friend grumbling all day.*

It wasn't the *fearful rough country* or the thorns of the scrub that curtailed McMillan's earliest attempt, but a hair-raising episode that left him fearing for his life.

It had taken weeks to secure Gibber's assistance. The Monaro tribe had scoffed when McMillan had first revealed his plan to explore Gippsland. One sceptical elder asked him if he wanted to be killed. The warrigals, the old man said, were much stronger men than they were. Such Ngarico scaremongering had unsettled the local settlers too, who were equally reluctant to join an expedition. *I again tried to get a European to accompany me but with no success; they were not to risk their lives in a country where the natives were reported as real giants, with red eyes and long red hair.*

Finally, after weeks of deliberation and a promise from McMillan to conquer the wild blacks so the Monaro tribe might live *in peace and quietness*, Gibber, a noted warrior, was dispatched to guide him, having been briefed by the few elderly Ngarico men who had seen this promised land.

Thus the pair, one keen and one reluctant, struck off south, but after only three days' travel Gibber's fear of the warrigal got the better of him. Growing steadily more spooked and unpredictable, he attempted to abandon McMillan in the bush, but was foiled. *He told me he was alarmed that the wild natives would come upon us, and that he would not be able to get away from them, as they could run faster than we could ride.*

Something about Gibber's panicked behaviour had the hair on the back of McMillan's neck prickling. That night he prepared himself to watch his companion, a pistol at each hand, *but being tired I soon dropped off asleep.* Later, a movement in the dark woke him with a start: *to my horror I saw my companion quietly picking up his waddy.* Both sprang to their feet at once, Gibber with his club in his hand. *In an instant my pistol was at his heart.*

A deadlock. Gibber attempted to deny that his intention had been to hurt McMillan, but the Scot did not believe him. He took possession of Gibber's club and axe, telling him that if anything happened to him while he was in the bush *he and all his tribe would suffer.*

McMillan would merrily recall this episode when relating tales of his daring exploits for the rest of his life. But, lying alone in the mountains with a hostile stranger, struggling to stay awake with a pistol under his pillow, must have been a formative experience for the young man. Not only had Gibber displayed that notorious Aboriginal bent for 'treachery' by his thwarted night-time attack, he had also demonstrated such a deep and deranging fear of the warrigals that, disregard it though he appeared to at the time, must have preyed on McMillan's mind during his earliest months and years in Gippsland.

*

Birdsong drifted from the gorge, the delicate strains of so many flautists practising their trills and scales. The sun was dipping quietly behind the distant mountains, taking with it the warmth of the day, and we stood gazing out into the depths, eyes straining as the light faded, until there was nothing more to be seen.

As the dusk rolled in, the wildlife emerged. Going was slow as Steve inched along the road, ready to brake if a kangaroo or wallaby leapt out in front of us. At the foot of a steep descent, a large deer stepped out of the shadows into the indigo twilight. It stared wide-eyed at the oncoming car, and froze, lit up like a stage performer. We slowed to a crawl, then stopped. There was a moment of respectful silence as we – humans and cervid – regarded each other with solemnity.

Steve slipped one hand back between the seats towards me. To touch my arm, I assumed, overcome by the wonder and beauty of the moment; but instead he stretched past me and closed his fingers on the empty air. Twisting, frowning, he looked back and located the barrel of the crossbow. I watched, horrified, as slowly, silently, he pulled it free from a tangle of fishing rods and slipped it through the gap between the seats, slotted in a bladed bolt and leaned out of the window to take aim. Slowly. Slowly.

Something in the movement must have spelled danger, for the deer took sudden fright and bounded out of the light and into the dark tangle of vegetation. 'Fuck,' said Steve. 'Fuck. I thought I had it.'

Cam scoffed. 'Good thing you didn't. What did you think we were going to do with a whole deer? We'd have been up all night gutting it. We'd have had to tie it to the *roof.*'

Steve was still cursing when he turned back to me, passing me the weapon and the bolt separately. I inspected the arrowhead – four mean metal blades, as on a kitchen knife, the sort of knife you need to keep in a guard – before wordlessly replacing it in a box on top of a heap of equipment.

We'd bought a carton of these bolts earlier, in a shop whose walls were lined with camouflage hunting suits, each printed with foliage as richly detailed as William Morris wallpaper, and glass display cases of weaponry worthy of *The Hunger Games*. I had dawdled, awkward as a husband in a lingerie department, looking sideways, out of the corners of my eyes, but not touching, reading the labels on the boxes. 'Dual side-by-side cutting blades and 6 razor-sharp cutting edges create up to a 250 per cent greater wound opening than traditional broadheads,' said one, before helpfully explaining: 'This means significantly greater blood loss, a better blood trail and ultimately, a faster kill.'

I frowned, contemplating the significance of 'a better blood trail'.

'Can I help you?'

I looked up to find a tall, tanned shop assistant smiling at me blandly from behind the counter. He dropped his eyes pointedly to the box, then raised them back to mine.

'Me?' I asked stupidly. 'Oh, no. No. No, thank you.'

We turned off at McKillop's Bridge to a camping spot far beneath its broad-shouldered span. The track was stony, steep, but as it levelled out the Snowy River came into view, huge and silver and calm in the moonlight.

We stopped repeatedly to allow more wildlife off the road: a fox, a large grey kangaroo, two dark-eyed wallabies, a fluffy possum that refused to be hurried. Several rabbits too, but Steve accelerated towards those, steering directly for them, trying to catch them under the wheels without taking us all over the precipice. But no such luck. Steve cursed again, Cam laughed.

The fire took quickly. Too tired to think, I listened to the boys talk as I lay back on my rucksack to look up at the stars, scattered across the night sky in their unfamiliar constellations. Cam had shown me how to find the Southern Cross, by joining the bright dots of Alpha Centauri and Beta Centauri and extending the line north, like a tail on the kite of Crux, its four bright points drawing the crossbars, its fainter fifth point, Epsilon Crucis, sitting on the edge of its sail. And beyond that, Carina, the keel of the great ship Argo that sailed the southern sky through the wash of the Milky Way, brighter here, shining with the lavender blue of a bruise.

My eyes, searching for a familiar handhold, alighted on my old friend Orion. Inverted from his usual posture, standing on his hands, but still reassuring in a sky that seemed so strangely foreign. Indigenous Australians saw him too, of course, but they interpreted him differently – some thought him not man but kayak, the three studs of his belt three hungry brothers, his sword not a sword but a fishing line, a kingfish on the end with a hook in its mouth.

Likewise, while Europeans saw Crux as the crucifix upon which hung the son of their god, the Gunai saw it as the head of an enormous emu, Ngooran, hunted nightly by Narran, the moon. Other Aboriginal groups saw the open talons of an eagle, or the prongs of a trident. The Maoris, across the Tasman Sea to the east, thought it a great aperture in the sky, through which wild winds would rush from another world.

A yowl broke the air, a melodic, haunting siren call. Then another, and another.

I sat up, eyes flitting nervously to the shadows that danced on the edge of our clearing, shadows that leapt and retreated in step with the flames.

Cam and Steve's eyes were wide, excited. 'Dingoes!'

The call came again, lupine voices joining together as one, then colliding and parting, rough, discordant, a dissonant choir. I lay back down to listen, pulled my jacket tighter around me, thoughts turning uneasily to the mysteries of the night beyond the clearing, beyond our circle of light. To bunyips, and doolagahs, and footsteps in the dark.

That night I dreamed about the massacres again. I heard those same shrill screams, the bloody thuds of spears hitting their targets. The crack of the guns, the rising panic of the reload, the blood spilling thick and wet across the ground, the animal groans of the wounded. It was the same scenario, the same sick thrill of fear and adrenaline. But this time they weren't killing me. I was killing them.

When I awoke I lay still, watching the light play across the sides of my tent. The leaves shifted in the breeze like kelp in a current. Birds called out and fell silent: rosellas, honeyeaters, the computerlike scramble of the magpie. Cockatoos gathered in a tree to complain, swearing and cursing, drunken revellers flashing their crests, then moved on as quickly as they had come. Bellbirds sounded their eerie sonar pulse, clear piercing tones, fingers drawn smoothly round the rim of a glass.

Steve cuts a shield from the bark of a gum tree, McKillop's Bridge.

I left Cam reading by the tents and wandered down through the straggly tail ends of the bush to the sand at the river's bank. Steve was fishing, bare-chested, his back to me. He didn't turn, but kept his eyes fixed on the point where his line met the water.

I shrugged off my clothes and waded into the river to bathe, the cold water hitting me like a slap in the chill morning air, making me gasp. Fresh air in my lungs. Clean white light on my skin. I dipped my head under like a baptism.

*

It was late by the time we left the Snowy, the early-morning clouds long burned off. By this time we were completely unanchored by anything so humdrum as schedules or obligations; we'd told Jeannie and Steve's parents to expect us back on Friday, and it was Sunday now, but it didn't seem to matter. Our phones had died days ago, and none of us had thought to bring an alarm. I didn't want to speak to anyone else, or know the date, or the time.

If anything, it was as though we were moving backwards in time. Not long after we crossed the border into New South Wales we came across an early settler's hut, restored, by the side of the road. It was the first permanent dwelling in the area, a sign said. It had been constructed in the 1840s. The smoke-blackened roof shingles were visible from the inside; on the walls flowery wallpaper peeled back to reveal newspaper print underneath, pasted there as a sort of plaster.

The bush here was dry, and made untidy by roots and the dry dropped limbs of the gums. Delegate, the nearest modern-day town to Currawong, was an old-style frontier settlement with false-fronted shopfronts of weathered clapboard and cracked tile terraces. Two old-fashioned petrol pumps sat beside the road, gleaming silver in the sunshine. A service station, or 'servo', as Australians call them. Long shut.

We stopped off at a bar before our last push up to Currawong, parking by an open-roofed horse trailer. As we got out of the car, three utes swerved off the road, windows down, music blaring, and their rugby-shirted drivers pushed in ahead of us, leaving their keys in the ignition and their windows open.

Inside it was dark, cool. A surly barmaid with frizzy hair was reading a newspaper behind the bar. 'NO CREDIT DON'T ASK' read a sign, not far from the 'BIRD SHIT TROPHY' and a list of its previous winners. Elsewhere, a flea-eaten dingo skin was mounted on the wall. 'Trapped May 1983 by John Coman,' read a plaque beneath it. 'Three legged yellow bitch with six yellow pups inside. Killed at the bottom of Tingiringi Mountain at the foot of a ribbony gum tree.'

I felt the eyes of the rugby shirted men on us. Me in my white dress, ragged now, my skin drawn with sharp raw lines where the sun had caught my forehead and cheekbones, my collarbones picked out by scarlet brush-strokes, my hair loose and tangled; Steve with his topknot and ironic T-shirt; Cam with a fancy camera around his neck, zoom lens jutting obscenely. City kids, I could hear them thinking.

I steered the boys to a table outside so we could speak freely. I was in low spirits, still uneasy from the night before, but Steve and Cam were fired up by our travels. As soon as we sat down they turned again to the events at the gully. Steve did most of the talking, his face set with righteous anger. Cam nodded fiercely along, and I did too, but emptily.

I recognised Steve's tone. It was one I'd used myself in pub discussions, when I hit my stride explaining to English friends and colleagues how messed-up my country was, *thanks to them*. It was the tone I used when I spoke about the battle at Culloden, where *the soil ran with blood*, and about the Clearances, when my countrymen were *pulled screaming from their houses*, those same houses sent up in flames behind them. The tone when I lectured strangers in bars on the massacre at Glencoe, when visiting loyalists killed their hosts in their beds for refusing to swear allegiance to their new English king. And, and, and ... I had more where those came from: my people, your people. The balance of payments.

And it was all true, or close enough. The English were the perpetrators, if not directly then indirectly, through their agents among the Scots. But I was more comfortable in those conversations when I was assuming the role of victim; now, here I was feeling defensive on behalf of my own people.

I didn't doubt what Steve was saying. God knows, I'd been on the same trail for weeks now, and uncovering the same narrative. But I was unhappy and uneasy with my new role as the representative of the aggressors, and I watched their conversation from the other side of the glass.

We had coasted high into rolling plains, our car now a tiny dot in a vast open expanse. Huge round rocks poked through the earth, fluorescent with lichen against the yellowing grass. Far to our left a man was herding sheep, broad-brimmed hat pulled low, silhouetted in the dust-cloud kicked up by his flock. He was the only figure in an enormous landscape that stretched out endlessly before us, baking in the sun. Straight-lined plantation forest tiled the valley sides in great flat blocks of bottle-green and tired, straggling brown. This was the Monaro, the starting point from which McMillan first struck off into the unknown.

We got out at a small redbrick church that stood alone on the plain. All the names in the tiny graveyard were

Irish. O'Hares, Tiernans. The grass had been cut recently, and had dried in clumps like hair in the prongs of the fence, but the windowpanes were dusty, and behind them we could see that the pews inside had been pulled together at the centre of the building. No numbers on the psalm board. Out back a timber outhouse listed at a steep angle, its corrugated-iron roof measled with oxidation, plank door hanging from a single rusted hinge.

The wind ramped up over the fells and blew through the long dry grass. The sound of the ocean. An incredible sense of scale.

James Atkinson, a settler arriving in the area in 1826, found it unbearable. 'The silence and solitude that reign in these wide spreading untenanted wastes, are indescribable,' he wrote. 'Nothing meets the eye of the traveller, with the exception of a few solitary Emus, to enliven the monotony of the dreary expanse. From the contemplation of this vacancy and solitude the mind recoils with weariness.'

Still, in 1840 this was comparative civilisation. This was where McMillan had ridden to seek assistance right at the start of the pioneer days of Gippsland, when he had first realised that the Gunai might be dangerous, and had been spurned. He had nowhere else to turn. With no help or support forthcoming from the state, he had little option but to return to his seedling Bushy Park and his terrified men. With orders from Macalister to carry out and his own ambition to attend to, he had no intention of backing down. They'd take care of the matter themselves, then.

George Faithfull, a squatter in Wangaratta, a hundred miles north of Gippsland, had a similar experience. In 1838, as McMillan was finding his feet at Camden, a party of Faithfull's men were attacked and eight of their number killed. After this, white–black relations deteriorated sharply. 'The government during all this time gave no help, no assistance of any kind, and at last threatened to hang anyone who dared to shoot a black, even in protection of his property,' he wrote later. 'This, instead of doing good, did much evil. People formed themselves into bands of alliance and allegiance to each other, and then it was the destruction of the natives really did take place.'

What would I have done in the same situation? I had to admit, I didn't know.

Such thoughts set bells ringing. Looking at things through McMillan's eyes had unsettled me; the ease with which I had found myself sympathising with the predicament the settlers found themselves in was unnerving. It was a problem all of their own making, of course. But what was the alternative? Give up on the dream of land? Give up on the mission they had sunk their money and the best years of their lives into? Abandon the whole project and go back to where they had come from, back to the established colony, and put the darker side of settlement from their minds?

I don't think I would have done that. The thought fluttered around in my head, a plastic bag caught by the wind.

Some did, of course, and in time they, with the other innocents, would move into the newly cleared country and condemn those who had come before them, and the wild work that had taken place in their absence.

And all the while, George Faithfull and his ilk watched from the sidelines with bitterness. 'No sooner was all fear of the blacks dissipated than the whites became almost as great a nuisance,' he wrote in 1853. 'Unfortunately the

Government gave too willing an ear to them as we were all branded as murderers of the blacks. They readily deprived us of portions of our runs to give them to the other squatters, who were considered peaceful men, as well they might be after the war was ended.'

'Ours was the danger,' he lamented. 'Theirs the reward.'

9

In Search of Elders

By the time the state of Victoria split off from New South Wales in 1851, the 'Black War' of Gippsland was, to all intents and purposes, over. The white man had won.

The surviving Gunai had either fled to the inaccessible, bush-fringed mountains, or gathered in shanty towns on the edges of white townships or cattle stations seeking employment or handouts. In a single decade the colonists had overseen the total collapse of a culture that had survived in its existing form for more than 30,000 years.

In this way, the events of Gippsland typify the collapse of Aboriginal culture across the continent, as tribe after tribe was extinguished in the face of the expansion of the British colony. The 'Omeo tribe' mentioned in McMillan's diaries, for example – more accurately, the Theddora-mittung branch of the Ya-itma-thang nation – saw their region settled around 1838. They survived this initial occupation in relatively rude health, but when gold was discovered in the region in 1852 the ensuing rush ensured that the once-populous tribe numbered a mere 'four or five' members only a decade later.

The original inhabitants of the land were falling at the hands of the newcomers, not only directly through open warfare, but indirectly by more stealthy killers. Men bearing arms may have been the most obvious of the invaders, but in many ways they were not the most insidious. What they carried with them – viruses – would prove far more destructive. Syphilis and influenza ran riot, but the most devastating of all was smallpox, a vicious, disfiguring disease that ripped through the vulnerable tribes without mercy.

Within a single year of the First Fleet's arrival, it had already cut swathes through the Eora people indigenous to the Sydney area. Watkin Tench described how their bodies piled up in every cove, 'thickly spread' with pustules. And the deaths did not stop. The whole country became one enormous petri dish where, dripped into a vast population without immunity, diseases morphed and massacred. The destructiveness of the epidemics multiplied the psychological effects of the more open warfare – the demoralising effect of seeing white men impervious to these invisible killers, as Aboriginal people succumbed in their hundreds of thousands.

Men like Angus McMillan – heading out into virgin territory, mingling with unknown tribes – were wreaking death upon their new companions even as they smiled and shook their hands. Today, 'first contact' interactions with new tribes across the world are very strictly controlled for exactly this reason, but in the 1840s there was little understanding of the transmission of disease; it was still widely thought that sickness was caused by odours and 'bad air'. The resulting plunge in the Aboriginal population echoed similar catastrophes that had tailed European conquest around the globe, notably the plagues of smallpox that so devastated the Native Americans and precipitated the downfall of the Aztec empire.

The damage was not confined to the human population: native plants and animals suffered too, as invasive species struggled for supremacy. Brambles and scotch thistles now flourish in their thickets, uncontested in temperate regions. Camels originally brought from India and Afghanistan for use as bulk transport in the desert regions roam feral in their hundreds of thousands. The wild brumbies, descended from those few horses shipped in across oceans, are now so numerous that the population must be managed by sharpshooters in helicopters. The whim of one Victorian settler who introduced twenty-four rabbits 'so as to provide a touch of home, in addition to a spot of hunting' in 1859 led inevitably to a nationwide explosion, and the notorious 'rabbit-proof fence' that stretches 1,100 unbroken miles across Western Australia.

Jeannie had told me about all this. Her latest play had been inspired by the real-life experiences of a friend, a man of hippyish disposition who had moved deep into the bush with his family. They wanted to get close to nature, but found themselves at close quarters with a far more ferocious environment than they had been prepared for. Wild dogs – an unholy hybrid of domestic dog and the native dingo – roamed the bush in packs, and as summer turned to drought, the soil to dust, and food dwindled, they skulked closer and closer to the house, eyeing first the chickens, then the family dogs – and finally, his children.

Not knowing what else to do, he bought a rifle, and went to a nearby shooting range to practise. When the dogs next appeared, rabid with hunger, he walked out onto the front step and, to the horror of his wife, gunned them down. Soon there came panicked calls from neighbours, and the lifelong pacifist found himself reinvented as the district dingo-hunter.

I had listened to this tale with an air of disbelief, but in the hills above Omeo we had stumbled across the evidence. As we slalomed down through the bush a grisly sight materialised at the side of the road. An aged gum stood with its boughs hanging heavy with the bodies of dead dogs, dozens of them, their hind legs trussed, forelegs and heads dangling lifelessly. We stopped for a closer inspection; the buzzing of the flies and the stench of putrid flesh hit us in a wall like humidity as we opened the car doors. I pulled my shirt up over my nose and mouth and advanced, searching for the cause of death. The corpses hung close together like pheasants for the pot, tan or dun-coloured, most of them, the shades of dried grass, but the occasional dark-brown, and one lucky white.

Gum tree hung with dead dogs, Omeo.

243

They'd been scalped. A long strip of fur, including the ears, had been peeled down the spine from each forehead. The tails were gone too. 'For the bounty,' explained Jeannie. The state of Victoria paid $100 per scalp. We were looking at thousands of dollars' worth of dead dog.

Ian exclaimed behind us — another tree, another haul. These ones were long-dead. Bones showed through the fur, tobacco-stain ribcages and interlocking vertebrae. Of some, whose joints had given way, only the feet were left, hanging from long ribbons of blue and purple baler twine, oddly festive.

Seeing all these corpses left hanging up on the roadside like trophies for all to see gave me an uneasy thrill. I didn't have to ask the reason: the dogs were vermin, they killed the sheep, they roamed wild and unconstrained across the countryside. I understood the concept easily enough. I'd heard the same arguments before, in a different context. It brought to mind an anecdote I'd read in the letters page of the *Sydney Gazette* dated 1841, an image I had since tried and failed to repress:

> I see by the Gazette of this day, that the blacks have again been spearing some white people to the southward, which we take amiss and call it an outrage; but, Sir, at this present moment while I am writing this to you, [name deleted] has forty-two human heads, stuck upon poles around his house, and nailed to his door posts. Pray, Sir, would you call this an outrage committed by us?

The state of the Aboriginal population soon grew so parlous – and things so comparatively comfortable for the newly respectable settlers – that public feeling shifted away from overt aggression towards something more closely resembling ridicule, or even pity.

By the mid-1850s, as the remaining Gunai emerged from the bush and appeared at the stations in greater and greater numbers, in search of employment or handouts, the very men who had masterminded their demise were at the vanguard of the movement to 'save' them, or at least to make their passage into the history books as painless as possible.

Tarra Bobby, a Gunai man assisted by McMillan when wrongly accused of murder.

245

Perhaps it was the manifestation of a guilty conscience, but Angus McMillan was considered a particularly charitable bleeding heart. As dozens of Gunai gathered in a humpy village by McMillan's homestead, the *Gippsland Guardian* wrote that 'his station at Bushy Park might well be called the Benevolent Asylum of Gippsland'. In 1858 he accompanied two Gunai men accused of murder – William Login and Tarra Bobby – to Melbourne, where he translated on their behalf. Soon enough he was appointed as an honorary protector for the region, and later as a member of a select committee tasked with the 'protection of Aborigines' – apparently with no irony intended.

And so they struggled on, until in 1859 a group of Gunai appealed to Assistant Protector William Thomas for a grant of land to be set aside for them, like that which had been granted to the Wurundjeri people of Goulburn the previous year. 'I tell them Mr McMillan will see & secure it,' Thomas wrote.

It took four years, but finally 2,300 acres were set aside for the remaining Gunai, in the form of a Christian mission where the struggling blacks could be fed and clothed and generally civilised. It was located at a site even McMillan had protested was singularly inappropriate: on a hillside overlooking Lake Wellington, close to Boney Point. It would be an unpopular choice, he said, as 'a great many Aborigines were killed [there] and as the bones lay about it got its gruesome name'. He made no mention of his involvement in their deaths.

His concerns went unheeded, and responsibility for the future of the surviving Gunai was taken out of his hands. The Ramahyuck mission station was established, led by the Reverend Friedrich Hagenauer, a German missionary. It was one of four such missions in Victoria, run by the Anglican or – like Ramahyuck – Moravian Churches. The station was located in what had traditionally been Tatungooloong country, but its residents were drawn from far and wide, resulting in an unhappy broth of tribal rivalries and miscommunication between dialect groups. Its organisers, however, were not concerned with the nuances of Aboriginal lifestyle; they planned to obliterate it.

The Ramahyuck mission station near Lake Wellington.

On arrival, the Reverend Hagenauer assembled his new Aboriginal charges and instructed them to place their traditional weapons and tools – waddies, boomerangs and so on – in a pile at the camp's centre, before setting fire to it. Corroborees, the traditional gatherings and festivals, were banned, and European dress made compulsory. To enable religious conversion, a basic education – 'reading, writing, singing and scripture' – was provided, and all tribal habits strictly forbidden. Aboriginal names were replaced with more appropriate Christian monikers; black, sun-ravaged faces bore names that could have been torn from the pages of a Jane Austen novel: Sophia Darby, Georgiana King, William Login, Percy Phillip, Mary Arnott. Hagenauer planned to record over the people like cassette tapes, and leave nothing of their original character.

The young Alfred Howitt, who moved to Gippsland in 1866, saw this, and realised that within a generation all the Gunai's age-old customs and knowledge would be lost. He began to invite the men to come and work on his hop farm on the Mitchell River, where he logged all they told him of the old ways. He did this, he wrote later, 'without definite aim', but these observations would form the foundation of his two pioneering works of ethnography, *Kamilaroi and Kurnai* (1880) and *The Tribes of South East Asia* (1904). These remarkable books detail the traditions and customs of the Aboriginal groups of Victoria and New South Wales, many of which have long since fallen into disuse. The sections concerning the Gunai are particularly fascinating, not least because they are the only written record ever made of many of their fantastical and other-worldly beliefs.

They believed that a great being, Mungan, had taught the Gunai everything they knew, and instituted the *jeraeil* (initiation) so that these secrets might be passed down, father to son, through the generations. Once, after the secrets of the *jeraeil* had been carelessly revealed to women, Mungan was so angry that he filled the entire space between the sky and the land with fire: 'Men went mad with fear, and speared one another, fathers killed their children, husbands their wives, and brethren each other. Then the sea rushed over the land and nearly all mankind were drowned.'

Some of those who survived became the ancestors of the Gunai; others became animals, birds and reptiles, which in turn were to become the familiars of the tribe, appearing to them in dreams or in bodily form to keep them safe. The crow, particularly, was a friend, who would follow them through the bush calling out advice and warnings. The Aurora Australis was an echo of the great fire. It signified that Mungan was growing angry again, and on nights when it appeared the elders – to whom prophecies were revealed in dreams – would order an exchange of wives to appease him.

The social system of the Gunai was as complex as the mythology, and equally unique. In almost all other instances, women were bound to fidelity, but men were not. Upon marriage the man must never again speak to his mother-in-law or use her name, referring to her only as 'that woman'; yet he must give the bulk of his booty from hunting to his wife's family. On his death his widow went to his brother – provided she gave her consent.

Howitt was captivated. As his relationship with the Gunai grew, he encouraged them to maintain their traditions, re-enacting their ceremonies and reviving the *jeraeil* for a last time. He recorded their song-charms, incantations and lullabies, as best as he was able. There was 'a wild and pathetic music' to their melodies, he wrote. 'With custom they grow upon one until at length one feels in some measure the effect which they produce upon an aboriginal audience in so powerful a manner ... As it is, white men know little of the black-fellow's songs, which to most people are unmeaning barbarous chants, and to the missionaries who have some knowledge of them they savour of heathendom, and must therefore be altogether pushed into oblivion and be forgotten. Thus before long all these songs, old and new, will be lost.'

Wa! – Wa! – Wa!
Stop! – Stop! – Stop!
Lelándū – mri – ngū
Sleep, – eyes of – thine

*

The Reverend Hagenauer's intention had been to destroy the traditional culture, but what his mission perhaps achieved more thoroughly was the obliteration of the Gunai people. They began to die, both young and old, with startling frequency. And with them, just as Howitt predicted, died all that they had known.

Peter Gardner has observed that 'the most frequent Christian ceremony, apart from Sunday observances, was the funeral': the mission's thirty-year registers reveal an average life expectancy of only twenty-five years, and a desperate infant mortality rate of 31 per cent. They died of strange, inexact conditions: 'exhaustion', 'abscess', 'teething', 'fits', 'decline'. Hagenauer showed little concern about the growing toll. Every death that followed conversion was to be celebrated, 'although all the victories which are here gained will bring us nearer to the end of the mission. The number of natives is small and every triumphant death which we have to record reduces the total.'

This apparent callousness reflected Hagenauer's belief, widely held at the time, that the Aboriginal Australians were a doomed race, destined for extinction. Theories of 'scientific racism' were entering the mainstream: in 1850 Robert Knox, a professor of anatomy at Edinburgh University, had published *Races of Men*, later described as 'one of the most articulate and lucid statements of racism ever to appear', in which he argued that the world's future would be decided by a 'war of extermination' in which 'the destruction of one race by another' was inevitable. Charles Darwin's seminal *On the Origin of Species* appeared in 1859, and was a favoured topic of discussion in the parlours of the day. His theory of 'natural selection' – the triumph of the strong over the weak – seemed applicable to the case of the unfortunate indigenous Australians; Darwin himself tackled the question of humanity in his 1871 book *The Descent of Man*, in which he assigned Aboriginals to the lowest rung on the ladder of humanity:

> the civilised races of man will almost certainly
> exterminate, and replace, the savage races
> throughout the world. At the same time the
> anthropomorphous apes ... will no doubt be
> exterminated. The break between man and his
> nearest allies will then be wider, for it will
> intervene between man in a more civilised state, as
> we may hope, even than the Caucasian, and some

ape as low as a baboon, instead of as now between the negro or Australian and the gorilla.

The future of the Aboriginal people seemed clear: there was none. The missionaries' purpose was thus also clarified: to make the death of a race as comfortable and as Christian as possible. In this, Hagenauer was highly successful. Even as the numbers at Ramahyuck dwindled, its school gained rave reviews from inspectors, and in 1877 it was declared the most successful of all the Victorian missions.

Hagenauer would play a key role in the institution of the 1886 Half-Caste Act, state legislation under which Aboriginal people of mixed descent were expelled from stations and reserves, in the hope that these lighter-skinned individuals would be quickly absorbed into white society as the reserves declined and eventually closed down – thus neatly solving the Aboriginal problem. The Act may have been based on a certain cold-blooded logic, but real human tragedy accompanied these expulsions: families were disrupted, married couples split apart, children forcibly removed from their parents and sent to orphanages or residential schools for 're-education' – the first of the so-called 'stolen generations', a nationwide practice of child-removal in the late nineteenth and early twentieth centuries that would see tens of thousands of Aboriginal children separated, either under duress or through deception, from their parents and placed in orphanages or 'fostered out' to white families. The practice continued in some areas up to the 1970s.

Earlier I had visited the Knob Reserve, a picturesque area of open, sun-dappled forest a short drive to the north of the Ramahyuck site, rising to a bluff that looked out over the long and languorous curves of the Avon River. Traditionally it was a meeting point between clans on important tribal occasions – corroborees, *jeraeils* and other ceremonies – but after the advent of the mission station it became the site of more melancholy gatherings, as bereft residents walked ten miles from the mission under cover of darkness to meet their exiled family members.

If it seems a cruel and unusual solution, the fact is that the approach taken by Hagenauer and his peers bears an eerie resemblance to policies that would be enacted not only in the rest of Australia over subsequent decades, but throughout the colonial world.

At around the same period, across the Pacific Ocean, the Canadian government was embarking on an aggressive programme of assimilation that also included a system of demarcated reserves and residential schooling. At one point, a third of all First Nation (indigenous) children were separated, sometimes by force, from their families, to be educated in institutions where they were indoctrinated in the English language, Christianity and the 'civilised' lifestyle, and where native languages, dress and cultural practices were banned.

In 2008, the then Prime Minister Stephen Harper made a national apology to surviving pupils and family members, conceding in his speech that the objectives of this system had been 'to remove and isolate children from the influence of their homes, families, traditions and cultures, and to assimilate them into the dominant culture. These objectives were based on the assumption aboriginal cultures and spiritual beliefs were inferior and unequal. Indeed, some sought, as it was infamously said, "to kill the Indian in the child".'

To the south, an analogous programme of 'Americanisation' was under way: more boarding schools, more plots of land where stubborn adults might be confined until they either died or changed their ways. In his State of the Union Address on 4 December 1871, President Ulysses S. Grant noted that 'many tribes of Indians have been induced to settle upon reservations, to cultivate the soil, to perform productive labor of various kinds, and to partially accept civilisation. They are being cared for in such a way, it is hoped, as to induce those still pursuing their old habits of life to embrace the only opportunity which is left them to avoid extermination.'

All across the globe, the pattern repeated as, again and again, one culture swallowed another as a python swallows an egg whole.

Perhaps there is a name for this systematic snuffing out of Aboriginal society: genocide.

Deployment of this word in terms of Australian history is divisive, and it is beyond the scope of this book to make an academic or legal study of whether it is appropriate. But it is worth touching upon the issue here, in the interests of considering the enormity of the events of the Gippsland frontier.

There are two definitions of the word that might come into play in the case of Aboriginal history. The 'standard' usage concerns the physical destruction of an ethnic group by violence or force, and there are two instances in which this is invoked in an Australian context.

The first is in terms of frontier massacres, when settlers driven by a homicidal frenzy set out to exterminate the indigenous population in their area. The most clear-cut example – often given as a 'classical example' of genocide – is the grim case of the Tasmanian 'Black War', a vicious struggle shortly before the discovery of Gippsland which saw the Aboriginal Palawa people almost entirely eradicated within a decade. At one point, a human chain 2,200 men strong, dubbed 'the Black Line', was organised to sweep the entire island – an area larger than Ireland – in an attempt to corral the remaining Palawa on a small, out-of-the-way peninsula. The notoriously violent Queensland frontier too, which the events of Gippsland closely echo, is often considered a possible case of genocide.

The second instance is the case of the 'stolen generations': an inquiry into the policy initiated by the Attorney General, which reported in 1997, concluded that it had indeed been an act of genocide, 'aimed at wiping out indigenous families, communities, and cultures' – or as one chief protector had put it, 'breeding out the colour'.

Still, many continue to reject these applications of the term. In the case of the massacres, some contest the basic facts, accusing those who have recorded such incidents of hyperbole; others, such as Richard Broome, hesitate to accept the term due to the lack of an official policy ordering the elimination of the Aboriginal population. As for the stolen generations, some fear that employing the word 'genocide' in such an instance somehow detracts from the seriousness of the charge – for example, the historian Inga Clendinnen: 'When I see the word "genocide", I still see Gypsies and Jews being herded into trains, into pits, into

ravines ... I believe that to take the murder out of genocide is to render it vacuous.'

On these points, the United Nations Convention on the
Prevention and Punishment of the Crime of Genocide is
clear: the state as perpetrator is not a prerequisite, and
execution is but one of five possible means of committing
genocide. As the historian Dirk Moses has noted, 'genocide is not a synonym for the Holocaust'. It is instead
defined as:

> any of the following acts committed with intent to
> destroy, in whole or in part, a national, ethnical,
> racial or religious group, as such:
>
> (a) Killing members of the group;
> (b) Causing serious bodily or mental harm to
> members of the group;
> (c) Deliberately inflicting on the group conditions
> of life calculated to bring about its physical
> destruction in whole or in part;
> (d) Imposing measures intended to prevent births
> within the group;
> (e) Forcibly transferring children of the group to
> another group.

By these definitions, it seems reasonable to regard Angus
McMillan's Gippsland – where the Crown Commissioner
spent his weekends 'hunting blacks' and Aboriginal men,
women and children were shot indiscriminately 'wherever
they can be met with' – and the settlement of Australia
more broadly, as being flecked with what Moses calls
'genocidal moments'.

An alternative usage, more applicable to the Ramahyuck mission station and the assimilation processes from the 1860s onwards, is one best understood as 'cultural genocide' – that is, the systematic destruction of the language, practices and customs that make a group distinct. The burning of cultural artefacts and the banning of tribal languages and ceremonies would seem to put Ramahyuck squarely in this camp. But this too is a highly contested area. Many commentators in Australia have taken umbrage at the concept that the actions of white missionaries and administrators, often undertaken in good faith, in the honest belief that their work would save Aboriginal communities – or, at the very least, their children – should be equated with genocide.

Because it would be amiss not to touch upon the fact that Victoria's half-caste laws, and others like them, were created out of – well, not exactly *love*, but often at least partly out of concern and a sense of responsibility. It is also worth acknowledging that even within the Aboriginal community itself there are mixed feelings towards the missions and missionaries. Some have expressed the sentiment that the missions saved their people from ruin, whether from death, disease or the dysfunction that was beginning to take hold of their families and communities.

Complex emotions had already begun to arise amongst the Gunai in 1846, at the height of the white woman hunt, as is revealed by the letters of Sergeant William Walsh, of the state-funded expedition. Having 'accompanied' a group of Gunai men and women to the native police station in Narre Warren, he was surprised to find that they wished to remain there: 'I have asked the Blacks several times if they would like to go back to the Lake where their tribe is – but they say no – that they would get nothing to Eat, and have to go naked,' he wrote. 'The last time I asked them they began to cry.'

For my part, I am ambivalent about the academic back-and-forthing over the use of the term 'genocide'. The debate surrounding its precise applications does not particularly interest me, given that all those accused are long dead, and will never face justice. Suffice it to say that whether or not the exact definitions are matched, their basic requirements have been fulfilled; certainly the 'spirit' of genocide shines through descriptions of 1840s Gippsland and its wildest work.

Whatever the technical term, and whatever the motivation, one of the saddest aspects is that this was a tried and tested method. McMillan's rival 'Count' Paweł Strzelecki noted:

The decrease and final annihilation of the great majority of indigenous races which has followed, and always does follow, the approach of the whites, – is a fact of such historical notoriety, that the melancholy instance of the Australian natives affords but a further corroboration of the fearfully destructive influence which the one race exercises upon the other.

For centuries the world had been regarded as an enormous game of Risk, as whole continents were conquered and lost by players who sat far away, directing counters on a map. One hears much about those great empires that conquered, but almost nothing of the growing toll of cultures that died away as collateral in the course of their rise: the remnants of people's past, the marginalia of humanity.

Groups like the Beothuk of Newfoundland, the original 'red Indians' who painted their bodies with ochre in the summer, who – like the Gunai – had no interest in befriending the Europeans when they arrived in the sixteenth century; instead, they moved inland, away from the colonists and their own main source of food. Starving, ravaged by disease, and trapped in a cycle of violence with the tribes upon whose land they had encroached, they died one by one. The last known full-blooded Beothuk, Shanawdithit, died of tuberculosis in 1829.

Or the Jangil people of the Andaman Islands, who tried to avoid all contact with mainland Indians and the British colonists, but who still disappeared sometime between 1907 and 1920, probably as the result of an introduced disease to which they had no immunity. There is no remaining record of their language or customs.

The Sharpheads of Alberta, Canada, nomadic until the late nineteenth century, when they were confined to a Christian mission. Their numbers fell dramatically, thanks to measles and influenza, until the last remaining few were redistributed among neighbouring reserves, and the land retaken by the Canadian government.

The Khodynts of northern Siberia, exterminated by smallpox in 1693. The Sadlermiut of Hudson Bay, wiped out by disease contracted from a British trading vessel in 1903. The Hachaath of Vancouver Island, who vanished off the face of the earth at some point in between.

And all those Australian Aboriginal nations that bloomed and withered barely recorded, wholly misunderstood, sometimes never even seen by the European outsiders. They were unknown then. Now they are unknowable.

'I have protested against the evident wrong of allowing whole tribes to perish out of existence without the slightest record being kept of their physical and moral characteristics,' the Melbourne journalist David Blair wrote in 1868. 'It is disgraceful that we should allow the original possessors of our magnificent territory to perish before our very eyes, without preserving any record of them, beyond, perhaps, a row of grinning skulls in the national museum.'

The only part of the Ramahyuck mission that remains is the cemetery. It is a small, square patch of dry grass, grown long in comparison to the cropped fields alongside, outlined by a neat picket fence. A sign: 'We ask that you do not leave the path, as you may be walking over many unmarked graves.' Pictures from the Hagenauer era show it as a forest of wooden crosses and posts, marking the sites of the bodies, but over the years they have all crumbled away, leaving only a single standing headstone: that of Nathaniel Pepper, Hagenauer's first and most loyal convert.

Sacred to the memory
of NATHANIEL PEPPER
who fell asleep in Jesus
7th of March 1877
aged 36 years

Pepper was a Wotjoballuk man, a convert from Hagenauer's first mission on the Wimmera River who followed the minister to his new project, where he married a local woman of the missionary's choice. But though his faith was strong, he was a sickly man. He grew frail and succumbed to consumption, like so many others at Ramahyuck. Hagenauer apparently felt only triumph at his young protégé's death: 'I was standing before his happy death-bed, and saw him, safe in the arms of Jesus, passing away from us to join the host of the redeemed in glory.'

What with all these 'victories' of the sickroom and the cemetery, and the removal of the 'quite whites', by 1908 there were few enough residents left to merit the closure of the mission at Ramahyuck. Hagenauer died the next year. This single headstone, therefore, might be seen as the culmination of his life's work. As the Gippsland author Donald MacDonald had observed a few years previously: 'When we came here, the aborigines covered these wide plains in thousands. Where are they today? We have civilized them – they are dead.'

The few remaining residents were bundled off to another mission at Lake Tyers, founded by John Bulmer, an Anglican missionary who on his arrival at the Victorian goldfields had been so shocked by the drunken and degraded state of the Aborigines that he made their improvement his life's work.

The mission station at Lake Tyers was centred on a pretty white clapboard church, and overlooked a glorious stretch of white sand and turquoise water. Its residents came from a mix of tribal backgrounds, including the Tatungooloong Gunai plus a few stragglers from the Omeo, Bidwelli and Monaro groups, but largely consisted of the Krowathunkooloong clan, who had only begun to emerge from the wildest parts of the bush and gorges to the east of Gippsland during the 1850s. This tangle of tribal loyalties caused terrible problems over the following decades; Bulmer wrote of 'almost daily' physical clashes that kept the mission in a 'continual state of excitement'.

Lake Tyers residents, 1890s. Traditional bark canoes can be seen in the background.

Although Bulmer was more sympathetic to, even admiring of, Aboriginal culture than Hagenauer, he and his pick-and-mix residents nevertheless witnessed the continued dying away of the old ways in favour of a bastardised 'Christian' lifestyle. The abandonment of Gunai culture, far from prompting acclaim from the adjacent white community, instead provoked a strange, ambivalent reaction amounting to a further loss of respect – even disgust – for the now detribalised, decultured and demoralised inhabitants. Even Bulmer himself was not immune: 'I must say there is nothing more repulsive than a half-civilised aboriginal,' he wrote. 'One cannot help looking back to the time when wild in the woods the noble savage ran, for after all, with all his civilization he was a very much superior individual in times gone by than he is today.'

He particularly grieved the loss of the last of the *birrarks*, the 'poets, prophets and spiritual mentors of the people': 'alas all these men have passed away, there was something interesting about them. They have left behind a nondescript lot who are neither fish, flesh nor good red herring. Education has been introduced but where there has been no change of heart it has made the aboriginal not in the least interesting. He may be athletic, so were their fathers even more so.'

In private he began to question the value of his work, as it became increasingly obvious that the 'improvement' to his charges had in many ways had deleterious effects at least equal to, and perhaps outweighing, the positive.

It is a realisation that has been faced by many engaged in charity and missionary work, particularly in a colonial context. For beyond the immediate trauma of assimilationist policies – after the loss of property or family members has been grieved for – there is a slower, more ponderous cruelty that continues to work in its shadow for years, and even generations, to come. After the old ways have been lost and the ceremonies fallen out of use, what it means to be 'native' becomes diluted; those who have been assimilated and their descendants often find themselves afflicted by a profound angst as they struggle for identity in a cultural limbo where they are no longer a discrete minority, nor yet truly of the majority.

Many of these 're-educated' masses develop complex feelings of alienation and contempt for their own culture

– what might be described as a 'cultural cringe' – which may endure for the rest of their lives. Such negative feelings (seen amongst Australian Aboriginal groups, and countless others worldwide) often manifest themselves in high levels of alcoholism, addiction, abuse and all kinds of societal self-harm, and a continuing rejection of one's own heritage even once more liberal policies are introduced.

Certainly in Australia, the government would soon discover that the blunt instrument of assimilation – applied with such force so soon after the horrors of conflict – had deeply unbalanced the Aboriginal societies it attempted to help. Over the following decades, the true damage that had been wrought would become clear. Deep social problems arrived, and never departed; indeed, the question of the long-term effects of dispossession has never been more pressing than it is today.

Aboriginal life expectancy is still a decade lower than the Australian average, and the unemployment rate three times higher. Aboriginal Australians are fifteen times more likely than the rest of the population to be imprisoned, thirty times more likely to suffer from childhood malnutrition, eight times more likely to die of alcohol-related causes, ten times more likely to be taken into care as a child, and more than twice as likely to commit suicide. Aboriginal men aged between thirty-five and forty-four have a mortality rate more than four times higher than their non-Aboriginal counterparts; for Aboriginal women between twenty-five and thirty-nine, it is five times higher.

Although life is complicated, and although there are many factors in play, it still seems inescapably the case that these statistics – and the comparable plight of innumerable indigenous peoples worldwide – are the present-day outcomes of Angus McMillan, the Reverend Friedrich Hagenauer and their peers' actions, the effects of which continue to ripple out across the ages.

Even as the earnest John Bulmer agonised over the value of his life's work, other anxieties arose. Like many 'do-gooders' before and after him, the disconnect between his vision and his residents' aspirations began to prompt in him the suspicion that he was being taken advantage of.

He dwelt frequently on such worries in his correspondence. 'They try to rely solely on the Government,' he complained. 'To them she is a good cow and they will milk her. Yet they fancy themselves independent and are impatient of control.' They were lazy too, he observed. When assigned menial tasks 'they go to work as if they were going to their deaths so they can make themselves as useless as possible'. Many made a mockery of what was, for a missionary, his *raison d'être*: his beliefs. 'I once reminded [an Aboriginal man] that he must die, perhaps sooner than he expected,' he recalled. 'Oh, said he, then I will look to Christ quick.'

Because many efforts to 'help' were rebuffed by the recipients, or repurposed to unexpected ends, resentment grew among even the more sympathetic elements of the white community, and with it a growing sense that the blacks *deserved* their poor lot in life became an ever more persistent undertone in the local discourse. As Commissioner Tyers complained to Governor La Trobe:

Notwithstanding the opportunities they have had by their increased intercourse with the settlers, I

cannot say they have made any progress in
civilization. They still conform to their savage
habits and mode of life. Too idle to cultivate the
soil and to lay up provision for tomorrow they
hold to their wandering propensities when
employed by the White population and are satisfied
with the scanty food which their indolent life
allows them to obtain from Gum Trees, or from
the Rivers and Lakes.

If all this sounds somehow familiar, it is because it is the
same language with which all societies denigrate their
underclasses. It is the way the British characterise those
who rely on the charity of food banks or the safety net of
social welfare; the way right-wing America vilifies the
youth of failing black neighbourhoods. It is the way many
Australians still portray Aboriginal people today: as lazy,
feckless scroungers who live off the largesse of the state.
(In 2014, a sixty-thousand-year-old Aboriginal cave painting in Western Australia was defaced when vandals carved
the phrase 'Go and work for a living' into the rock.)

The irony is that, at home in Britain, the very same
stereotypes were being trotted out and directed at the
dregs of society there: the Scottish Highlanders. Consider
this remarkable missive, published in 1845 in the *Glasgow
Herald* on the subject of the starving crofters, but which
might equally have been applied by men of Gaelic heritage
to the Aboriginal Australian in the very same year:

The apathy which through poverty stricken
generations had become part of their character
rendered these [charitable] efforts unavailing. They

preferred their habitual mode of life – their few days of desultory labour intermingled with weeks of lounging gossip – their half-clad, half-fed condition – to regular well repaid toil.

Or this most scathing of leaders in the *Fifeshire Journal*, in 1847:

It is not more notorious that the sons of Ethiopia are black, than it is to all who know them, that Highlandmen will not work if they can get their meat by any other means ... The destitution of the Highlanders is the natural and legitimate fruit of their national vices. There is abundant proof that laziness is the darling sin which the Highlandman cherishes amidst all his imagined piety.

Yet while the Lowland commentariat waxed lyrical upon the insufficiencies of the Gaelic race, Angus McMillan and his companions – the brave pioneers, the Highland Brigade – were reprising precisely the behaviour that had so devastated the lives and livelihoods of their own countrymen, but this time casting themselves in the principal role. They turfed the Aborigines out of their homelands to make way for sheep; enacted new, ever more brutal clearances upon the new land even as they grieved for the tragedies of the old one. And as the Gunai faced hopelessness head on, so the Gaels turned critical eyes upon them, and saw that they deserved it.

If nothing else, those rampaging Scotsmen are proof that all peoples are capable of atrocity. That there are no 'strong races' or 'weak races', only strong positions and weak ones.

'Morally and intellectually the Highlanders are an inferior race,' the *Scotsman* thundered in 1846. It was their 'mild nature', their 'meek and patient spirit' that destined them to domination by the tougher southerners, observed others. But elsewhere, with one lucky break, oh how the tables had turned.

Blessed are the meek, for they shall inherit the earth. But who is to say that, when they do, they shall not rule just as cruelly?

Bung Yarnda – or as it's now known, Lake Tyers. We stood on the sand, watching pelicans wheel overhead before silently alighting in squads upon the gentle waves.

We were early. I had heard that it was hard to find – mislabelled on maps, six miles off the nearest main road – so I'd overcompensated, and now we had half an hour to kill, basking in the bright sunlight like snakes, before the boys and I picked our way up from the water's edge, along a low row of white clapboard chalets and past the wooden spire of the church. Sweet-scented air swilled up off the water and through the wide avenue, painting my lips with faint traces of salt.

After all these years, the old mission station is now a township of around 150 Aboriginal residents, who own the land and buildings by way of a trust and run it as an agricultural cooperative. It was peaceful, quaint, a waterside community with a set of government buildings at its heart bearing fresh coats of paint. Not, I thought, an unpleasant place to live.

Yet the serene surroundings belied a turbulent history. After the escalation of assimilation policies in the early twentieth century, Aboriginal reserves were increasingly closed, with working-age residents ejected into adjacent communities to fend for themselves, and remits reduced to cover only the old and infirm. By 1924, Lake Tyers was the only staffed reserve left in Victoria.

Facilities were allowed to degrade. A 1957 inquiry found that its 150 remaining residents lived crammed into around thirty 'huts', with no running water, bathrooms or means of refuse disposal. Medical attention was insufficient, the nearest doctor being located fifty-five miles away and only visiting the reserve once a month. Residents were not allowed to own cars, and all visitors had to be approved by the manager. It was, in short, 'squalid, isolated and without hope'.

Closure was floated, but the proposal met stiff resistance. Despite the terrible living conditions, for many residents it was the only home they had ever had. It had become the final refuge for many of Victoria's Aboriginal people. A campaign to save the mission was born a few years later, calling for the management to be handed over to its indigenous residents.

The campaign came in the midst of a flurry of pro-indigenous sentiment, which had taken shape after a shocking 1957 documentary, *Manslaughter*, revealed to a horrified white audience for the first time the true scale of the deprivation suffered by indigenous people. Set among an Aboriginal community in the Warburton Ranges of Western Australia, it showed breastfeeding mothers so malnourished that their milk dried up and their babies died; blind women searching on their hands and knees for grass seeds to eat; children with scurvy bleeding from their mouths. 'Read this and see if you're still proud to be an Australian,' commanded the Melbourne *Mercury* above a report of the film's contents. 'If you're not, do something about it.'

Many did. A popular Aboriginal rights movement took hold in the 1960s, echoing similar sentiments that were being voiced internationally: the civil rights movement in the US, where Martin Luther King had a dream in 1963, and the introduction of the Race Relations Act in the UK in 1965, which outlawed discrimination for the first time. State by state, Aboriginal residents won the right to vote, the final one being Queensland in 1965, and in 1967 a national referendum over the removal of two discriminatory references to Aboriginal people in the Australian constitution was held, and passed with more than 90 per cent of the vote. For the first time, Aboriginal residents were included in the Australian census.

In Gippsland, the Lake Tyers campaign formed a key element in the burgeoning Aboriginal rights movement. When, in July 1971, the governor of Victoria finally handed over the deeds to the reserve to ninety-one shareholders, consisting of current and past Lake Tyers residents, it was the first time in Australian history that unconditional freehold title had been awarded to Aborigines. 'I express my sincere wish that history will record that today was a turning point in Aboriginal affairs,' the governor told a jubilant audience of seven hundred.

It appeared to make for a happy ending to a horrid story. But unfortunately there has been no happily ever after.

In 2005 the Victorian government took control of the trust, and sacked the entire management board. An administrator from the consultancy Deloitte was appointed and given wide-ranging powers and financial control of the trust. The shareholders were up in arms: 'Our elders fought for the land so that Aboriginal people at Lake Tyers could live without government control of our lives,' resident Leanne Edwards said six years later, during a blockade of the reserve's entrance. 'We now are in 2011 and [we continue to be] dictated to by a government whose policies on us have once again failed.'

I read about this with a sinking heart. 'Taking charge' of an Aboriginal group's welfare had ominous overtones of the earliest protectors and do-gooders – Angus McMillan among them, in his latter years – whose misguided 'help' had caused so much harm.

I had made an appointment to visit the trust, to see for myself, and the boys had decided to accompany me. Steve too doubted the government's motives – more white-man meddling, he suspected. I was pleased to have the company. I'd been advised not to go there alone, although now that I walked through the bright little seaside village such warnings seemed outlandish, perhaps even racist.

An hour in the office of the executive officer Leonie Cameron was enough to shatter my optimism. 'When the administration began in 2005, the trust had lost its way,' she told us. 'Things had gotten truly desperate. Drug and alcohol abuse, domestic violence and child abuse were all rampant. There were no working toilets, or sinks that drained. Children weren't going to school. Health workers said they were too scared to come here any more.' Later I would meet a former employee of the trust who confirmed Leonie's account. Doctors and nurses were threatened, he said. Rocks were thrown at social workers' cars. The 'creepiest, crawliest' paedophiles were allowed to stay on, unchallenged.

Leonie sighed. 'One of the problems was that, as it was private land, owned by shareholders, well – governments don't really step in to privately owned businesses, unless they're invited to.' The state felt unable to do anything, until a group of female elders – 'four old aunties' – appeared in Melbourne seeking help. They said they were scared to live at Lake Tyers.

The complaint amounted to an invitation to the government to intervene, Leonie said. A ten-year 'community renewal partnership' was announced, essentially a takeover accompanied by an influx of state investment. Hence the fresh paint, the newly dug sewers, the flashy public buildings. Despite the protests, 'the best thing that could have happened was to go under administration', she said. And though the ten years were almost up, the community showed no signs of being able to take back the reins. No one wanted to lead and take difficult decisions, because of the threat of violence and the repercussions on their family.

For these reasons, Leonie said, the way forward was unclear. 'Though the place has changed a lot, it's largely in terms of infrastructure. People don't change their ways so readily. Here they've been in survival mode for so long, they've learned to survive by force.'

We stood to soberly shake hands, then wandered aimlessly back through the township, whose tranquillity now seemed sterile and unreal. Steve was quiet. His indignation had leached away over the course of an hour, leaving him deep in thought. The church where Bulmer preached God's word had been left open, and we browsed the aisle. It had a clean, Spartan air. Stained glass filled the back wall; faint chalk graffiti in the font. High to my left, in a heavy wooden frame, a prayer of healing:

We live in faith that all people
will rise from the depths of despair and
hopelessness.

*

The information boards at the Gippsland and East Gippsland Aboriginal Co-Operative in Bairnsdale were an education. There were adverts for pre-employment courses, breakfast clubs and playgroups; factsheets explaining the functions of the dedicated Koorie Justice Unit and Aboriginal Medical Service; details of phone lines for Aboriginal gambling addicts and victims of domestic abuse. A poster offered help to those of the stolen generations still searching for their families ('Free call 1800 OUR MOB'). A brochure promoted Dreamtime Coffins (bark-effect or dot-painted) for 'culturally appropriate send offs'. Above it a bumper sticker pasted to the frame read 'Family violence is not part of our culture'. Stacks of leaflets offered medical advice written in simplified English: 'Hep C is a disease that will make the liver sick.'

'Hello?'

I looked up. Peter Ryan, the chief executive, stepped out to greet me with a firm handshake. He was white, tall, with closely cropped grey hair and dressed casually in a blue cotton shirt. He had an honest manner, friendly but forthright. 'So, what do you want to know?'

'I'm writing about Angus McMillan and the "Black War",' I said. 'So I suppose I'm interested in the longer-term consequences of all that, the state of the Gunai people today.'

'Ah,' he said, airily, motioning me to follow him through the carpark towards the museum. 'They're in a pretty rough shape. They won't mind me saying that.' As if to demonstrate his point, a battered car was parked haphazardly nearby, its windows down as far as they would go. An Aboriginal man sprawled in the front seat, almost horizontal, snoring loudly.

I felt slightly crestfallen. From what I'd heard, the isolated Lake Tyers 'mob' and the rest of the Aboriginal community in Gippsland lived quite separate existences. I had hoped to find a brighter picture among the more 'integrated' population of the cities. We took our seats in a meeting room in which a dozen photo-portraits of prominent elders glared balefully down at us. An office chair in the corner wore a possum-skin cloak, which my fingers yearned to stroke.

Peter spoke of a fractured community, one not short of people keen to improve the situation, but hampered by intergenerational rivalries, poor health and a lack of education. 'It's a hard job, this. It has so many heartbreaking aspects.' He interviewed everyone who came to work there, he said, to check that they were tough enough to handle it. Many who want to work in Aboriginal affairs do so because they think it will be rewarding. They think they will be thanked for their efforts. But it's not always so straightforward. Prejudice goes both ways; many of those they work with are suspicious of their methods and motivation.

A few weeks earlier, Peter had made a controversial decision to sack a prominent member of staff after a nasty scene outside working hours. I'd heard about it on the grapevine: drunk, disorderly, police in attendance, allegations of domestic violence. 'Some people said, "You know, it's different here. It's a cultural issue." But we can't ...'

He sighed. 'It put me in a difficult position. I'll always be the white chief executive who sacked a black officer.'

Locally, there is still a deep divide between the white and black communities. Bairnsdale has an Aboriginal population of around 4 per cent of the total, slightly higher than the national average. Generally they are young, with a median age of only nineteen compared to forty-three in the non-indigenous population, and poor, with a weekly income just two-thirds the white average. Relations with the police are shaky: in 2011, booze-fuelled violence prompted officers to order a blanket ban on selling alcohol to Aboriginal residents, raising the spectre of the notorious race-based 'interventions' of the Northern Territory. GEGAC filed a complaint to the Australian Human Rights Commission; police chiefs later blamed the controversy on a 'miscommunication'.

In many ways, the rift in Bairnsdale reflects the situation nationally. Racism is endemic in Australia; indeed, it is written into the country's DNA. Not only was the nation formed as a settler colony – white pitched against black in a desperate battle of attrition – but immigration legislation written at the time of Federation in 1901 was explicitly aimed at maintaining an overwhelming proportion of whites to ethnic minorities (the 'White Australia' policy, which made immigration from Asia or the Pacific Islands extremely difficult). Such policies were dismantled during the 1960s and 70s, but the underlying attitudes are still remarkably widespread; not only anti-immigrant, but anti-Aboriginal too.

In 2013 the *Sydney Morning Herald* posed the question 'Are you a casual racist?' to its readers. Of more than 11,000 respondents, 64 per cent admitted that the answer was yes. Of those, the majority answered bluntly: 'Yes, but I'm not going to change.'

To those on the receiving end, this amounts to an extraordinarily high incidence of race-related incidents. A 2012 survey of Aboriginal people in Victoria found that 97 per cent of respondents had been targets of verbal or physical abuse, or discrimination, over the previous year. Eighty-four per cent said they had been verbally abused, 67 per cent had been spat at or had objects thrown at them, 66 per cent told that they 'did not belong' in their home towns. Seventy per cent had suffered eight or more such attacks over that period.

But it's one thing to know that there's a problem. Another thing entirely to know how to solve it.

10

Reconciliation

Driving down from the Monaro south towards the coast we had travelled for a while through the ancient temperate rainforest of Errinundra, where stands of sassafras and black olive berry crowded together, overlooked by shining gums whose great, buttressed girths jutted from the canopy like the calves of giants. We stopped to walk amongst them, dwarfed in both scale and age, diminished by all that they had been alive to witness.

It was here that Steve showed me the smoking ceremony. It is an ancient custom, in which the perfumed smoke from native plants is used to cleanse an area, to ward off bad spirits. Traditionally the ceremonies mark major events, such as a significant death. In recent years they have been used to mark new public ventures. The Boon Wurrung and Woi Wurrung people were asked to perform such a ceremony at the site of the Melbourne Museum before it was built, so as to heal a troubled land. This was described as 'a historic step in recognising the desecration of spiritual, practical and cultural bonds with the land that occurred during invasion'.

Steve cut a section of bark about the size of an A4 sheet of paper from a gum tree, using his axe blade in a smooth movement to peel away the dry outer layers, leaving a perfect rectangle of pale new flesh on the trunk. I reached up to touch it, felt it soft and naked and slightly damp beneath my hand. This sheet became a tray, into which he shaved curls of wood in a small pile for tinder, then piled a few tiny sticks from the forest floor on top. It caught light easily enough, sending a thin line of smoke up through the branches above our heads. Immediately he smothered the flame, dropping a handful of the samphire-like leaves of the cherry ballart, a type of sandalwood, on it. They began to smoulder and steam, turning the elegant cigarillo whorl into a medicinal cloud. I shut my eyes. Breathed in. Solemnly he brought the bark sheet up to my chest, allowing the smoke to drift across my face on the lethargic breeze.

I imagined myself cleansed, loosing my layers of insincerity to let the smoke in underneath, exposing the least attractive parts of me to the air so they might be disinfected. I recalled a Gunai song that Alfred Howitt had recorded, a charm for driving away pain and bad magic. It was brought to the elder Tulaba by his late father in a dream, a 'curious tune' sung with extraordinary energy, the final syllable exploding from his mouth like the shot of a cannon:

Minyan – būlūn – ma naranke
Show – belly – moon to

'Show your belly to the moon.' This had struck a chord with me; perhaps it was a command that had been meant literally, but I heard it as a directive that one must display one's softest, most vulnerable parts, like a cat rolling over to show its tummy, ecstatic and terrified all at once, in order to be healed.

Steve demonstrates the smoking ceremony in the shade of a shining gum.

I felt a flush of envy, too – of those whose dreams were full of messages from the land beyond the clouds, from their dead elders. Healing charms, great truths. All my dreams seemed to consist of was adrenaline and recycled scraps from the wastepaper basket in my mind. All these gory re-enactments, the switching of perspectives. They were haunting me now, recurring, sometimes overlapping, sometimes overlaid upon other, more mundane reveries. These were no semaphores from the afterlife, I knew. Only the byproduct of my growing, waking preoccupation.

Still, I thought, now I knew how it felt to kill a man, or be killed by one. Maybe that was message enough.

'That should do it,' said Steve finally. 'Have to be careful. There might be a fire ban on. We can't let it actually catch light.'

Reluctantly we headed back towards the low country. But on the way we were struck by an idea: a ceremony of cleansing at the site of the worst massacre. To clear the air, clear the earth. A gesture of forgiveness, of reconciliation, that would mark the past with a full stop, ready for a new sentence to begin. We would organise it, invite all the elders, have speeches, make a day of it.

I called Libby to organise a return trip to the Warrigal Creek homestead, and we drove down with our proposal at the ready. I assumed that she would be excited, but to my surprise she seemed reluctant. Similar ventures had been floated before, she said. But not everyone in the community was ready to forgive. We needed to wait until everyone was united, or we would risk offending afresh.

When I introduced her to Steve, she said to him, 'Did you know your Pop has been out here?' She meant his grandfather, Uncle Albert.

'Oh? No.'

'Well, we've been batting ideas back and forth a long time. I really don't want to derail anything by rushing in. Things have to be done when the elders decide they are ready, I think.'

We were all disappointed, but we understood what she was saying. I felt young and rash, as if we were three cubs being gently batted away. You couldn't just smoke the pain away, I supposed. These things take time. The ceremony would one day be a symbol of the healing that has taken place, rather than itself the source of healing.

'Hey,' said Steve suddenly, rising from the table and wandering through to the next room to stare up at a framed print on the wall. 'I designed that!' It was the logo he'd drawn for the Gunaikurnai land rights movement spearheaded by his grandfather.

Libby followed him through, and took an ornate carved boomerang out of a cupboard. 'Recognise this?'

He smiled at it, then at her. 'Pop's work?' He turned it over, found the signature on the back. She smiled in return.

They hit it off. Libby was a charming hostess, interested in what we all had to say, deferring to Steve's knowledge of local Aboriginal politics. And both Steve and Cam were just as seduced by the beauty of the homestead as I had been. They cooed over the pressed tin ceiling, the hand-painted tiles, the rippling glass in the original Victorian windowpanes.

After tea, the boys and I walked out to the massacre site, and I watched Steve and Cam do the same mental restaging I had done, eyes flitting between strategic points, gauging the steepness of the banks.

'They're at the bottom of the waterhole. I can feel it.' Steve was certain. He stood on the bank, peering through the thick undergrowth into the pool beyond. Three pelicans paddled in leisurely circles, scooping their beaks through the water almost as an afterthought, Austen-era women trailing their hands from rowing boats.

'Saying that,' he continued, 'it doesn't feel so terrible, you know. I wasn't sure that I'd be able to come. Many people wouldn't. But it doesn't feel like there's anything malevolent still lurking here.'

Libby was waiting for us when we got back to the house, ready to take us out in the ute to some other spots named in Peter Gardner's book. First Gammon Creek, the site of one of the possible follow-up massacres, in the bend of another river marking the edge of an enormous field. We clambered out to stand on the bank in the fading light, the skyscape stretching before us painted in incredible colours, dip-dyed along its length the same blazing orange of the sun as, above, raspberry faded to lilac, streaked through with ripples of indigo cloud.

An agricultural track took us back to the coast behind the dunes to Freshwater Creek, another alleged site, and past Red Hill, a sandy hummock where the massacred bodies were said to have been carted down in their drayloads, burned, then crudely buried. Somewhere around here, a local schoolteacher and his friend stumbled over a cache of human remains in 1912. 'With our hands we scraped away the sand,' he wrote, 'and an inch or two below the surface discovered a quantity of human bones and skulls of men, women and children, even to very young children, all intermixed.'

But the bleakness I'd felt last time I'd come to this stretch of beach had washed away with the tide. In the gloaming, everything was beautiful. The waves sighed as they caressed the sand, keeping time, taking the pulse of the land.

We stood for a while in the cool salt air, not speaking much, then drove slowly back along the track to the house. Grey kangaroos, dozens of them, sprang out of the scrub away from the car and leapt ahead of us in the headlights. They were unsettlingly human: similar size, similar in expression. We found ourselves among them, travelling at the same speed, as if we were one of a crowd, all of us on our way to the same place.

I wanted to meet Uncle Albert Mullett for myself. I'd heard so much about him. He was a man with many strings to his bow: activist, cultural authority, government adviser, master craftsman, respected Gunai elder. Everyone I had spoken to so far had, at some point in our conversation, asked if I'd met him. 'You must,' they told me. 'He has such a wealth of knowledge.'

Still, Steve was reluctant to take me to see him. Uncle Albert was an old man now. He'd been unwell, I was given to understand. A heart attack several years previously had had a serious impact on his health, and these days he rarely left the house. Aunty Rachel, his wife and Steve's grandmother, had been acting the bouncer since he had taken ill, turning away the many who, like me, wanted an audience with the man himself.

But just as I'd given up hope, Steve relented and we stopped off at the pretty bungalow in Buchan where his grandparents were living out their retirement, clutching a box of cream cakes as an offering.

Aunty Rachel answered the door with a guarded expression. She was a slim, tan-skinned woman of around eighty, with long silver hair swept into a ponytail. 'I didn't know you were coming,' she chided Steve. He looked uncomfortable, and muttered something that sounded like an apology. She nodded at Cam, eyed me, then relented. 'All right,' she said, reluctantly accepting the box. 'But not long.'

Albert was born in 1933, as government attempts to force Aboriginal people to assimilate were intensifying, and lived much of his early life on the fringes of white society. His mother lived a transient lifestyle, moving between relationships, so he grew up under the care of his aunt and grandparents. The family were ejected from the Lake Tyers mission station when Albert was an infant, so they lived for a period on an island on the lake, making clandestine visits to friends who remained there, before moving on to temporary sites on riverbanks, near rubbish dumps, and at Jackson's Track, an unofficial camp that had sprung up by the sawmill at Drouin.

Albert left home at thirteen for a succession of seasonal jobs, later marrying his childhood sweetheart Rachel, a girl of Gunai-Ngarico descent, and settling in Bairnsdale, where they brought up their eight children. He became a well-known and very effective firebrand and activist, fighting for the recognition of Aboriginal rights and the preservation of Gunai culture. Among other things, he helped establish the 'keeping place' museum and archive I'd visited in Bairnsdale, and campaigned for fifteen years to have his people's right to the ownership of their traditional lands recognised. In 2013 he was inducted to the Indigenous Honour Roll of Victoria.

We found him propped up at the kitchen table watching television. I was taken aback by how much he'd aged since the last picture I'd seen of him, dated only a year or two previously. But his eyes were bright, and he was neatly dressed. A single bed had been pushed into the corner of the room, and adorned with cushions like a sofa.

At first I wasn't sure that he had noticed I was there. I smiled, as his eyes flickered away from the game show on the television to greet Steve and Cam and then returned to the screen. The volume was very loud. After a minute,

Aunty Rachel stepped forward and switched the set off. In the silence, Steve introduced me, and explained what we'd been doing. We'd been on a road trip, he said, of historical sites. I was a relative of Angus McMillan, visiting Australia to find out about his legacy.

Interest flickered in Uncle Albert's eyes, and he turned to look at me properly. 'McMillan?' he said. I nodded. He said something indistinct.

Aunty Rachel spoke from behind him. 'He said: "He was a butcher."'

'Oh!' I said, a bit taken aback. Then I turned back to him. 'Yes. He was, yes.'

He nodded once in approval. He might have been a frail man, but the anger was still raw. The inequalities devised by Angus McMillan's generation had still been very much in evidence during Uncle Albert's lifetime. Until the 1960s, he said, Aboriginal people had counted only as 'animals, vegetables or minerals' in Australian society. Haltingly, he recalled episodes from his earlier years when he and his family suffered from discrimination.

When he was a baby, two of his six brothers had been forcibly taken by the authorities and placed into care. He never saw them again. At school, white children had taunted them, told them they smelled – but, he added, raising his fists and weakly paddling the air, 'I gave them an education, all right.'

His speech was faltering, occasionally inaudible, and Rachel would interject to make his meaning clear. I craned to hear him, nodding to show that I had understood. Later, I watched an interview with him from some years previously, when he had been able to speak more clearly. In shops, he said, Aboriginal people wouldn't be served until last. In cinemas, attendants would force them to sit at the front. 'They ran us down like shit. Treated us like we weren't even human beings.'

He and Aunty Rachel had lived hand to mouth for many years, working every waking hour: in the sawmills, in the hayfields, bean-picking, at truckstops, in restaurants, at a hostel for Koorie children. And in the few scraps of free time they had, they campaigned for the rights of their people. When Gunai native title was recognised, Uncle Albert had fulfilled a lifetime's ambition.

I felt childlike and humbled, for the second time in only a few days. To me, and to Steve too, in many ways, reconciliation was simply a concept for discussion. But to Uncle Albert it had been his life's work. I wanted to beg for his forgiveness, on behalf of my relative, but what did he care for my second-hand guilt? All his life he had looked for solutions and action, not handwringing.

I knew that for me, struggling with a sense of shame that was not truly mine, action was only a small part of what I was searching for. But what use was that to anyone? Libby and I, I thought, and all those other uneasy descendants, were looking for an exoneration that will never come.

A few months after we met, Uncle Albert Mullett passed away, aged eighty-one. More than two thousand mourners gathered to pay their respects at his funeral, accompanied by a farewell smoking ceremony and the sound of the bullroarer, at the Knob Reserve near Stratford. I feel privileged to have met him.

*

So what can be done? If the past cannot be undone, and the wrongs never truly forgiven, what can be made right?

In recent decades there has been a rush of initiatives aimed at preserving and promoting Aboriginal culture, and raising awareness of the events of the past. Funding for Koorie art and oral-history projects has come in a flood, while the Australian government and academics have made ever greater efforts to ensure that Aboriginal viewpoints and experiences are represented. Strict laws have been enacted to protect and conserve archaeological sites, rather than simply allowing construction companies to build over them, by which so many have already been destroyed.

In 2008, Prime Minister Kevin Rudd made a national apology to Aboriginal Australians for the stolen generations. In his speech, Rudd repeated the phrase 'I am sorry' three times – on behalf of himself, the government and the parliament. The Melbourne *Age* reported that after he did so, 'there was, quite audibly, the exhalation of breath. That same release – the hope of an expulsion, really, of a national burden – could be felt across the country.'

Aboriginal ownership of the land has become far more explicitly accepted and proclaimed. Signs in public spaces now specify the land's traditional owners: in Gippsland, they pay tribute to the Gunaikurnai. Such tributes can also be found in the prologue to the text of many state and other official documents, while at public meetings or events a local elder often gives a short speech or performs a ceremony to open proceedings.

I stumbled upon this convention at an event at a local theatre near Drouin. At the start, without explanation, an Aboriginal woman took to the stage to give thanks to her ancestors and beseech them to welcome this roomful of white, middle-class retirees to the auditorium. I was bemused; even more so when Jeannie waved the woman over to a seat by us, only to be politely rebuffed. 'Sorry – can't!' she responded in a stage whisper. 'Got two more of these to give tonight!' To my eye it appeared tokenistic, but Aboriginal people I later spoke to disagreed. Finally, they said, their existence, their historic claim to the ownership of the lands was being acknowledged. Whatever form that took, it was an important step.

The Aboriginal claim to the land was acknowledged in a more concrete way through the advent of native-title legislation, an avenue of law that has sprung up since the landmark Mabo ruling in 1992, which struck down the colonial doctrine of *terra nullius*, thus undermining the entire basis of the Crown's claim to the Australian continent. Since then, Aboriginal groups that have been able to demonstrate an unbroken connection to their homelands since colonisation can lodge a claim with the federal court to have their status as traditional landowners recognised.

Uncle Albert Mullett spearheaded the native-title claim in Gippsland on behalf of the united 'Gunaikurnai' people, with the assistance of, among others, a younger Gunai man called Barry Kenny. They succeeded in 2010, becoming recognised as the traditional owners of almost 8,500 square miles of Gippsland, nearly a fifth of all the state of Victoria's Crown land. They were also awarded a $12 million settlement and joint control of ten national parks and reserves in the area, including the Knob Reserve and the temperate rainforest of Terra Bulga.

The land secured in this settlement is now managed via a statutory body called the Gippsland Land and Waters Aboriginal Corporation (GLaWAC), headed up by Barry

Kenny and based in Bairnsdale. I finally found its offices, in an unprepossessing glass-fronted building on MacLeod Street, an industrial thoroughfare full of paint and hardware stores. A crowd of Aboriginal men in matching shirts hung around the back of the building, loading tools into shiny four-wheel drives – the cultural rangers now employed to work alongside their government counterparts in the parks. Inside it was clean and corporate, maps of the area successfully claimed blown up huge on the walls. Stacks of newsletters were full of instructions for how those of Gunaikurnai origin could make the most of their new rights, by applying for free fishing permits and so on.

Barry sat down with me in a boardroom to talk me through the corporation's function. He saw GLaWAC not only as symbolic recognition of his people's history, but as a major opportunity to bring employment and income to a community that badly needs both. As native-title holder, the corporation has the power to oversee the exploitation of natural resources in the area; negotiations with mining companies, such as an iron-extraction group, have resulted in 'significant' income for a foundation that is used to pay for scholarships, educational equipment and funeral costs for community members.

It is relatively rare for such a body to be run by a member of the group it represents, Barry said. 'It's a difficult job. Everyone has a different opinion on every decision we have to make, and that can be hard when you know everyone socially.' This development in his career had taken him somewhat by surprise – as a young man he had, like many Gunai men, found employment as a labourer, picking beans and later working in sawmills.

Uncle Albert had recruited him to the cause and acted as a mentor during the native-title process, and now he found himself unexpectedly at its head.

Around 650 of the three-thousand-strong Gunai population had opted to join the organisation so far. To do so they had to fill in a form that detailed their family tree back three generations, specified the clan they belonged to, and which of the 'apical ancestors' they descended from – a list of twenty-five individuals or couples who appear in every *bona fide* Gunai family's lineage. Anyone who can't trace their ancestry back to one of these individuals is not recognised as Gunai and may not join, even if their family has lived in the region for generations, as might be the case with families imported to the Gippsland missions from elsewhere in Australia.

'Who is your apical ancestor?'

'Well my father was Krowathunkooloong, and we descend from ...' He ran his finger down a tick-list. I read it over his shoulder, a collage of traditional and Christian monikers: Tommy Bumberrah. Bungil Narran. Old Darby Tar-loomba. Mary Tur-un-gook. King Tom Kee-lum-bedin. James Scott. William McDougall. Jimmy. '... This man, George Thomas. He was one of two survivors of a massacre in the Lake Tyers area. He and another boy hid under a log. After they were found they were brought up on the Lake Tyers mission.'

I swallowed. Putting names to the victims of the massacres was a new development, and an uncomfortable one. It was in a different register from what I'd felt reading my history books, where the dead were rarely definitively identified and their numbers were debated, lending their accounts an airy, hypothetical aspect. In this way it had been possible for me to amass a vast amount of information, facts, figures, details, while still keeping a sort of intellectual distance from a lot of it. The questions I'd found myself considering! Like: How many deaths does it take to count as a massacre? (Six or more, apparently.) Or: Would it be better or worse to die in your sleep? (Better, probably.) But now I felt like a pathologist who, on rolling over a body, recognises its features as those of a friend.

I asked Barry whether, given his family story, he had any hesitation in dealing with the government and the wider white population, or in working at the coalface of the reconciliation process.

He pulled a conflicted face. 'Well,' he said, thinking aloud. 'A lot of our mob wouldn't do this job. They don't like white people, call 'em *gubbahs*. Just say, "They took our land," or "They killed our people," and keep themselves very separate. But I don't think that attitude helps. We got a bit of distance now. It wasn't you, and it wasn't me. Plus, you know, a lot of people don't know what really happened, with the massacres and the missions and everything. So we run cultural awareness courses for companies and government departments where we lay it all out.' A few years previously, he said, he had been helping to run one of these courses when one attendee, a girl from a prominent local farming family, had stood up partway through and simply walked out. Barry had followed her, irritated, only to find her in tears outside the front of the building.

'I'm so embarrassed. My family did that,' she told him, sobbing. 'It's too awful.'

He told her she didn't know that, not for sure, but she shook her head. 'Yes,' she said. 'I do.'

Seeing the tears streaming from her eyes, her trembling lips, her blotchy face, Barry had felt only compassion. 'Well,' he told her, 'you can't take it back.'

'It's quite something to meet a descendant.' Ricky Mullett, a cultural officer from GLaWAC, had come to meet me on his lunchbreak.

I shook the proffered hand, laughed to cover up my sudden rush of awkwardness. 'Great-great-great niece, actually. Not a direct descendant.'

There was a short pause while he seemed to be deciding whether or not to laugh. Then he led me across to a café, where he bought me lunch in a courtyard under trailing vines.

'I should really be buying you lunch,' I said, 'for taking time to meet me.'

His gaze crossed mine like a sword. 'You're a guest in my country. We, the Gunai people, are your hosts.'

'Thank you,' I said. 'But it's a strange situation.'

He inclined his head. 'Yes. Well. I don't really like to talk about any of this any more. I've had enough of it. But you did keep calling, and ... I believe in what you're doing. I think it's important.'

'Thank you,' I said again.

'This trip must have been confronting for you.'

Confronting: an adjective, not a verb. A word Australians use when discussing anything that deals with unsettling – often race-related – issues head-on. Modern art, human-rights reports, documentaries investigating Aboriginal health, that sort of thing. Issues that are easier to brush under the rug. It has a directness to it that I like.

'Confronting ... Yes, it's been that, I suppose.'

Too flippant. He looked at me a little oddly. 'You know what happened? That your ancestor and his men slaughtered my people? I say "slaughtered" on purpose, because that's what they did.'

I nodded mutely.

'You know the stories? You know that the official death toll is only a fraction of the true total? It was inhuman, what they did to my people. Killed them. Massacred them. Tortured them. Raped them. Murdered them. Your relative ... he decimated my people. And he got away with it.'

His eyes were shining. I felt him watching me for a response, but I didn't have one. I just nodded to show that I understood, agreed, didn't intend to argue the point. Sunlight streamed cleanly between the vine leaves, dappling his face and the table. A waitress stopped by to deliver him his milkshake, bringing a touch of the banal to the intense negotiations we seemed to be thrashing out.

'Now,' he continued, relenting, 'I don't hold any personal grudge against you or your family.'

'Why not?'

'Why?'

I blew out my cheeks. 'Don't we owe you something?'

'Owe what? Who's "we"?'

'I don't know, and I don't know. Me? The Australian descendants? More land? Private land? Land that's still in the hands of the old squatting families? Rule their original claims invalid?'

He shook his head, shutting his eyes as he did so. I already knew why. Native-title legislation was divisive enough when only Crown land was handed over, and in limited form. The process was still misunderstood by many landowners, who hung back from reporting archaeological finds for fear that their land might be taken away as a result. Striking down property deeds would cause outrage that could undo all the good work done in recent years to repair relations.

'Then what more can be done? How can it be fixed?'

There didn't seem to be an answer.

I kept on. 'How about efforts to reconcile within the community? I heard that there are groups that ...'

'"Reconciliation,"' he scoffed. 'It's just a political watchword. "Reconciliation" is a myth. The only reconciliation I believe in happens one on one. That's what we're doing now.' He gestured to the table, hands opening gracefully, conductor to orchestra.

'Which is?'

'Speaking to each other on a level. One on one. And this – me and you, sitting together at a table – this is very symbolic. Isn't it?'

I said I guessed it was. I didn't feel like a representative of my culture, meeting a representative of his in a great gesture of regret and forgiveness. I didn't feel qualified for that. I just felt like one of two people eating lunch together in a deli in Bairnsdale, on our second round of drinks. But maybe that was the point.

We sat talking in the courtyard for three hours. We discussed what I'd learned, the experiences he'd had, the problems that seemed so intractable, the past that seemed so irreversible. We got on. When Ricky asked me to name all the places I'd visited during my research, he seemed almost disappointed that he couldn't now show them to me himself. But there were a few lesser-known spots, he said, that I should visit.

On the way out, we stopped to pay the bill. Ricky knew the waitress well, and paused to introduce me. 'This is Cal Flyn,' he announced. 'Her great-great-great uncle, her *apical ancestor*, was Angus McMillan.'

'Ah yeah?' She smiled at me encouragingly.

'Her relative was responsible for the deaths of hundreds of my people, the Gunaikurnai people. She's come here all the way across the world, at great cost and personal discomfort. And emotional discomfort.'

The waitress nodded, smile fixed in place, not sure what the correct response was.

'Tomorrow we're going to go on a tour of massacre sites together.'

There was a pause. I wanted to make a joke to take the pressure off, but I managed to contain myself. Flippant, I rebuked myself. Don't be flippant.

'Well,' she said finally. 'You enjoy that. Bye now, Ricky. Bye, Carole.'

That night I thought about inherited guilt, about debts that transcend generations and cannot be repaid.

They have a word for it in Germany: *Erbschuld*. It is a particularly salient concept there, where the postwar generations have been forced to confront uncomfortable truths about their parents' or grandparents' role within the Nazi regime. The discomfort manifests itself in different ways; in the more extreme cases, such as of the offspring of former SS guards, there are children who have cut themselves off completely from their parents to make a 'fresh start' – for his 1987 book *Born Guilty: Children of Nazi Families*, Peter Sichrovsky interviewed a couple who had refused to invite their own parents to their wedding. Others choose to reimagine the past in more palatable form. As Dirk Moses has written, 'The imperative to insulate the family unit from the Nazi contamination is so strong [that] grandchildren imagine their grandparents as resisters or anti-Nazis despite evidence to the contrary.'

It is a theme dealt with in Bernhard Schlink's novel *The Reader*, which centres upon a young man who discovers that his former lover, an enigmatic older woman, is guilty of appalling war crimes. As well as an examination of an obsessive, cross-generational romance, the book serves as a parable for the postwar generation who, despite their youthful innocence, found themselves tarnished by association with their parents' generation. As Michael, the protagonist, reflects: 'The pain I went through because of my love for Hanna was, in a way, the fate of my generation, a German fate.'

Erbschuld is an abstract concept, but it is not a novel one, not for anyone who has had even the most cursory of Sunday school educations. It is also the term for the Christian concept of 'original sin', of the eating of the forbidden fruit by Adam and Eve, and the corruption of all subsequent generations.

Wherefore, as by one man sin entered into the world, and death by sin; and so death passed upon all men, for that all have sinned (Romans XV:12)

296

The Pentecostal Church's version is more elaborate, holding that sin is passed through blood down the generations. This belief is based on passages in scripture that refer to 'punishing the children for the sin of the parents to the third and fourth generation'. The principle is used to account for the apparent transmission of problems like alcoholism, depression or cancer between members of a family. To break these 'generational curses', believers are encouraged to create lists of all the sins of their ancestors for up to four generations, so they can confess to them on their relatives' behalf, and thus break free.

The state of North Korea takes a similarly literal approach to the idea of familial guilt, arresting the relatives of criminals and punishing them together or in the offender's place. One former prisoner, interviewed in 2011 after she had fled the country, told Reuters she had been detained at the age of thirteen, after her grandfather escaped to South Korea, and spent the next three decades in a notorious labour camp, where hangings and firing squads were commonplace.

These examples are extreme ones, of course, and few people subscribe to them. But the truth is that the notion of inherited guilt has no small amount of traction. What are national apologies, for instance, but admissions of a collective – if not inherited, precisely – guilt that continues generations later to stew? If this concept did not make a certain intuitive sense, their value would be very slight. Yet in 2008, as Kevin Rudd stood in the House of Representatives to make his apology to the Aboriginal people, many reported experiencing a profound sense of relief, of a 'weight' dropping away, or the dawning of a new sense of closure. My own trip to Australia, grounded in similar reasoning, seemed to appeal to my interviewees' senses of circularity.

The Gunai believe that the offences of an individual can bring a curse upon his relations, Ricky told me. Breaking the laws of the community – he gave the example of disobeying one's elders – is thought to bring bad fortune upon the family, over many years and in unpredictable ways.

'So,' I hazarded, 'although you say that you don't hate me, or the descendants of Angus McMillan, you do to some extent believe that we have been punished? That the entire family has been or will be forced to pay for his sins?'

He pursed his lips, nodded. 'Don't you think so? Has your family been afflicted with bad luck?'

I thought about it. 'Not really. Not my close family, anyway. Touch wood.'

'You're superstitious.'

I laughed. 'No, not really. Are you?'

'Yes.' He didn't elaborate.

'I've always thought that if you don't believe in it, it can't affect you. Sort of like the opposite of the placebo effect.'

I could tell he didn't agree with me, but he didn't argue the point. I was telling the truth, though: I'm not superstitious. I studied statistics for three years as part of my degree, and had drilled into me the folly of attaching significance to coincidence, of assuming causality where there is only correlation. Plus, I've been very fortunate in life, despite my lack of credence.

Angus McMillan's immediate family was not so lucky, I would later discover. His wife and children would be visited by tragedy again and again, decades after he had passed away.

After his death, Christina had a terrible time raising the children on no income – the pension promised to her by the government was never paid – and eventually became afflicted by a 'painful melancholia' that unhinged her mind. She was fixated by the idea of throwing herself into the river, twice attempting it, but finding, as she expressed it, that 'a hand seemed to draw her back'. Finally she disappeared, and her body was found face-down in the water.

The elder son, Ewen, grew up to become a capable bushman, but in 1926 he was 'burnt beyond recognition' while clearing a gorge of brambles. He survived despite 'being burned internally' and his limbs 'burnt to the bone', but died five years later, leaving only his younger brother Angus, who according to his obituary 'did not inherit the resource or enterprise of his father'. He 'lacked initiative', it continued, and had been 'mutually dominated by his brother'. After Ewen's death he turned to gold-prospecting, which he 'pursued without success for the remainder of his life', dying in 1936 after a long illness.

I didn't know any of that then. Still, I would have said, that doesn't prove anything.

Box's Creek is a small, sheltered inlet that cuts into the hillside behind a limestone bluff on the edge of Lake King. It is deep, picturesque, shielded from even the wildest of the winds that roar in off Bass Strait, and so it has become a firm favourite among the yachties who frequent the upmarket seaside village of Metung.

The owners of the cabins, whose roofs nudge up through the tea trees, live there for only a few weeks per year. When in residence they sit out on their verandahs of an evening to watch their neighbours pottering on the private jetty below, or turn instead to look out along the sweep of Bancroft Bay. It's a beautiful spot. Although it is debatable, perhaps, whether it would be quite so popular as a holiday destination had it retained its original name, Butcher's Creek.

'Can you see it?'

I aligned my gaze with Ricky's outstretched finger. 'Yes, I think so.'

'McMillan's men chased them all the way from Bushy Park, trapped them up on that bluff, and shot them down into the water. Crowds of them.'

Before European settlement, Gunai legend held that the creek was haunted by malevolent spirits, dead men who refused to stay dead. I suppose in Angus McMillan's time they must have believed it haunted too by the dozens of men shot down and killed there. Perhaps they were the same spirits, wandering, anchorless, through time.

'Are you all right with this?' Ricky studied my face, looking for shock or squeamishness. But I was only grim now, my teeth gritted, exhausted by the scale of it all. The endlessness of the horror that kept emerging from under every stone. I felt as if I'd been awake for a hundred years, my brain slowly turning over each thought one by one.

I recalled the words written by Henry Meyrick:

I remember the time when my blood would have run cold at the mention of these things but now I am become so familiarized with scenes of horror, from having murder made a topic of everyday conversation. I have heard tales told and some things I have seen that would form as dark a page as ever you read in the book of history.

Perhaps five hundred yards further along, just off the main road, was Legend Rock, an enormous rust-coloured meteorite that pokes from the shallows by the boardwalk. Gunai mythology holds that it was one of three fishermen who had eaten all their catch without sharing it with their dogs; for their greed, the womenfolk had turned them to stone. Two other rocks that completed the trio had sat nearby, but construction workers destroyed both in the 1960s to make way for the road we were driving on.

Directly between the two sites, two perfect case studies in the destruction of Aboriginal culture, was a luxury holiday resort. Its name: McMillan's of Metung. Of course it was. 'Relatives of yours!' Ricky crowed as we roared past, en route to our next stop on the massacre mystery tour.

'Tennis Court – Heated Pool – Private Marina – Spa', read a sign out the front.

One more stop. The top of a red limestone cliff. Eagle Point, it was called. The Mitchell River slid by sluggishly below, at the bottom of a sheer drop, fat and lazy and gathering the energy to empty itself into Lake King. We stood close to the edge, peering through a wire fence strung up to prevent suicides. The clifftop offered an unparalleled vista of the Gippsland low country, stretching out before us, golden and rippling in the breeze, illuminated with the gold leaf of the evening sun.

'Beautiful!' I gasped.

'Beautiful country ... yes. But stained.'

I'd never even heard of this massacre, but the story had been passed down in Ricky's family. It was the worst one yet. Here, the fleeing Gunai were herded together like cattle and forced from the clifftop, he said. Men, women and children. Think of the hysteria, the crush, the desperation, as feet scrabbled for purchase and hands grasped for handholds. Men stood on the opposite bank of the river below, shooting any survivors. The bodies all washed out to sea.

'And I haven't told you everything. About how else they were killed. I don't think I want to tell you.'

(I left it, allowing him to decide what he wanted and didn't want to talk about. But he told me later, anyway, over dinner. We were eating pie and mash, I was dangling his ten-month-old grandson over my knee. 'They cut the men's genitals off to see how far they'd run,' he told me calmly, watching my face. 'Stabbed women through their vaginas to see how much they'd bleed. Buried babies up to their necks and kicked their heads off.' '*Dad*,' complained his son Pat. 'We are *eating*.')

'It was your people who did this. But of course, the same happened to them. It was in their make-up, in their past as a people. The same that's in *your* make-up, in your *mother's* make-up.'

I scowled, thinking, 'Don't bring my mother into this.' Although, I realised, I had done that myself already, in pursuing my great theory of intergenerational guilt. But

Ricky must have seen my rebellious expression, because he backtracked, trying to defuse the tension.

'Not that I have bad feeling towards you. Or your mother. We won't *forget*, but we don't bear a grudge.' A pause, before he wondered out loud, 'But what is *your* motivation for all this? What question are you hoping to answer?'

My thoughts had crystallised now. 'I suppose what I really want to do is to understand how a person can do these things. *Evil* things. Because Angus McMillan was not evil. I've read his diaries. He seems like a normal guy. A bit like me in many ways –'

Ricky raised his eyebrows disbelievingly.

'It's true! He talks about this girl he fancies, he misses home. He makes resolutions about how to be a better man, he takes pity on convicts. He's frustrated because his boss doesn't trust his judgement. He's just a normal guy. Even ... a *good guy*. Relatable.'

'So, if you think he's like you – and part of him is *in* you, in your blood – you want to understand what it would take to turn you into a mass murderer?'

There was a long pause. 'Yes,' I admitted.

He shook his head at my folly. 'You won't understand. You'll never understand.'

But I didn't believe him.

I was running out of money. I'd been staying with people I'd met during my travels, or wild camping when possible, to cut costs. Towards the end of my trip I found myself setting up home in a rather dated static caravan just off the freeway near Bairnsdale. It was the best I could stretch to.

But I was beginning to find my boxy, cramped cabin quite reassuring: the murmurs of the other residents sitting out on their little porches; the small, high, net-curtained window that looked out on the featureless side of the caravan next door; the false timber 'panelling' on the walls, the false slate 'tiling' of the floor; the high, square bed, with its counterpane printed to look like a patchwork quilt. The flimsiness of the lock on my screen doors, less so.

I am rarely concerned by loneliness, usually finding more than enough amusement in books and navel gazing, but travelling alone can generate other, more pressing anxieties. At night in my box I drew the net curtains tight across the glass doors and policed my modesty like a Victorian spinster pulling her skirts around her legs.

Once I sat up all night doing an assignment for a magazine back home, battling the time difference as I conducted interviews and responded to queries, in the hope that I could beg them to pay up quickly and keep me from the bottom of my overdraft for another week or two. Blinking tired eyes and boiling my little kettle yet again, I concocted batches of soupy espresso from free sachets of freeze-dried coffee as I tried to focus on the task in hand. Outside the cicadas were as sleepless as me, endlessly tuning up ahead of some glorious insect symphony.

Halfway through, with restless legs, I stood and strode out across the crispy grass to the enormous, institutional toilet block. It had bare brick walls and echoed like a gym hall. I chose a cubicle and locked the door before realising that the lights, set off by a motion sensor, had already been lit when I'd come in.

'Hello?'

No answer. I froze, listening for the other person hiding in the row of stalls, my senses sent haywire by caffeine and lack of sleep. There's someone here to hurt me, I thought, madly.

I pissed quietly, against the side of the bowl to lessen the noise, my ears pricked for the sounds of breathing in the next cubicle. Nothing.

That fear is something that has been drilled into me. There's a certain unwelcome attention that shadows young women travelling alone for any length of time. I had become practised at deflecting conversations with strangers after nightfall with bland smiles and judicious use of my mobile phone. At walking odd looping routes down straight roads while watching for followers. At clocking and logging any curious or unusual glances from unknown men in hotel lobbies. These are all within the normal skillset of the urban woman. Standard practice. They would not, of course, throw off any determined pursuer, but that's not really the point. They're just to make yourself feel you're doing something useful.

Usually I can divorce myself from the unformed, unhinged fears that lurk behind the news reports and the unspoken presumptions of self-defence classes; but sometimes, when my logical brain is too busy or too tired to keep it at bay, the fear takes hold. Every man's eye seems to follow me, like portraits in a gallery – the ubiquitous gaze. Every rustle in the night is a stranger listening at the door. These are childish fears of monsters under the bed, fleshed out by true crime stories and statistics. A state-sanctioned paranoia, the sort of madness that can be taught.

Stumbling out of the fluorescent-lit toilet block, I paused, considering my caravan, wrestling with my doubts.

'There's no one,' I told myself sternly. But I hesitated by the small swimming pool. The water shone still and milky in the moonlight. I was so tired.

I vaulted silently over the locked gate and pulled off my clothes, slipped silently into the water. It was cold, calming. Up to my neck, I felt invisible as I trod water and breathed as quietly as possible. If anyone came out of the caravan, I reasoned, I would see them, and duck my head under. Or scream. It would be hard to get at me here.

My hands beat softly at my sides like fins, sending cool water spinning up, silky against my skin. I was acting like an insane person. I knew that. I pushed the churning fear back down my throat, forced myself to lie back and let the water inch up my cheeks and run its fingers through my hair. I began to feel safe again. I hate dealing with myself when I'm like this – irrational, full of fear, seeing silhouettes in every shadow. In reality I have never truly been at risk. I have always simply been able to trust that my fears are unfounded, *force* myself to believe that the worst is not going to happen. And it doesn't. My streets have always turned out to be safe ones, shadows only shadows, suspicious strangers only shy.

I waited for the fear to abate, there in the water in the dark, until I began to shiver. Then I pulled myself out and padded, dripping, across to the caravan's sliding doors. They were ajar, just as I'd left them. There was nobody inside.

11

Iguana Creek

There was one last aspect of Angus McMillan's life I had left to investigate: his final years.

Although he would be resurrected as a great local hero in the twentieth century, at the time of his death he had fallen on hard times.

In November 1860 he resigned his seat in the Legislative Assembly, citing 'failing health'. He addressed his constituents in a graciously worded letter in the *Gippsland Guardian*: 'Thanking you, Gentlemen, from my heart,' it began, 'for the honour you have done me in electing me as your representative ... I can assure you that nothing would have induced me to tender my resignation but the present cause, as I find myself from physical debility, quite unable to give a due attention to your interests.' This debility, though distressing, was left unlabelled.

Despite a convincing electoral triumph, his tenure had lasted only fourteen months, during which he attended only a third of divisions and failed to make a maiden speech in the house. He had also been moved to apologise after a public spat with the road board in the letters pages of the local papers, during which his record had come in for no small amount of criticism. He had not, it must be said, taken to public office with aplomb.

Still, his resignation produced little triumph from the *Gippsland Guardian*. Far from gloating, it ran an editorial with an almost apologetic, elegiac tone. 'Whatever feelings may have actuated our remarks from time to time on Mr. McMillan's public career must now lie buried in the regret which we, in conjunction with all who know the private worth of that gentleman, must feel at the reason assigned by him for thus placing in the hands of the electors the duty of again returning another representative.'

Quietly, he stepped aside. Financial ruin followed soon afterwards. Bushfire was blamed, but a series of poor financial investments were also a contributing factor. Suddenly the Laird of Gippsland found the ground crumbling beneath his feet. In 1862 he was declared insolvent and forced to sell almost his entire estate, including his beloved Bushy Park.

It was a terrible time. He was hit particularly hard by the loss of the Bushy Park homestead, which he had built quite literally with his bare hands, summoned it from the earth. Pride hurt, he retreated to a cottage at his remote Tabberabbera sheep station on the steep-sided hills near Dargo, the only remaining vestige of his once extensive property empire.

He was not the first or the last explorer to find it difficult to adapt to normal life, or to die in poverty. Good bushmen did not necessarily make good businessmen, and the Australian climate was unpredictable and unforgiving. As fast as riches arrived, they might depart, and in the New World, the wild world, far from family, there were no safety nets. Many saw the country they pioneered turn its back on them.

The Dargo Valley, near McMillan's Tabberabbera station, in 1865.

George Edward Mackay, he who complained of the 'œdematous swelling' brought on by the physical demands of overlanding, later wrote candidly of his regret that he had failed to attain the great riches the region had seemed to promise when he had settled there: 'These, Sir, are the salient points of my experience as a squatter: I have lost my capital. I have lost my health. I have lost fifteen years of the best period of my life. I have undergone many hardships, exposed myself to many dangers, and am now a poorer man than I was when I became a squatter.'

'The early squatters, their sufferings, and their services to the colony, are alike forgotten,' agreed the pastoralist and politician William Thomas Mollison in the same year, 1853. 'Men seem to regard them, as the new heir regards the furniture and portraits of the distant relative to whom he has succeeded, as something to be at once quietly consigned to the lumber room or the auction marts.'

Financial ruin had precipitated Angus McMillan's departure from Scotland; now it blighted his new life. This time he was the laird, undercut by other, more savvy businessmen. Meanwhile, whispers about his health and the exact nature of the 'debility' that had cut his parliamentary career so short began to circulate. The true nature of his health problems is not fully known, but reading contemporary accounts, one gets the sense of more being left unsaid than said.

There are several possibilities. McMillan was known to suffer from rheumatism, which became increasingly problematic towards the end of his life – but would that alone account for his giving up his political career so abruptly? It might, however, have been an excuse – a way of backing away from politics with his pride intact, after finding himself at sea among the legislative class.

For although Australia was in many ways a far more meritocratic country than the one he had fled, McMillan never truly broke through into the upper social circles outside of the relatively closed society of Gippsland. Decades later, a distant relation of Lachlan Macalister revealed that his family always believed that McMillan 'was at his best as a farm manager', and that his many achievements could be attributed to his employer's superior strategy and finances.

It is possible that such tensions may have underlain McMillan's lack of success in parliament, which was still dominated by the upper (or at least, upper-middle) classes. He 'did not enjoy' his time in politics, his contemporaries noted, was reportedly 'gravely offended by the criticism and manoeuvring that was a natural part of parliamentary politics', and largely confined his activities to backroom lobbying and the furthering of private projects, such as masterminding, as a member of the Royal Society of Victoria's exploration committee, the ill-fated attempt by Burke and Wills to cross the continent in 1860. The self-confessed 'man of few words' was more at home on horse-back than in an office or a debating chamber, it seemed.

There have also been some rumours of alcoholism, which are not easy to dismiss. A Highland man famed for his 'hospitality', who remunerated his men with whisky rations; a proud, capable outdoorsman who, risen to the top in his district, found himself disregarded by the polit-ical elite and pilloried in the local press by his constituents. Might a man in his position turn to the bottle to prop up his self-confidence? Yes, it is possible. With this in mind, a few asides in his friends' correspondence gave me pause.

Shortly after McMillan's death, the author John Shillinglaw would write to Commissioner Tyers, mention-ing somewhat euphemistically 'the well-known weakness of ... our late dear friend, McMillan'. He did not elabor-ate, but to my mind the implication looms large.

During this downturn in his fortunes, it must have been very hard for McMillan not to dwell upon the successes of his former rival Strzelecki, the man with whom his career had once run parallel. After his journey through Gippsland and subsequent celebrity in Melbourne, the Pole continued to Tasmania, where he undertook scientific explorations, before emigrating to London, where he became a natural-ised British citizen and was awarded fellowships of the Royal Geographical and Royal Societies. More acclaim was to follow: an honorary doctorate from Oxford University, elevation to the Order of the Bath for his charitable work during the Irish Famine, finally the title of Knight Commander. He would die in 1873, a few days after being informed by his friend, the prime minister William Gladstone, that Queen Victoria had expressed interest in meeting 'the famous count'.

Though he had succeeded in unseating his rival from the title of 'discoverer of Gippsland', McMillan may well have reconsidered the value of this victory in his later years, as with every new garland Strzelecki received, he saw his own fortunes recede. A silver tongue and gold-plated pretensions seemed, in the end, to have brought the so-called 'count' far more success than McMillan's steadfastness and loyalty ever had.

Still, life went on. In 1864, two years after the sale of Bushy Park, McMillan found his vocation once more when he was offered the role of leader of the Alpine Expedition, cutting tracks and mapping an area of high country to the north of Stratford that remained almost entirely unexplored and uncharted.

A series of gold discoveries – most recently at Good Luck Creek, by a party led by the anthropologist-to-be Alfred Howitt – had prompted a rush of incomers to the region, an ill-mannered rabble largely comprising inexperienced bushmen in search of fortune. Many had come to grief in the mountainous area lyrically described by Howitt as 'all frosted silver with black gorges and chasms running among their rugged spurs'. As a result, the government saw fit to commission McMillan to cut a route linking three main sites, totalling 280 miles of track. It may seem a menial sort of job for a former politician, but for McMillan it was both a much-needed source of income and an opportunity to return to prominence in the region.

In fact, it was a godsend. McMillan was back on top, and regaining some of his old swagger. Ahead of his departure he took a room at Scott's Hotel, the Melbourne lodgings of choice of the wealthy country set, where a correspondent for the *Mountaineer* spotted 'the redoubtable explorer' full of 'high hope and confidence in the future of what might very appropriately be called "McMillan's Land" instead of Gippsland'.

Savouring his return to favour, McMillan revived his journal, in which he distilled his relief into words. Others too seemed to share his delight. *Everyone glad to see that these unknown forest lands of Gippsland were at last to be penetrated into and thankful that I was to be the party that was to receive that honour, being the first European that first broke ground in the far famed land. I would not like another to carry the Laurels.* He directed his gratitude to the government that had given him another chance. *I hope they will find me do my duty.*

The party set out from the Dargo Inn, not far from McMillan's Tabberabbera run, in March 1864. Conditions were horrendous. Scrub so dense they were forced to dismount and proceed on foot, slashing at the undergrowth with long knives and axes. Heavy rain, for days at a time, sometimes so hard they were forced to abandon work to shelter under canvas and wait out the storm. Thunder, lightning, hail. McMillan's deputy, a man called Jones, branched off alone to clear a side path, and returned *like a drowned rat*, every item of clothing sodden, and streaked with blood; *even his forehead is bleeding with bites of leeches, which are always numerous at this altitude in thick damp underwood.*

Despite all this, morale was high. McMillan had seen worse; he was in his element. His men trusted his judgement. Pride and purpose were returning. He was older now, yes, but also more sure, more authoritative. He was back in control, leading by example, rising well before dawn at 4.30 a.m., getting the fire blazing and sounding a wake-up call at 5.30. By seven, the men would be at work. *Arrived back at camp at ½ past six, had supper and then our pipes cheered us with a few tunes, all hands in splendid spirits.* He found, to his delight, that the men continued to work in his absence; in return he gave them Sundays and Good Friday as rest days.

1864 engraving describing McMillan's party at work cutting tracks between the Alpine goldfields.

Happiness flooded back into him. It was in the bush, without domestic comforts, that he felt most at home. This was his kind of work; these were his kind of men.

He understood them, knew how to manage and motivate them. It was doing he was good at, not debating. *It is a great pleasure to one that they are so anxious to get on with the work and I make it my duty to keep them on the most friendly terms, as a party of explorers should be like one family, look on their leader as a father and the leader should behave to them as he would his children.*

Of course, his real children were many miles away. Now aged six and three, they were ensconced with Mrs McMillan in the remote cottage at Tabberabbera, and growing up in his absence. He had never spent much time at home. But he thought of them sometimes. The only hill on the Dargo road he christened Mount Ewen, after his eldest. *I hope he will deserve the honour one day. I hope, poor fellow, he will not have so many ups and downs in this cruel world as his papa has had.*

When McMillan left Barra he had cut himself loose from his roots, and in doing so had given himself the freedom to redefine himself as a man – a successful man. Now, after life had taken his measure and found him lacking, when he found himself fallen from grace, poor as on the day he began, disappointed by the way things had turned out, he cut himself loose once again.

Out in the bush, off the edge of the map, living on his wits, he rediscovered himself. He remembered his own strength and worth. He turned his face to the infinite sky, to his capricious God, and offered his thanks for all that he had endured.

6 May, 1864
Mr Bennison's stock men came to our camp this evening.
Mr. B's station is 8 miles lower down the river, near

what he called 'McMillan's coming' — where I camped 16 years ago. Those were happy days, but thanks to the Giver of all good and perfect gifts I am now contented with my lot, for he gives me strength according to my burden.

Despite everything I now knew about Angus McMillan as a man, I found myself happy for him. This tactical retreat, to a space where he might re-evaluate his life, was an impulse that I could understand. In a sense, my trip had fulfilled the same function for me.

The longer I spent away from home, the more I found myself a solitary figure. I drove long distances, camped in empty clearings, sat alone in bars. It was easier than lining up a constant stream of companions, and it allowed me to make my own timetable, going where I chose, sleeping when I wanted, eating at odd intervals and working for long stretches. More than that, I was finding that my thoughts came clearer, tauter, when I had time to digest what I had learned each day in the long hours of the lowering light, under canvas. Alone.

I was ever more out of sync with my old life back at home. This was not only due to the time difference — although the time difference was considerable, my friends and family asleep when I was awake, and vice versa — but emotionally too. I found it increasingly hard to explain to those I loved what I was hearing, seeing, reading, feeling, thinking. For months now I had been half-living in the nineteenth century, seeing the world through that prism, and it had unlinked me from my peers, broken the spell of the fears and stresses I had been labouring under. I had cut myself loose from normal life, and in doing so had found myself solid at the centre of it again, just as I had been all along, but had forgotten.

One night on the road at dusk, somewhere on the endless road between Melbourne and Sydney, I found euphoria. The roads were empty and I drove without clear direction, looking for either a place to camp or a motel to stop at for the night. An electrical storm was brewing in the cauldron of the sky, the air thick and crackling with anticipation, an unsettled wind pacing first one way and then the other. It had sent my GPS haywire; it kept telling me to turn off the road I was on, then abandoning me to my fate as soon as I did – 'Establishing satellite connection' so I had given myself up for lost, just followed my instincts. Leaving it to the horse, as the pioneers would have called it, I cork-screwed up an entry road and down again at the next exit, waiting for an answer to present itself.

I found myself in a long, wide valley, a fieldscape of waving green grasses. The sky bruised a deep, painful violet. Lightning flickered around me in all directions, long forking tails of it, the thunder drowned out by the noise of the car's engine. Along the verges of the road, silvery gums stood in lines, pressed against the barrier like spectators at a race. They reached to the sky, trunks split-ting then splitting again – into limbs, into branches, into twigs, until they formed thousands of pale twisting tendrils: ground lightning, a mirror image of the pyrotechnics above. To the side of the road, a fireman and a concerned man in overalls stood close together inspecting a patch of scorched, steaming earth.

All of this going on, and me watching from the other side of the window. I am here, I thought, but I will be gone again soon.

It filled me with a deep peace. I was both lost and found.

But while we loners are locking ourselves out of the world, turning inwards, the world does not stop spinning on its axis. While McMillan was out on the uncharted ranges, cutting tracks, Christina and their two sons were back home, getting on with things, making do with what little he had left them. They were getting used to life without him.

There was something destructive in this tendency to withdrawal, I was beginning to realise. Something selfish. It was the easy way out: just snip the ties and run off somewhere new, where nobody knows you. Like McMillan I had gone haring off, with little thought for what would happen in my absence, or when I got back. Behind me I had left a job, a relationship, a *life* trailing in my wake, and for the first time it occurred to me that it might no longer be waiting for me when I went home.

I had cut myself loose. Again. The realisation came over me in a flood of self-censure. Wasn't this part of a pattern? I had been constructing a rootless existence for myself. Wasn't that the reason I had found Angus McMillan's story so enchanting at the start of it all, as I stared at the map of Gippsland in the archive in Skye? Well, I'd made it. From Skye to the South Pacific, just as I'd imagined. To all those storybook placenames: I'd seen Snake Island from the mangrove-tangled shore near Port Welshpool; looked up the blue-grey peak of Mount Useful; bathed my feet in the warm, shallow waters of Sealer's Cove, lain back in the sand. I'd hiked there alone, weaving between the peaks of Wilsons Promontory, asked a stranger to take my picture when I got there.

But McMillan's generation had done so with reluctance. They had been tipped from their homeland by force or by finance, and once they had emigrated, home was a six-month sail and a lifetime away. But I was not rootless, not really. I had a family, a place to retreat to. Somewhere I could call and hear a voice tell me I could come home whenever I wanted. After years of trying to prove that I could do it all without them, I found that the thought of returning home to my parents, my brothers, the place I knew best of all, brought with it a stillness, a calmness, that I had never before traced back to its source. I was anchored to the place I was born by an invisible rope that had kept me steady, tugging hard at my heart when I stretched too far away. It was time to go home.

A wave of love broke over me. And something more melancholy, too. I understood, really understood, for the first time the significance of the Highlanders' dispossession. An appreciation of the pain of all those people who feel that same tug of longing and love for people and place, but have no way of returning; the ache of those whose families have been scattered, never to be reunited. How fiercely they must have felt the loss of their past selves: those once-worn paths now grown over; those once-blazing hearths now filled instead by grasses made heavy with seeds and droplets of rain.

I thought again of that lost town of Yallourn. I felt differently, now, about what it could teach us. Just as its residents reconstructed their virtual town so they might walk endlessly along old streets, and the modern-day Gunai reconstructed a lost language and laid claim to old hunting grounds, the Highland settlers of Gippsland kept their motherland alive by attaching old names to new places; by employing their fellow countrymen; by forming Caledonian Societies; by banding together in their Highland Brigades in times of strife. Because it is impossible to be truly rootless. Even if your roots lead to somewhere that no longer exists, even if they have been cut cleanly away, you still feel them as phantom pains. For everyone belongs to the land they were born in, the culture they were born into. It has helped form every aspect of who they are.

The new land, despite its many advantages, its opportunities, did not have the same emotional significance to the settlers. They were not invested in it in the same way, had no understanding or appreciation of the culture and the landscape they had stumbled upon. And so it was easy for them to destroy it without thought, like big boys jumping on sandcastles at the beach.

This story, the story of Angus McMillan and the Scotsmen and the Gunai and the guns, is, as much as anything, a study of nationalism. Of in-groups and out-groups, and of sticking with one's own people. The simple truth of it all is that when it came down to it, they chose to protect their own.

To McMillan, riding from the foothills of the Australian Alps, the broad, fertile flats of the Gippsland plains were a *Caledonia Australis: a country capable of supporting all my starving countrymen.*

Years later, in 1935, a group of Paweł Strzelecki's descendants led by New Yorker Boleslaw Strzelecki cabled Britain's King George V an extraordinary request. They were preparing a claim against the Australian government, they said. Would he lend his support? Not only did they want $560,000 as a refund of the cost of Strzelecki's Gippsland expedition, and the return of some £17 million of the count's money which had been left in British and Australian banks, but for Gippsland to be turned over to the family as a sanctuary for Polish refugees who were leaving their country, which found itself sharing its borders with two aggressive, expansionist regimes: the Soviet Union and Nazi Germany. The normal route out – the immigrant's American Dream – had been shuttered by the Great Depression. Their compatriots might arrive 'at a rate of 25,000 a year', they suggested.

A *Polonie Australis*, perhaps.

The Strzelecki family claim, fanciful though it was, caused an uproar in the region. Local author Hal Porter, himself of British immigrant stock, recalled the episode with outrage forty years later:

No mention of what was to happen to the inhabitants of all the towns and one-horse villages of Strzelecki Province; to the city of Sale; to the Bairnsdale Salvation Army which, in 1935, was celebrating its jubilee ... or how a Polish take-over would be regarded by a town with streets dubbed Buchanan, Moroney, Ballantyne, and Brown ...

Of course, one might ask the same of a province once inhabited by three thousand Gunai: the Tatungooloong of the lake country, the Bratowooloong of Corner Inlet and surrounds, the Brabawooloong who so haunted Bushy Park, the Krowathunkooloong of the Snowy River, the Brayakooloong of the high country. How was the British takeover regarded in a country where the Mitchell River was once the Wy-yung, the Avon the Dooyeedang, and the La Trobe the Tanjil?

But so it goes. We see only through our own eyes.

The '4x4 Adventure Map' I'd found in a petrol station was without contours, and vague in parts, but it was going to have to do. It was the only sufficiently detailed map I could find of the area, and it did at least label McMillan's walking track specifically. It had been picked out by a line of tiny diamonds, albeit interrupted by large gaps where the path could not be found. 'Track contains poorly defined and overgrown sections (Not recommended),' the map warned.

It was too hot to hike the whole length of it, and too risky, with the fire-danger rating inching up every day. But I wanted to get out onto his trail, following in his footsteps, to get an idea of his state of mind.

Cam had come along for the ride. It was getting dark by the time we turned off an unsealed road onto an even more rutted track – 'McMillan's Road', the GPS announced happily – that led us deep into the Grant Historic Area, home of the goldrush townships of Grant and Talbotville. Or, more accurately, the former goldrush townships of Grant and Talbotville. At the end of the nineteenth century both were hives of activity and excitement, as new houses sprang up every day. Today, however, it is as though they never existed.

'Jesus,' I said, as the headlamps of my hire car strobed the vacant ground; a clean-edged clearing in the woods about the size and shape of a village. 'What the hell is this?'

Cam snorted. 'I told you it would be underwhelming.'

I considered, slowing down to peer through the long grass. A faint depression ran off at right angles to the track, unnaturally straight: the outline of a street that no longer exists. My mind flitted to Sorley MacLean's 'Hallaig'. All those girls walking 'in silent bands', ghostly footsteps muffled by the moss grown over old roads. Right then, in our twilit clearing, in the crossover time between light and dark, past and present, I could feel our two realities brushing up against each other. Insects fluttered through the headlights' beams; I imagined the soft tread of feet, the press of cold hands against the window. 'I don't know if "underwhelming" is right,' I said. 'There's something sort of horrifying about it.'

'An actual ghost town.'

'Exactly. I'd say I wouldn't want to come here at night, except – well, here we are.'

'Camp?'

I sighed and pulled over. It was too late to look for anywhere else. We pitched up in a side clearing by the remains of a previous visitor's firepit, and I left Cam preparing a fire to wander back into the heart of old Grant, flicking a saucer-sized circle of torchlight ahead of me. Everything had vanished but the gravestones, which were real and solid, penned in by wooden rails as if they might make a break for it otherwise. Along what had once been Main Street, someone had recently, painstakingly, staked in plaques marking the former sites of shops, the post office, the old inn. Historical society stuff: more monuments to the mundane. 'We were here. We were here. We were here.'

The goldrush township of Grant in its heyday, 1865.

Now, after all that I had learned, I couldn't help but brood on the flipside: that secret history that has gone unrecorded, and too often forgotten. But what you don't know can't haunt you. I slept well that night, amid the shopkeepers and the tailors and the men panning for gold.

Morning found us in Talbotville; another blank space at the foot of the hill, another railed-off cemetery. The phantoms had evaporated off like water in the harsh sunlight, their place taken by a rowdy off-roading party, all of them men, who had parked their SUVs in a circle. Every so often another of their members careered by, mud and dirty water scraped by the windscreen wipers to create two shell-shaped look-holes. Each man clutched a can of beer in an insulated holder. All of them were clearly drunk. It was 11 a.m.

We prepared to walk. McMillan's track branched off from the 4x4 track somewhere around there, and I wanted to explore it on foot. Cam unfolded the map on the bonnet of the car and stooped to study it, but I was distracted. I felt eyes on me. When I looked up, I saw that two men had detached themselves from the party and were making their way, unsteadily, towards us.

'You lost?' The shorter, and drunker, of the pair swigged from his can as he peered over my shoulder. He wiped his mouth and offered me a swig.

We told them we were looking for McMillan's track. Yeah, said the other guy. He'd heard of it. But it was 'pretty crook'. Not much chance of getting the car along it. He eyed my shiny white rental vehicle. 'You done much off-roading before?'

'We're not going to drive. It's a walking track.'

'Bushwalking!' They both laughed openly. 'In this heat? You're going to die out there.'

We fended off their concerns and headed off along a track, looking for the turn-off, dodging the occasional SUVs that came roaring past like tanks on their way to battle, finally locating a tree marked with a small metal triangle denoting where the trail diverged.

The adventure map had not been lying when it warned of 'poorly defined and overgrown sections'. Fallen branches splayed across the path. Brambles totally choked the way. We struggled on into the thicket, bashing our way through with heavy sticks, not speaking except to exchange expletives and occasional groans of pain. The plan had been to follow the track for a few miles past the former Pioneer Racecourse, but after about an hour of fruitless hacking, stuck with thorns and bleeding from every bare patch of skin, we were ready to admit defeat.

'This is hopeless. How far do you reckon we've gone?'

Cam turned to size up the hillside. 'Less than a kilometre? We need a machete or an axe or a chainsaw. I don't envy them, those track-cutters.'

We turned and began to muddle our way back, but the path seemed to have sealed up just as tightly as before we had passed through. 'It's sad, isn't it?' I said, ducking under a fallen trunk. 'After all that effort, to allow it to grow over.'

Cam disagreed. He thought the trail should be allowed to disappear. 'It's not as if it's well-used, is it? And it's perverse to keep it as a monument to McMillan.'

'Do you think so?'

He paused from batting back a bramble that seemed determined to garrotte him, and looked back at me with a funny expression. 'Yes. Why, don't you?'

He had a point. It *was* perverse to have all these memorials to a man who had caused so much pain and damage. But it seemed wrong too to demolish them, or let them fade back into the bush as if they had never existed. Wasn't that just another sort of denial of the past?

A black cockatoo alighted on a branch far above my head. Its call came, harsh and rasping, the creaking of a door closing.

A few days previously, I had been driving through the hills in the hour before sunset when I came across another section of the track. I had come skidding along a dusty, unsealed road from Dargo High Plains down through a stand of straggling trees; they were torn limb from limb, branches arched off in strange poses like arms thrown up for protection. Just as the road straightened out, I passed a tree with a metal triangle nailed into its trunk. I slammed on the brakes, and twisted over the passenger seat to read the label: 'McMillan's Tk'.

Hello. I reversed back through my own dustcloud, pulled into a flat space just off the road beside a tumble-down corrugated-iron hut, tiger-striped with dark rust, and clambered out to wander in the evening sunlight, just in the flip-flops and shorts I'd been driving in. The path was clear enough up here on the plains, a bare track through sparse, burned-out bush, gnarled bare shrubs set far apart. There was little evidence that anyone had been up there recently. 'McMillans Walking Track', read another sign. 'Victoria River Via Mayford 25km 2 Days. Remote Walking – Please Use Intentions Book'.

I ignored the request, and set off along the track without a clear purpose in mind, feeling exposed and very alone in this sunbleached, windblasted clearing. The last woman on earth. The air was still, and silent. There were no sounds except for the muffled crunch of my footsteps on the dry earth. No birdsong. No wildlife that I could see –

I froze mid-step, a fraction of a second before I stepped on a fat-knuckled spider about the size of my hand. He sat brazenly in the middle of the path, as if expecting me. My breath caught in my throat and I swallowed a scream, carefully pedalling my foot backwards before taking two or three steps back in quick succession, like a spooked horse. The spider didn't move.

I watched it, heart pounding. What was it? Something venomous? I didn't recognise it, had no hope of identifying it, but it didn't look friendly, that was for sure. We stood at an impasse. A voice in the back of my head cackled and catcalled. 'Get on with it! Coward!'

Should I jump over it? I took one step closer, then immediately backed away again when the spider twitched a leg. Should I prod it with a stick? The thought made my stomach turn over. A lazy breeze played through the dry grass, across my bare ankles, my bare legs, the skin on the back of my neck. I glanced around in the dry undergrowth. Every stick and tree root looked like a snake, every clump of weeds a harbourer of some nasty predator.

Fight or flight? I swivelled my head to look back the way I'd come. I couldn't have gone further than half a mile. Flight was easier. I set off towards the car at a sprint, senses on full alert, leaping every suspicious rock and root, clawing my toes to keep the flimsy flip-flops on my feet.

Idiot. By the time I got back to the car I was giggling like a maniac. I gathered my wits, waited for my breath to slow, and wandered over to the metal locker that held the intentions book, hungry for human contact. It was a crumpled A4 notebook with a broken spine, the pages coming away in my hands. There were two and a half pages' worth of entries in the entire book. The first was dated 2010, and a handful of others were scattered throughout the following years. 'Pedersen's and Fyfe's had soup here 2/6/11'; '16-12-12 Manning and Graver ... Five horses with us, all good, heading to Mayford 2night.' According to the book, no one had passed this way on foot for months.

I looked at the sign again. 'Please Use Intentions Book'. It implied, but didn't say: 'So we know where to look for your body.'

Signpost where McMillan's track intersects with the road,
Dargo High Plains.

I thought about Angus McMillan, up here in his element. Bashing through the bush looking for new routes. Making up the maps. No tracks, no roads, no nothing. An hour or so in the bush and I was running for safety. Come on, come on, come on. Boots on.

I packed my rucksack quickly and set off again into the dusk, following the track through thousands of bleached trees, until I emerged at a flat spot with a view across the opposite hillside. A bushfire had rushed through years before; what must once have been a glorious lookout now offered an unbroken vista of the most incredible scene of devastation. For miles around, hills dropped and rose again, stubbled and wrecked and unrecovered after more than a decade. Dead trees carpeted the landscape as far as the eye could see, arms lifted in salvation, naked to the waist and streaked with scorch marks. They were silver and utterly bare, thin and leggy, javelins dropped into the hillside at speed.

On my own, I saw no point in lighting a fire. I just set up my tent, zipped myself in and climbed into my sleeping bag. I tried to read, but the battery in my head torch faded to nothing, so I switched it off and lay still in the dark, trying to shut out the noises of the night, the rustling in the grass beside my head. At some point, I slept.

I woke suddenly in the night, shivering. I was high up, I realised: the air was cold. I hadn't thought to bring a jumper with me. Desperate for the toilet, I reluctantly slid out of the bag and clambered from my tent to find the moon high and full in the sky. It flooded everything with a thin, clear light. Instantly, all fear was washed from me, replaced by wonder. Trees torn asunder were now curving, silver sculptures. The grass a carpet of white velvet. The stars piercing bright: the sky shot through with gossamer.

If ever there was to be a time of visitation, it was now. I felt drained of warmth, of colour, of worry. I waited patiently, my head upturned, letting the breath leave me in a long, low sigh. Who was I waiting for? Dark tribesmen, trailing pewter blood? Orphaned children, one-eyed, crying? Angus McMillan and his men, bearing arms? Bearing bodies? Offering explanations?

I didn't know, but I waited anyway, my mind still as the night, its surface unruffled by thoughts. I was heavy, pregnant with expectation, ready for answers.

I waited in the moonlight until the shivers came in violent pulses and my teeth clashed together. No one had come. Nothing. No answers. Perhaps there were none. I turned and let myself into the dark recess of the tent and my thin summer sleeping bag. My feet and hands were cold to the touch.

Not long after McMillan found his peace, things began to fall apart. His men struck gold near what would become the township of Grant, and though they honoured him by naming the reef 'Pioneer', for his new horse, most of the party deserted to stake their claims and chase their fortunes. McMillan hired a new team for the last leg and pushed on, but a delay in the delivery of government funds left him hard-pressed to pay their wages.

1864 engraving showing McMillan's party discovering a quartz gold reef.

As they inched towards the finish, McMillan grew taciturn. Funds were still short, the government were hanging back from paying him; they were nitpicking, he felt, over his scrappy bookkeeping. But the job was completed, was it not? With nothing else to be done, he sent the men home with his own money in their pockets; to raise it, he had been forced to sell his stake in the reef.

They were grateful for his efforts, at least. *All hands well and expressing themselves sorry to be so near the end of the journey. One of the men expresses that the expedition was more like a picnic for they never fared better. I always made it a rule to camp on a nice spot.*

But it was time to return to society, and he found himself a lonely figure. *I am now in the camp with only 1 man.* After four days, he sent the man home.

He could not follow, *being attacked with rheumatism.* The next day he was still *unable to move.* And the next. It was more than a week later, on Friday, 3 June 1864, before he could drag himself from the hut in which he had taken refuge to head slowly, painfully, back towards civilisation. On the way, yet another calamity would befall him. The packhorse he was leading slipped and fell from a rocky precipice, dragging the already aching McMillan down with it. The fall broke three of his ribs, and tore his right knee open, leaving him so badly injured that he found it difficult to walk. He struggled on for the remaining miles, tight eyes fixed upon the ground in front of his feet. He was in too much pain to record the details. *Arrived in camp on Sunday 5th June. Suffered fearfully on the road.*

He had accomplished his task, that was one thing at least. His friend John Shillinglaw wrote to Commissioner Tyers of his success: 'Mac has never looked better than he does now, and but for his bad knee, which is sometimes very bad, he would be able to enjoy the laurels he has lately won more heartily. The fact is that he is quite a hero just now, for there is every chance of a great rush during the spring and summer to the country he has newly opened.'

So it proved. Over the coming months, thousands rushed down McMillan's track to at least thirty-five more gold-quartz reefs that were discovered along its length, heralding an economic boom across all Victoria. McMillan was welcomed back into Gippsland society with open arms. But the cost had been very great.

Not only financially – although the government continued to drag their feet, leaving him out of pocket – but physically as well, and his failing health hung heavy upon the bushman who had always prided himself upon his strength and fortitude. McMillan was, as the *Gippsland Guardian* wrote later, 'broken in constitution and in spirit'. Still he did not return home, instead checking in to the Club Hotel in Sale, and later, perhaps when his money began to run out, to a down-at-heel inn on the road to Dargo, at a place called Iguana Creek.

It was there that he died on 18 May 1865, aged fifty-four. Neither his wife nor his children were present.

He never had made it back to Barra, despite his fervent hope all those many years ago, as he sat in his pitching bunk on board the *Minerva*, legs braced against the partition, casting his thoughts like a fishing line, first back, and then forward into the far-off future:

Farewell to the land where my first love is
A long farewell dear Barra to thee.
I think on thee while I write this
On the deep and stormy sea.

God grant that I may see your land and shore
In after years in other time
Again from thee to go no more
To other dear and distant time

But should He please my humble bones to lay
In foreign land, beneath a foreign sun
Why then, I have no more to say.
God's will be always done.

God's will be done. 'Endocarditis', the death certificate said. As a diagnosis, it made sense: a common complication of rheumatic fever. Still, a certain mystery surrounds Angus McMillan's death. Some have suggested suicide. Others that he drank himself to death. The coroner, his great friend Dr Arbuckle, declined to conduct a post mortem, and so a sliver of doubt survives.

I read all of this with sinking spirits. To die in a strange bed, in a dingy roadhouse, is a sad and anticlimactic exit for anyone. The Gippsland poet Laurie Duggan described McMillan's Iguana Creek: 'a few houses and a T-intersection;/proof only that the famous/die in ordinary places'.

Today, a memorial stands in the spot. I saw it as I came down the road from the high country, and made a sudden swerve onto the grassy flat alongside. A huge slab of orange sandstone poked toothily from the ground, lichen spread across the top like snowfall. Behind it the eponymous creek was a dry rocky bed, strangled by tall grass as high as my shoulders. A metal plaque bore a portrait of McMillan in relief, wearing a Highland cap and looking every bit the laird. I ran my fingers over his face: that same strong nose, that same strong brow. Above it was a chronological list of his explorations: the rivers he discovered, crossed and named. And beside his picture a legend:

DIED HERE
May 18, 1865

The plaque had been shot. There were three perfect round bulletholes in the metal: the first through his name, the second through the dedication. The third went through his face. Oh, Angus.

I thought of that young man sailing out from the Hebrides, drawing up in serpentine longhand his list of resolutions for a life to be lived the New World.

I resolve hereafter to do whatever I think to be my
duty and most for the good and advantage of
mankind.
I resolve to do this whatever difficulties I meet with.
I resolve to live with all my might while I do.
I resolve never to do anything which I should be
afraid to do if it were the last hour of my life.
I resolve never to do anything out of revenge.
I resolve I shall live as I shall wish I had done when
I come to die.

There was a dead tree on the hill, a whole, perfect skeleton. Its trunk split into thick muscled arms; at their tips, jointed twigs were crooked like bony fingers. Clumps of dried-out mistletoe hung from its branches as baubles.

Numbly, I got back into the car and drove on.

There was a danger in my quest, I realised now. By tying myself to McMillan, by submerging myself in his life and thoughts, I had begun to feel for him, care for him. Empathise with him, even. I had begun to allow my compassion for the man to colour my judgement of his actions.

A French proverb: *Tout comprendre, c'est tout pardonner.* To understand is to forgive.

But it is not my place to forgive. It is not my place, either, to become an apologist for a murderer, a defender of the indefensible. Whatever I recognise in McMillan, however engaging I find him as a man, it cannot be escaped that he must be defined by his worst actions. He was a murderer. A *mass* murderer. A proponent of genocide.

It is true that my improved knowledge of his situation, and the pressures it entailed, had engendered in me a better appreciation of how such wicked work might take place. I had begun to understand that many individuals might be capable of the same, under the right conditions. Myself, even. For can I truly say that in his position – far out on the frontier, where law and order is a distant construct, where white is good and black is evil – I would not behave in the same way? No. I can't say anything like that. Not for sure.

Yet that does not absolve him of guilt.

We must hold him, and others like him, accountable for their actions. It is important to look back with clear hindsight and see what havoc they wreaked, and know that it was wrong. That they should have acted differently, reacted more wisely to their fears, followed their ambition with more caution. But before we sermonise too loudly upon the moral weaknesses of our predecessors, we must remember too what things looked like to them, so we might understand why they behaved as they did, and in doing so, ask how such things might be prevented from happening again.

It we chalk this up as nothing but the actions of evil men, it will all have been for naught. We will not have confronted the moral ambivalence that lies at the heart of every person. Of this, McMillan is a better example than most: the conflicts between his actions and his ideals are obvious. He shot to kill; he handed out blankets. He lived in sin; he observed the Sabbath. He hunted those who speared his stock remorselessly; his generosity to his fellow men was renowned. He rallied to the rescue of the defiled white woman; he kept the mother of his bastard child as housekeeper for three years rather than marry her.

Contrast the barrowloads of bones he carted from Warrigal Creek, under cover of darkness, to be burned and disposed of in pits and under sandbanks, with the tidy grave he had dug for Clifton, his favourite horse, near the homestead at Bushy Park. The actions of both a cold-blooded killer and a soft-hearted fool. He was both.

That juxtaposition particularly called to mind a memory from another day, a long way from Gippsland. I was fishing with three others, bobbing in a small boat off the west coast of Scotland. After an hour of listless waiting we drifted through a shoal of mackerel, and suddenly we could not reel them in fast enough. Six hooks on every line; I had my feet braced against the side of the boat, cranking the reel, my rod bending with the weight of them. It was miraculous: the apostles fishing from the other side of the boat. Soon our catch had overflowed the buckets and we were wading through silver fish, which gasped and flipped between our feet.

I was laughing now, from shock, or joy, or something else entirely, holding my rod aloft with one hand, grasping ineffectually at their muscled bodies with the other, fingers slipping as they struggled and catching on the barbed hooks. Rob, the estate manager, teased me for my timidity, and leaned in to help. He grasped them roughly and pulled so the hooks ripped through their flesh, laughing when I winced. We were like merpeople, waterproofs caked in a thick layer of iridescent scales. Blood everywhere, from their torn mouths, our torn hands.

Finally it was still again. We had drifted out the other side. We slumped back, talking in undertones, regaining our composure. Rob watched his spaniel fondly as he crunched the head of a half-dead mackerel, which still lashed limply in its jaws. Its fur was foul with blood and fish guts. 'Good dog,' said Rob, addressing the top of his head. He thumped his tail half-heartedly, concentrating on the fish.

'I almost killed him once,' Rob recalled, wincing at the memory of it. 'When he was a puppy. Ran him over with a quad bike.' Thinking the dog was dying, he panicked, scooped him up in his arms and leapt into a powerboat, racing ten miles to Mallaig and the nearest vet with blood thudding in his ears. 'He was all right in the end.'

Rob put out a hand and rubbed the dog's haunches with a look of soft, familial pride. A fish flipped over at his feet. He lifted his boot and stamped it dead.

Isn't it strange, I thought then, how we see only certain kinds of pain? We tune in and out of them, choosing which to receive as if they were radio stations.

It was late summer now. The moisture had been sucked from the ground, the leaves were crisp and brittle on the trees, shifting in the wind with the sound of the ocean. Across the creek, a grass fire had swept through the fields not long before. The ground was scorched to a threadbare black-brown, what leaves remained on the shrubs were desiccated and curled. I had crossed into a world where it was forever autumn. The air was dry, woody: the smell of the sauna.

I headed south into thick, bitter air. Near Yallourn the fire had got into the coal seams, had been burning for a week. It was dark; evening had fallen though it was not yet noon. Dark particles swirled in the air, settled in the well behind the windscreen wipers like dirty snow. Cars appeared from the gloom, hazard lights blinking. Thick smoke rose up in a black wall ahead, and I drove into it.

Epilogue

GIPPS LAND.
(FROM OUR OWN CORRESPONDENT)
Port Albert, 6th March, 1856.
– Angus McMillan, Esq. –

The entertainment given to Angus McMillan, Esq., came off on Monday evening last, and brought together about fifty gentlemen. The dinner, which was entrusted to the care of Mr. Gellion, reflects the highest credit on that gentleman; and, in truth, it must be very gratifying to hear the praises of everyone lavished upon the excellence and good taste that characterised this – one of the most sumptuous entertainments ever given in Gipps Land.

After the cloth was withdrawn, the Chairman proposed the toast: 'Mr. McMillan, and discovery of Gipps Land.' The Chairman said:

Gentlemen – we are assembled here to-night to do honour to the man whose enterprise laid open to us the district we inhabit, – an enterprise, the difficulties of which can be but imperfectly appreciated by us who enjoy the fruits of it; but that we do appreciate the advantages thus afforded us, as well as the excellent qualities of the man to whom we are indebted for them, is shown by our presence here to-night. To those very obstacles which opposed a mighty barrier to the inroads of civilisation, and stayed the advancing progress of the white man, until McMillan, undeterred by difficulties and dangers, led the way, we are indebted for some of the principal advantages we enjoy as dwellers in Gipps Land.

The gigantic granite ramparts which seclude us from the rest of Australia shelter us also from the scorching winds of the desert, and give rise to numerous rivers, which, flowing in every direction through the land, fertilise the soil and give the superiority we claim for it as an agricultural and grazing district.

From our situation between those mountains and the sea, we enjoy a climate which I consider approaches more nearly to perfection than that of any spot on earth. Unchilled by severe frosts – sheltered from hot winds – knowing no dread of drought – the heat of the day followed invariably by cool refreshing nights; a climate to which not only no disease is to be ascribed, but which is calculated to retain the body in perfect health where no other disturbing cause is in action; a climate not only enabling a settler to endure the severe toil that ever must accompany the conversion of the forest into the farm, but fulfilling in the plenty of harvest the hopes with which he laboured in seedtime.

Epilogue

We have lately made a great stride in advance, and I confidently believe that the time is not far distant when the few gaps made in the forest by the present settlers will extend over the whole of the lower district, when in place of the sombre gum forest and tea-tree scrub, the makeshift hut, and the half-cleared paddock, the eye of the traveller will rest for miles on waving corn-fields, interspersed with the substantial dwellings and well stocked homesteads of a prosperous and happy race of families, whose industry will relieve us from our present state of dependence upon foreign countries for our food. When the vast mineral treasures of our granite ranges shall be worked by thousands instead of hundreds of sturdy miners, guided by science and aided by machinery, the valuable products of their industry and enterprise, brought to the coast by railway or canal, for the construction of which this country seems expressly formed.

When above all other resources we shall be found to possess in abundance, as I believe we do, that gift of provident nature, 'more precious than silver, more valuable than gold' – the food of the mighty steam-engine, coal.

Then, with an unequalled climate, a fertile soil, numerous and valuable mineral productions, safe and convenient harbours, it needs no prophetic vision to foresee that this district, the fortunate discovery of our honoured guest, shall hold a most important rank amongst Australian settlements. (Cheers.)

But I trust should we live to see Gipps Land rise from our present obscure to our future proud position, we may never see her people lose those characteristics which mark them now; the hospitality that welcomes everywhere the stranger and the traveller; the honesty that makes a locked door at night a rarity in the district; the energy that led the way, and has continued to distinguish the squatter and the farmer in their struggles ever since; the unity and friendly feeling that will never let a Gipps Lander stand by and see a neighbour beat for want of a helping hand either here, at home, or as I have often experienced myself, on the distant gold-fields.

Let us continue to cherish those feelings and we may then rejoice in the present and trust confidently in the future of the 'Land we live in', whilst our children's children shall learn to honour, as we do, the name of McMillan its discoverer. (Loud and continued cheers.)

Author's Note

I open this book with a dramatized account of the events of the Warrigal Creek massacre, the most significant violent clash between white settlers and indigenous people in the history of Gippsland – and one of the worst recorded in Australian history.

A great deal of secrecy surrounds the events of that day – as I have explained elsewhere, the participants were well aware that their actions were punishable by hanging – and so the sources are often coy or second-hand, and the true timeline is still a matter of some debate.

There is, for example, disagreement between sources over the exact location of the attack; others disagree on the nature of the injuries to Ronald Macalister (the *Port Philip Patriot* says the body and face were 'so totally disfigured that his countenance could not be recognized among his most intimate friends'; the source of early allegations of a massacre, William Hoddinott, described the Gunai 'driving spears into the body'; yet others state that he was beaten to death with sticks or waddies). There is also conflict among the sources as to who discovered the body: McMillan; an employee of his, John Morrison; or the Aboriginal station hand known as Boy Friday.

Author's Note

The scenario described in the prologue is necessarily a reconstruction of what seems, to my eyes, after carefully examining the available evidence, the most likely course of events that day. It must be underlined that I do not claim to have produced a 'definitive' account – although largely my scenario echoes that mooted by the historian Peter Gardner (who appears in person in Chapter 6) and outlined by Dirk Moses in his book *Genocide and Settler Society*.

I am aware that some voices in Australian historical circles are apt to focus on the uncertainty surrounding the attack at Warrigal Creek (and other cases both locally and nationwide), using it as evidence that these events did not take place. I find this denialism disingenuous and with the potential to cause great social harm.

In his book *The Gippsland Massacres*, Gardner compares and contrasts a wide range of sources – diaries, private correspondence, letters from the office of the Aboriginal Protector, interviews with the descendants of local settlers and so on – which, although not always in strict accordance with one another, in their volume, content and tone together paint a convincing picture of a brutal 'day of reckoning', and, more broadly, a region in the midst of a violent, unofficial conflict befitting the title 'black war'. (This term is commonly used to refer to the persecution of the Palawa in Tasmania between 1824 and 1831, but is also fastened to a series of earlier clashes in the Hawkesbury and Parramatta area, beginning in 1795; what they have in common is that they are outbreaks of racially motivated violence of such intensity as to resemble open warfare.) I encourage those who doubt the version of events recounted in my prologue to read that book and to make up their own minds.

346

I owe a great deal to Gardner's tireless research, and turned frequently to *The Gippsland Massacres*, *Through Foreign Eyes* and *Our Founding Murdering Father*. These works are not widely available but can be procured from Gardner directly through Ngarak Press or found in public libraries across Gippsland.

Other books that became essential texts include Don Watson's *Caledonia Australis*, Robert Hughes' extraordinary *The Fatal Shore*, and a fascinating compendium of first-hand accounts of frontier life written during McMillan's time at the request of Lieutenant-Governor Charles La Trobe, *Letters from Victorian Pioneers*. I also highly recommend Laurie Duggan's epic poem *The Ash Range*, in which he collages dozens of contemporary sources to create a haunting account of the founding of modern-day Gippsland.

McMillan's own journals, from which I have quoted liberally throughout the book, can be found in the archives of the State Library of Victoria in Melbourne. Several versions of the 'exploration journal' exist and it appears that McMillan reworked and revised his account of his early exploratory travels throughout his life. Each reiteration provides information not found elsewhere, and so I have not confined my quotations to one version, instead using whichever is most relevant and insightful in each case.

In terms of my own investigations, I conducted three separate trips to Gippsland of between four and six weeks in length between 2013 and 2015. The bulk of the 'action' in the book took place between November 2013 and February 2014, though the meetings with Ricky Mullet and Barry Kenny of GLaWAC took some time to set up and did not take place until I returned a year later in

February 2015 in the latter stages of writing this book. For the sake of narrative coherence, I have not referred to the intervening period. Similarly, a small number of other episodes did not occur in the order in which they are presented.

Dialogue is reproduced to the best of my ability, either from the use of my contemporaneous notes (in the case of more 'formal' interviews, such as my visit to Lake Tyers) or from detailed records of my activities and conversations entered in a daily journal during my travels.

I am extremely grateful to all of the people – historians, community leaders, writers and friends – who donated their time and knowledge. Any errors are mine and mine alone.

Spelling

McMillan

In modern accounts Angus is usually referred to as McMillan, and I have adopted this spelling to avoid confusion. In newspaper articles of the time he was often referred to as Angus M'Millan (or even Augustus M'Millan), which I consider a Victorian quirk and use only in direct quotations where necessary. However, in Chapter 1, I use Macmillan while discussing my mother's relatives. This is the spelling used by our branch of the family, which I'm told was settled upon by her grandfather. Prior to this, both Mc— and Mac— were used interchangeably, as in many Highland families in the nineteenth century.

Author's Note

Gunai

In recent decades there has been a linguistic split among the remaining Gunai people, some of whom refer to themselves as Kurnai, a derivation of the phonetic rendering of the tribe's name devised by the Victorian anthropologist Alfred Howitt (Kŭrnai). In the run-up to the native-title agreements in Gippsland, this disparity became a source of friction, and after a lengthy hearing the local community compromised on Gunaikurnai as a collective label (see Chapter 7). Nevertheless, I felt on reflection that this composite name would not reflect the original usage. Therefore, following discussion with indigenous language expert Dr Doris Paton and in accordance with independent expert testimony submitted during the native title hearings, I have opted for Gunai, which more closely follows the name's original pronunciation in McMillan's time.

Koorie

Aboriginal people from different regions of Australia refer to themselves as a group by several different names. Koorie is used in Victoria, while in New South Wales this is more often spelled Koori. Other words are in use in different regions, such as Murri in Queensland, Nyungar in the Perth area, and so on. Each word can be roughly translated to mean 'people'.

General comment on Aboriginal names

In the case of Aboriginal names (both for individuals like Bungelenc and Jackie Warren, and cultural groups such as Eora and Palawa), there are often several variants in texts dating from the period. I have tried to use what is, arguably, the most prevalent in each case, but with some caution.

Although apparently interchangeable to outsiders, in some cases these inconsistencies have become symbolic of deeper divisions between branches of cultural groups. Usually the issue arose only after Anglicised distortions were produced by Europeans attempting to record Aboriginal language and customs.

The settlers saw through European eyes and heard with European ears. As, of course, do I. I hope I have not caused offence by my choice of spellings: if I have, it was entirely unintended.

Sources

1. Blood Relatives

p. 16 almost a third: 2006 census: 288,180 respondents out of 903,090

p. 26 'A Scottish pioneer': 'Aborigines Vow to Wipe Pioneer Scot off the Map', *Scotsman*, 22 June 2005: http://www.scotsman.com/news/scotland/top-stories/aborigines-vow-to-wipe-pioneer-scot-off-the-map-1-1391101

p. 29 'O Flower of Scotland': 'Flower of Scotland' – unofficial national anthem of Scotland, by Roy Williamson of The Corries

p. 30 'every Scotch man': Quoted Linda Colley, *Britons: Forging the Nation 1707–1837* (1992), p. 120

p. 30 'skilful obstructions': Hugh Thomas, *The Slave Trade: The History of the Atlantic Slave Trade 1440–1870* (1997), p. 550

2. But for the Sea

p. 47 the novelist Catherine Sinclair: Don Watson, *Caledonia Australis: Scottish Highlanders on the Frontier of Australia* (2009), p. 54

p. 47 A fifth brother: 'A Dauntless Man: Angus McMillan', Traralgon and District Historical Society (1972)

p. 49 Until then, lairds: John Lorne Campbell, *A Very Civil People: Hebridean Folk, History and Tradition* (2014), p. 202

p. 50 £2 million and numerous estates: 'Legacies of British
Slave Ownership', University College London:
http://www.ucl.ac.uk/lbs/person/view/1301318774

p. 51 'a scene of horror': Eric Richards, *The Highland
Clearances* (2008), p. 209

p. 51 'in a state of absolute starvation': From a collection of
pamphlets assembled by James Maidment (Vol. 1,
p. 86) and held in Inverness Library: http://www.
ambaile.org.uk/en/item/item_narrative.jsp?item_
id=22818

p. 57 *Sporthail* (noun): Also features in 'Sound Poem' by
Rody Gorman, a collection of Gaelic descriptions
of sound

3. The Fever Ship

p. 66 'No parent, sister, brother': 'Written for Mr. George
Lang, the author's brother, on his embarking for New
South Wales. – London, April 25th, 1821'. Full text:
http://www.inspirationalstories.com/poems/
verses-i-john-dunmore-lang-poems/

p. 73 'overcrowded state': J.V. Thompson Esq., Deputy
Inspector General of Hospitals, writing from on board
the *Minerva*, 24 January 1838

p. 73 a third of the population: David Neal, *The Rule of Law
in a Penal Colony: Law and Politics in Early New South
Wales* (1991), p. 200

p. 74 New arrivals often: In 1790 the colony's chaplain,
Rev. Richard Johnson, wrote of the selfishness that
the depth of their penury engendered: 'Instead of
alleviating the distresses of each other, the weakest
were sure to go to the wall. In the night time, which
at this time is very cold, where [the convicts] had
nothing but grass to lay on and a blanket amongst the
four of them, he that was the strongest of the four
would take the whole blanket to himself and leave the
rest quite naked.' Quoted Robert Hughes, *The Fatal
Shore* (1987), p. 147

Sources

p. 75 'The colony that would': Ibid., p. 74

p. 75 'Famine ... was approaching': Watkin Tench, *A Complete Account of the Settlement at Port Jackson*, Chapter VI: http://www.gutenberg.org/files/3534/3534-h/3534-h.htm

4. The Cattle Station

p. 79 more than A$100 billion: Australian Bureau of Statistics, Yearbook 2012: http://www.abs.gov.au/ausstats/abs@.nsf/Lookup/by%20Subject/1301.0~2012~Main%20Features~Mining%20Industry~150

p. 83 'swans are black': *Caledonia Australis*, op. cit., p. 85

p. 84 'in the habit of': John Goodwin, quoted *The Fatal Shore*, op. cit., p. 311

p. 85 'I was put in': McMillan's account reprinted in the *Gippsland Times*, 3 January 1924, p. 2

p. 85 'accursed colony': Quoted Rev. J. Cox, *Notes of Gippsland History*, Vol. 1, *Exploration*, p. 44

p. 89 seventeen to one: P.J. Marshall (ed.), *The Cambridge Illustrated History of the British Empire* (1996), p. 258

p. 94 'The country looked very pleasant': From Bill Gammage, *The Biggest Estate on Earth: How Aborigines Made Australia* (2011; Kindle edition), p. 417

p. 94 'It may perhaps be doubted': Quoted ibid.

p. 94 'To clear the forest's': 'The Telegraph: A Consolatory Epistle', quoted *The Fatal Shore*, p. 179

p. 96 'Bathurst —': *South Australian Gazette and Colonial Register*, 11 May 1839

p. 103 'add fuel to the politics': Keith Windschuttle: 'Black and White Perspectives on the Apology', from *The Fabrication of Aboriginal History*, Vol. 3, *The Stolen Generations* (2009): http://www.stolengenerations.info/index.php?option=com_content&view=article&id=70&Itemid=22

353

5. First In, Best Dressed

p. 107 a nineteenth-century map: http://handle.slv.vic.gov. au/10381/116740

p. 109 'great care [had to] be exercised': Charles Browning Hall, recalling his time travelling from the Monaro to Port Phillip in 1840, quoted T.F. Bride (ed.), *Letters from Victorian Pioneers* (1898), p. 210

p. 110 'Mr [George] Blaxland': Quoted Laurie Duggan, *The Ash Range* (1987), p. 37

p. 111 *I looked to the S.W.*: From the *Gippsland Times* account (republished 1866 – first published 'nearly four years ago')

p. 115 'as wild as hares': Thomas Alexander Brown, *Robbery Under Arms* (1882). Full text: http://www.gutenberg. net.au/ebooks/e00008.txt

p. 118 'calls in various directions': Henry Reynolds, *The Other Side of the Frontier: Aboriginal Resistance to the European Invasion of Australia* (2006), pp. 14–15

p. 121 It put him in mind: http://www.trove.nla.gov.au/ ndp/del/article/65362111

p. 122 'I may mention': Letter recalling settlement of that region, dated 30 August 1853 and quoted *Letters from Victorian Pioneers*, op. cit., p. 187

p. 125 'the worst Governor': *Sydney Morning Herald*, 1846, quoted *The Australian Dictionary of Biography*: http:// www.adb.anu.edu.au/biography/gipps-sir-george-2098

p. 128 painted the panoramic view: http://www.beta. worldcat.org/archivegrid/collection/data/ 220087393

p. 128 'If hospitality be a virtue': Richard Mackay, writing in 1916, *Recollections of Early Gippsland Goldfields*, quoted P.D. Gardner, *Our Founding Murdering Father: Angus McMillan and the Kurnai Tribe of Gippsland, 1839–1865* (1990), p. 57

p. 128 'Chairman and Gentlemen': Melbourne *Argus*, Tuesday, 11 March 1856, p. 4

Sources

p. 131 recited poetry: The example given was 'The Pioneers', from Frank Hudson, *The Song of the Manly Men and Other Verses* (1908)

p. 131 'Let Onward, Onward, be the cry': Unknown author, 'To the Discoverer of Gippsland', quoted Rev. George Cox, *Notes on Gippsland History*, Vol. 1, p. 75

6. Black War

p. 142 'convenient situations': 'Secret Instructions for Lieutenant James Cook Appointed to Command His Majesty's Bark the Endeavour', 30 July 1768, National Library of Australia

p. 144 'every such treaty': Proclamation of Governor Bourke, 10 October 1835

p. 145 'suffering severely': *Letters from Victorian Pioneers*, op. cit., p. 133

p. 147 The region was 'infested': Ibid., p. 199

p. 147 'pandemonium upon earth': Rev. W. Bean's correspondence (1848–9), republished in the *Gippsland Standard and Alberton Shire Representative*, Wednesday, 4 March 1914, edited by Rev. J. Cox

p. 147 'We have learned': Quoted P.D. Gardner, *Through Foreign Eyes: European Perceptions of the Kurnai Tribe of Gippsland* (1994), p. 24

p. 148 'most beautiful': *Letters from Victorian Pioneers*, op. cit., p. 238

p. 149 'in the night, his father': L. Fison and A. Howitt, *Kamilaroi and Kurnai* (1880), p. 247

p. 149 'They are beautifully preserved': James Warman during the 'white woman' expedition, quoted Julie E. Carr, *The Captive White Woman of Gipps Land: In Pursuit of the Legend* (2001), p. 127

p. 154 'There was a desperate fight': P.J.C. Wallace writing in the *Gippsland Times*, 6 December 1923

p. 155 'It was scarcely to be': Quoted *Letters from Victorian Pioneers*, op. cit., pp. 177–8

355

p. 157 'Walked out ... to scrub': Diary entry, 1844, quoted *Through Foreign Eyes*, op. cit., p. 15

p. 159 'A.M. – rain[,] P.M. – fine': 27 January 1845, quoted ibid., p. 31

p. 159 'These things are kept': Letter dated 30 April 1846, quoted A. Dirk Moses (ed.), *Genocide and Settler Society: Frontier Violence and Stolen Aboriginal Children in Australian History* (2004), p. 202

p. 160 'most awful statement of doings': Quoted *Through Foreign Eyes*, op. cit., p. 51

p. 161 'GIPPSLAND: NUMBER OF ABORIGINES': *Letters from Victorian Pioneers*, op. cit., p. 79

p. 162 'melancholy anthropological footnote': Quoted Dr Mark McKenna, 'Different Perspectives on Black Armband History', Parliament of Australia (1997): http://www.aph.gov.au/About_Parliament/ Parliamentary_Departments/Parliamentary_Library/ pubs/rp/RP9798/98RP05

p. 162 'The charge of "political correctness"': Peter Gardner, 'Frontier Violence, Political Correctness and Memorials: Brief Comments on Henry Reynolds and Bill Bryson', http://petergardner.info/wp-content/ uploads/2012/11/Frontier-Violence-Political- Correctness-and-Memorials.pdf (2004)

p. 163 'so much garbage': From Gardner's collected notes: http://www.petergardner.info/wp-content/uploads/ 2012/11/Notes-on-Massacres-rev.ed_.pdf (2000–15)

p. 165 'Warrigal Creek: range 60–150': Ibid.

p. 166 'a fanatic': *Our Founding Murdering Father*, op. cit., p. 55

p. 171 'shot plenty of blacks': 'Bushman', quoted ibid., p. 38

7. The White Woman

p. 174 'The clue to the foregoing mystery': *Port Phillip Patriot*, 18 July 1841

p. 183 'Yallourn people bought': Peter Read, *Returning to Nothing: The Meaning of Lost Places* (1996), p. 99

Sources

p. 187 'Will *no one* come forward': *Port Phillip Herald*, 12 May 1846, quoted *The Captive White Woman of Gipps Land*, op. cit., p. 66

p. 188 'compelled to yield': Quoted Kate Darian Smith, 'Capturing the white woman of Gippsland: a frontier myth', Captured Lives: Australian Captivity Narratives: http://www.kcl.ac.uk/artshums/ahri/centres/menzies/research/Publications/Workingpapers/WP85-87Darian-Smithetal.pdf, p. 30

p. 189 'Unhappiest of the fairer kind': 'Homo' in the Melbourne *Argus*, quoted *Caledonia Australis*, op. cit., p. 203

p. 190 40 per cent nationally: Milton James Lewis, *The People's Health: Public Health in Australia, 1788–1950* (2003), p. 26

p. 192 'wandering about the bush': 'An Englishman', writing in the *Sydney Herald*, 10 September 1846, quoted *The Captive White Woman of Gipps Land*, op. cit., p. 95

p. 192 'a slave of savage lust': *Port Phillip Herald*, 1 October 1846, quoted *Our Founding Murdering Father*, op. cit., p. 47

p. 192 'total absence of women': Quoted *The Captive White Woman of Gipps Land*, op. cit., p. 26

p. 192 'well bro' up': John Pettit, quoted *Caledonia Australis*, op. cit., p. 204

p. 193 'like smoke': Ibid., p. 203

p. 195 'denounced in forcible terms': *The Captive White Woman of Gipps Land*, op. cit., p. 87

p. 196 'If Mr. La Trobe': 'Humanitas', writing in the *Port Phillip Herald*, 10 March 1846

p. 198 piles of black bodies: From sworn affidavits by de Villiers and Warman, 1847: http://www.prov.vic.gov.au/online-exhibitions/nativepolice/documents/00019_u094_47-1348_034.html

p. 198 'wanton barbarity': From a letter published in the *Port Phillip Patriot*, 22 January 1847. Emphasis in the original

Sources

p. 198 'have acted with a great want': Letter from clerk
William Elyard Jr on behalf of the Colonial Secretary,
5 March 1847 ('I am directed by the governor to
inform you ...')

p. 199 'tall, with a considerable stoop': De Villiers party
dispatches, quoted *The Captive White Woman of Gipps
Land*, op. cit., pp. 120–2

p. 199 'shouted with delight': H.B. Morris, quoted ibid.,
p. 119

p. 200 'As a proof': *Port Phillip Herald*, 18 February 1847

p. 200 'FORCE MUST BE USED': *Port Phillip Patriot*, 22
February 1847

p. 201 'upbraided him': Donald Mcleod, quoted *The Captive
White Woman of Gipps Land*, op. cit., p. 168

p. 202 'Of grief': Report on the death of Bungelene's son
Thomas, *Ballarat Star*, 14 January 1865, p. 2

p. 204 'The young Kũrnai man': Alfred Howitt, *The Native
Tribes of South East Asia* (1996), p. 273

8. Slaughterhouse Gully

p. 211 '"Some settlers gladly hailed"': L. Edgar, 1865, quoted
P.D. Gardner, *Gippsland Massacres: The Destruction of
the Kurnai Tribes 1800–1860* (1993), p. 98

p. 212 'The blacks who were living': Buchan resident Mr J.
Armstrong, recorded 1977 by P.D. Gardner, ibid.,
p. 80

p. 214 '"No bones have been found"': E. Whittaker, 1977,
quoted ibid., pp. 80–1

p. 214 '"The avenging party"': A. Macrae, 1966, quoted
ibid., p. 39

p. 217 'Here the offending tribe': C.H. Grove, quoted ibid.,
p. 82

p. 221 'unsurveyed country': Details from Map of Australia
Felix, 1847, compiled and engraved by Thomas
Ham

p. 221 'eyes like live coals': *Arrow*, Friday, 19 December
1924, p. 16

Sources

p. 222 'Their whole art of war': Quoted *The Other Side of the Frontier*, op. cit., p. 100

p. 226 'precipitous and broken country': Tyers writing in 1844, included in *Letters from Victorian Pioneers*, op. cit., p. 194

p. 237 'Nothing meets the eye': James Atkinson, *An Account of the State of Agriculture and Grazing in New South Wales* (1826), pp. 6–7

p. 238 'No sooner was all fear': *Letters from Victorian Pioneers*, op. cit., p. 153

9. In Search of Elders

p. 240 'four or five': *The Native Tribes of South East Asia*, op. cit., p. 78

p. 244 'I see by the Gazette': *Sydney Gazette*, 22 May 1841. Letter signed F.J. Sloman, quoted *The Captive White Woman of Gipps Land*, op. cit., p. 32

p. 246 'his station at Bushy Park': *Gippsland Guardian*, 16 September 1859, p. 3

p. 246 'I tell them': *Our Founding Murdering Father*, op. cit., p. 55

p. 248 'reading, writing, singing': *Through Foreign Eyes*, op. cit., p. 62

p. 250 'Wa! Wa! Wa!': Gunai lullaby, from A. Howitt, *Notes on Songs and Songmakers of Some Australian Tribes* (1887)

p. 250 'the most frequent': *Through Foreign Eyes*, op. cit.

p. 250 31 per cent: Ibid., pp. 65–6

p. 251 'one of the most articulate': Michael Banton, quoted http://www.core.ac.uk/download/pdf/9654087.pdf

p. 251 'the civilised races of man': Charles Darwin, *The Descent of Man* (1871), Vol. I, Chapter VI: 'On the Affinities and Genealogy of Man', pp. 200–1

p. 255 'When I see the word': Quoted *Genocide and Settler Society*, op. cit., p. 19

p. 256 'genocide is not a synonym': Ibid., p. 23

p. 256 'genocidal moments': Ibid., pp. 35–6

Sources

p. 257 'I have asked the Blacks': Letter to the Crown
Commissioner of Gippsland, dated 24 July 1846:
http://www.prov.vic.gov.au/online-exhibitions/
nativepolice/documents/00019_u092_47-907_027.
html

p. 260 'I have protested': Melbourne *Argus*, Saturday,
5 December 1868, p. 6

p. 261 'When we came here': Donald MacDonald, *Gum
Boughs and Wattle Bloom* (1887), quoted R. Evans, K.
Saunders and K. Cronin, *Exclusion, Exploitation and
Extermination: Race Relations in Colonial Queensland*
(2002), p. 65

p. 263 'I must say': Quoted *Through Foreign Eyes*, op. cit.,
pp. 75–6

p. 265 'Notwithstanding the opportunities': 15 January 1853:
http://www.parliament.vic.gov.au/papers/govpub/
VPARL1853-54NoC33.pdf

p. 266 'The apathy which': *Glasgow Herald*, 9 June 1845,
quoted 'Contempt, Sympathy and Romance: Lowland
perceptions of the Highlands and the clearances during
the Famine Years, 1845–1855': http://www.theses.
gla.ac.uk/842/1/1996fenyophd.pdf, p. 70

p. 267 'It is not more notorious': *Fifeshire Journal*, 23
September 1847, quoted ibid., pp. 111–12

p. 268 'Morally and intellectually': James Bruce in 1846,
quoted http://www.theses.gla.ac.uk/842/1/
1996fenyophd.pdf

p. 268 'mild nature': A. MacKenzie (ed.), *History of the
Highland Clearances* (2015), p. 21

p. 269 'squalid, isolated': Save Lake Tyers Committee
campaign leaflet (1965), quoted in 'A 1960s Campaign
to Save an Aboriginal Reserve: Lake Tyers in Victoria,
Australia', by Azita Shamsolahi, University of Bristol

p. 269 'Read this and see': Melbourne *Mercury*, 28 March
1957, p. 4

p. 275 Of more than 11,000 respondents: Poll published
online in 2013; these figures correct as of November

360

2014: http://www.smh.com.au/national/are-you-a-casual-racist-20130530-2ndyy.html#poll

p. 276 A 2012 survey: A VicHealth, Lowitja Institute, University of Melbourne and beyondblue survey, published at Congress Lowitja 2012, Melbourne: http://www.vichealth.vic.gov.au/Media-Centre/Media-Releases-by-Topic/Discrimination/Vast-majority-of-Aboriginal-Victorians-are-targets-of-racism-shows-new-survey.aspx

10. Reconciliation

p. 282 'With our hands': Mr Thomas, head teacher of Woodside School, to the *Gippsland Standard*, 9 October 1912, quoted *Gippsland Massacres*, op. cit., p. 58

p. 283 Albert was born in 1933: Doris Paton, 'A Journey with Woolum Bellum Koorie Open Door Education School. Its Life Cycle in Meeting the Educational Needs of Aboriginal Children', PhD thesis, RMIT university, pp. 15–16: https://www.researchbank.rmit.edu.au/view/rmit:6769/Paton.pdf

p. 286 'They ran us down like shit': Interview with Bobby Nicholls of Yarnin Pictures: https://www.vimeo.com/101897953

p. 288 Uncle Albert Mullett spearheaded: Mullett on behalf of the Gunai/Kurnai People vs. State of Victoria (2010)

p. 296 'The imperative to insulate': A. Dirk Moses, *German Intellectuals and the Nazi Past* (2007), p. 28

p. 299 'painful melancholia': *Maffra Spectator*, 31 January 1884, p. 3

p. 299 'burnt beyond recognition': *Gippsland Times*, 16 December 1926, p. 1

p. 299 'did not inherit': *Gippsland Times*, 20 January 1936, p. 1

Sources

11. Iguana Creek

p. 308 'Whatever feelings may have': *Gippsland Guardian*,
2 November 1860

p. 309 'These, Sir, are the salient points': *Letters from Victorian Pioneers*, op. cit., p. 188

p. 309 'The early squatters': Ibid., p. 185

p. 310 'was at his best': Letter from Norman Macalister,
dated 1982, held in Maffra Library

p. 310 'did not enjoy': *Our Founding Murdering Father*, op.
cit., p. 77

p. 313 'the redoubtable explorer': The *Mountaineer*, 24 May
1865, quoted *Caledonia Australis*, op. cit., p. 242

p. 321 'No mention of what was to happen': Hal Porter,
Bairnsdale (1977), p .61

p. 334 *'a few houses': The Ash Range*, op. cit., p. 115

p. 335 'I resolve hereafter': '*Minerva* journal', Monday, 13
November 1837

Epilogue

p. 341 'The entertainment given': Melbourne *Argus*, Tuesday,
11 March 1856 (cut for length and clarity)

Illustration Credits

State Library of Victoria: pp. ii, iii, 120, 129, 143, 156, 195, 197, 210, 245, 247, 262, 309, 314, 324 and 331

National Library of Australia: p. 17

© the author: pp. 90, 243 and 329

© Cameron James Cope: pp. 186, 233 and 279

© Steaphan Paton and Cameron James Cope: p. 206 (*gwin mooga (shame/someone's coming)*, 2015, photographic print from the series *Wallung Githa Unsettled*)

The author and publishers are committed to respecting the intellectual property rights of others and have made all reasonable efforts to trace the copyright owners of the images reproduced, and to provide appropriate acknowledgement within this book. In the event that any untraceable copyright owners come forward after the publication of this book, the author and publishers will use all reasonable endeavours to rectify the position accordingly.

Acknowledgements

I would like to express my sincere gratitude to a number of people who very generously assisted, advised and hosted me during the production of this book.

I am deeply indebted to Jeannie and Ian Haughton, Cameron Cope, Steaphan Paton, Ricky Mullett and Elizabeth Balderstone, who – as well as devoting hours to explaining Australian culture and discussing the modern-day legacy of settlement – fed me and put me up in their homes (and tents!). The historians Peter Gardner and Don Watson were both generous with their time and expertise, and our conversations directed my research in interesting directions. The same goes for Rachel Mullett, Doris Paton, Barry Kenny, Russell Mullett, Leonie Cameron, Peter Ryan, Kath and Mike Coggan, Ella and Jenny Jamieson, Ros Winspear at RANZCOG and the Maffra Historical Society: thank you.

Back in the UK, my agent Sophie Lambert of Conville & Walsh has been an endless source of ideas, encouragement and advice, and I owe her a great deal. Likewise, so many thanks to my brilliant editor Arabella Pike and others at William Collins: Stephen Guise, Robert Lacey, Joseph Zigmond, Katherine Patrick, as well as Catherine Milne of

HarperCollins Australia. Dr Naomi Parry, who saw the text in its later stages, also made many helpful observations.

I received financial awards from Creative Scotland and Arts Trust Scotland, without which I would not have been able to make the initial trip to Australia that enabled me to write a book proposal in the first place. The importance of support from such bodies in the development of a young writer cannot be overstated.

Thanks should go too to Alex Christofi and Charles Cumming, both of whom shared their experience and contacts at a crucial stage; Samira Shackle and Louise Gray, who provided insightful feedback and share daily with me the highs and lows of freelance life; my uncle Myles Macmillan and his wife Boo; Anna Blundy and Hope Mortimer, at whose beautiful home in Tuscany I wrote a good chunk of the first draft. Alex Kendall: apologies for taking your name in vain.

Most of all: to my parents, Fiona and Derek Flyn, and brothers, Rory and Martyn. Thank you for everything. And to Richard West, who makes me very happy.

Mediator

GRAVE DOUBTS & HEAVEN SENT

Meg Cabot is the author of the phenomenally successful The Princess Diaries series. With vast numbers of copies sold around the world, the books have topped the US and UK bestseller lists for weeks and won several awards. Two movies based on the series have been massively popular throughout the world.

Meg is also the author of the bestselling Airhead trilogy, *All American Girl*, *All American Girl: Ready or Not*, *How to Be Popular*, *Jinx*, *Teen Idol*, *Avalon High*, *Tommy Sullivan Is a Freak*, The Mediator series and the Allie Finkle series as well as many other books for teenagers and adults. She and her husband divide their time between New York and Florida.

Visit Meg Cabot's website at
www.megcabot.co.uk

Books by Meg Cabot

The Princess Diaries series

The Mediator series

The Airhead trilogy

All American Girl
All American Girl: Ready or Not

Avalon High
Avalon High manga: The Merlin Prophecy
Teen Idol
How to Be Popular
Jinx
Tommy Sullivan Is a Freak
Nicola and the Viscount
Victoria and the Rogue

For younger readers
The Allie Finkle series

For older readers
The Guy Next Door
Boy Meets Girl
Every Boy's Got One
Queen of Babble series
The Heather Wells series

Also available in audio

2 GHOSTLY *Mediator* BOOKS IN 1

Grave Doubts & Heaven Sent

Meg Cabot

MACMILLAN

Grave Doubts first published in the USA 2003 as *Haunted* by HarperCollins*Publishers*.
First published in the UK 2005 by Macmillan Children's Books

Heaven Sent first published in the USA 2005 as *Twilight* by
HarperCollins Children's Books, an imprint of HarperCollins*Publishers*.
First published in the UK 2006 by Macmillan Children's Books

This edition published 2010 by Macmillan Children's Books
a division of Macmillan Publishers Limited
20 New Wharf Road, London N1 9RR
Basingstoke and Oxford
Associated companies throughout the world
www.panmacmillan.com

ISBN 978-0-330-51952-6

1 3 5 7 9 8 6 4 2

A CIP catalogue record for this book is available from
the British Library.

Typeset by Intype Libra Ltd
Printed and bound in the UK by CPI Mackays, Chatham ME5 8TD

Mediator

GRAVE DOUBTS

For Benjamin

Many thanks to Jennifer Brown,
Laura Langlie, Abigail McAden
and Ingrid van der Leeden

Fog. That's all I can see. Just fog – the kind that pours in from the bay every morning, seeping over my bedroom window sills and spilling on to the floor in cold ropy tendrils . . .

Only here there are no windows, or even a floor. I am in a corridor lined with doors. There is no ceiling overhead, just coldly winking stars in an inky-black sky. The long hall made up of closed doors seems to stretch out forever in all directions.

And now I'm running. I'm running down the corridor, the fog seeming to cling to my legs as I go, the closed doors on either side of me a blur. There's no point, I know, in opening any of these doors. There's nothing behind them that can help me. I've got to get out of this hallway – only I can't, because it just keeps getting longer and longer, stretching out into the darkness, still blanketed in that thick white fog . . .

And then suddenly, I'm not alone in that fog. Jesse is there with me, holding my hand. I don't know if it's the warmth of his fingers or the kindness of his smile that banishes my fear, but suddenly I am convinced that everything is going to be all right.

At least, until it becomes clear that Jesse doesn't know the way out any more than I do. And now even the fact that my hand is in his can't squelch the feeling of panic bubbling up inside of me.

But wait. Someone is coming towards us – a tall figure striding through the fog. My frantically beating heart – the only sound I can hear in this dead place, with the exception of my own breathing – slows somewhat. Help. Help at last.

Except that when the fog parts, and I recognize the face of the person ahead of us, my heart starts pounding more loudly than ever. Because I know he won't help us. I know he won't do a thing.

Except laugh.

And then I'm alone again, only this time the floor beneath me has dropped away. The doors disappear, and I am teetering on the brink of a chasm so deep I cannot see the ground below. The fog swirls around me, spilling into the chasm and seeming intent on

1

taking me with it. I am waving my arms to keep from falling, grabbing frantically for something, anything, to hold on to.

Only there's nothing to grab.

A second later, an unseen hand gives a single push.

And I fall.

One

It was the first day of school after summer vacation, and everybody was pretty unhappy about it.

Everybody except me, that is.

Yeah, that's right. Me. The girl who, at her old school back in Brooklyn, was voted Most Likely to Dismember Someone. Me, Susannah Simon. *I* was happy to be back in school.

I know. It was freaking me out, too.

But the truth was, being at school beat being at home. Because while I'd never exactly been what you'd call popular at school, at home certain people were treating me like I had the plague. And I am not referring to my three step-brothers, either.

It was tough going, though, the whole back-to-school thing. Even I, happy to be anywhere but home, had to admit that. It wasn't eight in the morning yet and we were all standing around outside the Junipero Serra Mission in a thick September fog. It is sunny and pleasant almost every afternoon in the part of northern California my mom had dragged me to last year, but the mornings usually start out misty, thanks to the fog that rolls in every night from the Carmel Bay.

So there we were, all nine hundred of us, shivering in the

3

fog, waiting for morning assembly to begin so we could go inside our warm classrooms and start a whole new school year . . . another nine months of being taught things that would, I knew, have little or no use beyond the three-foot-thick walls of the seventeenth-century mission we were standing in front of. I mean, seriously, was it really going to be necessary for us to know how to diagram a sentence, or name all fifty states in alphabetical order, out in the real world?

No, there really wasn't anything to be happy about so early on such a grey, misty morning. Nothing at all.

And yet I couldn't really work up any kind of righteous indignation about the whole thing.

And I sort of had to, because my best friend CeeCee was telling me a story about her aunt that involved a lot of, you know, pathos.

'So she goes, "How dare you suggest that my niece can't parallel park?"' CeeCee, who resembled her aunt a lot more closely than she was willing to admit, did an imitation of her that involved a lot of hair-tossing and dramatic arm movement. As her aunt Pru was a professional medium, this was not entirely unwarranted. '"Don't you know that in a past life, my niece was Cleopatra?"'

'How come in people's past lives,' my other best friend, Adam, wanted to know, 'they were always somebody famous? I mean, how come nobody was ever a serf, or something?'

'Adam,' CeeCee said, letting her arms drop to her sides, 'you are completely missing the point.'

'No, I'm not,' he said. 'And the fact that you used to be Cleopatra in a past life doesn't exactly say much for your parking skills. I mean, Cleopatra didn't know how to drive.'

'The *point*,' CeeCee said, emphatically, 'is that now, thanks

4

to Aunt Pru doing her usual nutcase routine, I have no chance whatsoever of getting my licence for another six weeks.'

'Thanks to Aunt Pru's inherent wackiness,' Adam asked, 'or your inability to parallel park?'

CeeCee shook her head at him slowly, her long, white-blonde hair skimming her shoulders.

'You don't get it,' she said. 'Well, how could you? You come from a *normal* family. You have no idea what it's like to be constantly humiliated in public by your own relatives. Tell him, Suze. Tell him what it's like. Suze?'

I wasn't really listening, though. I mean, I'd heard CeeCee and all, but her words hadn't registered. Instead, I'd just stood there looking at them, CeeCee Webb and Adam MacTavish, my two best – and pretty much only – friends; the first people to express any sort of kindness towards me when, the year before, I'd joined the tenth grade at the Junipero Serra Mission Academy mid-semester. I'd heard a lot of things about California before moving out here with my mom, who'd decided to marry the star of a cable chan-nel's home improvement show and bring me three thousand miles from everything I had ever known or loved. Most of what I'd heard about California proved to be at least semi-erroneous. Like that there were no palm trees north of Los Angeles, and that it never rained . . . and that all the people who lived there were vacuous, self-centered, plastic-surgery addicts.

Nothing, it turned out, could have been further from the truth. Adam and CeeCee were two of the least self-absorbed people I had ever met. And vacuous? Hardly. They both got way better grades than I did.

And yeah, they were probably the least two popular people in our grade, despite the fact that CeeCee was editor

5

of the school paper, and Adam was the class clown. And yeah, whenever they got together – which was often – bickering ensued, on account of CeeCee carrying around a secret torch for Adam, and Adam being probably the only person in Carmel not aware of it.

But it was friendly bickering. I liked it. It was comforting.

And lately, I'd needed comforting. Which was strange, since for the first time in a long while, nobody, human or otherwise, was trying to kill me or any of my friends or family members. No supernatural forces were attempting to rip me from this dimension and fling me into another. No irate members of the undead were seeking to wreak justice by making me one of their own. All was quiet on both the spiritual as well as the material planes . . . which is something, you know, for someone in my line of work.

I should, of course, have taken this as a possible sign that all was not as it should be. You know what they say about things being quietest before a storm.

But can you blame me for being optimistic? I mean, for once in my life, things were actually going good for a change. I'd just turned sixteen, I was starting the eleventh grade, and hey – I was in love.

There was only one problem. The guy I was in love with? Yeah, he didn't appear to return the feeling.

'Suze?'

It was only after she'd said my name for what had to have been the fifth time that I finally noticed. Both CeeCee and Adam were staring at me uncomfortably.

'Suze,' Adam said, carefully. 'Are you all right?'

'Of course I'm all right,' I said, shaking myself. 'Don't I look all right?'

'Not really,' CeeCee said. 'I mean, you actually look kind of . . . weird.'

6

I looked down at myself. I had dressed with particular care since it was the first day back and I knew that Kelly Prescott and her cronies would have on all the Prada they had scored on their summer vacations in Europe. Not that I could compete with Prada, of course, on my babysitting budget – not since a big chunk of what I'd earned over the summer had gone to buy a headstone for my boyfriend.

Which was, you know, yet another not particularly bright spot in my little universe: the fact that Jesse, the guy I loved, was . . . well, technically speaking, anyway . . . dead.

But was I bumming? No. Because when you are in love – even if that love isn't returned and the object of your ardour happens to be a ghost – you don't quibble over things like whether or not the guy has a heartbeat.

And as for the clothes thing, with careful selections at one of the many outlet malls in Monterey, even on my limited budget I had come up with a new fall wardrobe that I had thought passable, at least.

Judging by Adam and CeeCee's expressions, however, I'd been wrong.

'What?' I said, fingering my black capris and pale blue sweater set. I knew the sweater set, something my mother had helped pick out, was a bit much, but I had wanted to make her happy. That's the thing about feeling the way I'd felt lately: I kept finding myself wanting to make other people happy, on account of the whole being in love thing, and ended up doing things I would never, in a million years, have done before in my pre-in-love-with-a-ghost state. Like buy pale blue sweater sets.

'It's too Renée Zellweger, isn't it?' I asked, worriedly.

'Not your clothes,' CeeCee said. '*You*. You're acting all . . . I don't know.'

'Creepy,' Adam suggested.

7

'Yeah,' CeeCee said. 'Creepy. Almost like you're happy to be back in school.'

Oh, what was the use? Why was I even trying to fight it?

'Look,' I said. 'I can't help it. I *am* happy to be back in school.'

CeeCee and Adam exchanged worried glances.

'Suze, why?' CeeCee wanted to know. 'What on earth do you have to be *happy* about? We still have two years of high school left. Two years of incarceration with a bunch of synaptically challenged individuals who actually care about – and have opinions on – lipgloss and organized sports. You can't seriously expect us to believe you've accepted this.'

'I can't help it,' I said again. 'I'm just happy to be back, OK?' To tell the strict truth, I was pretty happy to be *alive*, having had a particularly close shave with the Grim Reaper just a month earlier. Hey, you'd be happy to be starting eleventh grade, too, if the alternative was an urn. 'Can we please move on to another subject?'

CeeCee and Adam continued to stare at me, however.

'Maybe,' Adam offered, after a moment's silence, 'it's that Jake's gone off to college.'

CeeCee snorted. 'Jake hasn't gone anywhere. Has he, Suze? The only place he made it into was a junior college over in Pacific Grove. Am I right?'

'That's not true,' I said, finding myself in the odd position of defending my eldest stepbrother, Sleepy – known as Jake to the rest of the world. 'He made it into one of those tech schools in the Valley. It's just that his dad won't pay for him to go anywhere that isn't fully accredited.'

CeeCee rolled her violet eyes. 'Whatever. He's not even moving out. So it can't be that.'

Since I did not want CeeCee and Adam – even though they were my best friends on the West Coast . . . on any

8

coast, really, with the exception of Gina, back in Brooklyn – examining too closely the reasons I was so glad to be away from home, I started to say something about how I was just filled with eager anticipation for all the opportunities afforded by a new school year . . .

'That's it,' CeeCee said, when I was through. 'I'm drinking bottled water from now on because there's obviously something in the local tap that is turning formerly normal, clear-thinking individuals into gibbering idiots.'

'Speaking of which,' Adam muttered as Kelly Prescott, resplendent in beige suede, despite the fog, came bearing down upon us.

'Suze.' Kelly, though she had to have been bummed about what the mist was doing to all that suede, greeted us calmly. 'CeeCee. Adam.'

'Hi, Kel,' Adam said, with obviously forced enthusiasm. 'Have a nice summer? Didn't see you much around the country club.'

Kelly eyed him as if he were a caterpillar that had landed in her cobb salad. 'Yes,' she said. 'Well, we spent most of the summer in Majorca.'

'Oh, yeah?' Adam looked interested. 'I heard they've got lots of civil unrest down there. What were you on, some kind of peace-keeping mission?'

Kelly's look of disapproval deepened. 'Majorca is a resort island off the coast of Spain, you freak.'

'Oh.' Adam shrugged. 'I was wondering. You've never really struck me as the humanitarian type.'

'Yeah,' CeeCee said. 'How many sheep had to die to make that outfit you've got on, anyway?'

Kelly pointedly ignored what she tends to refer to as my 'little friends' and said to me, 'Listen, Suze, I just thought I'd let you know, in case you hadn't already heard, I'll be

9

supporting someone else as candidate for class vice-president in this year's election.'

I shrugged. Even if I had been capable of caring about anything besides Jesse, the information Kelly was imparting would not have ruffled me.

'Fine,' I said.

'I want you to know it's nothing personal,' Kelly said. 'I mean, except for the company you keep . . .' Her gaze slid towards Adam and CeeCee. '. . . I think we made a good team last year. I believe it's time for our class to move in a new direction, however, and I've found someone who will run with me as vice-president whose values are, shall we say, more reflective of my own.'

'Great,' I said. 'Go for it.'

Kelly blinked heavily mascaraed eyes. 'Are you serious? You don't mind?'

'You could kick her in the head,' I heard CeeCee mutter, 'and she wouldn't mind.'

While this wasn't strictly true – I hoped – it more or less summed up how I felt about the matter. My tenure as class vice-president had been brief – I'd been elected to the position shortly after starting midyear at the Mission Academy – and though I had enjoyed it, I would not miss it. It had seemed strange to me, at the time, that a group of people who did not even know me would elect me to a position of such power.

That, of course, was before I got to know them and realized they all assumed that anyone who talked faster than they did was automatically smarter than they were.

'I'm so glad there aren't any hard feelings,' Kelly gushed. 'I have to admit, I really didn't think you'd be this reasonable about it. I mean, you do have a reputation, Suze, for being a bit of a—'

10

A blast from a whistle sounded, long and shrill.

'All right,' Sister Ernestine, who'd been assistant principal at the Junipero Serra Mission School longer than any of us had been alive, shouted from the raised dais to one side of the flagpole. 'Lines, people. Lines!'

I had been shocked my first day at the Mission Academy to learn that first thing every morning the student body was expected to fall into lines outside the school according to grade and sex. Really. Then we had to stand there – outside – for the Pledge of Allegiance, morning prayer and announcements. Only during a downpour were we allowed to skip assembly and head straight indoors to our first-period class.

'I know you are all excited to see one another after summer vacation,' Sister Ernestine announced through the school megaphone, 'but that is no excuse for this kind of disorganization. Get . . . into . . . your . . . lines!'

As the Mission Academy hosts grades K through twelve, there was always a lot of confusion down at the far end of the courtyard while the younger kids tried to fall into line. This usually meant that the upper grades had a few extra minutes to chat before being commanded to silence.

'Really,' Kelly said, as we wandered over to where the rest of the eleventh grade was standing. 'I want to thank you for being so understanding about this.'

'No problem,' I said.

Kelly peered more closely at my face. 'Wait a minute. You *are* OK about it, aren't you?'

'Sure, I am,' I said. 'Why?'

'I don't know,' Kelly said. 'You just . . . I don't know. You look kind of . . . funny.'

CeeCee said, in a bored voice, 'She's been looking like that since she got here today. She won't let the rest of us in on the joke.'

11

'There's no joke,' I said. Because there really, really wasn't.

'Yeah,' Kelly said. 'Whatever, Simon. So listen. How's Jake doing? It must be pretty quiet at your house with him gone.'

It always took me a minute to figure out who people were referring to when they said the name Jake.

'Uh,' I said. 'Not really. Sleepy – I mean, Jake – has always been pretty quiet.' Excessive nappers tend to be this way. 'And anyway, he hasn't gone anywhere. He'll be commuting to college from home.'

Kelly was shocked – pleasantly so, you could tell.

'Really? Commuting? So is he keeping his job? You know, at Peninsula Pizza?' I could practically see the wheels of her mind spinning. Kelly's crush on Sleepy had reached almost legendary proportions around our house. Sleepy, who thought of only two things, sleeping and surfing – oh, yeah, and saving enough money to buy his own Camarro – paid Kelly no more mind than if she'd been, well, his kid step-sister's mortal enemy. 'So if, like, I ordered a pie, he might still be the one to deliver it?'

'Stranger things have happened,' I said.

But the truth was, I wasn't even paying attention to the conversation any more. This was because I'd spotted Father Dominic over by the flagpole. Since he was just about the last person I wanted to get into a conversation with these days, I ducked behind a pack of sophomores and tried to look as if I hadn't seen him. Although I could easily hide the true reason I was so happy to be back in school from my friends, I wasn't so sure I could keep it from Father Dom. He knew me – and Jesse – too well, damn it.

'So who do you think Kelly is planning on nominating for junior class vice-president?' CeeCee asked, careful to lower her voice so Kelly wouldn't overhear.

12

'Who do you think?' Adam sounded bored. 'Her hunch-backed assistant, Igor.'

CeeCee glanced in 'Igor's' direction. 'No way,' she said. 'Debbie Mancuso is not assistant chief executive material. Even Kelly must be able to see that. Besides, Debbie's not popular enough to swing the geek vote.'

While my friends assessed the political climate of the junior class, I continued to avoid Father Dominic's eye. I did this by scanning the people around me. The same old faces from last year. Maybe everyone was a little tanner. Some people were a little thinner, some a little heavier, some a little blonder, some a little darker. But overall, little seemed to have changed over the course of the three-month break.

Until I saw the new guy.

I wasn't the only one whose gaze was drawn to the tall, broad-shouldered boy standing off to one side of the junior class. I'm sure I wasn't the only one who noticed that his white Oxford T showed off his tan to perfection, and that the sleeves were just short enough to reveal a set of biceps that my body-building-obsessed stepbrother Brad – other-wise known as Dopey – was sure to envy. I doubt I was the only one who observed that crystalline droplets of fog had collected in his thick dark curls, or that his long black eye-lashes only enhanced the piercing blueness of his irises.

I was definitely not the only one, however, who knew who he was. Because when CeeCee, who'd noticed him at around the same time I did, went, in tones of wonder, 'Who is *that*?' Kelly Prescott replied, unable to keep her own admiration for this godlike apparition from her quavering voice, 'That's who's going to be your new vice-president. He's new, I just met him. Isn't he *hot*? His name's Paul. Paul Slater.'

Only, of course, Kelly didn't have any idea just how hot Paul Slater was. Whereas I knew only too well. Paul Slater

13

was New-York-City-sidewalk-in-July hot. Molten lava hot. Fiery pits of hell hot.

Because that's where he'd come from. Hell.

And that, I knew, was where he was going to try to drag me the very first chance he got: into hell.

Suddenly, I didn't feel so happy to be back at school any more.

Two

'Hi, Suze.'

That's what Paul Slater said to me. Hi, Suze. Like the last time I'd seen him, he hadn't been trying to off my boyfriend. Or the guy who would be my boyfriend, anyway, if he had a lick of sense.

Something like that doesn't tend to foster a sense of real good feelings about someone. You know what I mean?

'Hi,' I said back to him, then turned around and started digging blindly through my backpack, as if looking for a compact mirror. Really, though, I just wanted to avoid that ice-blue gaze of his . . .

And not let on that the very sight of him had set my heart beating faster than a rabbit's with fear.

'You *know* him?' CeeCee seized my arm in a grip that hurt as she came up and whispered into my ear. 'How do you know him?'

'I babysat for his little brother this summer,' I said. 'You know, while I was working at the resort.' Not only was I not smiling any more, but I actually felt a little queasy. Well, staring into the face of the devil can do that to you.

Not, of course, that I believed in that kind of thing. Devils and angels and all of that. But evil? That I believe in. Because Paul Slater pretty much epitomized it.

15

'Did you two go out or something?' CeeCee glanced over at Paul. 'Why is he looking at you like that?'

I found my compact, and opened it up. 'Like what?' I asked, aiming the little mirror so that I could see Paul in it, standing a little behind me, grinning as if at a secret all his own. I hoped he couldn't see how badly my hands were shaking.

'Like . . . I don't know.' CeeCee sounded suspicious. 'Like he *likes* you, or something.'

'He doesn't like me,' I said, snapping the compact shut and slipping it back into my bag.

'I don't know, Suze,' CeeCee said. 'He's totally staring. Kelly and Debbie are talking to him, but you're the one he's looking at.'

'He doesn't like me,' I repeated, firmly. 'And believe me, the feeling is mutual. Better stop talking, Ernestine's looking this way.'

Sister Ernestine had, indeed, aimed her megaphone in the direction of the eleventh grade, and suddenly called, 'Kelly Prescott, we're all waiting on *you.*'

Kelly, instead of being embarrassed – like a normal person would have been – simpered her way back into line, clearly delighted to be the centre of the entire school's momentary attention.

When Kelly had melted into her place in line, Sister Ernestine placed her right hand over her copious bosom and began the pledge. I, along with the rest of the student body of the Junipero Serra Mission Academy, dully recited the words along with her. But I wasn't thinking about what I was saying.

Instead, I was wondering, with an uncomfortably racing heart – I could feel its frantic pounding beneath my fingertips – what was going on. What was Paul Slater – a guy I'd

16

thought I was well rid of when he'd gone back to Seattle with the rest of his family, when their vacation at the Pebble Beach Resort was through – doing here? If the Slaters had enjoyed their stay in Carmel so much that they'd decided to move here, why had I not seen Paul's little brother, Jack, in line over by the fifth graders? Was Paul here on his own? And if so, why?

And why, out of all the schools in Carmel – the public high school, or Robert Louis Stevenson, where the kids of all the most fabulously wealthy families in Carmel went, a category into which Paul and his family would surely fall – had he had to pick *mine* to enroll in?

Even as I was thinking this, Father Dominic took the megaphone from Sister Ernestine, and, the pledge and morning prayers being over, started in on the morning announcements and his welcome-back speech. Father D's deep, rich voice, in contrast to Sister Ernestine's thin, shrill one, was like a restorative to my badly jangled nerves. I suddenly found myself wishing I'd spilled everything to him a long time ago – everything about me and Jesse, I mean.

Except, of course, that he'd never understand. How could he? I mean, Father Dominic's a mediator, like me (and Paul): a liaison between this world and the next for the spirits of the dead. You can imagine my surprise when, as a new student last year, I'd realized there was someone on earth besides me who could see and speak to – and even feel – ghosts. Our job, Father D's and mine, is to help those restless spirits who haven't yet moved on to their final destination, for whatever reason, to hurry it up. It takes an open mind, and sometimes a tight fist, but we get the job done, Father D and I. The peninsula is about as ghost-free as you can get thanks to us, with maybe one notable exception.

For a long time, of course, I'd assumed we were the only

17

ones, me and Father Dominic. Then along had come the Slaters, a family with not one but two mediators in it: Paul as well as his little brother Jack. How many others of us there might be out there we have no way of knowing, but, as far as I'm concerned, there's already one too many mediators as it is.

Still, open-minded as Father Dominic might be about the paranormal, a liberal thinker on the topic of boy-girl relations Father Dom is not. How could he be? Yeah, he's a mediator, but he's also, let's face it, a sixty-something-year-old Catholic priest. How jazzed was he going to be when he found out I'd been playing tongue hockey with a guy who'd been dead for two hundred years, give or take a few decades? Yeah, not so much.

I mean, Father D had gotten way bent out of shape the first time he'd ever even heard that the house my mom and stepdad had bought and renovated in the Carmel Hills had, unbeknownst to them, come complete with its own ghost – the spirit of a handsome mid-nineteenth-century Spanish rancher who'd been murdered in the room he'd rented for a night, back when our home had been a boarding house for lonesome cowboys and schoolmasters and the like.

Was it my fault the room Jesse had been murdered in just happened to be my bedroom? And was it my fault that I was now forced, for the first time in my life, to live with a roommate who happened to be of the spectral – but hot – variety? Father D had been way unsupportive of the whole thing . . .

At least until he'd finally met Jesse, who had, on several occasions, saved my life – not to mention Father Dominic's. After that, Jesse seemed to sort of grow on him.

Though I wasn't sure how thrilled Father D would be about the recent shift my heretofore platonic relationship with Jesse had taken.

18

Not that he really had anything to worry about. Father D, I mean. My virginity was in no great peril. Unfortunately. Not because Jesse happens to be a ghost. I mean, for anybody else that might be a problem. But for a mediator, it's no biggie. Because while to the rest of the world ghosts are ephemeral beings lacking in substantive matter, to a mediator a ghost is as solid as you or me. Jesse and I could, if we wanted to – and believe me, I did want to – do the nasty.

The only problem is that when the last time your boyfriend went out for a night on the town it was in a horse and buggy, and the fiesta ended at nine or whatever because everybody had to get up early the next day to feed the chickens, the chances of any pre-marital action taking place are exactly nil. Jesse's an old-fashioned guy. *Very* old-fashioned. Like no sex before marriage old-fashioned.

In fact, we'd been living together – well, more or less – for more than eight months before he ever even kissed me. And if it hadn't been for Paul and some of his dirty tricks, I might still be wondering what Jesse thought of me. You know, whether he liked me as just a friend or what.

Happily, thanks to Paul, I'd found out it was the latter. Or at least, it had been, until I'd managed to blow it somehow.

Come to think of it, I guess I owed a lot to Paul Slater. If he hadn't tried to have Jesse exorcized into nonexistence – for reasons I still don't think I fully understand – and if I hadn't had to risk my life to save him, Jesse might never have tried to kiss me that morning in my bedroom, when I'd been standing there trying to convince him that the only reason I'd done it – risked my life for his – was out of a sense of fair play. Not because I was in love with him. No way.

Which, of course, could not have been further from the truth.

Something I think both of us found out, the minute his

19

lips met mine. You know, that I was pretty much warm for his form, however much I might have pretended otherwise. Because you don't stand there with your tongue in someone else's mouth, the way Jesse and I were doing, for like five whole minutes, if you're not at least semi-attracted to the person.

Of course, the fact that that first kiss had yet to be followed by any others, and that Jesse seemed to be pointedly avoiding me, sort of leads me to believe that perhaps my ardour is not, in fact, returned.

Which I used to consider the worse thing that had ever happened to me . . .

Until now. Because Paul's showing up here at my school? Yeah, that did not bode particularly well. Not for Jesse, and not for me. Because Paul . . . well, let's just say that for a mediator, Paul isn't all that tolerant of the undead.

'Traditionally,' Father D was saying into the megaphone, 'autumn is a time for endings. Ending of summer. Ending of warmth. Ending, in the case of flowers and leaves, of life.'

Whoa, Father D, I started thinking. Way to bum us all out on the first day back at school.

But Father Dominic wasn't finished.

'For students and teachers, however,' he went on, 'autumn is an exciting time of learning and experiencing new things. Autumn, for those of us in the academic field, isn't an ending at all, but a time for new beginnings – a new start. So I beg you, children, not to squander this gift autumn has brought you. Take advantage of the fact that it is a new year, a new chance for you to excel, to show everyone what you can do. Make a fresh new beginning, starting now, today. I don't think any of us will regret it. Run along now.'

We were dismissed. The younger kids were led off in neat rows towards their classrooms in the single-storeyed, four-

20

hundred-year-old adobe building. The rest of us milled around comparing class schedules – we'd received them in the mail the week before – trying to see if we shared classes with any of our friends.

Except for me, of course. I was beating a path towards the dais, trying to catch Father Dom before he got back to his office and was too busy with the administrative tasks of being principal to see me.

Because what I had to ask him was why on earth he had ever let Paul Slater – who had only too recently tried to kill me (well, OK, maybe not directly, but he certainly hadn't done too much to try to save me) – into this school.

Only I guess I wasn't quick enough. Not because Father Dom left the dais before I got there, but because someone took hold of my arm and prevented me from getting to him at all.

'Hey,' Paul said with an easy smile, when I whipped my head around to see who had dared lay a finger on me. I am pretty much known throughout the school as a person you don't mess with physically. One too many tiffs with Brad, who was in my same grade, had made that pretty clear to everyone.

Everyone except, of course, Paul Slater, who'd never seen me in an altercation with my stepbrother.

'That's it?' he said, looking hurt as I only stared up at him dumbly. I was dumb, I have to admit, with fear. But fortunately, Paul didn't seem to realize that. 'That's all I get? No hi? No how have you beens? No what brings you to the neighbourhood, Paul? I thought friends as close as we are deserve better treatment than that.'

I looked down at the tanned fingers wrapped around my arm. I couldn't believe this guy even had the gall to talk to me. The last time I'd seen him had not been on this plane of

21

existence but on the spectral one, where I'd been forced to go in order to find Jesse, whom Paul had helped banish there. Considering how unhelpful the guy had been in getting me back to earth, he had some nerve, making out like I should be glad to see him.

I didn't, however, want to cause a scene right there in the assembly yard. So I just said to him (very calmly, considering how hard my heart was slamming into my ribs), 'Let go of me.'

'Now, Suze,' he said – though he did, in fact, drop his hand from my arm. 'Don't tell me you're still mad about that whole thing with Jesse. I mean, the two of you got out of there all right, didn't you?'

'No thanks to you,' I said acidly, and started to move on.

His tanned fingers shot out again, however, and prevented my escape.

'Suze,' he said, with a smile. Smiling – and probably even scowling, too – Paul Slater looked like a Calvin Klein underwear model. I knew. I'd seen him in a swimsuit back at the resort where we'd met. 'Don't be that way. Can't we do like the good father suggested and make a new start?'

'No,' I said, and jerked my arm from his grasp. 'We can't. You'd better stay away from me, Paul.'

He seemed to find this deeply amusing. 'Or what?' he asked, with another one of those smiles that revealed all of his white, even teeth – a politician's smile, I realized.

'Or you'll regret it.'

'Oh,' he said, his eyes widening in mock terror. 'You'll sic your boyfriend on me?'

It wasn't something I'd have joked around about, if I were him. Jesse could – and probably would, if he found out the guy was back – kill him.

And it wasn't like he could ever be prosecuted for it

22

because, to everyone but us mediators, Jesse was basically invisible.

Paul must have ascertained this from my expression, since he laughed and said, 'So that's how it is. Not one of Jesse's favourite people now, am I? What, the guy can't take a joke?'

Except there really hadn't been anything so funny about what Paul had done.

Only I didn't get to say so because right then Kelly came up to us, looking irritated but trying to hide it.

'You two already know each other?' she asked in a friendly way – though there was an undeniable edge to her voice.

'We've met,' I said, without enthusiasm.

Paul's reply was more effusive.

'Suze and I had a thing this past summer,' he told Kelly, whose eyes widened at the information.

'A thing?' she echoed. I could see the wheels in her mind spinning. It would take about nine minutes, I estimated, for it to get all over school that the new guy and I were an item.

'What *thing*?' I demanded, whirling on Paul. 'There was no *thing*. Unless you mean the *thing* where I hate your guts.'

Kelly's eyes got even wider. Only now they were filled with delight. 'Oh, so you guys broke up?'

'No, we didn't break up,' Paul said, with infuriating non-chalance.

'Because we were never going out,' I practically shouted. I realized I was attracting the attention of most of the eleventh grade, including my friends. CeeCee and Adam, over by the drinking fountain, were staring at me perplexedly. After all, I'd never mentioned Paul to them. How could I? They knew nothing about my being a mediator. And since that was, in essence, how I'd gotten to know Paul . . .

'I think,' I heard CeeCee say, though I'm pretty sure she

23

hadn't intended for me to overhear her, 'I know now why Suze looks so funny.'

Because you think I'm going out with *him*? I wanted to shriek. No freaking way!

Only I didn't get a chance, because as I drew in a breath to do just that, I was interrupted by a stern, 'Miss Simon! Miss Prescott! Miss Webb! Haven't you ladies got a class you should be getting to?'

Sister Ernestine – whose three-month absence from my life had not rendered her any less intimidating, with her enormous front chest and the even bigger crucifix adorning it – came barrelling down upon us, the wide black sleeves of her habit trailing behind her like wings.

'Get going,' she tut-tutted us, waving her hands in the direction of our lockers, built into the adobe walls all along the mission's beautifully manicured inner courtyard. 'You'll miss the first bell. Do you want to be late on the very first day of school?'

I couldn't, of course, reply the way I wanted to . . . that if it had been up to me, knowing what I knew now, I'd have been *absent* on the very first day of school. If I had known what I was going to find when I got here, that is.

24

Three

'How could this have happened?' I asked Father Dom, for what had to have been the thirtieth time that hour.

'Susannah, you've got to believe me.' Father Dominic sat behind his enormous mahogany desk, looking miserable. He blamed himself, of course. And if you asked me, he was right to. I mean, he's principal of the stupid school. How could he not have known that the guy who'd tried to kill me last summer had been admitted and enrolled?

'I've been so busy,' Father Dom went on, 'with preparations for the new school year – not to mention the Father Serra festival – I never glanced at the admission rosters. I am so, so sorry.'

I made an unladylike sound. He was sorry. *He* was sorry? What about *me*? *He* wasn't the one who had to be in the same classes with the guy. Two classes, as a matter of fact – homeroom and US history. Two whole hours a day I was going to have to sit there and look at the guy who'd tried to exorcize my boyfriend and more or less kill me. And that wasn't even counting morning assembly and lunch. That was another hour, right there!

'Although I don't honestly know what I could have done,' Father Dom said, riffling through Paul's file, 'to prevent his being admitted. His test scores, grades, teacher evaluations . . .

25

everything is exemplary. I am sorry to say that on paper, Susannah, the Slater boy comes off as a far better student than you did when you first applied to this school.'

'You can't tell anything,' I pointed out, 'about a person's moral fibre from a bunch of test scores.'

'No,' Father Dominic said tiredly, removing his glasses and cleaning them on the hem of his long black robe. There were, I noticed, purple shadows beneath his eyes. A hottie even though a senior citizen, Father Dom could still turn heads – though generally only when he was dressed in civilian clothes. It was a brave woman who would ogle a man in a priest's collar – at least in public. Still, if there'd been a bathing suit calendar for Roman Catholic hotties in the service of the Lord, Father D would have been in it for true. Against his will, of course.

'No, you cannot,' he said with a deep sigh, placing his wire rims back where they belonged, over the bridge of his perfectly aquiline nose. 'Susannah, are you really so certain this boy's motives are less than noble? Isn't it possible that perhaps he, like his younger brother, was duped by Jesse's former girlfriend, Maria de Silva, and her husband into exorcizing Jesse, and trying to kill you?'

I made a derisive noise. I hated remembering Maria de Silva and how she had treated Jesse. 'I'm going to let that one slide, Father D,' I said, 'considering the conk you got on the head at the time. Maybe you don't remember things as well as I do. But no, there is no chance Paul Slater was being duped. If anything, the three of them were in cahoots.' And with one goal in mind: to get rid of Jesse.

The real question – the thing I'd never been able to figure out later – was why. I mean, I knew why Maria and her dysfunctional hubby had come back from the netherworld

26

intent on taking Jesse with them: they'd wanted to hide forever the fact I'd stumbled across – that, a hundred and fifty years ago, the two of them had been the ones who'd killed him. Jesse, I mean.

But Paul? What could Paul have had against Jesse? A big fat load of nothing, since the two of them hadn't even known one another.

And what did Paul have against me? Nothing . . . not unless you counted the fact that I had straightened out his sweet younger brother, Jack, who, until I'd been assigned to babysit him, hadn't recognized his mediation skills for what they were, and had thought, basically, that he was a nutjob.

Was that it? Was that what I'd done to Paul Slater that had enraged him enough to exorcize Jesse and try to kill me? Because I'd explained to his neurotic little brother that he wasn't crazy, that the reason the spirits of the dead were approaching him all the time was because he, like me and Father Dom – and his big brother Paul, it had turned out – had been cursed from birth with the stigma of being a mediator, and that, though he might never have asked for the job, he was pretty much stuck with it for life like the rest of us?

That was the only thing I could think of that might make a guy like Paul take a murderous dislike to me. Well, that and the fact that Paul had asked me out and I'd said no.

But what kind of guy let something like *that* get him all bent out of shape?

Father Dom continued to look concerned. As well he might. We were, basically, screwed.

'Maybe,' he ventured, after a moment, 'Paul, like his little brother, is looking for guidance. It's possible that with the right influence, Paul might be made to see the error of his ways. After all, Suze, you certainly helped Jack. Perhaps Paul is looking for similar help.'

27

'Yeah, Father Dom,' I said, sarcastically. 'And maybe this year I'll get elected Homecoming Queen.'

Father Dominic looked disapproving. He was a mediator like me but, unlike me, Father Dominic tended always to think the best of people, at least until their subsequent behaviour proved his assumption in their inherent goodness to be wrong. You would think that, in the case of Paul Slater, he'd have already seen enough to form a solid basis for judgement on that guy's behalf, but apparently not.

'I am going to assume,' Father D said, 'until we've seen something to prove otherwise, that Paul is here at the Mission Academy because he wants to learn. Not just the normal eleventh grade curriculum, either, Susannah, but what you and I might have to teach him, as well. I am going to assume that Paul has realized the error of his past ways and truly wishes to make amends. I believe that Paul is here to make a fresh start. And it is our duty, as charitable human beings, to help him do just that. Until we learn otherwise, Susannah, I believe we should give Paul the benefit of the doubt.'

I thought this was the most horrible plan I had ever heard in my life. But the truth was, I didn't have any evidence that Paul was, in fact, here to cause trouble. Not yet, anyway. The fact that he'd tried to get rid of the guy I love – who, for reasons I felt were best left unexplored, was still here on earth when he should, by rights, have moved on to heaven or his next life or wherever a long time ago – might possibly have blinded me to Paul's better qualities. It was entirely possible the guy wasn't so bad.

Yeah. And it was entirely possible CeeCee's psychic Aunt Pru was playing with a full deck.

'Now,' Father D said, closing Paul's file and leaning back in his chair. 'I haven't seen you in a few weeks. How are you, Susannah? And how's Jesse?'

28

I felt my face heat up. Things were at a sorry pass when the mere mention of Jesse's name could cause me to blush, but there it was.

'Um,' I said, hoping Father D wouldn't notice my flaming cheeks. 'Fine.'

'Good,' Father Dom said, pushing his glasses up his nose and looking over at his bookshelf in a distracted manner. 'There was something of mine he mentioned wanting to borrow last time I talked to him . . .' Guiltily, I reflected that the last time Jesse and Father Dom had talked had been before we'd, you know, kissed.

'Oh, yes, here it is,' Father Dom said, and placed a giant, leatherbound book – it had to have weighed ten pounds at least – in my arms. '*Critical Theory Since Plato*,' Father D said in a pleased voice. 'Jesse ought to like that.'

I didn't doubt it. Jesse liked some of the most boring books known to man, including *Moby Dick* and *The Grapes of Wrath*. In fact, his favourite thing to do was to sit around and read out loud, apparently because this is how they used to entertain one another back home on the ranch when Jesse had been alive.

'Good, good,' Father D said, distractedly. You could tell he had a lot on his mind. Visits from the archbishop always threw him into a tizzy, and this one, for the feast of Father Serra, whom several organizations had been trying, unsuccessfully, to have sainted, was going to be a particularly huge pain in the ass, from what I could see.

'Let's just keep an eye on our young friend Mr Slater,' Father Dom said, 'and see how things go. He might very well settle down, Susannah, in a structured environment like the one we offer here at the Academy.'

I sniffed. I couldn't help it. Father D really had no idea what he was up against.

29

'And if he doesn't?' I asked.

'Well,' Father Dominic said, 'we'll cross that bridge when we get to it. Now run along. There's still some class time left.'

Didn't I know it? I'd managed to get out of Algebra 3–4 by claiming I'd had to go to the nurse. Unfortunately, I had not managed to use up all the allotted class time complaining to Father D about Paul.

I left the principal's office carrying the dusty old book he'd given me, thinking that if Jesse took it into his head that we were going to read this piece of garbage out loud, I might just have to put my foot down. *The Sound and the Fury*, at least as it was read aloud by Jesse, was worth missing *Friends* for. *Critical Theory Since Plato* was not.

The morning fog had dispersed, as it always did around eleven, and now the sky overhead was a brilliant blue. In the courtyard, hummingbirds busily worked over the hibiscus. The fountain, surrounded by a half-dozen tourists in Bermuda shorts – the Mission, besides being a school, was also a historic landmark and sported a basilica and even a giftshop that were must-see's on any touring bus's schedule – burbled noisily. The deep green fronds of the palm trees waved lazily overhead in the gentle breeze from the sea, and I was, once again, overcome with a feeling of contentment.

So what if Paul Slater had shown up at my school, and that his motives for doing so were most likely devious? So what if he had, in the past, done a few things I wouldn't exactly call admirable – that I might say were downright conniving, even cruel? What did it matter now? Everything had turned out all right in the end. Jesse and I were still together . . . more or less.

Why should I care about anything but that?

Suddenly, I was feeling all right again. How could I not? It had turned into a beautiful day. The drone of hummingbirds and the distant rumble of sea filled my ears, while the sweet smell of honeysuckle – there was a tree growing right outside of Father Dom's office door – was heavy in the air. It was gorgeous out. I was sixteen. I was in love.

But then an all-too familiar voice went, 'Well, well, well. If it isn't Susannah Simon.'

I guess he could read the fear in my eyes – carefully done up that morning with a brand-new combination of eye-shadows called Mocha Mist – when I whipped around to face him, because the grin that broke out across his good-looking face when I glanced in his direction was slightly crooked at one end.

'Suze,' Paul said, in a chiding tone. His teeth were dazzlingly white against his tennis tan. 'Here I am, nervous about being the new kid at school, and you don't even have a hello for me? What kind of way is that to treat an old pal?'

I continued to stare at him, perfectly incapable of speech. You can't talk, of course, when your mouth has gone as dry as . . . well, as the adobe brick building we were standing in front of.

Why did he have this effect on me? *Why?*

I don't know whether or not he sensed my fear. But he sure didn't like my pulling a prima donna act on him and not replying. His hand flew out as I attempted to sweep past him, and the next thing I knew, his fingers were wrapped around my upper arm in a vice-like grip.

I could, of course, have hauled off and slugged him. But I'd wanted to start this year off right: in Mocha Mist and my new black Club Monaco capris (coupled with the sweater set), not in a fight. And what would my friends and fellow schoolmates think if I began to freakishly pummel the new guy?

And then there was the unavoidable fact that I was pretty

31

convinced that, if I took a whack at Paul, he would not hesitate to whack me back.

Somehow I managed to find my voice. I only hoped he didn't notice how much it was shaking. 'Let go of my arm,' I said.

'Suze,' he said. He was still smiling, but now he looked – and sounded – slyly knowing. 'What's the matter? You don't look very happy to see me.'

'Still not letting go of my arm,' I reminded him. I could feel the chill from his fingers – he seemed to be completely cold-blooded in addition to being preternaturally strong – through my silk sleeve.

He dropped his hand.

'Look,' he said. 'I really am sorry. About the way things went down the last time you and I met, I mean.'

The last time he and I met. Instantly, I was transported in my mind's eye back to that long hallway – the one I had seen so often in my dreams, lined with doors on either side – doors that opened into who-knew-what . . .

. . . only this hallway hadn't existed in any hotel or office building known to man. It hadn't even existed in our current dimension.

And Paul had stood there, knowing Jesse and I had no idea how to find our way out of it, and laughed. Just laughed, like it was this big colossal joke that if I didn't return to my own universe soon I'd die, while Jesse would have been trapped in that hallway for ever. I could still hear Paul's laughter ringing in my ears. He had kept on laughing . . . right up until the moment Jesse had slammed a fist into his face.

I could hardly believe any of this was happening. 'You mean the part where you tried to kill me?' I croaked. This time, I know he heard my voice shake. I know because he

32

looked perturbed. In any case, he reached up and dragged one of those tanned hands through his curly hair.

'I never tried to kill you, Suze,' he said, sounding a little hurt.

I laughed. I couldn't help it. My heart was in my throat, but I laughed anyway. 'Oh,' I said. 'Right.'

'I mean it, Suze,' he said. 'It wasn't like that. I'm just . . . I'm just not very good at losing, you see.'

I stared at him. He was trying to pass the whole thing off as bad sportsmanship?

'I don't get it,' I said, shaking my head. 'What did you lose? You didn't lose anything.'

'Didn't I, Suze?' His gaze bore into mine. His voice was the same one I'd been hearing over and over in my dreams, laughing at me as I struggled to find my way out of the dark, mist-filled hallway, at either end of which was a precipice dropping off into a black void of utter nothingness, over which, right before I woke up, I teetered dangerously. It was a voice filled with hidden meaning . . .

Only I had no idea what that meaning could be, or what he was implying. All I knew was that this guy terrified me.

'Suze,' he said with a smile. 'Look, don't be this way. It's a new school year. I really do want to do as the old priest said and make a new start. Can't we?'

'No,' I said, glad that my voice didn't shake this time. 'We can't. In fact, you'd better stay away from me.'

He seemed to find this deeply amusing. 'Right. You said that before. Because if I don't, you'll sic your boyfriend on me, right?'

He must have figured out from my expression that all was not copacetic in Suze-and-Jesse-land, since he laughed and said, 'Oh, wait. So *that*'s how it is. Well, I never really thought Jesse was your type, you know. You need someone a little less—'

33

He didn't get a chance to finish his sentence because at that moment I breezed past him, heading purposefully for the lockers built into the adobe walls all along the mission's beautifully manicured inner courtyard. 'You better get back to class,' I warned him. 'You don't want to get detention your very first day.'

Unfortunately, Paul appeared to be immune to threats of detention.

'. . . dead,' he finished, referring to Jesse.

I could only stare at him as I fumbled with the combination to my locker. I couldn't believe this was happening, I really couldn't. What was Paul doing here, enrolling in my school, making my world – from which I'd thought I'd rid him for ever – a real life nightmare? Whatever his motives for coming back, I didn't want to know. I just wanted to get away from him.

'Well,' I said, slamming my locker door open. I hardly knew what I was doing. I had reached in and blindly grabbed the first books my fingers touched. 'Gotta go. Algebra calls.'

He looked down at the books in my arms, the ones I was holding almost as a shield, as if they would protect me from whatever it was – and I was sure there was something – he had in store for me. For us.

'You won't find them in there,' Paul said, with a cryptic nod at the textbooks bulging from my arms.

I didn't know what he was talking about. I didn't *want* to know. All I knew was that I wanted out of there – fast.

Still, even though I didn't want to, I heard myself asking, as if the words were being torn involuntarily from my lips, 'I won't find what in here?'

'The answers you're looking for.' Paul's blue-eyed gaze was intense. 'Why you, of all people, were chosen. And what, exactly, you are.'

34

This time, I didn't have to ask what he meant. I knew. As surely as if he'd said the words out loud. He was talking about the gift – the one we shared, he and I, the one about which he seemed to have such superior knowledge, and so much better control over, than I did.

Paul went on, smoothly, 'When you're ready to hear the truth about what you are, you'll know where to find me. Because I'll be right here.'

Four

I tried to tell myself that I was overreacting. That Father Dom was right, we didn't know what Paul's motives were in coming to Carmel. Perhaps he really had turned over a new leaf.

So why could I not get that image – the one from my nightmares – out of my head? Truthfully, I didn't know which was scarier: my nightmare, or what was happening now while I was awake. How was it that Paul seemed to know so much about the talent he and I shared? There's no mediator newsletter. No mediator conferences or seminars. I am as clueless now, practically, as I'd been back when I was little and known only that I was . . . well, different from the other kids in my neighbourhood.

But Paul seemed to think he had some kind of answers.

What could he know about it, though? Even Father Dominic didn't claim to know exactly what we mediators were and where we'd come from, and just what, exactly, was the extent of our talents . . . and he was older than both of us combined! Sure, we can see and speak to – and even kiss and punch – the dead . . . or rather, the spirits of those who had died leaving things untidy. I'd found that out at the age of six when my dad, who'd passed away from a sudden heart attack, came back for a little post-funeral chat.

36

But was that all mediators were capable of? Not according to Paul.

Despite Father Dominic's assurances that Paul likely meant well, I could not be so sure. People like Paul did not do anything without good reason. So what, exactly, was he doing back in Carmel? Could it be merely that, now that he'd discovered Father Dom and I, he wished to continue the relationship, out of some kind of longing to be with his own kind?

It was possible. Of course, it's equally possible that Jesse really does love me, and is just pretending like he doesn't, since a romantic relationship between the two of us really wouldn't be all that kosher . . .

Yeah. And maybe I really *will* get that Homecoming Queen nomination I've been longing for . . .

I was still trying not to think about this at lunch – the Paul thing, not the Homecoming Queen thing – when, sandwiched on an outdoor bench between Adam and CeeCee, I cracked the pull tab on a can of diet soda and then nearly choked on my first swallow after CeeCee went, 'So, spill. Who's this Jesse guy, anyway? Answer please.'

Soda went everywhere, mostly out of my nose. Some of it got on my Benetton sweater set.

CeeCee was completely unsympathetic. 'It's diet,' she said. 'It won't stain. So how come we haven't met him?'

'Yeah,' Adam said, getting over his initial mirth at seeing soda coming out of my nostrils. 'And how come this Paul guy knows him, and we don't?'

Dabbing myself with a napkin, I glanced in Paul's direction. He was sitting on a bench not too far away, surrounded by Kelly Prescott and the other popular people in our class, all of whom were laughing uproariously at some story he'd just told them.

37

I wanted to kill him. I'd had no idea CeeCee and Adam had overheard Paul's reference to my invisible would-be boyfriend.

'Jesse's just a guy,' I said, because I had a feeling I wasn't going to be able to get away with brushing their questions off. Not this time.

'Just a guy,' CeeCee repeated. 'Just a guy you are apparently going out with, according to this Paul.'

'Well,' I said, uncomfortably. 'Yeah. I guess I am. Sort of. I mean . . . it's complicated.'

Complicated? My relationship with Jesse made *Critical Theory Since Plato* look like *The Poky Little Puppy*.

'So,' CeeCee said, crossing her legs and nibbling contentedly from a bag of baby carrots in her lap. 'Tell. Where'd you two meet?'

I could not believe I was actually sitting there, discussing Jesse with my friends. My friends whom I'd worked so hard to keep in the dark about him.

'He, um, lives in my neighbourhood,' I said. No point in telling them the absolute truth.

'He goes to Robert Louis Stevenson?' Adam wanted to know, reaching over me to grab a carrot from the bag in CeeCee's lap.

'Um,' I said. 'Not exactly.'

'Don't tell me he goes to Carmel High.' CeeCee's eyes widened.

'He's not in high school any more,' I said, since I knew that, given CeeCee's nature, she'd never rest until she knew all. 'He, um, graduated already.'

'Whoa,' CeeCee said. 'An older man. Well, no wonder you're keeping him a secret. So, what is he, in college?'

'Not really,' I said. 'He's, uh, taking some time off. To kind of . . . find himself.'

38

'Hmph.' Adam leaned back against the bench and closed his eyes, letting the strong midday sun caress his face. 'A slacker. You can do better, Suze. What you need is a guy with a good solid work ethic. A guy like . . . hey, I know. Me!'

CeeCee, who had had her eye on Adam for as long as I had known them both, ignored him.

'How long have you guys been going out?' she wanted to know.

'I don't know,' I said, feeling pretty miserable now. 'It's all sort of new. I mean, I've known him for a while, but the whole dating angle of it . . . that's new. And it isn't really . . . Well, I don't really like to talk about it.'

'Talk about what?' A shadow loomed over our bench. Squinting, I looked up, and saw my younger stepbrother Doc – David, as he was known to everyone but me – standing there, his red hair glowing like a halo in the hot sun.

'Nothing,' I said, quickly.

Out of everyone in my family – and yes, I did think of the Ackermans, my stepdad and his sons as part of my family now, the little family that used to be just made up of my mom and me, after my dad died – thirteen-year-old David was the one closest to knowing the truth about me. That I wasn't merely the somewhat discontented teenaged girl I pretended to be, that is.

What's more, David knew about Jesse. Knew, and yet didn't know. Because while he, like everyone in the house, had noticed my sudden mood swings and mysterious absences from the family room every night, he could not even begin to imagine what was behind it all.

Now he stood in front of our bench – which was pretty daring, since the upperclassmen did not tend to take kindly to eighth-graders like David coming over to what they considered their side of the assembly yard – trying to look like

39

he belonged there, which, considering his hundred-pound frame, braces and sticky-out ears, could not have been further from the truth.

'Did you see this?' he asked now, shoving a piece of paper beneath my nose.

I took the paper from him. It turned out to be a flyer, advertising a hot tub party at Ninety-Nine Pine Crest Road on this coming Friday night. Guests were invited to bring a swimsuit if they wanted to have some 'hot 'n' frothy fun'. Or if they chose to forsake a suit, that was all right, particularly if they happened to be of the female persuasion.

There was a crude drawing on the flyer of a tipsy-looking girl with large breasts downing a can of beer.

'No, you can't go,' I said, handing the flyer back to David with a snort. 'You're too young. And somebody ought to show this to your class advisor. Eighth-graders shouldn't be having parties like this.'

CeeCee, who'd taken the flyer from David's hands, went, 'Um, Suze.'

'Seriously,' I continued. 'And I'm surprised at you, David. I thought you were smarter than that. Nothing good ever comes from parties like this. Sure, some people will have fun. But ten to one somebody will end up having to get their stomach pumped, or drown, or crack their head open, or something. It's always funny until someone gets hurt.'

'Suze.' CeeCee held the flyer up in front of my face, just inches from my nose. 'Ninety-nine Pine Crest Road. That's your house, isn't it?'

I snatched the flyer away from her with a gasp. 'David! What can you be thinking?'

'It wasn't me,' David cried, his already wobbly voice going up another two or three octaves. 'Somebody showed it to me

40

in Social Studies. Brad's passing them around. Some of the seventh graders got some, even . . .'

I narrowed my eyes in my stepbrother Brad's direction. He was leaning against the basketball pole, trying to look cool, which was pretty hard for a guy whose cerebral cortex was coated, as far as I could tell, with WD40.

'Excuse me,' I said, standing up. 'I have to go commit a murder.' Then I stalked across the playground, the bright orange flyer in my hand.

Brad saw me coming. I noted the look of naked panic that flitted across his features as his gaze fell upon what I had in my hand. He straightened up and tried to run, but I was too quick for him. I cornered him by the drinking fountain and held the flyer up so that he could see it.

'Do you really think,' I asked, calmly, 'that Mom and Andy are going to allow you to have this . . . this . . . whatever it is?'

The panic on Brad's face had turned to defiance. He stuck out his chin and said, 'Yeah, well, what they don't know isn't going to hurt them.'

'Brad,' I said. Sometimes I felt sorry for him. I really did. He was just such a dufus. 'Don't you think they're going to notice when they look out their bedroom window and see a bunch of naked girls in their new hot tub?'

'No,' Brad said ''Cause they aren't going to be around Friday night. Dad's got that guest lecture thing up in San Francisco, and your mom's going with him, remember?'

No, I did not remember. In fact, I wondered if I had ever even been told. I had been spending a lot of time up in my room lately, it was true, but so much that I'd missed something as important as our parents going away for an entire night? I didn't think so . . .

41

'And you better not tell them,' Brad said, with an unexpected burst of venom. 'Or you'll be sorry.'

I looked at him like he was nuts. '*I'll* be sorry?' I said, with a laugh. 'Um, excuse me, Brad, but if your dad finds out about this party you're planning, *you're* the one that's going to be grounded for the rest of your life, not me.'

'Nuh-uh,' Brad said. The look of defiance had been replaced by an even less attractive one of something that was almost venal. ''Cause if you even think about saying anything, I'll tell them about the guy you've been sneaking into your room every night.'

Five

Detention.

That's what you get at the Junipero Serra Mission Academy when you sucker punch your stepbrother on school grounds, and a teacher happens to notice.

'I can't understand what came over you, Suze,' said Mrs Elkins, who, in addition to teaching ninth- and tenth-grade Biology, was also in charge of staying after school with juvenile delinquents like myself. 'And on the first day back, too. Is this how you want to start out the new year?'

But Mrs Elkins didn't understand. And I couldn't exactly tell her, or anything. I mean, how could I tell her that it had all just suddenly become too much? That discovering my stepbrother knew something I had struggled to hide from the rest of my family for months now – on top of finding out that a monster from my dreams was currently stalking the halls of my own school, in the guise of an Abercrombie and Fitch-wearing hottie – had caused me to melt down like a Maybelline lipstick left in the sun?

I couldn't tell her. I merely took my punishment in silence, watching the minutes on the clock drag slowly by. Neither I nor any of the other prisoners would be released until four o'clock.

'I hope,' Mrs Elkins said, when that hour finally arrived, 'that you've learned a lesson, Suze. You aren't setting a very

43

good example for the younger children now, are you, brawling on school grounds like that?'

Me? I wasn't setting a good example? What about Brad? Brad was the one who was planning to have his own personal Oktoberfest in our living room. And yet Brad had *me* by the shorthairs. And did he ever know it.

'Yeah,' he'd said to me at lunch, when I'd stood there staring at him in utter dumbfoundedness, unable to believe what I'd just heard. 'Think you're so slick, don't you, letting the guy sneak up into your room every night, huh? How's he get in, anyway? That bay window of yours, the one over the porch roof? Well, I guess your little secret's blown now, huh? So you just keep quiet about my party, and I'll keep quiet about this Jesse guy.'

I'd been so flabbergasted by this news that Brad could hear – had heard – Jesse, I hadn't been able to formulate a coherent sentence for several minutes, during which time Brad exchanged greetings with various members of his posse who came up to high five him and say things like, 'Dude! Tub time. I'm so there.'

Finally, I managed to unlock my jaw and demanded, 'Oh, yeah? Well, what about Jake? I mean, Jake's not going to let you have a bunch of your friends over to get wasted.'

Brad just looked at me like I was nuts. 'Are you kidding?' he asked. 'Who you think's providing the beer? Jake's gonna steal me a keg from where he works.'

I narrowed my eyes at him. '*Jake?* Jake's getting *you* beer? No way. He would never . . .' Then comprehension dawned. 'How much are you paying him?'

'A hundred big ones,' Brad said. 'Exactly half of what he's shy on that Camarro he's been wanting.'

There was little Jake wouldn't do to get his hands on a Camarro all his own, I knew.

44

Stymied, I stared at him some more. 'What about David?' I asked, finally. 'David's going to tell.'

'No, he isn't,' Brad said, confidently. ''Cause if he does, I'll kick his bony butt from here to Anchorage. And you better not try to defend him, either, or your mom's gonna get a big fat helping of Jesse pie.'

That's when I hit him. I couldn't help it. It was like my fist had a mind of its own. One minute it was at my side, and the next it was sinking into Brad's gut.

The fight was over in a second. A half second, even. Mr Gillarte, the new track coach, pulled us apart before Brad had a chance to get in a blow of his own.

'Walk it off,' he ordered me with a shove, while he bent to tend a frantically gasping Brad.

So I walked it off. Right up to Father D, who was standing in the courtyard, supervising the stringing of fairy lights around the trunk of a palm tree.

'What can I tell you, Susannah?' he'd said, sounding exasperated, when I was done explaining the situation. 'Some people are more perceptive than others.'

'Yeah, but *Brad*?' I had to keep my voice down because a bunch of the gardeners were around, all helping to set up the decorations for the feast of Father Serra, which was happening on Saturday, the day after Brad's hot tub bacchanal.

'Well, Susannah,' Father D said. 'You couldn't have expected to keep Jesse a secret for ever. Your family was bound to find out sometime.'

Maybe. What I couldn't fathom was how Brad, of all people, knew about him, when some of my more intelligent family members – like Andy, for instance, or my mom – were totally clueless.

On the other hand, Max, the family dog, had always known about Jesse – wouldn't go near my room because of

45

him. And on an intellectual level, Brad and Max had a lot in common . . . though Max was a little bit smarter, of course.

'I sincerely hope,' Mrs Elkins said, when she'd released me and my fellow prisoners at last, 'that I won't see you here again this year, Suze.'

'You and me both, Mrs E,' I'd replied, gathering my things. Then I'd bolted.

Outside, it was a clear September afternoon in northern California, which meant that the sun was blinding, the sky was so blue it hurt to look at and, off in the distance, you could see the white surf of the Pacific as it curled up against Carmel Beach. I had missed all of my possible rides home – Adam, who was still eager to take anyone anywhere in his sporty green VW Bug, and of course Brad, who'd inherited the Land Rover from Jake, who now drove a beat-up Honda Civic, but only until he obtained his dream car – and it was a two-mile walk to Ninety-Nine Pine Crest Road. Mostly uphill.

I'd got as far as the gates of the school before my knight in shining armour showed up. At least, that's what I suppose he thought he was. He wasn't on any milk-white palfrey though. He drove a silver BMW convertible, the top already conveniently lowered. It so figured.

'Come on,' he said, as I stood in front of the Mission, waiting for the traffic light to change so I could cross the busy highway. 'Get in. I'll give you a ride home.'

'No, thank you,' I said, lightly. 'I prefer to walk.'

'Suze.' Paul looked bored. 'Just get in the car.'

'No,' I said. See, I had fully learned my lesson, in so far as the whole getting-into-cars-with-guys-who'd-once-tried-to-kill-me thing went. And it wasn't going to happen again. Especially not with Paul, who'd not only once tried to kill me, but who had frightened me so thoroughly while doing it

46

that I continuously relived the incident in my dreams. 'I told you. I'm walking.'

Paul shook his head, laughing to himself. 'You really are,' he said, 'a piece of work.'

'Thank you.' The light changed, and I started across the intersection. I knew it well. I did not need an escort.

But that's exactly what I got. Paul drove right alongside me, clocking a grand total of about two miles per hour.

'Are you going to follow me all the way home?' I enquired, as we started up the steep incline that gave the Carmel Hills their name. It was a good thing that that particular road was not highly trafficked at four in the afternoon, or Paul just might have made some of my neighbours mad, clogging up the only pathway to civilization the way he was driving.

'Yes,' Paul said. 'That is, unless you'll stop acting like such a brat and get into the car.'

'No, thanks,' I said, again.

I kept walking. It was hot out. I was beginning to feel a little moist in my sweater set. But no way was I going to get into that guy's car. I trudged along the side of the road, careful to avoid any plants that resembled my deadliest of enemies – before Paul had come along, anyway – poison oak, and silently cursing *Critical Theory Since Plato*, which seemed to be growing heavier and heavier in my arms with every step.

'You're wrong not to trust me,' Paul remarked, as he slithered up the hill alongside me in his silver snake-mobile. 'We're the same, you and I, you know.'

'I sincerely hope that isn't true,' I said. I have often found that with some enemies, politeness can be as strong a deterrent as a fist. I'm not kidding. Try it some time.

'Sorry to disappoint you,' Paul said. 'But it is. What'd Father Dominic tell you, anyway? He tell you not to spend any time alone with me? Not to believe a word I say?'

47

'Not at all,' I said, in the same distant tone. 'Father Dominic thinks I should give you the benefit of the doubt.'

Paul, behind his leather-covered steering wheel, looked surprised. 'Really? He said that?'

'Oh, yes,' I said, noticing a beautiful clump of buttercups growing alongside the road, and carefully skirting them in case they hid any dangerous stalks of poison oak. 'Father Dominic thinks you're here because you want to bond with the only other mediators you know. He thinks it's our duty as charitable human beings to allow you to make amends and help you along the path to righteousness.'

'But you don't agree with him?' Paul was staring at me intently. Well, and why not? Considering how slow he was going, it wasn't like he had to keep an eye on the road, or anything.

'Look,' I said, wishing I had a barrette or something I could put my hair up with. It was beginning to stick to the back of my neck. The tortoiseshell hairclip I had started out with that morning had mysteriously disappeared. 'Father Dominic is the nicest person I have ever met. All he lives for is to help others. He genuinely believes that human beings are, by nature, good, and that, if treated as such, will respond accordingly.'

'But you,' Paul said, 'don't agree, I take it?'

'I think we both know that Father Dom is living in a dream world.' I looked straight ahead as I trudged up the hill, hoping that Paul wouldn't guess that my staggering heartbeat had nothing to do with the exercise and everything to do with his presence. 'But because I don't want to let the guy down, I'm going to keep my personal opinion about you – that you're a user and a psychopath – to myself.'

'A psychopath?' Paul seemed delighted to hear himself described this way . . . further proof that he was, in fact,

48

exactly what I thought him. 'I like the sound of that. I've been called a lot of things before, but never a psychopath.'

'It wasn't a compliment,' I felt compelled to point out, since he seemed to be taking it that way.

'I know,' he said. 'That's what makes it so particularly amusing. You're quite a girl, you know that?'

'Whatever,' I said, irritated. I couldn't even seem to insult the guy successfully. 'Just tell me one thing.'

'Name it,' he said.

'That night we ran into each other . . .' I pointed towards the sky. '. . . you know, up there? The spirit world.'

He nodded. 'Yeah. What about it?'

'How'd you get there? I mean, nobody exorcized you, right?'

Paul was grinning now. I saw, to my dismay, that I'd asked him exactly the question he'd most wanted to hear.

'No, nobody exorcized me,' he said. 'And you didn't need anybody to exorcize you, either.'

This came close to flooring me. I froze in my tracks. 'Are you trying to tell me that I can just go strolling around up there whenever I want?' I asked him, truly stunned.

'There's a lot,' Paul said, still grinning lazily, 'that you can do that you haven't figured out yet, Suze. Things you've never dreamed of. Things I can show you.'

The silky tone of his voice didn't fool me. Paul was a charmer, it was true, but he was also deadly.

'Yeah,' I said, praying that he couldn't see how fast my heart was beating. 'I'm sure.'

'I'm serious, Suze,' Paul said. 'Father Dominic is a great guy. I'm not denying it. But he's just a mediator. You're a little something more.'

'I see.' I hitched my shoulders and started walking again. We had reached the crest of the hill, finally, and entered into

49

some shade afforded by the giant pine trees on either side of the road. My relief at finally being out of the heat was palpable. I only wished I could rid myself of Paul as easily. 'So, all my life people have been telling me I'm one thing, and all of a sudden you come along, and you say I'm something else, and I'm just supposed to believe you?'

'Yes,' Paul said.

'Because you're such a trustworthy person,' I quipped, sounding a lot more self-assured than I actually felt.

'Because I'm all you've got,' he corrected me.

'Well, that's not a real whole lot, is it?' I glared at him. 'Or do I need to point out that the last time I saw you, you left me stranded in hell?'

'It wasn't hell,' Paul said, with another one of his trademark eyerolls. 'And you'd have found your way out eventually.'

'What about Jesse?' I demanded. My heart was beating more loudly than ever, because this, of course, was what really mattered: not what he'd done – or tried to do – to me, but what he'd done to Jesse . . . what I was terrified he'd try to do again.

'I said I was sorry about that.' Paul sounded irritated. 'Besides, it all turned out OK in the end, didn't it? It's like I told you, Suze. You're much more powerful than you know. You just need someone to show you your true potential. You need a mentor. A real one, not a sixty-year-old priest who thinks Father Junipero Whoever is the be-all and end-all of the universe.'

'Right,' I said. 'And I suppose you think you're just the guy to play Mr Miagi to my Karate Kid.'

'Something like that.'

We were rounding the corner to Ninety-Nine Pine Crest Road, perched on a hill overlooking Carmel Valley. My

50

room, at the front of the house, had an ocean view. At night, fog blew in from the sea, and you could almost see it falling in misty tendrils over the sills if I left my windows open. It was a nice house, one of the oldest in Carmel, a former boarding house, circa 1850. It didn't even have a reputation for being haunted.

'What do you say, Suze?' Paul had one arm flung casually across the back of the empty passenger seat beside him. 'Dinner tonight? My treat? I'll tell you things about yourself – about what you are – that no one else on this planet knows.'

'Thanks,' I said, stepping off the road, and into my pine-needle-strewn yard, feeling insanely relieved. Well, and why not? I had survived an encounter with Paul Slater without being hurled into another plane of existence. That was quite an accomplishment. 'But no thanks. See you in school tomorrow.'

Then I waded through the heavy carpet of pine-needles to my driveway, while behind me I heard Paul calling, 'Suze! Suze, wait!'

Only I didn't wait. I went straight up the driveway to the front porch, climbed the steps, then opened the front door and went inside.

I did not look back. Not even once.

'I'm home,' I called, in case there was anybody downstairs who particularly cared. There did not appear to be. After seizing sustenance from the kitchen in the form of an apple and a diet soda, I climbed the steps to the second floor and flung open the door to my room.

There was a ghost sitting there on the window sill. He looked up when I walked in.

'Hello,' Jesse said.

51

Six

I didn't tell Jesse about Paul.

I probably should have. Except that I knew what would happen if I did: Jesse would want to rush into some big confrontation with the guy, and all it would result in was somebody getting exorcized again . . . that somebody being Jesse. And I really didn't think I could take it. Not again.

So I kept Paul's sudden matriculation at the Mission Academy to myself. I mean, things were weird between Jesse and me, it was true. But that didn't mean I was at all anxious to lose him.

'So how was school?' Jesse wanted to know.

'Fine,' I said. I was afraid to say anything more. For one thing, I was worried I might start blabbing about Paul. And for another, well, I'd found that the less said between Jesse and me, overall, the better. Otherwise, I had a tendency to prattle nervously. While I'd found that generally, prattling kept Jesse from dematerializing – as he tended to do more often now, with a hasty apology, whenever any awkward silences ensued between us – it did not seem to engender a similar desire to gab from him. Jesse had been almost unbearably quiet since . . .

Well, since the day we'd kissed.

I don't know what it is about guys that makes them French

you one day, then act like you don't exist the next. But that was the treatment I had been getting from Jesse lately. I mean, not three weeks ago he had pulled me into his arms and laid a kiss on me that I had felt all the way down to the base of my spine. I had melted in his embrace, thinking that at long last I could reveal to him my true feelings, the secret love I had borne for him since the minute – well, almost, anyway – I had first walked into my new bedroom and found it already occupied. Never mind that that occupant had breathed his last over a century and a half ago.

I should, I suppose, have known better than to fall in love with a ghost. But that's the thing about us mediators. To us, ghosts have as much matter as anyone living. Except for the whole immortal thing, there was no reason in the world why Jesse and I, if we wanted to, couldn't have the torrid affair I'd been dreaming of since he'd first resolutely refused to call me anything but my full name . . . Susannah, the name by which no one else but Father Dom ever referred to me.

Except that no torrid affair followed. After that first kiss – which had been interrupted by my youngest stepbrother – there'd been no other. Jesse had, in fact, apologized profusely for it, then seemed purposefully to avoid me, though I had made it a point to let him know that the whole thing had been all right . . . more than all right . . . by me.

Now I couldn't help wondering if maybe I'd been too accommodating. Jesse probably thought I was easy or something. I mean, back when he'd been alive, ladies slapped men who'd been as forward as he had. Even men who looked like Jesse, with flashing dark eyes, thick black hair, washboard abs, and irresistibly sexy smiles.

I still find it hard to believe anybody could have hated a guy like that enough to off him, but that's exactly how Jesse

53

ended up haunting my bedroom, the room in which he was strangled to death a hundred and fifty years ago.

Given the circumstances, I really didn't think there was much point in telling Jesse the details about my day. I just handed him *Critical Theory Since Plato* and said, 'Father Dominic says hello.'

Jesse seemed pleased by the book. Just my luck to be in love with a guy who gets more jazzed by critical theory than he seems to be by the idea of my tongue in his mouth.

Jesse thumbed through the book while I poured the contents of my backpack out on my bed. I was weighted down with homework already, and it was only the first day back. I could tell that eleventh grade was going to be just jam-packed with fun and adventure. I mean, between Paul Slater and trig, what could be more exciting?

I should have said something to Jesse about Paul then. I should have just been like, 'Hey, guess what? Remember that Paul guy whose nose you tried to break? Yeah, he goes to my school now.'

Because if I'd just been all casual about it, maybe it wouldn't have been a big deal. I mean, yeah, Jesse hated the guy – and with good reason. But I could have downplayed the whole fact that Paul might possibly be Satan's spawn. I mean, the guy *does* sport a Fossil watch. How malevolent could he be?

But just as I was kind of getting the guts up to go, 'Oh, yeah, and that Paul Slater dude, remember him? Yeah, he showed up in my homeroom this morning,' Brad shrieked up the stairs that dinner was ready.

Since my stepdad has this total thing about all of us gathering as a family at mealtimes and breaking bread together, I was forced to leave Jesse's side at that point – not that he seemed to care – and go downstairs and actually converse

54

with my relatives . . . a major sacrifice, considering what I could be doing instead: making myself available for more kisses from the man of my dreams.

Tonight, however, like most nights, didn't look as if it was going to yield any passionate embraces, so I went glumly down the stairs. Andy, I could tell from the aroma wafting through the house, had prepared steak fajitas, one of his best dishes. I had to give my mother credit for finding a guy who was not only handy around the house, but who was also practically a gourmet cook. Given that my mom and I had basically lived on takeout food back before she'd remarried, this was definitely an improvement.

The fact, however, that Mr Fix-It had come with three teenaged sons? Yeah, that part I was still sort of iffy about.

Brad burped as I entered the dining room. Only Brad had mastered the art of burping words. The word he burped as I walked in was, '*Loser*.'

'You're one to talk,' was my witty rejoinder.

'Brad,' Andy said, severely. 'Go and get the sour cream, please.'

Rolling his eyes, Brad slid out from his place at the table and trudged back into the kitchen.

'Hi, Susie,' my mother said, coming up and ruffling my hair affectionately. 'How was your first day back?'

Only my mother, out of all the human beings on the planet, is allowed to call me Susie. Fortunately I had already made this abundantly clear to my stepbrothers, so that they did not even snicker when she did it any more.

I didn't feel it would have been appropriate to have answered my mother's question truthfully. After all, she is unaware of the fact that her only child is a liaison between the living and the dead. She is not acquainted with Paul, or

55

with the fact that he once tried to kill me, nor is she aware of the existence of Jesse. My mother thinks merely that I am a late bloomer, a wallflower who will come into her own soon enough, and then have boyfriends to spare. Which is surprisingly naive for a woman who works as a television news journalist, even if it is only for a local affiliate.

Sometimes I envy my mom. It must be nice to live on her planet.

'My day was all right,' was how I responded to my mother's question.

''S not going to be so good tomorrow,' Brad pointed out, as he came back with the sour cream.

My mother had taken her seat at one end of the table and was flipping out her napkin. We only use cloth napkins. Another Andy-ism. It is more ecologically responsible and makes the presentation of the meal way more Martha Stewart.

'Really?' Mom said, her eyebrows, dark as mine, raised. 'How so?'

'Tomorrow's when we give the nominations for student body government,' Brad said, sliding back into his place. 'And Suze is going down as VP.'

Flipping out my own napkin and laying it delicately across my lap – along with the giant head of Max, the Ackermans' dog, who spent every meal with his muzzle resting on my thigh, waiting for whatever might fall from my fork and into my lap, a practice I was now so used to, I hardly even noticed any more – I said, in response to my mother's questioning gaze, 'It is so not a big deal.'

'What isn't?' my mother wanted to know.

Brad was the one who answered her. 'Kelly Prescott's asked someone else to be her running mate this year. That new guy, Paul Whatsit.' Brad shrugged his shoulders, from

56

which his thick wrestler's neck sprouted like a tree trunk from between a couple of boulders. 'So I guess Suze's reign as VP is *finito*.'

My mother glanced at me concernedly. 'Are you all right with this, Susie?'

It was my turn to shrug. 'Sure,' I said. 'I never really thought of myself as the student government type.'

This reply did not have the desired effect, however. My mother pressed her lips together, then said, 'Well, I don't like it. Some new boy coming in and taking Suze's place. It isn't fair.'

'It may not be fair,' David pointed out, 'but it's the natural order of things. Darwin proved that the strongest and fittest of the species tend to be the most successful, and Paul Slater is a superb physical specimen. Every female who comes in contact with him, I've noticed, has a distinct propensity to exhibit preening behaviour.'

My mother heard this last with some amusement. 'My goodness,' she said, mildly. 'And you, Suze? Does Paul Slater cause you to exhibit preening behaviour?'

'Hardly,' I said.

Brad burped again. This time when he did it, he said, '*Liar*.'

I glared at him. 'Brad,' I said. 'I do *not* like Paul Slater.'

'That's not what it looked like to me,' Brad said, 'when I saw the two of you in the breezeway this morning.'

'Wrong,' I said, hotly, to Brad. 'You could not be more wrong.'

'Oh,' Brad said. 'Give it up, Suze.'

'Enough,' my mother said, as I drew breath to deny this, too. 'Both of you.'

'I do not like Paul Slater,' I said again, just in case Brad hadn't heard me the first time. 'OK? In fact, I hate him.'

57

My mother looked aggrieved. 'Susie,' she said. 'I'm surprised at you. It's wrong to say you hate anyone. And how could you hate the poor boy already? You only just met him today.'

'She knows him from before,' Brad volunteered. 'From over the summer at Pebble Beach.'

I glared at him some more. 'How do *you* know *that*?'

'Paul told me,' Brad said, with a shrug.

Feeling a sense of dread – it would be just like Paul to spill the whole mediator thing to my family, just to mess with me – I asked, trying to sound casual, 'Oh, yeah? What else did he tell you?'

'Just that,' Brad said. Then his expression grew sarcastic. 'Much as it might come as a surprise to you to hear, Suze, people do have other stuff to talk about besides you, you know.'

'Brad,' Andy said, in a warning tone, as he came out of the kitchen carrying a tray of sizzling strips of beef and another of soft, steaming tortillas. 'Watch it.' Then, lowering the twin trays, his gaze fastened on the empty chair beside me. 'Where's Jake?'

We all glanced blankly at one another. It hadn't even registered that my eldest stepbrother was missing. None of us knew where Jake was. But all of us knew from Andy's tone that when Jake got home, he was a dead man.

'Maybe,' my mother ventured, 'he got held up in a class. You know it is only his first week of college, Andy. His schedule may not be the most regular for a while.'

'I asked him this morning,' Andy said, in an aggrieved tone, 'if he was going to be home in time for supper, and he said he was. If he was going to be late, the least he could have done was call.'

'Maybe he's stuck in some line at registration,' my mom

58

said, soothingly. 'Come on, Andy. You've made a lovely meal. It would be shame not to sit down and eat it before it gets cold.'

Andy sat down, but he didn't look at all eager to eat. 'It's just,' he said, in a speech we'd all heard approximately four hundred times before, 'when someone goes to the trouble to prepare a nice meal, it's only polite that everybody show up for it on time—'

It was just as he was saying this that the front door slammed, and Jake's voice sounded from the foyer, 'Keep your shirt on, I'm here.' Jake knew his father well.

My mom shot Andy a look over the bowls of shredded lettuce and cheese we were passing around. The look said, *See. Told you so.*

'Hey,' Jake said, coming into the dining room at his usual far less than brisk pace. 'Sorry I'm late. Got held up at the bookstore. The lines to buy books were unbelievable.'

My mom's *told you so* look deepened.

All Andy did was growl, 'You're lucky. This time. Sit down and eat.' Then, to Brad, he said, 'Pass the salsa.'

Except that Jake didn't sit down and eat. Instead, he stood there, one hand in the front pocket of his jeans, the other still dangling his car keys.

'Uh,' he said. 'Listen . . .'

We all looked up at him, expecting something interesting to happen, like for Jake to say that the pizza place had messed up his schedule again and that he couldn't stay for dinner. This generally resulted in some major fireworks from Andy's direction.

But instead, Jake said, 'I brought a friend with me. Hope that's OK.'

Since my stepfather would rather have a thousand people crowded around our dinner table than a single one of us

59

missing from it, he said, equably, 'Fine, fine. Plenty for everyone. Grab another place setting from the counter.'

So Jake went to the counter to grab a plate and knife and fork, while his 'friend' came slouching into view, having apparently dawdled in the living room, no doubt taken aback by the plethora of family photos my mother had plastered all over the walls there.

Sadly, Jake's friend was not of the feminine variety, so we could not look forward to teasing him about it later. Neil Jankow, as he was introduced, was nevertheless, as David would put it, an interesting specimen. He was well-groomed, which set him apart from most of Jake's surf buddies. His jeans did not sag somewhere midway down his thighs, but were actually belted properly around his waist, a fact which also put him a cut above most young men his age.

This did not mean, however, that he was a hottie. He wasn't, by any means. He was almost painfully thin, and pasty-skinned as well, with longish blond hair that badly needed trimming. Still, I could tell my mother approved of him, since he was excruciatingly polite, calling her ma'am – as in, 'Thank you very much for letting me stay for dinner, ma'am' – though his implication, that my mother had prepared the meal, was somewhat sexist, since Andy was the one who had done all the cooking.

Still, nobody seemed to take offence, and room was made for young master Neil at the table. He sat down and, following Jake's lead, began to eat . . . not very heartily, but with an appreciation that seemed unfeigned. Neil, we soon learned, was in Jake's Intro to English Literature seminar. Like Jake, Neil was just entering his first year at NoCal (the local slang for Northern California State Technical College). Like Jake, Neil was from the area. His family, in fact, lived in the Valley. His father owned a number of restaurants in the area,

60

including one or two at which I had actually eaten. Like Jake, Neil wasn't so sure what he wanted to major in, but, also like Jake, he was enjoying college much more than he had high school, since he'd arranged his schedule so that he didn't have a single morning class, and so could spend the a.m. hours sleeping in, or, if he happened to wake before eleven, taking advantage of a few waves over at Carmel Beach before his first class.

By the end of the meal, we knew just about all there was to know about Neil, except for one somewhat pertinent fact. It was something that, I was fairly certain, hadn't bothered anyone besides me. And yet I really felt that I was owed some sort of explanation, at least. Not that I could have said anything about it. Not with so many people around.

Which was part of the problem. There were too many people around. And not just the people gathered around the dinner table, either. No, there was the guy who'd come into the room and stood there during the entire course of our meal, right behind Neil's chair, watching him in complete silence with a baleful look on his face.

This guy, unlike Neil, was good looking. Dark-haired and cleft-chinned, you could tell that, beneath his Dockers and black polo, he was cut . . . he'd worked long and hard, I hadn't any doubt, to cultivate those triceps, not to mention what I guessed would be a killer set of washboard abs.

That wasn't the only difference between this guy and Jake's friend Neil, though. There was also the little fact that Neil, to the best of my knowledge, was noticeably alive, while the guy standing behind him was, well . . .

Dead.

61

Seven

It was so like Jake to bring home a haunted guest.

Not that Neil appeared to know he was being haunted. He seemed perfectly oblivious to the ghostly presence behind him – as was the rest of my family, with the exception of Max. The minute Neil sat down, Max took off for the living room with a whine . . . causing Andy to shake his head and say, 'That dog gets more neurotic every day.'

Poor Max. I so know how he felt.

Except that, unlike the dog, I couldn't slink from the dining room and go cower in another part of the house, the way I wanted to. I mean, doing so would only engender unnecessary questions.

Besides, I'm a mediator. Dealing with the undead is kind of unavoidable for me . . .

. . . though there are definitely times when I wish I could out of it. Now was one of those times.

Not that I could do anything about it. No, I was stuck at the table, trying to choke down steak fajitas while being stared at by a dead guy – a great end to my already way less than perfect day.

The dead guy, for his part, looked pretty peeved. Well, and why not? I mean, he was *dead*. I had no idea how he'd come to be parted with his soul, but it must have been

62

sudden, because he didn't seem very accustomed to the whole thing yet. Whenever anybody asked to be passed something that was near him, he reached for it . . .

. . . only to have it swept out from underneath his ghostly fingers by one of the living at the table. This caused him to look annoyed. But most of his animosity, I noticed, seemed reserved for Neil. Every bite of fajita Jake's new friend took, every chip he dipped into his guacamole, just seemed to enrage the dead guy more. His jaw muscles twitched, and his fists tightened convulsively each time Neil replied, in his quiet voice, 'Yes, ma'am,' or 'No, ma'am,' to any of the many questions my mom put to him.

Finally I couldn't stand it any more – it was *creepy*, sitting there at the table with this enraged ghost that only I could see . . . and I'm *used* to being stared at by ghosts – so I got up and started clearing everybody's empty plates, even though it was Brad's turn to do it. He gaped at me – providing us all with a very lovely view of some chewed-up steak he still had in his mouth – but didn't say anything about it. I think he was afraid that if he did so, it might snap me out of what-ever delusion I was under that it was my night to do the dishes. Either that, or he figured I was trying to stay in his good graces so he wouldn't tell on me about the 'guy' I was entertaining nightly in my room.

Anyway, my getting a move on with the dishes seemed to act as a signal that the meal was over, since everyone else got up and went out on to the deck to look at the new hot tub, which Andy was still showing proudly to every single person who walked through the front door, whether they asked to see it or not. It was while I was in the kitchen rinsing the plates before placing them in the dishwasher that Neil's walking shadow and I ended up alone together. He stood near enough to me – gazing through the sliding glass doors

63

at everybody out on the deck – that I was able to reach out with a sudsy hand and tug on his shirt without anybody noticing.

I startled him pretty badly. He swung around, his gaze furious and yet incredulous at the same time. Clearly, he hadn't been aware that I could see him.

'Hey,' I whispered to him, while everybody else was outside, chatting about chlorine and the flan Andy had made for dessert. 'You and I should talk.'

The guy looked shocked.

'You . . . you can see me?' he stammered.

'Obviously,' I said.

He blinked, then glanced out the sliding glass doors. 'But they . . . they can't?'

'No,' I said.

'Why?' he asked. 'I mean, why you and not . . . them?'

'Because I'm a mediator,' I explained.

He looked blank. 'A what?'

'Hang on a sec,' I said, because I could see my mother suddenly coming towards the sliding glass doors from the deck.

'Brr,' she said, as she pulled the door shut behind her. 'It gets cold out there when the sun starts to go down. How are you doing with those dishes, Suze? Do you need any help?'

'Nope,' I said, cheerfully. 'It's all good.'

'Are you sure? I thought it was Brad's turn to clear the table.'

'I don't mind,' I said, with a smile I hoped she didn't notice was completely forced.

It didn't work.

'Suze, honey,' she said. 'You aren't upset, are you? Over what Brad was saying – about this other boy being nominated for vice-president in your place?'

64

'Uh,' I said, with a glance at Ghost Boy, who looked pretty annoyed at the interruption. I couldn't really blame him. I guess it *was* kind of unprofessional of me to have a mother-daughter bonding session in the middle of a mediation. 'No, not really, Mom. I'm fine with it, actually.'

I wasn't lying, either. Not being in the student government this year was going to free up a lot of time for me. Time I had no idea what I was going to do with, of course, since it didn't look as if I'd be spending any of it being lifted to any romantic heights by Jesse. Still, hope springs eternal.

My mom continued to hover in the doorway, looking concerned.

'Well, Suze, honey,' she said. 'You're going to have to replace it with some other extra-curricular, you know. Colleges look for that sort of thing in their applicants. You're less than two years away from graduation. You'll be leaving us soon.'

Geez! My mom didn't even know about Jesse, and she was still doing all she could to keep the two of us apart, unaware of the fact that Jesse himself was taking care of that all on his own.

'Fine, Mom,' I said, eyeing Ghost Guy uncomfortably. I mean, I wasn't exactly thrilled that he was privy to all this. 'I'll join the swim team. Will that make you happy? Having to drive me to five a.m. practices every morning?'

'That wasn't even very convincing, Susannah,' my mom said, in a dry voice. 'I know perfectly well you'd never join the swim team. You're too obsessed with your hair, and what all those pool chemicals might do to it.'

Then she drifted off into the living room, leaving Ghost Guy and me alone in the kitchen.

'All right,' I said quietly. 'Where were we?'

65

The guy just shook his head. 'I still can't believe you can see me,' he said, in a shocked voice. 'I mean, you don't know . . . you can't know what it's been like. It's like everywhere I go, people just look through me.'

'Yes,' I said, tossing aside the dish towel I'd been using to dry my hands. 'That's because you're dead. The question is, what made you that way?'

Ghost Guy seemed taken aback by my tone. I guess it *was* a little curt. But then, I wasn't having the best day.

'Are you . . .' He eyed me sort of warily. '*Who* did you say you were again?'

'My name's Suze,' I told him. 'I'm a mediator.'

'A *what*?'

'Mediator,' I repeated. 'It's my job to help the dead pass on to the other side . . . their next life, or whatever. What's your name, anyway?'

Ghost Boy blinked again. 'Craig,' he said.

'OK. Well, listen, Craig. Something's screwy, because I highly doubt the cosmos intended for you to be hanging around my kitchen as part of your whole afterlife experience. You have got to move on.'

Craig knit his dark brows. 'Move on where?'

'Well, that's for you to find out when you get there,' I said. 'Anyway, the big question isn't where you're going, but why you haven't got there already.'

'You mean . . .' Craig's hazel eyes were wide. 'You mean this isn't . . . it?'

'Of course this isn't it,' I said, a little amused. 'You think after they die, everybody ends up at Ninety-Nine Pine Crest Road?'

Craig hitched his broad shoulders. 'No. I guess not. It's just that . . . when I woke up, you know, I didn't know where to go. Nobody could . . . you know. See me. I mean, I went

66

out into the living room and my mom was crying, like she couldn't stop, you know. It was kind of spooky.'

He wasn't kidding.

'That's OK,' I said, more gently than I'd spoken before. 'That's how it happens, sometimes. It's just not, you know, normal. Most people do go straight to the next . . . well, phase of their consciousness. You know, to their next life, or to eternal damnation if they screwed up during their last one. That kind of thing.' His eyes kind of widened at the words *eternal damnation*, but since I wasn't even sure there was such a thing I hurried on to, 'What we've got to figure out now is why you didn't. Move on right away, I mean. Something is obviously holding you back. We need to . . .'

But at that point, the examination of the hot tub — Andy's precious hot tub, which would, in less than a week from now, be filled with vomit and beer, if Brad's party went on according to plan – ended, and everyone came back inside. I gestured for Craig to follow me, and started up the stairs, where, I felt, we could continue talking uninterrupted.

At least by the living. Jesse, on the other hand, was another story.

'*Nombre de Dios*,' he said, startled from the pages of *Critical Theory Since Plato* when I came banging back into my bedroom, Craig close at my heels.

'Sorry about that,' I said, and seeing Jesse's gaze move past me and fasten on to the ghost boy, I made introductions: 'Jesse, this is Craig. Craig, Jesse. You two should get along. Jesse's dead, too.'

Craig, however, seemed to find the sight of Jesse – who, as usual, was dressed in what had been the height of fashion in the last year he'd been alive, 1850 or so, including knee-high black leather boots, somewhat tight-fitting black trousers, and a big billowy white shirt, open at the collar – a bit much.

67

So much so, in fact, that Craig had to sit down, heavily – or as heavily as someone without any real matter could sit, anyway – on the edge of my bed.

'Are you a pirate?' Craig asked Jesse.

Jesse, unlike me, did not find this very amusing. I guess I can't really blame him.

'No,' he said tonelessly. 'I'm not.'

'Craig,' I said, trying to keep a straight face and failing despite the look Jesse shot me. 'Really, you've got to think. There's got to be a reason why you are still hanging around here, instead of off where you're supposed to be. What do you think that reason could be? What's holding you back?'

Craig finally dragged his gaze away from Jesse. 'I don't know,' he said. 'Maybe the fact that I'm not supposed to be dead?'

'OK,' I said, trying to be patient. Because the thing is, of course, everybody thinks this. That they died too young. I've had folks who croaked at age one hundred and four complain to me about the injustice of it all.

But I try to be professional about the whole thing. I mean, mediation is, after all, my job. Not that I get paid for doing it, or anything, unless you count, you know, karma-wise. I hope.

'I can certainly see why you might feel that way,' I went on. 'Was it sudden? I mean, you weren't sick or anything, were you?'

Craig looked indignant. 'Sick? Are you kidding me? I can bench two forty, and I run four miles every single day. Not to mention, I was on the NoCal crew team. And I won the Pebble Beach Yacht Club's catamaran race three years in a row.'

'Oh,' I said. No wonder the guy seemed to have such a

68

wicked build beneath his polo. 'So your death was accidental then, I take it?'

'Damn straight it was accidental,' Craig said, stabbing a finger into my mattress for emphasis. 'That storm came out of nowhere. Flipped us right over before I had a chance to adjust the sail. Pinned me under.'

'So . . .' I said, hesitantly. 'You drowned?'

Craig shook his head . . . not in answer to my question, but out of frustration.

'It shouldn't have happened,' he said, staring unseeingly at his deck shoes, the kind guys like him – boaters – wear without socks. 'It wasn't supposed to have been me. I was on my high school swim team. I was first in the district one year in freestyle.'

I still didn't get it.

'I'm sorry,' I said. 'I know it doesn't seem fair. But things will get better, I promise.'

'Oh, really?' Craig looked up from his shoes, his hazel gaze seeming to pin me against the far wall. 'How? How are things going to get better? In case you haven't noticed, I'm *dead*.'

'She means things will get better for you when you've moved on,' Jesse said, coming to my rescue in a cool voice. He seemed to have gotten over the pirate remark.

'Oh, things will get better, will they?' Craig let out a bitter laugh. 'Like they have for you? Looks like you've been waiting to move on for a while, buddy. What's the hold-up?'

Jesse didn't say anything. There wasn't really anything he *could* say. He didn't, of course, know why he hadn't yet passed from this world to the next. Neither did I. Whatever it was that was trapping Jesse in this time and place had a pretty solid hold on him, though: It had already kept him here for over a century and a half, and showed every sign of

69

hanging on – I selfishly hoped for my lifetime anyway, if not for all eternity.

And while Father Dom kept insisting that one of these days Jesse was going to figure out what it was that was keeping him earthbound, and that I had better not get too attached to him, since the day would come when I would never see him again, those well-meaning warnings had fallen on deaf ears. I was already attached. Big time.

And I wasn't working too hard on extricating myself from that attachment, either.

'Jesse's situation is kind of unique,' I said to Craig, in what I hoped was a reassuring tone – for both his sake as well as Jesse's. 'I'm sure yours is nowhere near as complicated.'

'Damn straight,' Craig said. 'Because I'm not even supposed to be here.'

'Right,' I said. 'And I'm going to do my best to get you moving on to that next life of yours . . .'

Craig frowned. It was the same frown he'd been wearing all through dinner, as he'd gazed at Jake's friend Neil.

'No,' he said. 'That's not what I meant. I mean I'm not supposed to be here. As in, I'm not supposed to be dead.'

I nodded. I had heard this one before, countless times. No one wants to wake up and discover that he or she is no longer alive. No one.

'It's hard,' I said. 'I know it is. But eventually you'll adjust to the idea, I promise. And things will be better once we figure out what exactly is holding you back—'

'You don't get it,' Craig said, shaking his dark head. 'That's what I'm trying to tell you. What's holding me back is the fact that I'm not the one who's supposed to be dead.'

I said, hesitantly, 'Well . . . that may be. But there's nothing I can do about that.'

'What do you mean?' Craig rose to his feet and stood in

70

my bedroom, looking furious. 'What do you mean, there's nothing you can do about that? What am I doing here, then? I thought you said you could help me. I thought you said you were the mediator.'

'I am,' I said, with a hasty glance at Jesse, who looked as taken aback as I felt. 'But I don't dictate who lives or dies. That's not up to me. It's not part of my job.'

Craig, his expression turning to one of disgust, said, 'Well, thanks for nothing, then,' and started stalking towards my bedroom door.

I wasn't about to stop him. I mean, I didn't really want anything more to do with him. He just seemed like kind of a rude guy with a chip on his big swimmer's shoulders. If he didn't want my help, hey, not my problem.

It was Jesse who stopped him.

'You,' he said, in a voice that was deep enough – and commanding enough – to cause Craig to stop in his tracks. 'Apologize to her.'

The guy in the doorway turned his head slowly to stare at Jesse.

'No freaking way,' was what he had the lack of foresight to say.

A second later, he wasn't walking out – or even through – that door. No, he was pinned to it. Jesse was holding one of Craig's arms at what looked to be a fairly painful angle behind his back, and he was leaning heavily against him.

'Apologize,' Jesse hissed, 'to the young lady. She is trying to do you a kindness. You do not turn your back on someone who is trying to do you a kindness.'

Whoa. For a guy who seems to want nothing to do with me, Jesse sure can be testy sometimes about how other people treat me.

'I'm sorry,' Craig said, in a voice that was muffled against

71

the wood of the door. He sounded like he might be in pain. Just because you are dead, of course, does not mean you are immune to injury. Your soul remembers, even if your body is gone.

'That's better,' Jesse said, releasing him.

Craig sagged against the door. Even though he was kind of a jerk, I felt sorry for the guy. I mean, he had had an even tougher day than I had, what with being dead and all.

'It's just,' Craig said, in a suffering tone, as he reached up to rub the arm Jesse had nearly broken, 'that it isn't fair, you know? It wasn't supposed to have been me. I was the one who should have lived. Not Neil.'

I looked at him with some surprise. 'Oh? Neil was with you on the boat?'

'Catamaran,' Craig corrected me. 'And yeah, of course he was.'

'He was your sailing partner?'

Craig sent me a look of disgust . . . then, with a nervous glance at Jesse, quickly modified it to one of polite disdain.

'Of course not,' he said. 'Do you think we'd have tipped if Neil had had the slightest clue what he was doing? By rights, *he's* the one who should be dead. I don't know what Mom and Dad were thinking. *Take Neil out on the cat with you. You never take Neil out on the cat with you.* Well, I hope they're happy now. I took Neil out on the cat with me. And look where it got me. I'm dead. And my stupid brother is the one who lived.'

72

Eight

Well, at least now I knew why Neil had had so little to say all through dinner: he'd just lost his only brother.

'The guy couldn't swim to the other side of the pool,' Craig insisted, 'without having an asthma attack. How could he have clung to the side of a catamaran for seven hours, in ten-foot swells, before being rescued? How?'

I was at a loss to explain it as well. Much as I was at a loss as to how I was going to explain to Craig that it was his belief that his brother should be dead that was keeping his soul earthbound.

'Maybe,' I suggested, tentatively, 'you got hit on the head.'

'What if I did?' Craig glared at me. 'Freaking Neil – who couldn't do a chin-up to save his life – *he* managed to hold on. Me, the guy with all the swimming trophies? Yeah, I'm the one who drowned. There's no justice in the world. And that's why I'm here, and Neil's downstairs eating freaking fajitas.'

Jesse looked solemn. 'Is it your plan, then, to avenge your death by taking your brother's life, as you feel yours was taken?'

I winced. I could tell by Craig's expression that nothing of the kind had ever occurred to him. I was sorry Jesse had suggested it.

73

'No way, man,' Craig said. Then, looking as if he was having second thoughts, he added, 'Could I even do that? I mean, kill someone? If I wanted to?'

'No,' I said, at the same time that Jesse said, 'Yes, but you would be risking your immortal soul.'

Craig didn't listen to me, of course. Only to Jesse.

'Cool,' he said, staring down at his own hands.

'No killing,' I said, loudly. 'There will be no fratricide. Not on my watch.'

Craig glanced up at me, looking surprised.

'I'm not gonna kill him,' he said.

I shook my head. 'Then what?' I asked. 'What's holding you back? Was there . . . I don't know, something left unsaid between the two of you? Do you want me to say it to him for you? Whatever it is?'

Craig looked at me like I was nuts.

'Neil?' he echoed. 'Are you kidding me? I've got nothing to say to Neil. The guy's a tool. I mean, look at him, hanging around a guy like your brother. No offence, but Neil could do way better, if he'd just put himself out more.'

While I myself do not hold my stepbrothers in very high esteem – with the exception of David, of course – that didn't mean I could sit idly by while someone maligned them to my face. At least, not Jake, who was, for the most part, fairly inoffensive.

'What's wrong with my brother?' I demanded, a little hotly. 'I mean, my stepbrother?'

'Well, nothing against him, really,' Craig said. 'But, you know . . . well. He's not even in a frat. I mean, I know Neil's just a freshman and impressionable and all of that, but I warned him, you can't get anywhere at NoCal unless you're with the right crowd.'

74

I had, by that time, had about all I could take from Craig Jankow.

'OK,' I said, walking to my bedroom door. 'Well, it was great to meet you, Craig. You'll be hearing from me.' He would, too. I'd know how to find him. All I'd have to do would be to look for Neil and, ten to one, I'd find Craig trailing along behind.

Craig looked eager. 'You mean you're going to try to bring me back to life?'

'No,' I said. 'I mean like I'll determine why you are still here and not where you're supposed to be.'

'Right,' Craig said. 'Alive.'

'I think she means in heaven,' Jesse said. Jesse doesn't go much for the whole reincarnation thing the way I do. 'Or hell.'

Craig, who had taken to eyeing Jesse quite nervously since the whole incident by the door, looked alarmed.

'Oh,' he said, his dark eyebrows raised. '*Oh.*'

'Or your next life,' I said, with a meaningful look at Jesse. 'We don't really know. Do we, Jesse?'

Jesse, who'd stood up because I'd stood up – and Jesse was nothing if not gentlemanly in front of ladies – said, with obvious reluctance, 'No. We don't.'

Craig went to the door, then looked back at both of us.

'Well,' he said. 'See you around, I guess.' Then he glanced over at Jesse and said, 'And, um, I'm sorry about that pirate remark. Really.'

Jesse said, gruffly, 'That's all right.'

Then Craig was gone.

And Jesse let loose.

'Susannah, that boy is trouble. You must turn him over to Father Dominic.'

I sighed, and sank down on to the place on the window

75

seat that Jesse had just vacated. My cat Spike, as was his custom when I approached and Jesse was anywhere in the near vicinity, hissed at me, to make it clear to whom he belonged . . . namely, not me, even though I am the one who pays for his food and litter.

'He'll be fine, Jesse,' I said. 'We'll keep an eye on him. He needs a little time is all. He just died, for crying out loud.'

Jesse shook his head, his dark eyes flashing.

'He's going to try to kill his brother,' he warned me.

'Well, yeah,' I said. 'Now that you put the idea in his head.'

'You must call Father Dominic.' Jesse strode over to the phone and picked it up. 'Tell him he must meet with this boy, the brother, and warn him.'

'Whoa,' I said. 'Slow down, Jesse. I can handle this without having to drag Father Dom into it.'

Jesse looked sceptical. The thing is, even when looking sceptical, Jesse is the hottest guy I have ever seen. I mean, he's not perfect looking, or anything – there's a scar through his right eyebrow, clean and white as a chalk mark, and he is, as I think I've observed before, somewhat fashion impaired.

But in every other way, the guy is Stud City, from the top of his close-cropped black hair to his swashbuckling – I mean, riding – boots, and the six feet or so of extremely un-cadaverous-looking muscle in between.

Too bad his interest in me is apparently completely platonic. Maybe if I'd been a better kisser . . . But come on, it's not like I've had a lot of opportunity to practise. Guys – normal guys – don't exactly come flocking to my door. Not that I am a dog, or anything. In fact, I think I look quite passable, when fully made up with my hair nicely blown out. It is just that it is a bit hard to have a social life when you are constantly being solicited by the undead.

76

'I think you should call him,' Jesse said, thrusting the phone at me again. 'I am telling you, *querida*. There is more to this Craig than meets the eye.'

I blinked, but not because of what Jesse had said about Craig. No, it was because of what he'd called me. *Querida*. He hadn't called me that, not once, since that day we'd kissed. I had, in fact, missed hearing the word from his lips so much that I had actually got curious about what it meant, and looked it up in Brad's Spanish dictionary.

Dearest one. That is what *querida* means. Dearest one or sweetheart.

Which isn't exactly what you call someone for whom you feel mere friendship.

I hoped.

I didn't let on, however, that I knew what the word meant, any more than I let on that I'd noticed he'd allowed it to slip out.

'You're overreacting, Jesse,' I said. 'Craig's not going to do anything to his brother. He loves the guy. He just doesn't seem to have remembered that yet. And besides, even if he didn't – even if he did have homicidal intentions towards Neil – what makes you think all of a sudden that I can't handle it? I mean, come on, Jesse. It's not like I'm unaccustomed to bloodthirsty ghosts.'

Jesse put the phone down, so hard that I thought he'd cracked the plastic cradle.

'That was before,' he said, shortly.

I stared at him. It had grown dark outside, and the only light on in my room was the little one on my dressing table. In its golden glow, Jesse looked even more otherwordly than usual.

'Before what?' I demanded.

Except that I knew. I knew.

77

'Before *he* came,' Jesse said, with a certain amount of bitter emphasis on the pronoun. 'And don't try to deny it, Susannah. You have not slept a full night since. I have seen you, tossing and turning. You cry out in your sleep, sometimes.'

I didn't have to ask who *he* was. I knew. We both knew.

'That's nothing,' I said, even though of course it wasn't. It was something. It was definitely something. Just not what Jesse apparently thought it was. 'I mean, I'm not saying I wasn't scared when you and I thought we were trapped in that . . . place, I mean. And yeah, I have nightmares about it sometimes. But I'll get over it, Jesse. I'm getting over it.'

'You aren't invulnerable, Susannah,' Jesse said, with a frown. 'However much you might think differently.'

I was more than a little surprised that he'd noticed. In fact, I'd begun to wonder if perhaps it was because I didn't act vulnerable – or, OK, feminine – enough that he'd only grabbed and kissed me that once, and never tried to do it again.

Except, of course, as soon as he accused me of being vulnerable, I had to go and deny it was true.

'I'm fine,' I insisted. No point in mentioning to him that, in fact, I was far from fine. That the mere sight of Paul Slater had nearly caused me to have a heart attack. 'I told you. I'm over it, Jesse. And even if I wasn't, it's not like it's going to keep me from helping Craig. Or Neil, really.'

But it was like he wasn't even listening.

'Let Father Dominic take this one,' Jesse said. He nodded towards the door through which Craig had just walked – literally. 'You aren't ready yet. It's too soon.'

Now I wished I had told him about Paul . . . told him nonchalantly, as if it were nothing, to prove to him that's that what it was to me: nothing.

Except of course it wasn't. And it never would be.

'Your solicitude,' I said, sarcastically, in order to hide my discomfort over the whole thing – the fact that I was lying to him, not just about Paul but about myself, as well, 'is appreciated, but misplaced. I can handle Craig Jankow, Jesse.'

He frowned again. But this time, I could see, he really was annoyed. Were we ever actually to date, I knew it would take a lot of *Oprah* viewing before Jesse learned to get over his nineteenth-century machismo.

'I will go,' he said, threateningly, his dark eyes looking black as onyx in the light from my dressing table, 'and tell Father Dominic myself.'

'Fine,' I said. 'Be my guest.'

Which wasn't what I'd wanted to say, of course. What I'd wanted to say was, '*Why?* Why can't we be together, Jesse? I know you want to. Don't even bother denying it. I felt it when you kissed me. I may not have a lot of experience in that department, but I know I'm not wrong about that. You like me, at least a little. So what's the deal? Why have you been giving me the cold shoulder ever since? WHY?'

Whatever the reason might have been, Jesse wasn't revealing it just then. Instead, he set his jaw and went, 'Fine, I will.'

'Go ahead,' I shot back.

A second later, he was gone. *Poof*, just like that.

Well, who needed him, anyway?

All right. I did. I admit it.

But I tried resolutely to put him out of my head. I concentrated instead on my trig homework.

I was still concentrating on it when fourth period – computer lab, for me – rolled around the next day. I am telling you, there is nothing more devastating to a girl's ability to study than a handsome ghost who thinks he knows everything.

79

I was, of course, supposed to be working on a five-hundred-word essay on the Civil War, which had been punitively assigned to the entire eleventh-grade class by our adviser, Mr Walden, who had not appreciated the behaviour of a few of us during that morning's nominations for student government positions.

In particular, Mr Walden had not appreciated my behaviour, when, after Kelly's nomination of Paul for vice-president had been seconded and passed, CeeCee raised her hand and nominated me for vice-president as well.

'Ow,' CeeCee had cried, when I'd kicked her, hard, beneath her desk. 'What is *wrong* with you?'

'I don't want to be vice-president,' I'd hissed at her. 'Put your arm down.'

This had resulted in a good deal of snickering, which had not died down until Mr Walden, never the world's most patient instructor, threw a piece of chalk at the classroom door and told us we'd all better brush up on our American history – five hundred words on the battle of Gettysburg, to be exact.

But my objection came too late. CeeCee's nomination of me was seconded by Adam, and passed a moment later, despite my protests. I was now running for the position of vice-president of the junior class – CeeCee was my campaign manager, Adam, whose grandfather had left him a healthy trust, the main financial contributor to my bid for election – against the New Guy, Paul Slater, whose aw-shucks manner and stunning good looks had already won him almost every female vote in the class.

Not that I cared. I didn't want to be VP anyway. I had enough on my hands, what with the mediator thing and trigonometry and my dead would-be boyfriend. I did not need to have to worry about political infighting on top of all that.

80

It hadn't been a good morning. The nominations had been bad enough; Mr Walden's essay put a nice cap on it.

And then, of course, there was Paul. He'd winked suggestively to me in homeroom, as if to say hello.

As if all of that hadn't been enough, there was the fact that I had foolishly chosen to wear a brand-new pair of Jimmy Choo mules to school, purchased at a fraction of their normal retail cost at an outlet over the summer. They were gorgeous, and they went perfectly with the black Calvin Klein denim skirt I had paired with a hot-pink, scoop-neck top.

But of course they were killing me. I already had raw, painful blisters around the bases of all my toes, and the Band-Aids the nurse had given me to cover them so that I could at least hobble between classes, were not exactly doing the job. My feet felt like they were about to fall off. If I'd known where Jimmy Choo lived, I would have hobbled right up to his front door and popped him one in the eye.

So I was sitting there in the computer lab, my mules kicked off and my toes throbbing painfully, working on my trig homework when I should have been working on my essay, when a voice I had come to know as well as my own startled me by saying, close to my ear, 'Miss me, Suze?'

Nine

'Leave me alone,' I said, more calmly than, in fact, I felt.

'Aw, come on, Simon,' Paul said, reaching out for a nearby chair, swinging it around and then straddling it. 'Admit it. You don't hate me half as much as you pretend to.'

'I wouldn't bet on it,' I said. I tapped my pencil against my notebook with what I hoped he would take to be irritation, but which was, in fact, nervous tension. 'Listen, Paul, I have a lot of work to do—'

He plucked the notebook out from beneath my hands. 'Who's Craig Jankow?' he wanted to know.

Startled, I realized I had doodled the name in the margin of my worksheet.

'Nobody,' I said.

'Oh, that's good,' Paul said. 'I thought maybe he'd gone and replaced me in your affections. Does Jesse know? About this Craig guy, I mean?'

I glared at him, hoping he'd mistake my fear for anger and go away. He didn't seem to be getting the message, though. I hoped he couldn't see how rapidly my pulse was beating in my throat . . . or that if he did, he didn't mistake it for something it was not. Paul was not unaware of his good looks, unfortunately. He had on black jeans that fit him in all the right places and an olive-green polo, short-sleeved.

82

It brought out the deepness of his golf-and-tennis tan. I could see the other girls in the computer lab – Debbie Mancuso, for one – peeking at Paul speculatively, then looking quickly back at their computer monitors, trying to act as if they hadn't been trying to scope him out a minute before.

They were probably seething with jealousy over the fact that he was talking to me, of all people – the only girl in their class who didn't let Kelly Prescott tell her what to do, and who didn't consider Brad Ackerman a hottie.

Little did they know how much I would have appreciated it if Paul Slater hadn't chosen to grace me with his company.

'Craig,' I whispered, just in case anyone was listening, 'happens to be dead.'

'So?' Paul grinned at me. 'I thought that was how you liked 'em.'

'You . . .' I tried to snatch the notebook back from him, but he held it out of my reach. '. . . are insufferable.'

He looked meditative as he studied the problems on my worksheet. 'There's something to be said for having a dead boyfriend, I suppose,' he mused. 'I mean, you don't have to worry about introducing him to your parents, since they can't see him, anyway.'

'Craig's not my boyfriend,' I hissed at him, angry at finding myself in a situation where I was explaining anything to Paul Slater. 'I'm trying to help him. He showed up at my house yesterday—'

'Oh, God.' Paul rolled his expressive blue eyes. 'Not another one of those charity cases you and the good father are always taking on.'

I said, with some indignation, 'Helping lost souls find their way is my job, after all.'

'Who says?' Paul wanted to know.

83

I blinked at him. 'Well . . . it just . . . it just *is*,' I stammered. 'I mean, what else am I supposed to do?'

Paul plucked a pencil from a nearby desk and began swiftly and neatly to solve the problems on my worksheet. 'I wonder. It doesn't seem fair to me that we were just handed this mediator thing at birth without so much as a contract or list of employee benefits. I mean, I never signed up for this mediator thing. Did you?'

'Of course not,' I said, as if this was not something about which I complained, in almost those exact same words, every time I saw Father Dominic.

'And how do you know what your job responsibilities even consist of?' Paul asked. 'Yeah, you think you're supposed to help the dead move on to their final destination, because once you do, they stop bugging you and you can get on with your life again. But I've got a question for you. Who told you it was up to you? Who told you how it was done, even?'

I blinked at him. No one had told me that, actually. Well, my dad had, sort of. And later, a certain psychic my best friend Gina had taken me to back in Brooklyn. And then Father Dom, of course . . .

'Right,' Paul said, observing from my expression, apparently, that I didn't have a real straightforward answer for him. 'Nobody told you. But what if I said I knew. What if I told you I'd found something – something that dated back to the first days of actual written communication – that described mediators, though that wasn't what we were called back then, and their real purpose . . . not to mention techniques . . . exactly?'

I continued to blink at him. He sounded so . . . well, convincing. And he certainly looked sincere.

'If you really had something like that,' I said, hesitantly, 'I guess I'd say: show me.'

84

'Fine,' Paul said, looking pleased. 'Come over to my place after school today, and I will.'

I was up and out of my chair so fast, I practically tipped it over.

'No,' I said, gathering up my books and clutching them in front of my wildly beating heart, as if both to hide and protect it. '*No way.*'

Paul regarded me smilingly from where he sat, not seeming too surprised by my reaction.

'Hmmm,' he said. 'I thought as much. You want to know, but not enough to risk your reputation.'

'It isn't my reputation I'm worried about,' I informed him, managing to make my tone more acid than shaken. 'It's my life. You tried to kill me once, remember?'

I said these words a little too loudly, and noticed several people glance at me curiously over the tops of the computer monitors.

Paul, however, just looked bored.

'Not that again,' he said. 'Listen, Suze, I told you . . . Well, I guess it doesn't matter what I told you. You're going to believe what you want to believe. But seriously, you could have got out of there any time you wanted to.'

'But Jesse couldn't have,' I hissed at him. 'Could he? Thanks to you.'

'Well,' Paul said, with an uncomfortable shrug. 'No. Not Jesse. But, really, Suze, don't you think you're overreacting? I mean, what's the big deal? The guy's already dead.'

'You,' I said, my trembling voice giving the statement somewhat iffy conviction, 'are a pig.'

Then I started to stride away. I say started to because I didn't get very far before Paul's calm voice stopped me.

'Uh, Suze,' Paul said. 'Aren't you forgetting something?'

85

I turned my head to glare at him. 'Oh, you mean, did I forget to tell you not to speak to me again? Yes.'

'No,' Paul said, with a wry smile. 'Aren't those your shoes under there?' He pointed down at my Jimmy Choos, without which I'd been about to stalk from the room. Like Sister Ernestine wouldn't have had too big a coronary if she'd caught me wandering around school in my bare feet.

'Oh,' I said, mad that my dramatic exit had been spoiled. 'Yeah.' I went back to my desk so I could jam my feet into my mules.

'Before you go, Cinderella,' Paul said, still smiling, 'you might also want to take this.' He held out my trig homework. I could tell with a single glance that he'd finished it neatly and, I could only assume, correctly.

'Thanks,' I said, taking the notebook from him and feeling more and more sheepish with every passing second. I mean, why, exactly, was I always flying off the handle with this guy? Yeah, he'd tried to kill me – and Jesse – once. At least, I thought he had. But he kept saying I was wrong. What if I was wrong? What if Paul wasn't the monster I'd always thought him? What if he was . . .

What if he was just like me?

'About this Craig guy,' Paul added.

'Paul.' I sank down into the chair beside him. I had felt the gaze of Mrs Tarentino, the teacher assigned to supervise the computer lab, boring into me. Popping in and out of your chair in the lab is not strictly smiled upon, unless you are going back and forth from the printer.

But that wasn't the only reason I sat down again. I'll admit that. I was curious, too. Curious over what he'd say next. And that curiosity was almost stronger than my fear.

'Seriously,' I said. 'Thanks. But I do not need your help.'

86

'I think you do,' Paul said. 'What's this Craig guy want, anyway?'

'He wants what all ghosts want,' I said, tiredly. 'To be alive again.'

'Well, of course,' Paul said. 'I mean, what's he want besides that.'

'I don't know yet,' I said, with a shrug. 'He's got this thing with his little brother . . . thinks he should have been the one to die, not him. Jesse thinks . . .' I stopped talking, suddenly aware that Jesse was the last person I wanted to bring up in front of Paul.

Paul looked only politely interested, however. 'Jesse thinks what?'

It was, I saw, too late to keep Jesse out of it. I sighed and said, 'Jesse thinks Craig's going to try to kill his brother. You know. Out of revenge.'

'Which will, of course,' Paul said, not looking in the least surprised, 'get him exactly nowhere. When will they ever learn? Now, if he wanted to *be* his brother, that would be a different story.'

'*Be* his brother?' I looked at him curiously. 'What do you mean?'

'You know,' Paul said, with a shrug. 'Soul transference. Take over his brother's body.'

This was a little too much for a Tuesday morning. I mean, I had already had a pretty crummy night's sleep thanks to this guy. Then, to hear something like this come out of his mouth . . . well, let's just say I was not at my sharpest, so what happened next can hardly be described as my fault.

'*Take over his brother's body?*' I echoed. I had lowered my books until they rested in my lap. Now I reached out and gripped the arms of my computer chair, my nails sinking into the cheap foam-padded armrests. 'What are you talking about?'

87

One of Paul's dark eyebrows hiked up. 'Doesn't sound familiar, eh? What *has* the good father been teaching you, I wonder? Not much, from the sound of things.'

'What are you talking about?' I demanded. 'How can someone take over someone else's body?'

'I told you,' Paul said, leaning back in his chair and folding his hands behind his head, 'that there was a lot you didn't know about being a mediator. And a lot more that I could teach you, if you'd just give me the chance.'

I stared at him. I really had no idea what he was talking about with this body-swapping thing. It sounded like something from the Sci-Fi channel. And I wasn't sure if Paul was just feeding me a line – something, anything, to get me to do what he wanted.

But what if he wasn't? What if there was seriously a way to . . .

I wanted to know. My God, I wanted to know more than I had ever wanted anything in my life.

'All right,' I said, feeling the sweat that had broken out beneath my palms, making the chair's armrests slick with moisture. But I didn't care. My heart was in my throat and still I didn't care. 'All right. I'll come over to your place after school. But only if you'll tell me about . . . about that.'

Something flashed through Paul's blue eyes. Just a gleam, and I only saw it for a moment before it was gone again. It was something animal-like, almost feral. I couldn't say just what, exactly, it had been.

All I knew was that the next minute, Paul was smiling at me – smiling, not grinning.

'Fine,' he said. 'I'll pick you up by the main gate at three. Be there on time, or I'll leave without you.'

88

Ten

I wasn't, of course, going to meet him. I mean, despite ample evidence to the contrary, I am not stupid. I have, in the past, met various people at various appointed times and found myself, hours later, tied to a chair, thrust into a parallel dimension, forced to don one-piece swimsuits, or otherwise cruelly mistreated. I was not going to meet Paul Slater after school. I was so not.

And then I did, anyway.

Well, what else was I supposed to do? The lure was just too great. I mean, actual documented evidence about mediators? Something about people being able to take over other people's bodies? All the nightmares about long, fog-enshrouded hallways in the world were not going to keep me from finding out the truth, at last, about what I was and what I could do. I had spent too many years wondering just that to allow an opportunity like this to slip from my fingers. I had never, unlike Father Dominic, been able merely to accept the cards I'd been dealt. I wanted to know why they'd been dealt to me, and how. I *had* to know.

And if, in order to find out, I had to spend time with someone who regularly haunted my sleep, so be it. It was worth the sacrifice.

Or I hoped it would be, anyway.

89

Adam and CeeCee weren't too happy about it, of course. As the last class of the day let out, they met me in the hallway – I was visibly limping, thanks to my shoes, but CeeCee didn't notice. She was too busy consulting the list she'd drawn up in Bio.

'All right,' she said. 'We've got to head on over to Safeway for markers, glitter, glue and poster board. Adam, does your mom still have those dowel rods in the garage from when she went on that Amish chair-making kick? Because we could use them for the Vote for Suze placards.'

'Uh,' I said, hobbling along beside them. 'You guys.'

'Suze, can we take all the stuff over to your place to assemble it? I'd say we could take it to my place, but you know my sisters. They'll probably rollerskate over it, or whatever.'

'Guys,' I said. 'Look. I appreciate this and all. I really do. But I can't come with you. I've already got plans.'

Adam and CeeCee exchanged glances.

'Oh?' CeeCee said. 'Meeting the mysterious Jesse, are we?'

'Uh,' I said. 'Not exactly . . .'

At that moment, Paul came past us in the hall. He said to me, noticing my limp, 'Let me just pull the car around to the side door. That way you won't have to walk to the gate,' and breezed on by.

Adam gave me a scandalized look. 'Fraternizing with the enemy!' he cried. 'For shame, wench!'

CeeCee looked equally stunned. 'You're going out with *him*?' She shook her head so that her stick-straight, white-blonde hair shimmered. 'What about Jesse?'

'I'm not going out with him,' I said, uncomfortably. 'We're just . . . working on a project together.'

'What project?' CeeCee's eyes, behind the coloured lenses of her glasses, narrowed. 'For what class?'

90

'It's . . .' I shifted my weight from one foot to another, hoping to find some relief from my cruel shoes, all to no avail. 'It's not for school, really. It's more for . . . for . . . church.'

Even as the word came out of my mouth, I knew I'd made a mistake.

'*Church?*' CeeCee looked mad. 'You're Jewish, Suze, in case I need to remind you.'

'Well, not technically, really,' I said. 'I mean, my dad was, but my mom isn't . . .' A car horn sounded just beyond the ornately scrolled gate we were standing behind. 'Oops, that's Paul. Gotta go, sorry.'

Then, moving pretty quickly for a girl who felt shooting stabs of pain go up her legs with every step, I hightailed it out to Paul's convertible and slid into the passenger seat with a sigh of relief at being in a seated position once more, and a feeling that, at last, I was going to find out a thing or two about who – or what – I really was.

But I had an equally strong feeling that I wasn't going to like what I found out. In fact, a part of me was wondering whether or not I was making the worst mistake of my life.

It didn't help matters much that Paul, with his dark sunglasses and easy smile, looked like a movie star. Really, how could I have had so many nightmares about this guy who was so clearly any normal girl's dream date? I didn't miss the envious glances that were being shot in my direction from around the parking lot.

'Did I happen to mention,' Paul asked, as I fastened my seat belt, 'that I think those shoes are flickin'?'

I swallowed. I didn't even know what flicking meant. I could only assume from his tone that it meant something good.

Did I really want to do this? Was it worth it?

91

The answer came from deep within . . . so deep, I realized that I had known it all along: Yes. Oh, yes.

'Just drive,' I said, my voice coming out huskier than usual because I was trying not to let my nervousness show.

And so he did.

The house he drove me to was an impressive two-storied structure built into the side of a cliff right off Carmel Beach. It was made almost entirely of glass in order to take advantage of its ocean and sunset views.

Paul seemed to notice that I was impressed, since he said, 'It's my grandfather's place. He wanted a little place on the beach to retire to.'

'Right,' I said, swallowing hard. Grandpa Slater's 'little place' on the beach had to have cost a cool five million or so. 'And he doesn't mind having a roommate all of a sudden?'

'Are you kidding?' Paul smirked as he parked his car in one of the spaces of the house's four-car garage. 'He barely knows I'm here. The guy's gorked out on his meds most of the time.'

'Paul,' I said, uncomfortably.

'What?' Paul blinked at me from behind his Ray Bans. 'I'm just stating a fact. Pops is pretty much bedridden and should be in an assisted-living facility, but he put up this huge fuss when we tried to move him to one. So when I suggested I move in to kind of keep an eye on things, my dad agreed. It's a win-win situation. Pops gets to live at home – with health care attendants to look after him, of course – and I get to attend my dream school, the Mission Academy.'

I felt my face heat up, but I tried to keep my tone light.

'Oh, so going to Catholic school is your dream?' I asked, sarcastically.

'It is if you're there,' Paul said, just as lightly . . . but not quite as sarcastically.

92

My face promptly turned red as a cherry-dipped cone. Keeping it averted so that Paul wouldn't notice, I said, primly, 'I don't think this is such a good idea, after all.'

'Relax, Simon,' Paul drawled. 'That's Pop's day attendant's car parked down at the end of the driveway, in case you're, you know, suffering from any feminine misgivings about being alone in the house with me.'

I followed the direction Paul was pointing. At the end of the steep, circular drive sat a rusted-out Toyota Celica. I didn't say anything, but mostly only because I was kind of amazed at how easily Paul seemed to have read my mind. I had been sitting there suffering from second thoughts about the whole thing. I had never exactly raised the issue with my parents, but I was pretty sure I wasn't allowed to go to guys' houses when their parents weren't home.

On the other hand, if I didn't in this case, I would never find out what I needed – and I was convinced by now that this was something I actually really did need – to know.

Paul slid out from behind the wheel, then walked around to my side of the car and opened the door for me.

'Coming, Suze?' he asked, when I didn't move to undo my seatbelt.

'Uh,' I said, looking nervously up at the big glass house. It looked disturbingly empty, despite the Toyota.

Paul seemed to read my mind again.

'Would you get off it, Suze?' he said, rolling his eyes. 'Your virtue's in no danger from me. I swear I'll keep my hands to myself. This is business. There'll be plenty of time for pleasure later . . . that is, if I can ever manage to convince you to give one of us live guys a try.'

I tried to smile coolly, so he wouldn't suspect that I am not accustomed to people – OK, guys – saying this sort of thing to me every day. But the truth is, of course, I'm not. And it

93

bugged me, the way it made me feel when Paul did it. I mean, I did not even like this guy, but every time he said something like that – suggested that he thought I was, I don't know, special – it sent this little shiver down my spine . . . and not in a bad way.

That was the thing. *It wasn't in a bad way.* What was *that* all about? I mean, I don't even like Paul. I am fully in love with somebody else. And yeah, Jesse is presently showing no signs of actually returning my feelings, but it's not like because of that I am suddenly going to start going out with Paul Slater . . . no matter how good he might look in his Ray Bans.

I got out of the car.

'Wise decision,' Paul commented, closing the car door behind me.

There was a sort of finality in the sound of that door being snapped shut. I tried not to think about what I might be letting myself in for as I followed Paul up the cement steps to the wide glass front door to his grandfather's house, my Jimmy Choos in one hand and my book bag in the other.

Inside the Slaters' house, it was cool and quiet . . . so quiet you couldn't even hear the pounding surf of the ocean not a hundred feet below it. Whoever had decorated the place had taste that ran towards the modern, so everything looked sleek and new and uncomfortable. The house, I imagined, must be freezing in the morning when the fog rolled in, since everything in it was made of glass or metal. Paul led me up a twisting steel staircase from the front door to the high-tech kitchen, where all of the appliances gleamed aggressively.

'Cocktail?' he asked me, opening a glass door to a liquor cabinet.

'Very funny,' I said. 'Just water, please. Where's your grandfather?'

94

'Down the hall,' Paul said, as he pulled two bottles of designer water from the enormous Sub-Zero fridge. He must have noticed my nervous glance over my shoulder, since he added, 'Go take a look for yourself if you don't believe me.'

I went to take a look for myself. It wasn't that I didn't trust him. Well, OK, it was. Though it would have been pretty bold of him to lie about something I could so easily check for myself. And what was I going to do if it turned out his grandfather wasn't there? I mean, no way was I leaving before I'd found out what I'd come to learn.

Fortunately, it appeared I wouldn't have to. Hearing some faint sounds, I followed them down a long glass hallway until I came to a room in which a wide-screen television was on. In front of the television sat a very old man in a very high-tech wheelchair. Beside the wheelchair, in a very uncomfortable-looking modern chair, sat a youngish guy in a blue nurse's uniform, reading a magazine. He looked up when I appeared in the doorway, and smiled.

'Hey,' he said.

'Hey,' I said back, and came tentatively into the room. It was a nice room, with one of the better views in the house, I imagined. It had been furnished with a hospital bed, complete with an IV bag and adjustable frame, and metal bookshelves on which rested frame after frame of photographs. Black-and-white photographs, mostly, judging by their outfits, of people from the forties.

'Um,' I said, to the old man in the wheelchair. 'Hi, Mr Slater. I'm Susannah Simon.'

The old man didn't say anything. He didn't even take his gaze from the game show that was on in front of him. He was mostly bald and pretty much covered in liver spots, and he was drooling a little. The nurse noticed this and leaned over with a handkerchief to wipe the old man's mouth.

95

'There you go, Mr Slater,' the nurse said. 'The nice young lady said hello. Aren't you going to say hello back?'

But Mr Slater didn't say anything. Instead, Paul, who'd come into the room behind me, went, 'How's it going, Pops? Had another riveting day in front of the old tube?'

Mr Slater did not acknowledge Paul, either. The nurse said, 'We had a good day, didn't we, Mr Slater? Took a nice walk in the backyard, around the pool, and picked a few lemons.'

'That's great,' Paul said, with obviously forced enthusiasm. Then he took my hand and started to drag me from the room. I will admit he didn't have to drag hard. I was pretty creeped out, and went willingly enough. Which is saying a lot, considering how I felt about Paul, and everything. I mean, that there was someone who creeped me out more than he did.

'Bye, Mr Slater,' I said, not expecting a response – which was a good thing, since I got none.

Out in the hallway, I asked, quietly, 'What's wrong with him? Alzheimer's?'

'Naw,' Paul said, handing me one of the dark blue bottles of water. 'They don't know, exactly. He's lucid enough, when he wants to be.'

'Really?' I had a hard time believing it. Lucid people can usually maintain some control over their own saliva. 'Maybe he's just . . . you know. Old.'

'Yeah,' Paul said, with another of his trademark bitter laughs. 'That's probably it, all right.' Then, without elaborating further, he threw open a door on his right and said, 'This is it. What I wanted to show you.'

I followed him into what was, clearly, his bedroom. It was about five times as big as my own room – and Paul's bed was about five times bigger than mine, as well. Like the rest of

96

the house, everything was very streamlined and modern, with a lot of metal and glass. There was even a glass desk – or plexiglas, probably – on which rested a brand-new, top-of-the-line laptop.

There was none of the kind of personal stuff lying around Paul's room that always seemed to be scattered around mine – like magazines or dirty socks or nail polish or half-eaten boxes of Girl Scout cookies. There was nothing personal in Paul's room at all. It was like a very high-tech, very cold hotel room.

'It's here,' Paul said, sitting down on the edge of his boat-sized bed.

'Yeah,' I said, more spooked than ever now . . . and not just because of the bed, and the fact that Paul was sitting on, and patting, the empty space on the mattress beside him. No, it was also the fact that the only colour in the room, besides what Paul and I were wearing, was what I could see out the enormous plate glass windows . . . the blue, blue sky, and below it, the darker blue sea. 'Sure it is.'

'I'm serious,' Paul said, and he quit patting the mattress like he wanted me to sit beside him. Instead, he reached beneath the bed and pulled out a clear plastic box, like the kind you store wool sweaters in over the summer . . . or at least you would, if you lived in a place where it got cold enough for wool sweaters.

Placing the box beside him on the bed, Paul pulled off the lid. Inside were what looked to be a number of newspaper and magazine articles, each one carefully clipped from its original source.

'Check this out,' Paul said, carefully unfolding a particularly ancient newspaper article and spreading it out across the slate-grey bedspread so that I could see it. It came from the London *Times*, and was dated June 18, 1952. There was

97

a photograph of a man standing before what looked like the hieroglyphic-covered wall of an Egyptian tomb. The head-line above the photo and article ran, *Archaeologist's Theory Scoffed by Sceptics.*

'This is Dr Oliver Slaski,' Paul said, smoothing the yellowed paper out for me to read. 'He was an Egyptologist who worked for years to translate the complicated text on this particular wall here. Finally, he came to the conclusion that in ancient Egypt there was actually a small group of shamans who were considered essential to the successful passage of a king's soul into the spirit world. These were actual human beings who had the ability to travel in and out of the realm of the dead without, in fact, dying themselves. These shamans were called, as near as Dr Slaski could translate, shifters. They could shift from this plane of being to the next, and were hired as spirit guides for the deceased by the deceased's family, in order to ensure their loved one ended up where he was supposed to, instead of aimlessly wandering the planet.'

I had sunk down on to the bed as Paul had been speaking, so that I could get a better look at the picture he was indicating. I had been hesitant to do so before – I didn't really want to get near Paul at all, especially considering the whole bed thing.

Now, however, I hardly noticed how close we were sitting together. I leaned forward to stare at the picture until my hair brushed against the cracked and yellowed paper.

'Shifters,' I said, through lips that had gone strangely cold, as if I had put Carmex on them. Only I hadn't. 'What he meant was mediators.'

'I don't think so,' Paul said.

'No,' I said. I was feeling sort of breathless. Well, you would, too, if your whole life you had wondered where you'd

98

come from . . . what you were doing on this planet . . . why you were so different from everyone you knew . . . and then all of a sudden, one day you found out. Or at least got hold of a very important clue.

'That is exactly what it means, Paul,' I exclaimed. 'The ninth card in the tarot deck – the one called the Hermit – features an old man holding a lantern, just like this guy is doing. And the Hermit is a spirit guide, someone who is supposed to lead the dead to their final destination. And OK, the guy in the hieroglyphic isn't old, but they are both doing the same thing . . . He has to be a mediator, Paul,' I said, my heart thudding hard against my ribs. This was big. Really big. The fact that there was actual documented proof of the existence of people like me. I had never hoped to see such a thing. I couldn't wait to tell Father Dominic. 'He *has* to be!'

'But that's not all they were, Suze,' Paul said, reaching back into the acrylic box and bringing out a sheaf of papers, also brown with age. 'According to Slaski, who wrote a thesis about it, there's reason to believe there was a hierarchy within this group of shamans. There were ones you could hire merely to communicate with your dead family member – those are what we know traditionally as mediums, or, if you prefer, mediators. But then there was this whole other level of shamans – thought of as the most powerful mystic beings in Egypt – that you could hire actually to accompany your relative to the realm of the dead, get them all settled in, and then return. Those were the shifters. And that,' Paul said, looking at me very intently from across the bed (and not very far across the bed, either, as we were leaning only about a foot apart, the pages of Dr Slaski's thesis between us,) 'is what you and I are, Suze. Shifters.'

Again, I felt the chill. It raced up and down my spine, made the hair on my arms stand up. I don't know what it

99

was – the word, shifters, or the way Paul said it. But it had an effect on me . . . quite an effect on me. Like sticking my finger in a light socket.

I shook my head, vehemently enough that my hair brushed against the yellowed newspaper articles.

'No,' I said, in a panicky voice. 'Not me. I'm just a mediator. I mean, if I were a shifter, I wouldn't have had to exorcize myself that time—'

'You didn't have to,' Paul interrupted, his voice, compared to the high-pitched squeak mine had become, deep and calm. 'You could have got yourself there – and back – on your own, just by visualizing the place. You could do it right now, if you wanted to.'

I blinked at him. Paul's eyes, I noticed, above the crinkled pages of Dr Slaski's thesis, were very bright. They almost seemed to gleam, like cats' eyes. I could not tell if he was telling the truth or simply trying to mess with my head. Knowing Paul, either would not have surprised me. He seemed to get pleasure out of blurting things out, then seeing how people – all right, me – reacted.

'No way,' was how I responded to his suggestion that I was anything but what I'd always thought I was. Even though the whole reason I was even in his bedroom was because deep down, I knew I was not.

'Try it,' Paul urged. 'Picture it in your head. You know what the place looks like now.'

Did I ever. Thanks to him, I'd been trapped there for the longest fifteen minutes of my life. I was still trapped there, every single night, in my dreams. Even now, I could hear my heartbeat drumming in my ears as I tore down that long, dark corridor, fog swirling and then parting around my legs. Did Paul really think that, even for a second, I ever wanted to visit that place again?

100

'No,' I said. 'No, thanks.'

Paul's smile turned wry.

'Don't tell me Suze Simon is actually afraid of something.' His eyes seemed to glow more brightly than ever. 'You always act as if you were immune to fear the way some people are immune to chickenpox.'

'I'm not afraid,' I lied, with feigned indignation. 'I just don't feel like – what is it called again? Oh, yeah – shifting, right now. Maybe later. Right now I want to ask you about that other thing you mentioned. The thing where somebody can take over somebody else's body. Soul transference, or whatever.'

Paul's smile broadened. 'I thought that one might get your attention.'

I knew what he was referring to – or thought I did, anyway. I could feel my face heating up. I ignored my burning cheeks, however, and said, with what I hoped sounded like cool indifference, 'It sounds interesting, is all. Is it really possible?' I plucked at the crumpled pages of the thesis that lay between us. 'Does Dr Slaski mention it at all?'

'Maybe,' Paul said, laying a hand down over the typewritten sheets so that I could not lift them.

'Paul,' I said, tugging on the sheets. 'I'm just curious. I mean, have you ever done it? Does it actually work? Could Craig really take over his brother's body?'

But Paul wouldn't let go of Dr Slaski's papers.

'It's not because of Craig that you're asking, though, is it?' His blue-eyed gaze bore into me. There wasn't the slightest hint of a smile on his face any more. 'Suze, when are you going to get it?'

That was when I finally noticed how close his face was to mine. Just inches away, really. I started instinctively to pull away, but the fingers that had been holding down Dr Slaski's

101

paper suddenly lifted and seized my wrist. I looked down at Paul's hand. His tanned skin was very dark against mine.

'Jesse's dead,' Paul said. 'But that doesn't mean you have to act like you are, too.'

'I don't,' I protested. 'I—'

But I didn't get to finish my little speech, because right in the middle of it, Paul leaned over.

And kissed me.

Eleven

I won't lie to you. It was a good kiss. I felt it all the way down to my poor, blistered toes.

Which is not to say I kissed him back. I most definitely did not . . .

Well, OK. Not that much, anyway.

It was just that, you know, Paul was such a *good* kisser. And I hadn't been kissed in a very long time. It felt nice to know that *someone*, at least, wanted me. Even if that someone happened to be a person I despised. Or at least, someone I was pretty sure I despised.

The truth was, it was sort of hard to remember whether or not I despised Paul. Not while he was kissing me so thoroughly. I mean, it isn't every day – unfortunately – that hot guys go around grabbing and kissing me. In fact, it had really only happened a handful of times before.

And when Paul Slater did it . . . well, let's just say that the last thing I was expecting was to *like* it.

Now I really was in danger – not of being killed, but of completely losing my head for a guy who was bad for me in every way. Because that's exactly how Paul Slater's kiss made me feel. Like I'd do anything – *anything* – to be kissed by him some more.

Which was just plain wrong. Because I wasn't in love with Paul Slater. Granted, the guy I was in love with was

A) dead, and

B) apparently not real interested in pursuing a romantic relationship with me.

But that didn't mean it was permissible for me to fling myself at the very next hottie who happened to come along. I mean, a girl has to have some principles . . .

Such as saving herself for the guy she really likes, even if he happens to be too stupid to realize they are perfect for one another.

So even though Paul's kiss made me feel like throwing my free arm around his neck and kissing him back – which I may or may not, in the heat of the moment, actually have done   it would have been wrong, wrong, WRONG.

So I tried to pull away.

Only let me tell you, that grip he had on my wrist? Yeah, it was like iron. *Iron.*

And even worse, thanks to my having encouraged him by kissing him back a little, half his body ended up over mine, pressing me back on to the bed and probably wrinkling Dr Slaski's thesis pretty badly. I know it wasn't doing any good for my Calvin Klein jeanskirt.

So then I had like a hundred and eighty pounds or something of seventeen-year-old guy on top of me, which is not, you know, any picnic, when it isn't the guy you *want* to be on top of you. Or even if it is, but you are doing your best to stay true to someone else . . . someone who, to the best of your knowledge, doesn't even want you. But whatever.

I managed to wrestle my lips away from Paul's long enough to say, in a sort of a strangled voice, since he was crushing my lungs, 'Get off me.'

'Come on, Suze,' he said, in a tone that, I'm sorry to say, sounded as if it were heavy. With passion. Or something, anyway. I'm even more sorry to say that the sound of it

104

thrilled along every nerve in my body. I mean, that passion was for *me*. Me, Suze Simon, about whom no guy had ever felt all that passionate. At least so far as I knew. 'Don't tell me you haven't been thinking about this all afternoon.'

'Actually,' I said, pleased that I was able to answer this one truthfully, 'I really haven't. Now get off me.'

But Paul just went on kissing me – not on the mouth, because I had fully turned my head away – but on my neck and, at one point, part of one of my ears.

'Is this about the student government thing?' he asked, between kisses. 'Because I couldn't care less about being vice-president of your stupid class. If you're mad about it, just say the word and I'll drop out of the race.'

'No, this has nothing to do with the student government thing,' I said, still trying to wrench my wrist from his fingers, and also to keep my neck away from his mouth. His lips seemed to have a curious effect on the skin of my throat. They made it feel like it was on fire.

'Oh, God. It's not Jesse, is it?' I could feel Paul's groan reverberate through his entire body. 'Give it up, Suze. The guy's *dead*.'

'I didn't say it had anything to do with Jesse.' I sounded defensive, but I didn't care. 'Did you hear me say it had anything to do with Jesse?'

'You didn't have to,' Paul said. 'It's written all over your face. Suze, think about it. Where's it going to go with the guy, anyway? I mean, you're going to get older, and he's going to stay exactly the age he was when he croaked. And what, he's going to take you to the prom? How about movies? You guys go to the movies together? Who drives? Who *pays*?'

Now I was really mad at him. More, of course, because he was right than anything else. Also because he was assuming that Jesse even returned my feelings, which sadly I knew was

105

not true. Why else would he have stayed away from me so assiduously these past few weeks?

Then Paul drove the knife home.

'Besides, if the two of you were really right for each other,' he went on, 'would you even be here? And would you have been kissing me like you were a minute ago?'

That did it. Now I was furious. Because he was right. That was the thing. He was right.

And it was breaking my heart. Worse than Jesse already had.

'If you don't get off me,' I said, through gritted teeth, 'I will jab my thumb into your eye socket.'

Paul chuckled. Although I noticed he stopped chuckling when my thumb did actually meet with the corner of his eye . . .

'Ow!' he yelled, rolling off me fast. 'What the . . .'

I was up and off that bed faster than you could say paranormal activity. I grabbed my shoes, my bag and what was left of my dignity, and got the heck out of there.

'Suze!' Paul yelled, from his bedroom. 'Get back here! Suze!'

I didn't pay any attention. I just kept on running. I tore past Grandpa Slater's room – he was still watching an old rerun of *Family Feud* – then started down the twisting staircase to the front door.

I would have made it, too, if a three-hundred-pound Hell's Angel hadn't suddenly materialized between me and the door.

That's right. One minute my way was clear, and the next it was blocked by Biker Bob. Or should I say, the ghost of Biker Bob.

'Whoa,' I said, as I nearly barrelled into him. The guy had a handlebar moustache and heavily tattooed arms, which

106

he had crossed in front of him. He was also, I shouldn't need to point out, quite, quite dead. 'Where'd *you* come from?'

'Never you mind that, little lady,' he said. 'I think Mr Slater'd still like a word with you.'

I heard footsteps at the top of the stairs and looked up. Paul was there, one hand still over his eye.

'Suze,' he said. 'Don't go.'

'*Minions?*' I called up to him incredulously. 'You have ghostly *minions* to do your bidding? What *are* you?'

'I told you,' Paul said. 'I'm a shifter. So are you. And you are way overreacting about this whole thing. Can't we just talk, Suze? I swear I'll keep my hands to myself.'

'Where have I heard that before?' I asked.

Then, as Biker Bob took a threatening step towards me, I did the only thing that, under the circumstances, I felt that I could. I lifted up one of my Jimmy Choos and smacked him in the head with it.

This is not, I am sure, the purpose for which Mr Choo designed that particular mule. It did, however, work quite handily. With a very surprised Biker Bob incapacitated, it was only a matter of shoving him out of the way, throwing open the door and making a run for it. Which I did, with alacrity.

I was tearing down the long cement steps from Paul's front door to his driveway when I heard him calling after me, 'Suze! Suze, come on. I'm sorry for what I said about Jesse. I didn't mean it.'

I turned in the driveway to face him. I am sorry to say that I responded to his statement by making a rude, single-fingered gesture.

'Suze.' Paul had taken his hand down from his face, so that I could see that his eye was not, as I had hoped, dangling

107

out of its socket. It just looked red. 'At least let me drive you home.'

'No, thank you,' I called to him, pausing to slip on my Jimmy Choos. 'I prefer to walk.'

'Suze,' Paul said. 'It's like five miles from here to your house.'

'Never speak to me again, please,' I said, and started walking, hoping he wouldn't try to follow me. Because of course if he did, and attempted to kiss me again, there was a very good chance I would kiss him back. I knew that now. Knew it only too well.

He didn't follow me. I made it down his driveway and out on to the ocean-front road – imaginatively named Scenic Drive – with what was left of my self-esteem still more or less in tact. It wasn't until I was out of sight of Paul's house that I slipped off my shoes and said what I'd wanted to say the whole time I'd been striding, with as much hauteur as I could, away from him. Which was, 'Ouch, ouch, ouch!'

Stupid shoes. My toes were in shreds. No way could I walk in the torturous things. I thought about flinging them into the ocean, which would have been easy considering it was only about twenty feet below me.

On the other hand, the shoes were six hundred bucks, retail. Granted I had got them for a fraction of that, but still. The shopaholic in me would not allow so rash a move.

So, holding my shoes in my hand, I began to mince my way down the road barefooted, keeping a sharp eye out for bits of glass and any poison oak that might be growing alongside the street.

Paul had been right about one thing: it was a five-mile walk from his house to mine. Worse, it was about a mile walk from his house to the first commercial structure at which I

108

might reasonably expect to find a payphone where I could start calling around to see if I could get someone to pick me up. I could, I supposed, have gone up to one of the huge houses belonging to Paul's neighbours, rung the bell, and asked if I could use their phone. But how embarrassing would that be? No, a payphone. That was all I needed. And I'd find one soon enough.

There was only one real flaw in my plan, and that was the weather. Oh, don't get me wrong. It was a beautiful September day. There wasn't a cloud in the sky.

Which was the problem. The sun was beating down mercilessly upon Scenic Drive. It had to have been ninety degrees at least - even though the cool breeze from the sea didn't make it seem uncomfortable. But the pavement beneath my bare feet wasn't affected by the breeze. The road, which had seemed comfortably warm beneath the soles of my feet when I'd first come barrelling out of Paul's cold, cold house, was actually extremely hot. Burning hot. Like fry-an-egg-on-it hot.

There wasn't anything I could do about it, of course. I couldn't put my shoes back on. My blisters hurt more than the soles of my feet. Maybe if a car had gone by, I'd have tried to flag it down – but probably not. I was too embarrassed at my predicament, really, to have to explain it to a total stranger. Besides, given my luck, I'd probably manage to flag down a serial killer and find myself out of the frying pan – literally – and smack in the middle of the fire.

No. I kept walking, cursing myself and my stupidity. How could I have been so dumb as to have agreed to go to Paul Slater's house? True, the stuff he'd showed me, about the shifters, had been interesting. It was cool to know I might be a descendant of a race of Egyptian shamans. And that thing about soul transference . . . if there really was such a thing.

109

I didn't even want to let myself think about what *that* might mean. To put a soul in a someone else's body . . .

Shifting, I said to myself. Concentrate on the whole shifting thing. Better that, of course, than on the soul transference thing . . . or worse, the even more unpleasant topic of how it was that I could be so carried away by the kisses of someone other than the guy I happened to be in love with.

Or was it just that, after Jesse's seeming rejection, I was relieved to find that I was attractive to somebody, anyway . . . even somebody whom I did not particularly like? Because I did not like Paul Slater. I did not. I think the fact that I had been having bad dreams about him for the past few weeks was proof enough of that . . . no matter how fast my traitorous heart might beat when his lips were pressed against mine.

It felt good, as I walked, to concentrate on this instead of my extremely sore feet. It was slow going, walking down Scenic Drive without any protection from the shards of gravel and, of course, the hot pavement, beneath my soles. Of course, in a way I felt that the pain was punishment for my very bad behaviour. True, Paul had lured me to his house with promises that he would reveal some information I had very badly wanted. But I ought to have resisted just the same, knowing that someone like Paul would have to have a hidden agenda.

And that that agenda would most likely be my mouth.

What galled me was that for a minute or so back there, I hadn't cared. Really. I'd *liked* it, even. Bad Suze. *Very* bad Suze.

Oh, God. I was in trouble.

Then, finally, after about half an hour of painful mincing, I saw the most beautiful sight in the world: a seaside café. I

110

hurried towards it – well, as fast as I could on feet that felt as if they had been hacked off at the ankle – mentally ticking off who I could safely call when I got there. My mom? Never. She'd ask too many questions and probably kill me besides for agreeing to go to the house of a boy she'd never met. Jake? No. Again, he'd ask too many questions. Brad? No, he would just as soon leave me stranded, as he happened to hate my guts. Adam?

It was going to have to be Adam. He was the only person I knew who would not only happily drive out to get me, but who would relish his role as rescuer . . . not to mention also greatly enjoy hearing about how Paul had sexually harassed me, without afterwards desiring to beat Paul into a bloody pulp. Adam would have the sense to know that Paul Slater could kick his ass any day of the week. I would not mention to Adam, of course, the part where I'd sexually harassed Paul right back.

The Sea Mist Café – that was the restaurant I was limping towards – was an upscale restaurant with outdoor seating and valet parking. It was too late for lunch and too early for it to be serving dinner, so there were no diners, just the waiting staff setting up for the supper rush. As I came hobbling up a waiter was just writing the specials on the chalkboard by the door.

'Hey,' I said to him, in my brightest, least look-at-me-I-am-a-victim voice.

The waiter glanced at me. If he noticed my dishevelled, shoeless appearance, he did not comment upon it. He turned back to his chalkboard.

'We don't start seating for dinner until six,' he said.

'Um.' This was, I saw, going to be more difficult than I'd thought. 'That's fine. I just want to use your payphone, if you have one.'

111

'Inside,' the waiter said, with a sigh. Then, his gaze flicking over me scathingly, he added, 'No shoes, no service.'

'I've got shoes,' I said, holding up my Jimmy Choos. 'See?'

He just rolled his eyes and turned back to his chalkboard.

I don't know why the world has to be populated with so many unpleasant people. I really don't. It takes quite an effort to be rude, too. The amount of energy people expend on being a jerk astounds me sometimes.

Inside the Sea Mist, it was cool and shady. I limped past the bar, towards the little sign I'd seen, as soon as my eyes adjusted to the dim light – compared to the blazing sun outside – that said *Phone/Restrooms*. It was sort of a long walk to the Phone/Restrooms for a girl with what I was pretty sure were massive third-degree burns on the soles of her feet. I had got halfway there when I heard a guy's voice say my name.

I was sure it was Paul. I mean, who else could it have been? Paul had followed me from his house and wanted to apologize.

And probably make out some more.

Well, if he thought I was going to forgive him – let alone kiss him again – he had another thing coming, let me tell you.

I turned around slowly.

'I told you,' I said, keeping my voice even with an effort. 'I don't ever want to speak to you again . . .'

My voice trailed off. It wasn't Paul Slater standing behind me. It was Jake's friend from college, Neil Jankow. Craig's brother. He was standing there by the bar with a clipboard, looking thinner than ever . . . and now that I knew what he'd been through, sadder than ever, too.

'Susan?' he said, hesitantly. 'Oh, it is you. I wasn't sure.'

I blinked at him. And his clipboard. And the bartender

112

who was standing near him, holding a similar clipboard. Then I remembered what Neil had said, about his dad owning a lot of restaurants in Carmel. Craig and Neil Jankow's father, I realized, must own the Sea Mist Café.

'Neil,' I said. 'Hi. Yeah, it's me, Suze. How . . . um, how are you doing?'

'I'm fine,' Neil said, his gaze going to my Band-Aid-covered – and now extremely dirty – feet. 'Are you . . . are you all right?'

The concern in his voice was, I knew immediately, actually heartfelt. Neil Jankow was worried about me. Me, a girl whom he'd met only the night before. The fact that he could be so concerned about me, a girl he had only just met, while other people – namely Paul Slater, and yes, I was willing to admit it now, Jesse – could be so very, very mean, brought tears to my eyes.

'I'm OK,' I said.

And then, before I could stop it, the whole story came pouring out. Nothing about the ghosts and the whole mediator thing, of course. But the rest of it, anyway. I don't know what came over me. I was just standing there in the middle of Neil's dad's café, going, 'And then he made a move on me, and I told him to get off and he wouldn't so I had to jab my thumb in his eye, and then I ran away but my shoes really hurt and so I had to take them off and I don't have a mobile phone so I couldn't call anyone and this is the first place with a payphone that I could find . . .'

Before I'd finished, Neil was at my side, steering me towards the closest bar stool and making me sit on it. He said, 'Hey. Hey, it's all right now,' all nervously. It was clear he didn't have a whole lot of experience dealing with hysterical girls. He kept patting my shoulder and offering me things, like lemonade and free tiramisu.

113

'I'll . . . I'll take some lemonade,' I said, finally, worn down from my recital of all – well, OK, most – of my woes.

'Sure,' Neil said. 'Sure thing. Jorge, get her some lemonade, will you?'

The bartender hurried to pour me some lemonade from a pitcher he kept in a little fridge behind the bar. He put it in front of me, eyeing me warily, like I was some lunatic who might start spouting off New Age poetry at any minute. It was heartening to know this was the first impression I was giving people. Not.

I drank some of the lemonade. It was cool and tart. I put the glass down after a few gulps, and said to Neil, who was looking at me with concern, 'Thanks. I feel better. You're nice.'

Neil looked embarrassed. 'Um. Thanks. Look, I have a mobile phone. Do you want to borrow it? You can call someone. Maybe you could call, you know, Jake.'

Jake? Oh, God no. My eyes wide, I shook my head. 'No,' I said. 'Not Jake. He . . . he wouldn't understand.'

Neil was beginning to look panicky. You could tell all he wanted was to get rid of me. And who could blame him, really? 'Oh, OK. Your mom, then? How about your mom?'

I shook my head some more. 'No, no. I don't . . . I mean, I don't want them to know how stupid I was.'

Jorge, the bartender, went, 'You know, we're pretty much done here, Neil. You can go, if you want.'

And take her with you. He didn't say the words, but his tone implied them. It was clear that Jorge wanted the crazy girl with the sore feet out of his bar, and pronto – like before the first customers of the evening started to trickle in.

Neil looked pained. It was very gratifying to know that my appearance was so heinous at that moment that college boys hesitated to allow me into their vehicles. Really. I can't tell

114

you how much I appreciated that fact. He closed his mobile phone and stuck it back in the pocket of his Dockers.

'Um,' he said. 'I guess, you know. I could drive you home myself. If you want.'

The delivery left a little to be desired, but I don't think I could have been more grateful, even if he'd said he knew a place that sold Prada wholesale.

'That would be so, so great,' I gushed.

I guess my gushing was a little too effusive, however, since Neil's face turned as pink as my blisters, and he hurried away. Mumbling about how he just had to finish up a few things. I didn't care. Home! I was getting a ride home! No embarrassing phone calls, no more walking. Oh, thank God, no more walking. I don't think I could have stood on my feet for another minute. Just looking down at them made me feel a little light-headed. They were almost black with dirt, and let's just say the Band-Aids had taken a licking and sure weren't doing much sticking. Lovely oozing sores gleamed redly at me. I didn't even want to look at what was going on with the soles of my feet. All I knew was that I couldn't feel them any more. They were completely numb.

'That,' observed a voice at my elbow, 'is one wicked pedicure. You should ask for your money back.'

115

Twelve

I didn't even have to turn my head to see who it was.

'Hi, Craig,' I said, out of the corner of my mouth. Neil and Jorge were too deeply absorbed in the beverage order they were just finishing up discussing to pay attention to me, anyway.

'So.' Craig settled on to the bar stool next to mine. 'This is how you mediators work? Get your feet all wrecked, then mooch rides off the siblings of the deceased?'

'Not usually,' I said.

'Oh.' Craig fiddled with a book of matches from the bar. 'Because I was going to say, you know, great technique. Really making some stellar progress on my case there, aren't you?'

I sighed. Really, after everything I'd been through, I did not need some dead guy making wisecracks.

But I guess I deserved them.

'How are you doing?' I asked, trying to keep my tone light. 'You know, with the whole being dead thing?'

'Oh, jim dandy,' Craig said. 'Loving every minute of it.'

'You'll get used to it.' I said, thinking of Jesse.

'Oh, I'm sure I will,' Craig said. He was looking at Neil.

I should, of course, have got a clue then. But I didn't. I was too caught up in my own problems . . . not to mention my blisters.

Then Neil handed his clipboard to Jorge, shook his hand, and turned to me.

'Are you ready, Susan?' he asked.

I didn't bother to correct him about my name. I just nodded and slid down from the bar stool. I had to look to make sure my feet had hit the floor, because I couldn't feel it. The skin on the bottoms of my feet had gone completely numb.

'You really did a number on yourself,' was Craig's comment.

But he, unlike his brother, very helpfully slipped an arm around my waist and guided me towards the door, where Neil was waiting, his car keys in his hands.

I must have looked particularly peculiar as I approached – I was definitely leaning some of my weight into Craig, which must have given me an odd appearance, since of course Neil couldn't see Craig – because Neil said, 'Um, Susan, are you sure you want to go straight home? I think maybe you might want to pay a little visit to the emergency room.'

'No, no,' I said lightly. 'I'm fine.'

'Right,' Craig snickered, in my ear.

Still, with his help, I made it out to Neil's car all right. Like Paul, Neil had a convertible BMW. Unlike Paul, Neil's appeared to be secondhand.

'Hey!' Craig cried, when he saw the vehicle. 'That's *my* car!'

I looked at the little blue number. It was pretty sweet. Still, as I pointed out to Craig, 'It's not like you'll be needing it any more.'

Which might not, given what happened next, have been the most diplomatic thing to say. Still, Craig didn't seem that upset about it. True, he kept muttering, 'I can't believe they gave him my car.' But this was, I felt, the natural reaction of a guy who'd found his car in the possession of another. Jake

117

would undoubtedly have said the exact same thing. Over and over again.

Craig got over his indignation long enough to steer me into the front seat. I was about to give him a grateful smile when he then hopped into the backseat. Even then, of course, I didn't figure it out. I just assumed Craig wanted to come along for the ride. Why not? It wasn't like he had anything better to do, so far as I knew.

Neil started the engine, and Kylie Minogue began to wail from his CD player.

'I can't believe he's listening to this garbage,' Craig said disgustedly, from the backseat, 'in *my* car.'

'I like her,' I said, a little defensively.

Neil looked at me. 'You say something?'

Realizing what I'd done, I said, 'No,' quickly.

'Oh.'

Without another word – apparently he wasn't much of a conversationalist – Neil pulled his car out from the Sea Mist Café parking lot and headed down Scenic Drive for downtown Carmel, which we'd have to cut through to make it back to my house. Cutting through downtown Carmel was never a picnic, because it was usually crammed with tourists and the tourists never knew where they were going, because none of the streets had names . . . or stoplights.

But it can be especially dangerous navigating downtown Carmel-by-the-Sea when there happens to be a homicidal ghost in your backseat.

I didn't realize this right away, of course. I was attempting to do some, you know, mediation. I figured, as long as I had the two brothers together, I might as well try to patch things up between them. I had no idea at the time just how badly their relationship had disintegrated.

'So, Neil,' I said, conversationally, as we went down Scenic

Drive at a pretty good clip. The ocean breeze tugged at my hair and felt deliciously cool after the way the sun had beat down on me earlier. 'I heard about your brother. I'm really sorry.'

Neil didn't take his gaze off the road. But I saw his fingers tighten on the steering wheel.

'Thanks,' was all he said in a quiet voice.

It is generally considered rude to pry into the personal tragedies of others – particularly when the victims of said tragedy were not the ones who introduced the subject – but for a mediator, being rude is all part of the job. I said, 'It must have been really awful, out there on that boat.'

'Catamaran,' both Craig and Neil corrected me at the same time, Craig derisively, Neil gently.

'I mean catamaran,' I said. 'How long did you hang on for, anyway? Like eight hours, or something?'

'Seven,' Neil said softly.

'Seven hours,' I said. 'That's a long time. The water must have been really cold.'

'It was,' Neil said. He was clearly a man of few words. I did not allow that to dissuade me from my mission, however.

'And I understand,' I said, 'that your brother was what, a champion swimmer or something?'

'Damned straight,' Craig said, from the backseat. 'Made all-state four years in a—'

I held up a hand to silence him. It was not Craig I wanted to hear from just then.

'Champion swimmer,' Neil said, his voice not much louder than the purr of the BMW's engine. 'Champion sailor. You name it, Craig was better at it than anybody.'

'See?' Craig leaned forward. 'See? *He*'s the one that should be dead. Not me. He even admits it!'

'Shhh,' I said, to Craig. To Neil, I said, 'That must have

119

really surprised people, then. I mean, when you survived the accident and Craig didn't.'

'Disappointed them, is more like it,' Neil muttered. Still, I heard him.

So did Craig.

'Yeah,' he said, with feeling. 'Mom and Dad still haven't taken down any of my trophies or anything. Neil's room they've already turned into an office, but mine they left exactly how it was last time I was in it . . .'

'Shhh,' I said to Craig, again. If Neil noticed my constant shushing, he didn't say anything. 'Come on, Neil,' I said to him. 'You know that isn't true. No one was disappointed that you lived and not Craig.'

'Yeah,' Neil said. 'Right.'

'I'm serious,' I said. 'Your parents are probably so grateful not to have lost both of you—'

'Sure,' Neil said, with more emotion than he'd shown so far. 'That's why they've made Craig's room into a shrine, and mine's the one with the fax machine and computer in it.'

Craig settled back against the seat, looking triumphant. 'I told you so.'

'I'm sure your parents are sad about losing Craig,' I said, ignoring the ghost in the backseat. 'And you're going to have to give them some time. But they're happy not to have lost you, Neil. You know they are.'

'They aren't,' Neil said, as matter-of-factly as if he'd been saying the sky is blue. 'They liked Craig better. Everybody did. I know what they're thinking. What everybody is thinking. That it should have been me. I should have been the one to die. Not Craig.'

Craig leaned forward again. 'See?' he said. 'Even Neil admits it. He should be the one back here, not me.'

120

'Shut up,' I said to Craig. I was now more concerned for the living brother than I was for the dead one. 'Neil, you can't mean that.'

'Why not?' Neil shrugged. 'It's the truth.'

'It's not true,' I said. 'There's a reason you lived and Craig didn't.'

'Yeah,' Craig said, sarcastically. 'Somebody messed up. Big time.'

'No,' I said, shaking my head. 'That's not it. Neil lived because he was stronger. Plain and simple.'

Craig, in the back seat, hooted. '*Him?* Stronger than *me?* You have got to be kidding me. Look at him! He can't press more'n seventy-five pounds on a good day.'

But I was still shaking my head.

'I mean it, Neil,' I said. 'You lived because you were stronger than your brother. You may not have trophies and medals to prove it, but you were the strong one. That is nothing to be ashamed of.'

Neil looked, for a moment, like someone upon whom the sun had begun to shine after months of rain. Like he hardly dared believe it.

'Do you really think so?' he asked eagerly.

'Absolutely,' I said. 'You lived because you fought harder. That's all there is to it.'

But while this news appeared to have made Neil's day – possibly his week – it caused Craig to scowl.

'What is this bull?' he wanted to know. 'He's not stronger'n me. I fought. I fought just as hard as he did!'

'Not when it counted,' I said, quietly enough so that only Craig, and not Neil, could hear me.

This, however, did not prove to be the right answer. Not because it wasn't true – because it was – but because Craig did not like it. Craig did not like it one little bit.

121

'*He* should be dead,' he growled, from between gritted teeth, 'not *me*.'

'Maybe,' I said. 'But there's nothing you can do about it now.' I was glad Craig hadn't overheard the stuff Paul had mentioned about soul transference.

But it turned out it wouldn't have mattered if he had. Because he had another idea in mind.

'If I have to be dead,' Craig declared, 'then so should *he*.'

And with that, he lunged forward and seized hold of the steering wheel.

Neil was driving down a particularly quaint street, shady with trees and crowded with tourists. Art galleries and quilt shops – the kind my mother squeals over delightedly and I avoid like the plague – lined it on either side. We were crawling along at a snail's pace because there was an RV in front of us, and a tourist bus in front of that.

But when Craig grabbed the wheel, the back of the RV suddenly loomed large in our field of vision. That's because Craig also managed to bring a leg over the back seat and rammed his foot over Neil's, on the accelerator. If Neil hadn't reacted by slamming on the brake with his other foot, and I hadn't dived into the fray, yanking the wheel hard back the other way, we would have zoomed into the rear of that RV – or worse, into a thick knot of tourists on the sidewalk – killing ourselves, not to mention taking a few innocent bystanders out with us.

'What is *wrong* with you?' I shrieked at Craig. But it was Neil who responded, shakily, 'It wasn't me, I swear. The wheel just seemed to turn without my doing anything.'

But I wasn't listening. I was screaming at Craig, who seemed as stunned as Neil was by what had transpired. He kept looking down at his hands, like they had acted of their own volition, or something.

122

'Don't you ever,' I yelled at him, 'do that again. Not ever! Do you understand?'

'I'm sorry,' Neil cried. 'But it wasn't my fault, I swear it!'

Craig, with a pitiful little moan, suddenly gave a shimmer and disappeared. Just like that. He dematerialized, leaving Neil and me to deal with his mess.

Which fortunately wasn't that bad. I mean, a lot of people were looking at us, because we had stopped in the middle of the street and done a lot of screaming and yelling. But neither of us were hurt – nor, mercifully, was anyone else. We hadn't so much as tapped the back of the RV. A second later, it started rolling forward, and we followed it, our hearts in our throats.

'I better take this car in for an overhaul,' Neil said, clutching the steering wheel with white-knuckled fingers. 'Maybe the oil needs to be changed, or something.'

'Or something,' I said. My heart was drumming in my ears. 'That'd be a good idea. Maybe you should start taking the bus for a little while.' Or until I figure out what to do about your brother, I added, mentally.

'Yeah,' Neil said, faintly. 'The bus might not be so bad.'

I don't know about Neil, but I was still somewhat shaken by the time he pulled up in front of my house. I had had quite a day. It wasn't often I got French kissed and nearly murdered in the course of only a few hours.

Still, in spite of my own unease, I wanted to say something to Neil, something that would encourage him not to be so depressed over his being the sibling who'd lived . . . and also set him on his guard against his brother – though I didn't think Craig, judging by how he'd looked last time I'd seen him, was going to be up for another assault for some time, if ever.

But all I could come up with, when it came down to it, was a very lame, 'Well. Thanks for the ride.'

123

Really. That was it. *Thanks for the ride.* No wonder I was winning all those mediation awards. Not.

Neil didn't look as if he was paying much attention, anyway. He seemed to just want to get rid of me. And why not? I mean, what college boy wants to be saddled with a high school girl with giant blisters on her feet? None, that I know of.

He drove off the minute I'd stepped from the car, and tore down our deeply shaded, pine-tree-lined driveway, apparently unconcerned about the accident he'd nearly suffered just moments before.

Or maybe he was just so glad to be rid of me, he didn't care what happened to him . . . or his car.

All I know is, he took off, leaving me with the long, long walk up to my front door.

I don't know how I made it. I really don't. But going slowly – as slowly as a very, very old woman – I made it up the stairs to the porch, then through the front door.

'I'm home,' I yelled, in case there was anybody around who'd care. Only Max came running to greet me, sniffing me all over in hopes I had food hidden in my pockets. Since I didn't, however, he soon went away, leaving me to make my way up the stairs to my room.

I did it, step by agonizing step. It took me, I don't know, like ten minutes or something. Normally I bound up and down those stairs two steps at a time. Not today, however.

I was, I knew, going to have a lot of explaining to do, when I finally ran into someone besides Max. But the person I least wanted to have to face was going to be, I felt certain, the first person I'd see: Jesse. Jesse would be, more likely than not, in my room when I hobbled through the door. Jesse, who was not going to understand what I was doing at Paul Slater's house in the first place. Jesse, from whom I thought

124

it was going to be difficult to hide the fact that I had just been playing tonsil hockey with another guy.

And that I'd sort of liked it.

It was, I told myself, as I stood with my hand on the doorknob, Jesse's fault. That I'd gone off and made out with another guy. Because if Jesse had shown me the slightest shred of affection these past few weeks, I would never even have considered kissing Paul Slater back. Not in a million years.

Yeah, that was it. It was all *Jesse*'s fault.

Not that I was ever going to tell *him* that, of course. In fact, if I could possibly avoid it, I was going to keep from bringing up Paul's name altogether. I needed to think up some story – any story, other than the truth – to explain my poor, abused feet . . .

. . . not to mention my bruised lips.

But to my relief, when I threw open the door to my room, Jesse wasn't there. Spike was, sitting on the window sill, washing himself. But not his master. Not this time.

Alleluia.

I threw down my book bag and shoes and headed to my bathroom. I had one thing and one thing only on my mind, and that was to wash my feet. Maybe all they needed was a thorough cleaning. Maybe, if I soaked them long enough in warm, soapy water, some of the feeling in them would come back . . .

I opened the taps full blast, put the stopper in place and, sitting on the edge of the tub, swung my legs painfully over it and into the water.

It was all right for a second or two. In fact, it was a soothing relief.

Then the water hit my blisters, and I nearly keeled over with the pain. Never again, I vowed, clutching the side of the

125

tub in an effort not to pass out. No more designer shoes. From now on, it was strictly Aerosoles for me. I didn't care how ugly they might look. It wasn't worth it. Nothing was worth this.

The pain ebbed enough for me to make a tentative foray with a bar of Cetaphil and a body sponge. It wasn't until I had scrubbed for nearly five minutes before I got through the final layer of dirt and saw why the bottoms of my feet were so desensitized. Because they were covered, literally covered, with giant red burn blisters – some of them blood filled, and all of them getting bigger by the minute. I realized, with horror, that it was going to be days – maybe even a week – before the swelling was going to go down enough for me to walk normally again, let alone put on shoes.

I was sitting there cursing Paul Slater – not to mention Jimmy Choo and, oh, yeah, myself – for all I was worth when I heard Jesse utter a curse that, even though it was in Spanish, burned my ears.

Thirteen

'*Querida*, what have you done to yourself?'

Jesse stood at the side of the tub looking incredulously down at my feet. I had drained out all the dirty water and had run a new tubful to soak them in, so it was pretty easy to see through the clear water to the angry red blisters below it.

'New shoes,' I said. It was all the explanation I was capable of thinking up at the moment. The fact that I had had to flee in my bare feet from a sexual predator did not seem like the kind of thing that would sit too well with Jesse. I mean, I didn't exactly want to be the cause of any duels, or anything.

Yeah, yeah, I know: I wish.

Still, he'd called me *querida* again. That had to mean something, right?

Except that Jesse had probably called his sisters *querida*. Possibly even his mom.

'You did that to yourself on *purpose*?' Jesse was staring down at my feet in utter disbelief.

'Well,' I said. 'Not exactly.' Only instead of telling him about Paul, and our clandestine kisses on his dark grey bedspread, I said, talking about a hundred miles a minute, 'It's just that they were new shoes, and they gave me blisters and then . . . and then I missed my ride home, and I had to walk, and my shoes hurt so much I took them off, and I guess the

127

pavement was hot from the sun since I burned the bottoms of my feet . . .'

Jesse looked grim. He sat on the edge of the tub beside me and said, 'Let me see.'

I didn't want to show my hideously disfigured feet to the guy with whom I have been madly in love since the very first day I met him. I especially didn't want him to see them considering that he didn't know I had burned them in an effort to get away from a guy I shouldn't have been with in the first place.

On the other hand, you should be able to go over to boys' houses without them jumping on you and kissing you and making you want to kiss them back. It was all sort of complicated, even to me, and I am a modern young woman with twenty-first-century sensibilities. God only knew what a rancher from the 1850s would make of it all.

But I could see by Jesse's expression that he was not going to leave me alone until I showed him my stupid feet. So I said, rolling my eyes, 'You want to see them? Fine. Knock yourself out.'

And I pulled my right foot from the water and showed him.

I expected, at the very least, some revulsion. Chastisement for my stupidity, I felt quite sure, would soon follow – as if I didn't feel stupid enough.

But to my surprise, Jesse neither chastised me nor looked revolted. He merely examined my foot with what I would have to describe as almost clinical detachment. When he was through looking at my right foot he said, 'Let me see the other one.'

So I put the right one back in the water and pulled out the left one.

Again, no revulsion and no cries of 'Suze, how could you

be so stupid?' Which wasn't actually that surprising, since Jesse never calls me Suze. Instead, he examined my left foot as carefully as he had the other one. When he was through, he leaned back and said, 'Well, I have seen worse . . . but barely.'

I was shocked by this.

'You've seen feet that looked worse than *this*?' I cried. '*Where*?' I mean, I'd heard that during the Civil War a lot of the soldiers' boots had fallen apart and they'd had to march around in the snow with no shoes on and got frostbite and had to have their feet amputated. But Jesse had died before the Civil War.

'I had sisters, remember?' he said, his dark eyes alight with something – I wouldn't have called it amusement, because of course my feet weren't a laughing matter. Jesse wouldn't dare laugh at them . . . would he? 'Occasionally they got new shoes, with similar results.'

'I'll never walk again, will I?' I asked, looking down woefully at my ravaged feet.

'You will,' Jesse said. 'Just not for a day or two. Those burns look very painful. They'll need butter.'

'Butter?' I wrinkled my nose.

'The best treatment for burns like those is butter,' Jesse said.

'Uh,' I said. 'Maybe back in 1850. Now we tend to rely on the healing power of Neosporin. There's a tube of it in my medicine cabinet behind you.'

So Jesse applied Neosporin to my wounds. When he was through bandaging my feet – which, may I say, looked very attractive with about sixty-eight Band-Aids all over them – I tried to stand up . . .

But not for long. It didn't hurt, exactly. It was just that it felt so strange, like I was walking on mushrooms . . .

129

Mushrooms that were growing out of the soles of my own feet.

'That's enough of that,' Jesse said. Next thing I knew, he'd scooped me up – only instead of carrying me to my bed and setting me down on it all romantically, you know, like guys do to girls in the movies, he just dumped me on to it so I bounced around and would have fallen off if I hadn't grabbed on to the edge of the mattress.

'Thanks,' I said, not quite able to keep all of the sarcasm out of my voice.

Jesse didn't seem to notice.

'Not a problem,' he said. 'Would you like a book, or something? Your homework, maybe? Or I could read to you . . .'

He lifted *Critical Theory Since Plato* . . .

'No,' I said, hastily. 'Homework is fine. Just hand me my book bag, thanks.'

I was deeply absorbed in my essay on the Civil War – or at least, that's what I was pretending to be doing. What I was really doing, of course, was trying not to think about Jesse, who was over on the window seat reading. I was wondering what it would be like if he laid a couple of kisses like Paul's on me. I mean, if you thought about it, he had me in a really interesting position, considering that I couldn't walk. How many guys would have loved to have a girl basically trapped in their bedroom? Um, a lot of them. Except, of course, for Jesse – when Andy finally called me down to dinner.

I wasn't going anywhere, however. Not because I wanted to stick around and watch Jesse read some more, but because I really couldn't stand. Finally David came upstairs to see what was taking me so long to get to the table. As soon as he saw the blisters, he went running back downstairs for my mom.

May I just say that my mother was a good deal less

130

sympathetic than Jesse? She said I deserved every blister for being so asinine as to wear new shoes to school without breaking them in first. Then she fussed around my room, straightening it up (although since acquiring a roommate of the hot Latino male persuasion, I have become quite conscientious about keeping my room in a fairly neat condition. I mean, I don't exactly want Jesse seeing any of my stray bras lying around. And really, if anything, he was the one who was always messing things up, leaving these enormous piles of books and open CD cases everywhere. And then, of course, there was Spike).

'Honestly, Suze,' my mom said, wrinkling her nose at the sight of the big orange tabby sprawled out on my window seat. 'That cat . . .'

Jesse, who had politely dematerialized when my mom showed up, in order to afford me some modicum of privacy, would have been greatly disturbed to hear his pet disparaged so.

'How's the patient?' Andy wanted to know, appearing in my doorway with a dinner tray containing grilled salmon with dill and crème fraiche, cold cucumber soup and a freshly baked sourdough dinner roll. You know, unhappy as I'd been at the prospect of my mom remarrying and forcing me to move all the way across the country and acquire three stepbrothers, I had to admit, the food made it all worth it.

'She's definitely not going to be able to go to school tomorrow,' my mom said, shaking her head despairingly at the sight of my feet. 'I mean, look at them, Andy. Do you think we need to take her to . . . I don't know. Promptcare, or something?'

Andy bent down and looked at my feet. 'I don't know that they could do anything more,' he said, admiring Jesse's

131

excellent bandaging job. 'Looks like she's taken pretty good care of it herself.'

"You know what I probably do need,' I said. 'Some magazines and a six-pack of Diet Coke and one of those really big Crunch bars.'

'Don't push it, young lady,' my mom said severely. 'You are not going to loll around in bed all day tomorrow like some kind of injured ballerina. I am going to call Mr Walden tonight and make sure he gets you all of your homework. And I have to say, Suze, I am very disappointed in you. You are too old for this kind of nonsense. You could have called me at the station, you know. I would have come out to get you.'

Uh, yeah. And then she would have found out that I was walking home not from school, like I'd told everyone, but from the home of a guy who had dead Hell's Angels working for him and who had, oh yeah, tried to put the moves on me with his drooling grandpa right in the next room. Moves I had, at least up to a point, reciprocated.

No, thanks.

I overheard Andy, as the two of them left my room, say softly to my mom, 'Don't you think you were a little hard on her? I think she learned her lesson.'

My mom, however, didn't answer Andy back softly at all. No, she wanted me to hear her reply.

'No, I do not think I was too hard on her. She'll be leaving for college in two years, Andy, and living on her own. If this is an example of the kinds of decisions she'll be making then, I shudder to think what lies ahead. In fact, I'm thinking we should cancel our plans to go away Friday night.'

'Not on your life,' I heard Andy say, very emphatically, from the bottom of the stairs.

'But—'

'No buts,' Andy said. 'We're going.'

132

And then I couldn't hear them any more.

Jesse, who rematerialized at the end of all of this, had a little smile on his face, having clearly overheard.

'It isn't funny,' I said to him sourly.

'It's a little funny,' he said.

'No,' I said. 'It isn't.'

I wondered if he had thought, as I had been doing almost constantly of late, about just what, exactly, was going to happen in two years when I did leave for college. I mean, he'd never see me again. Well, OK, he'd see me when I came home for vacation, but that was it. Did he even care? Evidently not, since he sat right back down on the window sill and picked up his stupid book again. If things had been going a little differently between us, I might have said, 'Hey, Jesse, don't worry about it, I'll go to community college like Jake, and live at home, so we can always be together.' Or I might even have been all, 'Listen, Jesse, when I go off to Yale, why don't you come with me?'

But given the way he'd been treating me lately, I wasn't about to say either.

'I think,' Jesse said, cracking open the book Father Dom had loaned him, 'it's time for a little reading out loud.'

'No,' I groaned. 'Not *Critical Theory Since Plato*. Please, I am begging you. It's not fair, I can't even run away.'

'I know,' Jesse said, with a gleam in his eye. 'At last I have you where I want you . . .'

I have to admit, my breath kind of caught in my throat when he said that.

But of course he didn't mean what I *wanted* him to mean. He just meant that now he could read stupid Hazard Adams out loud and I couldn't escape.

'Ha ha,' I said wittily, to cover the fact that I thought he had meant something else.

133

Then Jesse held up a copy of *Cosmo* he'd hidden between the pages of *Critical Theory Since Plato*. While I stared at him in astonishment, he said, 'I borrowed it from your mother's room. She won't miss it for a while.'

Then he tossed the magazine on to my bed.

I nearly choked. I mean, it was the nicest – the *nicest* – thing anyone had done for me in ages. And the fact that Jesse – Jesse, whom I'd become convinced lately hated me – had done it positively floored me. Was it possible that he didn't hate me? Was it possible that, in fact, he *liked* me a little? I mean, I know Jesse *likes* me. Why else would he always be saving my life and all? But was it possible he liked me in that *special* way? Or was he only being nice to me on account of the fact that I was sick?

It didn't matter. Not just then, anyway. The fact that Jesse wasn't ignoring me for a change – whatever his motivation – was all that mattered.

Happily, I began to read an article about seven ways to please a man, and didn't even mind so much that I didn't have one . . . a man, I mean, of my very own. Because at last it seemed that whatever weirdness had existed between Jesse and me since the day of that kiss – that all too brief, sense-shattering kiss – was going away. Maybe now things would get back to normal. Maybe now he'd start to realize how stupid he'd been. Maybe now he'd finally get it through his head that he needed me. More than needed me. Wanted me.

As much, I now knew on no uncertain terms, as Paul Slater did.

Hey, a girl can dream, right?

And that was exactly what I did. For eighteen blissful hours, I dreamed of a life where the guy I liked actually liked me back. I put all thoughts of mediation – shifting and soul transference, Paul Slater and Father Dominic, Craig and

134

Neil Jankow – from my mind. The last part was easy. I asked Jesse to keep an eye on Craig for me, and he happily agreed to do so.

I won't lie to you: it was great. No nightmares about being chased down long, fog-enshrouded hallways, towards a bottomless drop-off. Yeah, it wasn't quite like the old, pre-kiss days, but it came close. Sort of. Until the next day, anyway, when the phone rang.

I picked it up, and CeeCee's voice shrieked at me through the receiver, loudly enough that I had to hold it away from my head.

'I cannot believe you decided to take a sick day,' CeeCee ranted. 'Today, of all days! How could you, Suze? We have so much campaigning to do!'

It took me a few seconds before I realized what she was talking about. Then I went, 'Oh, you mean the election? CeeCee, look, I—'

'I mean, you should see what Kelly's doing. She's handing out candy bars – candy bars – that say *Vote Prescott/Slater* on the wrappers! OK? And what are you doing? Oh, lolling around in bed because your feet hurt, if what your brother says is true.'

'Stepbrother,' I corrected her.

'Whatever. Suze, you can't do this to me. I don't care what you do. Put on some fuzzy bunny slippers if you have to. Just get here and be your usual charming self.'

'CeeCee,' I said. It was kind of hard to concentrate because Jesse was nearby. Not just nearby, but touching me. And OK, only putting more Band-Aids on my feet, but it was still way distracting. 'Look. I'm pretty sure I don't want to be vice-president—'

But CeeCee didn't want to hear it.

'Suze,' she yelled, into Adam's mobile phone. I knew she

135

was using Adam's mobile phone, and that she was on her lunch break, because I could hear the sound of gulls screaming – gulls flock to the school assembly yard during lunch, hoping to score a dropped French fry or two – and I could also hear Adam murmuring encouraging words to her. 'It is bad enough that Kelly-Mousse-For-Brains Prescott gets elected president of our class every year. But at least when you got elected vice-president last year, some semblance of dignity was accorded to the office. But if that blue-eyed rich boy gets elected – I mean, he is just Kelly's pawn. He doesn't care. He'll just do whatever Kelly says.'

CeeCee had one thing right: Paul didn't care. Not about the junior class at the Junipero Serra Mission Academy, anyway. I wasn't sure just what, exactly, Paul did care about, since it certainly wasn't his family or mediating. But one thing he definitely was not going to do was take his position as vice-president very seriously.

'Listen, CeeCee,' I said. 'I'm really sorry. But I truly did screw up my feet, and I really can't walk. Maybe tomorrow.'

'Tomorrow?' CeeCee squawked. 'The election's Friday! That gives us only one full day to campaign!'

'Well,' I said. 'Maybe you should consider running in my place.'

'*Me?*' CeeCee sounded disgusted. 'First of all, I was not duly nominated. And second of all, I will never swing the male vote. I mean, let's face it, Suze. You're the one with the looks *and* the brains. You're like the Reese Witherspoon of our grade. I'm more like . . . Tweety Bird.'

'CeeCee,' I said. 'You are way underestimating yourself. You—'

'You know what?' CeeCee sounded bitter. 'Forget it. I don't care. I don't care what happens. Let Paul Look-At-My-New-BMW Slater be our new class vice-president. I give up.'

136

She would have slammed the receiver down then, I could tell, if she'd been holding a normal phone. As it was, however, she could only hang up on me. I had to say hello a few more times, just to be sure, but when no one answered, I knew.

'Well,' I said, hanging up. 'She's mad.'

'It sounded like it,' Jesse said. 'Who is this new person, the one running against you, who she is so afraid will win?'

And there it was. The direct question – the truthful answer to which was, 'Paul Slater.' If I did not answer it that way – by saying 'Paul Slater' – I would really and truly be lying to Jesse, the person I cared about most in the entire world. Everything else I'd told him lately had been only half-truths, or maybe white lies.

But this one. This one was the one that later, if he ever found out the truth, was going to get me in trouble.

I didn't know then, of course, that later was going to be three hours later. I just assumed later would be, you know, next week, at the earliest. Maybe even next month. By which point, I'd have thought up an appropriate solution to the Paul Slater problem.

But since I thought I had plenty of time to sort the whole thing out before Jesse got wind of it, I said, in response to his question, 'Oh, just this new guy.'

Which would have worked out fine if, a few hours later, David hadn't knocked on my bedroom door – he had got very scrupulous about knocking, since the whole walking-in-on-Jesse-and-me-smooching thing – and went, 'Suze? Something just came for you.'

'Oh, come on in.'

David threw open my door, but I couldn't see him. All I could see from where I lay on my bed was a giant bouquet of red roses. I mean, there had to have been two dozen at least.

137

'Whoa,' I said, sitting up fast. Because even then, I had no clue. I thought Andy had sent them.

'Yeah,' David said. I still couldn't see his face, because it was blocked by all the flowers. 'Where should I put 'em?'

'Oh,' I said, with a glance at Jesse, who was staring at the flowers almost as astonishedly as I was. 'Window seat is good.'

David lowered the flowers – which had come complete with a crystal vase – carefully on to my window seat, shoving a few of the cushions aside first to make a place for them. Then, once he'd got them stable, he straightened and said, plucking a small white tag from the rich green leaves, 'Here's the card.'

'Thanks,' I said, tearing open the tiny envelope.

Get well soon! With love from Andy, was what I had expected it to say.

Or *We miss you, from the junior class of Junipero Serra Mission Academy*.

Or even, *You are a very foolish girl, from Father Dominic.*

What it said, instead, completely shocked me. The more so because of course Jesse was standing close enough to read over my shoulder. And even David, standing halfway across the room, could not have missed the bold, black script:

Forgive me, Suze, it read. *With love, Paul.*

Fourteen

So, basically, I was a dead woman.

Especially when David, who did not, of course, know that Jesse was standing right there – or that he is the man I happen to love with an all-consuming passion – went, 'Is that from that Paul guy? I thought so, he was asking me all these questions about why you weren't in school today.'

I couldn't even bring myself to look in Jesse's direction, I was so mortified.

'Um,' I said. 'Yeah.'

'What does he want you to forgive him for?' David wanted to know. 'The whole vice-president thing?'

'Um,' I said. 'I don't know.'

'Because you know, your campaign is really in trouble,' David said. 'No offence, but Kelly's handing out candy bars. You better come up with something gimmicky fast, or you might lose the election.'

'Thanks, David,' I said. 'Bye, David.'

David looked at me strangely for a moment, as if not sure why I was dismissing him so abruptly. Then he glanced around the room as if realizing for the first time that we might not be alone, turned beet red, and said, 'OK, bye,' and was out of my room like a shot.

Summoning all my courage, I turned my head towards Jesse and went, 'Look, it's not what you . . .'

But my voice trailed off, because beside me, Jesse was looking murderous. I mean, really, like he wanted to murder someone.

Only it was anybody's guess who he wanted to murder, because I think at that point I was as prime a candidate for assassination as Paul.

'Susannah,' Jesse said, in a voice I'd never heard him use before, 'what is this?'

The truth was, Jesse had no right to be mad. No right at all. I mean, he'd had his chance, hadn't he? Had it, and blown it. He was just lucky I am not the kind of girl who gives up easily.

'Jesse,' I said. 'Look. I was going to tell you. I just forgot—'

'Tell me what?' The small scar through Jesse's right eyebrow – not the result, I had learned, of a knife-fight in a saloon, as I had always rather romantically assumed, but from, of all things, a dog bite – was looking very white, a sure sign Jesse was very, very angry. As if I couldn't tell by the tone of his voice. 'Paul Slater is back in Carmel and you don't tell me?'

'He isn't going to try to exorcize you again, Jesse,' I said, hastily. 'He knows he'd never get away with it, not while I'm around.'

'I don't care about that,' Jesse said, scornfully. 'It's you he left for dead, remember? And this person is going to your school now? What does Father Dominic have to say about this?'

I took a deep breath. 'Father Dominic thinks we should give him another chance. He—'

But Jesse didn't let me finish. He was up and off my bed, pacing the room and muttering under his breath in Spanish. I had no idea what he was saying, but it did not sound pleasant.

140

'Look, Jesse,' I said. 'This is exactly why I didn't tell you. I knew you were going to fly off the handle like this.'

'Fly off the handle?' Jesse threw me an incredulous look. 'Susannah, he tried to kill you!'

I shook my head. It took a lot of guts, but I did it anyway.

'He says he didn't, Jesse,' I said. 'He says . . . Paul says I would have found my way out of there on my own. He says something about there being this thing called shifters, and that I'm one of them. He says they're different than mediators, that instead of just being able to, you know, see and speak to the dead, shifters can move freely through the realm of the dead, as well . . .'

But Jesse, instead of being impressed with this bit of news, only looked more angry.

'It sounds as if you and he have been doing a lot of talking lately,' he said.

If I hadn't known better, I might have thought Jesse sounded almost . . . well, jealous. But since I knew good and well as he had made only too clear that he did not feel about me the way that I felt about him, I simply shrugged.

'What am I supposed to do, Jesse? I mean, he goes to my school now. I can't just ignore him.' I didn't, of course, have to go over to his house and French kiss him, either. But that was one thing I was keeping from Jesse at all costs. 'Besides, he seems to know stuff, Jesse. Mediator stuff. Stuff Father Dominic doesn't know, maybe hasn't ever even dreamed of . . .'

'Oh, and I'm certain Slater is only too happy to share all he knows with you,' Jesse said, very sarcastically.

'Well, of course he is, Jesse,' I said. 'I mean, after all, we both have this sort of unusual gift . . .'

'And he was always so eager to share information about that gift with the other mediators of his acquaintance,' Jesse said. 'Like his own brother, for instance.'

141

I swallowed. Jesse had me there. There was no denying that Paul had shown a complete lack of interest in teaching Jack about the art of mediation. So why was he so keen on mentoring me? Judging by the way he'd jumped me in his bedroom, I had a pretty good idea. Still, it was hard to believe his motives could be entirely lascivious. There were way prettier girls than me who went to the Mission Academy whom he could have had with a lot less trouble.

But none of them, I knew, shared our, er, unique ability.

'Look,' I said. 'You're overreacting. Paul's a jerk, it's true, and I wouldn't trust him farther than I could throw him. But I really don't think he's out to get me. Or you.'

Jesse laughed, but not like he really found anything amusing in the situation. 'Oh, it's not me I think he's out to get, *querida*. I am not the one he's sending roses to.'

I glanced at the roses. 'Well,' I said, feeling myself blush. 'Yes. I can see your point. But I think he only sent those because he really does feel badly about what he did.' I didn't mention Paul's most recent transgression against me, of course. I let Jesse think I meant the stuff Paul had pulled over the summer.

'I mean, Jesse, he doesn't have anyone,' I went on. 'He really doesn't.' I thought of the big glass house Paul lived in, of the spare and uncomfortable furniture in it. 'I think . . . Jesse, I honestly think part of Paul's problem is that he's really, really lonely. And he doesn't know what to do about it, because no one ever taught him, you know, how to act like a decent human being.'

Jesse wasn't having any of that, though. I could feel sorry for Paul all I wanted . . . and a part of me truly did, and I don't even mean the part that considered Paul a really excellent kisser . . . but to Jesse the guy was, and always would be, dog meat.

142

'Well, for someone who doesn't know how to act like a decent human being,' he said, going over to the roses and flicking one of the fat, scarlet buds, 'he is certainly doing a good imitation of how one might behave. One who happens to be in love.'

I felt myself turning as red as the roses Jesse was standing beside.

'Paul is not in love with me,' I said. 'Believe me.' Because guys who were in love with girls did not send minions to try to keep them from fleeing the premises. 'And even if he were, he sure isn't now . . .'

'Oh, really?' Jesse nodded at the card in my hand. 'I think his use of the word love – not sincerely, or cordially, or truly yours – would indicate otherwise, would it not? And what do you mean, if he were, he isn't now?' His dark-eyed gaze grew even more intense. 'Susannah, did something . . . happen between the two of you? Something you aren't telling me?'

Damn! I looked down at my lap, letting some of my hair hide my face, so he couldn't see how deeply I was blushing.

'No,' I said, to the bedspread. 'Of course not.'

'Susannah.'

When I looked up again he was no longer standing by the roses. Instead, he was standing by the side of my bed. He had lifted one of my hands in his own and was looking down at me with that dark, impenetrable gaze of his.

'Susannah,' he said, again. Now his voice was no longer murderous. Instead, it was gentle, gentle as his touch. 'Listen to me. I'm not angry. Not with you. If there's something . . . anything . . . you want to tell me, you can.'

I shook my head, hard enough to cause my hair to whip my cheeks. 'No,' I said. 'I told you. Nothing happened. Nothing at all.'

143

But still Jesse didn't release my hand. Instead, he stroked the back of it with one callused thumb.

I caught my breath. Was this it? I wondered. Was it possible that after all these weeks of avoiding me, Jesse was finally – *finally* – going to confess his true feelings for me?

But what, I thought, with a wildly drumming heart, if they weren't the feelings I hoped? What if he didn't love me after all? What if that kiss had just been . . . I don't know. An experiment, or something? An experiment I'd failed? What if Jesse had decided he just wanted to be friends?

I would die, that's all. Just lie down and die.

No, I told myself. No one clutched someone else's hand the way Jesse was clutching mine and told her that he *didn't* love her. No way. It wasn't possible. Jesse loved me. He *had* to. Only something, or someone, was keeping him from admitting it . . .

I tried to encourage him into making the confession I so longed to hear.

'You know, Jesse,' I said, not daring to look him in the eye, but keeping my gaze instead on the fingers holding mine. 'If there's anything *you* want to tell *me*, you can. I mean, feel free.'

I swear he was about to say something. I *swear* it. I finally managed to lift my gaze to his, and I swear that when our eyes met, something passed between us. I don't know what, but *something*. Jesse's lips parted, and he was about to say who knows what when the door to my room burst open, and CeeCee, followed by Adam, came in, looking angry and carrying a whole lot of poster board.

'All right, Simon,' CeeCee snarled. 'Enough sloughing off. We need to get down to business, and we need to get down to business *now*. Kelly and Paul are whupping our butts. We have got to come up with a campaign slogan and we have to come up with it now. We have one day until the election.'

144

I blinked at CeeCee in astonishment, as Jesse was doing. He had dropped my hand as if it were on fire.

'Well, hi, CeeCee,' I said. 'Hi, Adam. Nice of you two to drop by. Ever heard of knocking?'

'Oh, please,' CeeCee said. 'Why? Because we might interrupt you and your precious Jesse?'

Jesse, upon hearing this, raised his eyebrows. Way up.

Blushing furiously – I mean, I didn't want him to know I'd been talking about him to my friends – I said, 'CeeCee, shut up.'

But CeeCee, who had dropped the poster board on the floor and was now scattering Magic Markers everywhere, went, 'We knew he wasn't here. There's no car in the driveway. Besides, Brad said to go on up.'

Of course he had. Brad had probably overheard Jesse and me talking.

Adam, spying the roses, whistled. 'Those from him?' he wanted to know. 'Jesse, I mean? Guy's got class, whoever he is.'

I have know idea how Jesse reacted upon hearing this, since I didn't dare glance in his direction.

'Yes,' I said. 'Listen, you guys, this really isn't a very good—'

'Ew!' CeeCee, on the floor by the poster board, was finally in a position to get a good look at my feet for the first time. 'That is disgusting! Your feet look just like the feet of those people they pulled down off Mount Everest . . .'

'That was frostbite,' Adam said, bending to scrutinize my toes. 'Their feet were black. Suze's got the opposite problem, I think. Those are burn blisters.'

Impressed in spite of myself that he knew this, I said, 'Yeah, they are. And they really hurt. So if you don't mind . . .'

'Oh, no,' CeeCee said. 'You are not getting rid of us that easily, Simon. We need to come up with a campaign slogan, and we need it pronto. If I'm going to abuse my photocopying privileges in my capacity as editor of the school paper by running off hand flyers – don't worry, I already got a bunch of my sister's fifth-grade classmates to agree to pass them out for us at lunch – I want to make sure they at least say something good. So. What should they say?'

I sat there like a lump, my mind completely filled with one thing and one thing only: Jesse.

'I'm telling you,' Adam said, uncapping a Sharpie and taking a deep, long sniff off its tip. 'Our slogan should be Vote Suze: She Doesn't Suck.'

'Kelly,' CeeCee said, with some disdain, 'would have a field day with that one. We'd be slapped with a defamation of character suit in no time for implying that Kelly sucks. Her dad's a lawyer, you know.'

Adam, done sniffing the Sharpie, said, 'How about Suze Rules?'

'That doesn't exactly rhyme,' CeeCee pointed out. 'Besides, then the implication is that the student government is a monarchy, which of course it is not.'

I risked a glance at Jesse, just to see how he was taking all of this. He did not appear, however, to be paying much attention. He was staring at Paul's roses.

God, I thought. When I got back to school, I was so going to kill that guy.

'How about,' I said, hoping to hurry CeeCee and Adam along, so that I could have some privacy with my would-be boyfriend again, 'Simon Says Vote for Suze.'

CeeCee, kneeling beside the poster board, cocked her head at me, the sun, slanting into my west-facing windows, making her white-blonde hair look bright yellow.

'Simon Says Vote for Suze,' she repeated, slowly. 'Yeah. Yeah, I like that. Good one, Simon.'

146

And then she bent down to start writing the slogan on the pieces of poster board scattered across my floor. It was clear that neither she nor Adam were going to be leaving any time soon.

I glanced in Jesse's direction again, hoping to signal to him, as subtly as I could, how sorry I was for the interruption.

But much to my chagrin, Jesse had disappeared.

Wasn't that just like a guy? I mean, you finally get him to a point where he's apparently ready to make the big confession – whatever it was going to be – and then, BAM. He disappears on you.

It's even worse when the guy happens to be dead. Because it wasn't even like I could have his licence plate traced, or whatever.

Not that I could blame him for leaving, I guess. I mean, I probably wouldn't have wanted to hang around in a room – that now smelled distinctly of Magic Marker – with a bunch of people who couldn't see me, either.

Still, I couldn't help wondering where he'd be back.

It wasn't until I glanced at Paul's roses again that the really horrible part of it all occurred to me. And that was that the question wasn't *when* Jesse would be back, it was really *if.* Because of course if you thought about, why would the guy bother coming back at all?

I told CeeCee and Adam that I wasn't crying. I told them my eyes were watering from all the marker fumes. And they seemed to believe me.

Too bad the only person I didn't seem able to fool any more was myself.

Fifteen

It didn't take me long to figure out where Jesse had disappeared to.

I mean, in the vast spectrum of things. Actually, it took me another day and a half. That's how long it was before the swelling in my feet went down and I was able to squeeze my feet into a pair of Steve Madden slides and go back to school.

Where I was promptly called to the principal's office.

Seriously. It was part of Father Dom's morning announcements. He went, into the megaphone, 'And let's all remember to remind our parents about the feast of Father Serra, which will take place here at the Mission tomorrow, starting at five o'clock. There will be food and games and music and fun. Susannah Simon, after assembly would you please come to the principal's office?'

Just like that.

I assumed Father Dom wanted to see how I was doing. You know, I had been out of school for two whole days, thanks to my feet. A nice person would naturally wonder if I was all right. A nice person would be concerned about my well-being.

And it turned out Father D was totally concerned about my well-being. But more spiritually than physically.

'Susannah,' he said, when I walked through his office door – well, walk might be too strong a word for how I was getting around. I was still sort of hobbling. Fortunately my slides were super cushioned, and the wide black elastic band that held them to my feet completely covered most of the unsightly Band-Aids.

I still sort of felt like I was walking on mushrooms, though. Some of those blisters along the soles of my feet had gone hard as rocks.

'When,' Father Dominic asked, 'were you going to tell me about you and Jesse?'

I blinked at him. I was sitting in the visitor's chair across from his desk where I always sit while we have our little chats. As usual, I had fished a toy out from the good father's bottom drawer, where he keeps the juvenile paraphernalia teachers confiscate from their pupils. Today I had hold of some Silly Putty. I didn't know they still made Silly Putty.

'About me and Jesse what?' I asked, blankly, because I genuinely had no idea what he was talking about. I mean, why would I ever suspect that Father Dom knew about me and Jesse . . . the truth about me and Jesse? I mean, who would ever have told him?

'That you . . . that you two . . .' Father Dom seemed to be having some trouble choosing his words.

That's how I got his meaning before he ever even got the whole sentence out.

'That you and Jesse are . . . I believe the term these days is *an item*,' he finally blurted.

I immediately turned as red as the robes of the archbishop who'd be descending upon our school at any moment.

I had been doing that a lot lately, I noticed, in some part of my brain that was detached from the current, quite mortifying situation. Blushing, I mean.

'We . . . we aren't,' I stammered. 'An item, I mean. Actually, nothing could be further from the truth. I don't know how . . .'

And then, in a burst of intuition, I knew. I knew exactly how Father Dom had found out. Or thought I did, anyway.

'Did Paul tell you that?' I demanded. 'Because I am really surprised at you, Father, for listening to a guy like that. Did you know that he is at least partly responsible for my blisters? I mean, he completely sexually harassed me . . .' I didn't feel it was necessary, under the circumstances, to mention the part where I'd sexually harassed him back. ' . . . and then when I tried to leave, he sicced this Hell's Angel after me—'

Father Dom interrupted me. Which is something Father Dominic does not do often. Interrupt someone, I mean.

'Jesse himself told me,' he said. 'And what is this about you and Paul?'

I was too busy gaping at him to pay attention to his question, however.

'*What?*' I exclaimed. '*Jesse* told you?' I felt as if the world as I knew it had suddenly been turned upside down, topsy-turvy and inside out. Jesse had told Father Dom that we were an item? That he had feelings for me? Before he'd even bothered to tell me? This could not be happening. Not to me. Because incredibly good things like this never happened to me. Never.

'What, exactly,' I asked, carefully, because I wanted to make sure that, before I got my hopes up, I got the story straight, 'did Jesse tell you, Father Dom?'

'That you kissed.' Father Dominic said the word so uncomfortably, you'd have thought there were tacks on the seat of his chair, or something. 'And I must say, Susannah, that I am disturbed that you said nothing of this to me the other day when we spoke. I have never been so disappointed

150

in you. It makes me wonder what else you are keeping from me.'

'I didn't tell you,' I said, 'because it was just one lousy kiss. And it happened *weeks* ago. And since then, nothing. I mean it, Father D.' I wondered if he could hear the frustration in my voice, and found that I didn't even care. 'Not even nothing. A big *fat* nothing.'

'I thought you and I were close enough that you would share something of this magnitude with me,' Father Dominic said, all glumly.

'Magnitude?' I echoed, smashing the Silly Putty in my fist. 'Father D, what magnitude? Nothing happened, OK?' Much to my everlasting disappointment. 'I mean, not what you're thinking, anyway.'

'I realize that,' Father Dominic said gravely. 'Jesse is far too honourable a young man to have taken advantage of the situation. However, you must know, Susannah, that I cannot in good conscience allow this to continue.'

'Allow *what* to continue, Father D?' I could not believe I was even having this conversation. It was almost as if I had woken up in Bizarro World, or something. 'I told you, nothing—'

'I owe it to your parents,' Father Dominic went on, as if I hadn't spoken, 'to look out for your spiritual welfare as well as your physical well-being. And I have an obligation to Jesse, as well, as his confessor—'

'As his *what?*' I yelled, feeling as if I might fall out of my chair.

'There is no need to shout, Susannah. I believe that you heard me perfectly well.' Father Dom looked about as miserable as I was just beginning to feel. 'The fact is, that in light of . . . well, the current situation, I have advised Jesse that he needs to move into the rectory.'

151

Now I did fall out of my chair. Well, I didn't fall out of it, exactly. I tumbled out of it. I tried to leap, but my feet were too sore for leaping. I settled for lunging at Father Dom. Except that there was this huge desk separating us, so I couldn't, as I wanted, grab big handfuls of his vestments and shriek, *Why? Why?* in his face. Instead, I had to grip the edge of his desk very tightly and go, in the kind of shrill girl voice I hate, but couldn't stop emitting at that point, 'The rectory? The *rectory?*'

'Yes, the rectory,' Father Dominic said, defensively. 'He will be perfectly content there, Susannah. I know it will be difficult for him to adjust to spending his time somewhere other than – well, the place where he died. But we live very simply at the rectory. In many ways, it will be much like what Jesse was accustomed to when he was alive . . .'

I was really having a lot of trouble processing what I was hearing.

'And Jesse *agreed* to this?' I heard myself asking in that same shrill girl's voice. Whose voice *was* that, anyway? Surely not my own. 'Jesse said he'd do it?'

Father Dominic looked at me in a manner I can only describe as pitying.

'He did,' he said. 'And I am more sorry than I can say that you had to find out this way. But perhaps Jesse felt . . . and I must say, I agree with him . . . that such a scene might . . . well, a girl of your temperament might . . . Well, you might have made it difficult . . .'

And then, from out of nowhere, the tears came. My only warning was a sharp tingle in my nose. The next thing I knew, I was fighting back sobs.

Because I knew what Father Dom was trying to say. It was all there, in hideous black and white. Jesse didn't love me. Jesse had never loved me. That kiss . . . that kiss had just been

152

an experiment after all. Worse than an experiment. A mistake, even. A horrible, miserable mistake.

And now Jesse knew that I loved him, that I'd always loved him and didn't want to lose him – he was moving out rather than telling me the truth. That he didn't return my feelings. Moving out! He would rather move out than have to spend another day with me! That's the kind of pathetic loser I am!

I fell back into the chair in front of Father Dom's desk, weeping. I didn't even care what Father Dom thought – you know, about me crying over a guy. It wasn't like I could just stop loving Jesse now that I knew – for absolute sure, once and for all – that he didn't love me back.

'I d-don't understand,' I said, into my hands. 'What . . . what did I do wrong?'

Father Dominic's voice sounded gently harassed. 'Nothing, Susannah. You did nothing wrong. It's just better this way. Surely you can see that.'

Father Dominic really isn't very good at dealing with love affairs. Ghosts, yes. Girls who've had their hearts stomped on? Yeah, not so much.

Still, he did his best. He actually got up from behind the desk, came around it, and laid one of his hands over my shoulder and patted it, kind of awkwardly.

I was surprised. Father D wasn't a real touchy-feely guy.

'There, there, Susannah,' he said. 'There, there. It will be all right.'

Except that it wouldn't. It would never be all right.

But Father Dom wasn't finished.

'You two cannot go on as you have been. Jesse's got to leave. It's the only way.'

I couldn't help letting out a humourless laugh at that one.

'The only way? To make him leave home?' I asked, angrily reaching up to wipe my eyes with the sleeve of my

153

suede jacket. And you know what salt water does to suede. That's how far gone I was. 'I don't think so.'

'It isn't his home, Susannah,' Father D said, kindly. 'It's your home. It was never Jesse's home. It was the boarding house where he was murdered.'

Hearing the word murder, I am sorry to say, only made me cry harder. Father D responded by patting my shoulder some more.

'Come now,' he said. 'You've got to be adult about this, Susannah.'

I said something unintelligible. Even I didn't know what it was.

'I have no doubt that you will handle this situation, Susannah,' Father Dom said, 'as you've handled all the others in your life, with . . . well, if not grace, then aplomb. And now you had better go. First period is nearly over.'

But I didn't go. I just sat there, occasionally letting out a pathetic sniffle as the tears continued to stream down my face. I was glad I'd worn waterproof mascara that morning.

But Father D, instead of taking pity on me, the way a man of the cloth is supposed to do, only looked at me a little suspiciously. 'Susannah,' he said. 'I hope . . . I don't believe I have to . . . well, I feel obligated to warn you . . . You are a very headstrong girl, and I do hope you will remember what I spoke to you about once before. You are not to use your, er, feminine wiles on Jesse. I meant it then and I mean it now. If you must cry about this, get it over with here in my office. But do not cry to Jesse. Don't make this harder on him than it already is. Do you understand?'

I stamped a foot, then, as pain shot up my leg, instantly regretted the action.

'God,' I said, not very graciously. 'What do you take me for? You think I'm going to beg him to stay, or something? If

154

he wants to go, that's fine by me. More than fine. I'm *glad* he's going.' Then my voice caught on another traitorous sob. 'But I just want you to know, it's not *fair*.'

'Very little in life is fair, Susannah,' Father Dominic said, sympathetically. 'But I shouldn't have to remind you that you have far, far more blessings in your life than many people. You are one very lucky girl.'

'Luck,' I said, with a bitter laugh. 'Yeah, right.'

Father Dominic just looked at me like I was a mental case. 'You seem better now, Susannah,' he said. 'So perhaps you won't mind running along. I have a lot of work to do concerning the feast tomorrow.'

I thought about how much I hadn't told him. I mean, about Craig and Neil Jankow, not to mention Paul, and Dr Slaski and the shifters. I should have told him about Paul. At the very least, I should have told him his whole fresh-start theory? Yeah, maybe not so sound. Paul was definitely up to no good, as my aching feet could attest.

But I was, I'll admit, a little bit peeved with Father Dominic. You would have thought he'd have shown me a bit more compassion. I mean, he'd basically just broken my heart. Worse, he'd done it on Jesse's order. Jesse didn't even have the guts to tell me to my face that he didn't love me. No, he had to make his 'confessor' do it. Nice one. Really made me sorry I'd missed out on life in the 1850s. Must have been sweet, everyone going around making priests do their dirty work.

Whatever.

I couldn't, of course, run along, as Father Dom had suggested. I couldn't technically *run* anywhere. But I hobbled out of his office, feeling extremely sorry for myself. I was still crying – enough so that when Father D's secretary saw me, she went, with motherly concern, 'Oh, hon. You all

155

right? Here, have a tissue,' which was a lot more comforting than anything Father D had done for me in the past half-hour.

I took the tissue and blew my nose, then took a few more for the road. I had a feeling I was going to be bawling my eyes out until at least third period.

Stepping out into the breezeway along the courtyard, I tried to get a hold of myself. OK. So the guy didn't like me. Lots of guys hadn't liked me in the past and I'd never lost it like this. And OK, this was *Jesse*, the person I loved best in all the world. But hey, if he didn't want me back, that was just fine. You know what it was? Yeah, it was *his* loss, that's what it was.

So why couldn't I stop crying?

What was I going to do without him? I mean, I had totally got used to having Jesse around all the time. And what about Spike? Was Spike going to go live at the rectory, too? I guess he would have to. I mean, that ugly cat loved Jesse as much as I did. Lucky cat, getting to go live with Jesse.

I wandered along the length of the breezeway, looking out at the sun-soaked courtyard without really seeing it. Maybe, I thought, Father D was right. Maybe it was better this way. I mean, let's say, just for a minute, that Jesse liked me back. Better than liked me. Loved me, even. Where was it going to go? It was like Paul had said. What were we going to do – date? Go to the movies together? I would have to pay, and it would just be for one ticket. And if anyone saw me, to all appearances sitting by myself, I would look like the biggest dork in the world. How lame.

What I needed, I realized, was a real boyfriend. Not just a guy people besides me could see, either, but a guy I liked, who actually liked me back. That was what I needed. That was exactly what I needed.

156

Because when Jesse found out about it, it might make him realize what a colossal mistake he had just made.

It's kind of funny that as I was thinking this, Paul Slater suddenly leapt out at me from behind a column and went, 'Hey.'

Sixteen

'Go away,' I said.

Because the truth was, I was still sort of crying, and Paul Slater was just about the last person in the world I wanted to see me doing so. I was totally hoping he wouldn't notice.

But as I'd informed Father Dominic, there is no such thing as luck. This was proved by the fact that Paul went, 'What's with the waterworks?'

'Nothing,' I said, wiping my eyes with my jacket sleeve. I'd used up all the tissues Father Dom's secretary had given me. 'Just allergies.'

Paul, looking scandalized, reached out and jerked my hand away. 'Are you insane?' he wanted to know. 'That's *suede*. Here, use this.'

And he passed me, of all things, a white handkerchief he'd pulled from his coat pocket.

Funny how, with everything else that was going on, all I could focus on was that white square of material. 'You carry a *handkerchief*?' I asked, in a voice that cracked.

Paul shrugged. 'You never know when you might need to gag someone.'

This was so not the answer I expected that I couldn't help laughing a little. I mean, Paul creeped me out a little . . . OK, a lot. But he could still be funny sometimes.

I mopped up my tears with the handkerchief, more conscious than I wanted to be of the proximity of its owner. Paul was looking particularly delectable that morning in a charcoal silk sweater and a chocolate-brown leather coat. I couldn't help looking at his mouth and remembering how it felt on mine. Which was good. More than good.

Then my gaze drifted towards his eye, the one I'd jabbed. No mark. The guy didn't bruise easily.

I wished the same could be said of me. Or of my heart, anyway.

I don't know if Paul noticed the direction of my gaze – I suppose it had been pretty obvious I'd been staring at his mouth. But all of a sudden, he lifted his arms and placed both hands against the three-foot-wide column I'd been leaning against – one of the columns that hold the roof of the breezeway up – sort of pinioning me in between them.

'So, Suze,' he said, in a friendly way. 'What did Father Dominic want to see you about?'

Even though I was definitely in the market for a new boyfriend, given that it turned out my old one apparently wanted nothing to do with me, I wasn't so sure Paul was the guy for me. For a start there was that whole thing where he'd tried to kill me. It's kind of hard just to let something like that go.

So I was sort of torn as I stood there, imprisoned between his arms. On the one hand, I wouldn't have minded reaching up and dragging his head down and laying a big fat one on his mouth.

On the other hand, giving him a good swift kick in the groin seemed equally appealing, given what he'd put me through the other day, what with the hot pavement and the Hell's Angel and all.

I didn't end up doing either. I just stood there, my heart

159

beating kind of hard inside my chest. This was, after all, the guy about whom I'd been having nightmares for the past few weeks. That kind of thing doesn't go away just because the guy put his tongue in your mouth and you sort of liked it.

'Don't worry,' I said, in a voice that didn't sound at all like my own, it was so hoarse from all the crying. I cleared my throat, then said, 'I didn't tell Father Dom anything about you, if that's what you're worried about.'

Paul visibly relaxed as my words soaked in. He even lifted one of his hands away from the wall and fingered a coil of my hair that had been curled against my shoulder.

'I like your hair better down,' he said, approvingly. 'You should always wear it down.'

I rolled my eyes in order to hide the fact that my heart rate, when he touched me, sped up considerably, and started to duck beneath the one arm he still had caging me in.

'Where do you think you're going?' he asked, moving to corner me once more, this time by taking a step closer so that our faces were only about three inches apart. His breath, I was close enough to note, still smelled of whatever tooth-paste he'd used that morning.

Jesse's breath never smells like anything because, of course, he's not even alive.

'Paul,' I said, in what I hoped was an even, completely toneless voice. 'Really. Not here, OK?'

'Fine.' He didn't move away, though. 'Where, then?'

'Oh, God, Paul.' I lifted a hand to my forehead. It felt hot. But I knew I didn't have a fever. Why was I so hot? It was cool in the breezeway. Was it Paul who was making me feel this way? 'I don't know, OK? Look, I have . . . I have a lot of stuff I have to figure out right now. Could you just . . . could you just leave me alone for a while so I can think?'

'Sure,' he said. 'Did you get the flowers?'

160

'I got the flowers,' I said. Whatever it was that was making me feel so feverish also forced me to add, even though I didn't want to, since all I wanted to do was run away and hide in the girls' room until it was time for classes to change, 'But if you think I'm going to forget about what you did to me, just because you sent me a bunch of dumb flowers . . .'

'I said I was sorry, Suze,' Paul said. 'I acted like an ass, I know. And I'm more sorry about your feet than I can say. You should have let me drive you home. I wouldn't have tried anything, I swear.'

'Oh, yeah?' I looked up at him. He was a head taller than me, but his lips were still only inches from mine. I could meet them with my own without much of a problem. Not that I was going to. I didn't think. 'What do you call what you're doing now?'

'Suze,' he said, playing with my hair again. His breath tickled my cheek. 'How else am I going to get you to talk to me? You've got this totally mistaken impression of me. You think I'm some kind of bad guy. And I'm not. I'm really not. I'm . . . well, I'm a lot like you, actually.'

'Somehow, I seriously doubt that,' I said. His proximity was making it difficult to talk. And not because he was scaring me. He still scared me, but in a different way now.

'It's true,' he said. 'I mean, we actually have a lot in common. Not just the mediator thing, either. I think our philosophy of life is the same. Well, except for the whole part where you want to help people. But that's just guilt. In every other way, you and I are identical. I mean, we're both cynical and mistrustful of others. Almost to the point of being misanthropic, I would go so far as to say. We're old souls, Suze. We've both been around the block before. Nothing surprises us and nothing impresses us. At least . . .' His ice-blue gaze bore into mine. ' . . . nothing until now. In my case, anyway.'

161

'That may very well be, Paul,' I said, as patronizingly as I was able – which wasn't very, I'm afraid, because his closeness was making it very difficult to breathe. 'The only problem is, the person I mistrust most in the world? Yeah, that'd be *you*.'

'I don't know why,' Paul said. 'When we're clearly meant for one another. I mean, just because you met Jesse first—'

'*Don't*.' The word burst from me like an explosion. I couldn't stand it. I couldn't stand hearing his name . . . not from those lips. 'Paul, I'm warning you . . .'

Paul laid a single finger over my mouth.

'Shhh,' he said. 'Don't say things you'll only regret later.'

'I am not going to regret saying this,' I said, my lips moving against his finger. 'You . . .'

'You don't mean it,' Paul said confidently, sliding his finger from my mouth, over the curve of my chin and down the side of my neck. 'You're just scared. Scared to admit your true feelings. Scared to admit that I might know a few things you and wise old Gandalf, aka Father Dominic, might not. Scared to admit I might be right, and that you aren't as completely committed to your precious Jesse as you'd like to think. Come on, 'fess up. You felt something when I kissed you the other day. Don't deny it.'

Felt something the other day? I was feeling something *now*, and all he was doing was running the tip of his finger down my neck. It wasn't right that this guy I hated – and I did hate him, I *did* – could make me feel this way . . .

. . . while the guy I loved could make me feel like such absolute—

Paul was leaning so close to me now his chest brushed the front of my sweater.

'You want to try it again?' he asked. His mouth moved

162

until it was only about an inch from mine. 'A little experiment?'

I don't know why I didn't let him. Kiss me again, I mean. I wanted him to. There wasn't a nerve in my body that didn't want him to. After being dissed so hard back there in Father Dom's office, it would have been nice to know someone – anyone – wanted me. Even a guy of whom I'd once been deathly afraid.

Maybe there was a part of me that still feared him. Or what he could do to me. Maybe that was what was making me feel so hot – making my heart beat so fast.

Whatever it was, I didn't let him kiss me. I couldn't. Not then. And not there. I craned my neck, trying to keep my mouth out of his reach.

'Let's not,' I said, tensely. 'I am having a very bad day, Paul. I would really appreciate it if you would *back off*.'

On the words back off, I laid both hands on his chest and shoved him away from me as hard as I could.

Paul, not expecting this, staggered backwards.

'Whoa,' he said, when he'd regained his balance – and his composure. 'What's the matter with you, anyway?'

'Nothing,' I said, twisting his handkerchief in my fingers. 'I just . . . I just got some bad news, is all.'

'Oh, yeah?' This had clearly been the wrong thing to say to Paul, since now he looked positively intrigued, which meant he might never go away. 'Like what? Rico Suavé dump you?'

The sound that came out of me when he said that was a cross between a gasp and a sob. I don't know where it came from. It seemed to have been ripped from my chest by some unseen force. It startled Paul almost as much as it did me.

'Whoa,' he said again, this time in a different tone. 'Sorry. I . . . Did he? Did he really?'

I shook my head, not trusting myself to speak. I wished Paul would go away – shut up and go away. But he seemed incapable of doing either.

'I kind of thought,' he said, 'that there might be trouble in paradise when he never showed up to kick my ass after, you know, what happened at my house.'

I managed to find my voice. It sounded ragged, but at least it worked. 'I don't need Jesse,' I said, 'to fight my battles for me.'

'You mean you didn't tell him,' Paul said. 'About you and me, I mean.'

When I looked away, he said, 'It has to be that. You didn't tell him. Unless you did tell him and he just doesn't care. Is that it, Suze?'

'I have to get to class,' I said, and turned around hastily to do just that.

Only Paul's voice stopped me.

'Question is, why didn't you tell him. Could it be because maybe, deep down, you're afraid to? Because maybe, deep down, you felt something . . . something you don't want to admit, even to yourself?'

I spun around. I don't know what was making me angrier, the fact that he'd guessed about Jesse and me, or the fact that he knew now how I felt about him.

'Or maybe,' I said, 'deep down, I didn't want a murder on my hands. Did you ever think about that, Paul? Because Jesse already doesn't like you very much. If I told him what you did to me – or tried to do to me, anyway – he'd kill you.'

This was, as I knew only too well, a complete fabrication. But Paul didn't know that.

Still, he didn't take it the way I'd meant him to.

'See,' Paul said, with a grin. 'You must like me a little or you'd have gone ahead and let him.'

164

I started to say something, realized the futility of it all, and spun around again to leave.

Only this time, classroom doors all around me were being flung open and students started streaming out into the breezeway. There is no bell system at the Mission Academy – the trustees don't want to disturb the serenity of the court-yard or basilica by having a claxon ring every hour, on the hour – so we just change classes every time the big hand reaches twelve. First period was over, I realized, as the hordes started to mill around me.

'Well, Suze?' Paul asked, staying where he was in spite of the sea of humanity darting past him. 'Is that it? You don't want me dead. You want me around. Because you like me. Admit it.'

I shook my head incredulously. It was, I realized, hopeless to argue with the guy. He was just too full of himself ever to listen to anyone else's point of view.

And then, of course, there was the little fact that he was right.

'Oh, Paul, there you are.' Kelly Prescott came up to him, flinging her honey-blonde hair around. 'I've been looking for you everywhere. Listen, I was thinking, about the voting, you know, at lunchtime. Why don't you and I stroll around the yard, passing out candy bars. You know, to remind people. To vote, I mean.'

Paul wasn't paying any attention whatsoever to Kelly, though. His ice-blue gaze was still on me.

'Well, Suze?' he called, above the clanging of locker doors and the hum of conversation – though we were supposed to be quiet during period changes so as not to disturb the tourists. 'Are you going to admit it, or not?'

'You,' I said, shaking my head, 'are in need of intensive psychotherapy.'

165

Then I started to walk past them.

'Paul.' Kelly was tugging on Paul's leather coat now, darting nervous glances at me the whole time. 'Paul. Hello. Earth to Paul. The election. Remember? This afternoon?'

Then Paul did something that would, I realized soon after, go down in the annals of the Mission Academy – and not just because CeeCee saw it, too, and filed it away for later reporting in the *Mission Bell*. No, Paul did something no one, with the possible exception of myself, had ever done in the whole of the eleven years Kelly had been attending the school.

He dissed her.

'Why can't you,' he said, pulling his coat out from beneath her fingers, 'leave me alone for five freaking minutes?'

Kelly, as stunned as if he had slapped her, went, 'W-what?'

'You heard me,' Paul said. Though he did not seem to be aware of it, everyone in the breezeway had stopped what they were doing suddenly, just so they could watch what he'd do next. 'I am freaking sick of you and this stupid election and this stupid school. Got me? Now get out of my sight before I say something I might regret.'

Kelly blinked as if her contact lens had slipped out. 'Paul!' she said, with a gasp. 'But . . . but . . . the election . . . the candy bars . . .'

Paul just looked at her. 'You can take your candy bars,' he said, 'and stick them up your—'

'Mr Slater!' One of the novices, who are assigned to patrol the breezeway between class periods to make sure none of us gets too noisy, pounced on Paul. 'Get to the principal's office, this instant!'

Paul suggested something to the novice that I was quite sure was going to earn him a suspension, if not expulsion. It was so inflammatory, in fact, that even *I* blushed on his

166

behalf, and *I* have three stepbrothers, two of whom use that kind of language regularly when their father isn't around.

The novice burst into tears and went running for Father Dominic. Paul looked after her fleeing, black-gowned little figure, then at Kelly, who was also crying. Then he looked at me.

There was a lot in that look. Anger, impatience, disgust.

But most of all – and I do not think I was mistaken about this – there was hurt. Seriously. Paul was hurt by what I'd said to him.

It had never occurred to me that Paul could be hurt. I had thought he was immune to feeling anything but superiority.

Maybe what I had said to Jesse – about Paul being lonely – had been right after all. Maybe the guy really did just need a friend.

But he certainly wasn't making many at the Mission Academy, that was for sure.

A second later, he'd broken eye contact with me, turned around and strode out of the school. Shortly after that, I heard the rev of the engine of his convertible, and then the squeal of his tyres on the asphalt of the parking lot.

And Paul was gone.

'Well,' CeeCee said, with no small amount of relish, as she came up to me. 'Guess that takes care of the election, doesn't it?'

Then she held up my wrist, prize-fighter-style. 'All hail Madam Vice-President!'

167

Seventeen

Paul didn't come back to school that day.

Not that anybody expected him to. A sort of all-points bulletin went through the eleventh grade, stating that, if Paul did come back, he would be put on automatic suspension for a week. Debbie Mancuso heard it from a sixth-grader who heard it from the secretary in Father Dom's office while she was in there handing in a late pass.

It seemed the best thing that Paul stayed away until things cooled down a little. The novice he'd cursed at was rumoured to have gone into hysterics and had had to go lie down in the nurse's office with a cool compress across her forehead until she recovered. I had seen Father Dom, looking grim-faced, pacing around in front of the nurse's office door. I'd thought about going up to him and being all, 'Told you so.'

But it seemed too much like shooting fish in a barrel, so I stayed away.

Besides, I was still mad at him about the whole Jesse thing. The more I thought about it, the angrier I got. It was like the two of them had conspired against me. Like I was just a stupid sixteen-year-old girl with a crush they'd had to figure out some way to handle. Stupid Jesse was too scared even to tell me to my face he didn't like me. What did he think I was

168

going to do, anyway? Pop him one in the face? Well, I sure felt like it now.

In between feeling like I just wanted to curl up somewhere and die.

I guess I wasn't alone in feeling that way. Kelly Prescott seemed to be feeling pretty bad, too. She handled her victimhood better than I did, though. She very dramatically tore the *Slater* part of the wrapper off all the candy bars she had left. Then she wrote Simon on the inside foil with a Sharpie instead. It appeared she and I were running mates once again.

I won the vice-presidency of the Junipero Serra Mission Academy junior class unanimously, except for a single write-in vote for Brad Ackerman. Nobody wondered very much who could have voted for Brad. He hadn't even tried to disguise his handwriting.

Everyone forgave him, though, on account of the party he was throwing later that night. Guests had been instructed not to arrive until after ten, at which point it was determined that Jake, getting off his shift at Peninsula Pizza, would arrive with the keg and several dozen pizzas. Andy and my mom had left a note on the refrigerator that morning listing where they could be reached and forbidding us from having guests over while they were gone. Brad had found it particularly hilarious.

For my part, I had more important things to worry about than a stupid hot tub party. And I'm not talking about the dumb election, either.

Except that CeeCee and Adam wanted to go out after school to celebrate my victory – which really had turned out to be a hollow one, since my adversary had basically been kicked out of school. But Adam produced a bottle of sparkling cider for the occasion, and I couldn't say no to that,

169

of course. He and CeeCee had both worked so hard on my campaign, to which I had contributed exactly nothing – well, except for a single slogan. I felt guilty enough that I rode with them to the beach after school and stayed there long enough to toast the sunset, a custom dating back to the first time I'd won a student election, way back when I'd first moved to Carmel, eight months earlier.

When I got home, I discovered several things. One, some of the guests had started arriving early, amongst them Debbie Mancuso who had always had a bit of a crush on Brad, ever since the night I caught the two of them making out in the pool house one time at Kelly Prescott's. And two, she knew all about Jesse.

Or at least she thought she did.

'So who's this guy Brad says you're seeing, Suze?' she wanted to know as she stood at the kitchen counter, artfully stacking plastic cups in preparation for the keg's arrival. Brad was outside with a couple of his cronies, giving the hot tub a heavy dose of chlorine, no doubt in anticipation of all the bacteria it was going to become filled with once some of his more unsavoury friends slid into it.

Debbie was in full-on party wear, which included a midriff-baring halter top and these balloony harem pants that I guess she thought hid the size of her butt, which was not small, but which really only made it look bigger. I don't like to be disparaging of members of my own sex, but Debbie Mancuso really was a bit of a parasite. She had been sucking Kelly dry for years. I just hoped she wouldn't turn her suckers on me next.

'Just a guy,' I said, coolly, moving past her to get a diet soda from the fridge. I was going to need a heavy duty caffeine buzz, I knew, to fortify myself for the evening – first confronting Jesse, then the party.

170

'Does he go to RLS?' Debbie wanted to know.

'No,' I said, cracking the soda open. Brad had, I saw, removed the note from Andy and my mom. Well, it was a little embarrassing, I guess. 'He isn't in high school.'

Debbie's eyes widened. She was impressed. 'Really? He's in college, then? Does Jake know him?'

'No,' I said.

When I did not elaborate, Debbie went, 'That was really weird today, huh? About that Paul guy, I mean.'

'Yeah,' I said. I wondered whether or not Jesse was upstairs, waiting for me, or if he was just going to leave without saying goodbye. The way things had been going lately I was betting on the latter.

'I kind of . . . I mean, some of the girls were saying . . .' Debbie, never the most articulate of people, seemed to be having more trouble than usual spitting out what she wanted to say. 'That that Paul seems to . . . like you.'

'Yeah?' I smiled without warmth. 'Well, at least someone does.'

Then I drifted up the stairs to my room.

On my way up, I met David, coming down. He was carrying a sleeping bag, backpack, and the laptop he had won at computer camp for designing the most progressive video game. Max followed on a leash at his heels.

'Where are you going?' I asked him.

'Todd's house,' he said. Todd was David's best friend. 'He said Max and I could spend the night. I mean, it's not like anybody's going to be able to get any sleep around here tonight.'

'A wise decision,' I said, approvingly.

'You should do the same thing,' David suggested. 'Stay over at CeeCee's.'

'I would,' I said, saluting him with my soda. 'But I have a little business to attend to here.'

171

David shrugged. 'OK. But don't say I didn't warn you.'

Then he continued down the stairs.

I was not surprised to find that Jesse was not in my room when I got there. Coward. I kicked off my slides, went into the bathroom and locked the door. Not that locked doors make any difference to ghosts. And not that Jesse was going to show up anyway. I just felt more secure that way.

Then I ran a bath, undressed, and sank into it, letting the warm water caress my battered feet and soothe my tired body. Too bad there was nothing I could do to comfort my aching heart. Chocolate might have helped, maybe, but I didn't happen to have any in my bathroom.

The worst part of it all was that, deep down, I knew Father Dom was right. I mean, about Jesse moving out. It was better this way. I mean, what was the alternative? That he stayed here and I just kept pining away for him? Unrequited love is all right in books and things, but in real life it completely sucks.

It was just that – and this was the part that hurt the most – I could have sworn, all those weeks ago, when he'd kissed me, that he'd felt something for me. Really. And I'm not talking about what I'd felt for Paul, which was, let's face it, lust. I'm warm for the guy's form, I'll admit it. But I don't love him.

I'd just been so sure – so, so sure – that Jesse loved me.

But, obviously, I'd been wrong. Well, I was wrong most of the time. So what else was new?

After I'd soaked for a while, I got out of the tub. I rebandaged my feet, then slid into my most comfortable, hole-filled jeans, the ones my mom told me I was never allowed to wear in public and was always threatening to throw away, coupled with a faded black silk T.

Then I walked back into my room – and found Jesse sitting in his usual place on the window seat, Spike on his lap.

172

He knew. I saw with a single glance that he knew Father Dom had talked to me and that he was just waiting – warily – to see what my reaction was going to be.

Not wanting to disappoint him, I said, very politely, 'Oh, you're still here? I thought you would have moved to the rectory by now.'

'Susannah,' he said. His voice was as low as Spike's got when he growled at Max through my bedroom door.

'Don't let me stop you,' I said. 'I hear there's going to be a lot of action over at the Mission tonight. You know, getting ready for the big feast tomorrow. Lots of piñatas left to stuff, I hear. You should have a blast.'

I heard the words coming out of my mouth, but I swear I don't know where they were coming from. I had told myself, back in the tub, that I was going to be mature and sensible about the whole thing. And here I was being peevish and childish, and it wasn't even a minute into the conversation.

'Susannah,' Jesse said, standing up. 'You must know it's better this way.'

'Oh,' I said, with a shrug to show him how very, very unconcerned I was with the whole thing. 'Sure. Give my regards to Sister Ernestine.'

He just stood there, looking at me. I couldn't read his expression. If I'd ever been able to, I'd have known better than to have let myself fall in love with him. You know, on account of the whole his not loving me back thing. His eyes were dark – as dark as Paul's were light – and inscrutable.

'So that's all,' he said, sounding, for reasons I couldn't begin to fathom, angry. 'That's all you have to say to me?'

I couldn't believe it. He had some gall! Imagine, him being mad at *me*!

'Yes,' I said. Then I remembered something. 'Oh, no, wait.'

173

The dark eyes flashed. 'Yes?'

'Craig,' I said. 'I forgot about Craig. How is he doing?'

The dark eyes were hooded once again. Jesse seemed almost to be disappointed. As if *he* had anything to feel disappointed about! *I* was the one whose heart was being ripped out of her chest.

'He's the same,' Jesse said. 'Unhappy about being dead. If you want, I can have Father Dominic—'

'Oh,' I said. 'I think you and Father Dominic have done quite enough. I'll handle Craig, I think, on my own.'

'Fine,' Jesse said, shortly.

'Fine,' I said.

'Well . . .' The dark-eyed gaze bore into mine. 'Goodbye, Susannah.'

'Yeah,' I said. 'See you around.'

But Jesse didn't move. Instead, he did something I completely wasn't expecting. He reached out one hand and touched my face.

'Susannah,' he said. His dark eyes – each one containing a tiny star of white, where my bedroom light reflected off them – bore into mine. 'Susannah, I—'

Only I never did find out what Jesse was going to say next, because the door to my bedroom suddenly swung open.

'Pardon me for interrupting,' Paul Slater said.

Eighteen

Paul. I had forgotten all about him. Forgotten about him and just what, exactly, he and I had been up to these past few days.

Which was a lot of stuff I did not particularly want Jesse to know about.

'Knock much?' I asked Paul, hoping he would not notice the panic in my voice as Jesse and I pulled apart from one another.

'Well,' Paul said, looking pretty smug for a guy who'd been suspended from school that day. 'I heard all the talking and figured you had guests. I didn't realize, of course, that you were entertaining Mr De Silva.'

Jesse, I saw, was meeting Paul's sardonic gaze with a pretty hostile stare of his own. 'Slater,' Jesse said, in a not particularly friendly voice.

'Jesse,' Paul said, pleasantly. 'How are you this evening?'

'I was doing better,' Jesse said, 'before you got here, frankly.'

Paul's dark eyebrows rose, as if he were surprised to hear this. 'Really? Suze didn't tell you the news, then?'

'What n—' Jesse started to ask, but I interrupted quickly.

'About the shifting?' I actually stepped in front of Jesse, as if by doing so I could shield him from what I had a very bad

175

feeling Paul was about to do. 'And the soul transference thing? No, I haven't had a chance to tell Jesse about all that yet. But I will. Thanks for stopping by.'

Paul just grinned at me. And something about that grin made my heart rate speed up all over again . . .

And not because anyone was trying to kiss me, either.

'That's not why I'm here,' Paul said, showing all of his very white teeth.

I felt Jesse tense beside me. Both he and Spike were behaving with extraordinary antagonism towards Paul. Spike had leapt on to the window sill and, all of his fur standing up, was growling at Paul pretty loudly. Jesse wasn't being quite that obvious about his contempt for the guy, but I figured it was only a matter of time.

'Well, if you're here for Brad's party,' I said, quickly, 'you seem to be a little lost. It's downstairs, not up here.'

'I'm not here for the party, either,' Paul said. 'I just came by to return this to you.' He dug into the pocket of his jeans and extracted something small and black from it. 'You left it in my bedroom the other day.'

I looked down at what he held in his outstretched palm. It was my tortoiseshell clip, the one I'd been missing. But not since I'd been in his room. I'd been missing it since Monday morning, the first day of school. I must have dropped it then, and he'd picked it up.

Picked it up and held on to it all week, just so he could fling it in Jesse's face as he was doing now.

And ruin my life. Because that's what Paul was. Not a mediator. Not a shifter. A ruiner.

A quick glance at Jesse showed me that those casually uttered words – *You left it in my bedroom the other day* – had hit home, all right. Jesse looked as if he'd been punched in the stomach.

176

I knew how he felt. Paul had that effect on people.

'Thanks,' I said, snatching the barrette from his hand. 'But I dropped it at school, not your place.'

'Are you sure?' Paul smiled at me. It was amazing how guileless he could look when he wanted to. 'I could have sworn you left it in my bed.'

The fist came out of nowhere. I swear I didn't see it coming. One minute I was standing there, wondering how in the world I was going to explain this one to Jesse, and the next thing I knew, Jesse's fist was ploughing into Paul's face.

Paul hadn't seen it coming, either. Otherwise he would have ducked. Taken completely off guard, like he was, he went spinning, right into my dressing table. Perfume and nail polish bottles rained down as Paul's body collided heavily with the ruffle-skirted desk.

'All right,' I said, stepping quickly between them again. 'OK. Enough. Jesse, he's just trying to get a rise out of you. It was nothing, all right? I went over to his house because he said he knew some stuff about something called soul transference. I thought maybe it was something that might help you. But I swear, that's all it was. Nothing happened.'

'Nothing happened,' Paul said, his voice filled with amusement as he climbed to his feet. Blood was dripping from his nose all over the front of his shirt, but he didn't seem to notice. 'Tell me something, *Jesse*. Does she sigh when you kiss her, too?'

I wanted to kill him myself. How could he? How *could* he?

The real question, of course, was how could *I*? How could I have been so stupid as to have let him kiss me like that? Because I *had* let him – I had even kissed him back. None of this would be happening if I had exercised a little more self-restraint. I had been hurt, and I had been angry, and I had been, let's face it, lonely.

177

Just like Paul was now.

But unlike Paul I had never purposefully meant to hurt anyone.

This time Jesse's fist sent him spinning into the window seat, where Spike, not too happy about anything that was going on, let out a hiss and bounded out through the open window on to the porch roof. Paul landed face down in the cushions. When he lifted his head, I saw blood all over the velvet throw pillows.

'That's *enough*,' I said again, grabbing Jesse's arm as he pulled it back to land another blow. 'God, Jesse, can't you see what he's doing? He's just trying to make you mad. Don't give him the satisfaction.'

'That is not what I am trying to do,' Paul said, from the floor. He had rolled his head back against the blood-smeared seat cushion and was pinching the bridge of his nose to stem the tide of blood that was flowing more or less freely from it. 'I am trying to point out to Jesse here that you need a real boyfriend. I mean, come *on*. How long do you think it's going to last? Suze, I didn't tell you before, but I'll tell you now because I know what you've been thinking. Soul transference only works if you toss out the soul that's currently occupying a certain body, then throw someone else's into it. In other words, it's *murder*. And I'm sorry, but you don't strike me as much of a murderer. Your boy Jesse's going to have to step into the light one of these days. You're just holding him back—'

I felt Jesse's arm move convulsively so I threw all my weight on it.

'Shut up, Paul,' I said.

'And what about you, Jesse? I mean, what the hell can you give her?' Paul was laughing now, in spite of the blood that was still dripping from his face. 'You can't even pay for her to have a damned cup of coffee—'

178

Jesse exploded from my grasp. That's the only way I can describe it. One minute he was there, and the next he was on top of Paul, and the two of them had their hands wrapped around one another's necks. They went crashing to the floor with enough force to jolt the entire house.

Not, I was certain, that anyone could hear them. Brad had turned on the stereo downstairs and music was now pulsing up through the walls. Hip-hop, Brad's favourite. I was certain the neighbours were going to enjoy being lulled to sleep tonight by its dulcet tones.

On the floor, Jesse and Paul rolled around. I thought about smashing something over their heads. The thing is, they were both so hardheaded it probably wouldn't do any good. Reasoning with them hadn't helped. I had to do something. They were going to kill one another. They were going to kill one another and it was all going to be my fault. My own stupid fault.

I don't know what put the idea of the fire extinguisher in my head. I was standing there, watching in dismay as Jesse sent Paul crashing very hard into my bookshelf, when suddenly I was just like, *Oh, yeah. The fire extinguisher.* I turned around and left my room, hurrying down the stairs, the pulse of the music getting louder and louder – and the sounds of the fight going on in my room growing further away – with each step.

Downstairs, Brad's party was in full swing. Dozens of scantily clad, gyrating bodies crowded the living room, dancing to the beat. Half of them I didn't even recognize. Then I realized that was because they were Jake's friends from college. In my hurry, I saw Neil Jankow holding on to one of those blue plastic cups Debbie Mancuso had been stacking so carefully on the kitchen counter. He sloshed foam everywhere as I tore past him. At least Craig hadn't got to him yet.

179

So Jake, I knew now, had arrived with the keg.

I had to flatten myself against the wall just to make it past the people crammed in the hallway to the kitchen. Once I got there, I saw that it, too, was packed with people I had never seen before. A glance out the sliding glass doors revealed that the hot tub, which had been designed to hold a total of eight people, was currently holding close to thirty, most of whom were straddling one another. It was like my house had suddenly become the Playboy Mansion. I couldn't believe it.

I found the fire extinguisher under the sink, where Andy kept it in case of grease fires on the stove. I had to shout 'excuse me' until I was hoarse before anybody would move enough to let me back out into the hallway. When I finally got there, I was shocked to hear someone screaming my name. I turned around and there, to my utter astonishment, stood CeeCee and Adam.

'What are you doing here?' I yelled at them.

'We were invited,' CeeCee yelled back – a little defensively, I noticed. I guessed that maybe the two of them had been getting some weird looks. They did not travel in the same social circle as my stepbrother Brad, by any means.

'Look,' Adam said, holding up one of Brad's flyers. 'We're legit.'

'Well, great,' I said. 'Have fun. Listen, I have kind of a situation upstairs . . .'

'We'll come with you,' CeeCee shouted. 'It's too noisy down here.'

It was not, I knew, going to be any quieter in my room. Plus there was the whole thing about Paul Slater fighting the ghost of my boyfriend in there.

'Stay here,' I told them. 'I'll be back in a minute.'

Adam, however, spied the fire extinguisher and said, 'Cool! Special effects!' and started after me.

180

There was nothing I could do. I mean, I had to get back upstairs if I was going to keep Paul and Jesse from killing each other – or at least Jesse from killing Paul, since Jesse, of course, was already dead. CeeCee and Adam were just going to have to deal with whatever they might see if they followed me.

I had hopes I might lose them on the stairs, but those hopes were dashed when, upon finally reaching the staircase, I saw Paul and Jesse tumbling down it.

That's what *I* saw, anyway. The two of them locked in a life-and-death struggle, rolling down the stairs on top of each other, each holding fistfuls of the other's clothing.

That's not what CeeCee and Adam – or anyone else who happened to be looking at that point – saw, however. What they saw was Paul Slater, bloody and bruised, falling down my stairs and seemingly hitting – well, himself.

'Oh my God!' CeeCee cried, as Paul – she couldn't see that Jesse was there, too – crashed heavily at her feet. 'Suze! What's going on?'

Jesse recovered himself before Paul did. He climbed to his feet, reached down, seized Paul by the arms and pulled him up – just so he could hit him again.

That was not, however, what CeeCee, Adam and everyone else who happened to be looking in the direction of the stairs at that moment saw. What they saw was Paul jerked up by some unseen force and then thrown, by an invisible blow, across the room.

Much of the gyrating stopped. The music pounded on, but nobody was dancing any more. Everybody was just standing there, staring at Paul.

'Oh, my God,' CeeCee cried. 'Is he on *drugs*?'

Adam shook his head. 'It would explain a lot about that guy,' he said.

181

Jake, meanwhile, apparently alerted by someone, pushed his way into the living room, took one look at Paul writhing on the floor – with Jesse's hands around his neck, though I was the only one who could see this – and went, 'Aw, Jesus.'

Then, seeing me standing with the fire extinguisher limp in my hands, Jake strode over, took it away from me and sent a jet of foamy white stuff spraying in Paul's direction.

It didn't do any good, really. All it did was cause the two of them to roll into the dining room – making a good many people jump out of the way – then crash into my mother's china cabinet, which of course teetered and fell, smashing all the plates inside.

Jake looked stunned. 'What the hell is wrong with that guy? Is he wasted, or what?'

Neil Jankow, who'd been standing nearby with his cup of beer still in his hand, said, 'Maybe he's having a seizure. Somebody better call an ambulance.'

Jake looked alarmed.

'No,' he cried. 'No, no cops! Nobody call the cops!'

At least, that's what he was saying right up until Jesse threw Paul through the sliding glass door to the deck.

It was the shower of glass that finally alerted all the people in the hot tub to the life-and-death battle that had been taking place inside. Screaming, they struggled to get out of the way of Paul's flailing body, only to find their escape dangerously impeded by shards of broken glass. Being barefooted, the people in the hot tub had nowhere to go as Paul and Jesse battered each other around the deck.

Brad, one of the people trapped in the hot tub – Debbie Mancuso hanging off him like a pilotfish – stared disbelievingly at the gaping hole where the sliding glass door had been. Then he thundered, 'Slater! You are paying for a new door, you freak!'

182

Paul, however, wasn't in a position to be paying much attention. That's because he was struggling just to breathe. Jesse had him by the neck and was holding him over the side of the hot tub.

'Are you going to stay away from her?' Jesse demanded as the lights from the jacuzzi floor cast them in an eerie blue glow.

Paul gurgled, 'No way.'

Jesse dunked Paul's head beneath the water and held it there.

Neil, who'd followed Jake out on to the deck, pointed and cried, 'Now he's trying to drown himself! Ackerman, you better do something, and quick.'

'Jesse,' I cried. 'Let him go. It's not worth it.'

CeeCee looked around. 'Jesse?' she echoed, confusedly. 'He's here?'

Jesse was distracted enough that he loosened his hold somewhat, and Jake, with Neil's help, was able to pull Paul up, gasping for air, with blood now mingling with chlorinated water all down his shirt front.

I couldn't take it any more.

'You have to stop it,' I said, to Jesse and Paul. 'That's enough. You've wrecked my house. You've made a mess of each other. And . . .' I added this last as I looked around and saw all the curious, half-frightened gazes aimed at me. '. . . I think you've pretty much destroyed what little good reputation I once had.'

Before either Jesse or Paul could reply, however, another voice broke in.

'I can't believe,' Craig Jankow said, materializing to the left of his brother, 'that you guys had a kegger and no one invited me. Seriously,' Craig went on, as I threw him an incredulous look. 'This is some good stuff. You mediators really know how to throw a party.'

183

Jesse wasn't paying any attention to the latecomer, however. He said to Paul, 'Don't come near her again. Do you understand?'

'Eat me,' Paul suggested.

Back he went into the hot tub with a splash. Jesse ripped him right out of Jake's grip.

The surprise was, this time Neil went under with Paul. That's because Craig, a quick learner, had decided to go ahead and follow through with his whole If-I'm-dead-my-brother-should-be-too thing, now that Jesse had shown him how.

'Neil!' Jake cried, trying to pull both Paul and his friend – who as far as he knew had just inexplicably plunged into the hot tub face first – up from the bottom of the jacuzzi. What he didn't know, of course, was that ghostly hands were holding both of them down.

I knew it, though. I also knew that there wasn't anything any of us could do to get them to let go. Ghosts have superhuman strength. There was no way any of us were going to get those two to give up their victims. Not until they were as dead as . . . well, as their killers.

Which was why I knew I was going to have to do something I really didn't want to do. I just didn't see any way out of it. Threats hadn't worked. Brute force hadn't worked. There was only one way.

But I really, really didn't want to take it. My chest was tight with fear. I could hardly breathe, I was so scared. I mean, the last time I'd been to that place, I'd nearly died. And I had no way of knowing whether or not Paul had told me the truth. What if I tried what he'd said and I ended up somewhere even worse than where I'd ended up before?

Although it would be hard to imagine any place worse.

Still, what choice did I have? None.

184

My heart in my throat, I thrust my hands into the hot, churning water and grabbed twin handfuls of shirt. I didn't even know whose clothes I had hold of. All I knew was, this was the only way I could think of to prevent a murder.

Then I closed my eyes and pictured that place in my head I had hoped never to see again.

And when I opened my eyes, I was there.

Nineteen

I wasn't alone. Paul was with me. And Craig Jankow, too.

'What the . . . ?' Craig looked up and down the long dark hallway, as eerily silent as Brad's party had been loud. 'Where the hell are we?'

'Where you should have gone a long time ago,' Paul said, carefully brushing lint off his shirt – though, since this was an alternative plane and only his consciousness, not his actual body, was on it, there was no lint to brush. To me, Paul said, with a smile, 'Nice work, Suze. And on your first try, too.'

'Shut up.' I was in no mood for pleasantries. I was somewhere I really, really didn't want to be: a place that, every time I returned to it in my nightmares, left me feeling completely physically and emotionally drained. A place that sucked the life out of me . . . not to mention my courage. 'I'm not exactly happy about this.'

'I can tell.' Paul reached up and felt his nose. Since we were in the spirit world, and not the actual one, it was no longer bleeding. His clothes weren't wet, either. 'You know the fact that we're up here means that our bodies, down there, are unconscious.'

'I know,' I said, glancing nervously up and down the long, fog-enshrouded hallway. Just like in my dreams, I couldn't

186

see what was at either end. It was just a line of doors that seemed to go on for ever.

'Well,' Paul said. 'That should get Jesse's attention, anyway. Your suddenly dropping off into a coma, I mean.'

'Shut up,' I said, again. I felt like crying. I really did. And I hate crying. Almost more than I hate falling into bottomless pits. 'This is all your fault. You shouldn't have antagonized him.'

'And you,' Paul said, with a spark of anger, 'shouldn't go around kissing—'

'Excuse me,' Craig interrupted. 'But could somebody maybe tell me exactly what—'

'Shut up,' Paul and I said to him, at the exact same time.

Then, to Paul, I said, a catch in my voice, 'Look, I'm sorry about what happened at your house. OK? I lost my head. But that doesn't mean that there's anything going on between us.'

'You lost your head,' Paul repeated tonelessly.

'That's right,' I said. The hairs on the back of my neck were standing up. I did not like this place. I didn't like the white plumes of fog that were licking my legs. I didn't like the tomblike stillness. And I especially didn't like that I couldn't see more than a few feet in front of me. Who knew where the floor might drop off from underneath?

Paul regarded me steadily with those ice-blue eyes of his.

'What if I want there to be something between us?' he asked.

'Too bad,' I said, shortly.

He glanced over at Craig, who was beginning to wander down the hall, regarding the closed doors on either side of him with interest.

'What about shifting?' Paul asked.

'What *about* it?'

187

'I told you how to do it, didn't I? Well, there's other stuff I can show you. Stuff you've never even dreamed you could do.'

I blinked at him. I thought back to what he'd said that afternoon in his bedroom, about soul transference. There was a part of me that wanted to know what that was all about. There was a part of me that wanted to know about this very, very badly.

But there was an equally big part of me that wanted nothing whatsoever to do with Paul Slater.

'Come on, Suze,' Paul went on. 'You know you're dying to know. All your life you've been wondering who – or what – you really are. And I'm telling you, I have the answers. I *know*. And I'll teach you, if you'll let me.'

I narrowed my eyes at him. 'And what do *you* get out of this magnanimous offer of yours?' I wanted to know.

'The pleasure of your company,' he said, with a smile.

He said it casually, but I knew there was nothing casual about it at all. Which was why, in spite of how much I was dying to find out more about all the other stuff he claimed to know, I was reluctant to accept his offer. Because there was a catch. And the catch was that I was going to have to spend time with Paul Slater.

But it might be worth it. Almost. And not because I'd finally be getting some insight into the true nature of our so-called gift, but because I might, at last, be able to guarantee Jesse's safety . . . at least where Paul was concerned.

'OK,' I said.

To say Paul looked surprised would have been the under-statement of the year. But before he could say anything, I added, gruffly, 'But Jesse is off limits to you. I really mean it. No more insults. No more fights. And no more exorcisms.'

188

One of Paul's dark eyebrows went up. 'So that's how it is,' he said, slowly.

'Yes,' I said. 'That's how it is.'

He didn't say anything for so long that I figured he wanted to forget the whole thing. Which would have been fine by me. Sort of. Except for the Jesse part.

But then Paul shrugged and went, 'Fine by me.'

I stared at him, hardly daring to believe my own ears. Had I just engineered – at great personal sacrifice, it had to be admitted – Jesse's reprieve?

It was Paul's nonchalance about the whole thing that convinced me I had. Especially after his response to Craig, when the latter reached out and rattled one of the doorknobs and called, 'Hey, what's behind these doors?'

'Your just rewards,' Paul said, with a smirk.

Craig looked over his shoulder at Paul. 'Really? My just rewards?'

'Sure,' Paul said.

'Don't listen to him, Craig,' I said. 'He doesn't know what's behind those doors. It could be your just rewards. Or it could just be your next life. No one knows. No one has ever come out through one of them. You can only go in.'

Craig looked speculatively at the door in front of him.

'Next life, huh?' he said.

'Or eternal salvation,' Paul said. 'Or, depending how bad you've been, eternal damnation. Go on. Open it and find out whether you were naughty or nice.'

Craig shrugged . . . but he didn't take his eyes off the door in front of him.

'Well,' he said. 'It's gotta be better than hanging around down there. Tell Neil I'm sorry I acted like such a . . . you know. It's just that . . . well, it's just that it really wasn't very fair.'

189

Then, laying a hand on the doorknob in front of him, he turned the handle. The door opened a fraction of an inch . . .

And Craig disappeared in a flash of light so blinding I had to throw up my hands to protect my eyes.

'Well,' I heard Paul saying, a few seconds later. 'Now that he's out of the way . . .'

I lowered my arms. Craig was gone. There was nothing left where he'd been standing. Even the fog looked undisturbed.

'Now can we get out of here?' Paul heaved a little shudder. 'This place gives me the heebie-jeebies.'

I tried to hide my astonishment that Paul felt exactly the way I did about the spirit plane. I wondered if he had nightmares about it, too. Somehow, I didn't think so.

But I didn't think I'd be having any more of them, either.

'OK,' I said. 'Only . . . only how do we get back?'

'Same thing,' Paul said, closing his eyes. 'Just picture it.'

I closed my eyes, feeling the warmth of Paul's fingers inside my arm, and the cool lick of the fog on my legs . . .

A second later, the awful silence was gone, replaced instead by the sounds of loud music. And screaming. And sirens.

I opened my eyes.

The first thing I saw was Jesse's face, hanging over mine. It looked pale in the flashing red and white lights of the ambulance that had pulled up alongside the deck. Beside Jesse's face was CeeCee's, and beside hers, Jake's.

CeeCee was the first one to go, 'She's awake! Oh my God, Suze! You're awake! Are you OK?'

I sat up groggily. I did not feel very good. In fact, I felt a little as if someone had hit me. Hard. I clutched my temples. Headache. Pounding headache. Nausea-inducing headache.

190

'Susannah.' Jesse's arm was around me. His voice, in my ear, was urgent. 'Susannah, what happened? Are you all right? Where . . . where did you go? Where's Craig?'

'Where he belongs,' I said, wincing as red and white lights caused my headache to feel a thousand times worse. 'Is Neil . . . is Neil all right?'

'He's fine, Susannah.' Jesse looked about as shaky as I felt . . . which was pretty shaky. I didn't imagine that the past few minutes had been all that great for him. I mean, what with me being slumped over, unconscious, and for no apparent reason, and all. My jeans were wet from where I'd landed in water from the hot tub. I could only imagine what my hair looked like. I feared passing a mirror. There was no telling what the reflection would reveal.

'Susannah.' Jesse's grasp on me was possessive. Delightfully so. 'What happened?'

'I'll tell you later,' I said. A few feet away, I could see that Paul, too, was sitting up. Unlike Neil, over where the sliding glass door used to be, he was doing so without the aid of an EMT. But like Neil, Paul was coughing up plenty of chlorinated water. And not just his jeans were wet. He was soaked, from head to toe. And his nose was bleeding profusely.

'What've we got here?' An Emergency Medical Technician knelt down beside me, and, lifting my wrist, began to take my pulse.

'She passed out cold,' CeeCee said, officiously. 'And no, she hadn't had anything to drink.'

'Lotta that going around here,' the EMT said. She checked my pupils. 'You hit your head, too?'

'Not that I know of,' I said, narrowing my eyes against the annoying glare of her little pen light.

'She might've,' CeeCee said. 'When she passed out.'

The EMT looked disapproving. 'When are you kids going

191

to learn? Alcohol,' she said, severely, 'and hot tubs do not mix.'

I didn't bother to argue that I hadn't been drinking. Or, for that matter, sitting in the hot tub. I was, after all, fully dressed. It was enough that the EMT let me go after telling me that my vitals checked out, and that I was to drink plenty of water and get some sleep. Neil, too, was given a clean bill of health. I saw him a little while later, calling for a cab on his mobile phone. I went up to him and told him that it was safe to use his car now. He just looked at me like I was crazy.

Paul wasn't as lucky as Neil and me. His nose turned out to be broken, so they trundled him off to the ER. I saw him moments before they wheeled him away, and he did not look happy. He peered at me from over the splint they'd taped to his face.

'Headache?' Paul asked, in a phlegmy voice.

'A killer one,' I said.

'Forgot to warn you,' he said. 'It always happens, post-shifting.' Paul grimaced. Then I realized he was trying to smile. 'I'll be back,' he said, in a pretty sad imitation of the Terminator. Then the EMTs returned to cart him away.

After Paul was gone, I looked around for Jesse. I had no idea what I was going to say to him . . . maybe something along the lines of how he wasn't going to have to worry about Paul any more?

Only it ended up not mattering anyway, because I didn't see him anywhere. Instead, all I saw was Brad, panting heavily and coming my way.

'Suze,' he cried. 'Come on. Some idiot called the cops. We've got to hide the keg before they get here.'

I just blinked at him. 'No way,' I said.

'Suze.' Brad looked panicky. 'Come on! They'll confiscate it! Or worse, arrest everybody.'

192

I looked around and found CeeCee standing over by Adam's car. I called, 'Hey, Cee. Can I come over and spend the night at your house?'

CeeCee called back, 'Sure. If you'll tell me everything there is to know about this Jesse guy.'

'Nothing to tell,' I said. Because there really wasn't. Jesse was gone. And I had a pretty good idea where he'd gone, too.

And there wasn't a thing I could do about it.

Twenty

'Face it, Suze,' CeeCee said, as she wolfed down her half of a cannoli we were sharing the next day at the feast of Father Serra. 'Men suck.'

'You're telling me,' I said.

'I mean it. Either you want them and they don't want you, or they want you and you don't want them.'

'Welcome to my world,' I said, glumly.

'Aw, come on,' she said, looking taken aback by my tone. 'It can't be *that* bad.'

I wasn't in any sort of mood to argue with her. For one thing, I had only just, a little less than twelve hours later, got over my post-shifting headache. For another, there was the little matter of Jesse. I wasn't all that keen to discuss the latest developments there.

It wasn't like I didn't have enough problems. Like, for instance, my mom and stepdad. They hadn't been *too* homicidal when they'd got home from San Francisco and discovered the shambles that had once been their home . . . not to mention the police summons. Brad was only grounded for life, and Jake, for going along with the whole party scheme – not to mention providing the alcohol – had his Camarro fund completely confiscated to pay whatever fines the party ended up costing. Only the fact that David had been safely

194

at Todd's the whole time kept Andy from actually killing either of his two elder sons. But you could tell he was totally thinking about it anyway . . . especially after my mom saw what had happened to the china cabinet.

Not that either Andy or my mom was particularly happy with me, either – not because they knew the busted-up china cabinet was my fault, but for not ratting my stepbrothers out in the first place. I would have intimated that blackmail had been employed, but then they would have known that Brad had something on me that was worthy of blackmailing.

So I kept my mouth shut, glad that for once I was more or less guiltless. Well, except where the china cabinet was concerned – though happily, no one but me knew it. Still, I knew I couldn't shirk my culpability there. I pretty much knew where any future babysitting earnings were going to go.

I am pretty sure they were thinking about grounding me, too. But the feast of Father Serra they could not keep me away from, on account of how, being a member of the student government, I was expected by Sister Ernestine to man a booth there. Which was how I'd ended up at the cannoli stand with CeeCee, who, as editor of the school paper, was also required to put in an appearance. After the preceding evening's activities – you know, massive brawl, trip to the netherworld, and then all-night gabfest accompanied by copious amounts of popcorn and chocolate – we were neither of us at our best. But the surprising number of attendees who plunked down a buck per cannoli didn't seem to notice the circles under our eyes . . . perhaps because we were wearing sunglasses.

'OK,' CeeCee said. It had been pretty dim of Sister Ernestine to put CeeCee and me in charge of a dessert booth, since most of the pastries we were supposed to be selling were disappearing down our throats. After a night like

195

the one we'd had, we felt like we needed the sugar. 'Paul Slater.'

'What about him?'

'He likes you.'

'I guess,' I said.

'That's it? You *guess*?'

'I told you,' I said. 'I like someone else.'

'Right,' CeeCee said. 'Jesse.'

'Right,' I said. 'Jesse.'

'Who doesn't like you back?'

'Well . . . yeah.'

CeeCee and I sat in silence for a minute. All around us, mariachi music was playing. Over by the fountain, kids were batting at piñatas. The statue of Junipero Serra had been adorned with flowered leis. There was a sausage-and-peppers stand right alongside the taco stand. There were as many Italians in the church community as there were Latinos.

Suddenly, CeeCee, gazing at me from behind the dark lenses of her sunglasses, went, 'Jesse's a ghost, isn't he?'

I choked on the cannoli I was scarfing down.

'Wh-what?' I asked, gagging.

'He's a ghost,' CeeCee said. 'You don't have to bother denying it. I was there last night, Suze. I saw . . . well, I saw stuff that can't be explained any other way. You were talking to him, but there wasn't anyone there. And yet someone was holding Paul's head under that water.'

I went, feeling myself turn beet red, 'You're nuts.'

'No,' CeeCee said. 'I'm not. I wish I were. You know I hate stuff like that. Stuff that can't be explained scientifically. And those stupid people on TV, who claim they can speak to the dead. But . . .' A tourist came up, drunk on the bright sunshine, the fresh sea air, and the extremely weak beer they were serving over at the German booth. He put down a

196

dollar. CeeCee handed him a cannoli. He asked for a napkin. We noticed that the napkin dispenser was empty. CeeCee apologized. The tourist laughed good-naturedly, took his cannoli and went away.

'But what?' I asked nervously.

'But where you're concerned, I'm willing to believe. And some day,' she added, picking up the empty napkin dispenser, 'you are going to explain it all to me.'

'CeeCee,' I said, feeling my heart start to return to its normal rhythm. 'Believe me. You're better off not knowing.'

'No,' CeeCee said, shaking her head. 'I'm not. I hate not knowing things.' Then she shook the empty dispenser. 'I'm going to go get a refill. You OK on your own for a minute?'

I nodded, and she went away. I don't know if she had any idea how badly she'd shaken me. I sat there, wondering what I ought to do. Only one other living person knew my secret – one other person besides Father Dom and Paul, of course – and even she, my best friend Gina, back in Brooklyn, didn't know all of it. I had never told anyone else because . . . well, because who would believe it?

But CeeCee believed it. CeeCee had figured it out for herself, and she believed it. Maybe, I thought. Maybe it wasn't as crazy as I'd always thought.

I was sitting there, trembling, even though it was seventy-five degrees and sunny out. I was so deeply absorbed in my thoughts, I didn't hear the voice that was addressing me from the other side of the booth, until he'd said my name – or a semblance of it, anyway – three times.

I looked up and saw a young man in a pale blue uniform grinning at me. 'Susan, right?' he said.

I looked from him to the face of the old man whose wheelchair he was pushing. It was Paul Slater's grandfather and his attendant. I shook myself and stood up.

197

'Um,' I said. 'Hi.' To say I was feeling a bit confused would have been the understatement of the year. 'What are you . . . what are you doing here? I thought . . . I thought . . .'

'You thought he was housebound?' the nurse asked, with a grin. 'Not quite. No, Mr Slater likes to get out. Don't you, Mr Slater? In fact, he insisted on coming down here today. I didn't think it was appropriate, you know, given what happened to his grandson last night, but Paul's at home, recuperating nicely, and Mr S was adamant. Weren't you, Mr S?'

Paul's grandfather did something that surprised me then. He looked up at the nurse and said, in a voice that was perfectly lucid, 'Go and get me a beer.'

The nurse frowned down at him. 'Now, Mr S,' he said. 'You know your doctor says—'

'Just do it,' Mr Slater said.

The nurse, with an amused glance at me, as if to say, *Well, what are you going to do?* went off to the beer booth, leaving Mr Slater alone with me.

I stared at him. The last time I had seen him, he'd been drooling. He wasn't drooling now. His blue eyes were rheumy, it was true. But I had a feeling they saw a lot more that was going on around him besides just *Family Feud* reruns.

In fact, I was sure of it when he said, 'Listen to me. We don't have much time. I was hoping you'd be here.'

He spoke rapidly and softly. In fact, I had to lean forward, over the cannolis, to hear him. But though his voice was low, his enunciation was crystal clear.

'You're one of them,' he said. 'One of those shifters. Believe me, I know. I'm one, too.'

I blinked at him. 'You . . . you are?'

'Yes,' he said. 'And the name's Slaski, not Slater. Fool son of mine changed it. Didn't want people to know he was

198

related to an old quack who went around talking about people with the ability to walk amongst the dead.'

I just stared at him. I didn't know what to say. What *could* I say? I was more astonished by this than by what CeeCee had revealed.

'I know what my grandson told you,' Mr Slater – Dr Slaski – went on. 'Don't listen to him. He's got it all wrong. Sure, you have the ability. But it'll kill you. Maybe not right away, but eventually.' He stared out at me from a grey, liver-spotted mask of wrinkles. 'I know what I'm talking about. Like that fool grandson of mine, I thought I was a god. No, I thought I *was* God.'

I blinked at him. 'But . . .'

'Don't make my mistake, Susan. You stay away from it. Stay away from the shadow world.'

'But . . .'

But Paul's grandfather had seen his nurse coming back, and he quickly lapsed back into his semi-catatonic state and would say no more.

'Here you go, Mr Slater,' the nurse said, carefully holding the plastic cup to the old man's lips. 'Nice and cold.'

Dr Slaski, to my complete disbelief, let the beer dribble down his chin and all over his shirt.

'Oops,' the attendant said. 'Sorry about that. Well, we'd better go get cleaned up.' He winked at me. 'Nice seeing you again, Susan. See you later.'

Then he wheeled Dr Slaski away towards the duck-shooting booth.

And that, as far as I was concerned, was it. I had to get out. I could not take it a minute longer in the cannoli booth. I had no idea where CeeCee had disappeared to, but she was just going to have to deal with the pastry sales on her own for a while. I needed some air.

199

I slipped out from behind the booth and strode, blindly, through the crowds packing the courtyard, darting through the first open door I came across.

I found myself in the Mission's cemetery. I didn't turn back. Cemeteries don't creep me out that much. I mean, though it might come as a surprise to learn, ghosts hardly ever hang out there. Near their graves, I mean. They tend to concentrate much more on the places they hung out while they were living. Cemeteries can actually be very restful, to a mediator.

Or a shifter. Or whatever it is that Paul Slater is convinced I am. Paul Slater who, I was beginning to realize, wasn't just a manipulative eleventh grader who happened to be warm for my form. No, according to his own grandfather, Paul Slater was . . . well, the devil.

And I had just sold my soul to him.

This was not information I could process lightly. I needed time to think, time to figure out what I was going to do next. I stepped into the cool, shady graveyard and turned down a narrow pathway that, by this point, had actually become sort of familiar to me. I went down it a lot. In fact sometimes, when I borrowed the hall pass, pretending I needed to visit the ladies' room during class, this was where I went instead, to the Mission cemetery, and down this very path. Because at the end of it lay something very important to me. Something I cared about.

But this time, when I got to the end of the little stone path, I found that I was not alone. Jesse stood there, looking down at his own headstone.

I knew the words he was reading by heart, because I was the one who, with Father Dom, had supervised their carving.

Here Lies Hector 'Jesse' De Silva, 1830–1850, Beloved Brother, Son and Friend.

200

Jesse looked up as I came to stand beside him. Wordlessly, he held his hand out over the top of the headstone. I slipped my fingers into his.

'I'm sorry,' he said, his gaze darkly opaque as ever, 'about everything.'

I shrugged, keeping my gaze on the earth above his coffin – dark as his eyes. 'I understand, I guess.' Even though I didn't. 'I mean, you can't help it if you . . . well, don't feel the same way about me as I do about you.'

I don't know what made me say it. The minute the words were out of my mouth, I wished the grave beneath us would open up and swallow me, too.

So you can imagine my surprise when Jesse demanded, in a voice I barely recognized as his, it was so filled with pent-up emotion, 'Is that what you think? That I *wanted* to leave?'

'Didn't you?' I stared at him, completely dumbstruck. I was trying very hard to remain coolly detached from the whole thing, on account of having had my pride stomped on. Still, my heart, which I could have sworn had shrivelled up and blown away a day or two ago, suddenly came shuddering back to life, even though I warned it firmly not to.

'How could I stay?' Jesse wanted to know. 'After what happened between us, Susannah, how could I stay?'

I genuinely had no idea what he was talking about. 'What happened between us? What do you mean?'

'That kiss.' He let go of my hand, so suddenly that I stumbled.

But I didn't care. I didn't care because I was beginning to think something wonderful was happening. Something glorious. I thought it all the more when I saw Jesse lift a hand to run his fingers through his hair, and I saw that they were shaking. His fingers, I mean. Why would his fingers be shaking like that?

201

'How could I stay?' Jesse wanted to know. 'Father Dominic was right. You need to be with someone your family and your friends can actually *see*. You need to be with someone who can grow old with you. You need to be with someone *alive*.'

Suddenly, it was all beginning to make sense. Those weeks of awkward silences between us. Jesse's stand-offishness. It wasn't because he didn't love me. It wasn't because he didn't love me at all.

I shook my head. My blood, which I'd begun to suspect had somehow frozen in my veins these past few days, seemed suddenly to begin flowing again. I hoped that I was not making another mistake. I hoped this was not a dream I was going to wake up from any time soon.

'Jesse,' I said, feeling drunk with happiness. 'I don't care about any of that. That kiss . . . that kiss was the best thing that ever happened to me.'

I was simply stating a fact. That's all. A fact that I'd been sure he'd already known.

But I guess it came as a surprise to him, since the next thing I knew, he'd pulled me into his arms and was kissing me all over again.

And it was like the world, which had, for the past few weeks, been off its axis, suddenly righted itself. I was in Jesse's arms and he was kissing me, and everything was fine. More than fine. Everything was perfect. Because he loved me.

And yeah, OK, maybe that meant he had to move out . . . and yeah, there was the whole Paul thing. I still wasn't too sure what I was going to do about that.

But what did any of that matter? He loved me!

And this time when he kissed me, no one interrupted.

Mediator

HEAVEN SENT

For Benjamin

Many thanks to Beth Ader, Jennifer Brown, Laura Langlie, Abigail McAden and especially Benjamin Egnatz, as well as all the readers who supported this series from the beginning

It had been a typical Saturday morning in Brooklyn. Nothing out of the ordinary. Nothing to make me suspect it was the day my life was going to change forever. Nothing at all.

I'd gotten up early to watch cartoons. I didn't mind getting up early if it meant I'd get to spend a few hours with Bugs and his friends. It was getting up early for school that I resented. Even back then, I hadn't been too fond of school. My dad had to tickle my feet on weekdays to get me out of bed.

Not on Saturdays, though.

I think my dad felt the same. About Saturdays, I mean. He was always the first one out of bed in our apartment, but he got up extra early on Saturdays, and instead of oatmeal with brown sugar, which he made me for breakfast on weekdays, he made French toast. My mom, who'd never been able to stomach the smell of maple syrup, always stayed in bed until our breakfast plates had been rinsed and put in the dishwasher, and all of the counters were wiped down, and the smell was gone.

That Saturday – the one right after I turned six – my dad and I had cleaned up the syrupy dishes and counters, and then I'd returned to cartoons. I can't remember which one I'd been watching when my dad strode in to tell me goodbye, but it had been a good enough one that I'd wished he'd hurry up and leave already.

'I'm going running,' he'd said, planting a kiss on the top of my head. 'See ya, Suze.'

'Bye,' I'd said. I don't think I even bothered to look at him. I knew what he looked like. A big tall guy with a lot of thick dark hair that had gone white in some places. That day, he'd been wearing grey jogging pants and a T-shirt that read HOMEPORT, MENEMSHA, FRESH SEAFOOD ALL YEAR ROUND, left over from our last trip to Martha's Vineyard.

Neither of us had known then they'd be the last clothes anyone would ever see him in.

'Sure you don't want to come to the park with me?' he'd asked.

'Da-ad,' I'd said, appalled at the thought of missing a minute of cartoons. 'No.'

'Suit yourself,' he'd said. 'Tell your mom there's fresh-squeezed orange juice in the fridge.'

'OK,' I said. 'Bye.'

And he'd left.

Would I have done anything differently, if I'd known it was the last time I'd ever see him again – alive, anyway? Of course I would have. I would have gone to the park with him. I'd have made him walk, instead of run. If I'd known he was going to have a heart attack out there on the running path and die in front of strangers, I'd have stopped him from going to the park in the first place, made him go to the doctor instead.

Only I hadn't known. How could I have known?

How could I?

208

One

I found the stone exactly where Mrs Gutierrez had said it would be, beneath the drooping branches of the overgrown hibiscus in her backyard. I shut off the flashlight. Even though there was supposed to have been a full moon that night, by midnight a thick layer of clouds had blown in from the sea, and a dank mist had reduced visibility to nil.

But I didn't need light to see by any more. I just needed to dig. I sunk my fingers into the wet soft earth and pried the stone from its resting spot. It moved easily and wasn't heavy. Soon I was feeling beneath it for the tin box Mrs Gutierrez had assured me would be there . . .

Except that it wasn't. There was nothing beneath my fingers except damp soil.

That's when I heard it – a twig snapping beneath the weight of someone nearby.

I froze. I was trespassing, after all; the last thing I needed was to be dragged home by the Carmel, California, cops.

Again.

Then, with my pulse beating frantically as I tried to figure out how on earth I was going to explain my way out of this one, I recognized the lean shadow – darker than all the others – standing a few feet away. My heart continued to pound in my ears, but now for an entirely different reason.

209

'You,' I said, climbing slowly, shakily, to my feet.

'Hello, Suze.' His voice, floating toward me through the mist, was deep, and not at all unsteady . . . unlike my own voice, which had an unnerving tendency to shake when he was around.

It wasn't the only part of me that shook when he was around, either.

But I was determined not to let him know that.

'Give it back,' I said, holding out my hand.

He threw back his head and laughed.

'Are you nuts?' he wanted to know.

'I mean it, Paul,' I said, my voice steady, but my confidence already beginning to seep away, like sand beneath my feet.

'It's two thousand dollars, Suze,' he said, as if I might be unaware of that fact. 'Two *thousand*.'

'And it belongs to Julio Gutierrez.' I sounded sure of myself, even if I wasn't exactly feeling that way. 'Not you.'

'Oh, right,' Paul said, his deep voice dripping with sarcasm. 'And what's Gutierrez gonna do, call the cops? He doesn't know it's missing, Suze. He never even knew it was there.'

'Because his grandmother died before she had a chance to tell him,' I reminded him.

'Then he won't notice, will he?' Despite the darkness, I could tell Paul was smiling. I could hear it in his voice. 'You can't miss what you never knew you had.'

'Mrs Gutierrez knows.' I'd dropped my hand so he wouldn't see it shaking, but I couldn't disguise the growing unsteadiness in my voice as easily. 'If she finds out you stole it, she'll come after you.'

'What makes you think she hasn't already?' he asked, so smoothly that the hairs on my arms stood up . . . and not because of the brisk autumn weather, either.

210

I didn't want to believe him. He had no reason to lie. And obviously, Mrs Gutierrez had come to him as well as me, anxious for any help she could get. How else could he have known about the money?

Poor Mrs Gutierrez. She had definitely put her trust in the wrong mediator. Because it looked as if Paul hadn't just robbed her. Oh, no.

But like a fool, I stood there in the middle of her back-yard and called her name just in case, as loudly as I dared. I didn't want to wake the grieving family inside the modest stucco home a few yards away.

'Mrs Gutierrez?' I craned my neck, hissing the name into the darkness, trying to ignore the chill in the air . . . and in my heart. 'Mrs Gutierrez? Are you there? It's me, Suze . . . Mrs Gutierrez?'

I wasn't all that surprised when she didn't show. I knew, of course, that he could make the undead disappear. I just never thought he'd be low enough to do it.

I should have known better.

A cold wind kicked up from the sea as I turned to face him. It tossed some of my long dark hair around my face until the strands finally ended up sticking to my lip gloss. But I had more important things to worry about.

'It's her life savings,' I said to him, not caring if he noticed the throb in my voice. 'All she had to leave to her kids.'

Paul shrugged, his hands buried deep in the pockets of his leather jacket.

'She should have put it in the bank, then,' he said.

Maybe if I reason with him, I thought. Maybe if I explain . . . 'A lot of people don't trust banks with their money—'

But it was no use.

'Not my fault,' he said with another shrug.

211

'You don't even need the money,' I cried. 'Your parents buy you whatever you want. Two thousand dollars is nothing to you, but to Mrs Gutierrez's kids, it's a fortune!'

'She should have taken better care of it, then,' was all he said.

Then, apparently seeing my expression – though I don't know how, since the clouds overhead were thicker than ever – he softened his tone.

'Suze, Suze, Suze,' he said, pulling one of his hands from his jacket pocket and moving to drape his arm across my shoulders. 'What am I going to do with you?'

I didn't say anything. I don't think I could have spoken if I'd tried. It was hard enough just to breathe. All I could think about was Mrs Gutierrez, and what he'd done to her. How could someone who smelled so good – the sharp clean scent of his cologne filled my senses – or from whom such warmth radiated – especially welcome, given the chill in the air and the relative thinness of my windbreaker – be so . . .

Well, evil?

'Tell you what,' Paul said. I could feel his deep voice reverberating through him as he spoke, he was holding me that close. 'I'll split it with you. A grand for each of us.'

I had to swallow down something – something that tasted really bad – before I could reply. 'You're sick.'

'Don't be that way, Suze,' he chided. 'You have to admit, it's fair. You can do whatever you want with your half. Mail it back to the Gutierrezes, for all I care. But if you're smart, you'll use it to buy yourself a car now that you finally got your licence. You could put a down payment on a decent set of wheels with that kind of change, and not have to worry about sneaking your mom's car out of the driveway after she's fallen asleep—'

'I hate you,' I snapped, twisting out from beneath his grip

212

and ignoring the cold air that rushed in to meet the place where his body had been warming mine.

'No, you don't,' he said. The moon appeared momentarily from behind the blanket of clouds overhead, just long enough for me to see that his lips were twisted into a lopsided grin. 'You're just mad because you know I'm right.'

I couldn't believe my ears. Was he serious? 'Taking money from a dead woman is the right thing to do?'

'Obviously,' he said. The moon had disappeared again, but I could tell from his voice that he was amused. 'She doesn't need it any more. You and Father Dom. You're a couple of real pushovers, you know. Now I've got a question for you. How'd you know what she was blathering about, anyway? I thought you were taking French, not Spanish.'

I didn't answer him right away. That's because I was frantically trying to think of a reply that wouldn't include the word I least liked uttering in his presence, the word that, every time I heard it or even thought it, seemed to cause my heart to do somersaults over in my chest, and my veins to hum pleasantly.

Unfortunately, it was a word that didn't exactly engender the same response in Paul.

Before I could think of a lie, however, he figured it out on his own.

'Oh, right,' he said, his voice suddenly toneless. '*Him.* Stupid of me.'

Then, before I could think of something to say that would lighten the situation – or at least get his mind off Jesse, the last person in the world I wanted Paul Slater to be thinking about – he said in quite a different tone, 'Well, I don't know about you, but I'm beat. I'm gonna call it a night. See you around, Simon.'

He turned to go. Just like that, he turned to go.

I knew what I had to do, of course. I wasn't looking forward to it . . . in fact, my heart had pretty much slipped up into my throat, and my palms had gone suddenly, inexplicably damp.

But what choice did I have? I couldn't let him walk away with all that money. I'd tried reasoning with him, and it hadn't worked. Jesse wouldn't like it, but the truth was, there was no other alternative. If Paul wouldn't give up the money voluntarily, well, I was just going to have to take it from him.

I told myself I had a pretty good chance at succeeding, too. Paul had the box tucked into the inside pocket of his jacket. I'd felt it there when he'd put his arm around me. All I had to do was distract him somehow – a good blow to the solar plexus would probably do the job – then grab the box and chuck it through the closest window. The Gutierrezes would freak, of course, at the sound of the breaking glass, but I highly doubted they'd call the cops . . . not when they found two thousand bucks scattered across the floor.

As plans went, it wasn't one of my best, but it was all I had.

I called his name.

He turned. The moon chose that moment to slip out from behind the thick veil of clouds overhead, and I could see by its pale light that Paul wore an absurdly hopeful expression. The hopefulness increased as I slowly crossed the grass between us. I suppose he thought for a minute that he'd finally broken me down. Found my weakness. Successfully lured me to the dark side.

And all for the low, low price of a thousand bucks.

Not.

The hopeful look left his face, though, the second he

noticed my fist. I even thought that, just for a moment, I caught a look of hurt in his blue eyes, pale as the moonlight around us. Then the moon moved back behind the clouds, and we were once again plunged into darkness.

The next thing I knew, Paul, moving more quickly than I would have thought possible, had seized my wrists in a grip that hurt and kicked my feet out from under me. A second later, I was pinned to the wet grass by the weight of his body and his face just inches from mine.

'That was a mistake,' he said, way too casually, considering the force with which I could feel his heart hammering against mine. 'I'm rescinding my offer.'

His breath, unlike my own, wasn't coming out in ragged gasps, though. Still, I tried to hide my fear from him.

'What offer?' I panted.

'To split the money. I'm keeping it all, now. You really hurt my feelings, you know that, Suze?'

'I'm sure,' I said as sarcastically as I could. 'Now get off me. These are my favorite low-riders, and you're getting grass stains on them.'

But Paul wasn't ready to let me go. He also didn't appear to appreciate my feeble attempt to make a joke out of the situation. His voice, hissing down at me, was deadly serious.

'You want me to make your boyfriend disappear,' he asked, 'the way I did Mrs Gutierrez?'

His body was warm against mine, so there was no other explanation for why my heart went suddenly cold as ice, except that his words terrified me to the point that my blood seemed to freeze in my veins.

I couldn't, however, let my fear show. Weakness only seems to trigger cruelty, not compassion, from people like Paul.

'We have an agreement,' I said, my tongue and lips

215

forming the words with difficulty because they, like my heart, had gone ice cold with dread.

'I promised I wouldn't kill him,' Paul said. 'I didn't say anything about keeping him from dying in the first place.'

I blinked up at him, uncomprehending.

'What . . . what are you talking about?' I stammered.

'You figure it out,' he said. He leaned down and kissed me lightly on my frozen lips. 'Good night, Suze.'

And then he stood up and vanished into the fog.

It took me a minute to realize I was free. Cool air rushed in to all the places where his body had been touching mine. I finally managed to roll over, feeling as if I'd just suffered a head-on collision with a brick wall. Still, I had enough strength left to call out, 'Paul! Wait!'

That's when someone inside the Gutierrez household flicked on the lights. The backyard lit up bright as an airport runway. I heard a window open and someone shout, 'Hey, you! What are you doing there?'

I didn't stick around to ask whether or not they planned on calling the cops. I peeled myself up from the ground and ran for the wall I'd scaled a half hour ago. I found my mom's car right where I'd left it. I hopped into it and started my long journey home, cursing a certain fellow mediator – and the grass stains on my new jeans – the whole way.

I had no idea that night how bad things were going to get between Paul and me.

But I was about to find out.

216

Two

He'd done it. Finally. Just like, deep down, I guess I'd always known he would.

You would think, what with everything I'd been through, I'd have seen it coming. I'm not exactly new at this. And it wasn't as if all the warning signs hadn't been there.

Still, the blow, when it came, seemed to strike like a bolt out of the clear blue.

'So where are you going for dinner before the Winter Formal?' Kelly Prescott asked me in fourth period language lab. She didn't even wait to hear what my answer was. Because Kelly didn't care what my answer was. That wasn't the point of her asking me in the first place.

'Paul's taking me to the Cliffside Inn,' Kelly went on. 'You know the Cliffside Inn, don't you, Suze? In Big Sur?'

'Oh, sure,' I said. 'I know it.'

That's what I said, anyway. Isn't it weird how your brain can slip into autopilot? Like, how you can be saying one thing and thinking something entirely different? Because when Kelly said that – about Paul taking her to the Cliffside Inn – the first thing I thought wasn't *Oh, sure, I know it*. Not even close. My first thought was more along the lines of *What? Kelly Prescott? Paul Slater is taking KELLY PRESCOTT to the Winter Formal?*

But that's not what I said out loud, thank God. I mean, considering that Paul himself was sitting just a few study booths away, futzing with the sound on his tape player. The last thing in the world I wanted was for him to think I was, you know, peeved that he'd asked someone else to the formal. It was bad enough that he noticed I was even looking in his direction, let alone talking about him. He raised his eyebrows all questioningly, as if to say, 'May I be of service?'

That's when I saw he still had on his headphones. He hadn't, I realized with relief, heard what Kelly had said. He'd been listening to the scintillating conversation between Dominique and Michel, our little French friends.

'It got five stars,' Kelly went on, settling into her booth. 'The Cliffside Inn, I mean.'

'Cool,' I said, resolutely ripping my gaze from Paul's and pulling out the chair to my own booth. 'I'm sure you two will have a really great time.'

'Oh, yeah,' Kelly said. She flipped her honey-blonde hair back so she could slip on her headphones. 'It'll be so romantic. So where're you going? To eat before the dance, I mean.'

She knew, of course. She knew perfectly well.

But she was going to make me say it. Because that's how girls like Kelly are.

'I guess I'm not going to the dance,' I said, sitting down at the carrel beside hers and putting on my own headphones.

Kelly looked over the partition between us, her pretty face twisted with sympathy. Fake sympathy, of course. Kelly Prescott doesn't care about me. Or anyone, except herself.

'Not going? Oh, Suze, that's terrible! Nobody asked you?'

218

I just smiled in response. Smiled and tried not to feel Paul's gaze boring into the back of my head.

'That's too bad,' Kelly said. 'And it looks like Brad's not going to be able to go, either, what with Debbie being out with mono. Hey, I've got an idea.' Kelly giggled. 'You and Brad should go to the dance together!'

'Funny,' I said, smiling weakly as Kelly tittered at her own joke. Because, you know, there isn't anything quite as pathetic as a girl being taken to the junior–senior Winter Formal by her own stepbrother.

Except, possibly, her not being taken by anyone at all.

I turned on my tape player. Dominique immediately began to complain to Michel about her *dormitoire*. I'm sure Michel murmured sympathetic replies (he always does), but I didn't hear what they were.

Because it didn't make any sense. What had just happened, I mean. How could Paul be taking Kelly to the Winter Formal when, last time I'd checked, *I* was the one he was hounding for a date . . . any date? Not that I'd been especially thrilled about it, of course. But I did have to throw him the occasional bone, if only to keep him from doing to my boyfriend what he'd done to Mrs Gutierrez.

Wait a minute. Was *that* what was going on? Paul was finally getting tired of hanging around with a girl he had to blackmail into spending time with him?

Well, good. Right? I mean, if Kelly wanted him, she could have him.

The only problem was, I was having a hard time not remembering the way Paul's body had felt as it had lain across mine that night in the Gutierrezes' yard. Because it had felt good – his weight, his warmth – despite my fear. Really good.

Right sensation . . . wrong guy.

219

But the right guy? Yeah, he wasn't a real pin-the-girl-to-the-grass kind of person. And warmth? He hadn't given off any in a century and a half.

Which wasn't his fault, really. The warmth thing, I mean. Jesse couldn't help being dead any more than Paul could help being . . . well, Paul.

Still, this asking-Kelly-to-the-dance-and-not-me thing . . . it was freaking me out. I'd been bracing myself for his invitation – and his reaction to my turning it down – for weeks. I'd even begun thinking I was finally getting the hang of the back-and-forth nature of our relationship . . . as if it were a tennis game at the resort where we'd met last summer.

Except that now I had a sinking feeling that Paul had just lobbed a ball into my court that I was never going to be able to hit back.

What was that all about?

The words floated before my eyes, scrawled on a piece of paper torn from a notebook, and were waved at me from over the top of the wooden partition separating my carrel from the one in front of it. I pulled the piece of paper from the fingers clutching it and wrote, *Paul asked Kelly to the Winter Formal*, then slid the page over the partition.

A few seconds later, the paper fluttered back down in front of me.

I thought he was going to ask you!!! my best friend, CeeCee, wrote.

I guess not, I scribbled in response.

Well, maybe it's just as well, was CeeCee's reply. *You didn't want to go with him, anyway. I mean, what about Jesse?*

But that was just it. What *about* Jesse? If Paul had asked me to the Winter Formal, and I'd responded with something less than enthusiasm to his invitation, he'd have let loose one

220

of his cryptic threats about Jesse – the newest one, in fact, about him apparently having learned of some way to keep the dead from having passed on in the first place . . . Whatever that meant.

And yet today he'd turned around and asked someone else to go to the dance with him instead. Not just someone else, either, but Kelly Prescott, the prettiest, most popular girl in school . . . but also someone I happened to know Paul despised.

Something wasn't right about any of this . . . and it wasn't just that I was trying to save all my dances for a guy who's been dead for 150-odd years.

But I didn't mention this to CeeCee. Best friend or no, there's only so much a sixteen-year-old girl – even a sixteen-year-old albino who happens to have a psychic aunt – can understand. Yes, she knew about Jesse. But Paul? I hadn't breathed a word.

And I wanted to keep it that way.

Whatever, I scrawled. *How about you? Adam ask you yet?*

I looked around to make sure Sister Marie-Rose, our French teacher, wasn't watching before I slid the note back toward CeeCee, and instead spotted Father Dominic waving at me from the language lab doorway.

I removed my headphones with no real regret – Dominique's and Michel's whining would hardly have been riveting in English; in French, it was downright unbearable – and hurried to the door. I felt, rather than saw, that a certain gaze was very much on me.

I would not, however, give him the satisfaction of glancing his way.

'Susannah,' Father Dominic said as I slipped out of the language lab and into one of the open breezeways that served as hallways between classrooms at the Junipero Serra

221

Mission Academy. 'I'm glad I was able to catch you before I left.'

'Left?' It was only then that I noticed Father D was holding an overnight bag and wearing an extremely anxious expression. 'Where are you going?'

'San Francisco.' Father Dominic's face was nearly as white as his neatly trimmed hair. 'I'm afraid something terrible has happened.'

I raised my eyebrows. 'Earthquake?'

'Not exactly.' Father Dominic pushed his wire-rimmed spectacles into place at the top of his perfectly aquiline nose as he squinted down at me. 'It's the monsignor. There's been an accident and he's in a coma.'

I tried to look suitably upset, although the truth is, I've never really cared for the monsignor. He's always getting upset about stuff that doesn't really matter – like girls who wear miniskirts to school. But he never gets upset over stuff that's actually important, like how the hot dogs they serve at lunch are always stone-cold.

'Wow,' I said. 'So what happened? Car crash?'

Father Dominic cleared his throat. 'Er, no. He, um, choked.'

'Somebody strangled him?' I asked hopefully.

'Of course not. Really, Susannah,' Father Dom chided me. 'He choked on a piece of hot dog at a parish barbecue.'

Whoa! Poetic justice! I didn't say so out loud, though, since I knew Father Dom wouldn't approve.

Instead, I said, 'Too bad. So how long will you be gone?'

'I have no idea,' Father Dom said, looking harassed. 'This couldn't have happened at a worse time, either, what with the auction this weekend.'

The Mission Academy is ceaseless in its fund-raising efforts. This weekend the annual antique auction would be

222

taking place. Donations had been flooding in all week and were being stashed for safekeeping in the rectory basement. Some of the more notable items that the fund-raising club had received included a turn-of-the-century Ouija board (courtesy of CeeCee's psychic aunt, Pru) and a silver belt buckle – estimated by the Carmel Historical Society to be more than 150 years old – discovered by my stepbrother, Brad, while he was cleaning out our attic, a task assigned to him as punishment for an act of malfeasance, the nature of which I could no longer recall.

'But I wanted to make sure you knew where I was.' Father Dominic plucked a cellphone from his pocket. 'You'll call me if anything, er, out of the ordinary occurs, won't you, Susannah? The number is—'

'I know the number, Father D,' I reminded him. Father Dom's cellphone was new, but not *that* new. May I just add that it totally sucks that Father Dominic, who has never wanted – nor has the slightest idea how to use – a cellphone has one and I don't? 'And by out of the ordinary, do you mean stuff like Brad getting a passing grade on his trig midterm, or more supernatural phenomena, like ecto-plasmic manifestations in the basilica?'

'The latter,' Father Dom said, pocketing the cellphone again. 'I hope not to be gone for more than a day or two, Susannah, but I am perfectly aware that in the past it hasn't taken much longer than that for you to get yourself into mortal peril. Kindly, while I'm away, see to it that you exercise a modicum of caution in that capacity. I don't care to return home, only to find another section of the school blown to kingdom come. Oh, and if you would, make sure that Spike has enough food—'

'Nuh-uh,' I said, backing away. It was the first time in a long time that my wrists and hands were free of angry red

223

scratches, and I wanted to keep it that way. 'That cat's your responsibility now, not mine.'

'And what am I to do, Susannah?' Father D looked frustrated. 'Ask Sister Ernestine to look in on him from time to time? There aren't even supposed to be pets in the rectory, thanks to her severe allergies. I've had to learn to sleep with the window open so that that infernal animal can come and go as it pleases without being spotted by any of the novices—'

'Fine,' I interrupted him, sighing gustily. 'I'll stop by PETCO after school. Anything else?'

Father Dominic pulled a crumpled list from his pocket.

'Oh,' he said after skimming it. 'And the Gutierrez funeral. All taken care of. And I've put the family on our neediest-case roster, as you requested.'

'Thanks, Father D,' I said quietly, looking away through the arched openings in the breezeway toward the fountain in the centre of the courtyard. Back in Brooklyn, where I'd grown up, November meant death to all flora. Here in California – even though it's northern California – all November apparently means is that the tourists, who visit the Mission daily, wear khakis instead of Bermuda shorts, and the surfers down on Carmel Beach have to exchange their short-sleeved wetsuits for long-sleeved ones. Dazzling red and pink blossoms still fill the Mission's flower beds, and when we're released for lunch each noon, it's still possible to work up a sweat under the sun's rays.

Still, temperatures in the seventies or not, I shivered . . . and not just because I was standing in the cool shade of the breezeway. No, it was a cold that came from inside that was causing the goose bumps on my upper arms. Because, beautiful as the Mission gardens were, there was no denying that beneath those glorious petals lurked something dark and . . .

224

. . . well, Paul-like.

It was true. The guy had the ability to cause even the brightest day to cloud over. At least, as far as I was concerned. Whether or not Father Dominic felt the same, I didn't know . . . but I kind of doubted it. After his somewhat rocky start to the school year, Paul had ended up not having nearly as much regular contact with the school principal as I did. Which, given that all three of us are mediators, might seem a little strange.

But both Paul and Father D seem to like it that way, each preferring to keep his distance, with me as a go-between when communication is absolutely necessary. This was partly because they were – let's face it – guys. But it was also because Paul's behaviour – at school, anyway – had improved considerably, and there was no reason for him to be sent to the principal's office. Paul had become a model student, making impressive grades and even getting appointed captain of the Mission Academy men's tennis team.

If I hadn't seen it for myself, I wouldn't have believed it. But there it was. Obviously, Paul preferred to keep Father D in the dark about his after-school activities, knowing that the priest was hardly likely to approve of them.

Take the Gutierrez incident, for instance. A ghost had come to us for help and Paul, instead of doing the right thing, had ended up stealing two thousand dollars from her. This was not something Father Dominic would have turned a blind eye to, had he known about it.

Only he didn't know about it. Father D, I mean. Because Paul wasn't about to tell him, and, frankly, neither was I. Because if I did – if I told Father Dominic anything that might make Paul seem less than the straight-A-getting jock he was pretending to be – what had happened to Mrs Gutierrez was going to happen to my boyfriend.

225

Or, you know, the guy who would be my boyfriend. If he weren't dead.

Paul had me, all right. Right where he wanted me. Well, maybe not exactly *right* where he wanted me, but close enough . . .

Which was why I'd had to resort to subterfuge in order to secure some form of justice for the Gutierrezes, who'd been robbed, even if they didn't know it. I couldn't go to the police, of course (*Well, you see, officer, Mrs Gutierrez's ghost told me the money was hidden beneath a rock in her backyard, but when I got there, I found out another mediator had taken it . . .What's a mediator, you ask? Oh, a person who acts as a liaison between the living and the dead. Hey, wait a minute . . . what're you doing with that strait jacket?*).

Instead, I'd placed the family's name on the Mission's neediest list, which had secured Mrs Gutierrez a decent funeral and enough money for her loved ones to pay off some of her debt. Not two thousand dollars' worth, though, that was for sure . . .

'—while I'm gone, Susannah.'

I tuned in to what Father Dominic was saying to me a little too late. And I couldn't ask, *What was that, Father D?* Because then he'd want to know what I'd been thinking about, instead of paying attention to what he was saying.

'Do you promise, Susannah?'

Father Dominic's blue-eyed gaze bore into mine. What could I do but swallow and nod?

'Sure, Father D,' I said, not having the slightest idea what I was promising.

'Well, I must say, that makes me feel better,' he said, and it was true that his shoulders seemed to lose some of the rigidity with which he'd been holding them as we'd talked. 'I know, of course, that I can trust the two of you. It's just

226

that . . . well, I would hate for you to do anything – er, stupid – in my absence. Temptation is difficult enough for anyone to resist, particularly the young, who haven't fully considered the consequences of their actions.'

Oh. Now I knew what he'd been talking about.

'But for you and Jesse,' Father Dominic went on, 'there would be especially catastrophic repercussions should the two of you happen to, er—'

'—give in to our unbridled lust for each other?' I suggested when he trailed off.

Father Dominic eyed me unhappily.

'I'm serious, Susannah,' he said. 'Jesse doesn't belong in this world. With any luck, he won't continue to remain here for much longer. The deeper the attachment you form for each other, the more difficult it's going to be to say goodbye. Because you will have to say goodbye to him one day, Susannah. You can't defy the natural order of—'

Blah blah blah. Father D's lips were moving, but I tuned him out again. I didn't need to hear the lecture again. So things hadn't worked out for Father Dominic and the girl-ghost he'd fallen in love with, way back in the Middle Ages. That didn't mean Jesse and I were destined to follow the same path. Especially not considering what I'd managed to pick up from Paul, who seemed to know a good deal more than Father Dom did about being a mediator . . .

. . . Particularly the little-known fact that mediators can bring the dead back to life.

There was just one little fly in the ointment: You needed to have a body to put the wrongfully deceased's soul into. And bodies aren't something I happen to stumble across on a regular basis. At least, not ones willing to sacrifice the soul currently occupying them.

227

'Sure thing, Father Dom,' I said as his speech petered out at last. 'Listen, have a real good time in San Francisco.'

Father Dominic grimaced. I guess people who are going to San Francisco to visit comatose monsignors don't necessarily get a lot of time off for touristy stuff like visiting the Golden Gate Bridge or Chinatown or whatever.

'Thank you, Susannah,' he said. Then he pinned me with a meaningful stare. '*Be good.*'

'Am I ever anything but?' I asked with some surprise.

He walked away, shaking his head, without even bothering to reply.

Three

'So what were you and the good father gabbing about during lab today?' Paul wanted to know.

'Mrs Gutierrez's funeral,' I replied truthfully. Well, more or less. I've found it doesn't pay to lie to Paul. He has an uncanny ability to discover the truth on his own.

Not, of course, that it means what I tell him is the strictest truth. I just don't practise a policy of full disclosure where Paul Slater is concerned. It seems safer that way.

And it definitely seemed safer not to let Paul know that Father Dominic was in San Francisco, with no known date of return.

'You're not still upset about that, are you?' Paul asked. 'The Gutierrez woman, I mean? The money's going to good use, you know.'

'Oh, sure, I know,' I said. 'Dinner at the Cliffside Inn's got to run, what, a hundred a plate? And I assume you'll be renting a limo.'

Paul smiled at me lazily from the pillows he was leaning against. Yes, we were on his bed. Together. Nothing was going on there – nothing more exciting than my usual Wednesday Mediator lesson, I mean, which I'm forced to take due to Paul's insistence that if I don't, he will send my boyfriend to the netherworld. Because Paul's room is all hard

229

tile and sharp angles, his bed is the only comfortable place to sit. I'm pretty sure he arranged it that way on purpose.

'Kelly told you?' he asked. 'Already?'

'First chance she got,' I said.

'Didn't take her long,' he said.

'When did you ask her? Last night?'

'That's right.'

'So about twelve hours,' I said. 'Not bad, if you consider that for about eight of them, she was probably sleeping.'

'Oh, I doubt that,' Paul said. 'That's when they do their best work. Succubi, I mean. I bet Kelly only needs an hour or two of shut-eye a night, tops.'

'Romantic.' I turned a page of the crusty old book lying between us on Paul's bed. 'Calling your date for the Winter Formal a succubus, I mean.'

'At least she *wants* to go with me,' Paul said, his face expressionless – with the exception of a single dark brow, which rose, almost imperceptibly, higher than the one next to it. 'A refreshing change, I must say, from the usual state of things around here.'

'You hear me complaining?' I asked, turning another page. I prided myself that I was maintaining – outwardly, anyway – a supremely indifferent attitude about the whole thing. Inside, of course, it was a whole other story. Because inside, I was screaming, *What's going on? Why'd you ask Kelly and not me? Not that I care about the stupid dance, but just what game do you think you're playing now, Paul Slater?*

It was amazing how none of this showed, however. At least, so far as I knew.

'It's just that I'd have appreciated some advance notice that I'd been stricken from the agenda,' was what I said aloud. 'For all you knew, I might have already blown a fortune on a dress.'

230

One corner of Paul's mouth flicked upward.

'You hadn't,' Paul said. 'And you weren't going to, either.'

I looked away. It was hard to meet his gaze sometimes, it was so penetrating, so . . .

Blue.

A strong, tanned hand came down over mine, pinning my fingers to the page I'd been about to turn.

'That's the one.' Paul doesn't seem to have the same problem looking into my eyes (probably because mine are green and about as penetrating as, um, algae) that I have looking into his. His gaze on my face was unwavering. 'Read it.'

I looked down. The book Paul had pulled out for our latest 'mediator lesson' was so old, the pages had a tendency to crumble beneath my fingers as I turned them. It belonged in a museum, not a seventeen-year-old guy's bedroom.

But that was exactly where it had ended up, pulled – though I doubted Paul knew I was aware of it – from his grandfather's collection. *The Book of the Dead* was what it was called.

And the title wasn't the only reminder that all things have an expiration date. It smelled as if a mouse or some other small creature had gotten slammed between the pages some time in the not-so-distant past, left to slowly decompose there.

'"If the 1924 translation is to be believed,"' I read aloud, glad my voice wasn't shaking the way I knew my fingers were – the way my fingers always shook when Paul touched me – '"the shifter's abilities didn't merely include communication with the dead and teleportation between their world and our own, but the ability to travel at will throughout the fourth dimension as well."'

231

I will admit, I didn't read with a lot of feeling. It wasn't exactly a barrel of laughs, going to school all day, then having to go to mediation tutoring. Granted, it was only once a week, but that was more than enough, believe me. Paul's house hadn't lost any of its sterility in the months I'd been coming to it. If anything, the place was as creepy as ever . . .

. . . and so was Paul's grandfather, who continued to live what he'd described, in his own words, as a 'half-life,' in a room down the hall from Paul's. That half-life seemed to be made up of around-the-clock health attendants, hired to see to the old man's many ailments, and incessant viewing of the Game Show Network. It isn't any wonder, really, that Paul avoids Mr Slater – or Dr Slaski, as the good doctor himself had confided to me he was really named – like the plague. His grandfather isn't exactly scintillating company, even when he isn't pretending to be loopy due to his meds.

Despite my less-than-inspired performance, however, Paul released my hand and leaned back once more, looking extremely pleased with himself. 'Well?' Another raised eyebrow.

'Well, what?' I flipped the page, and saw only a copy of the hieroglyph they were talking about.

The half smile Paul had been wearing vanished. His face was as expressionless as the wall behind him.

'So that's how you're going to play it,' he said.

I had no idea what he was talking about. 'Play what?' I asked.

'I could do it, Suze,' he said. 'It can't be hard to figure out. And when I do . . . well, you won't be able to accuse me of not having stuck by our agreement.'

'What agreement?'

Paul set his jaw.

'Not to kill your boyfriend,' he said tonelessly.

232

I just stared at him, genuinely taken aback. I had no idea where this was coming from. We'd been having a perfectly nice – well, OK, not nice, but ordinary – afternoon, and all of a sudden he was threatening to kill my boyfriend . . . or not to kill him, actually. What was going on?

'Wh-what are you talking about?' I stammered. 'What does this have to do with Jesse? Is this . . . is this because of the dance? Paul, if you'd asked, I'd have gone with you. I don't know why you turned around and asked Kelly without even—'

The half grin came back, but this time, all Paul did was lean forward and flip the book closed. Dust rose from the ancient pages, almost right up into my face, but I didn't complain. Instead, I waited, my heart in my throat, for him to reply.

I was destined for disappointment, however, since all he said was, 'Don't worry about it,' then swung his legs over the side of the bed and stood up. 'You hungry?'

'Paul.' I followed him, my Stuart Weitzmans clacking loudly on the bare tile floor. 'What's going on?'

'What makes you think anything's going on?' he asked as he made his way down the long, shiny hallway.

'Oh, gee, I don't know,' I said, fear making me sound waspish. 'That crack you made the other night about Jesse. And letting me off the hook for the Winter Formal. And now this. You're up to something.'

'Am I?' Paul glanced up at me as he made his way down the spiral staircase to the kitchen. 'You really think so?'

'Yes,' I said. 'I just haven't figured out what yet.'

'Do you have any idea what you sound like right now?' Paul asked as he pulled open the Sub-Zero refrigerator and peered inside.

'No,' I said. 'What?'

'A jealous girlfriend.'

I nearly choked. 'And how *are* things on Planet You Wish?'

He found a can of Coke and cracked it open.

'Nice one,' he said in reference to my remark. 'No, really. I like that. I might even use it myself someday.'

'Paul.' I stared at him, my throat dry, my heart banging in my chest. 'What are you up to? Seriously.'

'Seriously?' He took a long swig of soda. I couldn't help noticing how tanned his throat was as I watched him swallow. 'I'm hedging my bets.'

'What does *that* mean?'

'It means,' he said, closing the refrigerator door and leaning his back against it, 'that I'm starting to like it around here. Strange, but true. I never thought of myself as the captain-of-the-tennis-team type. God knows, at my last school' – he took another long pull at the soda – 'Well, I won't get into that. The truth is, I'm starting to get into this high school stuff. I want to go to the Winter Formal. Thing is, I figure you won't want to be around me for a while, after I . . . well, do what I plan on doing.'

He'd closed the refrigerator door, so that couldn't have been what caused the sudden chill I felt all along my spine. He must have seen me shiver, since he went, with a grin, 'Don't worry, Susie. You'll forgive me eventually. You'll realize, in time, that it's all for the be—'

He didn't get to finish. That's because I'd strode forward and knocked the Coke can right out of his hand. It landed with a clatter in the stainless-steel sink. Paul looked down at his empty fingers in some surprise, like he couldn't figure out where his drink had gone.

'I don't know what you're planning, but let me make one thing clear: If anything happens to him,' I hissed, not much louder than the soda fizzing from the can in the sink, but

234

with a lot more force, 'anything at all, I will make you regret the day you were born. Understand?'

The look of surprise on his face twisted into one of grim annoyance.

'That wasn't part of our deal. All I said was that I wouldn't—'

'*Anything,*' I said. 'And don't call me Susie.'

My heart was banging so loudly inside my chest that I didn't see how he couldn't hear it – how he couldn't see that I was more frightened than I was angry . . .

Or maybe he did, since his lips relaxed into a smile – the same smile that had made half the girls in school fall madly in love with him.

'Don't worry, Suze,' he said. 'Let's just say that my plans for Jesse? They're a lot more humane than what you've got planned for me.'

'I—'

Paul just shook his head. 'Don't insult me by pretending like you don't know what I mean.'

I didn't have to pretend. I had no idea what he was talking about. I didn't get a chance to tell him that, though, because at that moment a side door opened, and we heard someone call, 'Hello?'

It was Dr Slaski, along with his attendant, back from one of their endless rounds of doctor's appointments. The attendant was the one who'd let out the greeting. Dr Slaski – or Slater, as Paul referred to him – never said hello. At least, not when anybody but me was around.

'Hey,' Paul said, going out into the living room and looking down at his wheelchair-bound grandfather. 'How'd it go?'

'Just fine,' the attendant said with a smile. 'Didn't it, Mr Slater?'

235

Paul's grandfather said nothing. His head was slumped down on to his chest, as if he were asleep.

Except that he wasn't. He was no more asleep than I was. Inside that battered and frail-looking exterior was a mind crackling with intelligence and vitality. Why he chose to hide that fact, I still don't understand. There's a lot about the Slaters that I don't understand.

'Your friend staying for dinner, Paul?' the attendant asked cheerfully.

'Yes,' Paul said at the same time I said, 'No.'

I didn't meet his gaze as I added, 'You know I can't.'

This, at least, was true. Mealtime is family time at my house. Miss one of my stepfather's gourmet dinners, and you'll never hear the end of it.

'Fine,' Paul said through teeth that were obviously gritted. 'I'll take you home.'

I didn't object. I was more than ready to go.

Our ride should have been a lot more enjoyable than it was. I mean, Carmel is one of the most beautiful places in the world, and Paul's grandfather's house is right on the ocean. The sun was setting, seeming to set the sky ablaze, and you could hear waves breaking rhythmically against the rocks below. And Paul, who isn't exactly painful to look at, doesn't drive any old hand-me-down car, either, but a silver BMW convertible that I happen to know I look extremely good in, with my dark hair, pale skin and excellent taste in footwear.

But you could have cut the tension inside that car with a knife, nonetheless. We rode in utter silence until Paul finally pulled up in front of 99 Pine Crest Drive, the rambling Victorian house in the Carmel hills that my mother and stepfather had bought more than a year ago, but still hadn't finished refurbishing. Seeing as how it had been built at the

236

turn of the century – the nineteenth, not the twentieth – it needed a lot of refurbishing . . .

But no amount of recessed lighting could rid the place of its violent past, or the fact that, a few months earlier, they'd dug up my boyfriend's skeleton from the backyard. I still couldn't set foot on the deck without feeling nauseated.

I was about to get out of the car without a word when Paul reached over and put a hand on my arm.

'Suze,' he said, and when I turned my head to look at him, I saw that his blue eyes looked troubled. 'Listen. What would you say to a truce?'

I blinked at him. Was he kidding? He'd threatened to off my boyfriend; stole from people he'd been asked to help; and neglected to invite me to the school dance, humiliating me in front of the most popular girl in the whole school in the process. And now he wanted to kiss and make up?

'Forget it,' I said as I gathered up my books.

'Come on, Suze,' he said, flashing me that heart-melting smile. 'You know I'm harmless. Well, basically. Besides, what could I do to your boy Jesse? He's got Father D to protect him, right?'

Not really. Not now, anyway. But Paul didn't know that. Yet.

'I'm sorry about the thing with Kelly,' he said. 'But you didn't want to go with me. Can you blame me for wanting to take someone who . . . well, actually likes me?'

Maybe it was the smile. Maybe it was the way he blinked those baby blues. I don't know what it was, but suddenly, I found myself softening toward him.

'What about the Gutierrezes?' I asked. 'You'll give the money back?'

'Uh,' Paul said. 'Well, no. I can't do that.'

'Paul, you can. I won't tell, I swear . . .'

237

'It's not that. I can't because . . . I, er, need it.'

'For *what*?'

Paul grinned. 'You'll find out.'

I threw open the car door and got out, my heels sinking deep into the pine-needle-strewn lawn.

'Goodbye, Paul,' I said, and slammed the door behind me, cutting off his 'No, Suze, wait!'

I turned around and headed toward the house. My step-father, Andy, had started a fire in one of the house's many fireplaces. The rich smell of burning wood filled the crisp evening air, tinged with the scent of something else . . .

Curry. It was tandoori chicken night. How could I have forgotten?

Behind me, I heard Paul throw the car into reverse and drive away. I didn't look back. I headed up the stairs to the front door, stepping into the squares of light thrown on to the porch from the living room windows. I opened the door and went inside, calling 'I'm home!'

Except that I wasn't, really. Because home meant something else to me now, and had for quite a while.

And he didn't live there any more.

Four

The handful of pebbles I'd thrown rattled noisily against the heavy, leaded glass. I looked around, worried someone might have heard. But better for them to hear tiny rocks hitting a window than me whispering the name of someone who wasn't even supposed to be living there . . .

Someone who, technically speaking, wasn't living at all.

He appeared almost at once, not at the window, but by my side. That's the thing about the undead. They never have to worry about the stairs. Or walls.

'Susannah.' The moonlight threw Jesse's features into high relief. There were dark pools in the place where his eyes should have been, and the scar in his eyebrow a dog bite wound from childhood – showed starkly white.

Still, even with the tricks the moon was playing, he was the best-looking thing I had ever seen. I don't think it's just the fact that I'm madly in love with him that makes me think so, either. I'd shown the miniature portrait of him I'd accidentally-on-purpose snagged from the Carmel Historical Society to CeeCee, and she'd agreed. *Hottie extraordinaire* was how she'd put it, to be exact.

'You don't have to bother with these,' he said, reaching out to brush the remaining pebbles from my hand. 'I knew you were here. I heard you calling.'

239

Except, of course, that I hadn't. Called him. But whatever. He was here now and that's what mattered.

'What is it, Susannah?' Jesse wanted to know. He'd moved out of the shadows of the rectory, so that I could finally see his eyes. As usual, they were darkly liquid and full of intelligence . . . intelligence, and something else. Something, I like to think, that's just for me.

'Just stopped by to say hi,' I said with a shrug. It was chilly enough that when I spoke, I could see my breath fog up in front of me.

This didn't happen when Jesse spoke, however. Because, of course, he has no breath.

'At three in the morning?' The dark eyebrows shot up, but he looked more amused than alarmed. 'On a school night?'

He had me there, of course.

'Father D asked me to pick up some cat food,' I said, brandishing a bag. 'I didn't want Sister Ernestine to see me smuggling it in. She's not supposed to know about Spike.'

'Cat food,' Jesse said. Now he *definitely* looked amused. 'Is that all?'

It wasn't all and he knew it. But it also wasn't what he thought. At least, not exactly.

Still, when he pulled me toward him, I didn't precisely object. Especially not considering that there's only one place in the world I feel completely safe any more, and that's where I was just then . . . in his arms.

'You're cold, *querida*,' he whispered into my hair. 'You're shivering.'

I was, but not because I was cold. Well, not *only* because I was cold. I closed my eyes, melting in his embrace as I always did, reveling in the feel of his strong arms around me, his hard chest beneath my cheek. I wished I could have

240

stayed that way forever – in Jesse's arms, I mean, where nothing could ever hurt me. Because he'd never let it.

I don't know how long we stood like that in the vegetable garden behind the rectory where Father Dom lived. All I know is that eventually Jesse, who'd been stroking my hair, pulled back a little, so that he could look down into my face.

'What is it, Susannah?' he asked me again, his voice sounding strangely rough, considering the tenderness of the moment. 'What's wrong?'

'Nothing,' I lied, because I didn't want it to end . . . the moonlight, his embrace, any of it . . . all of it.

'Not nothing,' he said, reaching up and pulling a strand of hair from where the wind had blown it, so that it was sticking to my lip gloss. I always seem to have that problem. 'I know you, Susannah. I know there's something the matter. Come.'

He took me by the hand and pulled. I went with him, even though I didn't know where we were going. I'd have followed him anywhere, even into the bowels of hell. Only of course he'd never take me there.

Unlike some people.

I did balk a little when I saw where he had led me, though. It wasn't exactly hell, but . . .

'The *car?*' I stared at the hood of my mom's Honda Accord.

'You're cold,' Jesse said firmly, opening the driver's side door for me. 'We can talk inside.'

Talking wasn't really what I'd had in mind. Still, I figured we could do what I *had* had in mind just as easily in the car as in the rectory's vegetable garden. And it *would* be a lot warmer.

Only Jesse wasn't having any of it. He seized both my

241

hands as I tried to slip them around his neck, and placed them firmly in my lap.

'Tell me,' he said from the shadows of the passenger seat, and I could tell by his voice that he was in no mood for games.

I sighed and stared out the windshield. As far as romance went, this was not exactly what I'd call a prime make-out spot. Big Sur, maybe. The Winter Formal, definitely. But the rectory parking lot at the Junipero Serra Mission? Not so much.

'What is it, *querida*?' He reached out to sweep back some of my hair, which had fallen over my face.

When he saw my expression, however, he pulled his hand back.

'Oh. *Him*,' he said in an entirely different voice.

I guess I shouldn't have been surprised. That he'd known, I mean, without my having said anything. There was just so much I hadn't told Jesse – so much that I'd decided I didn't dare tell him. My agreement with Paul, for instance: that, in return for Paul not removing Jesse to the great beyond, I'd meet with him after school every Wednesday under the auspices of learning more about our unique skill . . . although truthfully, most of the time it seemed all Paul wanted to do was get his tongue in my mouth, not study mediator lore.

Jesse would not have been particularly enthused had he known of the lessons . . . less so, if he'd had an inkling of what they actually entailed. There was no love lost between Jesse and Paul, whose relationship had been rocky from the start. Paul seemed to think he was superior to Jesse merely because he happened to be alive and Jesse was not, while Jesse disliked Paul because he'd been born with every priv-ilege in the world – including the ability to communicate

242

with the dead – and yet chose to use his gifts for his own selfish purposes.

Of course, their mutual disdain for each other might also have had something to do with me.

Back before Jesse had come into my life, I used to sit around and fantasize about how great it would be to have two guys fighting over me. Now that it was actually happening, though, I realized what a fool I'd been. There was nothing funny about the grounding I'd gotten the last time the two of them had gone at it, destroying half the house in the process. And that fight hadn't even been my fault. Much.

'It's just,' I said, careful not to meet his gaze because I knew if I looked into those twin dark pools I'd be lost, as usual, 'Paul's been . . . worse than usual.'

'Worse?' The glance Jesse shot me was stiletto sharp. 'Worse in what way? Susannah, if he's laid a hand on you—'

'Not that,' I interrupted quickly, realizing with a sinking heart that the speech I'd been up half the night rehearsing – the speech that I'd convinced myself was so perfect, I needed to hurry right down to the rectory to say it now, at once, even though it was the middle of the night and I'd have to 'borrow' my mom's car to get there – wasn't perfect at all . . . In fact, it was completely wrong. 'What I mean is, lately, he's been threatening . . . well, to do something I don't really understand. To you.'

Jesse looked amused. Which was not exactly the reaction I'd been expecting.

'So you came rushing down here,' he said, 'in the middle of the night to warn me? Susannah, I'm touched.'

'Jesse, I'm serious,' I said. 'I think Paul's up to something. Remember Mrs Gutierrez?'

243

'Of course.' Jesse had translated the dead woman's frantic message for me because my Spanish is pretty much confined to *taco* and, of course, *querida*. 'What about her?'

Quickly, I told him about having met Paul in Mrs Gutierrez's backyard. Even though I skimmed over the bit about Paul having stolen the money before I'd been able to get my hands on it, Jesse's outrage was obvious. I saw a glint of steel in his eyes, and he said something in Spanish that I couldn't understand, but I'm guessing it wasn't complimentary to Paul's parentage.

'Father D's going to take care of it,' I hastened to assure him, in case Jesse was getting any ideas about trying to take Paul on – something I'd warned him repeatedly would be foolhardy in the extreme. I didn't say that Father D was unaware of Paul's theft . . . only that the Gutierrezes were in need. I knew what Jesse would say if he found out I'd left Father Dominic in the dark about Paul's latest transgression.

I also knew, however, what Paul would do if he found out I'd narced on him.

'But that's not what I'm worried about,' I added hastily. 'It's something Paul said when I . . . when I tried to get him to give the money back.' I thought it better to leave out the part about when I'd gone for Paul's solar plexus. Also the thing Paul had said earlier in the day, about how his plans for Jesse were more humane than my own plans for himself. Because I had a feeling now that I knew what he'd meant by that. Though he couldn't have been more wrong. 'It was something about you and what he was going to do to you. Not kill you—'

'That,' Jesse interrupted dryly, 'would be difficult, *querida*, given that I'm already dead.'

I glared at him. 'You know what I mean. He said he *wasn't*

244

going to kill you. He was going to . . . I think he said he was going to keep you from having died in the first place.'

Even in the darkness of the car's interior, I saw Jesse's eyebrow go up.

'He has a very high opinion of his own abilities, that one' was all he said, however.

'Jesse,' I said. I couldn't believe he wasn't taking Paul's threat seriously. 'He really meant it. He's said it to me a couple of times, now. I seriously think he might be up to something.'

'Slater is always going to be up to something where you're concerned, Susannah,' Jesse said, in a voice that suggested he was more than a little tired of the subject. 'He's in love with you. Ignore him, and eventually he'll go away.'

'Jesse,' I said. I couldn't, of course, tell him that I'd have liked nothing better than to turn my back on Paul and his manipulative ways, but that I couldn't because I'd promised him I wouldn't . . . in return for Jesse's life. Or at least his continued presence in this dimension. 'I really think—'

'Ignore him, Susannah.' Jesse was smiling a little now as he shook his head. 'He's only saying these things because he knows they upset you, and then you pay attention to him. *"Oh, Paul! No, don't, Paul!"*'

I looked at him in horror. 'Was that supposed to be an imitation of *me*?'

'Don't gratify him by paying attention,' Jesse continued as if he hadn't heard me, 'and he'll grow tired of it and move on.'

'I don't sound anything like that.' I chewed my lower lip uncertainly. 'Do I really sound like that?'

'And now, if that's all,' Jesse went on, ignoring me exactly the way he'd told me to ignore Paul, 'I think you should be getting home, *querida*. If your mother should wake and

245

find you gone, you know she'll worry. Besides, don't you have school in a few hours?'

'But—'

'*Querida.*' Jesse leaned over the gearshift and slipped a hand behind my neck. 'You worry too much.'

'Jesse, I—'

But I didn't get to finish what I'd started to say – nor, a second later, could I even recall what I'd meant to tell him. That's because he'd pulled me – gently, but inexorably – toward him, and covered my mouth with his.

Of course, it's impossible when Jesse's lips are on mine to think about anything other than the way those lips make me feel . . . which is unbelievably cherished and desired. I don't have a whole lot of experience in the kissing department, but even I know that what happens every time Jesse kisses me is . . . well, extraordinary.

And not just because he's a ghost, either. All the guy has to do is lower his lips to mine and it's like a Fourth of July sparkler going off deep inside me, flaming brighter and brighter until I can hardly bear the white-hot heat any more. The only thing that seems as if it might put the fire out is pressing myself closer to him . . .

But, of course, that only makes it worse, because then Jesse – who usually seems to have a fire of his own burning somewhere – ends up touching me someplace, beneath my shirt, for instance, where, of course, I *want* to be touched, but where he doesn't think his fingers have any business roaming. Then the kissing ends as Jesse apologizes for insulting me, even though insulted is the *last* thing I feel, something I've made as clear to him as I can, to no apparent avail.

But that's what I get for falling in love with a guy who was born back when men still treated women as if they were

246

dainty breakable figurines instead of flesh and blood. I've tried to explain to him that things are different now, but he remains stubbornly convinced that everything below the neck is off-limits until the honeymoon . . .

Except, of course, when we're kissing, like now, and he happens, in the heat of the moment, to forget he's a nineteenth-century gentleman.

I felt his hand move along the waistband of my jeans as we kissed. Our tongues entwined, and I knew it was only a matter of time until that hand slipped beneath my sweater and up toward my bra. I uttered a giddy prayer of thanks that I'd worn the front-closing one. Then, my eyes closed, I did a little exploration of my own, running my palms along the hard wall of muscles I could feel through the cotton of his shirt . . .

. . . until Jesse's fingers, instead of dipping inside my 34B, seized my hand in a grip of iron.

'Susannah.' He was breathing hard and the word came out sounding a little ragged as he rested his forehead against mine.

'Jesse.' I wasn't breathing too evenly myself.

'I think you'd better go now.'

How had I known he was going to say that?

It occurred to me that we would be able to do this – kiss like this, I mean – a lot more often and more conveniently if Jesse would get over the absurd idea that he has to stay with Father Dominic, now that we are, for want of a better word, an item. It was my bedroom, after all, that he'd been murdered in, way back when. Shouldn't it be my bedroom he continues to haunt?

I didn't couch it in those terms, though, since I knew Jesse, who's an old-fashioned guy, doesn't exactly approve of couples living together before wedlock. I also put resolutely

247

from my mind the warning Father Dominic had given me, just before he'd left for San Francisco, about not giving into temptation where Jesse is concerned. It's all very well for Father D to talk. He's a *priest*. He has no idea what it's like to be a red-blooded teenage mediator. Of the female variety.

'Jesse,' I said, still a little breathlessly, from all the kissing, 'I can't help thinking . . . well, this thing with Paul. I mean, who knows if maybe he really has come up with some new way to . . . to keep you and me apart? And now, with Father Dom gone for who knows how long, I . . . Well, don't you think it might be better if you came back to my house for a while?'

Jesse, even though he'd almost just had his hand up my shirt, didn't like that idea at all. 'So you can protect me from the nefarious Mr Slater?' Was it my imagination or did he sound more amused than, er, aroused? 'Thank you for the invitation, *querida*, but I can take care of myself.'

'But if Paul finds out Father D is gone, he might come after you. And if I'm not around to stop him—'

'This may come as a surprise to you, Susannah,' Jesse said, lifting his head and placing my hand in my lap once more, 'but I can handle Slater without your help.'

Now he *definitely* sounded amused.

'And now you're going home,' he went on. 'Good night, *querida*.'

He kissed me one last time, a brief peck goodbye. I knew that any second he was going to disappear.

But there was still something else I needed to know. Ordinarily, I'd have asked Father Dominic, but since he wasn't around . . .

'Wait,' I said. 'Before you go . . . one last thing.'

Jesse had already started to shimmer. 'What, *querida*?'

248

'The fourth dimension,' I blurted out.

He had begun to dematerialize, but now he looked solid again.

'What about it?' he asked.

'Um,' I said. I'm sure he thought I was just asking to keep him there for a few more precious seconds. And truthfully? I probably was. 'What is it?'

'Time,' Jesse said.

'Time?' I echoed. 'That's it? Just . . . time?'

'Yes,' Jesse said. 'Time. Why do you ask? For school?'

'Sure,' I said. 'For school.'

'The things they teach now,' he said, shaking his head.

'Cat food,' I said, holding out the bag. 'Don't forget.'

No wonder we can't seem to make it past second base.

He took the bag from me.

'Good night, *querida*,' he said.

And then he was gone. The only sign that he'd been there at all were the badly fogged windows, steamed by our breath.

Or rather, by my breath, since Jesse doesn't have any.

Five

Mr Walden held up a stack of Scantron sheets and said, 'Number-two pencils only, please.'

Kelly Prescott's hand immediately shot up into the air.

'Mr Walden, this is an outrage.' Kelly takes her role as president of the junior class extremely seriously . . . especially when it has to do with scheduling dances. And, apparently, aptitude testing. 'We should have been given at least twenty-four hours' notice that we'd be undergoing state testing today.'

'Relax, Prescott.' Mr Walden, our homeroom teacher and class advisor, began passing out the Scantron sheets. 'They're career aptitude tests, not academic. Your scores won't show up on your permanent record. They're to help you' – he picked up one of the test booklets lying on his desk and read from it aloud – '"determine which careers are best suited to your particular skills and/or areas of interest and/or achievement." Got it? Just answer the questions.' Mr Walden slapped a pile of answer sheets on to my desk for me to pass down my row. 'You've got fifty minutes. And no talking.'

'"Which do you enjoy more, working while a) outdoors? or b) indoors?"' I heard my stepbrother Brad read aloud from across the room. 'Hey, where's c) heavily intoxicated?'

'You loser,' Kelly Prescott chortled.

'Are you a "night person" or a "day person"?' Adam McTavish looked mockly shocked. 'This test is totally biased against narcoleptics.'

'"Do you work best a) alone or b) in a group?"' My best friend, CeeCee, could hardly seem to contain her disgust. 'Oh my God, this is *so stupid*.'

'What part of "no talking,"' Mr Walden demanded, 'do you people not understand?'

But no one paid any attention to him.

'This *is* stupid,' Adam declared. 'How is this test going to determine whether or not I'm qualified for a career?'

'It measures your *aptitude*, stupid.' Kelly sounded disgusted. 'The only career you're qualified for is working the drive-through window at In-N-Out Burger.'

'Where you, Kelly, will be working the fryer,' Paul pointed out dryly, causing the rest of the class to crack up . . .

Until Mr Walden, who'd settled behind his desk and was trying to read his latest issue of *Surf Magazine*, roared, 'Do you people want to stay after school to finish up those tests? Because I'll be happy to keep you here; I've got nothing better to do. Now, shut up, all of you, and get to work.'

That had a significant impact on the amount of chit-chat going on around the room.

Miserably, I filled in the little bubbles. My misery didn't just stem, of course, from the fact that I was operating on zero sleep. While that didn't exactly help, there was the more pressing concern than career aptitude tests. Yeah, they don't much apply to me. My fate is already laid out for me . . . has been laid out for me since birth. I'm destined to be one thing when I grow up and one thing only. And any other career I choose is just going to get in the way of my true calling, which is, of course, helping the undead to their final destinations.

I glanced over at Paul. He was bent over his Scantron sheet, filling in the answer bubbles with a little smile on his face. I wondered what he was putting down as fields of interest. I hadn't noticed any entries for extortion. Or felony theft.

Why, I wondered, was he even bothering? It wasn't like it was going to do us any good. We were always going to be mediators first, whatever other careers we might choose. Look at Father Dominic. Oh sure, he had managed to keep his mediator status a secret . . . a secret even from the church, since, as Father D put it, his boss is God, and God invented mediators.

Of course, Father D isn't *just* a priest. He'd also been a teacher for years and years, winning some awards, even, until he'd been promoted to principal.

But it's different for Father Dom. He really believes that his ability to see and speak to the dead is a gift from God. He doesn't see it for what it really is: a curse.

Except . . . except, of course, that without it, I never would have met Jesse.

Jesse. The little blank bubbles in front of me grew decidedly blurry as my eyes filled up with tears.

Oh, great. Now I was crying. At *school.*

But how could I help it? Here I was, my future laid out in front of me . . . graduation, college, career. Well, you know, pseudo-career, since we all know what my *real* career was going to be.

But what about Jesse? What future did *he* have?

'What's wrong with you?' CeeCee hissed.

I reached up and dabbed at my eyes with the sleeve of my Miu Miu shirt. 'Nothing,' I whispered back. 'Allergies.'

252

CeeCee looked sceptical, but turned back to her test booklet.

I'd asked him once what he'd wanted to be. Jesse, I mean. You know, before he'd died. I'd meant what he'd wanted to be as far as a career went, but he hadn't understood. When I'd finally explained, he'd smiled but in a sad way.

'Things were different when I was alive, Susannah,' he'd said. 'I was my father's only son. It was expected that I would inherit our family's ranch and work it to support my mother and sisters after my father died.'

He didn't add that part of the plan had also included his marrying the girl whose dad owned the farm next door, so that their land would be united into one supersized ranchero. Nor did he mention the fact that she was the one who'd had him killed, because she'd liked another fella better, a fella her dad hadn't exactly approved of. Because I already knew all of that.

Things were tough, I guess, even way back in the 1850s.

'Oh,' was what I'd said in response. Jesse hadn't spoken with any detectable rancour, but it seemed like a raw deal to me. I mean, what if he hadn't *wanted* to be a rancher? 'Well, what would you have *liked* to be? You know, if you'd had a choice?'

Jesse had looked thoughtful. 'I don't know. It was different then, Susannah. *I* was different. I did think . . . sometimes . . . that I might have liked to have been a doctor.'

A doctor. It made perfect sense – at least to me. All those times I'd staggered home with various parts of me throbbing in pain – whether from poison oak or blisters on my feet – Jesse had been there for me, his touch soft as cashmere. He'd have made a great doctor, actually.

'Why didn't you, then?' I'd wanted to know. 'Become a doctor? Just because of your dad?'

253

'Yes, mostly that,' he'd said. 'I'd never even dared mention it to anyone. I could barely be spared from the ranch for a few days, let alone the years medical school would have taken. But I would have liked that, I think. Medical school. Though back when I was alive,' he'd added, 'people didn't know nearly as much about medicine as they do today. It would be more exciting to work in the sciences now, I think.'

And he would know. He'd had 150 years to hang around and watch as inventions – electricity, automobiles, planes, computers . . . not to mention penicillin and vaccines for diseases that in the past had routinely killed millions – changed the world into something unrecognizable from the one in which he'd grown up.

But rather than clinging stubbornly to the past, as some would have, Jesse had followed along excitedly, reading whatever he could get his hands on, from paperback novels to encyclopedias. He said he had a lot to catch up on. His favourite books seem to be the non-fiction tomes he borrows from Father Dom, everything from philosophy to explorations on emerging viruses – the kind of books I'd have given to my dad on Father's Day, if my dad wasn't, you know, dead. My stepdad, on the other hand, is more the cookbook type. But you get my drift. To Jesse, stuff that seems dry and uninteresting to me is vitally exciting. Maybe because he'd seen it all unfolding before his eyes.

Sighing, I looked down at the hundreds of career options in front of me. Jesse was dead, but even *he* knew what he'd wanted to be . . . would have been, if he hadn't died. Or not been, considering what he'd said about his father's expectations for him.

And here I was, with every advantage in the world, and all I could think that I wanted to be when I grew up was . . .

Well, with Jesse.

254

'Twenty more minutes.' Mr Walden's voice boomed out across the classroom, startling me from my thoughts. I found that my gaze had become fixed on the sea less than a mile from the Mission and viewable through most of the school's classroom windows . . . to the detriment of students like me. I hadn't grown up, like most of my classmates, around the sea. It was a constant source of wonder and interest to me.

Kind of, I realized, like Jesse's fascination with modern science.

Only unlike Jesse, I actually had a chance to *do* something with my interest.

'Ten more minutes,' Mr Walden announced, startling me again.

Ten more minutes. I looked down at my answer sheet, which was half empty. At the same time, I noticed CeeCee shooting me an anxious look from her desk beside mine. She nodded to the sheet. *Get to work,* her violet eyes urged me.

I picked up my pencil and began to haphazardly fill in bubbles. I didn't care what answers I chose. Because, truthfully, I didn't care about my future. Without Jesse, I *had* no future. Of course, with him, I had no future, either. What was he going to do, anyway? Follow me to college? To my first job? My first apartment?

Yeah. That'll happen.

Paul was right. I'm so stupid. Stupid to have fallen in love with a ghost. Stupid to think we had any kind of future together. Stupid.

'Time's up.' Mr Walden pulled his feet from the top of his desk. 'Lay your pencils down, please. Then pass your answer sheets to the front.'

I wasn't all that surprised when Paul came up to me after Mr Walden had dismissed us for lunch. 'That was

255

pointless,' he said in a low voice, as we made our way toward our lockers. 'I mean, we have our career paths cut out for us, don't we?'

'Well, you can't really make a living doing what we do,' I said, then remembered, too late, that Paul certainly seemed to have managed to.

'An *honest* living,' I amended.

But instead of feeling ashamed of himself, as I'd meant him to, Paul just grinned.

'That's why I've decided on a career in the legal profession,' he said. 'Your dad was a lawyer, right?'

I nodded. I don't like talking about my dad with Paul. Because my dad was everything that was good. And Paul is everything that . . . isn't.

'Yeah, that's what I thought,' Paul went on. 'Nothing's black and white with the law. It's all sort of grey. So long as you can find a precedent.'

I didn't say anything. I could easily see Paul as a lawyer. Not a lawyer like my dad had been, a public defender, but the kind of lawyer who'd defend rich celebrities, people who thought they were above the law . . . and because they had limitless funds to pay for their defence, they *were* above it, in a way.

'You, on the other hand,' Paul said. 'I think you're destined for a career in the social services. You're a natural-born do-gooder.'

'Yeah,' I said, as I stopped beside my locker. 'Maybe I'll follow in Father D's footsteps, and become a nun.'

'Now that,' Paul said, leaning against the locker next to mine, 'would just be a waste. I was thinking more along the lines of a social worker. Or a therapist. You're very good, you know, at taking on other people's problems.'

Wasn't that the truth? It was the reason I was so bleary-

256

eyed and tired today. Because after I'd left Jesse the night before, I'd driven home and gone up to bed . . . only not to sleep. Instead, I'd lain awake, blinking at the ceiling and mulling over what Jesse had told me. Not about Paul, but about what Paul had made me read aloud earlier that day: *The shifter's abilities didn't merely include communication with the dead and teleportation between their world and our own, but the ability to travel at will throughout the fourth dimension as well.*

The fourth dimension. Time.

The very word caused the hairs on my arms to stand up, even though it was another typically beautiful autumn day in Carmel and not cold at all. Could it really be true? Was such a thing even possible? Could mediators – or shifters, as Paul and his grandfather insisted on calling us – travel through time as well as between the realms of the living and the dead?

And if – a big if – it *were* true, what on earth did it *mean*?

More important, why had Paul been so intent on making sure I knew about it?

'You look strung out,' Paul observed as I stowed my books away and reached for the paper bag containing the lunch my stepfather had made me: tandoori chicken salad. 'What's the matter? Trouble sleeping?'

'You should know,' I said, glaring at him.

'What'd *I* do?' he asked, sounding genuinely surprised.

I don't know if it was my exhaustion, or the fact that the career aptitude test had got me thinking about my future . . . my future and Jesse's. Suddenly, I was just very tired of Paul and his games. And I decided to call him on the latest one.

'The fourth dimension,' I reminded him. 'Time travel?'

He just grinned, however. 'Oh, good, you figured it out. Took you long enough.'

257

'You really think shifters are capable of time travel?' I asked.

'I don't think so,' Paul said. 'I *know* so.'

Again, I felt a chill when I shouldn't have. We were standing in the shade of the breezeway, it was true, but just a few feet away in the Mission courtyard, the sun was blazing down. Hummingbirds flitted from hibiscus blossom to hibiscus blossom. Tourists snapped away with their digital cameras.

So what was up with the goosebumps?

'Why?' I demanded, my throat suddenly dry. 'Because you've done it?'

'Not yet,' he said, casually. 'But I will. Soon.'

'Yeah,' I said, fear making me sarcastic. 'Well, maybe you could travel back to the night you stole Mrs Gutierrez's money and *not* do it this time.'

'God, would you let it go already?' He shook his head. 'It was two thousand lousy bucks. You act like it was two million.'

'Hey, Paul.' Kelly Prescott broke away from her clique – the Dolce and Gabbana Nazis as CeeCee had taken to calling them – and sauntered over, fluttering her heavily mascaraed eyelashes. 'You coming to lunch?'

'In a minute,' Paul said to her . . . not very nicely, considering she was his date for next weekend's dance. Kelly, though stung, nevertheless pulled herself together enough to send me a withering glance before heading for the yard where we dined daily, alfresco.

'So I don't get it.' I stared at him. 'What if we *can* travel through time? Big deal. It's not like we can *change* anything once we get there.'

'Why?' Paul's blue eyes were curious. 'Because Doc from *Back to the Future* said so?'

258

'Because you can't . . . you can't mess up the natural order of things,' I said.

'Why not? Isn't that what you do every day when you mediate? Aren't you interfering with the natural order of things by sending spirits off to their just reward?'

'That's different,' I said.

'How so?'

'Because those people are already dead! They can't do anything that might change the course of history.'

'Like Mrs Gutierrez and her two thousand dollars?' Paul's glance was shrewd. 'You think if you'd given it to her son, it wouldn't have changed the course of history? Even in some small way?'

'But that's different than entering another dimension to change something that already happened. That's just . . . wrong.'

'Is it, Suze?' A corner of Paul's mouth lifted. 'I don't think so. And you know what? I think this time, your boy Jesse is going to agree. With me.'

And suddenly, it seemed to get even colder than ever under that breezeway.

Six

Please be home, please be home, please be home, I prayed as I waited for someone to answer the doorbell. *Please please please please* . . .

I don't know if someone heard my prayer, or if it was just that invalid archaeologists don't get out that much. In any case, Dr Slaski's attendant answered the front door, recognition dawning when he saw that it was me who'd been ringing the bell with so much urgency.

'Oh hi, Susan,' he said, getting the name wrong, but the face that went with it right. Sort of. 'You looking for Paul? Because far as I know, he's still in school—'

'I know he's still at school,' I said, stepping hurriedly inside the Slaters' foyer, before the attendant could close the door. 'I'm not here to see him. I stopped by to see his grandfather, if that's all right.'

'His *grandfather?*' The attendant looked surprised. And why shouldn't he? For all he knew, his patient hadn't had a lucid conversation with anyone in years.

Except that he had. And it had only been a few months ago. With me.

'You know, Susan, Paul's grandpa isn't . . . He's not real well,' the assistant said slowly. 'We don't like to talk about it in front of him, but his last round of tests . . . Well, they

260

didn't look so good. In fact, the doctors aren't giving him all that much longer to live . . .'

'I just need to ask him a question,' I said. 'Just one little question. It'll only take a second.'

'But . . .' The attendant, a young guy who, judging from his sun-bleached dreads, probably used whatever spare time he got to hit the waves, scratched his chin. 'I mean, he can't . . . he doesn't really talk all that much any more. The Alzheimer's, you know . . .'

'Can I just try?' I asked, not caring that I sounded like a whacko. I was *that* desperate. Desperate for answers that I knew only one person on earth could give me. And that person was just right upstairs. 'Please? I mean, it couldn't hurt, could it?'

'No,' the attendant said slowly. 'No, I guess it couldn't hurt.'

'Great,' I said, slipping past him and starting up the stairs two at a time. 'I'll just be a couple of minutes. You won't mind leaving us alone, will you? I'll call you if he looks like he might need you.'

The attendant, closing the front door in a distracted sort of way, went, 'OK. I guess. But . . . shouldn't you be in school?'

'It's lunchtime,' I informed him cheerfully, as I made my way up the stairs and then down the hall toward Dr Slaski's room.

I wasn't lying, either. It *was* lunchtime. The fact that we weren't technically supposed to leave school grounds at lunch? Well, I didn't feel that was important to mention. I was less worried about facing the wrath of Sister Ernestine when she found out I was skipping school than I was about explaining to my stepbrother Brad why I'd so desperately needed the keys to the Land Rover. Just because Brad had

261

happened to get his driver's licence about five seconds before I'd gotten mine (well, OK, a few weeks before I'd gotten mine, actually), he seems to feel that the ancient Land Rover, which is supposed to be the 'kids' car', belongs solely to him, and that only he's allowed to ferry the two of us, plus his little brother, David, to and from school every day.

I'd had to resort to using the words 'feminine hygiene products' and 'glove compartment' just to get him to surrender the keys. I had no idea what he was going to do when I didn't return before the end of lunch and he discovered the car was gone. Narc on me, doubtlessly. It seemed to be his one joy in life.

Sadly, I never seem able to return the favour, thanks to Brad generally having some kind of goods on me.

In any case, I wasn't going to squander what precious little time I had wondering what Brad was going to say about my taking the car. Instead, I hurried into Paul's grandfather's bedroom.

As usual, the Game Show Network was on. The attendant had parked Dr Slaski's wheelchair in front of the plasma screen television. Dr Slaski himself, however, appeared to be paying no attention whatsoever to Bob Barker. Instead, he was staring fixedly at a spot in the centre of the highly polished tile floor.

I wasn't fooled by this, however.

'Dr Slaski?' I picked up the remote and turned the TV volume down, then hurried to the doctor's side. 'Dr Slaski, it's me, Suze. Paul's friend, Suze? I need to talk to you for a minute.'

Paul's grandfather didn't respond. Unless you call drooling a response.

'Dr Slaski,' I said, pulling up a chair so that I could sit

262

closer to his ear. I didn't want the attendant to overhear our discussion, so I was trying to keep my voice low. 'Dr Slaski, your nurse isn't here and neither is Paul. It's just the two of us. I need to talk to you about something Paul's been telling me. About, er, mediators. It's important.'

As soon as he heard that neither Paul nor his attendant was nearby, a change seemed to come over Dr Slaski. He straightened up in his chair, lifting his head so he could fix me with a rheumy-eyed stare. The drooling stopped right away.

'Oh,' he said when he saw it was me. He didn't exactly look thrilled. 'You again.'

I didn't think that was completely fair, seeing as how the last time the two of us had spoken, *he* had sought *me* out . . . sought me out to deliver a cryptic warning about his own grandson, whom he'd equated to the devil, no less.

But I decided to let that slide.

'Yes, it's me, Dr Slaski,' I said. 'Suze. Listen. About Paul.'

'What's that little jerk been up to now?'

Clearly there is very little love lost between Dr Slaski and his grandson.

'Nothing,' I said. 'Yet. At least, so far as I can tell. It's what he says he can do.'

'What's that, then?' Dr Slaski asked. 'And this better be good. *Family Feud* comes on in five minutes.'

Good God. Was I, I wondered, going to end up wheel-chair bound and addicted to game shows when I was Dr Slaski's age? Because Dr Slaski – or Mr Slater, as Paul wanted everyone to think of him – is also a mediator, one who'd gone to the ends of the earth looking to find answers about his unusual talent. Apparently, he'd found what he was looking for in the tombs of ancient Egypt.

Problem is, nobody believed him. Not about the existence

263

of a race of people whose sole duty it was to guide the spirits of the dead to their ultimate destinations, and certainly not that he, Dr Slaski, was one of them. The old man's many writings on the subject, most of them self-published, went ignored by the scientific and academic communities, and were now gathering dust in plastic bins beneath his grandson's bed.

Worse, Dr Slaski's own family seem to be trying to sweep *him* under the bed, as well, Paul's father even having gone so far as to change his name to avoid being associated with the old man.

And what had Dr Slaski gotten for all his efforts? A terminal illness and his grandson, Paul, for company. The illness, or so Dr Slaski claimed, had been brought on by spending too much time in the 'shadowland' – that way station between this world and the next. And Paul?

Well, he had brought Paul on all by himself.

I guess he had a reason to feel bitterly toward the human race. But why he felt that way toward Paul, I was only just learning.

I tried to start out slowly, so he'd be sure to understand.

'Paul says mediators—'

'Shifters.' Dr Slaski insisted people like him and Paul and me are more properly called shifters, for our (in my case, newly discovered) ability to shift between the dimensions of the living and the dead. 'Shifters, girl, I told you before. Don't make me say it again.'

'Shifters,' I corrected myself. 'Paul says that shifters have the ability to time travel.'

'Indeed,' Dr Slaski said. 'What of it?'

I gaped at him. I couldn't help it. If he'd hit me in the back of the head with a piñata stick, I could not have been more surprised. 'You . . . you *knew* about this?'

264

'Of course I know about it,' Dr Slaski said acidly. 'Who do you think wrote the paper that gave that fool grandson of mine the idea?'

This is what I got for not paying more attention during my mediator sessions with Paul.

'But why didn't you *tell* me?'

Dr Slaski looked at me very sarcastically. 'You didn't ask,' he said.

I sat there like a lump staring at him. I couldn't believe it. All this time . . . all this time I'd had *another* skill I'd known nothing about. But what would I have ever needed the ability to time travel for, anyway? I guess there were a few bad hair days I wouldn't have minded going back and fixing, but other than that . . .

Then, like a bolt of lightning, it hit me.

My dad. I could go back through time and save my dad.

No. No, it didn't work that way. It couldn't. Because if it could . . . if it could . . .

Then everything would be different.

Everything.

Dr Slaski coughed, hard. I shook myself and touched his shoulder.

'Dr Slaski? Are you all right?'

'What do you think?' Dr Slaski demanded, not very graciously. 'I've got six months to live. Maybe less, if those damned doctors have their way and keep bleeding the life out of me. You think I'm all right?'

'I . . .' It was selfish of me, I knew, but I didn't have time to listen to his health problems. I needed to know more about this new power he – and possibly I – had.

'How?' I demanded eagerly. 'How do you do it? Travel through time, I mean.'

Dr Slaski glanced at the TV. Fortunately the credits for

265

The Price Is Right were still rolling. *Family Feud* hadn't started yet.

'It's easy,' he said. 'If my idiot grandson can figure it out, any moron can.'

We didn't have much time. *Family Feud* was going to start at any second.

'How?' I asked him again. '*How?*'

'You need something,' the doctor said with exaggerated patience, like he was talking to a five-year-old. 'Something of the time you want to go to. To anchor you to it.'

I thought of a time-travel movie I had seen. 'Like a coin?' I asked.

'A coin would do it,' Dr Slaski said, though he looked sceptical. 'Of course, you'd need to use a coin that had once been owned by a specific person who existed in the time you want to go to, and who'd once actually stood where you're standing. And you need to pick a spot you can get back to without shifting onto some innocent bystander.'

'You mean—' I blinked. 'You mean when you go back, *all* of you goes back? Not just—'

'Your soul?' Dr Slaski snorted. 'Lot of good that what do, wandering around in some other century without any body. No, when you go, you *go*. That's why you've got to be smart about it. You can't just go hopping through time and space all willy-nilly, you know. Not if you want to keep your guts from spilling out. You've got to go to a spot where you knew the person once stood, hold the object they once owned, and—'

'And?' I asked breathlessly.

'Close your eyes and shift.' Dr Slaski looked back at the television, bored by the whole conversation.

'And that's it?' It *was* easy. 'You mean I can just pop back through time and visit anyone I want?'

266

'Of course not,' Dr Slaski said, his gaze glued to the TV screen. It was almost as an afterthought that he added, 'He's got to be dead, of course. And someone you've mediated. I never determined why, but it must have something to do with that person's energy, or being. Must be the link . . .' Dr Slaski trailed off, lost in research done decades before.

'You mean . . .' I blinked in confusion. 'We can only go back through time if it's to help a ghost?'

'Give the girl a prize,' Dr Slaski drawled, turning his gaze back toward the television.

For once I didn't mind his sarcasm. Because ghosts . . . Ghosts I can deal with. Ghosts like . . .

. . . well, my dad, for instance.

And I had plenty of stuff that once belonged to Dad. I still had the shirt he'd been wearing the day he died. I had plucked it from the pile of things the hospital had given us and kept it under my pillow for months after he'd died . . . right up until the day I finally saw him again, when he appeared to me, and told me exactly why it was that I, but not Mom, could see him.

I thought my mom hadn't known about it – the shirt, I mean – but now I knew she must have. She surely would have found it when she was making my bed or playing tooth fairy.

But she had never said anything. To be fair, she *couldn't* say anything, because she kept Dad's ashes in his favourite beer stein for years before we finally got the guts to scatter them in the park where he'd died, the park he'd loved so much, just before her wedding to Andy.

A park, I realized, I'd have to go to if I wanted to go back through time to save him, because the apartment we'd lived in had been sold and I couldn't very well walk up to the new owners and be all 'Can I stand in your living room for a

267

minute? I just need to pop back through time to save my dad's life.'

Of course, both the park and the apartment were all the way across the country. But I had some babysitting money saved up. Maybe even enough for a plane ticket . . .

I could do it. I could totally keep my dad from dying.

'What else?' I asked Dr Slaski, with a glance at the TV. A commercial, thank God. 'When you have the . . . thing that belonged to the ghost, and you're standing in a spot where he once stood? What do you do then?'

Dr Slaski looked annoyed. 'You hold the object – that's your anchor – and nothing else. That's important, you know. You can't be touching anything else or you could end up taking it with you. Then you picture the person. And then you go. Easy as pie.' Dr Slaski nodded at the TV. 'Turn it up. *Feud*'ll be on in a minute.'

I couldn't believe it was so easy. Just like that, I could go back through time and keep someone I loved from dying.

'Of course,' Dr Slaski said casually, 'once you get there – to where you're going – you have to watch yourself. You don't want to be changing history . . . at least, not too much. You have to weigh the consequences of your actions very carefully.'

I didn't say anything. What possible consequences could my saving my dad have? Except that my mom, instead of crying into her pillow every night for years after he died – right up until she met Andy, actually – would be happy? That *I* would be happy?

Then it hit me. Andy. If my dad had lived, my mother would never have met Andy. Or rather, she might have met him, but she would never have married him.

And then we would never have moved to California.

And I would never have met Jesse.

268

Suddenly, the full impact of what Dr Slaski had said sunk in. 'Oh,' I said.

His gaze – despite the glaucoma that clouded his blue eyes, which otherwise were like a photocopy of Paul's – was sharp.

'I thought there'd be an *oh* in there somewhere,' he said. 'Not as easy as you thought, shifting through time, is it? And keep in mind the fact that the longer you stay in a time not your own, the longer your recovery time when you do get back to the present,' Dr Slaski added not very pleasantly.

'Recovery time? You mean like . . . it gives you a headache?' Which was what shifting gave me. Every time.

Dr Slaski looked amused about something. His gaze wasn't on the television screen, so I knew it was something to do with what I'd just said.

'Little worse than a headache,' he said dryly, and patted the mattress beneath him. 'Unless you mean that as a euphemism for losing a host of brain cells. And that's the least of what could happen to you. Time shift too many times and you'll be a vegetable before you're old enough to buy beer, I can guarantee.'

'Does Paul know that?' I asked. 'I mean, about the . . . losing brain cells thing?'

'He should,' Dr Slaski said, 'if he read my paper on it.'

And yet he still wanted to try it.

'Why would Paul want to go back through time?' I asked. He could hardly be motivated by a desire to help anyone, as the only person Paul Slater had ever been interested in helping was . . . well, Paul Slater.

'How should I know?' Dr Slaski looked bored. 'I don't understand why you spend any time at all with that boy. I told you he was no good. Just like his father, that one is, ashamed of me . . .'

269

I didn't pay attention to Dr Slaski's diatribe against his grandson. I was too busy thinking.

What was it Paul had said the other night, in the Gutierrezes' backyard? That he wouldn't kill Jesse . . .

. . . but that he might do something to keep Jesse from having died in the first place.

That was when it finally dawned on me. Standing there in Dr Slaski's bedroom, while he fumbled for the remote, found the volume button, and cried, 'Dammit, we missed the first category!'

Paul was going back through time. To Jesse's time.

And not to kill him.

To save his life.

Seven

'Father Dominic?' My voice seemed frantic, even to my own ears. 'Father D, are you there?'

'Yes, Susannah.' Father Dominic sounded frazzled. But then, that could be because he still hadn't figured out how to work his cellphone. 'Yes, I'm here. I thought you had to hit the Send button to answer, but apparently—'

'Father Dominic, something terrible has happened.' I didn't wait for him to respond, but just plunged ahead. 'Paul's figured out a way to go back through time, and he's going to go back to the day Jesse died and save his life.'

There was a long pause. Then Father Dominic said, 'Susannah. Where are you?'

I looked around. I was standing in Paul's kitchen, using the wall-mounted phone I had found there. I'd asked Dr Slaski's attendant after I'd left his patient, if I could use the phone. He'd told me to go right ahead.

'I'm at Paul's house,' I said. 'Father Dominic, did you hear me? Paul's figured out a way to keep Jesse from dying.'

'Well,' Father Dominic said, 'That's wonderful news. But shouldn't you be in school? It's only just a little past one o'clock—'

'Father D!' I practically screamed. 'You don't understand! If Paul keeps Jesse from dying, *then Jesse and I will never meet!*'

'Hmmm.' Father Dominic took his sweet time to consider what I'd said. 'Altering the course of history is never a good idea, I suppose. Look what happened in that film. What was it? Oh, yes. *Back to the Future*.'

'*Father Dominic*.' I was practically crying with frustration. 'Please, this isn't a movie. It's my *life*. You've got to help me. You've got to come back here and help me stop him. He won't listen to me. I know he won't. But he might listen to you . . .'

'Well, I couldn't possibly come back now, Susannah,' Father Dominic said. 'The monsignor isn't – well, the, er, hot dog appeared to be lodged in his throat for longer than anyone thought . . . Susannah, did you say Paul's figured out a way to *travel through time*?'

'Yes,' I said from between gritted teeth. I was beginning to regret having kept Father Dominic in the dark about so much of what I'd learned from Paul during our Wednesday afternoons together.

'Goodness,' Father Dominic said. 'How interesting. And how do you suppose he does that?'

'All he needs is something old,' I said. 'Something belonging to the person, you know, he wants to travel back to see. The person has to be a ghost, a ghost that he's met. And then he just has to stand in a place he knows that person will be – in his head, you know – and he's there.'

'Good heavens,' Father Dominic said. 'Do you know what this means, Susannah?'

'Yes,' I said, miserably. 'It means that I'm going to move to Carmel, and there isn't going to be anybody haunting my bedroom because Jesse will never have been killed there.'

'No,' Father Dominic said. 'Well, I mean, yes, I suppose it does mean that. But more important, it means we could

272

prevent the deaths of all of the ghosts we encounter, just by popping back through time and—'

'We can't,' I interrupted flatly. 'Unless we want to end up with six months left to live, like Paul's grandfather. It isn't like shifting to the spirit plane. Your whole body goes . . . and, I guess, suffers the consequences. But Paul's just planning the one trip.'

'Yes,' Father Dominic said, sounding distant – more distant than San Francisco, anyway. 'Yes, I see.'

'Father Dominic!' I cried. I was losing him . . . and not just because our phone connection wasn't the best. 'You've got to stop him!'

'But why should I, Susannah?' Father Dominic asked. 'What Paul plans on doing is quite generous, actually.'

'*Generous*?' I cried. 'What's so *generous* about it?'

'He's giving Jesse another chance at life,' Father Dominic said. 'And, from what you say, risking his own life in the process. I'd say it's quite noble of him, actually.'

'Noble!' I couldn't believe my ears. 'Father Dom, I can assure you, Paul's motives are far from noble. He's only doing it . . .'

'Yes?' Father Dominic was suddenly all ears.

But how can you explain to a priest that a guy is trying to off your boyfriend so he can get into your pants?

Especially when Paul wasn't trying to off Jesse at all, but to save his life, actually? 'It's just . . .' I wasn't making any sense, but I didn't care. 'Can't you expel him or something?'

'No, Susannah,' Father Dominic said. Was it my imagination or was there a slight chuckle in his voice. 'I can't expel him. Not for that, anyway.'

'But we have to stop him,' I said. My protests, even to my own ears, were starting to grow faint. 'It's . . . it's *unnatural*, what he's planning on doing.'

273

'That may very well be,' Father Dominic said, 'but it isn't immoral. It isn't even illegal, as far as I can tell.'

This had to be a first. Paul doing something that could actually be construed as moral, I mean.

'—But I do wonder,' Father Dominic went on thoughtfully, 'just how he's planning on accomplishing this little miracle.'

'I told you,' I said bitterly. 'All he has to do is get something the person once owned, and then stand in a place he once stood, and—'

'Yes,' Father Dominic said. 'But what belonging of Jesse's does Paul have?'

This shut me up for a minute. Because Father Dominic was right. Paul didn't have anything of Jesse's. He couldn't stop Jesse's murder, because he didn't own anything from Jesse's past.

'Oh,' I said, beginning to feel a little less like I had a slowly tightening noose around my neck. 'Oh. You're right.'

'Of course I am,' Father Dominic said. Was it my imagination or did he sound distracted? 'Although it's something you might think of doing, Susannah. If he'll teach you how, I mean.'

'What?' I twisted the phone cord around my finger. 'Go back through time and save Jesse from dying?'

'Exactly,' Father Dominic said. 'It might, for all you know, be the reason why he's still here on earth. Because he was never meant to die in the first place.'

I was so appalled that, for a moment, I couldn't say anything. Unbidden, my mind flashed back to that poster my ninth grade English teacher had hung up in her classroom, of two seagulls flying over a beach . . . A poster I always seemed to remember at the most inconvenient moments. IF YOU LOVE SOMETHING, LET IT GO, the words beneath the

274

seagulls read. IF IT WAS MEANT TO BE, IT WILL COME BACK TO YOU.

The imaginary noose around my neck tightened to a choking point.

'That's bull, Father D,' I yelled into the phone. 'Do you hear me? *Bull!*'

'Susannah—' Father Dominic sounded startled.

'That is NOT why Jesse is still here,' I shouted. 'It's NOT. Jesse and I are meant to be together, and if you can't see that, well, that's your own damn problem!'

Now Father Dominic sounded more than startled. He sounded angry. 'Susannah,' he said. 'There's no reason to use that kind of language—'

'No, there's not,' I agreed with him. 'Especially since I have nothing more to say to you.' I slammed the phone back down into its cradle. A second later, Dr Slaski's attendant appeared, looking worried.

'Susan?' he asked. 'You all right?'

'I'm fine,' I said, horrified to find that my cheeks were damp.

Great. So, on top of everything else, I'd been crying.

'It's just,' the attendant said, 'I heard shouting . . .'

'It's nothing,' I said. 'I'm leaving. Don't worry.'

And I did, without saying goodbye to Dr Slaski. I had no more to say to him than I did to Father Dom. There was only one person, I realized, who could stop Paul from doing what I now knew he was going to do.

And that person was me.

Of course, knowing that fact wasn't the same as actually having a plan for how I was going to stop him. That's what I tried to come up with as I drove back to school. A plan.

It wasn't until I was pulling into the Mission Academy's student parking lot that what Father Dominic had said

275

really began to sink in. Paul didn't have anything of Jesse's that could bring him back to that horrible night when Jesse had died. I was almost sure of it. Jesse had been murdered and his body never found – until recently, that is. His own family had believed he'd run away to escape an unwanted marriage.

What could Paul possibly have of Jesse's that could help him get back to the day leading up to his death? Nothing. Because the only things that still existed from that time were a miniature portrait of Jesse – which I kept safe at home – and some letters he'd written to his fiancée. But those were on display at the Carmel Historical Society museum.

There was nothing of Jesse's that Paul could possibly have that he could use to hurt him. Or rather, to save him. Nothing. Jesse was safe.

Which meant that *I* was safe.

The relief I felt was short-lived, however. Oh, not my relief about Jesse. That remained. It was as I was attempting to sneak back into school that my newly restored equilibrium was shaken again. Only this time, it wasn't by Paul. No, it was Sister Ernestine who shattered my hard-won sense of calm, just as I was trying to blend in with my fellow students as they made their way to their next class, pretending like I'd been there with them all along.

'Susannah Simon!' The vice principal's shrill voice caused several doves that had been roosting in the beams overhead to take off in startled flight. 'Come to my office immediately!'

My youngest stepbrother, David, happened to be nearby. When he heard the sister's command, he visibly paled . . . an accomplishment for him, seeing how pale he was already, being a redhead.

'Suze,' he asked me, looking a bit freaked. And why not?

276

Usually when I get into trouble, it isn't for mere tardiness. No, more often, it's along the lines of destruction of property . . . and someone usually ends up unconscious, if not dead. 'What did you do *now*?'

'Never mind,' I said, a little chagrined that I'd been busted for so minor an offence as skipping class. I was really losing my touch.

I followed Sister Ernestine into her office, which, unlike Father Dominic's, didn't have any teaching awards on the shelves. No one would consider Sister Ernestine an exemplary educator. She's a disciplinarian, plain and simple.

I got off lightly, I suppose. She'd noticed I'd been gone during religion class, which I was supposed to have right after lunch. I told her I'd had a slight medical emergency, and needed to go to the drugstore, once again invoking the 'crimson tide' in the hopes she'd drop the subject. It didn't have the same effect on Sister Ernestine as it had on Brad, however.

'Then you should have gone to the nurse's office,' was Sister Ernestine's terse response.

For my crime, I was assigned to write a thousand-word essay on the importance of honouring one's commitments. Additionally, I was told to be at Saturday's antique auction to help man the eighth graders' bake sale table.

All in all, I suppose it could have been worse.

Or so I thought. Before I ran into Paul Slater.

He was lurking behind one of the stone supports that hold up the breezeway, which is why I didn't spot him on my way from Sister Ernestine's office to my trig class. He stepped out from the shadows just as I was hurrying by.

'The wanderer returneth,' he said.

I flattened a hand to my chest, as if doing so would cause my heart, which had practically jumped through my ribs at the sight of him, to beat normally again.

'Why do you have to do that?' I demanded testily. 'You scared the pants off me.'

'I wish.' Paul's smile was decidedly irreligious, considering the fact that we were standing only a few hundred feet away from a church. 'So. Where'd you disappear to?'

I could have lied, I suppose. But what would have been the point? He'd learn the truth as soon as he got home and his grandfather's attendant told him I'd stopped by.

So I stuck out my chin and, ignoring my stuttering pulse, plunged. 'Your place,' I said.

Paul's dark eyebrows came down in a rush as he frowned. '*My* place? What'd you go to *my* place for?'

'To have a chat,' I barrelled on, 'with your grandfather.'

Paul's scowl grew even deeper. 'My grandfather?' He shook his head. 'What the hell would you want to go see him for? The guy's a complete gork.'

'He's not well,' I agreed. 'But he's still capable of carrying on a conversation.'

'Yeah,' Paul said with a sneer. 'About game shows, maybe.'

'Well, that,' I said, knowing what I was about to say next would enrage him, but also knowing that really, I didn't have any other choice, 'and time travel.'

Paul's eyes widened. As I'd expected, I'd shocked him.

'Time travel? You talked about *time travel*? With Grandpa Gork?'

'With Dr Slaski,' I corrected him. 'And yes, I did.'

The two words – doctor and Slaski – seemed to hit him like physical blows. He certainly looked as stunned as if I'd hit him.

'Are you . . .' He couldn't seem to find the right words to express himself. 'Are you crazy?' is what he seemed to settle for.

278

'No,' I said. 'And neither is your grandfather. But I think *you* might be,' I went on – recklessly, I knew, but no longer caring. Not now that I knew what he was after.

'I know your grandfather is Oliver Slaski,' I stated. 'He told me so himself.'

He just stared at me. It was as if, right before his eyes, I was turning into a completely different person than the Suze he'd known. And maybe I was. I was certainly angrier at him than I'd ever been before – more than the first time, even, that he'd tried to get rid of Jesse. Because he hadn't known then what he surely knew by now . . . That Paul and me?

Yeah, that was *never* going to happen.

'He didn't talk to you,' Paul said finally, his blue eyes flat and cold as the Pacific in November. 'He doesn't talk to anybody.'

'Not to you, maybe,' I said. 'Why should he, when you treat him the way you do . . . like he's a big inconvenience, a – what do you call him? – Oh, yeah. A gork. I mean, your own father changed his name, he was so ashamed of him. But if you'd ever taken the time to find out, you'd know Dr Slaski isn't as far gone as you think . . . and he has some pretty interesting things to say about you.'

'I'm sure,' Paul said with a smirk. 'In fact, I'm pretty sure I can guess. I'm the spawn of Satan. I'm up to no good. And you should stay away from me. That about sum it up?'

'Pretty much,' I said. 'And considering that you plan on travelling back through time and keeping Jesse from dying? I'd say he's one hundred percent right.'

At that, the flatness left his eyes – but not the coldness. He even smiled a little, though it was with just half his mouth. 'So you finally figured it out, huh? Took you long enough—'

279

But I didn't let him finish. I took a step forward until my face was just inches below his, and said as fiercely as I could, 'Well, I've figured it out now. And all I can say is that if you think making it so Jesse and I never met will change my feelings about you, you're dreaming.'

Paul looked hurt. But I knew it was all just a put-on. Because Paul doesn't have feelings. Not if he really intends to do what I suspect.

But he was doing his best to prove me wrong.

'But, Suze,' he said, his blue eyes wide and innocent. 'I'm just doing what you want. After that whole thing with Mrs Gutierrez, you got me thinking . . . I'm really trying to tread the path of righteousness. And isn't saving Jesse's life the right thing to do? I mean, if you really love him, you must want what's best for him, don't you? And wouldn't his living a long and happy life be what's best for him?'

I blinked at him, completely thrown by the way he'd twisted everything around.

'That isn't— I—' I couldn't seem to get the words out. All I could do was stand there and stammer.

'That's OK, Suze,' Paul said, reaching up and laying a hand on my arm – to comfort me, I suppose, in my hour of need. 'You don't have to thank me. Now, don't you think we'd better get back? You don't want Sister Ernestine to find you skipping class again, now, do you?'

I stared at him, dumbfounded. I had never in my life met anyone as manipulative as he was . . . with the exception, maybe, of my stepbrother Brad. Only Brad didn't have Paul's smarts and was rarely able to pull off anything more twisted than a house party . . . and even that had gotten busted by the cops.

'You're – you're high,' I finally managed to stammer, 'if you think saving Jesse that night – the night he died – will

280

guarantee him a long life. Who's to say Diego won't try again the next night? Or the next? What are you going to do, stay in 1850 and become Jesse's personal bodyguard?'

'If that's what it takes,' Paul said in a sickeningly sweet voice. 'You see, I'd do anything – anything it takes – to make sure Jesse dies peacefully in his sleep at a ripe old age, so that he never, ever has need of a mediator.'

The colours in the courtyard – the red roof tiles along the Mission, the pink hibiscus blossoms, the deep green of the palm fronds – spun dizzyingly around me as his words sunk in. I tasted something awful rising in my throat.

'Why are you doing this?' I stared up at him in horror. 'You must know it will never work. Getting rid of Jesse won't make me care about you. *I don't like you in that way.*'

'Don't you?' Paul asked with a smile that was as cold as his gaze. 'Funny, I could have sworn, the last time we kissed, that you did. At least a little. Enough, anyway—'

His voice trailed off suggestively . . . but just what he was suggesting, I couldn't imagine.

'Enough for what?' I demanded.

'Enough,' Paul said, 'that you're thinking about transferring my soul out of my body and throwing Jesse's in here instead.'

281

Eight

'Don't bother denying it,' Paul said as I stared up at him in utter shock. 'I know that's what you've been planning ever since I first made the mistake of telling you about it.' The heat from the hand he'd placed on my arm seemed to singe my skin. 'My saving Jesse's life is more a pre-emptive strike than anything else. Because the truth is, I kind of like my body. I don't really want to give it up for him.'

My mouth was moving – I know it was, because Paul seemed to be waiting for some kind of reply.

Only I couldn't make a sound. I was *that* stunned.

Because it finally made sense, now. That accusation Paul had hurled at me the other day in his kitchen. That his plans for Jesse were a lot more humane than what I'd had planned for Paul. Because he was planning on saving Jesse, whereas I, apparently, am planning on killing Paul.

Except, of course, that I'm not.

But that didn't seem to matter to him.

'It's OK,' Paul assured me. 'I mean, it's kind of flattering in a way, really. That you think I'm hot enough to put your boyfriend's soul into. It proves that, whatever you say, you do like me, a little. Or at least that you like making out with me.'

'That is so—' I found my voice at last. Unfortunately, it

282

came out shrill as a banshee's. I didn't care, though. All I cared about was proving to him how very, very wrong he was. '—so untrue! How could you even – what could have given you the idea that I—'

'Oh, come on, Suze,' Paul said. 'Admit it. With me, it's the real thing. Don't tell me that when you're with Jesse, you aren't thinking about the fact that, cozy as things might get between the two of you, it's all an illusion. That isn't *really* his heart you hear beating in his chest. His skin isn't *really* warm. Because he doesn't *have* skin. It's all in your head . . . Not like this,' he added, gently stroking my arm with his thumb.

Until I wrenched my arm away, that is, and fell back a step. He looked taken aback, but held up both hands to indicate he wouldn't touch me again. 'Whoa, OK, Suze. Sorry. But you can't deny it's true that, when we kiss, you don't exactly fight me off. At least, not right away—'

I felt my cheeks flame. I was so embarrassed. I couldn't believe he was bringing this up here, at *school*, of all places . . .

Especially considering that Jesse . . . Yeah, this was his new stomping ground. He was undoubtedly around somewhere nearby.

But I couldn't deny what Paul was saying. I mean, I could, but I'd be lying.

'Of course I like it when you kiss me,' I said, though I practically had to cough out every word, they stuck in my throat so badly. 'You're a good kisser and you know it.' What else could I say? It was true. 'But that doesn't mean I like *you*.'

Which was also true.

But it didn't seem to bother Paul.

'Proving my point,' he said smugly, 'that you want my body, but with Jesse's soul in it.'

283

'I think what happened to Jesse was horrible,' I said slowly, referring to the murder. 'And OK, there pretty much isn't anything I wouldn't do if I thought it would bring him back to life. *But not that.*'

'Why not?' Paul asked with a shrug. 'I mean, what's stopping you? As you've pointed out numerous times, I'm a reprehensible human being with no redeeming qualities . . . except for my kissing abilities, apparently. So why not just give my soul a yank and let the all-perfect Jesse have a second chance at life?'

The truth was, I really was innocent of what he was accusing me. It had never once occurred to me to do what he was insisting I'd been plotting for some time to do. Oh, OK, maybe I'd considered it in passing every now and then. But I'd always instantly dismissed the idea.

But now – perhaps because he was goading me into it – a part of me actually seemed to perk up and go *Why not?* Paul *didn't* deserve all the great things he had. He didn't even appreciate them! He stole from people less fortunate than he was, he didn't treat his family with anything like respect, and he certainly hadn't been very nice to me . . . or to Jesse.

Why *couldn't* I send Paul off to the great unknown, and let Jesse have Paul's body . . . and his life? Jesse deserved a second chance, and he'd certainly be a better Paul Slater than Paul had ever been . . .

Of course, Jesse wouldn't like it. He would definitely think it was wrong to rob Paul of the life that was rightfully his, just so he could have a chance to live again.

And it *would* be weird, looking into Paul's blue eyes and knowing Jesse was looking out of them.

But it wouldn't *really* be like I was killing Paul. His body would still be alive. And his soul would be . . . well, right

284

where Jesse's was now, aimlessly wandering the earth, with no idea what was going to happen to him next.

But then sanity returned, cold and dampening as the water burbling in the fountain in the centre of the Mission's courtyard. And I heard myself answering Paul's question – *So why not just give my soul a yank and let the all-perfect Jesse have a second chance at life?* – every bit as coolly as he'd asked it.

'Um,' I said sarcastically, 'because that would be *murder*, maybe?'

Some muscles in Paul's jaw tightened. 'Justifiable homicide at best,' he said. 'And we both know I wouldn't really be dead. And I would deserve it, wouldn't I? For my sins?'

'Maybe so,' I said, feeling the way I usually did after long session with my kick-boxing exercise video. You know, the endorphins rushing in. Because I really had, in a way, just had a major workout. This one just happened to be an emotional one. 'But the fact is, I'm not the one to judge.'

'Why not?' Paul asked. 'You don't seem to have a problem when it comes to judging *me.*'

But he wasn't going to get me with that one. 'Your grandfather warned me once that when he'd realized all the things we mediators could do, he'd made the mistake of thinking he was God,' I told him. 'And look where that got him. I won't be making the same mistake.'

Paul just blinked at me. I really think he'd believed I'd meant to do it. The soul transference thing, I mean. Now that I'd taken all the wind out of his sails, he seemed . . . well, as stunned as I'd been earlier.

'So you see,' I said while I still had the advantage, 'your whole going-back-through-time-to-save-Jesse scheme? It's kind of pointless. Because for one thing, you can't travel back through time unless the person you're going back to

285

see actually wants your help . . . which Jesse most definitely does not. And, for another, I was never going to steal your body and give it to Jesse, Paul. But, you know, you can keep on flattering yourself that I was, if it makes you happy.'

I shouldn't, I realized a moment too late, have been quite so flippant. At least not then. Because when I attempted to stroll by him after that last remark – even giving my hair a toss to show my disdain for him – something inside him seemed to snap. Next thing I knew, his hand had shot out and caught my arm in a grip that hurt.

'Oh no, you don't,' he snarled. 'You're not getting away that easily—'

But he was wrong. Because the very next second, Paul's hand had been pried off me and his arm was bent behind his back in what looked to be a pretty painful position.

'Hasn't anyone ever told you,' Jesse asked, in a semi-amused voice, 'that a gentleman never lays a hand on a lady?'

Which I thought was kind of funny, considering where Jesse had had *his* hand the last time I'd seen him. But I thought it better to let that slide.

'Jesse,' I said. 'I'm OK. You can let him go.'

But Jesse didn't loosen his grip. If anyone had happened to walk by, they'd have seen Paul bent over at a peculiar angle, his face white with pain. Because of course, only he and I could see the ghost who had hold of him.

'I wasn't gonna do anything to her,' Paul insisted in a strangled voice. 'I swear!'

Jesse looked at me for confirmation of this.

'Did he hurt you, Susannah?' he asked.

I shook my head. 'I'm all right,' I said.

Jesse held on to Paul for a second or two longer – just, I think, to prove he could – then he let go, so suddenly that

286

Paul lost his balance and fell to his hands and knees, on to the stone slabs that made up the floor of the breezeway.

'You didn't have to call *him*,' Paul said to me, with wounded dignity.

'I didn't.' I was telling the truth, too.

'She didn't have to,' Jesse said, going to lean against one of the breezeway's support pillars. He folded his arms across his chest and looked at Paul dispassionately as he climbed to his feet and brushed himself off.

'What'd you, sense a disturbance in the Force, or something?' Paul asked testily.

'Something like that.' Jesse looked from Paul to me and then back again. 'Is there anything going on here that I should know about?'

'No,' I said quickly. Too quickly, maybe, since one of Jesse's eyebrows – the one with the scar through it – went up inquisitively.

Paul, to my fury, burst out into scornful laughing.

'Oh yeah,' he said. 'You two have a *great* relationship. It's really great how *honest* you are with each other.'

Jesse narrowed his dark eyes in Paul's direction. That seemed to cause some of his laughter to dry up, without Jesse even having to say a word.

Then Jesse turned his penetrating gaze on me.

'It's nothing,' I blurted, feeling a little panicky all of a sudden. 'Paul was just . . . he was thinking of doing something to you. But he changed his mind. Didn't you, Paul?'

'Not really,' Paul said. 'Hey, I have an idea. Let's ask *Jesse* what he'd want, shall we? Say, Jesse, how would you feel if I told you I could—'

'No,' I interrupted with a gasp. Suddenly, it was getting very difficult to breathe. 'Paul, really, that's not necessary. Jesse won't—'

'Now, Suze,' Paul said as if he were speaking to a three-year-old. 'Let's allow Jesse to decide. Jesse, what if I told you that in addition to all the many other wonderful things that we mediators can do, it turned out we can also travel through time? And that I had generously offered to travel back to your time – the night you died, I mean – and save your life. What would you say to that?'

Jesse's dark gaze didn't leave Paul's face, nor did his expression waver from cold disdain. Not even for a second.

'I would say that you're a liar' was Jesse's preternaturally calm response.

'See, I thought you might say that.' Paul had the smooth patter and the self-confidence of a travelling salesman giving his spiel. 'But I'm here to tell you it's the absolute truth. Think about it, Jesse. You didn't have to die that night. I can go back through time and warn you. Well, you won't know me, of course, but I think if I tell you – the past you – that I'm from the future and that you're going to die if you don't do what I tell you, you'll believe me.'

'Do you?' Jesse asked in the same deadly calm voice. 'Because I don't.'

That stumped Paul for a second or two, during which my breathing became easy again. My heart swelled with affection for the man leaning against the stone pillar beside me. I shouldn't have worried about hiding this from Jesse. Jesse would never choose life over me. Never. He loves me too much.

Or so I thought, before Paul started his patter once again.

'I don't think you understand what I'm saying here.' Paul shook his head. 'I'm talking about giving you back your *life*, Jesse. None of this wandering around in a sort of half-life for a hundred and fifty years, watching the people you love grow older and die, one by one. No way. You'll *live*. To a ripe

288

old age, if I can, you know, get rid of that Diego guy who killed you. I mean, how can you say no to an offer like that?'

'Like this,' Jesse said tonelessly. 'No.'

Yes! I thought, flushing with joy. *Yes!*

Paul blinked. Once. Twice.

Then he said, his voice devoid of the friendliness that had been in it moments before, 'Don't be an idiot. I'm offering you a chance to live again. *Live.* What are you going to do, hang around here for the rest of eternity? Are you going to watch *her* get old' – he thrust a finger at me – 'and eventually turn to dust like you did with your family? Don't you remember how that felt? You want to go through all that again? You want her to sacrifice having a normal life – marriage, kids, grandkids – just to be with you, when you can't even support her, can't even—'

'Paul, stop it,' I commanded because I could see Jesse's face growing less and less expressionless with every word.

But Paul wasn't done. Not by a long shot.

'You think you're doing *her* any favours by sticking around?' he demanded. 'Man, you're only keeping her from leading a normal life—'

'Stop it!' I shouted at Paul as I reached out and grasped Jesse by the arm.

Two things happened at once then. The first was that classroom doors suddenly flew open all around us and students began streaming out into the breezeway as they changed classes for the next period.

The next was that I seized Jesse's arms with both my hands and, looking up anxiously into his face, said, 'Don't listen to him. Please. I don't care about those things, marriage and kids. All I want is you.'

But it was too late. I could tell it was too late. Some of what Paul had said was already starting to sink in. Jesse's

289

expression had grown troubled, and he seemed unable to look me in the eye.

'I mean it,' I said, giving him a frustrated shake. 'Don't pay attention to a word he says!'

'Um, hello, Suze.' Kelly Prescott's voice rose above the noise of slamming lockers and chit-chat. 'Talk to the wall much?'

I flung a glance over my shoulder and saw her standing there with the rest of the Dolce and Gabbana Nazis, smirking at me. I knew, of course, what they were seeing. Me with hands raised, clutching nothing but air, and speaking to one of the pillars in the breezeway.

Like I don't have enough of a reputation for being a freak. Now I *really* looked like I was going around the bend.

But when I turned my head back to tell Jesse we'd finish this conversation later, I saw that I was too late. He'd already disappeared.

I dropped my hands and turned to face Paul, who still stood there looking angry and defensive and pleased with himself at the same time.

'Thanks a lot,' I said to him.

'Don't mention it.' He walked away, whistling to himself.

Nine

'Is there wheat in this?' a petite woman with a bob and huge dark sunglasses asked me as she held up a chocolate chip cookie.

'Yes,' I said.

'What about this?' She held up a brownie.

'Yes,' I said.

'What about this?' A Mexican wedding cookie.

'Yes.'

'Are you telling me,' she demanded, looking outraged, 'that there is wheat in *all* of these baked goods?'

I lowered my chair. I'd been tilting it out of boredom, to see how far back I could lean without falling.

'Because Tyler doesn't eat wheat,' the woman went on, her hand going to cradle the chubby-cheeked face of a kid standing beside her. His blue eyes blinked out at me past his mother's perfectly manicured nails. 'I'm raising him on a gluten-free diet.'

'Try one of those,' I said, pointing to some lemon bars.

'Is there dairy in it?' the woman asked suspiciously. 'Because I'm raising Tyler lactose-free, as well.'

'Dairy- and gluten- free, I promise,' I said.

The woman slipped me a dollar, and I handed her the lemon bars. She passed one to Tyler, who inspected it, bit into it . . . then gave me a dazzling smile – his first of the day, no doubt – as his mother took his hand and led him away. Beside me, Shannon, my fellow bake sale attendant, looked appalled.

'There's wheat *and* dairy in those lemon bars,' she said.

'I know.' I rocked my chair back again. 'I felt bad for the little guy.'

'But—'

'She didn't say he was allergic. She just said she was raising him without it. Poor kid.'

'Suu-uuze,' the eighth grader said, giving my name multiple syllables. 'You are so cool. Your brother Dave said you were cool, but I didn't believe him.'

'Oh, I'm cool, all right,' I assured her. It was weird to hear someone call David 'Dave.' He was such a David to me.

'You so are,' Shannon said with perfect seriousness.

Whatever. It was so the story of my life to be stuck running a school bake sale while the rest of the world was enjoying such a perfect Saturday. The sky overhead was so blue and cloudless, it was almost painful to look at. The temperature was hovering at an extremely comfortable seventy degrees. A beautiful day for the beach or cappuccino at an outdoor café, or even just a walk.

And where was I? Yeah, that'd be manning the eighth grade bake sale booth at the Mission's charity antique auction.

'I couldn't believe it when Sister Ernestine told us *you* would be helping out at the booth,' Shannon was saying. Shannon, I'd discovered, was not shy. She likes to talk. A lot. 'I mean, you being an eleventh grader and all. And, you know. So cool.'

Cool. Yeah, right.

I hadn't expected so many people to show up at the auction. Oh, sure, a few parents, eager to look like they cared about their kids' school. But not, you know, hordes of eager antique collectors.

But that's exactly who was here. There were people everywhere, people I'd never seen before, all wandering around, peering at the items that would be auctioned off, and whispering conspiratorially to one another. Occasionally, some of them stopped by our booth and shelled out a buck for a Rice Krispies treat or whatever. But mostly they had their eyes on the prize . . . in this case, a hideously ugly wicker birdcage, or some old Mickey Mouse watch, or a snow globe of the Golden Gate Bridge, or some other equally non-designer thing.

The bidding got started late because the monsignor was supposed to have been acting as auctioneer. Because he was still in a coma up in San Francisco, there appeared to have been some frantic phone calls on the part of Sister Ernestine, as she looked for someone worthy to fill in.

You can imagine my surprise when she got up on to the dais at the end of the courtyard and announced into the microphone, in front of all the many antique collectors gathered there, that in the monsignor's absence, the auction would be called by none other than Andy Ackerman, well-known host of a home repair show on cable . . .

. . . and my stepdad.

I saw Andy climb the dais, waving modestly and looking abashed at all the applause he was getting. Not sure if there could possibly be anything more embarrassing than this, I started to slink down in my chair . . .

Oh but wait, there *was* something more embarrassing than my stepfather calling the school antique auction.

293

There was also the fact that most of the applause he was getting was coming from a woman in the front row.

My mother.

'Hey,' Shannon said. 'Isn't that—'

'Yes,' I interrupted her. 'Yes, it is.'

A few minutes later the auction began, with Andy doing a very good imitation of those auctioneers you see on TV, the ones who talk really fast. He was gesturing to an ugly orange plastic chair and declaring it 'authentic Eames' and asking if anyone would be willing to bid a hundred dollars for it.

A hundred dollars? I wouldn't have traded a Rice Krispies treat for it.

But wouldn't you know it, people in the audience were lifting their paddles, and soon the chair went for 350 bucks! And nobody even complained about what a rip-off it was.

Clearly Sister Ernestine had impressed upon this audience just how badly the school needed its basketball court repaved, because people were just throwing their money away on the most worthless pieces of garbage ever. I saw CeeCee's aunt Pru and my own homeroom teacher Mr Walden both bidding against each other for an extremely hideous lamp. Aunt Pru finally won it – for 175 bucks – then walked over to Mr Walden, apparently to gloat. Except that a few minutes later, I saw them having lemonade together and overheard them laughing about sharing custody of the lamp, like it was a kid in a divorce settlement. Shannon, observing this, went, 'Aw, isn't that cute?'

Except that it totally wasn't. It totally isn't cute when your best friend's weird aunt and your homeroom teacher make a love connection, and you yourself can't get the guy you like to call you, because, oh guess what, he's a ghost and doesn't have a phone.

294

Not that if Jesse'd call, I'd have had anything much to say to him. What was I going to do, be all *'Oh, yeah, by the way, Paul wants to travel through time and make it so you never died. But I plan on stopping him. Because I want you to roam around in the netherworld for a hundred and fifty years so you and I can make out in my mom's car. OK? Buh-bye.'*

Besides, it wasn't like it was going to happen. Paul going back through time, I mean. Because he didn't have that anchor thing his grandpa had been talking about. The thing to anchor him to the night Jesse died.

Or that's what I was telling myself – reassuring myself – right up until Andy held up the silver belt buckle Brad had found while he'd been cleaning out the attic. When he'd found it – wedged between the floorboards beneath the attic window – it had been this tarnished, crusty old thing I'd barely glanced at twice. Andy had thrown it into the box marked MISSION AUCTION, and I hadn't really thought about it again.

When he held it up now, I saw it winking in the afternoon sunlight. Someone had washed and polished it. And now Andy was going on about how it was an artifact from when our house had been the area's only hotel – a fancy way of saying that it had really been a boardinghouse – and that the Carmel Historical Society had put its age at close to 150 years.

About as long, actually, as my boyfriend had been dead.

'What'll I get for this sterling silver buckle?' Andy wanted to know. 'A real piece of old-fashioned craftsmanship. Look at the detail in the ornate D carved into it.'

Shannon, sitting beside me, suddenly went, 'Does your brother ever talk about me? Dave, I mean.'

I was idly watching my stepfather. The sun was beating down on us kind of hard, and it was difficult to think about anything except how much I wished I was at the beach.

295

'I don't know,' I said. I could understand Shannon's pain, of course. She had a crush on a guy. All she wanted to know was whether or not she was wasting her time.

As the sister of the object of her affections, however, all I could think was . . . *ew*. Also, that David is *way* too young to have a girlfriend.

'One of the members of the historical society – don't think I don't see you there, Bob,' Andy went on laughingly, 'even ventured that this belt buckle might have belonged to someone in the Diego clan, a very old, very respected family that settled in this area nearly two hundred years ago.'

Respected, my butt. The Diegos – or at least, the ghost of the one member of the family I had had the misfortune to meet – had all been thieves and murderers.

'I believe that for that reason and not just because of its intricate beauty,' Andy continued, 'this piece is going to be highly sought after by collectors some day . . . and, who knows, maybe even today!'

'David doesn't really talk about girls at home all that much,' I said to Shannon. 'At least, not to me.'

'Oh.' Shannon looked dejected. 'But do you think . . . well, do you think if Dave *did* like a girl, it'd be, you know, someone like me?'

'Let's start the bidding for this fine piece of authentic period jewelry at a hundred dollars,' Andy said. 'A hundred dollars. OK, we have a hundred. How about a hundred and twenty-five? Does anybody bid a hundred and twenty-five?'

I thought about what Shannon had asked me. *David, a girlfriend?* The youngest of my stepbrothers, I could no more picture David with a girlfriend than I could picture him behind the wheel of a car or even playing soccer. He just isn't that kind of guy.

296

'Three fifty,' I heard Andy say. 'Do I hear three fifty?'

But I supposed that one day David *would* drive a car. I mean, *I* could drive now, and there'd been a time when my whole family had despaired of *that* ever happening. It made sense that some day David would be sixteen and do all the same things that his older brothers Jake and Brad and I were doing . . . You know, drive. Take trig. Make out with members of the opposite sex.

'My goodness, Bob,' Andy said into the microphone. 'You weren't kidding when you mentioned how important you thought this piece was going to be to our auction today, were you? I have seven hundred dollars. Does anyone – OK, seven fifty. Do I hear eight?'

'Sure,' I said to Shannon. 'I mean, why *wouldn't* David like you? I mean, if he liked anyone better than anybody else. Which I'm not saying he does. That I know of.'

'Really?' Shannon looked worried. 'Because Dave's really smart. And I think he'd probably only like smart girls. But I'm not doing all that well in math.'

'I'm sure David wouldn't care about something like that,' I said even though I wasn't sure of it at all. 'So long as, you know, you're a nice person, and all.'

'Really?' Shannon flushed prettily. 'Do you really think so?'

My God, what had I said?

Fortunately at that moment, Andy brought his auctioneer's hammer down hard, and distracted Shannon by shouting, 'Sold for eleven hundred dollars!'

'Wow,' Shannon said. 'That's a lot of money.'

She wasn't the only one in shock. There was an astonished hum through the crowd. Eleven hundred dollars was the most any item on the block had brought in so far. I craned my neck to see what kind of fool had that much

297

money to burn on a piece of junk, and was a little startled to see that Andy was still holding up the belt buckle Jake had found in the attic . . .

. . . and that Paul Slater, of all people, was striding up through the crowd to claim it.

I watched as Paul, looking pleased, shook Andy's hand, took the belt buckle, then whipped out his cheque book. *What a loser*, I thought. I mean, I had known Paul was a weirdo for a long time. But to throw away his hard-earned money – well, not so hard-earned, actually, because I was pretty sure he was paying for the belt buckle with funds stolen from the Gutierrezes – on a piece of junk like that . . . Well, that was just insane.

It didn't make any sense. Why would Paul Slater spend 1,100 bucks on a banged-up old belt buckle . . . even if it *had* been polished and its lineage could be traced back to its original owner, someone in the Diego clan?

And then, as if someone had brought Andy's auctioneer's hammer down on my head, finally banging some sense into me, it all became clear.

And I began to feel as if I might throw up all those baked goods we'd secretly been scarfing down behind Sister Ernestine's back. I guess it must have shown on my face, since Shannon suddenly sucked in her breath and went, 'Are you all right?'

'Bad lemon bar,' I said. 'I'll be right back.' I got up and hurried away from the bake sale table, around the back of the rows of folding chairs, and then up the aisle, toward the dais where Paul was standing, collecting his bounty.

But before I could get anywhere close to him, someone grabbed me by the arm.

My heart was beating so fast on account of the whole

298

Paul-trying-to-keep-my-boyfriend-from-dying thing, that I almost jumped a mile in the air, I was so startled.

But it turned out it was only my mother.

'Susie, honey,' she said, smiling beatifically up at Andy, behind his podium. 'Isn't this fun? Isn't Andy doing great?'

'Uh,' I said, 'yeah, Mom.'

'He's a real natural, isn't he?' She's so in love with this guy. It's totally gross. In, like, a nice way, I guess. But still gross.

'Yeah,' I said. 'Look, I have to—'

But I shouldn't have worried. Because Paul found me.

'Suze,' he said, coming down the steps from the dais. I was too late. The transaction had been completed. In his hand was the belt buckle. 'Fancy meeting you here.'

'I need to talk to you,' I said more intensely than I'd meant to, because both my mother and Sister Ernestine, who was standing nearby with Paul's cheque still hot in her hands, turned to look at me.

'Susie, honey,' my mom said. 'You all right?'

'I'm fine,' I said quickly. Could they tell? Could they tell my heart was hammering a mile a minute and that my mouth was as dry as sand? 'I just need to talk to Paul really fast.'

'And who is minding the bake sale table?' Sister Ernestine wanted to know.

'Shannon's got it under control,' I said, reaching out and taking Paul's arm. He was watching us – my mom, Sister Ernestine, and me – with a slightly sardonic smile, as if everything we were saying was amusing him very much.

'Well, don't leave her alone too long,' Sister Ernestine said severely. I could tell that wasn't what she'd wanted to say, but just as far as she was willing to go in front of my mom.

299

'I won't, Sister,' I said.

And then I dragged Paul away from the dais and folding chairs, and over behind one of the display tables holding the rest of the stuff that was to be auctioned.

'What do you think you're doing?' I hissed at him the moment we were out of earshot.

'Well, hey, Suze,' he said, looking as if he was still finding plenty about the situation to amuse him. 'Nice to see you, too.'

'Don't give me that,' I said. It was kind of hard to talk with my mouth feeling so dry and all, but I wasn't about to give up. 'What did you buy that belt buckle for?'

'This?' Paul opened his fist and I saw silver flash in the bright sun for a second before his fingers closed over it again. 'Oh, I don't know. I just thought it was pretty.'

'Eleven hundred dollars' worth of pretty?' I glared at him, hoping he couldn't see how badly I was shaking. 'Come on, Paul, I'm not stupid. I know why you bought that thing.'

'Really?' Paul's grin was more infuriating than ever. 'Enlighten me.'

'Only it's not going to work.' My heart was slamming into my ribs now, but I knew there was no going back. 'Jesse's last name is de Silva. That's an S, not a D. That isn't his buckle.'

I'd expected this news to wipe the insufferable smile right off Paul's face.

Only it didn't. The corners of his mouth didn't even waver.

'I know it isn't Jesse's buckle,' he said evenly. 'Anything else, Suze? Or can I go now?'

I stared at him. I could feel my pulse slowing down, and the roaring sound that had filled my ears since I'd realized he was the buckle's new owner suddenly disappeared.

300

For the first time in several minutes, I was able to take a deep breath. Before, I'd only been able to manage shallow ones.

'Then . . . then you know,' I said, feeling ridiculously relieved, 'you know you won't be able to use that to go . . . to go back through time to save Jesse.'

'Of course,' Paul said, his smile growing broader than ever. 'Because I'm going to use it to go back through time to stop Jesse's murderer. See you, Suze.'

Ten

Diego. Felix Diego, the man who'd killed Jesse, because Jesse's fiancée, the heinous Maria, asked him to. She had wanted to marry Diego, a slave-runner and mercenary, rather than the man her father had picked out for her to marry, her cousin (*ew*) Jesse.

But Jesse never made it to the wedding. That's because he was killed on his way there. Killed by Felix Diego, though no one at the time knew that. His body was never found. People – Jesse's own family, even – assumed that he'd chosen to run away rather than marry a girl he didn't love and who didn't love him. Maria had gone on to marry Felix, and they'd produced a whole bunch of kids who later grew up to be murderers and thieves themselves.

And, not too long ago, the pair of them had paid a little visit to me, at Paul's behest. He'd met Diego's ghost. In fact, Paul was the one who'd summoned him.

Now Paul was going to stop Diego from killing Jesse . . . probably by killing Diego himself. It's easy for shifters to kill people. All we have to do is remove their souls from their bodies, escort them to that spiritual way station where their fate – whatever it was, heaven, hell, next life – was decided, and boom: back on earth, another unexplained death, another body in the morgue.

Or, in Diego's case, the ice house, because they didn't have morgues in California circa 1850.

Except that it wasn't going to happen like that. I wasn't going to let Paul do it. Oh sure, Diego deserved to die. He was the scum of the earth. He'd killed my boyfriend, after all.

But if Diego died, that meant Jesse wouldn't.

And then I'd never meet him.

I knew, of course, that I couldn't stop Paul on my own – short of killing him myself. I needed back-up.

Fortunately, I knew just where to find it. As soon as the auction was over, and Sister Ernestine dismissed Shannon and me with a curt, 'You may go now,' I headed for my mom's car, which she'd graciously allowed me to borrow for the day, in light of my 'volunteering' to help out at the Mission. Paul had left the second after he'd dropped his little bomb about stopping Felix Diego. I had no way of knowing, really, where he'd disappeared to.

But I had a pretty good idea who might know.

The sun was just starting to set as I pulled out on to Scenic Drive, painting the western sky a deep burnt orange, and turning the sea the color of flames. The windows in the expensive seaside homes I passed reflected the light from the setting sun, so you couldn't see inside them.

But I knew that behind the glowing glass, families were just sitting down to dinner . . . families like my own. I was going to be in big trouble for what I was doing . . . not for trying to keep Paul from saving my boyfriend's life, but for missing dinner. Andy's a real stickler about family meal-times.

But what choice did I have? There was a life at stake here. And OK, so the life belonged to a heinous killer who deserved to die. That was beside the point. Paul had to be stopped.

303

And I knew of only one person he might possibly listen to.

But when I pulled into the Slaters' driveway, I saw that my panic had been for nothing. Not only was Paul's silver BMW convertible there, but it had been joined by a red Porsche Boxster that I recognized only too well.

Paul wouldn't, I knew, be hurtling through alternative dimensions any time soon.

I parked behind the Boxster, then hurried up the long flight of stone steps to the modern house's front door, where I leaned on the bell. A cool, crisp breeze was blowing in from the sea. Inhaling it, you almost felt like all was right with the world . . . anything that could smell that clean and fresh had to be good, right?

Wrong. So wrong. The water in Carmel Bay can be treacherous, with dangerous rip tides that had swept hundreds of hapless vacationers to their deaths. It was fitting that Paul would live just yards away from something so deadly.

Paul answered the door himself. You could tell he was expecting some kind of food delivery, and not me, because he had his wallet out.

To his credit, when he saw it was me, and not, say, my stepbrother Jake delivering a pie from Peninsula Pizza, Paul didn't skip a beat. He slipped his wallet back into the pocket of his perfectly pressed chinos and said with a slow smile, 'Suze. To what do I owe the pleasure?'

'Don't get your hopes up,' I said. With luck he'd mistake my sudden hoarseness for gruff disconcern, and not what it actually was, which was fear. 'I'm not here to see you.'

'Paul?' A familiar voice tinkled like wind chimes from somewhere deep in the house. 'Make sure he gives you extra of those, you know. Whaddyacall'ems. Hot sprinkles.'

Paul looked over his shoulder, and I saw Kelly Prescott – barefoot, with the straps of her extremely skimpy Betsey Johnson dress slipping off her shoulders – coming down the stairs.

'Oh,' she said when she saw it was me at the door and not a pizza. 'Suze. What are *you* doing here?'

'Sorry to interrupt,' I said, hoping they couldn't see how fast my heart was racing beneath the conservative white blouse I'd worn to appease Sister Ernestine. 'But I really need to have a word with Paul's grandfather.'

'Grandpa Gork?' Kelly looked up at Paul inquisitively. 'You told me he couldn't talk!'

'Apparently,' Paul said, the amused smile never leaving his face, 'he does. But only to Suze.'

Kelly flicked a scathing glance at me. 'Geez, Suze,' she said. 'I didn't know you were so into old people.'

'That's me,' I said with a laugh I hoped didn't sound as nervous to their ears as it did to my own. 'Friend to the old people. So . . . can I come in?'

I half expected Paul to say no. I mean, he had to have known why I was there. He had to have known I only wanted to talk to Dr Slaski so I could see if he knew of some way I could stop his grandson from playing with the past . . . and messing up my present.

But instead of looking angry about it or even mildly annoyed, Paul opened the door wider and said, 'Be my guest.'

I stepped inside and managed a smile at Kelly as I went by her and up the stairs to the main floor. Kelly didn't return the smile. I could see why when I stepped into the living room. There was a fire going in the fireplace and, from the placement of the brandy snifters on the chrome-and-glass coffee table in front of the long low couch, it

305

appeared that I'd interrupted a 'moment' between her and Paul.

I tried not to take it personally that Paul had never broken out the brandy or firewood during the many times I'd been over. I am, after all, taken. Still, the whole thing smacked of overkill. Kelly had been warm for Paul's form for so long, she'd have been happy with beef jerky and a Slurpee, let alone a fire and Courvoisier.

I hurried past the living room and down the long hallway that led to Dr Slaski's room. I could hear the Game Show Network blaring away. That must have been a nice accompaniment to Kelly and Paul's make-out session. The dulcet tones of Bob Barker. *Smack, smack.*

When I got to Dr Slaski's room, I stopped and knocked, just to make sure I wasn't interrupting a sponge bath or anything. When no one called for me to come in, I went ahead and pushed the partly open door. Dr Slaski's attendant was sprawled in a chair in one corner, taking what was probably a well-earned nap. Dr Slaski himself, propped up in his hospital bed, appeared to be dozing as well.

I hated to wake him, of course, but what choice did I have? Was I wrong in thinking that he might want to know that his own grandson was thinking of tampering with the course of history, something he himself had warned me was perilous in the extreme?

'Dr Slaski?' I whispered, since I didn't want to wake the attendant, as well. 'Dr Slaski? Are you awake? It's me, Suze. Suze Simon. I have something really important I need to ask you.'

Dr Slaski opened one eye and looked at me. 'This,' he wheezed – his breathing didn't sound right – 'had better be good.'

306

'It's not,' I assured him. 'I mean, it's not good news, anyway. It's about Paul.'

Dr Slaski looked toward the ceiling. 'Why am I not surprised?'

'It's just,' I said, slipping onto the chair beside his bed, 'that I found out why Paul wants to go back through time.'

Dr Slaski's eyelids opened a little wider. 'To save mankind from the atrocities of Stalin?' he rasped.

'Um,' I said. 'No. To keep my boyfriend from dying.'

Paul's grandfather blinked his rheumy eyes at me. 'And this is a bad thing because . . . ?'

'Because if Paul goes back through time and saves Jesse,' I whispered, to keep the attendant from overhearing, 'I'll never meet him!'

'Paul?'

'No.' I couldn't believe this. '*Jesse!*'

Dr Slaski licked his cracked lips. 'Because,' he wheezed, 'Jesse is . . .'

'Dead, all right?' I shot the still-dozing attendant a careful look. 'Jesse is dead. My boyfriend is a ghost.'

Slowly, Dr Slaski closed his eyes. 'I don't,' he sighed, 'have the patience for this. I'm not feeling very well today.'

'Dr Slaski!' I leaned forward and prodded his arm. 'Please, you have to help me. Tell Paul he can't do this. Tell him he can't play around with time travel, the way you told me. Tell him it's dangerous, that he'll end up like you. Tell him something, *anything*. But you've got to get him to stop before he ruins my life!'

Dr Slaski, his eyes still closed, shook his head slowly from side to side. 'You've come to the wrong person,' he said. 'I can't control that boy. Never could. Never will.'

'But you can still *try*, Dr Slaski,' I cried. 'Please, you've *got* to! If he saves Jesse . . . if he succeeds . . .'

307

'Your heart will break.' Dr Slaski had opened his eyes and was gazing at me. 'Your life will be over.'

'Yes!'

'How old are you?' Dr Slaski wanted to know. 'Fifteen? Sixteen? You really think your life will be over if a boy you have a crush on – not even a boy, a *ghost*! – happens to disappear? Next year, you won't remember him, anyway.'

'That isn't true,' I hissed at him through gritted teeth. 'What Jesse and I have . . . it's something special. Paul knows that. That's why he's trying to ruin it.'

Dr Slaski looked interested in that.

'Is he?' he said with a little more animation. 'And why would he want to do that, do you think?'

'Because . . .' I was embarrassed to admit it, but what choice did I have, really? I took a deep breath. 'Because he thinks we should be together. Him and me. Because we're mediators.'

A slow smile broke out across Dr Slaski's dry, liver-spotted lips.

'Shifters,' he corrected me.

'Shifters,' I said. 'Whatever. Dr Slaski, it's not right, and you know it.'

'On the contrary,' Dr Slaski said with a phlegmy cough. 'It's probably the smartest thing that boy's ever done. Romantic, too. Almost gives me faith in him.'

'Dr Slaski!'

'What's so wrong with it, anyway?' Dr Slaski glared at me. 'Sounds to me like he's doing you a favour. Or the boyfriend, anyway. You think this Jessup—'

'Jesse.'

'You think this Jesse likes being a ghost? Hanging around for all eternity, watching you live your life, while he hovers in the background, never ageing, never feeling an ocean

308

breeze on his face, never again tasting blueberry pie. Is that the kind of life you wish for him? You must love him a lot, if that's true.'

I felt heat rising in my cheeks at his tone.

'Of course that's not what I want for him,' I said fiercely. 'But if the alternative is never having known him at all – well, I don't want that, either. And neither would he!'

'But you haven't asked him, have you?'

'Well, I—'

'Have you?'

'Well.' I looked down, unable to meet his gaze. 'No. No, I haven't.'

'I didn't think so,' Dr Slaski said. 'And I know why, too. You're afraid of what he'll say. You're afraid he'll say he'd rather live.'

I looked up sharply. 'That isn't true!'

'It is and you know it. You're afraid he'd say he'd rather live out the rest of his life, the way he was supposed to, never having known you—'

'There has to be another way!' I cried. 'It can't just be one thing or the other. Paul said something about soul transference—'

'Ah,' Dr Slaski said. 'But for that, you need to have a body available to take the soul you want to transfer into it.'

I thought darkly of Paul. 'I think I know of one,' I said.

As if he'd read my thoughts, Dr Slaski said, 'But you won't do that.'

I raised my eyebrows. 'Won't I?'

'No,' he said. His voice was beginning to sound fainter and fainter. 'No, you won't. *He* would. If he thought it'd get him what he wanted. But not you. You don't have it in you.'

'I *do*,' I said as fiercely as I was able.

But Dr Slaski only shook his head again. 'You're not like

309

him,' he said. 'Or me. No need to get huffy about it. It's a good thing. You'll live longer.'

'Maybe,' I said, tears filling my eyes as I looked down at my hands. 'But what's the point, if I'm not happy?'

Dr Slaski didn't say anything for a while. His breathing had grown so raspy that, after a minute or so, I began to think he was snoring, and looked up, fearing he'd fallen asleep.

But he hadn't. His gaze on me was steady.

'You love this boy?' Dr Slaski asked finally.

'Jesse?' I nodded, unable to say more.

'There is *one* thing you could do,' he wheezed. 'Never tried it myself, but I heard it could be done. Wouldn't recommend it, of course. Probably put you into an early grave, like I'll be, soon enough.'

I leaned forward in my chair.

'What is it?' I cried. 'Tell me, please. I'll do anything . . . anything!'

'Anything that doesn't involve killing someone, you mean,' Dr Slaski said and broke down into a coughing fit from which it seemed to take him ages to recover. Finally, lying back on his hospital bed, the horrible, body-wracking spasms finished, he wheezed, 'When you go back . . .'

'Back? Through time, you mean?'

He didn't respond. He just looked up at the ceiling.

'Dr Slaski? Go back through time? Is that what you meant?'

But Dr Slaski never finished that sentence. Because midway through it, his jaw went slack, his eyes closed, and he fell sound asleep.

Or at least that's what I assumed.

I couldn't believe it. He's about to give me some really valuable tip on how I might be able to save Jesse, and

310

suddenly his sleeping pill kicks in? What's the deal with *that*?

I reached out to touch his hand, hoping that might wake him. 'Dr Slaski?' I called a little more loudly. When he still didn't respond, panic set in.

'Dr Slaski?' I cried. 'Dr Slaski, wake up!'

My scream brought the attendant snorting back into consciousness. He was up and out of his chair at once, crying, 'What? What is it?'

'I don't know,' I stammered. 'He – he won't wake up.'

The attendant's fingers flew over Paul's grandfather's body, feeling for a pulse, adjusting IVs

Next thing I knew, he'd straddled the old man and was pounding on his chest.

'Call nine-one-one,' he yelled at me.

I just stood there, not understanding. 'He was just talking to me,' I said. 'We were having a totally normal conversation. I mean, he was coughing a lot, but . . . but he was fine. And then all of a sudden—'

The attendant had to say it twice.

'Call nine-one-one! Get an ambulance!'

That's when I noticed that there was a phone right there in the room. I picked it up and dialled. When the operator came on, I told her that we needed an ambulance and gave her the address. Meanwhile, behind me, the attendant had placed an oxygen mask over Dr Slaski's face, and was filling a syringe with something.

'I don't understand this,' he kept saying. 'He was fine an hour ago. Just fine!'

I didn't understand it, either. Unless Dr Slaski was much more ill than he'd ever let on.

There didn't seem to be much else I could do to help, so I figured I'd better go and tell Paul his grandfather had had

311

some sort of attack. I got back to the living room just in time to see Kelly, seated beside Paul on the couch, her legs draped over his like a throw, stick her tongue in his mouth . . . A sight I actually would have paid money to have been spared.

'Ahem,' I said, from the hallway.

Kelly pulled her face off Paul's and looked at me sourly.

'What do *you* want?' she demanded. Given her animosity toward me, you'd hardly have guessed that we were currently president and vice-president of the junior class, and had to work daily (well, weekly) together in order to decide such important issues as where to go for a class trip and what kind of flowers to order for the spring formal.

Ignoring Kelly, I said, 'Paul, your grandfather appears to be having a heart attack or something.'

Paul looked at me through eyes that were half lidded. That Kelly sure has some sucking power.

'What?' he said stupidly.

'Your grandfather.' I lifted a hand to push some hair from my eyes. I hoped he didn't notice how much my fingers were shaking. 'An ambulance is on the way. He's had like a stroke or something.'

Paul didn't look surprised. He said, 'Oh,' in kind of a disappointed voice . . . but more like he was bummed that his make-out session with Kelly had been interrupted than that his grandfather was, for all we knew, dying.

'Be right there,' Paul said and started to disentangle himself from Kelly's legs.

'Paul,' Kelly cried. She managed to give his name two syllables, so it came out sounding like *Paw-wol*.

'Sorry, Kel,' Paul said, giving one of her calves a good-natured pat. 'Grandpa Gork's OD'd on his meds again. Gotta go take care of business.'

312

Kelly pouted prettily. 'But the pizza's not even here yet!'

'We'll have to take a rain check, babe,' he said.

Babe. I shuddered.

Then realized what he'd said. As he moved past me to get to his grandfather's room, I reached out and seized his arm. 'What do you mean, he's OD'd on his meds?' I hissed.

'Uh,' Paul said, looking down at me with a half smile. 'Because that's what happened?'

'How do you know? You haven't even seen him yet!'

'Uh,' he said, the smile growing broader. 'Because maybe I helped make it happen.'

I dropped my hand as if his skin had suddenly burst into flames. '*You* did this?' I couldn't believe what I was hearing.

Except that I should have. I really should have. Because it was Paul.

'For God's sake, Paul, *why*?'

'I knew you'd be coming over to see him after what happened today at the auction,' he said with a shrug. 'And frankly, I didn't need the hassle from the old man. Now if you'll excuse me . . .'

He went sauntering down the hall in the direction of his grandfather's room. I stared after him, not quite believing what I'd just heard.

And yet . . .

And yet it made sense. It was Paul, after all. Paul, a guy whose morals were more than a little askew.

Feeling numb, I wandered back out into the living room, where Kelly was pulling on her shoes and squawking into her cellphone. 'No, I'm telling you, she came busting in here, demanding to know what I was doing with *her* boyfriend. Well, OK, she didn't say it *quite* like that. She made up some story about wanting to talk to Paul's grandfather. Yeah, I know, the one who can't talk. I know, have

313

you ever heard a lamer excuse? Then she—' Looking up, Kelly saw me. 'Oh, sorry, Deb, gotta go, call you later.' She hung up and just stood there, glaring at me. 'Thanks,' she said finally, 'for spoiling what otherwise might have been a really nice evening.'

I was tempted to tell her the truth – that I hadn't spoiled anything. Paul was the one who'd apparently overmedicated his grandfather. At least, that seemed to be what he wanted me to believe.

But what would have been the point? She wouldn't have believed me, anyway.

'Sorry' was all I said and started for the door.

When I opened it, however, I saw my stepbrother Jake standing there, a pizza box in his hand.

'Peninsula Pizza, that'll be twenty-seven ninety . . .' His voice trailed off as he recognized me. 'Suze? What are *you* doing here?'

'Just leaving,' I said.

'Yeah, well, you'd better.' Jake glanced at his watch. 'You're gonna be late for dinner. Dad'll kill you.'

Yet another thing to look forward to.

'Kelly,' I called up the stairs. 'Your pizza's here!' To Jake I said, 'Hope you remembered the hot pepper flakes.'

Then I left.

Eleven

Because of the auction, Andy was late putting dinner on the table, so I ended up getting home just in time. My mom couldn't understand why I was so quiet during the meal, though. She thought maybe I'd gotten too much sun sitting out at the bake sale table.

'Sister Ernestine should at least have given you an umbrella,' she said as she dug into the pork tenderloin Andy had prepared. 'That little girl you were sitting with . . . what was her name again?'

'Shannon.'

Only it wasn't me who said it. It was David.

'Yes, Shannon,' my mother said. 'She's a redhead, like David. That much sun can be very damaging to redheads. I hope she was wearing sunscreen.'

I half expected David to come up with one of his usual comments – you know, the exact statistical incidents of skin cancer occurring in eighth graders in northern California, or something. His head was filled with all sorts of useless information like that. Instead, he just flicked his mashed potatoes around his plate, until Brad, who'd finished all of his own mashed potatoes, as well as what was left in the bowl, went, 'Man, are you going to eat that or play with it? Because if you don't want it, give it to me.'

'David,' Andy said. 'Finish what's on your plate.'

David picked up a spoonful of mashed potatoes and ate it.

Brad's gaze immediately flickered over to my plate. But the hopeful look in his eye faded when he saw how clean it was. Not, of course, that I'd felt like eating. At all.

But I had Max, the family dog-slash-garbage disposal, by my side, and I'd grown expert at slipping him what I couldn't choke down myself.

'May I be excused?' I asked. 'I think maybe I did get a little too much sun—'

'It's Suze's turn to put the plates in the dishwasher,' Brad declared.

'No, it isn't.' I couldn't believe this. Didn't these people realize I had *way* more important things to do than worry about household chores? I had to make sure my boyfriend died, like he was supposed to. 'I did it last week.'

'Nuh-uh,' Brad said. 'You and Jake traded weeks, remember? Because he had to work the dinner shift this week.'

Since this was indisputably true – I'd seen the evidence myself over at Paul's – I couldn't argue any more.

'Fine,' I said, scooting my chair back, nearly running over Max in the process, and standing up. 'I'll do it.'

'Thank you, Susie,' my mom said with a smile as I took her plate.

My reply wasn't exactly gracious. I muttered, 'Whatever,' and went into the kitchen with everybody's plates, Max following closely at my heels. Max loves it when I have plate-clearing duty, because I just scrape everything into his bowl, rather than into the trash compactor.

But on that night, Max and I weren't alone in the kitchen.

Even though I didn't notice anyone else in there right away, I knew something was up when Max suddenly lifted

316

his head from his bowl and fled, his food only half finished, and his tail between his legs. Only one thing had the power to make Max leave pork uneaten, and that was a visitor from beyond.

He materialized a second later.

'Hey, kiddo,' he said. 'How's it going?'

I didn't scream or anything. I just poured Lemon Joy into the pot Andy had used to cook the potatoes, then filled it with hot water.

'Nice timing, Dad,' I said. 'You just stop by to say hi, or did someone on the ghost grapevine alert you to my extreme mental anguish?'

He smiled. He looked no different than he had the day he died . . . No different from the dozens of times he'd visited me since then. He was still wearing the shirt he'd died in – the shirt I'd slept with for so many years.

'I heard you were having some . . . issues,' my dad said. That's the problem with ghosts. When they aren't haunting people, they sit around in the spectral plane, gossiping. Dad had even met Jesse . . . A prospect I found too horrifying to even contemplate sometimes.

And of course, when you're dead . . . well . . . there isn't a whole lot to do. I knew my dad spent a goodly portion of his free time basically spying on me.

'Been a while since we had a chat,' Dad went on, looking around the kitchen appreciatively. His gaze fell on the sliding glass doors and he noticed the hot tub. He whistled appreciatively. 'That's new.'

'Andy built it,' I said. I started in on the glass dish Andy had roasted the pork in.

'Is there anything that guy can't do?' my dad wanted to know. But he was, I knew, being sarcastic. My dad doesn't like Andy. At least, not that much.

317

'No,' I said. 'Andy is a man of many talents. And I don't know what you've seen – or heard – but I'm fine, Dad. Really.'

'Wouldn't expect you to be anything else.' My dad looked more closely at the kitchen counters. 'Is that real granite? Or imitation?'

'Dad.' I nearly threw the dish towel at him. 'Quit stalling and say what you came to say. Because if it's what I think you're here to say, no deal.'

'And what do you think that is?' Dad wanted to know, folding his arms and leaning back against the kitchen counter.

'I'm not going to let him do it, Dad,' I said. 'I'm not.'

My dad sighed. Not because he was sad. He sighed with happiness. In life, Dad had been a lawyer. In death, he still relished a good argument.

'Jesse deserves another chance,' he said. 'I know it. You know it.'

'If he doesn't die,' I said, attacking the potato pot with perhaps more energy than was strictly necessary, 'I'll never meet him. Same with you.'

Dad raised his eyebrows. 'Same with . . . oh, you mean you thought about saving me?' He looked pleased. 'Suze, that's the sweetest thing you've ever said to me.'

That did it. Just those ten little words. Suddenly, something inside of me seemed to break, and a second later, I was sobbing in his arms . . . only silently, so no one else in the house could hear.

'Oh, Dad,' I wept into his shirt front. 'I don't know what to do. I want to bring you back. I do, I really do.'

Dad stroked my hair and said in the kindest voice imaginable, 'I know. I know you do, kiddo.'

That just made me cry harder. 'But if I save you,' I choked, 'I'll never meet *him*.'

318

'I know,' my dad said again. 'Susie, I know.'

'What should I do, Dad?' I asked, lifting my head from his chest and attempting to control myself – his shirt was practically soaked already. 'I'm so confused. Help me. Please.'

'Susie.' Dad grinned down at me, still tenderly brushing back my hair with his hands. 'I never thought I'd see the day when you, of all people, would actually admit you need help. Especially from me.'

I used a fist to swipe at the tears that were still rolling down my face. 'Of course I need you, Dad,' I whispered. 'I've always needed you. I always will.'

'I don't know about that.' My dad, instead of stroking my hair, rumpled it now. 'But I do know one thing. This time-shifting thing. It's dangerous?'

I sniffled. 'Well,' I said. 'Yeah.'

'And do you really think,' Dad went on, the skin around his eyes crinkling, 'that I'd let my little girl risk her life to save mine?'

'But, Dad—'

'No, Suze.' The crinkles deepened and I could tell he was more serious than he'd been in a long time. 'Not for me. I'd give anything to live again' – and now I saw that, along with the crinkles, there was moisture there, as well – 'but not if it means anything bad might happen to you.'

I gazed up at him, my eyes as bright with tears as his own.

'Oh, Dad,' I said, unable to keep the throb from my throat.

He reached up to lay a hand on either side of my wet face.

'And I wouldn't presume to speak for Jesse,' he said, tilting my head so that we were looking straight into each other's eyes. 'But I think I can safely say that he's not going

319

to like the idea of you risking your life to save his any more than I do. Knowing him, in fact, he'll probably like it even less.'

I reached up and placed my hands over his own. Then I said, 'I get it, Dad. Really, I do. And I won't go back for you if you really don't want me to. But . . . I still can't let him do it, Dad. Paul, I mean.'

'Can't let him save the life of the guy you supposedly love,' Dad said, not looking too happy to hear it. 'Something's very wrong with that picture, Suze.'

'I know, Dad,' I said, 'but I love him. You know it. You can't ask me to just sit back and let Paul do this. If he succeeds I won't even remember having *met* Jesse.'

'Right,' my dad said reasonably. 'So it won't hurt.'

'It *will*,' I insisted, 'It *will* hurt, Dad. Because deep down, I'll know. I'll know there was someone . . . someone I was supposed to have met. Only I'll never meet him. I'll go through my whole life waiting for him to come along, only he never will. What kind of life is that, Dad, huh? What kind of life is *that*?'

'And what kind of life,' my dad asked gently, 'is it for Jesse to spend all of eternity as a ghost – especially if something goes wrong and you end up dead right along with him?'

'Then,' I said with a feeble attempt at humour, 'at least we'll be able to haunt people together for the rest of eternity.'

'With Jesse having to live forever with the guilt of knowing he's the reason you died in the first place? I don't think so, Suze.'

He had me there. I stared up at him, unable to think of a single thing to say in reply.

'Suze, your whole life,' my dad went on, not without sympathy, 'you've always made the right decisions. Not necessarily the easiest ones. The right ones. Don't mess that

320

up now, when you're facing what's probably the most important decision you'll ever have to make.'

I opened my mouth to tell him he was wrong . . . that I was making the right decision . . . that I was doing what I knew Jesse would want . . .

Only I knew there was no point.

So instead I said, 'All right, Dad. But there's just one thing I don't understand.'

He nodded. 'Why Maroon 5 is so popular?'

'Um,' I said, grinning in spite of myself. 'No. I don't understand why, if you feel that way . . . that you had a good life and that you've learned so much since you died . . . If you really feel that way, then why are you still here?'

'You should know,' he said.

I blinked at him. 'I should? How?'

'Because you said it yourself.'

'When did I—'

'Um . . . Suze?'

I whirled around and found myself looking not into my dad's gentle brown eyes but David's anxious blue ones.

'Are you OK?' David's pale face was pinched with concern. 'Were you . . . were you just crying?'

'Of course not,' I said, hastily snatching up a dish towel – seeing, as I did so, that my dad had vanished – and scrubbing my cheeks with it. 'I'm fine. What's up?'

'Um . . .' David looked around the kitchen, his eyes wide. 'Are you . . . are you not alone?'

Outside of my dad, David is the only one in my family who knows the truth about me . . . or at least, most of the truth. If I had told him all of it . . . well, he'd probably be able to handle it, with his scientific, orderly mind.

But I don't think he'd have liked it.

'I am now,' I said, knowing what he meant.

'I just came in for dessert,' David said. 'Dad said . . . Dad said he made a fruit tart.'

'Right,' I said. 'Well. I'm through here. I'll just be going upstairs.'

I turned to go, but David's voice – it had changed lately, gone from squeaky to deep in the course of a few months – stopped me by the door. 'Suze. Are you sure you're all right? You seem . . . sad.'

'Sad?' I looked back at him over my shoulder. 'I'm not sad. Well, not that sad. Just . . . there's just something I have to do.' Because I had already decided that, despite my dad's concerns, I wasn't giving Jesse up just yet. Not without a fight. 'Something I'm not exactly looking forward to.'

'Oh,' David said. Then his face brightened. 'Then just do it quick. You know, like pulling off a Band-Aid.'

Do it quick. I'd have loved to. But I had no way of knowing when Paul was going to make his trip back through time. For all I knew, I could wake up tomorrow with no memory of Jesse whatsoever.

'Thanks,' I said to David, managing a semblance of a smile. 'I'll keep that in mind.'

But I wasn't smiling a half hour later, when I finally managed to get Father Dominic – my last hope – on the phone.

Father Dom wasn't exactly as sympathetic to my plight as I'd hoped he'd be. I'd thought the information I had to impart – about Paul buying Felix Diego's belt buckle, and then possibly drugging his own grandfather – would spark a little righteous indignation in the old guy.

But Father Dominic's sentiments seemed right in line with my dad's. Jesse had died too young, too violently. He had a right to a second chance at life. It was morally reprehensible of me to stand in the way of that.

Maybe Father D had other reasons to be feeling upbeat.

322

The monsignor had come out of his coma and seemed to be recuperating nicely.

'Huh,' I said as Father D imparted this supposedly joyous news. 'That's great, Father D. Now, about Paul—'

'I wouldn't worry too much about it, Susannah,' he said. 'I'll admit it was wrong, what he did to his grandfather – if, indeed, he really did—'

'He said he did, Father D,' I interrupted. 'Well, almost.'

'Yes,' Father Dominic said. 'Well, the two of you do have a tendency to, er, exaggerate the truth somewhat—'

'Father Dom,' I said, my fingers tightening on the receiver. 'I called the ambulance myself.'

'So you said. Still, Susannah, for Paul to do this thing – this time-travel thing you spoke of – I understand he'd have to put himself in the exact spot where the person he wishes to see was once standing during the exact time he wishes to travel back to.'

'Yeah,' I said. 'So?' I wasn't usually so rude to Father Dom, but this was, you have to admit, an extenuating circumstance.

'So wouldn't that mean Paul would have to travel from your bedroom?' Father Dominic sounded a bit distracted. That's because he was. He was packing to come back home. He was planning on driving back to Carmel that very night. 'Isn't that where Diego killed Jesse? Your room? It's rather unlikely Paul is going to be able to get into your bedroom, Susannah,' he went on. 'Not without your permission.'

I nearly dropped the phone. I couldn't believe it. I couldn't believe this hadn't occurred to me before.

Because Father Dominic was right. There was no way Paul was travelling back to the night Jesse died . . . not unless he did a little breaking and entering. Because that was the only way he was getting into my room. The *only* way.

323

'I hadn't thought of that,' I said with a growing feeling of relief. 'But you're right. Oh my God, you're totally right. Father Dominic, you're a genius!'

'Er,' Father Dominic said. 'Thank you, Susannah. I suppose. Although if you were to do the right thing, you'd allow Paul in and let Jesse live out his life naturally, as he was meant to—'

'Um,' I said. I'd heard this tune before, one too many times. Fortunately, the call-waiting went off at that very moment. Perfect timing.

'Oops, that's my other line, Father D,' I said. 'Gotta go. See you when you get back.'

I hung up the phone, feeling better than I had since . . . well, since the auction that afternoon. Jesse was safe. Paul couldn't make him disappear, because to do so, he'd have to have access to my bedroom. How else was he going to find his way back to 1850?

He needed to have a place to stand, somewhere that existed in both 1850 and the present. Somewhere Felix Diego had once stood. Where was he going to go? The mall?

'Hello?' I said, clicking over to the other call.

'Suze?' It was CeeCee, sounding breathless with excitement. 'Oh my God, you'll never believe what just happened.'

'What?' I asked, not actually paying attention. Because, really, where else could Paul go, if not my bedroom?

'He asked me.' CeeCee's voice was actually trembling. 'Adam. Adam asked me to the Winter Formal. We're just at the Coffee Clutch, you know, having cappuccinos – we'd have asked you, only I know you were at the auction all day—'

'Uh-huh,' I said.

'—and he just asked me. Out of the blue. I had to run

324

outside and call you. He's still inside. I just . . . Oh, my God. I had to tell someone. He asked me.'

Besides, it isn't like Paul is going to be able to do it anytime soon, anyway. Go back through time, I mean. Not with his grandfather in the hospital.

'That is so great, CeeCee,' I said into the phone.

'I guess I should go back in and say yes,' CeeCee said. 'I should say yes, right? Or should I play hard to get? I don't want him to think I'm too eager. And it *is* next weekend. Technically, he should have asked me a long time ago—'

Suddenly, I focused on what CeeCee was saying.

And laughed.

'CeeCee,' I said. 'Are you nuts? Hang up the phone, go inside and say yes.'

'I should, shouldn't I? I just . . . I mean, I've been wanting this to happen for so long, and now it is, and I . . . well, I just can't believe it . . .'

'CeeCee.'

'Hanging up now,' CeeCee said. And the line clicked.

He and Kelly had looked pretty . . . *friendly* on that couch. Maybe he'd given up. Maybe he was over the whole 'us' thing.

Maybe now my life would go back to normal.

Maybe . . .

Twelve

'This is by the same director who made *Jaws*?' Jesse wanted to know. 'I don't believe it.'

Saturday night. Date night.

And, OK, though technically Jesse and I can't exactly go out (how could we, really?), Jesse does come over most Saturday nights. True, it isn't as romantic as dinner and a movie. And true, we have to be really quiet, so my family won't suspect I'm not alone in my room.

But at least we get to be together.

And yeah, on this particular Saturday night, I had a lot on my mind, none of which I had any intention of mentioning to Jesse.

But that didn't mean we couldn't spend a couple of hours watching videos. Jesse has a lot of catching up to do, movie-wise, considering the fact that they hadn't even been invented back when he'd been alive.

His favourite so far is *The Godfather*. I was hoping to cure him of this weakness by showing him *E.T.* How could anyone prefer Don Corleone over a six-year-old Drew Barrymore?

But Drew barely managed to hold Jesse's attention.

'*Jaws* is much better than this,' Jesse said.

Jaws is another one of Jesse's favourites. He doesn't even

326

like the right parts, either. He likes the part where all the men are showing one another their scars. Don't ask me why. I guess it's a guy thing.

Finally, I turned *E.T.* off and went, 'Let's just talk.'

By which, of course, I meant 'Let's make out.'

Which was working out very nicely until Jesse quit kissing me at one point and said, 'I almost forgot. What was Paul doing at the Mission tonight? Has he found religion?'

This was so outlandish that I pulled my arms from around his neck and went, '*What?*'

'Your friend Paul,' Jesse said. I may have let go of him, but he wasn't letting go of me. While this was nice, it was also just a little distracting. Especially the way his lips were still moving along mine. 'I saw him a little while ago in the basilica . . . which was closed, you know. Why would he be there after hours, do you think? He hardly seems the type to be considering a career in the priesthood. Unless he suddenly received his calling . . .'

I wrenched myself away from him.

Well, if you'd suddenly been seized by stark white terror, you'd have done the same thing.

'Susannah?' Jesse stared at me, concern filling his dark brown eyes where just a few seconds earlier there'd been . . . well, not concern. 'Are you all right?'

'Oh, God.' How could I have been so stupid? How, how, *how*? Here I was, watching movies – *movies* – with my boyfriend, never suspecting a thing. Thinking Paul would have to come here to the house if he wanted to travel back to Jesse's time. Thinking he wouldn't be able to go back if he didn't. Thinking he wouldn't dream of going back tonight, with his grandfather in the hospital. Thinking he and Kelly were together now, so why would he bother?

327

Paul didn't care about his grandfather. He didn't care about anyone in his family and never had.

And he certainly didn't care about Kelly. Why should he? Kelly didn't understand him, Kelly didn't know what he really was . . .

And, of course, there was another landmark in this century that had existed in Jesse's as well. A place Felix Diego had probably gone often, during his day.

The Mission. The Junipero Serra Mission, which had been built back in the 1700s.

'I have to go,' I said, stumbling to my feet and diving for my jacket. I felt sick to my stomach. 'I'm sorry, Jesse, but I have to—'

'Susannah.' Jesse was on his feet as well, taking hold of my arm in a grip that was as strong as it was gentle. Jesse would never hurt me. On purpose. 'What is it? What is this about? Why do you care if Paul is in the basilica?'

'You don't understand,' I said. I really did think I was going to be sick. I really did. It must have shown on my face because Jesse's grip on my arm suddenly got a good deal tighter . . .

. . . just as the expression his face got a lot grimmer.

'Try me, *querida*,' he said in a voice that was as hard as his grasp.

And then – don't ask me how or what I was thinking because, truthfully, I don't think I was – it all came spilling out.

I hadn't wanted to tell him. Not because I didn't want to upset him. God, nothing like that. No, I didn't want him to find out for the most selfish of all reasons: I hadn't wanted to tell him for fear he'd agree with Father Dominic and my dad – that he'd prefer another chance at life than eternity as a ghost.

328

But out it poured, everything, from what Dr Slaski had told me to what Father Dom had said on the phone just a few hours ago. It was a raging flood that couldn't be stopped, the torrent of words coming from my mouth. I wanted to stuff them back as quickly as they spilled out.

But it was too late. It was way too late.

Jesse listened unflinchingly, not interrupting me, even when I told him the part about my deal with Paul: our secret arrangement in which I endured Wednesday afternoon 'mediator lessons' with him in exchange for his not sending my boyfriend to the netherworld.

'Only now he doesn't want to kill you, Jesse,' I told him bitterly. 'He wants to *save* you, save your life. He's going back through time to stop Felix Diego from killing you. And if he does that . . . if he does that . . .'

'You and I will never meet.' Jesse's expression was calm, his voice its normal deepness.

Never had any statement sounded as chilling to me. It felt like a stab wound to the heart.

'Yes,' I said frantically. 'Can't you see, I've got to go down there – now. Right now – and stop him.'

'No, *querida*,' Jesse said, still in that unhurried voice. 'You can't do that.'

For a second, the terror that was gripping my heart seemed to squeeze it until it stopped. I thought I would die, right there on the spot.

Jesse wanted to live. My dad, Father Dominic, Dr Slaski, Paul . . . they had been right. They had all been right, and *I* was the wrong one, *me*. Jesse would prefer to live than to have met me, to have known me . . .

. . . to have loved me . . .

I should have known, of course. And I think deep down, I *did* know. What kind of person – especially one who'd died

329

the age Jesse had been, just twenty – wouldn't want a chance to go back and live again, if he could? What kind of person wouldn't be willing to give up everything he had for that chance?

And what did Jesse have? Nothing. Nothing at all. Just me.

My dad had accused me long ago of being the thing that was holding Jesse back, keeping him from moving on. Father Dominic had said it, as well . . . that if I really loved him, I'd set him free.

And now I knew. Jesse himself would rather be free than be with me.

God. I'd been such a fool. Such a total fool.

Then Jesse let go of my arm.

But instead of saying what I'd expected him to – *You can't go after him, because I want the chance. I want the chance to live again, if I can* – he said in a voice gone suddenly as cold as the wind outside, 'You can't go after him. He's too dangerous. I'll go. I'll stop him.'

I wasn't sure I'd heard him right. Had he said – could he possibly have said – what I thought he'd said?

'Jesse,' I said. 'I don't think you understand. He wants to save you. To keep you from . . . from dying that night.'

'I understand,' Jesse said. 'I understand that Paul is a fool who thinks he's God. I don't know what makes him think it's his right to play with my destiny. But I do know he's not going to succeed. Not if I can stop him.'

My circulation seemed to spring to life. Suddenly, I could breathe again. Relief washed over me in waves.

He wanted to stay. Jesse wanted to stay. He would rather stay than live. *He would rather stay* – with me – *than live.*

'You can't,' I said, my voice sounding freakishly high-pitched even to my own ears. That was the relief I felt, making me giddy. 'You can't stop him, Jesse. Paul will—'

330

'And just what do *you* intend to do, Susannah?' he demanded sharply. And if I hadn't been convinced before of the sincerity of his wish to remain in this place and time, his gruff tone then would have been enough. '*Talk* him out of what he plans? No. It's too dangerous.'

But love had given me courage I'd never even known I had. I shrugged into my leather motorcycle jacket and said, 'Paul won't hurt me, Jesse. I'm the reason he's doing this, remember?'

'I don't mean Paul,' Jesse said. 'I mean time travelling. Slaski says it's dangerous?'

'Yes, but—'

'Then you're not doing it.'

'Jesse, I'm not afraid—'

'No,' Jesse said. There was a look in his eye I had never seen before. 'I'm going. You're staying here. Leave everything to me.'

'Jesse, don't be—'

But a second later, I saw that I was talking to thin air.

Because Jesse was gone.

I knew where he'd disappeared to, of course. He'd gone to the basilica, to have a word with Paul.

And I was betting that that word would be accompanied by a fist.

I was also betting Jesse was going to be too late. Paul wouldn't be at the Mission any more by the time Jesse got to him.

Or rather, he would be. But not the basilica as we knew it.

There was only one thing, really, that I could do then. And that wasn't, as Jesse had urged, to leave everything to him. How could I, when I could quite possibly wake up in the morning with no memory of Jesse whatsoever?

331

I knew what I had to do.

And this time, I wasn't going to make the mistake of consulting with anybody beforehand.

I strode across the room, lifted my pillow and pulled out the miniature portrait of Jesse – the one he'd given to his one-time fiancée, Maria. The one that I'd been sleeping on since the day I'd stolen – er – been given it.

Looking down into Jesse's dark, confident gaze, I closed my eyes and pictured him . . . pictured Jesse in this very room, only not looking as it did now, with a frilly canopy bed and princess phone (thanks, Mom).

No, instead I pictured it as it must have looked 150 years earlier. No ruffled white curtains over the bay window. No window seat scattered with fluffy pillows. No carpet over the wood floor. No – ack! – bathroom, but maybe one of those, what were they called? Oh yeah, chamber pots.

No cars. No cell phones. No computers. No microwaves. No refrigerators. No televisions. No stereos. No aeroplanes. No penicillin.

Just grass. Grass and trees and sky and wooden wagons and horses and dirt and . . .

And I opened my eyes.

And I was there.

332

Thirteen

It was my room, but it wasn't.

Where the canopy had stood sat a bed with a brass stand. The bed was covered with a brightly coloured quilt, the kind of quilt that my mom would have gone nuts over if she'd seen it in some craft shop. Instead of my vanity table, with its big light-up mirror, was a chest of drawers with a pitcher and bowl on it.

There was no mirror anywhere, but on the floor was a rug woven from . . . well, lots of different stuff. It was kind of hard to see really well, because the only light was what little moonlight spilled in from the bay windows. There was no electric switch. I felt for it instinctively the minute I opened my eyes to so much darkness. Where the light switch had been was just wood.

Which could only have meant one thing.

I'd done it.

Whoa.

But where was Jesse? This room was empty. The bed didn't look as if it had been slept in anytime recently.

Had I come too late? Was Jesse already dead? Or had I come too early and Jesse hadn't yet arrived?

There was only one way to find out. I laid my hand on

the doorknob – only, of course, there was no knob now, but a latch instead – and went out into the hallway.

It was nearly pitch-black in the hallway. There was no electric switch here, either. Instead, when I groped for it, my hand touched a framed picture, or something . . .

. . . that promptly fell off the wall with a banging sound, although no glass broke. I didn't know what to do. I couldn't find the thing I'd knocked over, it was too dark. So I continued down the stairs, navigating the various twists and turns by memory alone, since I had no light to guide me.

I saw the glow before I heard the quick footsteps approaching the bottom of the stairs. Someone was coming . . . someone holding a candle.

Jesse? Could it possibly be?

But when I reached the bottom of the stairs, I saw that it was a woman who was coming toward me, a woman holding not a candle but some kind of lantern. At first, I thought she must be enormously fat, and I was like, God, what could she have been eating? It's not like they had twinkies back in Jesse's day . . . er, now, I mean.

But then I saw that she was wearing some sort of a hoop-skirt, and that what I'd taken for girth was really just her clothes.

'Mary, Mother of God,' the woman cried when she saw me. 'Where did you come from?'

I thought it better to ignore that question. Instead, I asked her as politely as I could, 'Is Jesse de Silva here?'

'What?' The woman held the lantern higher and really peered at me. 'Faith,' she cried. 'But you're a girl!'

'Um,' I said. I would have thought this was obvious. My hair, after all, is pretty long, and I always wear it down. Plus, as always, I had on mascara. 'Yes, ma'am. Is Jesse here? Because I really have to speak to him.'

But the woman, instead of appreciating my politeness, pressed her lips together very firmly. Next thing I knew, she was reaching for the door, holding it open and trying to shoo me through it.

'Out,' she said. 'Out with you, then. You should know we don't allow the likes of you in here. This is a respectable house, this is.'

I just stood there gaping at her. A respectable house? Of course it was. It was MY house.

'I don't mean to cause trouble, ma'am,' I said, since I could see how it would be a little weird to find a strange girl wandering around your house . . . even if it was a boarding house. That happened to belong to me. Or at least to my mother and her new husband. 'But I really need to speak to Jesse de Silva. Can you tell me if he—'

'What kind of fool do you take me for?' the woman demanded not very nicely. 'Mr de Silva wouldn't give the time of day to a . . . creature like you. Need to speak to Jesse de Silva, indeed! Out! Out of my house!'

And then, with a strength surprising for a woman in a hoopskirt, she grabbed me by the collar of my leather motorcycle jacket, and propelled me out the door.

'Good riddance to bad rubbish,' the woman said and slammed the door in my face.

Not just any door, either. My *own* door. My *own* front door, to *my* house.

I couldn't believe it. From what I'd been led to believe, from Jesse and those *Little House on the Prairie* books, things back in the 1800s had been all butter churns and reading out loud around the fire. Nothing about mean ladies throwing girls out of their own houses.

Chagrined, I turned around and started down the steps from the front porch . . .

335

. . . and nearly fell on my face. Because the steps weren't where they used to be. Or would be one day, I mean. And except for the moonlight, which was sadly lacking just then, due to a passing cloud, there was no light whatsoever to see by. I mean it, it was spookily dark. There was no reassuring glow of streetlights – I wasn't even sure there *was* a street where Pine Crest Road ought to have been.

And, turning my head, I could see no lights on in any nearby windows . . . for all I could tell, there *were* no nearby windows. The house I was standing in front of might have been the only house for miles and miles . . .

And I'd just been thrown out of it. I was stranded in the year 1850 with no place to go and no way to get there. Except, I guess, the old-fashioned way.

I could, I supposed, have walked to the Mission. That's where Paul had supposedly gone. I craned my neck, looking for the familiar red dome of the basilica, just visible from my front porch, perched as it was in the Carmel Hills.

But instead of seeing Carmel Valley stretched out below me, all winking lights stretching to the vast darkness of the sea, all I saw was dark. No lights. No red dome, lit up for the tourists. Nothing.

Because, I realized, there *were* no lights. They hadn't been invented yet. At least, not light bulbs.

God. How could anybody find their way anywhere? What did they use to guide them, freaking stars?

I looked up to check out the star situation, wondering if it would help me, and nearly fell off the porch again. Because there were more stars in the sky than I had ever seen before in my life. The Milky Way was like a white streak in the sky, so bright it almost put the moon, finally flitting out from behind some clouds, to shame.

336

Whoa. No wonder Jesse was unimpressed whenever I successfully located the Big Dipper.

I sighed. Well, there was nothing else I could do, I supposed, but start hoofing it in the general direction of the Mission, and hope I ran into Paul – or Jesse . . . Past Jesse, I mean – on the way.

I had just found my way off the porch – down a set of rickety wooden steps, unlike the cement ones in place there now . . . I mean, in the present . . . *my* present – when it hit me. The first heavy, cold drops of rain.

Rain. I'm not kidding. No sooner had I looked up to see if it was really rain, or someone dumping their chamber pot out on me (*ew*) from the second floor, than I saw the bank of big black clouds rolling in from the sea. I had been so distracted by all the stars, I hadn't noticed them before.

Great. I travel more than a century and a half through time, and what do I get for my efforts? Getting thrown out of my own house, and rain. A lot of it.

Lightning flashed, high up in the sky. A few seconds later, thunder rumbled, long and low.

Fabulous. A thunderstorm. I was stuck in an 1850 thunderstorm with nowhere to go.

Then the wind picked up, carrying with it a scent I couldn't place right away. It took me a minute to remember it. Then, all at once, I did: my occasional forays into Central Park back when I'd lived in Brooklyn.

Horse. There were horses nearby.

Which meant there had to be a barn. Which might be dry. And which might be unguarded by hoopskirted women who consider me bad rubbish.

Ducking my head against the rain, which was coming down harder now, I ran in the direction of the horse smell and soon found myself behind the house, facing an enormous barn, right where Andy had said he was going to have a pool installed one day, after we'd all finished college and he could afford it.

The barn doors were closed. I hurried toward them, praying they wouldn't be locked . . .

They weren't. I heaved one open and slipped inside just as another bolt of lightning streaked through the sky, and thunder sounded again, more loudly, this time.

Inside the barn it was dry, at least. Black as tar, but dry. The horse smell was strong – I could hear them moving uneasily around in their stalls, startled by the thunder – but the smell of something else was stronger. Hay, I think it was. Not exactly being a country girl, I couldn't say for sure. But I thought the stuff that crunched and rolled a little beneath my boots might be hay . . .

Well, this was just great. I'd come to save my boyfriend's life – or rather, to keep someone else from saving it – and all I'd accomplished so far was to enrage his landlady.

Oh and I'd been rained on. And found a barn.

Perfect. Dr Slaski hadn't been kidding when he'd warned me against time travel. It sure hadn't been any picnic so far.

And when, a second later, I'd reached up to wring some of the water from my hair and felt a heavy hand on my shoulder—

Well, I had definitely had enough of the mid-1800s.

Fortunately for me, a roll of thunder drowned out my scream. Otherwise, the landlady – or worse, her husband, if she had one – would have been out here in a flash. And I probably would have gotten a lot more than just a bad scare.

'Shut up!' Paul whispered. 'Do you want to get us both shot?'

I whirled around. I could only dimly make out his figure

338

there in the darkness. But it was enough to send my pulse, which had been racing before, to a near standstill.

'What are you doing here?' I demanded, hoping he couldn't hear the confusion in my voice. I was feeling an odd mix of emotions at seeing him: anger, that he'd gotten there before me; fear, that he was there at all; and relief, at seeing a familiar face.

'What do you *think* I'm doing here?' Paul tossed something rough and heavy at me.

I caught it inexpertly. 'What's this?'

'A blanket. So you can dry yourself off.'

I gratefully threw the blanket around my shoulders. Even though I still had my motorcycle jacket on, I was shivering beneath the leather. I don't think it was from the rain, either.

The blanket smelled strongly of horse. But not in a bad way. I guess.

'So,' Paul said and moved into the sliver of light thrown through the still-open barn door, so that I could finally see his face. 'You made it.'

I sniffled miserably. I tried not to pay attention to the fact that I was cold, wet and inside a barn. In the year 1850.

'I can't believe you really thought you would get away with it,' I said, glad I'd finally seemed to get the trembling of my voice under control. My chattering teeth were another story. 'Did you think I wouldn't try to stop you?'

Paul shrugged. 'I figured it was worth a try. And there's still a chance I'll succeed, you know, Suze. He isn't here yet.'

'Who isn't?' I asked stupidly. I was still busy trying to figure out how I could possibly ditch Paul and get to Jesse without him noticing.

'Jesse,' Paul said as if I were mentally impaired. And you know what? Probably I am. 'We're a day early. He gets here tomorrow.'

339

'How do you know?' I asked, wiping my dripping nose on the back of my wrist.

'I talked to that lady,' he said. 'Mrs O'Neil. The one who owns your house.'

'She talked to you?' I couldn't hide my surprise. 'She wouldn't talk to me. She threw me out.'

'What'd you do, materialize in front of her?' Paul asked with a sneer.

'No,' I said. 'Well, not *right* in front of her.'

Paul shook his head. But I could see that he was grinning a little. 'Bet you gave her a coronary. What'd she think of your get-up?' He gestured at my clothes.

I looked down at myself. In my jeans and motorcycle jacket, I guess I didn't really resemble any nineteenth-century miss I'd ever seen in the movies. Or, more important, in pictures from the era.

'She said she ran a respectable house and I should know better than to show my face there,' I admitted and was stung when Paul laughed out loud.

'What?' I demanded.

'Nothing,' Paul said. But he was still laughing.

'Just tell me.'

'OK. But don't get mad. She thought you were a lady of the evening.'

I glared at him. 'She did not!'

'She did so. And I told you not to get mad.'

'I'm not exactly dressed like a hoochie mama,' I pointed out. 'I'm wearing *pants*.'

'That's the problem,' Paul said. 'No respectable woman in this century wears pants. Good thing Jesse didn't see you. He probably wouldn't even have talked to you.'

I had had about all I could take of Paul. I said hotly, 'He would so. Jesse's not like that.'

340

'Not the Jesse you know,' Paul said. 'But we're not talking about the one you know, are we? We're talking about the one who's never met you. Who hasn't sat around for a hundred and fifty years, watching the world go by. We're talking about the Jesse who's on his way to Carmel to marry the girl of his—'

'Shut up,' I said before he could finish that sentence.

Paul's grin got broader. 'Sorry. Well, we've got a while to wait. No sense spending it arguing. Come up to the loft with me, and we'll sit out this storm together.'

He slipped back into the shadows, and I heard a foot scrape on a wooden rung. One of the horses whinnied.

'Don't be scared, Suze,' Paul called down to me from a few feet in the air. 'They're just horses. They won't bite. If you don't get too near them.'

That wasn't why I was scared. Not that I was about to admit any such thing to him.

'I think I'll stay down here,' I said into the darkness his voice had come from.

'Fine by me,' Paul said, 'if you want to get caught. It'll just make my job easier. Mr O'Neil came by a little while ago to check on the horses. I'm sure he wouldn't shoot a girl, though. If he realized you were a girl in time, I mean.'

This got me moving toward the ladder.

'I hate you,' I commented, as I started to climb.

'No, you don't,' Paul said from the darkness above me. I could tell by his voice that he was grinning again. 'But you go right on telling yourself that, if it makes you feel better.'

341

Fourteen

It was warm in the loft. Warm and dry. And not just because of all the hay. No, also because Paul and I were sitting so close together – for body-heat purposes only, I'd informed him, when he'd shown me the hole he'd dug in the giant pile of hay at one end of the loft.

'Because I don't want to die of hypothermia' was what I'd said, since the horse blanket didn't seem to be doing the job. At least, my teeth hadn't stopped chattering. My jeans weren't drying as fast as I'd have liked them to.

'I'll keep my hands to myself,' Paul had assured me.

And so far, he'd been true to his word.

'What I don't get,' I said as the rain pelted down outside, with occasional flashes of lightning, though the thunderstorm portion of the evening seemed to be mostly over, 'is what you're doing here. Aren't you supposed to be looking for Felix Diego? To stop him?'

'Yeah.' In the darkness of the loft, I could only make out Paul's profile by the light that crept in from chinks and knotholes in the wood that made up the barn walls.

'So . . . why aren't you? Unless' – my blood ran cold – 'you already found him. But then why—'

'Relax, Simon,' Paul said. 'I didn't find him. Yet. But we both know he's due to show up here tomorrow, same as Jesse.'

I did relax then. Well, just a little. So Paul hadn't gotten to Diego yet. Which meant there was still time . . .

To do what, though? What was I going to do when I found Jesse? I couldn't tell him not to stay at Mrs O'Neil's boarding house or he'd be killed, because the truth was, I *wanted* him to be killed. How else was I ever going to get to meet him – OK, date him – in the twenty-first century?

I was just going to have to stick to Paul, was all. Stick to Paul and keep him from stopping Diego. Maybe I wouldn't even see Jesse. Which would probably be just as well. Because if I did, what on earth was I going to say to him? What if he, like Mrs O'Neil, mistook me for some random hoochie mama? I didn't think I could bear it . . .

Which reminded me . . .

'Are people going to notice we're gone?' I asked. 'In our own time, I mean? Or when we get back, will it be like no time has gone by?'

'I don't know.' I got the feeling Paul had been trying to get some sleep when I'd shown up. He seemed to be attempting to get back to it now and my endless questions were only serving to irritate him. 'Why didn't you ask my grandfather? You two are so close and all . . .'

'I didn't exactly get a chance, now, did I?' I stared at him – or tried to, anyway – in the darkness. I still wasn't sure why Dr Slaski had chosen me as his confidante and not his own grandson. Well, except for the fact that Paul is a user. And a thief. And, oh yeah, had possibly purposefully drugged him.

'He's not who you think he is, Paul,' I said, meaning Dr Slaski. 'He's not your enemy. He's just like us.'

'Don't say that.' Paul's blue-eyed gaze suddenly bore into me from the darkness. 'Don't ever.'

343

'Why? He's a mediator, Paul. A shifter. He's probably who you got it from. He knows a lot. And one thing he knows is that the more we play around with . . . with our powers . . . the better our chances of ending up like him—'

'I told you not to say that,' Paul snapped.

'But if you'd just give him a chance, instead of calling him a gork and purposefully—'

'We're not like him, all right? You and I? We're nothing like him. He was stupid. He tried to tell people. He tried to tell people that mediators – shifters – whatever – that we exist. And everyone laughed at him. My dad had to change his name, Suze, because no one would take him seriously, knowing he was related to someone they all said was a quack. So don't you ever – *ever* – say we're like him or that we're going to end up like him. I already know how I'm going to end up.'

I just blinked at him. 'Oh, really? And how's that?'

'Not like him,' Paul assured me. 'I'm going to be like my dad.'

'Your dad isn't a mediator,' I reminded him.

'I mean I'm going to be rich, like my dad,' Paul said.

'How?' I asked with a laugh. 'By stealing from the people you're supposed to be helping?'

'There you go again,' Paul said, shaking his head. 'Who told you we're supposed to help the dead, Suze? Huh? Who?'

'You know perfectly well it was wrong of you to take that money. It wasn't yours.'

'Yeah,' Paul said. 'Well, there's more where it came from and, unlike you, I suffer no moral compunctions in taking it. I'm going to be rich some day, Suze. And, unlike Grandpa Gork, in control.'

'Not if you kill all your brain cells flitting in and out of the past,' I pointed out.

'Yeah, well,' Paul said. 'This is a one-time trip. After this, I shouldn't need to go back again.'

I stared at his profile. Only our sides were touching beneath the horse blanket we shared. Still, Paul radiated a lot of heat. I was getting a little hot under the blanket.

That was when I realized the only other guy I'd ever lain this close to was Jesse, and that the heat he gave off . . . Yeah, a lot of that was in my mind. Because ghosts can't give off heat. Even to mediators. Even to mediators who happen to be in love with them.

'It's wrong,' I said quietly to Paul as I looked at his closed eyelids. 'What you're doing to Jesse. He doesn't want it.'

Paul's eyes opened at that.

'You *told* him?'

'Of course I told him,' I said. 'And he doesn't want it. He doesn't want you to interfere, Paul. He was going down to the Mission to stop you when I left.'

Paul looked at me for a few seconds, his blue eyes unreadable in the darkness.

'Are you sleeping with him?' he asked bluntly.

I gaped at him, feeling heat flood my cheeks. 'Of course not!' Then, realizing what I'd said, stammered, 'N-not that it's any of your business.'

But Paul, rather than grinning over his so fully discomfiting me, as I would have expected him to, was gazing down at me very seriously.

'Then I don't get it,' he said simply. 'Why him? Why not me?'

Oh. *That.*

'Because he's honest,' I said. 'And he's kind. And he puts me ahead of everything else—'

345

'So would I,' Paul said. 'If you'd give me the chance.'

'Paul,' I said. 'If we were in an earthquake or something, and you had a chance to save me but it was at the risk of your own life, you would save yourself, not me.'

'I would not! How can you even say that?'

'Because it's true.'

'But you're saying that your perfect Jesse would save you, at the risk of his own life?'

'Yes,' I said with absolute certainty. 'Because he has. In the past.'

'No, he hasn't, Suze,' Paul said with equal certainty.

'Yes, he has, Paul. You don't even know—'

'Yes, I do know. Jesse could never possibly have risked his own life to save yours, because in all the time you've known him, he's been dead. So he hasn't been risking anything, all those times he's saved you. Has he?'

I opened my mouth to deny this, then realized that Paul was right. It was the truth. A screwed-up version of the truth, but the truth just the same.

'What have you got to be so bitter about?' I demanded instead. 'You've always gotten everything you've ever wanted your whole life. You've only had to ask for it, and it was yours. But it's like it's never enough for you.'

'I haven't gotten *everything* I've ever wanted,' Paul said pointedly. 'Although I'm working to correct that.'

I shook my head, knowing what he meant.

'You only want me because you can't have me, Paul,' I said. 'And you know it. I mean, my God. You've got Kelly. All the guys in school want her.'

'All the guys in school,' Paul said, 'are idiots.'

I ignored that.

'You would be a lot better off,' I said, 'if you'd just be

346

happy with what you have, Paul, instead of wanting what you'll never get.'

But Paul kept right on grinning. Grinning and rolling back over so he could sleep. 'I wouldn't be so sure of that, if I were you, Suze,' he said in a tone that sounded way too smug to me.

'You—'

'Go to sleep, Suze,' Paul said.

'But you—'

'We've got a long day ahead of us. Just sleep.'

Amazingly, I did. Sleep, I mean. I hadn't expected that I'd be able to. But maybe Dr Slaski was right. Travelling through time DOES wear you out. I don't think I'd have fallen asleep otherwise . . . you know, given the hay, the horses, the rain, and, oh yeah, the hot-but-totally-deadly guy lying next to me.

But I laid my head down, and next thing I knew, lights-out.

I woke with a start. I hadn't even realized I'd been asleep. But there was light streaming through the slits between the wood planks that made up the sides of the barn. Not the grey light of dawn, either. It was full-on sunlight, revealing that I'd slept way past 8:00 . . .

And kneeling in front of me was Paul, with breakfast.

'Where'd you get *that*?' I asked, sitting up. Because in Paul's hands was a pie. A whole pie. Apple, from the smell of it.

And it was still warm.

'Don't ask,' he said, pulling, of all things, two forks from his back pocket. 'Just eat.'

'Paul.' I could hear movement below. Paul had been speaking in hushed tones. I knew why now.

We were not alone.

347

A man's voice said, 'Git along there.' He appeared to be speaking to the horses.

'Did you steal this?' I asked, even as I was taking the fork and digging in. Time travel doesn't just make you sleepy. It makes you hungry, too.

'I told you not to ask,' Paul said as he, too, shovelled a forkful of pie into his mouth,

Stolen or not, it was good. Not the best I'd ever had, by any means – I don't know if, out in the Wild West, they really had access to the best sugar and stuff.

But it satisfied the rumbling in my stomach . . . and soon made me aware of another urge.

Paul seemed to read my mind.

'There's an outhouse behind the barn,' he informed me.

'A *what* house?'

'You know.' Paul grinned. 'Watch out for the spiders.'

I thought he was joking.

He wasn't. There were spiders. Worse, what they had to use as toilet paper back then? Let's just say that today, it wouldn't be considered fit to *write on*, let alone . . . you know . . . anything else.

Plus I had to hurry, so no one would see me in my twenty-first-century clothes and ask questions.

But it was hard because once I'd slipped out of the barn, I was flabbergasted by what I saw . . .

Which was nothing.

Really. Nothing, in all directions. No houses. No telephone poles. No paved roads. No Circle Ks. No In-N-Out Burger. Nothing. Just trees. And a dirt track that I suppose passed for a street.

I could, however, see the red dome of the basilica. There it was, down in the valley below us, with the sea behind it. That, at least, hadn't changed in the last 150 years.

Thank God plumbing has, however.

When I crept back up to the loft, there was no sign of Mr O'Neil. He appeared to have taken his horses and gone off to do whatever it was men like him did all day in 1850. Paul was waiting for me with an odd look on his face.

'What?' I asked, thinking he was going to tease me about the outhouse.

'Nothing,' was all he said, however. 'Just . . . I have a surprise for you.'

Thinking it was another food-related item, although I was quite full from the pie, I said, 'What? And don't tell me it's an Egg McMuffin, because I know they don't have drive-through here.'

'It's not,' Paul said.

And then, moving faster than I'd ever seen him move before, he took something else from his back pocket – a length of rope. Then he grabbed me.

People have, of course, tied me up before. But never somebody whose tongue was once in my mouth. I really wasn't expecting Paul to do something so underhanded. Save my boyfriend's life so I'd never meet him, yes. But hog-tie my hands behind my back?

Not so much.

I struggled, of course. I got in a few good elbow jabs. But I couldn't scream, not if I didn't want Mrs O'Neil to show up and go running for the sheriff or whatever. I wouldn't be able to help Jesse from jail.

But it appeared I wouldn't be much help to him for the time being, either.

'Believe me,' Paul said as he tightened knots that were already practically cutting off my circulation. 'This hurts me a lot more than it hurts you.'

'It does not,' I said, struggling. But it was hard to struggle

349

when I was on my stomach in the hay, and his knee was in the small of my back.

'Well,' he said, going to work on my feet now. 'You're right, I guess. Actually, this doesn't hurt me at all. And it'll keep you out of trouble while I go find Diego.'

'There's a special place for people like you, Paul,' I informed him, spitting out hay. I was getting really sick of hay.

'Reform school?' he asked lightly.

'Hell,' I informed him.

'Now, Suze, don't be that way.' He finished with my feet and, just to be sure I wouldn't get it into my head to, I don't know, roll out of the hayloft, he tied one end of the rope to a nearby post. 'I'll be back to untie you just as soon as I kill Felix Diego. Then we can go home.'

'Where I'll never speak to you again,' I informed him.

'Sure you will,' Paul said cheerfully. 'You won't remember any of this. Because we won't have gone back through time to save Jesse. Because you won't even know who Jesse is.'

'I hate you,' I said, really meaning it this time.

'You do now,' Paul agreed. 'But you won't when you wake up tomorrow in your own bed. Because without Jesse, I'll be the best thing that ever happened to you. It'll just be you and me, two shifters against the world. Won't that be fun?'

'Why don't you go—'

But I didn't get to finish that sentence, because Paul took something else out of his pocket. A clean white handker-chief. He'd told me once that he always carried one because you never know when you might need to gag someone.

'Don't you dare!' I hissed at him.

But it was too late. He wadded the handkerchief into my mouth and secured it there with another piece of rope.

If I had never hated him before, I did then. Hated him

350

with every bone in my body, every beat of my heart. Especially when he gave me a pat on the head and said, 'See ya.'

Then disappeared down the ladder to the barn floor.

Fifteen

I don't know how long I lay there like that. Long enough to start wondering whether I could just close my eyes and shift home. Who knew where I'd end up? Somewhere in the backyard, anyway. Possibly in a big bunch of poison oak, since there was no barn there now. But anything had to be better than lying in a very cramped position on the floor of a hayloft, with who knew what crawling through my hair and the blood pounding in my temples.

But a world without Jesse? Because that's what I'd be guaranteeing myself if I gave up now. A world without my one purpose for living. Well, more or less. I mean, I know women need men like fish need bicycles, and all of that. Except . . .

Except I love him.

I couldn't do it. I was too selfish. I wasn't going to give up. Not yet. There were still plenty of hours of daylight left, or at least, there had been when Paul had left. The shadows, I couldn't help noticing, were growing longer.

Still, if Mrs O'Neil had told Paul the truth, and Jesse was expected that night, there was still time. Paul might not find Diego. He might have to come back with his task unaccomplished. And when he did, and he untied me . . .

Well, he was going to learn a lot about pain, that was for sure. Because this time, I'd be ready for him.

I don't know how much time passed while I lay there, plotting my revenge on Paul Slater. Death was too good for him, of course. An eternity as a ghost – floating shiftlessly through this dimension and the next – was what would suit him best. Give him a little taste of what it had been like for Jesse all of these years. That ought to teach him . . .

I could do it, too. I could pull Paul's soul out of his body and make it so that he could never return to it . . .

. . . by giving that body to someone else. Someone who deserved a chance to live again . . .

But I couldn't. I knew I couldn't. I couldn't kiss Paul's lips, even if I knew it was Jesse inside them, kissing me back. It was just too . . . gross.

It was as I was lying there thinking this that I heard it, a sound my ears had become so finely attuned to over the past year that I could have been at the Super Bowl, a million rows away, and I still would have heard it.

Jesse's voice.

He was calling to someone. I couldn't hear what, exactly, he was saying. But he sounded, I don't know. Different, somehow.

He was getting closer, too. His voice, I mean.

He was coming toward the barn.

He'd found me. I don't know how – Dr Slaski hadn't said anything about ghosts being able to travel through time. But maybe they could. Maybe they could, just like shifters, and Jesse had done it, he'd come back through time looking for me. To save me. To help me save him.

I closed my eyes, thinking his name as hard as I could. This worked, more often than not. Jesse would materialize in front of me, wondering what on earth was so urgent.

Only he didn't. Not this time. I opened my eyes, and . . . nothing.

353

Only I could still hear his voice below me. He was saying, 'No, no, it's all right, Mrs O'Neil.'

Mrs O'Neil. Mrs O'Neil could see Jesse?

The barn door opened. I heard it creak. Then . . .

Footsteps.

But how could Jesse have footsteps? He's a ghost.

Wriggling as far toward the edge of the hayloft as I could, I craned my neck, trying to see what I could only hear. But the rope Paul had used to tie my feet to the post wouldn't let me wiggle more than a few feet from my original position. I could hear him now, though – really hear him. He was speaking in a soft, soothing tone to . . . to . . .

To his horse.

Jesse was talking to a horse. I heard it whinny softly in reply.

Which was when I finally knew. This wasn't Ghost Jesse, come to rescue me. This was Alive Jesse, who didn't even know me. Alive Jesse, come to meet his fate in my room tonight.

I froze, feeling pins and needles all over – and not just because I'd been lying in such a cramped position for so long. I needed to see him. I *needed* to see him. Only how?

Then he moved and I turned my head, following the sound . . .

. . . and saw, through a chink in the floorboards of the loft, a spot of color. His horse. It was his horse. I saw his hands moving over the saddle, unstrapping it. It was Jesse. He was right beneath me. He was –

Why I did what I did next, I'll never know. I didn't want Jesse to know I was there. If Jesse found me, it could throw off everything. Who knew, he might not even be murdered that night. And then I'd never get to meet him.

But the urge to see him – alive – was so strong, that with-

354

out even thinking about it, I banged my feet as hard as I could on the hayloft floor.

The hands moving over the saddle grew suddenly still. He'd heard me. I tried to call to him, but all that came out, thanks to Paul's gag, was *gnnh, gnnh*.

I banged my feet harder.

'Is someone there?' I heard Jesse call.

I banged again.

This time, he didn't call out. He started climbing the ladder to the loft. I heard the wood strain beneath his weight.

His weight. Jesse had *weight*.

And then I saw his hands – his large, brown, capable hands – on the top rung of the ladder, followed, a second later, by his head . . .

The breath froze in my lungs.

Because it was him. It was Jesse.

But not Jesse as I'd ever seen him before. Because he was alive. He was . . . *there*. He was so solidly and unquestionably *there*, taking up space like he *owned* it, like the space better get out of *his* way, as opposed to the other way around.

He wasn't glowing. He was radiating. Not the spectral glow I was used to seeing around him, either, but instead an undeniable aura of health and vitality. It was like the Jesse I had known was a pale replica – a reflection – of the one I was looking at now. Never had I been so aware of the way his dark hair curled against the back of his tanned neck; the deep brown of his eyes; the whiteness of his teeth; the strength in those long legs as he knelt down beside me; the tendons in the back of his brown hands; the sinews in his bare arms . . .

'Miss?'

And his voice. His voice! So deep, it seemed to reverberate

355

down my spine. It was Jesse's voice all right, but suddenly, it was in surround sound, it was THX, it was . . .

'Miss? Are you all right?'

Jesse was gazing down at me, his dark eyes filled with concern. One of his hands moved to his boot, and the next thing I knew, a long and shiny blade was gleaming in his hand. I watched in fascination as the blade came nearer and nearer to my cheek.

'Don't be afraid,' Jesse was saying. 'I'm going to untie you. Who did this to you?'

Suddenly, the gag was gone. My mouth was raw from where the rope had cut into it. Then my hands were free. Sore, but free.

'Can you speak?' Jesse's hands were on my feet now, his knife neatly slicing through the ropes Paul had tied me with. 'Here.'

He laid the knife aside and lifted something else toward my face. Water. From a flask. I took it from him and sucked greedily. I'd had no idea how thirsty I'd been.

'Easy,' Jesse said in that voice – *that voice!* 'I can get you more. Stay here and I'll get help—'

On the word *help*, however, my hands, as if of their own volition, dropped the flask and flew out to seize his shirt front instead.

It wasn't the shirt I was used to seeing Jesse in. It was similar, the same soft, white linen. But this one was higher at the neck. He was wearing a vest, too – a waistcoat, I think they were called back then – of a sort of watered silk.

'No,' I croaked and was startled at how raspy my voice sounded. 'Don't go.'

Not, of course, because I was worried he was going to go and get Mrs O'Neil, who'd recognize me as the strumpet she'd found wandering around her front parlour the night

356

before. But because I couldn't bear the thought of him leaving my sight. Not now. Not ever.

This was Jesse. This was the *real* Jesse. This was who I loved.

And who was going to die shortly.

'Who are you?' Jesse asked, lifting the flask I'd dropped and, finding it not quite empty, handing it back to me. 'Who did this – left you here like this?'

I drank what was left of the water. I'd known Jesse long enough to see that he was outraged – outraged at whoever had left me like that.

'A . . . a man,' I said. Because, of course, Jesse – this Jesse – wouldn't know who Paul was . . . Didn't know who *I* was, clearly.

His eyebrows furrowed, the one with the scar in it looking particularly adorable. The scar wasn't as obvious, I noticed, on Live Jesse as it was on Ghost Jesse.

'And did this same man put you in these outlandish clothes?' Jesse wanted to know, looking critically at my jeans and motorcycle jacket.

Suddenly, I wanted to laugh. He seemed like a different Jesse entirely – or rather, a hundred times more real than the Jesse I had known – but his disgust with my wardrobe? That hadn't changed a bit.

'Yes,' I said. I figured it would be more believable to him than the real explanation.

'I'll see him horsewhipped,' Jesse said as matter-of-factly as if he had people horsewhipped for dressing girls up in odd outfits and leaving them tied up in haylofts every day of the week. 'Who are you? Your family must be looking for you—'

'Um,' I said. 'No, they aren't. I mean . . . I doubt it. And my name is Suze.'

357

Again the dark brow furrowed. 'Soose?'

'Suze,' I said with a laugh. I couldn't help it. Laughing, I mean. It was so wonderful to see him like this. 'Susannah. As in "Oh, Susannah, Don't You Cry for Me."'

It was what I had said to him, I realized with a pang, back in my bedroom, the very first time I'd met him, the day I'd arrived in Carmel. I hadn't known then what I knew now – that that moment had been a turning point in my life – everything before it was BJ: Before Jesse. Everything afterward, AJ: After Jesse. I hadn't known then that this guy in the puffy shirt with the tight black pants would one day mean more to me than my own life . . . Would one day be my everything.

But I knew it now, just as I knew something else:

I had it wrong. I had it all wrong.

But it wasn't, I knew, too late to fix it. Thank God.

'Susannah,' Jesse said, as he sat beside me in the straw. 'Susannah O'Neil, perhaps? You are related to Mr and Mrs O'Neil? Let me get them. I know they'll want to see that you're safe—'

'No,' I said, shaking my head. 'My, um, family is far away.' *Really* far away. 'You can't get them. I mean, thank you, but . . . you can't get them.'

'Then this man . . .' Jesse looked excited. And why not? It probably wasn't every day the guy stumbled over a sixteen-year-old girl who'd been left bound and gagged in a hayloft. 'Who is he? I'll fetch the sheriff. He must pay for what he's done.'

Much as I would have liked to set Jesse – Live Jesse – on Paul, it didn't seem like the appropriate thing to do. Not when Jesse was going to have so many problems of his own to handle very soon. Paul was my problem, not his.

'No,' I said. 'No, that's OK.' Then, seeing his puzzled

358

look, I said, 'I mean, that's all right. Don't get the sheriff—'

'You needn't fear him any more, Susannah,' Jesse said, gently. He clearly did not know he was speaking to a girl who had kicked a lot of butt in her day. Ghost butt, mostly, but whatever. 'I won't let him hurt you again.'

'I'm not afraid of him, Jesse,' I said.

'Then—' Jesse's face clouded suddenly. 'Wait. How did you know my name?'

Ah. Well, there was the rub, wasn't it?

Jesse was looking at me curiously, that dark-eyed gaze raking my face. I'm sure I must have looked a picture. I mean, what girl wouldn't after having been left for hours with her head in the straw and her mouth gagged?

It didn't matter, of course. What Jesse thought of me. But I felt self-conscious just the same. I reached up and shoved some hair out of my eyes, trying to tuck it back behind an ear. Just my luck, the first time I meet my boyfriend – while he's still living – and I look like a complete train wreck.

'Do I know you?' Jesse asked, his gaze searching. 'Have we met? Are you . . . are you one of the Anderson girls?'

I had no idea who the Anderson girls might be, but I felt a stab of envy for them, whoever they were. Because they were girls who'd gotten to know Jesse – Live Jesse. I wondered if they knew how lucky they were.

'We haven't met,' I said. 'Yet. But . . . I know you. I mean, I know . . . about you.'

'You do?' Recognition dawned at last in his gaze. 'Wait . . . yes! Now I know. You're friends with one of my sisters. From school? Mercedes? You know Mercedes?'

I shook my head, fumbling around in the pocket of my leather jacket.

'Josefina, then?' Jesse studied me some more. 'You must

359

be close to her age, fifteen, yes? You don't know Josefina? You can't know Marta, she's too old—'

I shook my head again, then held out what I'd fished from my pocket.

He looked down at what I held in my hand.

'*Nombre de dios*,' he said softly, and took it from me.

It was the miniature portrait of Jesse, the one I'd stolen from the Carmel Historical Society. I saw now how poor a portrait it actually was. Oh, the painter had gotten the shape of Jesse's head right and his eye colour and expression were close enough.

But he'd completely failed to capture what it was that made Jesse . . . well . . . Jesse. The keen intelligence in his dark brown eyes. The confident twist of his wide, sensuous mouth. The gentleness of his cool, strong hands. The power – just now leashed, but coiled so close to the surface, it might rise up at any moment – of those muscles, honed from years of working alongside his father's ranch hands, beneath that soft linen shirt and those black pants.

'Where did you get this?' Jesse demanded, his fist closing over the portrait. Sparks seem to fly from his dark eyes, he was that angry. 'Only one person has a portrait like this.'

'I know,' I said. 'Your fiancée, Maria. You're here to marry her. Or at least, that's the plan. You're on your way to see her now, but her father's ranch is still pretty far off, so you're staying here for the night before you go on to her place in the morning.'

Anger turned to bewilderment as Jesse lifted his free hand and raked his fingers through his thick dark hair – a gesture I had seen him perform so many times when he was completely frustrated with me, that tears actually sprang to my eyes, it was so familiar . . . and so adorable.

'How do you know all this?' he asked desperately.

360

'You're . . . you're friends with Maria? Did she . . . give you this?'

'Not exactly,' I said.

And took a deep breath.

'Jesse, my name is Susannah Simon,' I said all in a rush, wanting to get it out before I changed my mind. 'I'm what's called a mediator. I'm from the future. And I'm here to keep you from being murdered tonight.'

Sixteen

Because, in the end, I couldn't do it.

I thought I could. I really did think I could sit back and let Jesse be murdered. I mean, if the alternative was never to meet him? Sure, I could do it. No problem.

But that had been before. Before I'd seen him. Before I'd spoken to him. Before he'd touched me. Before I'd known what he was, what he could have been, if he'd only lived.

I knew now I could no more stand by and let Jesse be killed than I could have . . . well, shoved my little step-brother David out in front of a speeding car or fed my mother poison mushroom caps. I couldn't let Jesse die, even if meant never seeing him again. I loved him too much.

It was as simple as that.

Oh, I knew I was going to hate myself later. I knew I was going to wake up and, if I even remembered what I'd done, hate myself for the rest of my natural life.

But what else could I do? I couldn't stand idly by while someone I loved was walking into mortal danger. Father Dominic, my dad, all of them – even Paul – were right. I had to save Jesse, if I could.

It was the right thing to do.

But not, of course, the easy thing. The easy thing would have been to point a finger in his face as he stared down at me, completely disbelieving, and gone, 'Ha! Fooled ya! Just kidding.'

Instead, I said, 'Jesse. Did you hear me? I said I'm here from the future to save you from being—'

'I heard what you said.' Jesse smiled at me gently. 'Do you know what I think would be best? If you would let me get Mrs O'Neil. She'll take good care of you while I go to town to get the doctor. Because I think the man who did this to you – tied you like this – might also have hit you on the head—'

'Jesse,' I said flatly. I couldn't believe this. Here I was, making this tremendous sacrifice, saving the love of my life and knowing that I would never be with him again, and he was accusing me of being bonkers. 'Paul didn't hit me in the head. All right? I'm fine. A little thirsty still, but otherwise fine. I just need you to listen to me. Tonight Felix Diego is going to sneak into your room here at the boarding house and strangle you to death. Then he's going to throw your body into a shallow grave, and no one is going to find it until a century and a half later, when my stepdad installs a hot tub on our deck.'

Jesse just looked down at me. I couldn't be sure, but I think I saw pity in his gaze.

'Jesse, I'm serious,' I said. 'You've got to go home. OK? Just get back on your horse and turn around and go home, and don't even think about marrying Maria de Silva.'

'Maria did send you,' Jesse said, finally. His face darkened with a sudden anger. 'This is her way of trying to save face, is it? Well, you can go back to your mistress and tell her it won't work. I won't have her family thinking I wasn't gentleman enough to break it off in person – no matter who she sends with strange tales to frighten me off. I'm going to see her tomorrow whether she likes it or not.'

363

I blinked up at him, completely dumbfounded. What was he talking about?

Then, too late, I remembered the secret Jesse had once confided in me, the secret only I knew . . . that he had been on his way to the de Silva ranch all those years ago not to marry Maria, but to break things off with her . . .

. . . Which explained why all of her letters to him had been discovered alongside his remains last summer, when my stepbrother accidentally dug them up. Nineteenth-century manners demanded that couples breaking off their engagements returned the letters each had written the other. Diego had murdered Jesse before such an exchange could take place in order to prevent Maria's father from asking any uncomfortable questions concerning the break-up – like what Jesse had heard about his fiancée that had made him want to end their engagement.

'Wait,' I said. 'Hold on. Jesse, Maria didn't send me. I don't even know Maria. Well, I mean, we've met, but—'

'You have to know her.' Jesse looked down at the framed portrait in his hand. 'She gave this to you. She must have. How else could you have gotten it?'

'Um,' I said, with a shrug. 'Actually, I stole it.' Then I saw his face change, and knew I'd made a mistake.

'Oh, no,' I said, holding up both hands, palms toward him. 'Down, boy. I didn't steal it from your precious Maria, believe me. I stole it from the Carmel Historical Society, OK? A museum, where it had been sitting for God knows how long. In fact, I bet if you check with good old Maria, she still has hers. Her portrait of you, I mean.'

'There were no duplicates made,' Jesse said, in a hard voice.

'I know that.' God, this was hard. 'But look at the one you're holding, Jesse. Look how old it looks, how cracked

364

the paint is, how tarnished that frame's gotten. That's because it's nearly two hundred years old. I stole it in the *future*, Jesse. I used it to help me get back here, to the past, so I could warn you . . .' This wasn't strictly true, of course, but close enough. 'You've got to believe me, Jesse. Paul – the guy who tied me up – will back me up on this. He's out looking for Felix Diego right now to try to stop him before he can get to you—'

Jesse shook his head.

'I don't know who you are,' he said in a low, even tone unlike any he'd ever used with me before. 'But I'm returning this—' He dangled his portrait in my face. '—to its rightful owner. Whatever game you're playing, it ends *now*. Do you understand?'

Game? I couldn't believe this. Here I was, risking my neck for him, and he was *mad* at me for stealing a stupid portrait of him? 'There's no game, Jesse, OK? If this were just a game if Maria really did send me – how would I know the stuff I know? How would I know that Maria and Diego are secretly in love? How would I know that your girlfriend – who is quite the skank, by the way – doesn't want to marry you at all? And that her dad doesn't approve of Diego and thinks if she marries you she'll forget about him eventually? How do I know that the two of them have cooked up a scheme to kill you tonight and hide your body so it looks as though you skipped out on the engagement—'

'*Nombre de dios*.' Jesse was on his feet and swearing. I couldn't help noticing how the loft shook a little under his footsteps. This was not something that would have happened with Ghost Jesse, and was just more proof of how very far I'd come from the world I knew.

But that wasn't the only thing that wouldn't have happened with Ghost Jesse. I realized this a second later when

365

Alive Jesse bent down and siezed me by my arms, and gave me a frustrated shake.

'You know all this because Maria told you!' he said, from between gritted teeth. 'Admit it! She told you!' As quickly as he'd snatched me up, he let go and turned away. Uttering a groan of pent-up annoyance, Jesse dragged a hand through his hair.

My arms, where he'd touched me, tingled.

'Look, I'm sorry,' I said, meaning it. I knew how he felt, after all. His wasn't the only heart in that barn that was breaking. 'I mean, about your girlfriend wanting to kill you and all. Even if you were going to, you know, break up and all. But if it's any consolation, I do think you're a lot better off without her. I mean, the only times I ever met her, she was trying to kill me, too, but still. Better you find out she's a skank now, you know, and break it off cleanly, than find out after you're married. Because I don't even know if they let people get divorced in, you know, your time.'

'Stop saying that!' Both of Jesse's hands went to grasp his hair now.

'What? Skank?' Maybe I *was* being a little harsh. 'Well, OK. But the girl seems like major bad news.'

'No.' Jesse turned around to stare down at me, and I was surprised at the intensity with which his gaze burned into mine. '*Your time. The future.* You . . . you . . . I'm sorry, Miss Susannah. But I'm afraid I'm going to have to get the sheriff after all. Because you are very clearly not right in the head.'

'*Miss* Susannah!' To my utter horror, tears pricked at the corners of my eyes. But I couldn't help it. It was just so . . . so . . .

Unfair.

'So it's Miss Susannah, is it?' I asked him, ignoring my

366

tears. 'Oh, that's just great. I come all the way back here, risking major brain cell burnout, and you don't even believe me? I'm basically guaranteeing myself a lifetime of heart-break, and all you have to say is that you think I'm not right in the head? Thanks a lot, Jesse. No, really. That's just fine.'

I broke off with a sob. Suddenly, it was all too much. I couldn't even look at him, because every time I did, he dazzled my eyes, like he was the most glorious Christmas tree that had ever existed. I buried my face in my hands and wept.

Maybe I had done enough, I told myself. Maybe tipping him off about Maria and Diego's plan would make him turn around tonight and go home. Even though the tip had come from what he obviously considered an unreliable source. I couldn't do anything more, could I? I mean, how else could I get him to believe me?

Then I remembered.

I dropped my hands from my face and looked up at him, not caring if he saw my tears.

'Doctor,' I said.

'Yes.' Jesse had fished a handkerchief from somewhere and handed it to me, his anger apparently dissipated. 'Let me get one for you. I really feel that, despite what you say, Miss Susannah, you are unwell—'

'No.' I pushed the handkerchief away impatiently. 'Not for me. You.'

A small smile appeared at the corners of his lips. '*I* need a doctor? I assure you, Miss Susannah, I have never felt fitter in my life.'

'No.' I stumbled to my feet. It was the first time I'd tried to stand since he'd untied me, and I wasn't exactly steady.

Still, I managed to get up without his help. Now I stood

367

in front of him, breathing hard – but from emotion not exertion.

'A doctor,' I said, looking up into his confident, concerned face. He was a good six inches taller than me, but I didn't care. I kept my chin up.

'You secretly want to be a doctor,' I said. 'You haven't asked him, but you know your father won't let you. He needs you to run the ranch, because you're the only boy. They couldn't spare you long enough for you to get through medical school, anyway.'

Something happened to Jesse's face then. The glint of suspicion that I'd seen in his eye since I'd shown him the miniature portrait dropped away, and in its place came something else . . .

Something like wonder.

'How . . . ?' Jesse stared down at me in utter incredulity. 'How could you possibly have . . . ? I have never told any-one that.'

I reached out and took one of his hands . . .

. . . and was shocked by how warm it felt in mine. All those times Jesse had held me . . . all those times he'd stroked my hair and I'd marvelled at his heat . . . I knew now it hadn't been real, that heat. It had all been in my head. This, *this* heat was real. This hand was real. The hard calluses I knew so well . . . they were real. Really Jesse.

'You told me,' I said to him. 'You told me in the future.'

Jesse shook his head, but not hard. Just a little.

'That . . . that's not possible,' he said.

'Yes,' I said. 'Yes, it is. You see, what happens tonight is that Diego kills you. But only your body dies, Jesse. Your soul doesn't go anywhere, because . . . well, because I think it wasn't supposed to happen like that.' I gazed up at him

368

tenderly, still holding his hand. 'I think you were supposed to live. But you didn't. So your soul hung around until I came along, about a hundred and fifty years later. I'm someone who helps . . . well, people who've died. You told me you wanted to be a doctor, Jesse. You told me in the future. Do you believe me now? Will you *please* go away from here and never come back?'

Jesse looked down at our entwined fingers, mine so pale against his sun-darkened skin, so soft against his calluses. He didn't say anything. What *could* he have said, really?

But because he was Jesse, he thought of something to say . . . the exact right thing to say.

'If you know something like that about me,' he said softly, 'about my wanting to be a doctor – something I have never told Maria – or any living person – then I must . . . I suppose I must . . . believe you.'

'So,' I said. 'Now you know. You've got to get out of here, Jesse. Just get on your horse and ride.'

'I will,' he said.

We were standing so close, all he'd have had to do was reach out, and he could have cupped my face in his hand.

He didn't, of course.

But I could feel the warmth radiating from him, not just from the hand I held, but along the course of his entire body. He was so vibrant, so alive, that he made me feel aware of every hair on my head, every corpuscle in my skin. I loved him so much . . .

. . . and he'd never, ever know it.

But that was all right. Because at least he'd be able to go on living.

'But not,' Jesse said, suddenly dropping my hand and turning away, 'tonight.'

I stood there, feeling as if I'd been kicked. Cool air rushed

369

into all the places that, moments before, had been warmed by his body heat.

'W-what?' I stammered stupidly. 'Not what?'

'Not tonight,' Jesse said with a nod toward the barn doors, through which, I could see, the lengthening shadows were gone. The sun had set. There were no shadows any more. 'Tomorrow I will ride to the de Silvas' ranch to speak with Maria and her father. But not tonight. It's growing late. Too late to travel. I'll stay here tonight, and leave in the morning.'

'But you can't!' The words were wrenched from the depths of my soul. 'You've got to leave now, Jesse, tonight! You don't understand, it's too dangerous—'

An all-too-familiar smile crept across those lips I knew so well. 'I can take care of myself, Miss Susannah,' he said. 'I am not afraid of Felix Diego.'

I couldn't believe what was happening right before my eyes.

'Well, you should be!' I practically screamed. 'Considering that he kills you!'

'Ah,' Jesse said. 'But if I understand you correctly, that was before you came to warn me . . . for which I thank you.'

I couldn't believe how badly this was going.

'Jesse,' I said, making one last desperate attempt to reason with him. 'You can't spend the night in that house. Do you understand? It's way, way too dangerous.'

But Jesse surprised me. Well, why not? He always had.

'I understand,' he said.

'You do?' I stared at him. 'Really? Then you'll go?'

'No,' he said, 'I won't go.'

'But—'

'I will stay here,' he said, nodding to indicate the loft. 'With you. Until morning.'

I gaped at him.

'Here?' I echoed. 'Here . . . in the barn?'

'With you,' Jesse said.

'With me?'

'Yes,' he said.

It took me until that moment to realize what he was doing. Here I was, traveling back 150 years to protect him – well, *now* that's what I was doing, anyway – and *he* was trying to protect *me*.

That was just so pure Jesse that I almost started to cry. Really.

But only almost.

Because his next question distracted me. 'I have to ask, though . . . Why?' His dark-eyed gaze raked my face.

'Why what?' I murmured, hypnotized as ever, by his gaze on mine.

'Why did you do this – come all this way – to warn me about Diego?'

Because I love you.

Four simple words. Four simple words that there was no way I could say. Not to this Jesse, who was virtually a stranger to me. He already thought I was nuts. I didn't want to make things even worse.

'Because it isn't right, what happened to you. That's all.'

That's what I started to say, anyway, when a man's voice called, 'Señor de Silva?'

And let's just say that it wasn't Mr O'Neil.

371

Seventeen

I felt the blood in my veins run cold.

I knew that voice. Knew it only too well. The man who owned it had tried to kill me once.

'It's him,' I whispered. Unnecessarily, of course, since Jesse obviously knew perfectly well who it was.

Jesse stood up and moved from the shadows that had cloaked his face. He wore an expression, I was relieved to see, of intense distrust. He was starting to believe me now.

'Who's there?' he called, lifting the lantern and turning a knob that brought what had been a tiny flame to a more powerful one.

The man below said something in Spanish that I didn't understand. Except for the last two words. And they were easy enough for even me to decipher.

Felix Diego.

This is it, I thought. There was no going back now.

Jesse said something in Spanish to Diego, who replied in tones that, though I could not understand the words he spoke, sounded too silky-smooth to be trustworthy. He appeared to be inviting Jesse to do something.

And Jesse, for his part, was clearly declining.

'Well?' I whispered anxiously when the conversation ended and I heard Diego finally leave.

Jesse held up a hand, though, clearly not as convinced as I was that the man was well and truly gone.

Then, as the evening turned irrevocably to night and I could no longer see beyond the golden rays shooting out from the lamp Jesse held, he said, 'It was Felix Diego. He said his master – Maria's father – had sent him to see that I had everything I needed to be comfortable and to escort me on the remainder of my journey tomorrow.'

'Has Maria's father ever done that when you've come to visit before?' I asked.

'No' was Jesse's terse reply to that question.

'What did you tell him?'

'I told him that I was fine,' Jesse said. He was answering my questions, but it was clear from the expression on his face that his mind was a thousand miles away. He was putting the extraordinary tales I'd been telling him together with what had just happened, and not liking what he was coming up with.

'I told him I'd be here all night,' he went on. 'Because my horse was sick. He said my horse looked fine to him and suggested I join him outside for a bottle—'

I sucked in my breath. 'You didn't say yes, did you?'

'Of course not.' For the first time, Jesse seemed really to *see* me as he looked at me. 'I think you're right. I think he does mean to kill me.'

I didn't reply with a hearty *Told you so*, because what would have been the point? Besides, Jesse looked upset enough. Not upset really – stunned. And something else, too. Something I couldn't put my finger on . . .

At least, not until a second later, when I heard footsteps scrape for a second time on the ladder to the loft. Thinking it was Diego returning, I started toward the ladder, ready to fling the guy's soul back to kingdom come . . .

373

But Jesse stepped in front of me, throwing out an arm to stop me from coming any closer.

And I realized what that 'something' was that I'd seen in his eye.

But it turned out the person climbing toward us wasn't Felix Diego after all.

'Oh, great,' Paul said, when he finally pulled himself up to the top of the ladder and saw us. 'Oh, this is just great. What's *he* doing here?' Paul was glaring at Jesse, who glared right back.

'He just found me, Paul,' I said. I didn't mention the part where I'd sort of *made* him find me.

Paul just glared at Jesse some more. If he noticed how different Jesse looked alive than he did dead, he didn't exactly mention it.

Jesse, for his part, simply nodded to Paul and asked me, 'Is this him? The man who tied you up?'

I should have said no, of course. I should have seen what was coming.

But I didn't think. I just went, 'Yeah, that's him.'

It wasn't until I saw Jesse's hands clench into fists that I realized what I'd done. 'No, wait!' I started to cry.

But it was too late. Jesse had launched himself at Paul like a linebacker, tackling him to the floor of the hayloft, and causing an enormous crash that sent the horses below whinnying and thumping around in their stalls.

'Stop it!' I cried, darting forward and trying to separate them.

But it was like trying to pull apart a couple of mountains.

Paul, at least, wasn't as into the fight as Jesse was, since I could hear him crying, 'Get him off me! Suze, get him *off*—'

On the word *off*, Jesse let go of his own accord and

374

backed away, breathing hard. His shirt had gotten unbuttoned a little in the melee, and I caught a glimpse of his strong hard abs. It was impossible, even given the gravity of the situation, not to appreciate the sight.

'What the—' Paul scrambled up from the hay, brushing bits of it off him. 'God, Suze. What did you tell him about me? Doesn't he know *I'm* the good guy here? You're the one who was going to let him get—'

'He knows,' I interrupted, quickly.

Paul quit brushing himself and sent me a quizzical look. 'He knows?' he echoed. 'As in . . . *knows* knows?'

'He knows,' I repeated grimly.

'Well,' Paul said, looking intrigued. 'What brought about that little change of heart? I thought—'

'That was before,' I said quickly.

'Before *what?*' Paul found a piece of straw in his hair and pulled it out.

'Before I saw him,' I said softly, not looking at either of them.

Paul didn't say anything – which for him was unusual. Jesse, of course, didn't know what we were talking about. He was still mad at Paul for tying me up.

'I don't know if it's considered normal in the time you come from to leave women bound and gagged,' Jesse said severely. 'But in this day and age, allow me to assure you that such behaviour would generally land a gentleman in jail.'

Jesse said the word *gentleman* like it was the last thing he actually thought Paul was.

Paul just looked at him. 'You know,' he said. 'I think I like your ghost better.'

I felt it wise to change the subject. 'He's here,' I said to Paul. 'Felix Diego, I mean.'

375

'I know,' Paul said. 'I followed him back here.'

'I thought you were going to get rid of him!'

'Yeah, well, I couldn't just walk up to him and suck out his soul in front of everyone.'

'Why not?'

'Because I would've gotten shot, that's why not.'

'But you could just have shifted back to the future—'

'Uh, and left you tied up in Mrs O'Neil's hayloft? I don't think so. I'd have had to come back and rescue you.' His gaze shifted toward Jesse's. 'I didn't know, of course, that Prince Charming here had come along and done it for me.'

'So what are we going to do?' I asked. Paul looked at Jesse.

'Well,' he said. 'What does Wonderboy want to do?'

'Wonderboy?' Jesse glared menacingly in Paul's direction. 'Is this person a friend of mine in the future?' he asked me.

'No,' I said to Jesse. To Paul I said, 'I tried to get him to leave, but he won't go.'

Paul looked at Jesse. 'Buddy,' he said. 'I'm not telling you this because I like you. Believe me. But if you stay here, you're gonna get iced. Simple as that. That Diego guy? He means business.'

'I'm not afraid of him,' Jesse said as if we were morons for not believing him.

'See what I mean?' I said, to Paul.

'Great.' Paul sat down on a hay bale, looking pained. 'This is just great. So when Diego comes to kill him, he can take a crack at you and me, too.'

I opened my mouth to insist this wouldn't happen, but Jesse interrupted.

'If you think I would leave you alone with her again,' he said, his gaze never wavering from Paul's face, 'you don't know me at all in this future you speak of.'

376

'Don't worry,' Paul said, holding up a hand wearily. 'I wouldn't expect anything else from you, Jesse. Well, that's it then.' Paul leaned back in the hay, making himself more comfortable. 'We wait. And if he comes back, thinking you've fallen asleep and he can do the job out here, we take him.'

'No.' Jesse's jaw was set. He didn't raise his voice. Not at all. His tone was hard as steel, however. '*I* will take him.'

'Uh, no offence,' Paul said, 'but Suze and I, we came here especially just to—'

'I said I'll do it,' Jesse said in that same ice-cold voice – the one I had come to recognize as the voice Jesse used only when he was truly angry about something 'I'm the one he's come to kill. I am the one who will stop him.'

Paul and I exchanged glances. Then Paul sighed, lifted the horse blanket, and stretched out across the hay in a dark corner of the loft.

'Fine,' he said. 'Wake me when it's time to shift home.'

And to my utter disbelief, he closed his eyes and seemed to doze off.

I glanced at Jesse and saw that he was eyeing Paul with distaste. When he noticed the direction of my gaze, he asked, his tone less hard than before, 'You two are friends in the place you come from?'

'Uh,' I said. 'Not really. More like . . . colleagues. We both have the same . . . gift, I guess you'd call it.'

'For travelling through time,' Jesse said.

'Yes,' I said. 'And . . . other things.'

'And when I kill Diego' – I noticed he said *when* and not *if* – 'you'll go back where you came from?'

'Yes,' I said, trying not to think about how incredibly hard that moment was going to be.

'And you want to help me,' Jesse said, just as quietly as I'd spoken to him, 'because . . . ?'

377

I realized I hadn't actually answered his question the first time he'd asked it. In the soft glow of the lamp – he'd turned the flame down to make sure Diego really did think he was sleeping, so he could take him unawares – Jesse had never looked as handsome as he did then. Because, of course, he'd never been alive any other time I'd seen him. His brown eyes looked soft, the lashes around them dark as the shadows all through the loft. His lips – those strong, soft lips that hadn't kissed mine nearly as often as I'd have liked, and, in all likelihood, never would again – looked hypnotically appealing. I had to tear my gaze from them and keep it instead on a threadbare spot on the knee of my jeans.

'Because it's what I do,' I said, only something was happening in my throat, making the words come out more huskily than I'd intended them to.

I coughed.

'And you do this—' Jesse seemed to mean travel back through time to warn potential murder victims of their impending doom. ' – for all who die before their time?'

'Uh, not exactly,' I said. 'Yours is kind of . . . a special case.'

'And are all girls from your time,' Jesse went on, thoughtfully, apparently not noticing my discomfort or my fascination with his mouth, 'like you?'

'Like me? Like . . . that they're mediators?'

'No.' Jesse shook his head. 'Unafraid, like you. Brave, like you.'

I smiled a little ruefully. 'I'm not brave, Jesse,' I said.

'You're staying here,' he said, indicating the loft. 'Even though you know – or think you know – something terrible is going to happen.'

'Well, sure,' I said. 'Because that's the whole reason I came. To make sure it doesn't. Although, to be truthful . . .'

378

I threw a cautious glance at Paul, in case – and he probably was – he was listening. ' – really I came here to stop him. Paul, I mean. From stopping Diego. Because you see, if you don't die tonight, you and I – in the future, where I come from – will never meet. And I couldn't bear to let that happen. And you even – in the future – said you didn't want that to happen. Only . . . only . . . here I am, letting it happen. So you see, I'm not brave at all.'

I doubt he'd understood a word I'd said. It didn't matter, though. It was as close to an apology as the Jesse I had known and loved was going to get. And I felt I owed him one. An apology. For what I had done.

Which was destroy everything we'd had together.

'I think you're wrong,' Jesse said. About my not being brave.

But what did he know about any of it, really?

I just smiled at him.

Which is when I heard it.

379

Eighteen

Don't ask me how. I wasn't born with superhearing or anything. I just . . . heard it.

The scrape of the barn door.

And Jesse, over by the ladder, froze. He had heard it, too. A second later, I saw Paul sit up. He hadn't been sleeping. Not at all.

We waited in tense silence, each of us hardly daring to breathe.

Then I heard another scrape. This time, it was of a boot on a ladder rung.

Diego. It had to be. Diego was coming to kill Jesse.

Jesse must have sensed my unease, since he lifted a single hand toward me, palm out, in the universal signal for 'Stay'. He wanted Paul and me to leave Diego to him.

Yeah. Right.

And then I saw them – Diego's head and shoulders, looming massive and black against the lighter dark of the rest of the barn. His head was turned in the direction of Jesse's supine form – he didn't see anything else.

Slowly, obviously fearful of waking his prey, Diego climbed into the loft, his footfalls softened by all the hay. As he crept closer and closer – now he was five feet away . . . now four . . . now three – I leaned forward, ready to pounce.

I had no idea what I was going to do to stop him. He was not a small man, and I'm no black belt. But shifting definitely came to mind.

Paul had his hand on me now, though, holding on to the sleeve of my motorcycle jacket, keeping me back so that Jesse could have a chance at taking care of the problem himself. Funny how, in this one thing, Paul should be on Jesse's side, when he'd never taken Jesse's side on any other occasion.

One foot. Diego was now one foot from Jesse's supposedly sleeping form. He reached for something at his waist – his belt. I saw the gleam of his buckle . . . the same buckle that, in my own time, had somehow ended up in the attic . . .

Then, just as Diego had wrapped both ends of the belt around either fist and yanked the part in the middle taut, to use as a kind of garrote, Jesse's voice, cool and assured, cut through the silence.

In Spanish. He said something in Spanish.

Why? Why had I taken French and not Spanish?

Diego, caught totally off guard, stumbled back a step.

I couldn't stand it.

'What did he say?' I hissed at Paul.

Paul, not looking too happy about playing translator, said, 'He said, "So it IS true." Now shut up so I can hear.'

Diego recovered nicely, however. He didn't lower the hands that clutched the belt. Instead, he said something.

In *Spanish*.

This time, Paul didn't need any urging.

'He said, "So you know. Yes, it's true. I'm here to kill you."'

Jesse said something else. The only word I recognized was a name.

'He said, "Maria sent you?"'

381

Diego laughed. Then he nodded. Then he lunged.

I don't think I screamed. I know I sucked in a ton of air and was going to let it out in a shriek. But I found myself holding my breath instead. Because Jesse, instead of rolling out from under Diego, as I would have done, rose up to meet his assailant.

The two men teetered dangerously on the edge of the hayloft floor, just before the twelve-foot drop to the ground below. It was hard to see exactly what was happening in the semi-darkness, but one thing was certain: Diego had the advantage, weight-wise.

Now Paul and I were on our feet, completely unnoticed by the two men struggling at the edge of the loft. I tried to rush forward to help, but again Paul wouldn't let me.

'It's a fair fight,' he said to me.

But when, a second later, the two men broke apart, and Diego threw aside his belt with a chuckle, I saw that there was nothing fair about the fight at all. Because Diego had suddenly produced a knife. It gleamed wickedly in the light from the lantern, sitting on the loft floor a few feet away from them.

Now the air in my lungs came out in a rush. 'Jesse!' I shrieked. 'Knife!'

Diego whirled. 'Who's there?' he asked in English.

The distraction gave Jesse just enough time to pull from his boot his own knife . . . the one he'd used to cut me loose from Paul's ropes.

'OK, that's it,' I said when I saw this. 'Somebody's going to get—'

'That's what we want,' Paul said, keeping a firmer grip on me than ever. 'So long as it's the right guy.'

I couldn't understand what Paul was doing, what he was thinking. Jesse and Diego were circling each other warily

382

now, coming within inches with every other step of the loft ledge. We could stop it. We could stop it so easily. Why wasn't he—

Then it hit me. Was Paul on *Diego's* side? Was this whole thing some kind of weird setup? Had he really failed to find Diego during the day or had he only pretended to go and look for him, so he could have the pleasure of watching Jesse die later? Because that could be the only reason he'd have gone to these elaborate lengths – so that he could watch Jesse die—

I wrenched myself free of him.

'You want Jesse to die,' I shrieked at him. 'You want him to, don't you?'

Paul looked at me like I was nuts. 'Are you kidding? The whole reason I came back was to make sure he didn't.'

'Then why aren't you helping him?'

'I don't need—' Jesse ducked as Diego took a swing at him. '—any help!'

'Who are those people?' Diego snarled, lunging at Jesse again.

'No one,' Jesse said. 'Pay no attention to them. This is between you and me.'

'See?' Paul said to me, not without some self-righteousness. 'Would you chill?'

But how could I, when I was standing there watching my boyfriend – OK, well, he wasn't exactly my boyfriend, yet – in a struggle for his life? I stood there, my heart in my mouth, barely able to breathe, watching the flash of cold hard metal as the two men circled each other . . .

And then it happened. Diego suddenly reached behind him, and in a flash had grabbed hold of—

Me.

I was caught so off guard, I couldn't think. All I knew was

383

that one minute I was standing there next to Paul, barely able to watch what was happening, I was so scared . . .

. . . and the next, I was in the middle of it, an arm crushing my throat as Diego held me in front of him, the tip of his silver blade at my neck.

'Drop the knife,' he said to Jesse. He was standing so close to me, I could feel his voice reverberating through his body. 'Or the girl dies.'

I saw Jesse blanch. But he never hesitated. He dropped his knife.

Paul screamed, 'Suze! Shift!'

It took me a second to realize what he meant. Diego was touching me. Diego was touching me. All I had to do was picture that hallway I hated so much – that way station between existences – and he and I would both be transported there . . .

. . . and we'd be rid of him forever.

But before I could so much as close my eyes, Diego threw me away from him and lunged at Jesse. I tried to scream as I fell, but my throat was so sore from the force with which he'd held me, nothing came out.

I didn't fall from the loft, however. Instead, I fell against something metal – and glass. Something that broke beneath my weight. Something that soaked the straw beneath me.

Something that burst into flames.

The lantern. I'd fallen on the lantern, and broken it. And set the hay on fire.

The flames broke out more quickly than I ever could have imagined they would. Suddenly, I was separated from the others by a wall of orange. I could see them standing on the other side, Paul staring at me in dumb horror, while Jesse and Diego—

384

Well, Jesse was trying to keep Diego from plunging a knife into his heart.

'Paul,' I shrieked. 'Help him! Help Jesse!'

But Paul just stood there looking at me for some reason. It was Jesse who finally broke Diego's grip on him. Jesse who twisted the arm that held the knife until Diego, with a cry of pain, let go of it. And Jesse who hauled off and struck Diego with a blow to the face that sent him reeling—

Right over the ledge.

I heard his body hit the barn floor, heard the unmistakable snap of breaking bones . . . breaking neck bones.

The horses heard it as well. They whinnied shrilly and kicked at the doors to their stalls. They could smell the smoke.

So, I realized, could the O'Neils. I heard shouts coming from outside the barn.

'You did it,' I cried, gazing at a panting Jesse through the smoke and fire. 'You killed him!'

'Suze.' Paul was still staring at me. 'Suze.'

'He did it, Paul!' I couldn't believe it. 'He's going to live.' To Jesse, I said, joyfully, 'You're going to live!'

Jesse didn't look too happy about it, though. He said, 'Susannah. Stay where you are.'

Then I saw what he meant. The fire had completely cut me off from the rest of the loft. Even from the ledge. I was cornered by flames. And smoke. Smoke that was getting so thick, I could barely see them.

No wonder Paul had been staring at me. I was caught in a fire trap.

'Suze,' Paul said. But his voice sounded faint. Then he cried, 'Jesse, no—'

But it was too late. Because the next thing I knew, a large object hurtled at me through the smoke and flame – hit me, as a matter of fact, and knocked me to the ground. It took me a second to realize the object was Jesse and that he'd wrapped himself in the horse blanket I'd slept under the night before . . .

A horse blanket that was now smoldering.

'Come on,' Jesse said, throwing down the blanket, then grabbing my hand and pulling me back to my feet. 'We haven't much time.'

'Suze!' I heard Paul yelling. I could no longer see him, the smoke was so thick.

'Get down,' Jesse yelled to Paul. 'Get down and help them with the horses.'

But Paul didn't appear to be listening.

'Suze,' he yelled. 'Shift! Do it now! It's your only chance!'

Jesse had turned and was kicking at the planks that made up the closest wall. The boards shuddered under the assault.

Shift? My mind seemed to be working only murkily, maybe due to all the smoke. But it didn't seem like I could shift just then. What about Jesse? I couldn't leave Jesse. I hadn't gone to all this trouble to save him from Diego just to have him die in a barn fire.

'Suze,' Paul yelled once more. 'Shift! I'm doing it, too. I'll meet you on the other side!'

Other side? What was he talking about? Was he insane?

Oh, right. He was Paul. Of course he was insane.

I heard a crash. Then Jesse was taking my hand.

'We're going to have to jump,' he said, his face very close to mine.

I felt something cool lick my face. Air. Fresh air. I turned my head and saw that Jesse had kicked out enough boards in the barn wall for a person to squeeze through. It was dark through that hole. But lifting my face a little to better feel the deliciously cool breeze, I saw stars in the night sky.

386

'Do you understand me, Susannah?' Jesse's face was very close to mine. Close enough to kiss me. Why didn't he kiss me? 'We'll jump together, on the count of three.'

I felt him reach out and grab me by the waist, bringing me close to him. Well, that was better. Much better for kissing—

'One . . .'

I could feel his heart drumming hard against mine. Only how was that possible? Jesse's heart had stopped beating 150 years ago.

'Two . . .'

Hot flames were licking my heels. I was so hot. Why didn't he hurry up and kiss me already?

'Three . . .'

And then we were flying through the air. Not because he was kissing me, I realized. No, because we were really flying through the air.

And as if the fresh cool wind had cleared the smoke from my brain, I realized what was happening. Jesse and I were hurtling toward the ground, which looked extremely far away.

And so I did the only thing I could. I clung to him, closed my eyes and thought of home.

Nineteen

I landed with such force, all the wind was knocked out of me. It was like being hit in the back with a railroad tie – which has actually happened to me before, so I would know. I lay there, completely stunned, unable to breathe, unable to move, unable to do anything but be aware of the pain.

Then, slowly, consciousness returned. I could move my legs. This was a good sign. I could move my arms. Also good. Breathing returned – painfully, but there, none the less.

Then I heard it.

Crickets.

Not the shrieks of horses as they protested being dragged from their burning stalls. Not the roaring of fire all around me. Not even my own labored breathing.

But crickets, chirping away like they had nothing better to do.

I opened my eyes.

And instead of smoke and fire and burning barn, all I saw were stars, hundreds of them, glowing coldly millions of miles away.

I turned my head.

And saw my house.

Not Mrs O'Neil's boarding house, either. But my house. I

was in the backyard. I could see the deck Andy had built. Someone had left the lights on in the hot tub.

Home. I was home.

And I was alive. Barely, but alive.

And I was not alone. Suddenly, someone was kneeling beside me, blocking my view of the hot tub lights, and saying my name.

'Suze? Suze, are you all right?'

Paul was tugging on me, pushing me in places that hurt. I tried to slap his hands away, but he just kept doing it until finally I said, 'Paul, quit it!'

'You're OK.' He sank down into the grass beside me. His face in the moonlight looked pale. And relieved. 'Thank God. You weren't moving before.'

'I'm fine,' I said.

Then remembered that I wasn't. Because . . . Jesse . . . I had lost Jesse. We had saved him, so that I could lose him forever. Pain – much worse pain than I'd felt during my landing on the cold hard ground – gripped me like a vise.

Jesse. He was gone. Gone for good . . .

Except . . .

Except if that were true, why did I remember him?

I rose up on to my elbows, ignoring the jolt of pain that rose from my ribs when I did so.

That's when I saw him. He was lying on his stomach in the grass a few feet away, totally unmoving, totally not . . .

Glowing.

He wasn't glowing.

I looked at Paul. He blinked back at me.

'I don't know,' he said as if the words had been wrung from him. 'All right, Suze? I don't know how it happened. You were both here when I showed up just now. I don't know how it happened—'

389

And then I was on my hands and knees, crawling through the wet grass toward him. I think I was crying. I don't know for sure. All I know was, it was hard to see all of a sudden.

'Jesse!' I reached his side.

It was him. It was really him. The real Jesse, Alive Jesse.

Only he didn't seem too alive just then. I reached out and felt for a pulse on his throat. There was one – my breath caught as I felt it – but it was faint. He was breathing, but barely. I was afraid to touch him, afraid to move him . . .

But more afraid not to.

'Jesse!' I cried, rolling him over and shaking him by the shoulders. 'Jesse, it's me, Suze! Wake up. Wake up, Jesse!'

'It's no good, Suze,' Paul said. 'I already tried. He's there . . . but he's not. Not really.'

I had Jesse's head in my arms. I cradled it, looking down at him. In the moonlight, he looked dead.

But he wasn't. He wasn't dead. I'd have known if he was.

'I think we screwed up, Suze,' Paul said. 'You weren't – you weren't supposed to bring him back.'

'I didn't mean to,' I said. My voice was so faint, it was practically drowned out by the crickets. 'I didn't do it on purpose.'

'I know,' Paul said. 'But . . . I think maybe you need to put him back.'

'Put him back where?' I raged. Now my voice was much louder than the crickets. So loud, in fact, that the crickets were startled into silence. 'In the middle of that fire?'

'No,' Paul said. 'I just – I just don't think he can stay here, Suze, and . . . live.'

I continued to cradle Jesse's head, thinking furiously. This wasn't fair. No one had warned us about this. Dr Slaski hadn't said a word. All he'd said was to picture in your head the time and place you wanted to be in, and . . .

390

And not to touch anything you didn't want to bring through time with you.

I groaned and dropped my face to Jesse's. It was my fault. It was all my fault.

'Suze.' Paul reached out and rested a hand on my shoulder. 'Let me try. Maybe I can get him back—'

'You can't.' I lifted my head, my voice cold as the blade Diego had pressed to my throat. 'It'll kill him. He's not like us. He's not a mediator. He's . . . he's human.'

Paul shook his head. 'Maybe he was meant to die, then, Suze,' he said. 'Like you said. Maybe we aren't supposed to mess with this stuff, just like you warned me.'

'Great.' I let out a bitter little laugh. 'That's just great, Paul. *Now* you agree with me?'

Paul just stood there, looking anxious. If I could have been capable of feeling anything except despair, at that point, I would have hated him.

But I couldn't. I couldn't hate him. I couldn't think of anything but Jesse. I had not, I told myself, saved him just so I could sit and watch him die.

'Go to the carport,' I said in a low, even voice. 'And inside the house through the door there. They never remember to lock it. Hanging on a hook by the door are my mom's car keys. Get them and then come back and help me take him to the car.'

Paul looked down at me like I was a crazy woman.

'The car?' He sounded dubious. 'You're going to . . . drive him somewhere?'

'Yes, you fool,' I snarled. 'To the hospital.'

'The hospital.' Paul shook his head. 'But Suze—'

'Just do it!'

Paul did it. I know he thought it was futile, but he did it. He got the keys, then came back and helped me carry Jesse

391

to my mom's car. It wasn't easy, but between the two of us, we managed. I'd have dragged him the whole way by myself if I'd had to.

Then we were on the road, Paul driving while I continued to hold Jesse's head in my arms. I didn't think then that what I was doing was futile. Maybe, I kept thinking, the hospital could save him. Medicine had made so many advances in the past 150 years. Why couldn't it save a man who'd just traveled to another time, through another dimension? Why couldn't it?

Except that it couldn't.

Oh, they tried. At the hospital. They came running out with a gurney when Paul went in to tell them we had an unconscious man in the car. They hooked Jesse up to an oxygen mask while the emergency room doctor grilled me. Had he taken drugs? Had too much to drink? Had a seizure? A headache? Complained of pain in his arm?

There was no medical explanation for the coma Jesse was in. That's what the doctor came out and told me, hours later. None that he had been able to determine so far. A CT scan might tell him more. Did I happen to know what kind of insurance Jesse had? His Social Security number, maybe? A phone number for his next of kin?

At 6:00 in the morning, they admitted him. At 7:00, I called my mother, and told her where I was – at the hospital with a friend. At 8:00, I phoned the only person I could think of who might possibly have some idea what to do.

Father Dominic had gotten back from San Francisco the night before. He listened to what I had to say without remark. 'Father Dominic, I did . . . I think I did something awful. I didn't mean to, but . . . Jesse's here. The real Jesse. The live one. We're at the hospital. Please come.'

He came. When I saw his tall, strong figure approaching

392

the hard plastic seat I'd been sitting in for hours, I nearly collapsed all over again.

But I didn't. I stood up and, a second later, was in his arms.

'What did you do?' he kept murmuring over and over. He wasn't talking to just me, either. Paul was there, too. 'What did you two do?'

'Something bad,' I said, lifting my tear-stained face from his shirt. 'But we didn't mean it.'

'We were trying to save him,' Paul said sheepishly. 'His life. We almost did—'

'Until I brought him back,' I said. 'Oh, Father Dominic—'

He shushed me and went into the room where Jesse lay, so still, the blanket over him barely stirring with each shallow breath. Ghost Jesse, I now realized, would have looked better – more alive – than Alive Jesse did.

Father Dominic crossed himself, he was so startled by what he saw. A nurse was there, taking Jesse's pulse and writing the results down on a clipboard. She smiled sadly when she saw Father Dominic, then left the room.

Father Dominic looked down at Jesse. For the first time, I noticed that the lenses of his glasses were kind of fogged up.

He didn't say anything.

'They want to know what kind of insurance he has,' I said bitterly, 'before they do more tests.'

'I . . . see,' Father Dominic said.

'I don't see what more tests are going to tell them,' Paul said.

'You don't know,' I snapped, lashing out at Paul because I couldn't lash out at the person who most deserved it . . . myself. 'Maybe there's something they can do. Maybe there's—'

'Isn't your grandfather here somewhere?' Father Dominic asked Paul.

Paul lifted his gaze from Jesse's unconscious form.

'Yeah,' he said. 'I mean, yes, sir. I think so.'

'Perhaps you should go and pay him a visit.' Father Dominic's voice was calm. His presence, I had to admit, was soothing. 'If he's conscious, perhaps he'll be able to offer us some advice.'

Paul's chin slid out truculently. 'He won't talk to me,' Paul insisted. 'Even if he *is* awake—'

'I think,' Father Dominic said quietly, 'that if there is a lesson to be learned from all of this, it's that life is fleeting and if there are fences to mend, you had best mend them quickly, before it's too late. Go and make amends with your grandfather.'

Paul opened his mouth to protest, but Father Dominic shot him a look that snapped his lips shut. With one final glance at me, Paul left the room, looking aggrieved.

'Don't be too angry with him, Susannah,' Father Dominic said. 'He thought he was doing right.'

I was too tired to argue. Much.

'He thought he was robbing me of Jesse,' I said. 'Even his memory.'

Father Dominic shrugged. 'In the end, Susannah, that might actually have been kinder, don't you think? Kinder than this, anyway.' He nodded his head at Jesse's unconscious form.

Well, that much was true.

'He would have had to leave, anyway, Susannah,' Father Dominic said. 'Some day.'

'I know.' The knot in my throat throbbed.

Which was when I remembered. There'd been a ghost in

394

Father Dom's life, as well. The ghost of a girl he'd loved, maybe even as much as I loved Jesse.

'I . . .' I could barely speak, the lump in my throat had swelled to such gigantic proportions. 'I'm sorry, Father Dominic. I forgot.'

Father Dom just smiled sadly and touched my arm.

'Don't be too hard on him,' he said, meaning Paul. Then, with a final glance at Jesse, he said, 'There isn't much I can think of to do. But the insurance situation. That I think I can take care of. I'll be back soon. Can I bring you anything? Have you eaten?'

The thought of trying to swallow anything down past the mass in my throat was so ludicrous, I actually laughed a little.

'No, thanks,' I said.

'All right.' Father Dominic started from the room. At the doorway, however, he paused and looked back.

'I'm sorry, Susannah,' he said quietly. 'I'm sorry I wasn't there for you when . . . it happened. And I'm more sorry than I can say that it had to end this way.'

And with that, he was gone.

I stood there for a moment, not doing anything, not thinking a thing. Then the true meaning of his words sunk in.

And I lost it.

Because Father Dominic was right. This *was* the end. I could deny it as much as I wanted, but this was it. Jesse was dying, right before my eyes, and there was nothing, nothing on earth, that I could do for him.

And it was *my* fault. My own fault he was leaving me. Sure, I could comfort myself that wherever he was, it had to be better than the half-life he'd had with me.

But that didn't make it hurt any less.

I fell into the chair beside Jesse's hospital bed. I couldn't see, I was crying so hard. Not out loud. I didn't want any nurse to come running with a bunch of tranquilizers or anything. What I really wanted, I realized, was my mom. No, not my mom. My dad. Where was my dad now, when I really needed him?

'Susannah.'

I thought about Jesse's grave, the one marked by the headstone Father Dominic and I had paid for. What was in that grave now, if Jesse's body was here? Nothing. It was empty.

But not for long. No, not for long.

'Susannah.'

And back in his own time? What were Mr and Mrs O'Neil doing right now? Probably combing through the rubble of what had been their barn. They'd find one skeleton for sure. But would they know it wasn't Jesse's? Would Jesse's family have closure or would they wonder forever what had happened to their beloved son and brother?

No. They had no way of knowing the body was Diego's. They'd think it was Jesse. The de Silvas would have a funeral. But for the wrong man.

I felt a hand on my shoulder. Great. Someone was there. Someone was watching me cry my eyes out. Nice. Let the girl have a little time to grieve, would you, please?

'Go away,' I snapped, lifting my head. 'Can't you see I'm—'

That's when I noticed that the figure beside me was glowing.

396

Twenty

I must have jumped about a mile and a half into the air, I was that startled. I know I sprang from the chair, so fast that I knocked it over. I stood there, my chest heaving, my eyes suddenly bone dry, and stared.

Because standing there beside the bed, looking down at Jesse's prone body, was . . .

Jesse.

I looked from one Jesse to the other, not quite believing what I was seeing.

But it was true. There were two Jesses, the dead one and the live one.

Or, I suppose it would have been more correct to say the dead one and the dying one.

'J-Jesse?' I swiped at the tears coating my cheeks with the back of my smoky sleeve.

But Jesse wasn't looking at me. He was staring down at . . . well, at himself, on the bed.

'Susannah,' he whispered. 'What . . . what did you do?'

I was so overjoyed to see him, I wasn't thinking straight. I went to him and grabbed his hand.

'Jesse, I went. Back through time, I mean,' I babbled.

He tore his gaze from the figure on the bed and focused all of that intense dark gaze on me. He didn't look too happy.

397

'You *went?*' He glared at me. 'You went after Slater? After I told you I could take care of myself?'

He was furious. I was so happy to see that fury, however, that I let out a little burble of laughter. I didn't realize, then, what seeing him here in the hospital meant.

'You did take care of yourself,' I assured him. 'I-I told you – the past you – about Diego, and he didn't kill you, Jesse. You killed him. But then . . . then . . . there was a fire.' I swallowed, not feeling like laughing any more. 'In the barn. The O'Neils' barn . . .'

His eyes narrowed.

'The O'Neils,' he murmured. He appeared to be in as much of a daze as I was. 'I remember them.'

'Yes,' I said. 'There was a fire, and Jesse . . . Jesse, you saved me. Or, at least, you tried to. But . . . but . . .'

My voice trailed off. Jesse had dropped my hand. He was moving closer to the bed, looking down at the body that lay there, barely breathing.

'I don't understand,' Jesse said. 'How did this happen?'

I bit my lip. There was no time for explanations. Not when, any minute, I knew we were going to have to be saying goodbye . . .

'I did it,' I blurted. 'I didn't mean to. I meant to save you, Jesse, not . . . not this. But I was still touching you when I shifted back to the future, and you . . . you just got caught.'

Jesse finally looked at me like he was really seeing me, maybe for the first time since he'd come into the room.

'You really went back?' He stared at me. 'To the past? My past?'

I nodded. What was there to say?

He shook his head. 'And Paul? I went to the basilica to look for him, but he was gone. You followed him?'

I nodded again.

398

'I wanted to stop him,' I said. 'From . . . from keeping you from dying. But in the end . . . I couldn't, Jesse. It wasn't right. What Diego did to you. I couldn't let it happen again. So I told you. And you killed him. You killed Diego. But then there was the fire and . . . ' I looked down at the figure in the bed. I couldn't stifle a sob. 'And now I think this is goodbye. I'm sorry, Jesse. I'm so, so sorry.'

My vision clouded over again with tears. I couldn't believe any of this was happening. I had always thought of my 'gift' as a curse, but never, never had I hated it as much as I did just then. I wished I had never heard of mediators. I wished I had never seen a single ghost. I wished I had never been born.

Then I felt Jesse's hand on my cheek.

'*Querida,*' he said.

He placed his other hand on the bed to balance himself as he leaned across it to kiss me. One last kiss before he was ripped from me forever. I closed my eyes, anticipating the feel of those cool lips against mine. *Goodbye, Jesse. Goodbye.*

His mouth had barely touched mine, however, when I heard him gasp. He jerked his head from mine and looked down.

His hand had touched his living body's leg.

Something seemed to jolt through him, then. He flared more brightly for a second, his gaze on mine more intense than it had ever been in all the time I'd known him.

And then he was sucked down into his body, like smoke pulled into a fan.

And was gone.

Oh, his body was still there. But the ghost of Jesse – the ghost I had loved – was gone. In his place was . . .

Nothing. I reached out, desperate to grab some small piece of him, but my hand clutched only air.

399

Jesse was gone. He was truly gone. He was back inside the body he'd left so long ago . . . the body that, even as I watched, shuddered all over as if to reject the soul that had just entered it . . .

Then went still as death.

I knew then what had happened. Jesse's body had come forward through time, yes. But not his soul, because two of the same souls could not exist in the same dimension. Jesse's body had been without a soul just as, for so many years, Jesse's soul had been without a body.

Now the two were united at last . . .

But too late. And now I was going to lose them both.

I don't know how long I must have stood there, holding Jesse's hand, gazing down at him in utter despair. Long enough, I know, that Father Dominic came back, and said, 'Don't worry, Susannah, it's all taken care of. Jesse will get the tests he needs.'

'It doesn't matter,' I murmured, still holding his hand . . . his cold hand.

'Don't give up hope, Susannah,' Father Dominic said. 'Never give up hope.'

I let out a bitter laugh. 'And why is that, Father D?'

'Because it's all we have, you know.' He placed a hand on my shoulder. 'You did what you did because you loved him, Susannah. You loved him enough to let him go. There's no greater gift you could have given him.'

I shook my head, my vision still blurred with tears.

'That's not how it's supposed to go, Father Dominic.'

'What's not, Susannah?' he asked gently.

'The saying. It's supposed to be, If you love something, set it free. If it was meant to be, it will come back to you. Don't you know? Haven't you read it?'

When I looked up at Father Dominic to see what he

400

thought of this, I saw that he wasn't even looking at me. He was staring down at Jesse on the bed. Father Dominic's blue eyes, I noticed, were as tear-filled as my own.

'Susannah,' he said in a strangled voice. 'Look.'

I looked. And as I moved my head, felt the fingers of the hand I was holding suddenly tighten around mine.

Colour that hadn't been there a minute before had flooded Jesse's face. His face was no longer the same colour as the sheets. His skin was the same olive tone it had been when I'd first seen him, back in the O'Neils' barn.

And that wasn't all. His chest was rising and falling visibly now beneath the blanket that covered him. A pulse thrummed visibly in his neck.

And, as I stood there, staring down at him, his eyelids lifted . . .

. . . and I was falling, as hard as I did every time he looked at me, into the deep dark pools that were Jesse's eyes . . . eyes that weren't just seeing me, but knew me. Knew my soul.

He lifted the hand I wasn't clutching, plucked aside the oxygen mask that had been covering his nose and mouth, and said just one word.

But it was a word that set my heart singing.

'*Querida.*'

Twenty-one

'Suze!'

I heard my mother's voice calling from downstairs. 'Suze!'

I was sitting at my dressing table, admiring my blowout. CeeCee and I had spent the afternoon getting our hair and nails done. CeeCee hadn't needed a blowout . . . her white-blonde hair is straight on its own. But she'd gotten an updo, then fretted all afternoon that it wouldn't hold.

My blowout, however, apparently had staying power, because my hair looked as dark and shimmery as it had when I'd stepped from the salon.

'Suze!' my mom called a third and final time.

I glanced at the clock. I'd made him wait nearly five minutes. That seemed long enough.

'Coming,' I yelled and grabbed my evening bag and the filmy white stole that went with my dress.

I went to my bedroom door and threw it open. Coming up the stairs as I was about to head down them was Jake, carrying a heavy backpack filled with books. From the library.

'Has hell frozen over?' I asked him as he went by me on his way to his room.

'Don't start with me, I've got finals,' he growled. Then,

402

just as he got to the door of his room, he turned and, with all apparent sincerity, said, 'Nice dress,' and disappeared into the confines of his bachelor cave.

I couldn't help smiling. It was the first compliment I'd ever managed to wring from Jake.

I started down the stairs, one hand lifting the hem of my gown. They were the exact same stairs, I realized, as the ones Mrs O'Neil had chased me down about, oh, 150-something years ago. I wondered if, in my current ensemble, she'd have mistaken me for a hoochie mama. Somehow, I doubted it.

It's nice, I thought, that we have stairs like this. Stairs a girl can really make an entrance on. I got to the last landing, the one that basically served as a stage for girls who were going to their first Winter Formal to pivot and show off their dress to the people waiting in the living room, and paused, preparing to do just that.

But it was no use. I saw that at once. My stepfather was running around with a spoon filled with something green, urging everyone he encountered to taste it, just taste it. My mom was trying to figure out how her new digital camera worked and not doing the world's best job at it. My youngest stepbrother, David, was talking a mile a minute to my date about some new advances in aeronautics he'd seen on the Discovery Channel.

And Max, the family dog, had his nose buried in the front of my date's tuxedo pants.

I guess it was a pretty typical familial scene, one that I'm sure occurs in millions of homes every night.

So why did tears spring to my eyes at the sight of it?

Oh, not at Andy and his spoon, or my mom and her camera, or David and his complete conviction that anyone wanted to hear the entire transcript of the show he'd watched.

403

No, it was the fact that the family dog kept thrusting his nose into inappropriate places on my date, and that my date had to keep shoving Max away, that made the tears well up.

Because Max could smell my date. Max could finally smell Jesse.

David noticed me standing there on the landing first. His voice trailed off and he dried up, and just stood there staring. After a minute, everyone was staring.

I hastily blinked my tears away. Especially when Max rushed over and tried to thrust his big furry head beneath my skirt.

'Oh, Susie,' my mom cooed and to everyone's surprise – especially her own – managed to snap a picture. 'You look beautiful.'

Andy, spying another victim, raised his spoon toward me, but my mother cut him off at the pass.

'Andy, don't you go near her with that stuff while she's in that dress,' she warned.

That made me smile. When I looked at Jesse, I saw he was smiling, too. A secret smile, just for me – even though now, of course, everyone else could see it, too.

It still took my breath away, same as ever.

'So,' I said as casually as I could with a giant lump in my throat. But this one was from joy. 'I see you've met Jesse.'

Andy summed up their introduction in two words before heading back to the kitchen with his spoon. 'He'll do.'

My mother was beaming. 'So nice to meet you,' she said to Jesse. 'Now come down here, I want to get your picture together.'

I came down the rest of the stairs and went to stand by Jesse's side in front of the fireplace. He looked so tall and handsome in his tux, I could hardly stand it. I didn't even care that my mother was completely mortifying me in front

404

of him. I guess those kind of things don't really matter when you nearly lose your reason for living, then get it back again, against all odds.

'This is for you,' Jesse said when I came close enough. He handed me something he'd been holding. It was a single white orchid, the kind you usually only see at funerals. Or on graves.

I took it from him with a wry smile. Only he and I realized the flower's significance. To my mother, who came rushing over to pin it to my dress before she took the picture, it was just a corsage.

'Now, say cheese,' she said and took the picture, thankfully without actually making us say it.

Andy re-emerged from the kitchen, this time without his spoon, and started looking parental.

'Now, you have her home by midnight, understand, young man?' he said, clearly enjoying being father to a girl instead of a boy for a change.

'I will, sir,' Jesse replied.

'One,' I said to Andy.

'Twelve thirty,' Andy countered.

'Twelve thirty,' I agreed. I'd only argued because, well, that's what you do. It didn't really matter what time Jesse had to bring me home by. Not when we had our whole lives together ahead of us.

'Suze,' my mom whispered as she fussed with my shawl, 'we like him, don't get us wrong. But isn't he a little, well, old for you? After all, he's in college – Jake's age.'

If only she knew.

'That makes us about even,' I assured her. 'Girls mature faster than boys.'

Brad chose that moment to come barrelling in from the TV room, where he'd been playing video games. When he

405

saw we were still in the doorway, his face twisted with annoyance.

'Haven't you guys left yet?' he demanded and stormed back into the kitchen.

I looked at my mother.

'I see what you mean,' she said and patted me on the back. 'Have a nice time.'

Outside in the crisp evening air, Jesse looked over his shoulder to make sure my parents weren't watching. Then he took my hand.

'Between doing that again and an eternity in hellfire,' he said, 'I'd take the hellfire.'

'Well, you'll never have to do it again,' I said with a laugh. 'Now that they know you. And besides, they liked you.'

'Your mother didn't,' Jesse assured me.

'Yes, she did,' I said. 'She just thinks you're a little old for me.'

'If only she knew,' Jesse said, voicing, as he so often did, exactly what I'd been thinking.

'Your stepfather, on the other hand, invited me to dinner tomorrow night.'

'Sunday dinner?' I was impressed. 'He really *must* like you.'

We'd reached Jesse's car – well, really, it was Father Dom's car. But Father D was letting Jesse borrow it for the occasion. Not, of course, that Jesse had a licence. Father Dom was still working on getting him a birth certificate . . . and a Social Security card . . . and school reports, so he could start applying for colleges and for student loans.

But, the good father had assured us, it wouldn't be hard. 'The church,' he'd said, 'has ways.'

'Madam,' Jesse said, opening the front passenger door for me.

406

'Why, thank you,' I said, and slid in.

Jesse went around to the driver's seat, slid into it, then reached for the ignition.

'You're sure you know how to drive one of these things?' I asked him, just to make sure.

'Susannah.' Jesse started the engine. 'I did not sit idly by eating bonbons for the 150 years I was a ghost. I did make a few observations now and then. And I most definitely know—' He started backing the car out of the driveway. '—how to drive.'

'OK. Just checking. Because I could always take over if you need—'

'You will sit where you are,' Jesse said, turning on to Pine Crest Road without nearly hitting the mailbox, which was something even I, a driver with an actual licence, rarely managed to do, 'and look pretty, as a young lady ought to.'

'Wait, which century is this?'

'Humour me,' he said, looking pained. 'I'm doing it for you, in this monkey suit.'

'Penguin.'

'Susannah.'

'I'm just saying. That's what it's called. You need to get hip with the lingo if you're going to fit in.'

'Whatever,' Jesse said in such a perfect imitation of – well, me – that I was forced to mock punch him in the arm.

I sat and looked pretty for the entire rest of the two-mile ride to the Mission. When we got there, I even waited and let him come around to open the car door for me. Jesse thanked me, mentioning that his male ego had taken enough blows over the past week.

I knew what he meant and didn't blame him a bit for feeling that way. He had basically walked out of the Carmel Hospital a man newly born, without a past, at least, not one

407

that was going to help him in this century, without family – except for me, of course, and Father Dominic – and without a cent to his name. If it hadn't been for Father Dominic, in fact, who knew what might have happened? Oh, I suppose my mom and Andy might have let him move in with us . . .

But they wouldn't have been wild about it. Instead Father Dominic had found Jesse a small – but clean and nice – apartment, and he was looking into a job. College would come later, after Jesse had studied for and taken the SATs.

But when we ran into Father D at the entrance to the dance – it was being held in the Mission courtyard, which had been transformed for the occasion into a moonlit oasis, complete with white fairy lights twisted around every palm tree and multicolored gels over the lights in the fountain – he pretended he and Jesse were meeting for the first time, for the sake of Sister Ernestine, who was standing nearby.

'Very nice to meet you,' Father Dominic said, shaking Jesse's hand.

Jesse was unable to keep a smile from his face. 'Same with you, Father,' he said.

After Sister Ernestine left with a sniff at my dress – I suppose she'd been waiting for me to show up in something slit to my navel, not the very demure white Jessica McClintock number I was wearing instead – Father Dominic dropped the pretence and said to Jesse, 'I have good news. The job's come through.'

Jesse looked excited. 'Really? What is it? When do I start?'

'Monday morning, and though the pay won't be much, it's something I think you'll be unusually well-suited for –

giving talks about old Carmel at the Historical Society Museum. Do you think you can stand to do that for a while? Until we can get you into medical school, anyway?'

Jesse's grin seemed – to me, anyway – even more brilliant than the moon.

'I think so,' he said.

'Excellent.' Father Dominic pushed his glasses up his nose and smiled at us. 'Have a nice evening, children.'

Jesse and I assured him we would, then went into the dance.

It wasn't any mid-nineteenth-century ball or anything, but it was still very nice. There were punch and cookies and chaperones. And OK, there was also a DJ and a smoke machine, but whatever. Jesse seemed to be enjoying himself, especially when CeeCee and Adam came up to us, and he was able to shake both their hands and say, 'I've heard a lot about you both.'

Adam, who'd had no idea about Jesse's existence, scowled.

'Can't say I can return the compliment,' he said.

But CeeCee, who'd turned pale as her dress when she heard me say Jesse's name, was more friendly. Or at least enthusiastic.

'B-but,' she stammered, looking from Jesse's face to mine and then back again, 'are – aren't you—'

'Not any more,' I said to her and, though she still looked confused, she smiled.

'Well,' she said. Then, more loudly, 'Well! That's wonderful!'

That's when I noticed her aunt standing nearby, chatting with Mr Walden.

'What's she doing here?' I asked CeeCee.

Adam laughed and, before CeeCee could say a word,

409

explained, 'Mr Walden's chaperoning. And guess who he brought as his date?'

'They aren't dating,' CeeCee insisted. 'They're just friends.'

'Right,' Adam said with a grin.

'Suze.' CeeCee pulled her lace shawl more tightly over her bare shoulders. 'Come to the ladies' room with me?'

'I'll be right back,' I said to Jesse.

'How—' CeeCee began as soon as she'd dragged me into the ladies.

But she couldn't get out anything more than that, because a bunch of giggling freshmen came in and crowded around the mirror over the sink, checking their hair.

'I'll tell you some day,' I said to her with a laugh.

CeeCee screwed up her face. 'Promise?'

'If you'll tell me how it's going with Adam.'

CeeCee sighed and checked out her own reflection. 'Dreamy,' she said. Then looked at me. 'It is for you, too. I can tell by your face.'

'Dreamy's a good word for it,' I said.

'I thought so. Well, come on. No telling what Adam might be saying to him.'

We turned to leave just as the bathroom door swung open, and Kelly Prescott came in. She shot me a supremely dirty look, which I didn't understand until she was followed by Sister Ernestine, who had a measuring tape in her hand. That's when I saw the slit in Kelly's designer gown. It was much higher than the regulation knee-length.

CeeCee and I slipped past the nun and fell giggling into the breezeway.

At least, I was giggling until I saw Paul.

He was standing in the shadows, looking coolly handsome in his tuxedo. He was obviously waiting for Kelly to

410

emerge with her slit adjusted. He straightened when he saw me.

'Uh, tell Jesse I'll be right there, will you, Cee?' I said.

CeeCee nodded and went back to the dance. I walked up to where Paul was leaning against one of the stone pillars, and said, 'Hi.'

Paul took his hands from his pockets. 'Hi,' he said.

Then neither of us seemed to be able to think of anything to say.

Finally, Paul said, 'I ran into Jesse out there.'

I raised my eyebrows. 'I ran into Kelly in there.'

'Yeah,' Paul said, flicking a glance at the door to the ladies' room. Then he said, 'I . . . my grandfather asked about you.'

'Really?' I had heard Dr Slaski had come home from the hospital. 'Is he—'

'He's better,' Paul said. 'A lot better. And . . . and you were right about him. He isn't crazy. Well, he is, but not in the way I thought. He actually knows a lot of stuff about . . . people like us.'

'Yeah,' I said. 'Well, tell him I said hi.'

'I will.' Paul looked incredibly uncomfortable. I couldn't blame him, really. It was the first time we'd been alone together since the fire . . . and the hospital. I'd seen him in school the following week, but he'd seemed to do everything possible to avoid me. Now he looked very much like he'd have liked to run away.

But he didn't. Because it turned out he still had something to say.

'Suze. About . . . what happened.'

I smiled at him. 'It's all right, Paul,' I said. 'I already know.'

He looked confused. 'Know? About what?'

411

'About the money,' I said. 'The two thousand dollars you donated anonymously to the church's neediest fund, specially earmarked for the Gutierrezes. They got it and, according to Father Dominic, they were deeply grateful.'

'Oh,' Paul said. And he actually blushed. 'Yeah. That. That's not what I meant. What I meant is . . . you . . . you were right.'

I blinked at him. 'I was? About what?'

'My grandfather.' He cleared his throat. I could tell how much it was costing him to admit this. I could also tell, however, that he needed to say it, very badly. 'Well, not just about my grandfather, but about . . . well, everything.'

I raised my eyebrows. This was more than I'd ever dared hope for.

'Everything?' I echoed, hoping he meant what I thought he meant.

He seemed to. 'Yeah. Everything.'

'Even about' – I had to be sure – 'you and me?'

He nodded, but not very happily.

'I should have known it all along,' he said slowly, as if the words were being forced out of him by some unseen force. 'How you felt about him, I mean. You told me enough times. But it didn't . . . it didn't really hit me until that night in the barn, when you . . . you told him. Why we were there. The fact that you'd have rather let him live—'

'We don't need to talk about this,' I said, because just thinking about that night made my chest feel tight. 'Really.'

'No,' Paul said, his blue-eyed gaze boring into me. 'You don't understand. I've got to. I've never – Suze, I've never felt that way about anybody. Not even you. Which you, uh, probably noticed. When I didn't exactly come to your rescue. During the fire and all.'

'But you were great afterward,' I said, sticking up for him,

412

because I felt like somebody should. 'Helping me get Jesse to the hospital and all.'

He shrugged miserably. 'That was nothing. What Jesse did – jumping through those flames – and he barely even knew you—'

'It's all right, Paul,' I said. 'Really.'

He didn't look convinced. 'Really?'

'Really,' I said, meaning it. Then I nodded toward the ladies' room door. 'Besides, I always thought you two are much better suited, anyway.'

'Yeah,' Paul said, following my gaze. 'I guess.'

Then, to my surprise, he stuck out his right hand. 'No hard feelings, Simon?'

I looked down at his hand. It seemed incredible, but I really didn't have any. Hard feelings toward him, I mean. Not now. Not any more.

I slipped my fingers into his.

'No hard feelings,' I said.

Then the bathroom door burst open and Kelly came out, her gait considerably altered because Sister Ernestine had stitched the slit in her dress to just above the knee.

Kelly had some pretty unpleasant things to say about the nun as she approached us.

'But at least she didn't make you go home and change,' I interrupted her to point out.

Kelly just blinked at me. 'Who's that guy?' she wanted to know.

I looked over my shoulder. Jesse was approaching us from down the breezeway. My heart, as always when I saw him, turned over in my chest.

'Oh, him?' I said casually. 'That's just Jesse, my boyfriend.'

My boyfriend. *My boyfriend.*

413

Kelly's eyes widened to their limits as Jesse stepped into the pool of moonlight in which we were standing, and took my hand.

'Paul,' he said with a nod.

'Hey, Jesse,' Paul said, looking uncomfortable. Then, remembering Kelly, he made uneasy introductions.

'Very nice to meet you,' Jesse said, shaking Kelly's hand.

She, however, seemed too stunned to reply. She was just staring up at Jesse as if she'd seen . . .

Well, not a ghost, exactly. More like something she couldn't quite understand. I could almost hear her wondering, *What's a guy like* that *doing with* Suze Simon?

Hey, she didn't know what I'd been through for the guy . . . or what he'd been through for me.

Trying not to look too smug, I took Jesse's arm and said, 'Well, see you around.' And led him to the dance floor.

'Things with Paul are . . . ?' Jesse raised his eyebrows questioningly as I slid my arms around his neck.

'Fine,' I said.

'And you know that because . . . ?'

'He told me.'

'And you believe him?'

'You know what?' I lifted my head from where I'd been resting it on Jesse's shoulder. 'I do.'

'I see.' Jesse stood there as I swayed to the music. 'Susannah? What are you doing?'

'I'm dancing with you.'

Jesse looked down at our feet, but couldn't see them, because my long skirt was swaying above them.

'I don't know this dance,' he said.

'It's easy,' I said. I let go of his neck and took his hands and brought them around my waist. Then I put my arms back around his neck. 'Now sway.'

414

Jesse swayed.

'See?' I said. 'You're doing it.'

Jesse's voice in my ear sounded a bit strangled. 'What's this dance called?' he asked.

'Slow,' I said. 'It's called a slow dance.'

Jesse didn't say anything much after that. He really was catching on fast to twenty-first-century social customs.

I don't know how much later it was that I lifted my head and saw my dad standing there.

This time, I didn't jump out of my skin. I'd sort of been expecting to see him.

'Hey, kiddo,' he said.

I stopped dancing and said to Jesse, 'Could you just excuse me a minute? There's just somebody I have to, um, have a word with.'

Jesse smiled. 'Of course.'

My heart swelling with adoration for him, I hurried over to the palm tree my dad was lurking behind.

'Hey,' I said to him, a little breathlessly. 'You came.'

'Of course I came,' Dad said. 'My little girl's first real dance? You think I'd miss it?'

'That's not why I'm glad you came,' I said, reaching out to take his hand. 'I wanted to say thanks.'

'Thanks?' Dad looked bewildered. 'For what?'

'For what you did for Jesse.'

'For Jesse?' Then comprehension dawned and he made as if to drop my hand, looking embarrassed. 'Oh. That.'

'Yes, *that*,' I said, holding his fingers more tightly. 'Dad, Jesse told me. If you hadn't made him come to the hospital when you did, I'd have lost him forever.'

'Well,' he said, looking as if he wished he was someplace – anyplace – else. In fact, he looked . . . well, almost as if he already *was* someplace else. He was much less opaque than

415

usual. 'I mean, you were crying. And calling me. When it was Jesse you should have been calling.'

'I thought Jesse was gone,' I said. 'So I called you. Because you've always been there when I really needed you. And you were there for me then, too. You saved him, Dad. And I just wanted to let you know how much that meant to me. Especially since I know you didn't agree with my going – you know – in the first place.'

My dad reached up to straighten my orchid. But for some reason, instead of being able to grab on to it, his fingers seemed to go right through the waxy petals. Suddenly, I realized what was happening. And there was nothing I could do but stand there, looking up at him, tears gathering beneath my eyelids.

'Yeah, sorry about that,' Dad went on, meaning our disagreement about my going back through time to 'save' Jesse. He was growing physically fainter and fainter with every word. And it wasn't just because I was looking at him through a veil of tears. 'It's just that if you'd gone back and saved my life, it would have been like . . . well, like I'd died – and been hanging around for the past ten years for nothing.'

'It wasn't for nothing, Dad,' I said, holding as tightly as I could to the hand that, even as I spoke, I could feel slipping away. 'It was for Jesse. And for me. That's why you're finally ready to move on. See for yourself.'

Dad looked down at himself and then at me, clearly stunned.

'It's OK, Dad,' I said, reaching up with my free hand to wipe the tears from my face.

He was almost impossible to see now . . . just a shimmer of colour and light, and a faint pressure on my hand. But I could tell he was grinning. Grinning and crying at the same time. Just like I was. 'I'll miss you.'

'Take care of your mother for me,' he said quickly, as if he was afraid of being snatched away before he could get the words out.

'I will,' I promised.

'And be good,' he said.

'Am I ever anything but?' I asked, my voice breaking.

Then, with a shimmer, he disappeared.

Forever.

It was a long time before I could go back to where Jesse was standing. I'd had to cry for a while behind one of the palm trees, then repair the damage those tears had done with the make-up from my bag. When I finally returned to Jesse's side, he looked down at me, and smiled.

'He's gone?' he asked.

'He's gone,' I said automatically. Then I gasped.

'Jesse . . .' I stared up at him. 'Can you . . . did you . . . ?'

'See you talking to your father just then?' he asked, the corners of his lips twitching a little. 'Yes.'

'Then you can . . .' I was completely dumbfounded. 'You can . . .'

'See and speak to ghosts?' Jesse grinned in the moonlight. 'Apparently so. Why? Is that a problem?'

'No. Except that . . . that would mean—' I could barely believe what I was saying. 'That means you're a—'

'*Querida*,' Jesse said, pulling me toward him. 'Let's just dance.'

But I was still too stunned to think of anything else. Jesse – my Jesse – was no longer a ghost. He was a mediator.

Like me.

'The only thing I don't understand,' Jesse was saying, his breath warm in my ear, 'is why it took him all this time.'

I swayed in Jesse's arms, barely registering what he was

417

saying. *Jesse is a mediator*, was all I could think. *Jesse's a mediator now.*

'Your father,' Jesse said. 'His moving on, I mean. Why now?'

I put my arms around his neck. What else could I do?

'Do you really not know?' I asked him.

He shook his head.

I smiled because I felt as if my heart might burst with joy.

Mediator

Love You to Death & High Stakes

Meet Susannah Simon – the sassiest ghost-hunter ever!

In *Love You to Death*: Suze has just arrived in California and needs to unpack, make friends, look around . . . and exorcise a vicious ghost, hell-bent on making her life a complete nightmare. Oh, and the sexiest spook in existence just happens to haunt her new bedroom . . .

In *High Stakes*: When a screaming spirit wakes Suze in the middle of the night with an important message, she finds herself on the trail of a very creepy businessman. One who doesn't like sunshine and only drinks a weird red liquid . . . Suze may have met her match, but his cute son Tad makes it hard for her to stay away.

Mediator

MEAN SPIRITS & YOUNG BLOOD

Meet Susannah Simon – the sassiest ghost-hunter ever!

In *Mean Spirits*: School is out! And Suze is set to spend the summer at the beach with her best friend, Gina. But four vengeful ghosts are out to wreak havoc – Suze must use all her skills to try to stop them, before they turn on her . . .

In *Young Blood*: Suze never meant to fall in love with Jesse – the heart-stoppingly gorgeous ghost who haunts her bedroom. It just sort of happened. But how can she make him love her back? And what will she discover when she digs up his mysterious past?

JINX
Meg Cabot

Does Jinx have bad luck – or special powers?

Misfortune has followed Jean Honeychurch all her life – which is why everyone calls her Jinx. And now her parents have shipped her off to New York to stay with relatives – including her sophisticated cousin, Tory – until the trouble she's caused back home dies down.

Could she even be . . . a WITCH?

Tory is far too cool to bother with Jinx – until Jinx's chronic bad luck wreaks havoc in Tory's perfect life. Only then does Jinx discover that beneath Tory's big-city glamour lies a world of hatred and revenge. Now it seems that the jinx that's driven Jean crazy may just be the only thing that can save her life . . .

meg cabot

air head

She's a brainiac trapped inside the body of an airhead...

Teenagers Emerson Watts and Nikki Howard have nothing in common. Em's a tomboy-brainiac who couldn't care less about her looks. Nikki's a stunning supermodel, the world's most famous airhead. But a freak accident causes the girls' lives to collide in the most extraordinary way – and suddenly Em knows more about Nikki's life than the paparazzi ever have!

The first book in a spectacular romantic trilogy with a spine-tingling twist!

air head
Being Nikki
meg cabot

Em Watts is gone. Nikki Howard is here to stay.

Teen-supermodel Nikki Howard has a secret. She's not the gorgeous golden airhead she seems – on the inside she's someone else. Literally. Em Watts is stuck in the body of glamazon celebutante Nikki. And it's not easy. Especially when Nikki's past is about to catch up with her, her boss is spying on her, and Em's heart wants one thing but her lips keep kissing someone else . . .

The funny, crazy, super-glamorous sequel to *Airhead*.